American Games

Comprehensive

Collector's Guide

Featuring the Alex G. Malloy Game Collection

by Alex G. Malloy

Antique Trader Books
A Division of Krause Publications
Iola, Wisconsin

Technical Editor: Eric Percival

Color Plates Editor: Stuart Wells

Cover design by Heather Ealey

ISBN: 00-930625-60-9

Library of Congress Catalog Card Number: 98-71056

To order additional copies of this book or to
obtain a free catalog, please contact:

Krause Publications
700 E. State Street
Iola, WI 54990-0001
1-800-258-0929

Contents
American Games
Comprehensive Collector's Guide

Preface

This book was conceived years ago. A book on games for enthusiasts to look up their favorite, or find one they vaguely remembered from childhood. I recall a game I played in Miami Beach when I was five years old. Neighbors, two teenage boys and their ten-year-old sister, invited me over to play a game. It was during World War II, and I was infatuated with both the subject and action of the game: countries and the procurement of goods and armies. For over fifty years I looked for this game, not knowing its name. In the early nineties, I found the game at a giant outdoor antique fair called Renningers, in eastern Pennsylvania. I thought it was the game I had been looking for! I had done research on all games published in pre- and early World War II. I had seen an advertisement for a game in a Selchow and Righter catalogue called **The Game of Empires**. After purchasing the game and opening the box, a rush of delight swept over me. This indeed was that elusive game. The rest of the day I did not touch the ground!

This book is intended to list most games that a collector will encounter. There are other books that list certain categories and ages, or provide an overview of games, but none that provides a comprehensive guide along with accurate values. A fine set of 112 color pages has been added, featuring games from all ages of American games.

The basis of this book began with my collection, started in 1954. The collection has grown to 4,650 games. The American games, both card and board, span from 1811 to 1998. Two additional groups, one of foreign games and the other of ancient gaming pieces, round out the collection. Examples of all types of games have been added to try to complete the collection in scope. All games pictured are from this collection.

Over the years, many people who have become friends have helped me in adding to this collection and in sharing their knowledge. Thank you, Paul and Davia Fink, for your support and fun times at conventions and Club Get-A-Way; to Debby, Marty, and Stephanie Krim for our special sessions in West Peabody; to Susan Stock and David Oglesby at the early Hartford conventions (remember our dinner at the jazz restaurant in Atlantic City); to Mary Lou Alpert, and waiting for John Overall before the Katonah Museum Game exhibition; to Bruce Whitehill, and our times at your home in New Jersey, and selling games at Liberty Park; to John and Anna Ellerbe, and our luncheon at the first AGCA convention in Essex Connecticut; to David Galt, and our three-hour trip home from Long Island with the car filled to the top with games purchased at the auction; to John and Mildred Spear, and their guidance into the Presidency of the AGCA; to Anne Williams, and her support and help in running the AGCA; to Mike "Old Games" and Margaret Johnson, and our searching Stormville for goodies; to Peter Coddles, disguised as Wayne Saunders; to Lea and Steve Horvath, and our *tête-à-têtes* regarding AGCA finances; to Helen Andrews, and her acceptance speech at the Worcester AGCA convention; to Joe Angiolillo, and our love for Parker Brothers and old games; to Harry Rinker, and his guidance in making books; to Alfonzo Smith, and his auction antics at the LA AGCA convention; and to Hugh and Laura Bell, and our Danbury Sunday brunches with the other Gameaholics. Also, sincere thanks to Peter Freitag, Bob Finn, Debby Leo, Ryan Brown, Jim Polczynski, Rick Russack, Dave Bausch, Mark Cooper, Geraldine Goodwin, Dave Deayton, Stuart Kaplan, Jeff Lowe, Paul Meyer, Steve Olin, Roy and Grace Olsen, Phil Orbanes, Jerry Slocum, Lindy and Jim Van Fleet, and Bill Alexander. Thanks also to Eric Percival, Camden Percival, Phillis Schlemmer, and Stuart Wells for your computer expertise. Thank you, Paul Fink and David Oglesby, for their suggestions and help in the valuing of games.

Special thanks to Elaine Malloy for her help in the preparation of this book, as well as her support and patience in my collecting of games.

Alex G. Malloy
December 1999

Those desiring information regarding games, or who would like to sell games, please contact me at:
P.O. Box 38, South Salem N.Y
914-533-2661, Fax 203-438-6744,
E-mail alexmalloy@aol.com

GAMES THROUGH THE AGES

With the beginning of civilization and man's advent into community, came man's interest in competition and the invention of games. Five thousand years ago in Sumer, situated between the Tigris and Euphrates Rivers, came **The Royal Game of Ur**. Found in the excavations of the royal palace at Ur this game was complete with an inlaid ivory board and playing tokens.

One thousand years later in Old Babylon, the game of **Tjal** or **"Game of Twenty Squares"** was produced. During this same period in Egypt, during the New Kingdom, the popular game of **Senet** was played. A beautiful example of Senet was found in King Tut's tomb. The Greeks in Troy and the Celts in Bronze Age Ireland played the game of **Nine Men's Morris**, which had originated in Egypt in 1400 B.C. It was also found in the burial sites of Viking Kings dating from 900 A.D. This game was played throughout medieval Europe. An illuminated manuscript from the thirteenth century Spain depicts Alfonso X, king of Castile and Leon, playing this game. By the medieval period the game was known as **Morris** in Spain and England, **Mühle (Mill)** in Germany and **Jeu de Moulin (Game of Mill)** in France.

Dice was played as early as 1500 B.C. in Egypt. Nero, the Roman emperor, reportedly wagered 15,000 sestertii or 15,000 dollars a throw in **Dice**. Examples of Roman dice carved in bone or ivory look exactly the same as today's dice. During the Renaissance Henry VIII of England was an ardent **Dice** enthusiast. **Knucklebones**, so called as the game pieces were made of sheep's knucklebones, was a similar game to dice. Homer mentioned the game in both The Iliad and The Odyssey. Sophocles attributed the invention of the game to Palamedes, who taught the game to the Greeks during the Trojan War. The Romans knew the game as **Astragaloi**. They produced **Astragaloi** in many materials including: glass, bronze, silver, terra cotta, and stone. The emperor Claudius was reputably an excellent player.

Backgammon originated in China during the second century. In ancient Rome, where the game was known as **Tabula**, beautiful multicolored playing pieces were produced and highly prized. The Parthians and the Sassanians in Persia also played Backgammon. Many Islamic kingdoms adopted the game and played it extensively. In medieval times it was known as **Tables**.

During the first century A.D. the Chinese developed the game of **Go**. Introduced into Japan in 735 A.D., the game gained great popularity. For hundreds of years Go was the rage in the East, but was not introduced to the West until the twentieth century.

Pachisi was invented in India in the sixth century A.D. in the Deccan region. During the sixteenth century the Moghul emperor Akbar played it. Its popularity spread through out the world. **Chess** was also developed in India in the seventh century. Known as **The Royal Game**, it spread throughout the world with the spread of Islam. The Sanskrit word for chess, **Chaturanga**, refers to the game components as the army of elephants, chariots, horses, and the pawns as the foot soldiers. Changes both to the names and pieces occurred as the game spread throughout medieval Europe, becoming one of the most popular games in history.

Checkers, developed in Europe during the twelfth century, is a game derived from Backgammon's playing tokens and Chess's game board. **Lotto** was the national game of Italy and was played as early as 1530. **Bingo**, a variation of lotto, is the American variation of Keno. **Fox and Geese**, a game from Scandinavia, developed during the Middle Ages. Edward IV (1461-1483) King of England was an enthusiast. **Game of Goose** was made famous by Francesco de Medici of Florence (1574-1587) who presented the game as a gift to Phillip II of Spain. By the turn of the sixteenth century it was very popular on continental Europe and in England.

ANCIENT GAMING PIECES

Sumerian   Price

1. 3000 B.C., White marble gaming token, cylindrical terminating to a point, base flat. $350

Early Dynastic

2. 2000 B.C., White chalcedony gaming token, four sloping flat sides to a pointed top. 250

3. 2000 B.C., White chalcedony gaming token, four sloping sides with two narrower. 250

Babylonian

4. 1800 B.C., Grey-black steatite gaming token, cylindrical with sloping flat sides to rounded top, flat splayed base. 250

Syrian

5. 1800-1500 B.C., Black steatite gaming token, cylindrical shape near top carved ridge giving a button top; carved vertical lines at sides. 300

6. 1800-1500 B.C., Black steatite gaming token, disc with flat base and top design carved with thin rays. 150

7. 1800-1500 B.C., Black steatite gaming token, Disc with flat base, top with carved swirl ray pattern, circle dot in center. 150

Neo Assyrian

8. 800-600 B.C., Variegated striped orange and beige stone gaming token, cylindrical sloping inward sides to shoulder, neck with flare rim, flat top and base. 500

Neo Babylonian

9. 700-600 B.C. Cream and Translucent chalcedony gaming token, Short cylindrical sloping to sharp pointed top, flat base. 250

Egyptian

10. Middle Kingdom, 2133-1786 B.C., Cream alabaster gaming token, pedestal base sloping inward, sides to pointed knob. 600

11. Middle Kingdom, 2133-1786 B.C., Cream alabaster gaming token, wide pedestal base sloping inward to wide knob with three-line hieroglyphic inscription. 1200

12. New Kingdom, 1567-1085 B.C., Light-green faience gaming token, flat base, sides sloping to rounded knob. 200

13. New Kingdom, 1567-1085 B.C., Blue-green faience gaming token, flared flat base with sides sloping inward and up to button knob. 300

14. New Kingdom, 1567-1085 B.C., Blue-white faience gaming token, flare flat base, sloping sides inward and up to tall neck terminating in button top with round rosette on top. 500

15. New Kingdom, 1567-1085 B.C., Light blue faience gaming token, flare base with inward sloping sides up to button knob. $200

16. New Kingdom, 1567-1085 B.C., Blue faience gaming token, stubby base with inward sloping sides to large button knob. 300

17. New Kingdom, 1567-1085 B.C., Light-blue faience gaming token, wide flare base with inward sloping sides to large cone knob. 200

18. New Kingdom, 1567-1085 B.C., Light-blue faience gaming token, flare base with inward sloping sides to tall neck termination in cone knob. 200

19. New Kingdom, 1567-1085 B.C., Baby blue faience gaming token, Male head wearing bagwig terminating in solar disc, flat base. 1500

20. New Kingdom, 20th Dynasty, 1200-1085 B.C. Limestone game board of *Senet*, with grid of twenty spaces of incised lines, five decorated with two of *nefer* (good) signs; a boat for upon the water, Three *neter* (good) signs, two more *neter* signs, and a single Horus falcon.cf. Scott, *Yale*, 60. 15000

21. Late Period, 1085-332 B.C., Limestone carved game board of *Tjal*, or the "game of twenty squares" one third board present with a grid of six squares and part of a third register of squares within which all have large incised circles, the central square has a large drilled dot. The game originated in Mesopotamia but this example was found in Abydos, Egypt. 3500

22. Late Period, 25th-30th Dynasty, 760-341 B.C., Carved red-stained ivory gaming piece, tall cylindrical shape sloping slightly inward to the top. Cf. Scott, *Yale* 60a. 300

23. Ptolemaic, 300-100 B.C., Dark blue faience gaming token with bright blue knob in center, ridges radiating from center to edge. 350

Greek

24. 2nd-1st century B.C., Carved ivory gaming tessera, Disc the tragic mask of diadem male head with mouth open in tragic look, two curled locks of hair at side, reverse, three line inscription VIII/AφPOΔITH/H-Translates to number 8, Aphrodite, H. 1500

Greek continued

25. 1st century B.C., Carved ivory gaming tessera, carved disc with youthful male head diadem in three circles, reverse is blank with centration mark. 1200

Ancient Israel

26. 300-100 B.C., Opaque baby blue glass gaming token, rounded cone. 400

Roman Egypt

27. 1st century A.D., Ivory carved gaming tessera glazed light green, edge incised with two scalloped outer concentric circles, central raised knob. 200

Roman

28. 1st- 3rd century B.C., Bone and ivory dice cubes with circle and dot numbers on each surface. 200

29. 1st century A.D., Clear blue-aqua glass knucklebone gaming piece. 250

30. 1st century A.D., Clear glass knucklebone gaming piece. 225

31. 1st century A.D., Clear glass green-aqua knucklebone gaming piece. 250

32. 1st century A.D., Opaque glass yellow knucklebone gaming piece. 250

33. 1st century A.D., Opaque glass dark blue knucklebone gaming piece. 250

34. 1st-2nd century A.D., Bronze knucklebone gaming piece, three dots drilled on one side. 500

35. 1st-3rd century A.D., Red-brown sard gaming token, dome. 200

36. 1st-3rd century A.D., Brown-grey conglomerate stone gaming token, dome. 200

37. 1st-3rd century A.D., Bronze square gaming tessera, inscribed NIT, horse prancing right. 500

38. 1st-3rd century A.D., Bronze square gaming tessera, inscribed MPV, galley traveling left. 400

39. 1st-3rd century A.D., Bronze square gaming tessera, inscribed AC/AI. 300

40. 1st-3rd century A.D., Bronze square gaming tessera, Togate male figure standing. 400

41. 3rd-4th century A.D., Bronze square gaming tessera, Roma standing left in helmet and holding figure of Victory. 450

42. 1st century A.D., Bronze round gaming tessera, head of Augustus right, Reverse has V in wreath, Ex. Professor T. O. Mabbott collection # 5251. 600

43. 1st century A.D., Bronze round gaming tessera, Laureate head of Augustus right, in circle, reverse has VII in wreath. Ex. Professor T.O. Mabbott collection #5250. 600

44. 1st century A.D., Bronze round gaming tessera, Radiate head of Augustus left, reverse has XI in wreath. Ex. T.O. Mabbott collection # 5258. 600

45. 1st century A.D., Bronze round gaming tessera, incised XII reverse has two drilled dots, ex-Professor T.O. Mabbott collection #5266. 250

46. 1st century A.D., Bronze round gaming tessera, Biga galloping right, reverse large II. Ex T.O. Mabbott collection # 5290. 400

47. 1st century A.D., Bronze round gaming tessera, man on horseback to right, reverse is blank. 400

48. 1st century A.D., Milleflori green with yellow glass gaming token, disc flattened dome, ten eyes from edge with nine eyes in center of yellow field. 250

49. 1st century A.D., Milleflori red, black and white short lines glass gaming token, dome. 250

50. 1st century A.D., Milleflori red, black and white irregular sections glass gaming token, dome. 250

51. 1st century A.D., Milleflori blue, green and yellow glass gaming token, dome. 250

52. 1st century A.D., Milleflori blue, green and yellow glass gaming token, dome. 250

53. 2nd-3rd century A.D., Amber glass gaming token, swirl dome. 100

54. 2nd-3rd century A.D., Aqua glass gaming token. rounded end disc, heavy iridescence. 100

55. 2nd-3rd century A.D., Black glass gaming token, rounded end disc. 75

56. 2nd-3rd century A.D., Opaque cream glass gaming token, rounded end disc. 75

57. 2nd-3rd century A.D., Clear aqua-yellow glass gaming token, rounded end disc. 100

Greco-Roman

58. 2nd-3rd century A.D., Red sard dodecagon gaming die, in each pentagon a Greek letter, Ν,Ρ,Ι,Α,Π,Θ,Λ,Δ,Κ,Ρ,Η,Λ. 1000

Medieval

59. 10th-13th century, Jadeite dark green gaming token, rectangular sides sloping inward to triangular top, short pedestal base. + with dot in each angle. Inscribed on base. 350

Islamic

60. 12th-14th century, Clear green glass gaming token, disc with indented circle inscription in kufic. 12

1   2   4   5   8   9

11

12, 13, & 14

15

16, 17, & 18

19

24

25

23 & 27

30, 33, 29, 31, & 32

34 & 36

58

41, 37, 38, & 39

45, 46, & 43

47 & 48

51 & 52

59

FOREIGN GAMES

Arabic   Price

**60a. Arabic Game of Chutes and Ladders and
Parcheesi.** Circa 1960s. Board Game. $25

Australia

61. Squatter, Australian Wool Game. J. Sands Pty.
© 1961. Economic, Board Game. 75

62. Triple Up. Thorpe, Australia. © 1985.
Card Game. 5

Austria

63. Animal Families. Platnik, #279. Circa 1970s.
Animal, Card Game. 7

64. Art Memo. Platnik, Vienna. © 1989. Art, Board
Game. 7

65. Die Vier Jahreszeiten, Les Quatre Saisons,
Austrian. Anton Paterno. 1840. Time, Board Game. 600

66. Grimms Fairy Tales. Platnik Vienna #285. Circa
1930s. Literary, Card Game. 20

67. Tops & Tails. Platnik & Sons, Austria. Circa
1970s. Animal, Card Game. 7

Canada

68. Big Bucks, The Word of Business. Gestion
Group, Canada. © 1987. Economic, Board Game. 25

69. Condomania 2000, French Edition. Games
Galore, Canada. © 1979. Architecture, Board
Game. 30

70. Crude, One of the best designed games, 1st
Edition. St. Laurent. 1974. Economic, Board Game. 200

71. Five Thousand. Reid Ent. Canada. © 1949.
Economic, Board Game. 60

72. Jeu De Cartes Sur L'Environement. G. Raphia,
Quebec. © 1990. Geography, Card Game. .... CRP

73. Jeu Super M Expos Baseball Game. Jeu Super
Baseball. © 1979. Sports, Baseball Board Game. 50

74. Journey Through Disneyland. Ontex, Canada.
Circa 1950s. Disney, Board Game. 200

75. Land Grab. House of Games, Canada. 1974.
Economic, Board Game. 45

76. Nations, Game of. The Canada Game Co. Circa
1900. Geography, Card Game. 65

77. Nations, The Game of. Waddington, Canada.
©1973. Military, Board Game. 50

78. Nobel, World Peace Game. Richard Maruist,
Quebec. 1988. International, Board Game. 35

79. Quebec Election Puzzle Game. Circa 1890s.
Political Board Game. 80

80. Saguenay-Lac-Saint-Jean. D.M.De Chicoutimi
Inc. © 1990. Travel, Board Game. 20

81. Warzon. Warzon M Co. © 1940. Military, World
War II, Board Game. 300

82. Wonderful Game of Oz, The. Copp Clark.
© 1939. Literary, Board Game. 500

Denmark

83. Kobenhaun. Seven Touns, Denmark. Circa 1970s.
Cities, Board Game. 25

France

84. Babar 7 Families Card Game, The. Lide
Brunhoff, France. © 1981. Literary, Card Game. 35

85. Business, French Business Game. Fenwick. 1976.
Economic, Board Game. 50

86. Expansion. French Trade Union Game.
Fenwick. 1978. Economic, Board Game. $50

87. Gendarmes et Voleurs. D.D.F., Paris. Circa
1880-90. Law & Order, Board Game. 200

88. Jardin D'Acclimatation, Le. S. C. Paris. Circa
1890s. Card Game. 100

**89. Jeu De Cartes Historiques De L'Histoire,
Grecae.** E. Jouy-Vanachere-Nicole. Circa 1760.
History, Card Game. 250

**90. Jeu De Cartes Historiques De L'Histoire,
Romaine.** E. Jouy-Vanachere-Nicole. Circa 1760.
History, Card Game. 250

91. Jeu de L'Araignee. M-D, Paris. Circa 1900s.
Board Game. 200

92. Jeu Du Grand-Homme, (Life of Napoleon) Me
Ve Turgis, Paris. Circa 1850. Historical, Board
Game. 750

93. Jeu Du Monde, Le. P. Du Val, Paris. 1650.
Geography, Board Game. 1000

94. Jeux De Société, French, 8 Game Set. Jeux et
Jovets, Paris. Circa 1900. Classic, Combination,
Board Game. 300

95. La Pêche au Trésor. Ticet Patte, Circa 1960s.
Animal, Board Game. 40

**96. Le Loto De La Maternelle, 1re Série,
(Jean Perrot).** F. Nathan, Paris. Circa 1900s.
Board Game. 200

97. Les Ascensionnistes. L. & A. Cresson, Paris. Circa
1880s. Adventure, Board Game. 250

98. Les Presidents Directeurs Generaux, About
selling cars. Miro. 1967. Travel, Cars, Board Game. 100

99. Les Routiers Sont Sympa Max Meynier. Ematec.
1977. Travel, Economic, Board Game. 75

100. L'Histoire De France, 1re Parte. F.N., Paris.
Circa 1890s. History, Board Game. 125

101. Monopoly, French Edition. Parker Bros. © 1985.
Economic, Board Game. 40

102. Monopoly, French Edition. Miro, Paris. © 1961.
Economic, Board Game. 60

103. Moto-Cross, Motorbike scrambling, Nathan. 1977.
Travel, Road, Board Game. 75

104. Pigeon Courrier. Hirne et Cie., Paris. Circa 1900.
Animal, Board Game. 150

105. Renard et Cmiens. M.D. Paris-Imp. Roche. Circa
1900. Board Game. 125

106. Stragone. Polyajeu. 1979. Strategy, Board Game. 50

107. Superman Le Film. Miro, Paris. © 1979. Super
Heroes, Board Game. 45

108. Tableau Chronologique de l'Histoire Universelle. 1715. Historical, Board Game. $800
109. Walt Disney Jeu Des 7 Families. Nathan, France. © 1990. Card Game. Disney. 20
110. Zoologie, La. Circa 1910s. Animal, Card Game. 75

Germany
111. Atravers La Suisse. Jos. Scholz Mayence. Circa 1910. Geography, Card Game. 150
112. Barbacan. PTN:5913. Circa 1900s. Board Game. 100
113. Ben Her. German chariot racing game. Jean du Poel. 1985. Literary, Board Game. 75
114. Berlinspiel. Promotional City Game. Jumbo. Circa 1985. Geography, Board Game. 100
115. Big Roller, The. Ravensburg. Circa 1930s. Strategy, Board Game. 65
116. Boerenschroom. German Mfg. Circa 1850-60. Board Game. 400
117. Bomben Über England. Nazi air battle over England. D. R. O. M. 1940s. Military, World War II, Board Game. 350
118. Boomers, Fighters & Bombers. Schmid, Munich. Circa 1970s. Military, World War II, Card Game. 50
119. Cash and Carry. German Business Game. Hanje. 1986. Economic, Board Game. 50
120. Climbing Monkey's, The. Spear's Games. Circa 1920s. Animal, Board Game, made for US market. 200
121. Cross Country Race. Clover, Bavaria. Circa 1920s. Sports, Board Game, for the English speaking Market.** 200
122. Das Ist Des Deutschen Vaterland. Hallsser, Circa 1910s. Geography, Board Game. 250
123. Der Siegeszug unferer Jungen Wehrmacht. Nazi Air Game. D. M. Hausser. Circa 1940s. Military, World War II, Board Game. 350
124. Dus Gansespiel, [The Game of Goose]. Anonymous, Circa 1820s. Animal, Board Game. 350
125. Endangered Species, Antarctica-Africa. Altenboro. Circa 1980s. Animal, Card Game. 20
126. Endangered Species, Asia-Australia. Altenboro, Circa 1980s. Animal, Card Game. 20
127. Endangered Species, North American-Arctic. Altenboro, Circa 1980s. Animal, Card Game. 20
128. Falsches Speil Mit Roger Rabbit. Schmidt Spiele, © 1987. Disney, Board Game. 125
129. Forum Romanum. Franckh, German. 1988. Historical Board Game. 100

130. Fox, Game of. (with dice). R. Deder, Berlin. Circa 1830s. Animal, Card Game. $250
131. Gulliver. Ravensburg Games. © 1971. Literary, Card Game. 30
132. Hitlerjugend Geländespiel, Nazi War Game. D. M. Hausser. 1940s. Military World War II, Board Game. 350
133. I Ching Cards. A. G. Muller, West Germany. © 1971. Card Game. 20
134. Journey Round the World. "B", Bavaria. Circa 1910s. Geography, Board Game, made for English speaking countries. 225
135. Liliputians, The Game of. Germany. Circa 1900. Social, Card Game. 200
136. Lutiges 1x1. Germany, Circa 1890s. Board Game. 150
137. Manhattan. Hans im Glück, © 1994. Architecture Board Game. 50
138. Menschärgere Dich Nichti. Jos. Friedr. Schmidt. Circa 1930s. Mystic, Board Game. 45
139. Miraculum. German. Circa 1930s. Mystic, Board Game, circulated in the US. 100
140. Modern Art. Hans im Glück, © 1992. Art, Board Game. .... CRP
141. Monopoly, German Edition. Parker Bros. © 1991. Economic, Board Game. 40
142. Monte Carlo, The Game of. J.W. & S., Bavaria. Circa 1900. Chance, Board Game. 75
143. Motor Race Game. B. Germany. Circa 1920s. Sports, Car, Board Game, for the English speaking. 135
144. Off to the Tower. Ravensburger, Germany. © 1978. Fantasy, Board Game. 50
145. Onkel Tom's Bütte, [Uncle Tom's Cabin]. Anonymous, Germany. Circa 1850s. Literary, Ethnic, Board Game. 2500
146. Romans Against Carthaginians. From the movie Hannibal. Hausser. 1960. Military, Movie, Board Game. 85
147. Shopping Center. Otto-Maier Verlag. © 1972. Economic, Board Game. 60
148. Shopping Center. Ravensburg, © 1972. Economic, Board Game. 60

149. South Sea Adventures. Spears Games. © 1928. Adventure, Board Game, made for English speaking countries. 200
150. Spion Vs. Spion, German version of Mad's Spy vs. Spy. Milton Bradley. 1987. Comics, Board Game. 35

Germany continued

151. **Sports, The Game of.** Circa 1900. Sports, Card Game. $75
152. **Steeple Chase.** J.W. Spear, Circa 1920s. Sports, Horse Racing, Board Game, made for England. 125
153. **Super Top Trumpf "Helden".** Berliner, Spielicarten. © 1988. Card Game. 20
154. **Super Top Trumpf "Schurken".** Berliner, Spielicarten. © 1988. Card Game. 20
155. **Trip Through the British Isles, A.** Clover. Circa 1920s. Geography, Board Game, made for English market. 150
156. **Uber Stadt Und Land.** Airship playing pieces. Wickuler. 1965. Travel, Board Game. 125
157. **Wonders of the Deep, The.** B. Bavaria. Circa 1920s. Animal, Sea, Board Game, made for English market. 150

Israel

158. **Seejeh.** Orda Ind., Israel. © 1978. Strategy, Board Game. 35

Italy

159. **Al Parlamento,** Italian politics. Alam. Circa 1975. Political, Board Game. 150
160. **Diletovole Gioco Del'Ocha,** Very early game. Italian. 1625. Classic, Board Game. 950
161. **Monopli.** Italian Edition. Editirice Giochi. © 1979. Economic, Board Game. 50
162. **Ruma-Rita.** O.M.H.L. Circa 1930s. Board Game. 75

Ireland

163. **Discovering Ireland.** Gosling Games Ltd. © 1987. Geography, Board Game. 25

Japan

163a. **Hawaii Game.** In Japanese. Circa 1970s. Travel, Board Game. 50
163b. **Monopoly.** Parker. Circa 1990s. Economic, Board Game. 50

New Zealand

164. **Cathedral.** Robert Moore. © 1985. Architecture, Strategy, Board Game. 150

Portugal

165. **Descobrimetos.** Majorica Porto © 1980. Travel, Board Game. 30

Spain

166. **El Juego de las Elecciones.** Spanish elections. Mirol. 1987. Political, Board Game. 75
167. **La Batalla De Vitoria.** Spanish 19th century Army. Fournier. 1988. Military, Card Game. 30
168. **La Ruta Del Tesoro.** Spanish Monopoly type game. Cefa. 1988. Economic, Board Game. 40
169. **Monopoly.** Parker Bros., Spain. 1982. Economic, Board Game. 40
170. **Por Las Carreteras De España.** Didacta. Circa 1960s. Travel, Board Game. 35

Switzerland

171. **Holidays in Switzerland.** Carlit. Circa 1960s. Travel, World, Board Game. 40

172. **Matterhorn Spiel.** Verlag Spes, Lausanne. Circa 1920s. Geography, Board Game. $125

United Kingdom

173. **A Voyage of Discovery, or the Five Navigators.** William Spooner. 1836. Geography, Board Game. 1000
174. **Aerial Attack.** Ilex Series. Circa 1939-40. Military, World War II, Board Game. 150
175. **Airport Flying Game.** Fairylite. Circa 1935-9. Travel, Air Board Game. 55
176. **Alibi, The Game of.** Tor Productions Ltd. Circa 1950s. Law, Card Game. 55
177. **Alice in Wonderland.** PHS-Jmm. Circa 1900. Literary, Board Game. 150
178. **Alice in Wonderland.** Thomas De La Rue. Circa 1930s. Literary, Card Game. 125
179. **Ambassadors.** Bee Hive for Israel. Circa 1930s. Religious, Board Game. 65
180. **America West, The.** Fax-Pax, © 1992. Western, Card Game. 25
181. **Amusement in English History.** William Sallis. © 1840. History, Board Game. 750
182. **Attack, Game of.** J.W. Spear, London. Circa 1910s. Military, World War I, Board Game. 85
183. **Auto Race.** D. M. Co. Circa 1920s. Sports, Car, Board Game. 85
184. **Aviation.** H.P. Gibson & Sons. Circa 1940s. Military, World War II, Board Game. 125
185. **BBC Antiques Road Show.** San Serif Print Promo. © 1988. Economic, Board Game. 50
186. **Bowles's British Geographical Game.** C. Bowles, © 1780. Geography, Board Game. 750
187. **Buy British.** Geographia, Ltd. Economic, Board Game. 75
188. **Cabinet of Knowledge Opened, The.** John Wallis, London. © 1797. History, Card Game. 300
189. **Cabinet of New Maps Games.** Geographia, Ltd. Circa 1940s. Geography, Board Game. 75
190. **Cardora National Dog Race Game, The.** Cardora. Sports, Board Game. 125
191. **Cathedrals and Abbeys of England, Game of.** Satterlee. © 1893. Geography, Card Game. 50
192. **Cathedrals, Abbeys & Ministers.** Fax-Pax. © 1989. Geography, Card Game. 25
193. **Cattle Drive.** Jackman Studios. © 1974. Western, Board Game. 50
194. **Commonwealth Trader.** Metal boats. Geographia. 1930. Economic, Board Game. 125
195. **Contraband.** Pepys. Circa 1946-50. Economic, Card Game. 65
196. **Convoy.** Tree Brand. Circa 1940s. Military, World War II, Card Game. 150
197. **Cottage of Content or Right Roads and Wrong Ways.** W. Spooner. 1848. Geography, Board Game. 900
198. **Counties of England, The.** John Jaques. Circa 1890s. Geography, Card Game. 75
199. **Countries of Empire.** J. Jacques. Circa 1930s. Geography, Card Game. 60
200. **Dennis Wheatley's Invasion.** Geographia. 1930. Military, Board Game. 200
201. **Destruction of Jerusalem, The.** E. Wallis. © 1824. Historical Board Game. 1000
202. **Discovering London.** Gosling Games Ltd. © 1988. Geography, Board Game. 50

United Kingdom continued

203. **Donald Duck.** Pepys. Circa 1930s. Disney, Card Game. $45
204. **Dover Patrol.** Gibson & Sons. Circa 1915-9. Military, World War I, Board Game. 150
205. **Election X.** British Election Game. Intellect. Circa 1972. Political, Board Game. 100
206. **England Expects.** England. Circa 1940s. Military, World War II, Card Game. 60
207. **English Kings, Game of.** England. Circa 1875. History, Card Game. 200
208. **Ergo.** Invicta Games. © 1977. Board Game. 20
209. **Escalado.** Chad Valley. Circa 1970s. Board Game. 25
210. **Escape from Colditz.** Parker. © 1970. Military, World War II, Board Game. 50
211. **Exploration.** Spiring. © 1967. Adventure, Board Game. 65
212. **Flight Around the World, A.** J.W. Spear & Son. © 1928. Travel, Air, and Board Game. 200
213. **Flight.** British Mfg. Circa 1945-50. Travel, Air, Card Game. 40
213a. **Frog Race.** © 1973. Spears. Animal, Board Game. 75
214. **Garden Game, The.** Sarah Ponsonba. © 1984. Plant, Board Game. 50
215. **Geography Game,** Hand made and finely painted. Anonymous Circa 1890. Geography, Card Game. 5000
216. **Gooban's Game of Musical Characters.** Goulding. 1818. Musical, Board Game. 1200
217. **Goulash, For Gourmets.** Calla. © 1987. Food, Card Game. 25
218. **Goulash, For Veggies.** Calla. © 1987. Food, Card Game. 25
219. **Goulash,** Calla. © 1987. Food, Card Game. 25
220. **Grandmamm's New Game of Natural History.** English Mfg. Circa 1866. Animal, Board Game. 1000
221. **Green Game, The.** Octogo Games. Circa 1980s. Plant, Board Game. 50
222. **Halma.** T.S.L. Circa 1900s. Classic, Board Game. 30
223. **Happy Families.** Chad Valley Games. Circa 1900. Card Game. 30
224. **Happy Families.** Anonymous, U. K. Circa 1900. Social, Card Game. 25
225. **Hazard.** Past Times. © 1995. Board Game. 20
226. **Hide & Seek with Kings of England, Henry IV-Charles I,** A Game. John Jaques. Circa 1870s. History, Card Game. 250
227. **Hide & Seek with Kings of England, William I. & Richard II,** A Game. John Jaques. Circa 1870s. History, Card Game. 250
228. **Highwaymen.** Chad Valley. Circa 1930s. Law & Order, Board Game. 75
229. **International Mail, The.** J. W. Spear. Circa 1895. Communication, Board Game. 125

230. **Jolly Postman, The.** Michael Stanfield. © 1986. Occupations, Card Game. $25
231. **Jolly Snap, The Game of,** (Sports). Anonymous, Circa 1900. Sports, Card Game. 125
232. **Jumping Rabbits.** Glevum. 1920. Animal, Board Game. 75
233. **Junior Motor Race.** Peter Pan Series. Circa 1930s. Sports, Car, Board Game. 50
234. **Kingdoms Europe, The.** John Jaques, London. Circa 1890s. Geography, Card Game. 50
235. **Kings & Queens of England.** Fax-Pax. © 1989. History, Card Game. 25
236. **Knock-Knock.** Chad Valley. Circa 1930s. Ethnic, Card Game. 35
237. **Kon-Tiki.** Spear's Games. © 1964. Historical Board Game. 60
238. **L'Attaque.** H.P. Gibson & Sons, Ltd. © 1916. Military, World War I, Board Game. 150
239. **Laughable Game of What D'ye Buy, The.** Anonymous London. Circa 1846. Economic, Card Game. 400
240. **London Cabbie Game.** Intellect Ltd. © 1971. Travel, Car, Board Game. 50
241. **Lord Calvert Game.** Lord Calvert Coffee House. © 1900. Advertising, Card Game. 50
242. **Manufactures of the Counties of England.** J. Passmore, © 1842. Geography, Board Game. 900
243. **Market, or Convent Garden.** Kum-Bak M Co. London. Circa 1940s. Economic, Card Game. 50
244. **Mickey and the Beanstalk Card Game.** Pepys. Circa 1930s. Disney, Card Game. 40
245. **Mickey Mouse Ludo.** Chad Valley. Circa 1930s. Disney, Board Game. 150
246. **Millionaire.** Wm. Sessions Ltd. Circa 1930s. Economic, Board Game. 125
247. **Money Game, The, Book & Game,** by N. Angeil. Dent & Sons, London. © 1928. Economic, Board Game. 100
248. **Monopoly.** John Waddington. Circa 1970s. Economic, Board Game. 50
249. **My Word.** Waddington. Circa 1970s. Word, Card Game. 20
250. **National Gallery Card Game.** National Gallery. © 1987. Art, Card Game. 20
251. **National Gallery, The.** Jaques & Son, London. Circa 1890s. Art, Card Game. 70
252. **Naturalist, The.** E. Wallis, London. 1820. Animal, Board Game. 1000
253. **New and Elegant Game of Birds and Beasts.** William Darton. 1821. Animal, Board Game. 1000
254. **New Game Spring Heeled Jack, The.** Novelty Passing Co. Circa 1900. Board Game. 100
255. **New Moral and Entertaining Game of the Reward of Merit.** John Harris. 1801. Educational, Board Game. 1200
256. **Old West from A to Z, The.** Fax-Pax. © 1992. Western, Card Game. 20
257. **On Spec, The Game of.** J. Jacques, London. Circa 1920s. Stock Market, Card Game. 40
258. **Oscar.** Perry & Co. © 1949. Movie, Board Game. 150
259. **Patchesi, The Game of.** J. Jaques & Sons, London. Circa 1870s. Classic, Board Game. 150
260. **Paths and Burrows, The World of Beatrix Potter.** Traditional Games. © 1988. Literary, Board Game. 75

United Kingdom continued

261. Piccadilly, The New Game of. G.W. & Co. Circa 1920s. Board Game. $75

262. Picturesque Round Game of the Produce & Manufactures of the Counties of England. J. Passmore, London. © 1842. Geography Board Game. 1000

263. Pilgrim's Progress Game. Castell Bros. © 1943. Religious, Card Game. 35

264. Plantit. Garden Game. Geographia. 1935. Plant, Board Game. 40

265. Pop Game of Monte Carlo. Mahco Line. Circa 1920s. Board Game. 45

266. Queen Mary. Harlesden Games. Circa 1930s. Travel, Sea, Board Game. 75

267. Raise the Titanic. Withdrawn from sale early. Hoyle. 1987. Travel, Sea, Board Game. 50

268. Really Nasty Horse Racing Game, The. Upstarts. © 1989. Sports, Horse Racing, Board Game. 35

269. Rich Uncle. Red-brown cover. Waddington. © 1946. Stock Market, Board Game. 60

270. Road Race Game. Fairylite. Circa 1930s. Travel, Land, Board Game. 75

271. Road to the Temple of Honour and Fame, The. John Harris. 1810. Educational, Board Game. 1200

272. Round Britain. Pepys. Circa 1950s. Geography, Card Game. 35

273. Royal and Most Pleasant Game of Y Goose. John Overton. 1660. Animal, Board Game. 1500

274. Royal Game of British Sovereigns, The. Wallis, London. Circa 1820s. History, Board Game. 1000

275. Royal Game of Ur. Merit. Circa 1960s. Classic, Board Game. 50

276. Royalle Pass-Tyme of Cupid, The. A game of snake. John Garrett. 1690. Classic, Board Game. 1500

277. Rush Hour. Universal Pub. London. Circa 1930s. Travel, Card Game. 35

278. Save the President! J. Jaffee. © 1994. Political, Board Game. 25

279. Science is Sport or Pleasures of Astronomy. Wallis, London. Circa 1803. Space, Board Game. 1500

280. Scoop. England. 1920s. Card Game. 35

281. Scoop! The Game. Publish Your Own Newspaper. Waddington. © 1955. Communications Board Game. 65

282. Scramble, Air Battle Game. Vic-Toy. Circa 1970s. Military, Board Game. 35

283. Scripture Cards. J. Moore. Circa 1790s. Religious, Card Game. 250

284. Seaside Frolics. Halcyon Games Ltd. © 1987. Travel, Board Game. 45

285. Secret Agent. English version of G-Men. Parker, UK. 1945. Law & Order, Board Game. 65

286. Shuffled Symphonies. Pears Soap. Circa 1930s. Disney, Adventure, Card Game. 35

287. Snap, Game of. Milk Premium, Variant. Cow & Gate. Circa 1930s. Premium, Card Game. 35

288. Snap, Game of. Milk Food Premium. Cow & Gate. Circa 1930s. Premium, Card Game. 35

289. Snow White and the Seven Dwarfs. Pepys. Circa 1940s. Disney, Card Game. 25

290. Soccer Pontoon. Soccer Pontoon Syn, London. Pat 1938. Sports, Card Game. $65

291. Speed Card Game. Pepys. © 1946. Travel, Road, Card Game. 35

292. Spy Ring, International Spy Game. J. Waddington. © 1965. Spy, Board Game. 50

293. Station to Station. Chad Valley. 1918. Travel, Rail, Board Game. 75

294. Tabula, The Roman Game. Oxford Games. © 1990. Classic, Board Game. 20

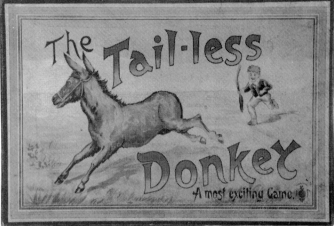

295. Tail-Less Donkey, The. Globe Series of Games. Circa 1900s. Animal, Skill Game. 45

296. Tour of Britain. Waddington. © 1978. Geography, Card Game. 25

297. Tour of Knowledge. Waddington. © 1978. History, Card Game. 25

298. Tour of London. Waddington. © 1979. Geography, Card Game. 25

299. Tour Through Europe, A. John Betts, London. Circa 1850. Geography, Board Game with teetotum. 1100

300. Touring Scotland. Geophia Ltd. Circa 1950s. Geography, Board Game. 50

301. Transport. H. P. Gibson & Sons, Ltd. Circa 1930s. Travel, Card Game. 35

302. Tweedledum. Gibson Games. © 1989. Literary, Board Game. 75

303. Victory, New War Game. Tonknousin. Circa 1910s. Military, World War I, Board Game. 150

303b. Voyage Through the Clouds, A. Zeppelin cover and metal playing pieces. Spear for U.K. market. Circa 1900s. Travel, Board Game. 1500

304. Wallis's Elegant and Instructive Game, Wonders of Art. Edward Wallis. 1818. Art, Board Game. 1000

305. Wallis's New Geographical Game. John Wallis. © 1802. Geographical, Board Game. 1000

306. Wild West. Pepys. Circa 1950s. Western, Card Game. 30

307. Winkle's Wedding. Chad Valley. Circa 1930s. Social, Card Game. 50

279

145

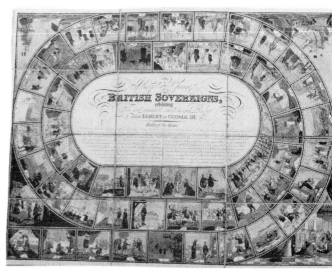

124

274

201

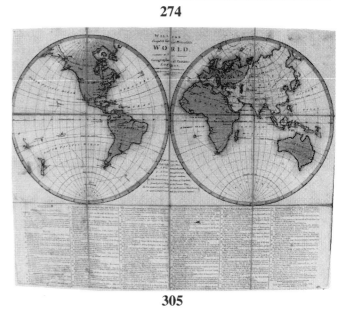

305

THE AGES OF AMERICAN GAMES

American game production, which started in colonial times, mirrors history in an astonishing way. Every major and significant change in American life has been captured in games. Games in the nineteenth century were largely religious in nature, revealing strong moral values. This influence declined as modern America emerged onto the world scene. Every American war has been documented in games along with the political and economic stresses associated with war-time. By the turn of the nineteenth century, the number of different games being manufactured was at an all time high. High production continued into the first decade but economic conditions then slowed game production. The economics of America entered into the equation resulting in a leaner and savvier game industry. An increase in leisure time among the working class corresponded with an increased interest in games. This has grown through the twentieth century with staggering results. Out of the depths of the Depression **Monopoly** became the largest selling game in history with millions of copies sold. Early production of TV games in the 1950s also resulted in millions sold. Today game companies are at an all time high and so are sales.

The ages of American games can be divided into five segments, the last two running concurrently. The first, the Early Age, saw the development of card and board games from the colonial period to post-centennial America. The Golden Age comprises the pinnacle of game art and with it American games as an art form. The Silver Age, spanning the World War years, realized the idea that playability as well as art were important factors in games. The Modern Age followed America's love of television and resulted in the vicarious television game, usually child-oriented. Action games and games about social concerns also gained popularity during the Modern Age. Close on its heels, Simulation and Role-Playing games were developed for the young adult and adult.

The Early Age of American Games (1744-1880)

The first American game was the colonial card game **Der Frommen Lotterie**. Produced in 1744 by Christoph Sauer for the Pennsylvania Dutch community in Germantown, the game taught Bible verses. This card game was probably patterned after a German prototype.

During the early Federal period, American games followed English prototypes. Card games such as **Conversations** and board games such as **Reward of Virtue** and **Mansion of Happiness** were redesigned and reprinted by American printers and booksellers. Early Age game manufacturing can be divided into two categories: card and board games. The preponderance of the former in the pre-Civil War era and Reconstruction period is striking: 437 card games and fewer than 88 different type board games are known to exist.

America saw little game production in the years immediately following the nationwide financial panic of 1837, during which ninety percent of the Eastern factories had closed. Hard times continued until the depression ended in 1843, when board games with purely American content started to appear. Three such games were W & S. B. Ives', **The National Game of National Eagle**, L. Burge's, **American Revolution**, and L. I. Cohen's, **The National Game of Star Spangled Banner**. In 1843, Ms. Abbot invented and Ives produced the card game **Dr. Busby**. This was one of the most successful games of the mid-nineteenth century. A. A. Smith developed the greatest game craze of all in 1861 with **Authors**. This card game became one of the most played and printed games in the later 19th century, and is still played today. **Authors** was so popular that almost every game company had to have a version of the game in its line.

John McLoughlin started a fine game company in New York City in the early 1850s and by the Civil War his brother had joined him to create McLoughlin Bros. This company went on to create some of today's most sought after and collected games.

In 1860 Milton Bradley, after being primarily a game distributor, developed his famous game, **The Checkered Game of Life**, which was very popular throughout the Civil War. Bradley had a small but steady line of board games and a larger line of card games during the later Victorian era.

Card games continued to predominate during the Reconstruction and Indian Wars period (1865-1880). West and Lee produced a small series of popular card games during the 1870s including an attractive game called **Society**, which depicted American life in card form. West & Lee's successors, Noyes, Snow & Co., continued the tradition. This early age of games saw the emergence and development of the American game.

The Golden Age of American Games (1880 - 1913)

The blossoming of the Golden Age of American games started in the late 1870s, but full bloom was not achieved until the 1890s. With the development of chromolithography, a multicolor printing process, game producers jumped at the opportunity to make large, colorful game boxes and boards. The last decade of the nineteenth century saw some of the most exquisite games ever produced in the world.

McLoughlin Brothers was the king of games at this time. In the 1870s, the company produced colorful wood-sided boards in a bookshelf game series, but by the 1890s had switched primarily to production of chromolithographic game covers. McLoughlin Brothers early on realized that very colorful and artistic covers would sell games. Publishing colorful books in addition to producing games, McLoughlin Brothers had many color plates available that they used over time and again.

George Parker as a young man in Salem, Massachusetts developed the game **Banking** in 1883 and started one of the most successful game companies. His company became an even stronger competitor in 1888 after his brother Charles joined the firm. Parker Brothers quickly established itself as a producer of games with good graphics and fine playability.

Various other game manufacturers, such as Singer and Ottman, were producing smaller fine quality games. Bliss also manufactured games, often with wood components, but they are scarce on today's market. Chaffee & Selchow produced an exceptional series of large-board, colorful and gilded games in the late 1890s. Their games rivaled Mcloughlin's best. The same rise in quality was seen in card games. McLoughlin Bros. led the field with their multicolored card pictures and beautifully illustrated boxes.

During the Golden Age it seemed that each manufacturer wanted to outdo the other, but the bubble burst at the turn of the century. By 1905 both Singer and R. Bliss had stopped manufacturing games; Chaffee & Selchow was gone; Ottman had virtually ceased production. McLoughlin was struggling financially and, except for a few standouts, their quality was declining. Parker Bros. traversed the turn of the century well and was forging ahead into new development and innovation. Suddenly, Parker was the new giant expanding its horizons from Salem to New York and then to London.

Milton Bradley also had entered the picture in a large way by the turn of the century. They produced an inexpensive line of games with less dramatic covers than those of other Golden Age companies. Bradley's games showed a decline in both quality of artwork and production. However, the games were priced right for the period and sold well for the company. Many of Milton Bradley's popular games continued to be produced for a period of twenty years or more unchanged. The result today is that their games tend to be more common than their counterparts.

Competition in the industry was stiff and by 1920 McLoughlin Bros. sold out its game line to Milton Bradley. With the great McLoughlin Bros. departed, the Golden Age was at an end.

The Silver Age of American Games: (1915 - 1945)

The Silver Age of American games coincides with the beginning of World War I, and culminates with the Japanese signing of the peace treaty on the USS Missouri in 1945. This period saw the most devastating economic shifts in world history. Game making realized vast changes in production, style, art, and new innovative game play. The old giant McLoughlin died and the new giants, Parker Brothers and Milton Bradley, reached new heights.

Many companies arose to challenge the giants. Included among the challengers were All-Fair, known for snappy names, good quality, and timely subjects, and Noble-Stoll-Einson group, who developed a reputation for producing literary games. Selchow & Righter, an old standard, by the 1920s produced colorful, fun, and playable games. Smith, Kline & French, a short-lived company, produced an innovative line of games. Wilder, a large game company from the Midwest, produced a line of games that followed Mcloughlin in art style with colorfully painted covers. Zulu Toy Co. of Chicago produced a few excellent games. Russell, primarily a card game manufacturer, entered the game later with line drawing covers. Embossing Co. produced an innovative line of games with die-cut wood pieces. Henriksen Mfg. Co., along with Willis G. Young, created a series of games in thin and narrow cardboard boxes.

The later newcomers of the deep Depression and subsequent recovery included Rosebud Art, known for its generally inexpensive line of two- or three-color boxed games. Whitman was known for very colorful boxed games with little substance inside. They also produced a multitude of comics related games including many Dis-

ney card games. Transogram, a small company, along with Pressman, Gabriel, Saalfield, and Cadaco-Ellis came onto the scene and tried to challenge. Jim Prentice and his Electric Game Co. produced games that were certainly forerunners to the printed circuit with batteries and lights.

Several companies began game production at the beginning of and during World War II. Corey Game Company produced very colorful games in large formats, and many of their games were oriented to the war in progress. American Toy Works created colorful large format games many created by Arthur Dritz. Dritz also created games for other Long Island game companies such as Game Makers and Vitaplay Toy Co. Toy Creations were known for their patriotic games during the war. Master Toy Co., Craig-Hopkins & Co., and Advance Games, all from New York, produced games that are prized by collectors today. Not one of these companies outlasted the War.

During the Silver Age, box production changed from a single four-color sheet top to four-, three- and even two-color cover wrap-around box tops; apron graphics increased. Separate boards rather than bottom of the box boards became the norm. Inside build-ups became standard. Art Deco permeated game design. Comic character games were everywhere and mostly by the innovation of Milton Bradley. New game topics mirrored the exciting new phenomena of the time: radio, flight in every aspect, speed, movies, and the Depression and World War II.

During the depths of the Depression, Monopoly, the most popular American game of all time, appeared on the retail marketplace. Originally developed from **The Landlord's Game**, patented by Elizabeth J. Magie (Phillips) in 1904, it became known as **Monopoly** after 1910. The game gained popularity on the college scene. It was copied and recopied by individuals who would localize the place names found in the game. Charles Darrow copied his game from a group of Quakers in Atlantic City. He attempted to sell it to Parker Brothers who initially declined the game. Darrow finally produced it himself and introduced his game at the Philadelphia Wanermakers Department Store. **Monopoly** sold so well that Parker Brothers purchased the game the next year. Parker personalized it with the great and popular Rich Uncle Pennybags character.

The **Monopoly** craze resulted in a number of similar games from other companies. Milton Bradley produced **Easy Money**; Transogram made **Big Business**; and Finance Games produced **Finance**. Game makers had finally realized that the public would buy and play new games designed for adults and older children, with more intricate play. The Silver Age reflected the United States and its coming of age.

Modern Age of Games (1946-1999)

The seeds of television games began germinating in the Twenties when Milton Bradley began licensing and using comic characters in games. Milton Bradley became the master of the licensed character. By the late 1930s, Whitman was also successfully licensing top comic and radio characters. Parker Brothers, Bradley, and Whitman were licensing movies beginning in the mid-1930s. Quiz shows were made into games, but it was with the emergence of TV that the nature of games changed. Except for the old standbys by the big manufacturers, television games became the norm.

The television craze began in 1950 when Milton Bradley produced the popular **Hopalong Cassidy** game. Robert Whitman, founder of Bettye-B Company, was one of the first game manufactures to license a TV game show with **Masquerade Party**. By 1955, some twelve game companies were producing TV games, the peak number of companies at any time since. Lowell Toy of New York City was one of the first and most prolific producers of TV games. In the mid-1950s they produced **Beat the Clock, Groucho's You Bet Your Life**, and **What's My Line** among their TV titles. Lowell's distribution was not as good as others during this period, resulting in the fact that they are scarcer today. Transogram entered the TV game business in 1955 with one of the most popular TV shows, **Dragnet**. They became, along with Milton Bradley, one of the most prolific producers of TV games. George E. Mousley, a small company from Rhode Island, made some rare TV games in 1956 including **Fury** and **The Count of Monte Christo**. Ideal Toy Corporation, a giant in the toy industry, entered the game market in the early 1960s. They produced TV Games from 1963 to the late 1970s, including **The Addams Family, Dr. Kildare**, and **Bullwinkle and Rocky**. Both Game Gems, a division of T. Cohn Inc., and Standard Toycraft Inc. produced good but scarce TV Games during the 1960s. Cadaco-Ellis, Kohner Brothers, Pressman Toy Co, Dexter Wayne, Lizbeth Whiting, Knickerbocker Plastic, Marx, Ed-U-Cards, Remco, Hasbro, Sears, and Parks Plastic all licensed TV games. The newer TV Game companies in the 1980s and 1990s were Apple Street, Reiss Games, Cardinal, and Warren. From the Fifties to the present, over 300 television games were produced. The popularity peaked for the ten-year period from 1955-65. TV games remain a mainstay in game collecting today.

A multitude of action games began production by the mid-1960s. **Mouse Trap**, released in 1963 by Ideal, became an overnight sensation. Designer Marvin Glass originally offered **Mouse Trap** to Ideal as a toy. Sid Sackson was responsible for converting Glass's design to a game. Other popular action games included Milton Bradley's **Operation** and **Ker Plunk** from Ideal. Plastic objects became the mainstay in action games and are still manufactured in large quantities.

In the early 1970s many small entrepreneurs invented games of social relevance in tune with the political unrest in the United Stares. Many of these games are scarce today and are beginning to be collected. Along with them were games that portrayed the many avenues of American life. Farming games, trucking games, games about lawyers and politicians were all manufactured. The sexual revolution and politics were both the subjects of games. Political spoof games are popular to collect now.

Anti-Monopoly, a game produced in the late 1960s, was the subject of a lawsuit over the name "monopoly." During the dispute the game had to be called merely **Anti-,** but the company won and Anti-Monopoly was made again. This lawsuit has resulted in many **Monopoly** look alikes. Parker Brothers has now realized its great potential and is marketing Monopoly and Rich Uncle Pennybags with McDonalds, many off-shoot games, and licensing various **Monopoly** games. This is a potential great new collectible game category for the future.

Smaller but still popular collecting areas include games about cities and towns. These games started for the most part in the 1970s and were used by local chambers of commerce for fund-raising. This type of game has gained popularity with the general public. It has now overflowed to the production of university and college games. The overall pattern is a **Monopoly-**type game with the local known habitats as visiting spaces.

Simulation and Role-Playing Games (1958-1999)

Simultaneously, another game phenomenon was emerging as television games were blossoming. The simulation game began with Charles Roberts and his Avalon Hill Game Co. In 1958 he launched the company with a small group of war games that he developed into his now large line of simulation games. His early games were patterned after some World War II games, using a square grid field and various playing pieces. Roberts deviated from these earlier games and produced variable cardboard playing pieces. With **Gettysburg** he superimposed the historical situation, creating the simulation game. These games were popular, and the innovative hexagonal game board provided even greater challenges for players. No simulation games were made in great quantity like the mass-media games but their popularity has increased year after year; the new simulation game titles are now produced in the many hundreds per year. A big press run from these smaller companies might have been two thousand copies. The target audience was an older clientele and thus a far higher proportion of the games has survived.

Simulation games differ from their mass-media game counterparts in that they were often offered without boxes and instead sold in plastic ziplock bags. Maps were often found unmounted and playing pieces were made of laminated and die-cut cardboard. Most of these games have a dual value that is collectibility and playability. Collectors go for games they remember or are enticed into a game that has a reputation for high simulation.

Role-playing games can be divided into fantasy, science fiction, superheroes, espionage, and historical games. **Dungeons and Dragons**, a fantasy game introduced by TSR in 1973, was followed by thousands of off-shoots of its role-playing concept. A new and strong game craze, collectible card games, has developed alongside these role-playing games. This started with Wizards of the Coast's extremely popular **Magic the Gathering** game. The more rare and unusual cards one can amass, the more proficient and better player one can become. The search for the rarer cards has created this current phenomenon.

These two game categories, simulation and role-playing, have developed a strong following with large conventions devoted to the games and there play.

Collecting Games

Game collecting is a hobby which has seen enormous growth in the last ten years. It has become a new and widely accepted pastime. There are several rules of thumb that novice game collectors should familiarize themselves with before encountering the chutes and ladders of the hobby.

One of the important concerns for game enthusiasts is the buying or trading of unseen games from auctions or fixed price lists, or through correspondence via e-mail, mail or phone. Grading is then very important to the

buyer. The grading of games is, at best, subject to one's own individual opinions. So many factors come into play that a single grade can never truly tell the story.

Dealers and collectors, however, have set down guidelines. The standard grades for games break down as follows: Mint, Near Mint, Excellent, Very Good, Good, Fair, and Poor. The box exterior, the colors, the box interior, completeness, and the condition of the pieces are all factors that determine the grading of games. Paper and cardboard are the main ingredients in games, but the occasional metal spinner, tokens and wooden tokens must also be judged where grading is concerned. The chart at the end of this chapter provides guidelines to assist the collector in grading games.

Games deteriorate more quickly than other collectibles such as plastic and metal toys, cards, stamps and coins. Boxes flatten, parts are lost, and mildew, water, and light take their toll. Games do not hold up well under ordinary conditions.

A game played only five or six times will usually show decisive wear and even careful storage of games can result in warped boxes or sagged centers. In addition, misplaced game pieces, die, and instructions present continual roadblocks in game collecting. The popular and pricey game, Milton Bradley's **Dark Shadows**, was issued with white plastic fangs to be worn by players. These fangs are rarely found with the game today.

On the positive side, families rarely threw out their games but stored them in attics and basements. As a result, interesting and rare games are always surfacing for sale. This aspect is what allows the hobby to remain exciting and fresh. Primarily, it is a hobby still in its infancy and it is not uncommon to find a game that no expert ever knew to exist.

The outside box is the collector's first and prime concern in terms of grading. The points on the corners of the box should be the primary focal point as it is here that the game shows the first signs of wear. From this point, the other areas of the outside box should be examined including the state of the box top graphics. If the box is totally damaged and defaced, it is hardly collectible and a game without a box top is good for playing only. Collectors of early American games will be happy to have just the board and many times it will be hard to find a full deck of cards.

The inside contents of the game are also important. A great box without a board is of very limited value as the board is the foremost collectible component in a game. Even early boards (pre-1940), in and of themselves, have a value. Minor parts missing from inside the box can lessen the value, but major parts missing can devastate game's value to a collector. Items which are unique to a game, such as the scales or special spinner found in the **Game of Justice** by Lowell, can decrease the value of a game significantly if missing. Lack of special metal tokens or punched cardboard graphic images can also lessen the value. Instructions are important in the higher grades, but Xerox copies are often acceptable in the lesser conditions. Remember that you can <u>not</u> play a game without the instructions.

Ways of procuring games can be as vast as your persistence. Toy conventions are one of the best places to purchase games. Here you can see the games and inspect them. This is also true of auctions that you attend. Buying games through magazine and newspaper advertisements can be another avenue. A new phenomenon is buying games on the Internet. Often the games are pictured and graded which helps make decisions in purchasing. A special warning is to know your dealer when you can. Dealers will often be free with information on how and what to collect, and will often find games you might be looking for.

Now that you have some idea of the aspects that are integral to game collecting, investing in reference guides and newsletters will help you go to the head of the class. Rick Polizzi has printed numerous quality books on games including *Spin Again* by Rick Polizzi and Fred Schaefer and his companion book *Baby Boomer Games, Identification and Value Guide*. Desi Scarpone's book *Board Games with Price Guide* and Stephanie Lane and David Diley's *Board Games of the 50s, 60s & 70s* are also useful books. These books are devoted to board games of the fifties, sixties, and the seventies and have good photo illustrations. *American Board Games and their Makers 1822-1992 with Values* by Bruce Whitehill is an excellent companion reference to this book. It explains the historical aspects of game companies and includes many indexes that guide the collector along with an excellent overview of games.

Publications such as these, as well as toy catalogs, continue to create new collectors. The formation of groups devoted to the game cause, such as the Association of Game and Puzzle Collectors, has also helped nurture new enthusiasts.

Association of Game and Puzzle Collectors

In 1985, a diverse group of people who had found each other visiting the now-defunct Game Preserve museum in New Hampshire, digging through piles of games at auctions and flea markets, and answering each other's advertisements for old games, gathered together to form the Association of Game and Puzzle Collectors.

Potential members were contacted using addresses gleaned from Lee and Rally Dennis, owners of The Game Preserve. Under the auspices of founder Bruce Whitehill, a board of advisors developed a framework of purposes and goals. A charter was drawn that created an international organization dedicated to the collection and preservation of American games, and to the research of American game history. Thirty-one charter members gave the AGPC the strength and impetus to hold its first convention only eight months after the organization's inception.

Since its modest beginnings the AGPC has grown steadily. The AGPC is the only international organization for collectors and researchers who share a common interest in the history and preservation of American games. No longer a small haven for collectors of antique American games, the club's members represent individual collectors as well as museums, game manufacturers, publishers, and research institutions. The club's interests have grown to include not only games, but all types of jigsaw puzzles, dexterity puzzles, tops, marbles, tiddley winks, crokinole boards, game and company histories, manufacturing and marketing, and other related topics.

Owning one of the most extensive archives of game-related information, the AGPC offers its members and the public access to over 1800 sets of game rules. The Game Catalog, an all-inclusive listing of known games and their publishers, is a one-of-a-kind documentation of game history and game manufacturers. Copies of game publications, and game catalogs from current, as well as long-gone game and puzzle manufacturers, are available for members and researchers.

Whether your interest is primarily in games, or whether it centers on related pastimes, the AGPC offers many opportunities to network and to broaden your knowledge and your collections. Continuous publication of newsletters and research information keeps members up-to-date on auctions, recent finds, personal collections, exhibitions, and scheduled events of interest, as well as historical research and ongoing study. Classified advertising allows members to buy and sell games and related items within this active club. The annual AGPC convention, which includes seminars, auctions, sales and trading, game playing, and networking with fellow members, offers some of the best opportunities to immerse yourself in game fun and lore. Regional meetings held during the year across the United States allow smaller groups of local collectors to get together and concentrate on specific topics of interest.

Whatever your interest in games, collecting, or history, the AGPC will enhance your knowledge and enjoyment. For membership information contact the AGPC at P. O. Box 44, Dresher, PA 19025, or visit the AGPC web site at www.AGCA.com.

Good research and exposure to game conventions will ensure that the road to collecting will not be a trivial pursuit. Who knows, perhaps you'll even be able to monopolize the games' market without passing go!

Values

The values of games can range from twenty thousand dollars to as little as one or two dollars. Within this vast range, a collector must determine his or her level of collecting. For the most part collectors start with the games they remember from their childhood, or with a category that they enjoy such as Disney games, or military games.

The values presented are for games that have sold over a period of ten years. The values of older games sold have been updated to the current national market. The prices one will encounter can be higher or lower, depending on condition, and circumstances in how one buys. Remember, these values are only a guide and can change. The prices are what a game dealer would ask, not what a dealer would pay. A dealer will usually pay about half the retail value for general games but will pay higher for better quality games.

The values listed in this book are for games in conditions most widely encountered and collected today. The conditions also reveal the various time periods. Collecting Early and Golden Age games, a vast leeway in grades is more accepted and encountered by collectors.

How to use this book

The American game listings start with the Early Age and follow sequentially through the Golden Age, the Silver Age, and the Modern Age. The listings are presented alphabetically by game manufacturer. The game title is listed first, followed by the date or known period each was published. The game category is listed next. Categories relate to the different themes found in the games such as animals, economics, and sports. The type of game (board, card, action, etc.) and the game's U.S. dollar value are listed last. At the end of all the listings an extensive cross-reference of games by category is listed alphabetically for the specialist collector.

The simulation game section is listed under manufacturer, and the role-playing game section is listed alphabetically by category. Collectible card games are listed with values by set, starter box and booster box.

Conditions of Listed Games

Early Age Games are valued in **very good** condition.

Golden Age Games are valued in **very good** condition

Silver Age Games are valued in **near excellent** condition.

Modern Age Games are valued in **excellent** condition.

Simulation Games are in **excellent** condition.

Role-Playing Games are in **excellent** condition.

Modern Games from 1990 on are in **near mint** condition.

Foreign Games are valued as above.

Game Dealers

The following are game dealers I have dealt with and are members of the Association of Game and Puzzle Collectors. They all can be visited at various conventions or through the mail. There are many other fine dealers doing business but these are the ones I have dealt with on a regular basis.

Paul Fink
Fun and Games
P O Box 488
Kent, CT 06757
Phone 860-927-4001
E-mail; gamesandpuzzles@mokawk.net

David Oglesby
57 Lakeshore Dr.
Marlboro, Ma 01752
Phone 508-481-1087
E-mail; Doglesby@shipley.com

Jeff Lowe
5005 Tamara La.
West Des Moines, IA 50265
Phone 515-267-8768
E-mail; gamesguy1@aol.com

Roy and Grace Olsen
PO Box 8232
Radnor, Pa 19087
Phone 610-688-4919

Debbie and Marty Krim
New England Auction Gallery
PO Box 2273
West Peabody, Ma 01960
Phone 978-535-3140
E-mail; dlkrim@star.net

John and Mildred Spear
8336 Millman St.
Chestnut Hill, Pa 19118
Phone 215-247-7112

GAME GRADING GUIDE

	OUTSIDE BOX				INSIDE BOX				COMPONENTS		
	Corners	Edges	Box Top	Aprons	Build Ups	Board Game	Card Game	Die Cuts	Implements	Instructions	
MINT - PRISTINE A game that shows no sign of wear	Mint	Mint	Mint	Mint	Mint	Mint	Mint	Unpunched	Ming	Mint	Complete
NEAR MINT A game that has been played just a few times with little actual wear or deterioration	Slight wear	Slight wear	Superb - not noticeable	Superb	Superb	Superb	Superb	Punched or unpunched	Superb	Superb	Complete
EXCELLENT A game that shows some stress but no discernable problems	Definite wear	Discernible wear	Minor marks + very slight fading OK	Slight bowing	Slight warping OK	Board signs of wear	Card wear	Punched	Can show wear	Can have slight creases	Complete
VERY GOOD Still a collectible game but strong signs of use and deterioration. Collectible in pre-1970 games	Heavy wear	Worn and one or two edges torn	Minor pencil + pen marks. Some fading	Bowing and wear OK	Can be warped	Heavy stress at folds	Cards some slight creases	Punched	Show wear	Slight tears acceptable	Some minor implements can be missing
GOOD A game wtih definite problems and wear. Still very collectible in pre-1960 games	Heavy wear and cracks	Worn and separation	Minor tears, possible fading. Marks	Some split aprons but intact	Signs of deterioration. Tears and creases	Heavy stress at folds	Cards with creases	Punched	Worn	Xerox or copy instructions acceptable	Some implements missing
FAIR Major problems. Collectible in pre-1950 games	Partially crushed	Separation	Tears, fading. Strong marks	Split aprons + separation	Partially crushed	Close to separation	Cards with minor tears	Punched and many missing	Worn and missing	Partial or Missing	Many missing parts
POOR A rough game. Only partially collectible. Collectible in pre-1940 games	Crushed	Separation	Tears, heavy marks + fading	Torn. Some separate + missing	Missing or crushed	Partial separation	Tears and missing	Most missing	Broken or missing	Missing	Most implements missing

EARLY GAMES

Charles Ackerman
308. Goose, The. Game of. © 1855. Animal,
Board game. $800

Josiah Adams
309. Errand Boy, The; or Jack at All Trades. © 1845.
Communications, Card game. 500

309a. Game of Kings, The. ©1845 instruction book
white cards, History, Card game. 400

310. Game of Kings, The. © 1846. History, Card game,
yellow cards. 400

310a. Game of Kings, The. Date 1845 on instructions
book, yellow cards, flap pouch box, Card game. 400

311. Kings of France, The Game of the. Circa 1845.
History, Card game. 500

312. New World, A Game Of American History, The.
© 1845. History, Card game. 500

313. Romance of American History, The. Circa 1845.
History, Card game. 600

314. Young Traveler, or Geographical Cards. © 1846.
Geography, Card game. 500

Adams & Co.
315. Bobbing Around. Circa 1860s. Miscellaneous,
Card game. 150

316. Bottle Imp, The. Circa 1860s. Social, Card game. 150

317. Chopped-Up Monkey, The. Circa 1860s. Animal,
Card game. 200

318. Christmas Pudding. Circa 1860s. Holiday,
Card game. 250

319. Colored Fires. Circa 1860s. Social, Card game. 150

320. Eskimo. Circa 1860s. Ethnic, Card game. 200

321. Feast of Flowers, A Floral Game of Fortune.
Circa 1860s. Plant, Card game. 250

322. Forced Confessions. Circa 1860s. Social, Card
game. 150

323. Fun Alive. Circa 1860s. Social, Card game. 150

**324. Go-Bang, Japanese Verandah Game, Tay-Bang
Slam-Bang.** Circa 1860s. Combination,
Board game. 750

325. House That Jack Built. Circa 1860s. Nursery
Rhymes, Card game. 200

326. Humorous Authors. © 1868. Literary,
Card game. $200

327. Japanese Scintillities, or Parlor Fireworks.
Circa 1860s. Social, Card game. 150

328. Joker's Bond, The. Circa 1860s. Social,
Card game. 150

329. K K K, Komical Konversation Kards. © 1856.
Social, Card game. 175

330. Lively Monkey, The. Circa 1860s. Animal,
Card game. 200

331. Love Chase. Circa 1860s. Social, Card game. 150

332. Match & Catch. Circa 1860s. Romance, Card
game. 150

333. Mixed Pickles. Circa 1860s. Plant, Card game. 200

**334. Most Laughable Thing on Earth, The, or A Trip
to Paris.** Circa 1860s. Geography, Card game. 150

335. Oliver Twist. Circa 1860s. Literary, Card game. 175

336. Popping the Questions. Circa 1860s. Social,
Card game. 175

337. Santa Claus' Magical Box. Circa 1860s.
Holidays, Card game. 250

338. Shakespearean Oracle, The. Circa 1860s.
Literary, Card game. 200

339. Squails. Circa 1860s. Skill, Card game. 150

340. Squirming Fish, The. Circa 1860s. Animal,
Card game. 150

341. Three Merry Men. Circa 1860s. Reading, Social,
Card game. 200

342. Tom Thumb's Comical Fortune Teller.
Circa 1860s. Mystic, Card game. 150

343. Trade and Dicker. Circa 1860s. Economic,
Card game. 175

344. Trip to Paris, A. © 1865. Reading, Card game. 150

345. Tumble Down Dick. Circa 1860s. Action,
Board game. 150

346. Which Is the Largest? Circa 1860s. Q & A,
Card game. 175

347. Wizard's Pack of Playing Cards, The. Circa
1860s. Mystic, Card game. 150

348. Zarofiel (author Harriet Adams). Circa 1860s.
Card game. 200

David Allison
**349. Geography and Amusement or Geographical
Cards.** Circa 1800's. Geography, Card game. 500

350. Geography and Entertainment. Circa 1800.
Geography, Card game. 500

Amsden & Co.
351. Three Merry Men. © 1865. Reading, Card game. $175
352. Trip to Paris. © 1857. Reading, Card game. 150

Andrus & Starr
353. Conversation Cards. Circa 1810s. Social,
Card game. 500

Anonymous
354. Boston Game of Authors. © 1850. Literary,
Card game. 300
355. Buried Cities. Circa 1850s. History, Card game. 400
356. Conversation Cards. Large Cards. Circa
1810-15. Social, Card game. 250
357. Conversation Cards. Small Cards. Circa
1810-15. Social, Card game. 250
358. Fortress, The Game of. Circa 1850s. Military,
Board game. 1500
359. Gifts, Uses and Consequences, Game of. Circa
1850s. Social, Card game. 500
360. History for Young and Old, Games of. Circa
1829. History, Card game. 500
**361. Improved and Illustrated Game of Dr. Fuzby,
The.** Circa 1845-50. Social, Card game. 300
362. Laughable Game of What D'ye Buy, The.
Circa 1845-6. Economic, Card game. 500
363. Merry Goose Game, The. Circa 1850s. Nursery
Rhymes, Card game. 400
364. Musical Garlands and Landscape Alphabet.
Circa 1850s. Plant & Musical, Card game. 500
365. Our Army, A Solders Game. © 1863. Military,
Civil War, Card game. 1000
366. Sociable Snake, The Game of the. Circa1830s.
History, Board game. 1200

Anonymous (McLoughlin)
367. Merry Game of Old Maid, The. Hand painted
cards, cover. Circa 1860s. Classic, Card game. 600

D. Appleton & Co.
368. Flower Game, The © 1857. Plant, Card game. 400
369. Pocket Chess-Board, The © 1858. Classic, Board
game. 400

J. P. Beach
370. Jolly Game of Goose, The. © 1851. Animal,
Board game. 800

A. C. Beaman
371. Sabbath School Cards. © 1850. Religious,
Card game. 400

S. Beman
372. New York Counting Cards, The. Circa 1841.
Numbers, Card game. 250

Bence & Recother
**373. Snip, Snap, Snorum, New and Illustrated, Game
of.** Circa 1850s. Social, Card game. $350

Blakeman & Mason
**374. House of Washington and the Palace of Santa
Claus, The.** Circa 1870s. History, Block game. 1500
375. King's of England & House that Jack Built, The.
Circa 1863. History, Block game. 1000
**376. (Rabbit) that Lived in the Garden of Flowers,
The.** Circa 1860s. Plant, Animal, Board game. 1200

Bliss
377. Snap Dragon. Circa 1870s. Social, Board game. 300

Milton Bradley & Co.
378. American Jack Straws. Circa 1870s. Classic,
Skill game. 150
379. Authors Improved. © 1872. Literary, Card game. 150
380. Backgammon, Japanese. © 1870. Classic, Board
game. 150
381. Bamboozle, Game of. © 1872. Strategy, Board
game. 300
382. Checkered Game of Life, The. © 1866. Social,
Board game, beige and red squares. 250
382a. Checkered Game of Life, The. Circa 1870s,
Blue and red squares. 200
383. Figaro, Game of. Circa 1872. Music, Card game. 200
384. I Down Know. Circa 1860s. Social, Card game. 175
385. Japhet Jenkins & Sally Jones Visit to Boston.
Circa 1868. Reading, Card game. 150
386. Magic Squares and Mosaic Tablets. © 1869.
Mystic, Card game. 150
387. Modern Hieroglyphics. © 1868. Mystic, Card
game. 150
388. Nationalia. Circa 1872. Geography, Card game. 175
389. Poetical Pot Pie, or Aunt Hilda's Courtship. ©
1868. Literary, Card game. 150
390. Popular Characters From Dickens. Circa 1872.
Literary, Card game. 175
391. Queen's Guards. © 1873. History, Card game. 175
392. Round the World. © 1873. Geography, Board
game. 500
**393. Sam Slick From Weathersfield to Paris and the
Great Exposition, The Travels of.** © 1871.
Geography, Card game. 150
**394. Scripture Game, or Who Knows? (by Mrs.
J. Thurber).** © 1869. Religious, Card game. 150
395. Sequences, The Game of. Circa 1872. Card game. 150
396. Squails. © 1877. Skill, Card game. 150
397. Visit to the Gypsies. Circa 1870s. Mystic,
Card game. 175
**398. What is it or the Way to Make Money, The
Game.** Circa 1869-73. Economic, Card game. 250
399. Words and Sentences, Game of, Early Edition.
Circa 1870s. Word, Card game. 150
400. Words and Sentences, Game of. Circa 1870s.
Word, Card game. 125

D. B. Brooks & Brother
401. Quack Doctor, Game of. Circa 1850s. Animal,
Card game. 350

Brown & Co.
402. New Centennial Game! A Trip to Philadelphia.
© 1876. Social, Card game. $200

Brown, Taggert, and Chase
402a. The Game of Coquette and Her Suitors.
© 1858. Social, Board game. 1800

L. Burge
403. New Game of American Revolution, The.
© 1844. History, Military, American Revolution,
Board game. 2000

J. G. Chandler
404. Laughable Game of What D'ye Buy, The. Black
cover. Circa 1845. Economic, Card game. 400

H. G. Clarke & Co.
405. Mixed Pickles. © 1850. Plant, Card game. 350

Claxton, Remsen & Finger
406. Authors, The New Game of. Circa 1850s.
Literary, Card game. 200
407. Courtship and Marriage, The Game of. Circa
1850s. Romance, Card game. 200
408. Familiar Quotations, The Game of. Circa 1850s.
Literary, Card game. 225
409. Great Events, The Game of. Circa 1850s. History,
Card game. 250
410. Great Truths, The Game of. Circa 1850s.
Literary, Card game. 200
411. Shakespearean Game, The. Circa 1850s. Literary,
Card game. 250
412. Stratford Game of Characters and Quotations.
Circa 1850s. Literary, Card game. 200

L. I. Cohen & Co.
413. National Game of the Star Spangled Banner,
Geographical Historical Tour Through the
United States and Canada. © 1844. History,
Board game. $2000

William Crosby
414. Races, The Game of the. © 1844. Sport, HR,
Board game. 1800
415. Strife of Genius, By a Lady. © 1844. Social,
Card game. 500

Crosby & Nichols
416. Fanny Gray. © 1845. Paper dolls. 150

Crosby, Nichols-Saxon
417. Robinson Crusoe and His Man Friday © 1845.
Literary, Card game. 1000

Davis, Porter & Co.
418. Happy Family, A New Illustrated Game of the.
Circa 1860s. Social, Card game. 200

E. A. Day & Co.
419. Tipsy Philosophers, or Language Game of
Words Bewitched. © 1859. Literary, Card game. 200

Degen, Estes & Co.
420. Card Dominoes. Circa 1860s. Classic, Card
game. 150
421. Patriot Heroes. Circa 1860s. History, Card game. 350
422. Puck's Portfolio. © 1866. Literary, Card game. 200

A. A. Dugan
423. Railroad Game or Clear the Track. © 1851.
Travel, Rail, Board game. 2500

Edson C. Eastman
424. Commanders of Our Forces, The. Circa 1862-4.
Military, Civil War, Card game. 1000
425. Historical Topics. © 1879. History, Card game. 250
426. Planting, The Game of. © 1865. Plants,
Card game. 350

A. J. Fisher, Publisher
427. Artists. Circa 1860s. Art, Card game. 200
428. Authors. Circa 1860s. Literary, Card game. 150
429. Beauties of Mythology. Circa 1860s. Literary,
Card game. 200
430. Birds, Fact & Fables about. Circa 1860s.
Animals, Birds, Card game. 200
431. Cats & Mice. Circa 1860s. Animal, Card game. 175
432. Combinique. Circa 1860s. Combo, Card game. 150
433. Fashionable Boarding House, The Game of.
Circa 1860s. Social, Card game. 250
433. Heroines of History. Circa 1860s. History,
Card game. 400
435. Intelligence Office, Game of an. © 1874.
Miscellaneous, Card game. 200
436. Jack and the Bean Stalk. Circa 1860s. Nursery
Rhymes, Card game. 200

A. J. Fisher, Publisher, continued
437. Matrimonial Bureau. © 1874. Social,
Card game. $200
438. Merry Foxes. Circa 1860s. Animal, Card game. 200
439. Musical Composers. Circa 1860s. Music,
Card game. 250
440. Old Maid. Circa 1860s. Classic, Card game. 200
441. Old Woman Who Lived in a Shoe. Circa 1860s.
Nursery Rhymes, Card game. 200
442. Puss in the Corner. Circa 1860s. Animal,
Board game. 1000
443. Snake Game. Circa 1860s. Political, Board game. 1000
444. Studies from Shakespeare. Circa 1874. Literary,
Card game. 250
445. Verbilude. Circa 1860s. Word, Card game. 150

G. W. Fisher
446. New Military Game, The. © 1859. Military,
Card game. 1000

Fisher & Denison
447. Chameleonoscope. © 1870. Strategy, Card game. 150
448. Moorish Fort, Game of the. © 1870. Military,
Board game. 400
449. Railway Traffic, Game of. © 1870. Travel, Rail,
Board game. 500

A. Flanagan Co.
449. Auctioneer, (© D. Eckley Hunter). © 1866.
Economic, Card game. 350
451. Banker, (© D. Eckley Hunter). © 1866.
Economic, Card game. 400
452. Biographer, (© D. Eckley Hunter). © 1866.
Literary, Card game. 350
453. Chronographer, (© D. Eckley Hunter). © 1866.
History, Card game. 350
454. Chronologist, (© D. Eckley Hunter). © 1866.
Time, Card game. 350
455. Double Snap, (© D. Eckley Hunter) © 1866.
Action, Card game. 250
456. Fortune Teller, (© D. Eckley Hunter). © 1866.
Mystic, Card game. 250
457. Historian, (© D. Eckley Hunter). © 1866.
History, Card game. 350
458. Librarian, (© D. Eckley Hunter). © 1866.
Literary, Card game. 350
459. Patriot, (© D. Eckley Hunter). © 1866. History,
Card game. 400
460. Philosopher, (© D. Eckley Hunter). © 1866.
History, Card game. 350
461. Recitation, (© D. Eckley Hunter). © 1866.
Miscellaneous, Card game. 300
462. Schoolmaster, (© D. Eckley Hunter). © 1866.
Education, Card game. 300
463. Sentiment, (© D. Eckley Hunter). © 1866. Social,
Card game. 250
464. Sentimental Biographer, (© D. Eckley Hunter).
© 1866. Literary, Card game. 350
465. Snap, (© D. Eckley Hunter). © 1866. Action,
Card game. 200

466. Statesman, (© D. Eckley Hunter). © 1866.
History, Card game. $375
467. Statesman, Variant, (© D. Eckley Hunter).
© 1866. History, Card game. 375
468. War, (© D. Eckley Hunter). © 1866. Military,
Card game. 350
469. War, Variant, (© D. Eckley Hunter). © 1866.
Military, Card game. 350

C. S. Francis & Co.
**470. Interrogatory Geographical Game of the World,
W.G. Evans.** © 1830. Geography, Card game. 500
471. Multiplication Merrily Matched. © 1846.
Numbers, Card game. 400
472. Pickwick Card. © 1845. Literary, Card game. 650
472. Races, Game of the. Circa 1840s. Sports,
Horseracing, Board game. 1800
474. Shakespeare in a New Dress. © 1845.
Literary, Card game. 500

H. M. Francis
475. Aesop, New Game of. © 1861. Literary,
Board game. 1200

Fuller, Upham & Co.
476. Pinafore, Game of. © 1879. Literary, Card game. 350

Charles T. Gill
477. Expanding Fortune Teller, The. © 1849.
Mystic, Skill game. 350

J. S. Goodman
478. Tyche: The Fireside Oracle (author C.B.B.).
© 1876. Mystic, Card game. 200

Goodnow Brothers
479. Figurette. © 1875. Miscellaneous, Card game. 200

D. O. Goodrich
480. Presidential Quartets, A New Game. © 1859.
Politics, Card game. 600

J. Jay Gould
481. Age Cards. Circa 1870s. Social, Card game. 150
482. Key to the King's Garden, The. Circa 1870s.
Social, Card game. 200
483. Shadows on the Wall. Circa 1870s. Kiddie,
Card game. 150
484. What, the Battle with Letters (© J. Jay Gould).
© 1876. Letters, Card game. 150
485. Who Do You Love Best? (© J. Jay Gould).
© 1876. Social, Card game. 150

Wm. R. Gould
**486. Anybody and Everybody; Somebody and
Nobody.** Circa 1875. Social, Card game. 150

Gould & Lincoln
487. Peter Coddle's Trip to New York. © 1858.
Reading, Card game. $450

Hammet & Hammet
488. Word Making & Talking. © 1877. Word,
Card game. 150

S. Hart & Co.
**489. What D'ye Buy, Laughable Game of (Professor
Punch).** Circa 1860s. Social, Card game. 400

W. P. Hazard
490. Conquest of Nations, The (Game of Nations).
© 1853. History, Card game. 500

Glay Herrick
491. Quotations, Game of. © 1878. Literary, Card
game. 150

Albert A. Hill
492. Right and Wrong, or The Princess Belinda.
© 1876. Social, Card game. 165

William H. Hill, Jr., & Co.
493. Portfolio of Social Games. © 1864. Social,
Combination, Card games. 300

L. J. Hodges
**494. Travels and Sojourn of Ichabod Solo, Esquire,
Among the Pee-Wee Indians.** © 1858. Social,
Card game. 500

Hoffman & Knickerbocker
495. American Eagle, or Bird Chase, Game of the.
© 1855. Animal, Birds, Card game. 350
496. Little Corporal, The World and Its People.
© 1854. History, Card game. 450

Henry Holt & Co.
497. Auteurs, Le Jeu des. © 1873. Literary,
Card game. 1500
498. Scripture Cards. © 1860. Religious, Card game. 150
499. Scripture Characters. Circa 1860s. Religious,
Card game. 250

E. I. Horsman
500. Letters, The Original Game of. © 1878. Letters,
Card game. $150
501. Portrait Authors. © 1873. Literary, Card game. 150

D. Eckley Hunter
502. Helps to History © 1866. History, Card game. 250

D. P. Ives & H. P. Ives
503. Miser, The Game of. Circa 1840s. Social,
Card game. 600

Henry Ives, Selchow & Righter
504. Dr. Busby, Game of. Circa 1840s. Literary,
Card game. Lady at piano cover. 500

John M. Ives & Co.
505. Travellers, Game of the. © 1856. Travel, Land,
Sea, Rail, Board game. 400

S. B. Ives, M. Bradley Co.
506. Dr. Busby, Game of. Circa 1840s. Literary,
Card game. Lady with child cover. 500

W. & S. B. Ives
507. Characteristics, An Original Game. © 1843.
Social, Card game. 350
508. Christmas Game of the Months. Circa 1853.
Holiday, Card game. 500
509. Circles, The Game of. Circa 1852. Miscellaneous,
Card game. 400
510. Comical Converse. Circa 1849. Social, Card
games. 400
511. Dr. Busby, Game of, beige cover. © 1843.
Literary, Card game. 1st edition, small symbols. 450
511a. Dr. Busby, Game of, green cover. © 1843
2nd. Edition, small symbols, card game. 300
512. Dr. Busby, Game of, green cover. © 1843.
Literary, Card game. 3rd edition, large symbols. 250
512a. Dr. Busby, Game of, green cover. Circa 1850s.
Published with Milton Bradley & Co. Larger box,
Lady ironing cover. 500
513. Fireside Game. Circa 1852. Social, Card game. 350
514. Flags of Nations. Circa 1852. Geography,
Card game. 350
515. French Puzzle Brain Game. © 1851. Puzzle,
Card game. 300
516. Fusby Cards. Circa 1849. Social, Card game. 300

W. & S. B. Ives continued

517. Heroes, The Game of. © 1845. History,
Card game. $1000

518. Mahomet and Saladin (The Battle of Palestine).
Circa 1846. Military, Board game. 2000

**519. Mansion of Happiness w/Selchow & Righter,
Hosford, and Adams.** © 1844. Social, Board
game. 450

**520. Mansion of Happiness, golden spaces, 1st
Edition.** © 1843. Social, Board game, fine line
engraving. 1200

**521. Mansion of Happiness, green spaces, 2nd
Edition.** © 1844. Social, Board game, fine line
engraving. 800

**521a. Mansion of Happiness, green spaces, 3rd
Edition and later,** © 1844. Bold line engraving. 400

**522. Mansion of Happiness, published with, Milton
Bradley & Co.** © 1844. Published in 1850s,
Social, Board game. Bold line engravings. 450

523. Master Rodbury and His Pupils. Circa 1844.
Social, Card game. 500

524. Meangerie or Game of Beasts. Circa 1846.
Animal, Card game. 600

525. Merelles, or Nine Men's Morris. Circa 1852.
Strategy, Board game. 800

526. National Game of American Eagle, The.
Circa 1844. History, Board game. 3500

527. Pope and Pagan, Game of. © 1844. Strategy,
Board game. 2000

528. Reward of Virture, The. © 1850. Social,
Board game. 1500

529. Scripture History. Circa 1845. Religious,
Card game. 400

530. Spanish Fairy Tale Game. Circa 1850s.
Nursery Rhymes, Card game. 400

531. States, The Game of. © 1845. Geography,
Card game. 500

532. Tivoli, The Game of. Circa 1850. Social,
Card game. 400

533. Uncle Tom's Cabin. Circa 1840s. Literary,
Card game. 1200

534. Yankee Trader or What D'ye Buy by Dr. Busby.
© 1848. Economic, Card game. 500

M. Jacobs & Co.

535. 16 Merry Face. Circa 1870. Kiddie, Card game. 150

A. N. Jordan-S.W. Chandler

536. Yacht Race, Franklin and Great Republic.
© 1853. Sports, Sea, Board game. $2500

Alexander S. Jorden

537. Diamond Game, The. Circa 1850s. Skill,
Board game. 2000

C. H. Joslin

538. Amusette. Circa 1870. Social, Card game. 150

A. S. Lanceton

539. Universe, Game of. © 1874. Space, Card game. 250

Wm. Chancy Langdon

540. American Story and Glory, The Game of.
© 1846. History, Card game. 600

541. English Blood Royal, Game of. © 1846. History,
Card game. 500

Thomas Lawrence

542. Chief. © 1851. Card game. 500

Lee and Shepard

543. Jolly Exempts, The. Circa 1860s. Social,
Card game. 750

544. Old Pampheezle and His Comical Friends.
Circa 1840. Classic, Card game. 500

545. Planting, Game of. © 1865. Plants, Card game. 250

Miss Leslie

546. History of Philadelphia. © 1831. History,
Card game. 600

Levi J. Lewis

547. Conversation Game. Circa 1830s. Social,
Card game. 300

Lindsay & Blakiston

548. Sybelline Leaves. © 1852. Mystic, Card game. 350

B. Lindsey

549. Conversation Cards. © 1811. Social, Card game. 600

F. & R. Lockwood
550. Astronomical Cards. Circa 1822-23. Space,
Card game. $2000
551. Botanical Cards. Circa 1822-23. Plant,
Card game. 1500
552. Cabinet of Knowledge. Circa 1822-23. Learning,
Card game. 1000
553. Geographical Cards. Circa 1822-23. Geography,
Card game. 600
554. Philosophical Cards. Circa 1822-23.
Miscellaneous, Card game. 750
555. Scripture Cards. Circa 1822-23. Religious,
Card game. 600
556. Traveller's Tour Round the World, The.
Circa 1822-23. Geography, Board game. 3000
557. Traveller's Tour Through Europe, The.
Circa 1822-23. Geography, Board game. 3000
**558. Traveller's Tour Through the United States,
The.** Circa 1822-23. Geography, Board game. 6000
559. Venacular Cards, The. Circa 1822-23. Word,
Card game. 600

A. E. Lyman & Son
560. American Tivoli Game, Lyman's Improved.
Circa 1875. Miscellaneous, Board game. 200
**561. New Railroad Game, or Trip Around the World,
The.** Circa 1873. Travel, Board game. 900

Charles Magnus and Co.
562. American Fortune-Telling Cards. © 1877.
Mystic, Card games. 150
563. Atlantic Telegraph. Circa 1860. Communications,
Board game. 2500
564. Boa Constrictor. Circa 1860. Animal, Board
game. 1000
565. Bonaparte's Oraculum, Non-Portrait cover.
Circa 1854-67. Mystic, Card game. 600
**566. Bonaparte's Oraculum, Portrait cover of
Napoleon.** Circa 1854-67. Mystic, Card game. 750
567. Checquers and the Game of Mill Morris.
Circa 1860. Classic, Board game. 550
568. Children's Arithmetic Game of 1000 Changes.
Circa 1860. Numbers, Card game. 200
569. Comic Leaves of Fortune, the Sibyl's Prophecy.
Circa 1860s. Mystical, Card game. 200
570. Conquer, The Game To. Circa 1860s. Military,
Board game. 1300
571. Conversation. Circa 1860s. Social, Card game. 250
572. Cottage of Content. Circa 1860. Social, Board
game. 250
573. English Farm: Twenty Rural Scenes, The.
Circa 1860. Travel, Board game. 1000
574. Fox Chase. Circa 1860s. Animal, Board game. 550
**575. Humorous Queries and Solutions, Brother
Jonathon's.** Circa 1860. Q & A, Card game. 350
**576. Masquerade Game, The (inv. by Wm. Frederick
Balch).** Circa 1859. Social, Card game. 500
577. Miracle. Circa 1860. Social, Board game. 300

578. National Jubilee Snake Game. © 1851. History,
Board game. $1500
579. New National Snake Game. Circa 1855. History,
Board game. 1200
**580. Pigs and Kittens, Comical Game of
(Grand-Father Fisher).** Circa 1860. Animals,
Board game. 300
581. Rising Star, The. Circa 1860. Board game. 1200
582. Running the Blockade. Circa 1862. History,
Board game. 3500
583. Sociable Snake, The Game of. Circa 1860s.
History, Board game. 1200
584. Steeple Chase. Circa 1860s. Animal, Board game. 1200
585. Uncle Sam's Game of Six Corners. Circa 1860.
Strategy, Board game. 1800

Many & Delameter
586. Zouave, Game of the. Circa 1861. Military,
Card game. 1000

M. A. Mayhew
**587. King of the Golden River, or The Black
Brothers.** Circa 1860s. Social, Card game. 400
588. Old Pamphezzle and his Comical Friends.
© 1861. Classic, Card game. 400
**589. Sea of Ice, or The Arctic Adventurers (Percy B.
St. John).** Circa 1860s. Social, Card game. 650
**590. Willis the Pilot, or Sequel to Swiss Family
Robinson.** Circa 1860s. Literary, Card game. 400

Mayhew & Baker
591a. Dissected Comical Dominoes, The Game.
© 1859. Card game. 800
591. Gypsy Fortune Teller, The Game of the. © 1859.
Mystic, Card game. 400
592. School in An Uproar, The Game of the. © 1859.
Education, Card game. 400
593. Tournament, The New Game of. © 1858.
Military, Board game. 800
594. Yankee Land, The Game of. © 1859. Historic,
Card game. 500
**595. Young Peddlers, or Learning to Count in a
Pleasant Manner.** © 1859. Numbers, Card game. 300

McCleary & Pierce
596. Counties of the State of New York, A Game.
© 1849. Geography, Card game. 350

A. A. McCormick
597. Marque, or Triple-Score. © 1879. Miscellaneous,
Card game. 150

John McLoughlin
598. Amusing Game of Conundrums, The. © 1853.
Social, Card game. 1500
599. Yankee Pedler. Circa 1850. Economic,
Card game. 1500
599a. Poor Old Soldier and His Dog, The. © 1853
Card game. 1000

McLoughlin Brothers

600. Addem Up and Dividem. Circa 1870s. Numbers,
Card game. $100

601. Ambuscade, Bounce, & Constellation, Games of.
© 1877. Combination, Board game. 350

602. Arithmetical Game, Grandmama's Improved.
Circa 1875. Numbers, Card game. 200

603. Authors, Cribbage. Circa 1870s. Literary,
Card game. 150

604. Authors, Musical. © 1879. Music, Card game. 175

605. Authors, Star. © 1875. Literary, Card game. 125

606. Authors. © 1875. Literary, Card game. 125

607. Bear Hunt, Game of. © 1870. Animals,
Card game. 250

608. Black Cat, Game of. Circa 1875. Animals,
Card game. 300

**608a. Bobbing Around the Circle, Tri Bang,
Robbing the Miller, Games of.** Circa 1870s,
Combination Board game. 300

609. Bugle Horn or Robin Hood, The. Circa 1860s.
Literary, Adventure, Card and Board game. 1200

610. Captive Princess, The. © 1875. Strategy,
Board game. 500

611. Cats & Mice; Gantlope; Lost Diamond. © 1877.
Combo, Board game. 350

612. Centennial Presidential Game. Circa 1875.
History, Card game. 600

613. Checkers, Back-Gammon and Tousel. © 1877.
Classic, Board game. 200

614. Chinese Puzzle. Circa 1850s. Puzzle Game. 500

615. Chiromagica. Circa 1879's. Mystic, Board game. 450

616. Cinderella, or Hunt the Slipper. Circa 1875.
Literary, Card game. 200

617. City Traveler, The. Circa 1875. Travel,
Card game. 200

618. Cock Robin. Circa 1875. Nursery Rhyme,
Card game. 150

619. Cock Robin. Hand painted cover. Circa 1860s.
Nursery Rhyme, Card game. 500

620. Comical Conversation Cards. Circa 1875. Social,
Card game. 125

621. Conundrums. Circa 1870. Social, Card game. 125

622. Conversations on Love. Circa 1875. Social,
Card game. 150

623. Conversations on Marriage. Circa 1875. Social,
Card game. 150

624. Croquet. Circa 1875. Classic, Board game. 100

625. Dr. Fusby, Game of. Circa 1875. Social,
Card game. 150

626. Duck Shooting. Circa 1875. Animal,
Action Game. 125

627. Falconry. Circa 1875. Animal, Card game. 200

**628. Familiar Quotations from Popular Authors,
New Game.** Circa 1875. Literary, Card game. 125

629. Familiar Quotations. Circa 1870s. Literary,
Card game. $125

630. Farmer Trot and His Family. Circa 1875.
Social, Card game. 150

631. Farmer Trott, Game of. Circa 1860s. Social,
Card game. 400

632. Fashion and Famine. Circa 1875. Social,
Card game. 200

633. Fishing. Circa 1875. Animal, Board game. 150

634. Gifts, Uses and Consequences, Game of.
Circa 1870. Social, Card game. 150

**635. Go-Bang, Russian Tivoli, Fox & Geese,
Solitaire,** © 1878. Combo, Board game. 250

636. Going to Sunday School. Circa 1875. Religious,
Card game. 150

637. Good and Bad Scholar. Circa 1870. Educational,
Card game. 150

638. Grandmama's Game of Useful Knowledge.
Circa 1860s. History, Card game. 125

639. Grandmama's Games of Riddles. Circa 1865-70.
Reading, Card game. 300

640. Grandmama's Geographical Game. Circa 1860s.
Geographical, Card game. 300

641. H.M.S. Pinafore, Game of. © 1879. Literary,
Card game. 175

642. Happy Family, The New Illustrated Game of.
Circa 1875. Social, Card game. 150

643. Hens and Chickens, Game of. © 1875.
Animal, Card game. 125

644. Hocus Pocus Conjurocus. Circa 1875.
Mystic, Card game. 150

645. House that Jack Built, The. Circa 1875.
Nursery Rhyme, Card game. 150

646. Jerome Park Steeplechase. © 1875. Sports,
Horseracing, Board game. 1000

647. John Gilpin, Rainbow Backgammon, Games of.
© 1876. Combo, Board game. 400

648. Ladies & Gentlemen's Conservation Cards.
Circa 1875. Social, Card game. 125

649. Leap Frog. Circa 1870. Animal, Board game. 500

650. Life. Circa 1870s. Social, Board game. 150

651. Life's Mishaps, A Merry Game. © 1875.
Social, Board game. 300

**652. Life's Mishaps, Domino Rex and Diamonds
and Hearts.** Circa 1875. Combination, Social,
Board game. 400

653. Little Red Riding Hood. © 1867. Nursery Rhyme,
Card game. 400

654. Logomachy. © 1874. Words, Card game. 100

McLoughlin Brothers, continued

655. Lost Diamond. © 1870. Strategy, Board game. $250
656. Loves & Likes. Circa 1875. Social, Card game. 150
657. Merry Game of Old Maid, The. Circa 1870s. Classic, Card game. 200
658. Merry Goose Game. Circa 1875. Nursery Rhymes, Card game. 175
659. Monopolist, Ten Up, and Mariner's Compass. © 1878. Economic, Board game. 1200
660. Mother Hubbard, A Game. Circa 1875. Nursery Rhymes, Board game. 400
661. Mystic Thirty-One, The. © 1876. Mystic, Card game. 125
662. Nations, or Quaker Whist, Game of. Circa 1875. Geography, Card game. 350
663. Naval Engagement. © 1870. Military, Board game. 350
664. New Testament Game, Grandma's. Circa 1875. Religious, Card game. 150
665. New Yankee Letter Cards. © 1879. Word, Card game. 125
666. Old Maid, Game of. Circa 1870s. Classic, Card game. 200
667. Old Maid, The New. Circa 1870s. Classic, Card game. 150
668. Old Testament Game, Grandma's. Circa 1870s. Religious, Card game. 150
669. Old Testament Questions & Answers, Grandma's. Circa 1870s. Religious, Card game. 150
670. One, Two, Three, Game of. Circa 1870s. Numbers, Card game. 125
671. Oriental Color Game. Circa 1870s. Miscellaneous, Card game. 125
672. Pearl Divers, The. Circa 1870s. Adventure, Card game. 150
673. Phantoms, or Delusive Visions. © 1875. Social, Card game. 150
674. Philosopher's Travels or Game of Nations, The. Circa 1860s. Geography, Card game. 1200
675. Pilgrim's Progress Going to Sunday School, Tower of Babel. © 1875. Religious, Board game. 400
676. Pilgrim's Progress, Game of the. © 1875. Religious, Board game. 400
677. Poor Old Soldier and His Dog. Circa 1870s. Social, Card game. 200
678. Quizzical Questions and Quaint Replies. © 1869. Q & A, Card game. 175
679. Quoits. Circa 1870s. Skill, Board game. 125
680. Rabbit Hunt, The Game of. © 1870. Animals, Card game. 150
681. Scripture Cards. © 1877. Religious, Card game. 150
682. Six Nations, Game of. Circa 1867. Geography, Card game. 550
683. Speculation. Circa 1870. Economic, Card game. 200
684. Spider and the Fly. © 1870. Nursery Rhymes, Board game. 250
685. Tight-Rope, Game of. © 1870. Circus, Board game. 400

686. Tight Rope Dancing. Circa 1875. Circus, Board game. $450
687. Uncle Sam's History of the U.S. Circa 1870. History, Card game. 500
688. Uncle Sam's Game of American History. © 1851. History, Card game. 1250
689. Valdevia, or Central Park Game. Circa 1870s. Card game. 300
690. Visit to Camp. Circa 1864-5. Military, Card game. 1000
691. Where is Johnny? Circa 1870s. Social, Card game. 150
692. Where's Johnny, A Game. Painted cards & cover. Circa 1860s. Social, Card game. 400
693. Yankee Letter Blocks. © 1879. Letters, Card game. 200
694. Yankee Letter Cards. © 1879. Letters, Card game. 125
695. Yankee Pedlar. Circa 1860s. Economic, Card game. 600

Chester Metcalf
696. Events and Dates of U.S. Colonial History. © 1876. History, Card game. 350

Charles L. Mores
697. Multiplication, An Arithmetical Game. Circa 1850s. Numbers, Card game. 400

Munroe & Francis
698. Cards of Boston. © 1831. Geography, Card game. 600

National Art Co.
699. Centennial Games of the Revolution. Circa 1870s. History, Card game. 350

Nora Norwood
700. American Revolution. Circa 1850s. Military, American Revolution, Card game. 750

Novelty Game Co.

701. Old Curiosity Shop. © 1869. Economic, Card game. 250

Henry D. Noyes & Co.
702. Old Hunter and His Game, The. © 1880. Animal, Card game. 300

Noyes, Snow, & Co.
703. Anybody and Everybody; Somebody and Nobody. Circa 1870s. Social, Card game. 150
704. Bible Questions, Game of. Circa 1873-6. Religious, Card game. 150
705. Chivalrie. © 1873. Military, Card game. 250
706. Chronicles of Uncle Sam's Family. © 1876. History, Card game. 250

Noyes, Snow, & Co. continued

707. Donny-Brook Fair. © 1877. Social, Card game. $200
708. Great Republic, The. Circa 1870s. History,
   Card game. 250
709. Harlequin Circle. © 1877. Circus, Card game. 200
710. Letters Improved. © 1878. Word, Card game. 125
711. Letters, Game of. © 1876. Letters, Card game. 125
712. Letters, The Original Game of. © 1872. Letters,
   Card game. 125
713. Lost Heir, The. Circa 1870s. Strategy, Card game. 150
714. Lucky Traveller. Circa 1870s. Travel, Card game. 150
715. Original Game of Letters, The. © 1878. Word,
   Card game. 125
716. Royal Comedy. Circa 1870s. Royal, Card game. 150
717. Royalty, Game of. Circa 1870s. Royal,
   Card game. 150
718. Snap. © 1872. Social, Card game. 125
719. Trio. Circa 1870s. Card game. 150
720. Uncle Sam's Family, Chronicles of. © 1876.
   History, Card game. 250
721. Who Can Tell?, The Scripture Game of.
   Circa 1870s. Religious, Card game. 150

Oakley & Mason

**722. House of Washington and the Palace of Santa
   Claus, The.** Circa 1870s. History, Block game. 1500
723. Parlor Monuments to the Illustrious Dead.
   Circa 1870s. History, Block Game. 1500

Orange Judd Co.

724. Billiardette. © 1879. Miscellaneous, Board game. 225
725. Pedestrians. © 1879. Travel, Board game. 750

Owens & Agar

726. Artists, Game of. Circa 1850s. Art, Card game. 350

H. B. Palmer

727. Grand National Victory. Circa 1864-5. Military,
   Civil War, Board game. 2000

V. S. W. Parkhurst

**728. Lamplighter, Game of the; or Uncle True and
   Little Gerty.** Circa 1850s. Social, Card game. 500
729. Uncle Tom and Little Eva, The Game of. © 1852.
   Social, Literary, Card game. 1000

Richard H. Pease

730. Biographical Amusement. Circa 1840s. History,
   Card game. 600
**731. Capital Fun or New Game of Geographic
   Charades.** © 1855. Geography, Card game. 500
732. Comic Game of Multiplication Table. © 1846.
   Numbers, Card game. 400

733. Five Navigators, or A Voyage of Discovery, The.
   Circa 1853-4. History, Geography, Board game. $3500
734. Historical Amusements. © 1846. History,
   Card game. 600
735. Laughable Game of What D'ye Buy, The.
   Circa 1840s. Economic, Card game. 600
736. Odd Figures, The Merry Game of. Circa 1840s.
   Social, Card game. 400
**737. Peter Puzzlewig's Mirthful Game of Happy Hits
   at Useful.** Circa 1840s. Social, Card game. 500
738. Poor Old Soldier and His Dog. Circa 1840s.
   Social, Card game. 500
739. Round Game of the Jew, The. Circa 1840s.
   Board game. 800
740. Trades or Knowledge is Power. Circa 1850s.
   Economic, Card game. 1200

Pease & Warren

741. Anagrams, The Game of. Circa 1853-4. Letters,
   Card game. 250

A. Phelps

742. Alphabet of Nations, The New. Circa 1840s.
   Geography, Card game. 400

D. S. Pillsbury

743. Geographical Game of the Old World. © 1875.
   Geography, Card game. 200

Porter & Coates

744. Authors, Game of. Brown Cloth Box. © 1872.
   Literary, Card game. 150
745. Instructive Game of Authors. © 1873. Literary.
   Card game. 150
746. Mythology, Game of. © 1873. Religious,
   Card game. 200
747. Poets, Game of. © 1872. Literary, Card game. 200

L. Prang & Co.

**748. Courtship of Jonathan Peas and Salley
   Marrowfat, The.** Circa 1870s. Social, Card game. 150
749. Game of Fortune Telling. Circa 1870s. Mystic,
   Card game. 125
750. Magic Cards. Circa 1870s. Mystic, Card game. 125

M. Redgrave

751. Patent Parlor Bagatelle Table, pat. 1871. Skill,
   Board game. 500

Richards & Kibbe
752. Signers of America's Independence, The.
© 1877. History, Card game. $350

Richardson & Co.
753. Martelle. © 1867. Miscellaneous, Card game. 300

Russell & Richardson SF
754. Fish Pond, Early wooden boxed set. Circa 1860s.
Animal, Sea, Board game. 600

Sage, Sons & Co.
755. Author's Game. Circa 1860s. Literary,
Card game. 350

M. Salom
756. Conversation Cards, Loves & Likes, Salom's.
Circa 1860s. Social, Card game. 250
757. Divination Cards, Salom's. Circa 1860s. Mystic,
Card game. 200
758. Dr. Kane's Trip, Salom's New Game.
Circa 1860s. Social, Card game. 300
759. Draft Enforced, The. © 1863. Military, Civil War,
Card game. 500
760. Young Banker, The, Salom's Game. Circa 1860s.
Economic, Card game. 500
761. Young Compositor, The, Salom's Game.
Circa 1860s. Learning, Card game. 350

Wm. Thomas Sater
**762. Parallels of History (author Wm. Thomas
Sater).** © 1876. History, Card game. 200

Christoph Saur, Mfg., Germantown, PA
762a. Der Frommen Lotterie. In German. © 1744.
Holy Lottery. 3500

Saxon & Miles
763. Amusing Game of Consequences by Uncle John.
Circa 1840s. Social, Card game. 500

F. P. Schmitthenner
764. Alphabet Game. © 1877. Letters, Card game. 150

E. G. Selchow & Co.
765. Chopped Up Monkey, The. Circa 1870s. Animal,
Card game. 200
766. Corn & Beans. © 1873. Social, Card game. 250
767. Crescent. Circa 1870s. Miscellaneous, Card
game. 200
768. Grand Mother Haphazard's Carnival.
Circa 1870s. Social, Card game. 300
769. Parcheesi. © 1874. Classic, Board game. 150
770. Parcheesi (© John Hamilton). © 1869. Classic,
Board game. 200
771. Popping the Question. Circa 1870s. Social,
Card game. 200

772. Quartette Union War Game. © 1874. Military,
Card game. $400

Selchow & Righter Co.
773. Anagrams or Word's Alive. Circa 1870s.
Word, Card game. 125
**774. Carnival of Characters from Dickens (author
Albert Hill).** © 1876. Literary, Card game. 300
775. Croquet (© S. F. Cramer). © 1878. Classic,
Board game. 200
**776. Parlor Race, or Dickens on the Turf (© D. E.
Fisk).** © 1877. Sport – Horseracing, Card game. 250
777. Pigs in Clover. Circa 1870s. Animals, Card game. 250
778. Vignette Authors. © 1874. Literary, Card game. 100
779. Vignette Authors. Variant cover. © 1874. Literary,
Card game. 100

W. C. Smith
780. Centennial Seventy-Six (author W. C. Smith).
© 1876. History, Card game. 300

A. H. Smythe & Co.
781. Century Game. © 1872. History, Card game. 250
782. Painters. © 1883. Art, Board game. 125

Snow Brothers Publishers
783. Snap, Game of. © 1872. Social, Card game. 200

Stevens Patent
784. Liberty, Law, Protecton, Habeas Corpus.
© 1869. Law & Order, Card game. 200

William Stodart
785. Sybil's Leaves for 1833. © 1833. Mystic,
Card game. 500

Albert B. Swift
786. Bezique. Circa 1865. Classic, Card game. 250

John H. Tingsley
787. Authors, The New Game of. Circa 1850s.
Literary, Card game. 350
788. Courtship and Marriage, The Game of. © 1864.
Romance, Card game. 350
789. Familiar Quotations, The Game of. Circa 1850s.
Literary, Card game. 300

E. B. Treat
790. Centennial Games 1776-1876. © 1874. History,
Card game. 300
791. Races to the White House. © 1881. Politics,
Card game. 350

L. W. Turner
792. National Game of States. © 1878. Geography, Card game. $150

Turner & Fisher
793. Courting Cards. © 1847. Romance, Card game. 500
794. Ladies and Gentlemens Improved Sibylline Leaves (© W. Mather). © 1839. Mystic, Card game. 500

James Vick
795. Botany, The Game of. Circa 1878. Plants, Card game. 250

F. S. Weeks & Co.
796. Paul Pry, The Game of. Circa 1850s. Social, Card game. 350

Samuel Weller
797. Pickwick Cards, The, Cloth Cover. © 1844. Literary, Card game. 500
798. Pickwick Cards, The, Cupid Cover. © 1844. Literary, Card game. 600
799. Pickwick Cards, The, Pickwick Standing Cover. © 1844. Literary, Card game. 600
800. Pickwick Cards, The. © 1844. Literary, Card game. 500

West & Lee
801. Avilude, Game of Birds. © 1873. Animal, Card game. 200
802. Ferrilude or Game of Beasts. © 1873. Animal, Card game. 200
803. Portrait Authors. © 1873. Literary, Card game. 150
804. Society. © 1873. Social, Card game. 250
805. Totem. © 1873. Card game. 250

C. M. Whipple & A. A. Smith
806. Ah Sin, the Heathen Chinese, The New Game of. © 1871. Religious, Card game. 200
807. Anybody & Everybody; Somebody & Nobody, The Game. © 1861. Social, Card game. 300
808. Authors, Game of, The. © 1861. Literary, Card game. 200
809. Contest for the Capital, The. Circa 1860s. History, Card game. 350
810. Garrison Game. Circa 1860s. Military, Card game. 500

811. Gypsy Oracles for the Drawing Room. © 1867. Mystic, Card game. $300
812. Guerrillas, The. Circa 1860s. Military, Card game. 500
813. Letters, The Game of. Circa 1860s. Letters, Card game. 200
814. Noted People and Places. Circa 1860s. History, Card game. 250
815. Old Curiosity Shop, The. Circa 1860s. Literary, Card game. 300
816. Old Flag or 1776, The. © 1863. History, Card game. 500
817. Olympus, or A Feast with the Gods. © 1867. Literary, Card game. 400
818. Originations of Shakespeare. Circa 1860s. Literary, Card game. 450
819. Peggy, New Game of. Circa 1860s. Skill, Skill game. 350
820. Race Course. © 1868. Sports - Horseracing, Board game. 1200
821. Showman, The. Circa 1860s. Card game. 350
822. Squails. © 1865. Skill, Card game. 250
823. Tipsy Philosophers, or Laughable Game of Words Bewitched. © 1860. Literary, Card game. 400

H. Whipple & Son
824. Letters, The Game of. © 1876. Word, Card game. 200

J. M. Whittemore
825. Christmas Game or "Dickens", The. Circa 1840s. Holiday & Literary, Card game. 750

A. Williams & Co
826. Auctioneer, The Game of. © 1850. Economic, Card game. 500
827. Rebellion, The Game of. Circa 1860s. Military, Civil War, Card game. 800
828. Trip to Paris. © 1857. Travel, Card game. 350

F. A. Wright
829. Logomachy, or War of Words. © 1874. Words, Card game. 150
830. Logomachy, Or War of Words, Variant box. © 1875. Word, Card game. 125

Wright & Hasty
831. Scripture Characters. © 1852. Religious, Card game. 400

Edward R. Young
832. Gems of Wisdom. © 1855. Literary, Card game. 450

GOLDEN AGE GAMES

Acme Card Co.   Price
875. **Battles of the Republic.** Circa 1915. Military,
      Card Game. $100

Frederick J. Allen
876. **Boston Game, The.** © 1905. Geography, Card
      Game. 75
877. **Somerville.** © 1904. Travel, Card Game. 65

Allison Mfg. Co.
878. **Chi-Chi.** © 1915. Miscellaneous, Card Game. 50

American Parlor Baseball
879. **Parlor Base Ball.** © 1903. Sports, Baseball,
      Board Game. 150
880. **Parlor Base Ball, Wooden Box Edition.** © 1903.
      Sports, Baseball, Board Game. 300

American Play Games Co.
881. **Button, Button** (© Frank F. Honeck). © 1910.
      Skill, Board Game. 75
882. **Hearts, The Society Game also known as Heart
      Dice** (© Frank F. Honeck). © 1909. Skill, Board
      Game. 75
883. **Parlor Base Ball.** © 1903. Sports, Baseball,
      Board Game. 250

American Printing Co.
884. **Teddy Bear, Game of.** © 1906. Political, Card
      Game. 1200

American Publishing Co.
885. **Rambles Through Our Country.** © 1881.
      Travel, Board Game. 400

American Toy Co.
886. **Klondike, or a Trip to the Gold Fields of Alaska**
      (by Chas. W. Kennard, author of Oiuja). ©
      1897. Travel, Board Game. 300

American Toy Mfg. Co.
887. **Boston-New York Motor Tour.** Circa 1920s.
      Travel, Board Game. 150
888. **Marble Muggins.** Circa 1890s. Marble, Skill
      Game. 75

Animate Toy Co.
889. **Bugville Games.** © 1915. Animal, Insect, Board
      Game. 200

Anonymous
890. **American Sports.** Circa 1880s. Sports, Card
      Game. $300
891. **Comical Game of Atta Boy, A.** Circa 1910s.
      Social, Card Game. 100
892. **Hunting Big Game.** Circa 1910s. Animal, Board
      Game. 150
893. **Lost Heir, Game of.** Circa 1890s. Social, Card
      Game. 100
894. **Muggins, Hand Made Game, cf. Happy Family.**
      Circa 1900s. Social, Card Game. 250
895. **New Game of Tiddledy Winks, Earliest edition.**
      Circa 1880s. Classic, Skill Game. 300
896. **Panama Canal Game.** Circa 1910. History,
      Board Game. 300
897. **Race, Game of the.** Circa 1880s. Sports,
      Horseracing, Board Game. 350
898. **Rambles.** © 1881. History, Travel, Board Game. 500
899. **Steeple Chase Game, The.** Circa 1880s. Sports,
      Horseracing, Board Game. 350
900. **Steeplechase, The Game of.** Circa 1890s. Sports,
      Horseracing, Board Game. 300

Anonymous (Milton Bradley)
901. **Beast, Bird or Fish.** Circa 1890s. Animal, Card
      Game. 100
902. **Old Maid.** Circa 1905. Social, Card Game. 75

Geo. Apfel
903. **Diamond, or The Game of Short Stop, The.**
      Circa 1885. Sports, Baseball, Board Game. 350

Archarena Game Co.
904. **25 New Top Games: Cuban Battle Spin;
      Cushion Orange Diagonal Pins; Five Back
      Spin; Five Pin Cuban Top Game; Four Pin
      Circle; Half Minute Battle; Half Orange Pins;
      Head Pin Four Back Circle; Long End Battle;
      Long End Tipsy; Pyramid Pins; Seven Up
      Spin; Spinette; Spinning Battle; Spinoza; Spot
      Games; Ten-Pin Top Game; Three Minute
      Battle; Three Pin Circle; Tipsy; Tipsy Topsy
      Turvy; Topsy; Triangle Top Game; Turvy.** Circa
      1895. Combination, Board Game. 150
905. **Archarena Combination Boards.** Circa 1900.
      Combination, Board Game. 150
906. **Flag Travelette.** Circa 1900. Combination, Board
      Game. 150

C. B. Arnold
907. **Caesars, Game of.** 1903. History, Card Game. 125

31

C. E. Akins
908. **Parlor Quoits.** © 1891. Skill, Board Game. $100

Atkins & Co., Inc.
909. **Cortella.** © 1913. Miscellaneous, Board Game. 25

Atlantic Co.
910. **No-Jump-O.** © 1899. Strategy, Board Game. 25

Atlas Game Co.
911. **Piggle Wiggle.** © 1910. Miscellaneous, Board
       Game. 200

Austin & Craw
912. **Tit-Tat-Toe, Three in a Row.** © 1896. Strategy,
       Board Game. 100

Aviation Game Co.
913. **Aviation Game.** © 1911. Travel, Air, and Card
       Game. 125

Aydelott
914. **Aydelott's Base Ball Cards, The.** © 1910.
       Sports, Baseball, Card Game. ....:............................... 250

Bailey, Banks & Biddle Co.
915. **Women are Trumps.** © 1914. Social, Card
       Game. 200

Baker & Bennett Co.
916. **Coontown Shooting Gallery.** Circa 1909. Ethnic,
       Board Game. 1000

Lizzie Ballou
917. **Royal (author Lizzie Ballou).** © 1887. History,
       Board Game. 250

J. S. Barcus & Co.
918. **Literature, The University Game of (series 1).**
       Circa 1890s. Literary, Card Game. 75
919. **University Game of Literature, The.** Circa
       1900. Literary, Card Game. 75

C. W. Bardeen
920. **Our Country (© A. M. Edwards).** © 1891.
       Travel, USA, Card Game. 100
921. **Historical Game "Our Country".** © 1891.
       History, Card Game. 100

Leavitt Bartlett
922. **Chronology (author Leavitt Bartlett).** © 1875.
       History, Card Game. 250

Base Balline Publishing Co.
923. **Base Balline.** Circa 1888. Sports, Baseball, Board
       Game. 250

Baseballitis Game Co.
924. **Baseballitis.** © 1906. Sports, Baseball, card
       Game. $250

Batter Up Co., Fennenberg.
925. **Batter Up, Game of.** © 1908. Sports, Baseball,
       Card Game. 250

J. H. Beach
926. **Amusing Instructor, The.** © 1887.
       Miscellaneous, Card Game. 75

Welcome L. Beckley
927. **Quotations.** © 1889. Literary, Card Game. 60

N. J. Beeching
928. **N. J. Bible Game, The.** © 1912. Religious, Card
       Game. 40

Fred H. Behring
929. **Golf Bug.** © 1915. Sports, golf, Board Game. 150

C. E. Begerow
930. **Our Cinderella Party.** © 1896. Nursery Rhymes,
       Board Game. 75

J. C. Bell Co.
931. **Uncle Sam's Baseball Game.** © 1890. Sports,
       Baseball, Board Game. 800

Berkley Card Co.
932. **Busy Work Picture Cards.** Circa 1900.
       Miscellaneous, Card Game. 50

E. P. Best Mfg. Co.
933. **Greased Pigs.** © 1875. Animals, Board Game. 150
934. **Peek-a-Boo.** © 1875. Kiddie, Board Game. 125
935. **Wild Indians.** ©1875. Western, Board Game. 175

H. A. Biereley
936. **Biereley's Arithmetical Cards.** © 1895.
       Numbers, Card Game. 75

Harry S. Bird
937. **Scratch.** Circa 1910s. Animal, Board Game. 125

R. Bliss Manufacturing Co.
938. **A B C, Game of.** © 1896. Word, Card Game. 125
939. **Arena, Game of.** © 1896. Strategy, Board Game. 400
940. **Attack, Game of.** Circa 1890s. Military, Board
       Game. 1800
941. **Bad Boy's Little Game, The.** © 1891. Kiddie,
       Board Game. 500
942. **Ball Toss Game.** © 1896. Skill, Board Game. 200

R. Bliss   continued

943. Balloon, Game of. © 1889. Skill, Board Game. $1500

944. Base Ball Game, League Parlor. Circa 1889. Sports, Baseball, Board Game. 1500

945. Detective, Game of. © 1889. Law & Order, Board Game. 3000

946. Domino Pool, Game of. Circa 1891. Miscellaneous, Board Game. 500

947. Dudes, Game of the. © 1890. Western, Board Game. 1500

948. Fish Pond Game, Improved. Circa 1889. Animal, Board Game. 500

949. Good Luck, Game of. Circa 1895. Miscellaneous, Board Game. 350

950. Great Railroad Game, The. Circa 1891. Travel, Rail, and Board Game. 4000

951. Humpty-Dumpty, Game of. Circa 1896. Nursery Rhymes, Board Game. 700

952. Hunting Match. Circa 1891. Animal, Board Game. 700

953. Lawn and Parlor Ring Toss. Circa 1880. Skill, Board Game. 350

954. Life in the Wild West. Circa 1894. Western, Board Game. 2500

955. Man in the Moon. Circa 1885. Space, Board Game. 3000

956. Milk Maid. Circa 1885. Social, Card Game. 350

957. Minnehaha, Game of. © 1891. Western, Indians, Board Game. 1500

958. Mother Goose Ten Pins. Circa 1896. Skill, Board Game. 1200

959. Newsboy, Game of. © 1890. Communication, Board Game. 1200

960. Noah's Ark, Game of. Circa 1891. Religious, Animal, Board Game. 500

961. Open Sesame, Game of. Circa 1891. Miscellaneous, Board Game. 500

962. Parlor Floor Croquet. Circa 1880. Skill, Board Game. 500

963. Perfection Game Board. Circa 1896. Combination, Board Game. 400

964. Punch and Judy Ten Pins. Circa 1895. Skill, Board Game. 1200

965. Ring Toss, Game of. Circa 1890. Skill, Board Game. 400

966. Rough Rider Ten Pins. Circa 1896. Military, Board Game. 2000

967. Runaway Sheep. © 1892. Animal, Board Game. 500

968. Sailor Boy Ring Toss. Circa 1896. Military, Board Game. 500

969. School's Out. Circa 1896. Kiddie, Board Game. 500

970. Shopping, Game of. © 1891. Economic, Board Game. 2200

971. Solitaire & Siege Boards. Circa 1889. Miscellaneous, Board Game. 500

972. Stanley Africa Game, The. © 1891. History, Board Game. 2000

973. Stars and Stripes, Game of. Circa 1896. Political, Board Game. 1500

974. Table Croquet. Circa 1889. Skill, Board Game. $200

975. Visit to The Farm. © 1893. Animal, Board Game. 750

976. Wall Ring Game, The. Circa 1896. Skill, Board Game. 350

977. Wild West, Game of. © 1889. Western, Board Game. 2000

978. World's Columbia Exposition, Game of the. Circa 1895. Fair, Board Game. 2000

E. L. Bonnet

979. Citations Des Auteurs Francais. © 1896. Literary, Card Game. 100

Robert K. Bonsall

980. Bible Animals and Plants. © 1898. Religious, Card Game. 65

981. Bible Books. © 1898. Religious, Card Game. 50

982. Bible Customs & Ceremonies. © 1898. Religious, Card Game. 65

983. Bible Events. © 1898. Religious, Card Game. 65

984. Bible Localities. © 1898. Religious, Card Game. 65

985. New Testament Characters. © 1898. Religious, Card Game. 50

986. Old Testament Characters, The Game of. © 1898. Religious, Card Game. 50

John D. Boroff

987. Gems of Thought (author John D. Boroff). © 1884. Literary, Card Game. 75

Boston Globe

988. Boston Globe's Bicycle Game of Circulation, The. © 1895. Premium, Sport, Board Game. 1000

Boston Herald, The

989. Success, The Game of. Circa 1906. Economic, Board Game. 500

Boston Loan Co.

990. Base Ball with Cards. Circa 1887. Sports, Baseball, Card Game. 250

Bowers & Hard

991. Teddy's Bear Hunt. © 1907. Political, Board Game. 1250

992. Vanderbilt Cup Race Game, The. Circa 1920s. Sports, Car, Board Game. 1800

Geo. H. Bowman Co.

993. Teddy Bear (by Newbern H. Lewis). © 1907. Political, Card Game. 750

Milton Bradley

994. A.D.T. Messenger Boy. © 1890. Communications, Board Game. 200

995. A.D.T. Messenger Boy. Circa 1900s. Occupation, Communication, Small Board Game. 75

Milton Bradley   continued

996. Across the Border. Circa 1910s. Military, Spanish American War, Board Game. $200

997. Across the Sea. Circa 1910s. Travel, World, Board Game. 200

998. Across the Yalu. Circa 1905. Military, Board Game. 200

999. ADT Messenger, Robinson Crusoe & Little Miss Muffet. © 1911. Combination, Board Game. 200

1000. Advance and Retreat, Game of. Circa 1900. Strategy, Board Game. 150

1001. Aesop. © 1890. Nursery Rhyme, Animal, Card Game. 125

1002. Ally Sloper. © 1907. Miscellaneous, Board Game. 100

1003. American Boys. © 1916. Organizations, Board Game. 200

1004. American Jack Straws. Circa 1880s. Miscellaneous, Skill Game. 50

1005. American Politics, The Game of. © 1888. Politics, Board Game. 250

1006. An Account of Peter Coddles Visit to New York. Circa 1890. Social, Card Game. 65

1007. Anagrams, Variant cover. Circa 1910s. Word, Card Game. 25

1008. Anagrams. Circa 1910s. Word, Card Game. 25

1009. Animal Ten Pins. Circa 1905. Skill, Board Game. 150

1010. Authors Improved, Illustrated Edition. Circa 1890s. Literary, Card Game. 40

1011. Authors William Shakespeare, Game of. Circa 1900. Literary, Card Game. 75

1012. Authors, Household (4051). Circa 1900. Literary, Card Game. 40

1013. Authors. © 1890. Literary, Card Game. 40

1014. Auto Game, The. Circa 1906. Travel, Road, Board Game. 325

1015. Backgammon, Japanese. © 1870. Skill, Board Game. 150

1016. Bamboozle, Game of. © 1872. Strategy, Board Game. 250

1017. Beauty and the Beast, The Game of. © 1905. Animal, Nursery Rhyme, Board Game. 150

1018. Bible Objects, Game of. © 1900. Religious, Card Game. $50

1019. Bible Questions, Game of. Circa 1910s. Religious, Card Game. 50

1020. Bicycle Game. Circa 1895. Sports, Miscellaneous, Board Game. 450

1021. Bicycle Race. © 1910. Sports, Bike, Board Game. 200

1022. Billie's Dream. © 1912. Mystic, Card Game. 75

1023. Black Beauty. Circa 1900. Literary, Board Game. 150

1024. Blockade. Circa 1898. Military, Board Game. 250

1025. Boy Scouts, Game of. Circa 1910s. Organizations, Board Game. 300

1025a. Boy Scouts. Circa 1910s, three scouts doing semi-four, organizations Board Game. 200

1026. Buccaneers, Game of. © 1908. Adventure, Board Game. 200

1027. Bull Board, Bradley's. Circa 1900. Stock market, Board Game. 150

1028. Bull in a China Shop. © 1906. Animal, Board Game. 125

1029. Cadet Game (4036). © 1905. Military, Board Game. 250

1030. Captive Princess, The. © 1905. Adventure, Board Game. 300

1031. Carromette, The New Game of. Circa 1872. Strategy, Board Game. 125

1032. Checkered Game of Life. Circa 1910s. Social, Board Game. 250

1033. Choice Thoughts from Longfellow. © 1890. Literary, Card Game. 125

1034. Chuba. Circa 1895. Mystic, Card Game. 60

1035. Cinderella, A Game. © 1909. Literary, Board Game. 150

1036. Cinderella. Circa 1900. Literary, Card Game. 100

1037. Circus Game. Circa 1910s. Circus, Board Game. 150

1038. Cock-a-Doodle-Do (4079). Circa 1913. Nursery Rhymes, Board Game. 100

1039. Columbus. Circa 1891. History, Card Game. 100

1040. Conette. Circa 1900s. Strategy, Board Game. 25

1041. Costumes and Fashions, Game of. © 1881. History, Card Game. 75

1042. Crokinole. © 1900. Classic, Board Game. 150

1043. Crown Cards, Inc.: Aviation; Baffle; Crown Baseball; Flique; Goal; Grafto; Jack-Daw; Kid-O; Prince and Pauper; Quenette; Rustle; Secret Seven. © 1911. Combination, Card Game. 100

1044. Days, Game of. © 1905. Time, Card Game. 100

1045. Dickens, Game of. Circa 1890s. Literary, Card Game. 125

1046. Donkey Race. Circa 1895. Animal, Board Game. 125

1047. Down the Pike with Mrs. Wiggs at the St. Louis Exposition. © 1904. Fair, Card Game. 75

1048. Dr. Busby. © 1905. Social, Card Game. 65

1049. Dreamland. © 1910. Miscellaneous, Card Game. 125

1050. Drummer Boy, Game of. © 1910. Military, Board Game. 350

1051. Duck and Eggs. Circa 1895. Animals, Board Game. 125

Milton Bradley   continued

1052. Duck on the Rock (4136). Circa 1910s. Animal,
Board Game. $125

1053. Eckha. © 1889. Strategy, Board Game. 125

1054. Enchanted Forest. Circa 1910s. Fantasy,
Board Game. 300

1055. English Literature. Circa 1895. Literary,
Card Game. 75

1056. Evening Party. Circa 1895. Social, Card Game. 125

1057. Excursion to Coney Island. Circa 1885. Travel,
Board Game. 250

1058. Fairyland Game. Circa 1910s. Nursery Rhyme,
Board Game. 250

1059. Fast Mail, The. Circa 1900. Travel, Rail, and
Board Game. 800

1060. Figaro, Game of. Circa 1872. Literary, Card
Game. 100

1061. Fire Fighters. © 1910. Occupation, Board
Game. 350

1062. Fish Pond, 10 fish cover. Circa 1910s. Animal,
Sea, Board Game. 175

1063. Fish Pond. Circa 1890s. Animal, Sea,
Board Game. 150

1064. Fish Pond. Circa 1910s. Animal, Sea,
Board Game. 125

1065. Flags, The Game of (4061). Circa 1901.
Geography, Card Game. 75

1066. Fortune Teller, The. © 1905. Mystic,
Board Game. 125

1067. Forty Five. Circa 1895. Skill, Card Game. 75

1068. Fox and Geese, Game of. Circa 1900s. Animal,
Board Game. 150

1069. Fox Hunt. © 1905. Sports, Miscellaneous,
Board Game. 250

1070. Freddie the Frog, Game of. © 1910. Animal,
Reptile, Board Game. 150

1071. Funny Conversation Cards, Game of. © 1906.
Social, Card Game. 50

1072. Funny Fortunes. Circa 1895. Literary,
Card Game. 50

1073. Genii. Circa 1895. Mystic, Card Game. 65

1074. Get Busy, Game of. © 1906. Social, Card Game. 65

1075. Globe Trotter, The. Circa 1880s. Travel,
Board Game. 150

1076. Go Bang. © Circa 1890. Miscellaneous,
Board Game. 100

1077. Gold Hunter, The. Circa 1900. Adventure,
Board Game. 125

1078. Golf. Circa 1890s. Sports, Golf, Board Game. 900

1079. Golliwogg. © 1907. Ethnic, Card Game. 250

1080. Grandma's Game of Riddles (4928). Circa
1910. Literary, Card Game. 50

1081. Grandma's Geographical Game (4930). Circa
1910. Geography, Card Game. 50

1082. Grandma's New Testament Game (4933). Circa
1910s. Religious, Card Game. 75

1083. Grandma's Old Testament Game (4932). Circa
1910s. Religious, Card Game. 75

1084. Grandma's Arithmetical Game. Circa 1910s.
Numbers, Card Game. 50

1085. Grandma's Game of Useful Knowledge. ©
1910. History, Card Game. $50

1086. Happy Days in Old England, The Game of.
Circa 1895. History, Card Game. 75

1087. Happy Harry Ring Toss. Circa 1900. Skill,
Skill Game. 75

1088. Hee Haw (4057). © 1905. Miscellaneous,
Board Game. 100

1089. Hide and Seek. Circa 1880s. Miscellaneous,
Board Game. 225

1090. Hippodrome. Circa 1900s. Circus, Board Game. 350

1091. Hold the Fort. © 1909. Military, Board Game. 200

1092. Home History Game. © 1909. History,
Card Game. 65

1093. Honey Bee Game. © 1913. Animal, Insect,
Board Game. 150

1093a. Honey Gatherers, The. Circa 1890s, Animal,
Insect, Board Game. 300

1094. Hurdle Race. © 1905. Sport, Comics,
Board Game. 350

1095. India, Game of. Circa 1910s. Classic,
Board Game. 60

**1096. Interchangeable Combination Circus,
Bradley's.** © 1882. Combination, Board Game. 400

1097. Jack and Jill. © 1900. Nursery Rhyme,
Card Game. 85

1098. Jack and Jill. © 1906. Nursery Rhyme,
Board Game. 75

1099. Jack and Jill. © 1909. Nursery Rhyme,
Board Game. 65

1100. Jack O'Lantern. Circa 1913. Nursery Rhyme,
Board Game. 250

1101. Jack Straws. Circa 1890s. Classic, Skill Game. 40

1102. Jolly Tumblers. © 1910. Animal, Board Game. 175

1103. Junior Combination Board (4927), incl.:
American Corners; Bicycle Race; Checkers;
Cornering the Pig; Fortune Telling; Hop;
India; Johnny Jumps; Puss in the Corner;
Railroad Game; Steeplechase; Yacht Race. ©
1905. Strategy, Board Game. 50

1104. Kakeba, or Japanese Backgammon. Circa
1895. Strategy, Board Game. 125

1105. Kerion. Circa 1895. Strategy, Board Game. 250

1106. Komical Kats. © 1909. Animal, Card Game. 175

1107. Kornelia Kinks at Jamestown. © 1907. Social,
Card Game. 100

1108. Life Savers. © 1905. Adventure, Board Game. 250

1109. Little Boy Blue. © 1910. Nursery Rhyme, Board
Game. 150

1110. Little Jack Horner. © 1909. Nursery Rhyme,
Board Game. 200

1111. Little Knight, The. Circa 1910s. Military, Board
Game. 150

1112. Little Miss Muffett. Circa 1910s. Nursery
Rhyme, Board Game. 200

1113. Little Nemo. Circa 1913. Comic, Card Game. 1000

1114. Little Red Men. Circa 1910s. Indian,
Card Game. 100

1115. Little Red Riding Hood. Circa 1910. Nursery
Rhymes, Board Game. 200

Milton Bradley   continued

1116. Lively Frog. Circa 1913. Animal, Board Game. $200

1117. Logomachy or War of Words, Premium Game. Circa 1890s. Word, Card Game. 50

1117a.Louusa, Knight on horseback cover. Circa 1900, Board Game. 250

1118. Luck, Game of. Circa 1913. Miscellaneous, Card Game. 65

1119. Magic Fortunes. Circa 1872. Mystic, Card Game. 65

1120. Magnetic Fish Pond. Circa 1915-9. Animal, Sea, Board Game. 75

1121. Mail, Express or Accommodations, Game of. © 1895. Communications, Board Game. 250

1122. Merry Christmas Game. © 1907. Holiday, Christmas, Board Game. 800

1123. Merry Go Round. © 1906. Circus, Card Game. 150

1124. Merry-Go-Round. © 1910. Animal, Card Game. 75

1125. Mice and Cheese. © 1905. Animal, Board Game. 300

1126. Military Table Game, A. © 1911. Military, Card Game. 250

1127. Mind Reading. Circa 1895. Mystic, Card Game. 65

1128. Modern Authors. Circa 1890. Literary, Card Game. 50

1129. Modern Hieroglyphics. © 1868. Words, Card Game. 125

1130. Mother Goose, Game of Melodious. Circa 1895. Nursery Rhyme, Board Game. 300

1131. Mother Goose, Game of. © 1909. Nursery Rhyme, Board Game. 300

1132. Mother Goose. © 1905. Nursery Rhyme, Board Game, Yellow background and dressed goose. 400

1133. Motor Cycle Game. © 1905. Travel, Board Game. 600

1134. Mounting the Camel in Cairo. Circa 1895. Animal, Board Game. 300

1135. Myriopticon, The. Circa 1880. Mystic, Card Game. 100

1136. National Standards. Circa 1895. Advertising, Card Game. 150

1137. Nationalia. Circa 1872. Geography, Card Game. 125

1138. Nations, Game of. Circa 1900s. Geography, Card Game. 150

1139. Nations, The Game of. © 1908. History, Card Game. 100

1140. O'Grady's Goat. © 1906. Animal, Card Game. 100

1141. Old Gypsy Fortune Teller. © 1913. Mystic, Card Game. 65

1142. Old Mill Fortune Teller, The. Circa 1890s. Mystic, Card Game. 150

1143. Old Mother Hubbard. © 1910. Nursery Rhyme, Card Game. 100

1144. On Guard. Circa 1913. Military, Board Game. 200

1145. Over the Garden. © 1911. Plant, Board Game. 125

1146. Over There. Circa 1915-18. Military, World War I, Board Game. 225

1147. Palmistry. © 1895. Mystic, Card Game. 75

1148. Peter Coddle's Trip. Circa 1900. Reading, Card Game. 75

1149. Peter Rabbit. Circa 1910s. Animal, Board Game. 150

1150. Pick Up, The New Game. Circa 1905. Social, Card Game. $75

1151. Pirate & Traveler. © 1911. Adventure, Board Game. 175

1152. Progressive Words. Circa 1895. Words, Card Game. 75

1153. Puss in Boots, Game of. Circa 1920s. Nursery Rhymes, Board Game. 200

1154. Puss, the Funny Game of. © 1919. Nursery Rhymes, Board Game. 150

1155. Queer Heads and Odd Bodies. Circa 1880. Social, Card Game. 200

1156. Races. Circa 1900. Sports, Horseracing, Board Game. 125

1157. Rip Van Winkle. © 1909. Literary, Card Game. 100

1158. Robinson Crusoe, Game of. Different color cover. Circa 1920s. Literary, Adventure, Board Game. 75

1159. Robinson Crusoe, Game of. Circa 1910s. Literary, Adventure, Board Game. 100

1160. Round the World. © 1890. Travel, Board Game. 400

1161. Round the World. © 1910. Geography, Board Game. 175

1162. Round Up, Game of. Circa 1910s. Western, Board Game. 300

1163. Royal Jack Straws. © 1900. Skill, Skill Game. 50

1164. Rummie, with: Argentina; Baffles; Flique; Goop; Grafto; Quenette; Reno; Rummie Baseball; Secret Seven; Turkette. © 1914. Combination, Board Game. 150

1165. Rummie. © 1914. Classic, Card Game. 40

1166. Safety Target. Circa 1900. Skill, Action Game. 125

1167. Sailor Boy. © 1905. Military, Board Game. 250

1168. Santa Claus Game. Circa 1913. Holidays, Board Game. 300

1169. Scouts and Indians. © 1912. Western, Cowboys & Indians, Board Game. 300

1170. Siege, Game of. Circa 1910s. Military, Board Game. 300

1171. Signs, The Game of. Circa 1890. Social, Card Game. 85

1172. Snap. ©1905. Classic, Card Game. 50

1173. Spelka, The Great Word Game. Circa 1908. Words, Card Game. 35

1174. Spelling School. Circa 1895. Word, Card Game. 40

1175. Sports. Circa 1910. Sports, Board Game. 300

1176. Springfield Football Game. © 1895. Sports, Football, Board Game. 650

1177. Stars and Stripes. Circa 1895. Military, Board Game. 300

1178. Steeple Chase, Game of. Circa 1910s. Sports, Horseracing, Board Game. 250

1179. Stubborn Pigs, Game of. Circa 1910s. Animal, Board Game. 250

1180. Table Croquet. Circa 1890s. Skill, Board Game. 60

1181. Telegraph Game, Bradley's. Circa 1905. Combination, Board Game. 200

1182. Three Bears. © 1909. Animal, Board Game. 150

Milton Bradley continued

1183. Three Little Kittens, The. Circa 1910s. Nursery Rhyme, Animal, Board Game. $150

1184. Three Little Pigs. Circa 1943. Animals, Board Game. 25

1185. Through the Locks to the Garden Gate. © 1905. Geography, Board Game. 350

1186. Tiddledy Winks (4455). Circa 1905. Skill, Skill Game. 25

1187. Timothy Tuttle. Circa 1895. Social, Card Game. 75

1188. Tip-Top Four Game Combination. Circa 1910s. Combination, Board Game. 50

1189. Tommy Tenderfoot's Western Trip. Circa 1895. Western, Card Game. 65

1190. Tourist, A Rail Road Game, The. Circa 1910s. Travel, Rail, and Board Game. 300

1191. Tourist, The, A Railroad Game. Circa 1900. Travel, Rail, and Board Game. 350

1192. Toy Town Target with Foxy Grandpa. © 1911. Comics, Skill Game. 150

1193. Transportation, Game of. Circa 1895. Travel, Board Game. 350

1194. Trip to Washington. © 1884. Travel, Board Game. 350

1195. Twelve Game Combination Board (4469). 1937. Combination, Board Game. 40

1196. Two Game Combination, Steeple Chase and Checkers. Circa 1910. Combination, Board Game. 250

1197. Two Game Combination, U.S. Mail and Checkers. Circa 1920. Combination, Board Game. 200

1198. Uncle Sam's Mail. Circa 1910. Communications, Board Game. 250

1199. Uncle Silas at the Fair. Circa 1900. Reading, Fair, Card Game. 125

1200. War of Nations. Circa 1900. Military, Board Game. 200

1201. War of Nations. Circa 1900. Military, Board Game. 200

1202. War, Game of. Circa 1910s. Military, Board Game. 200

1203. War, Game of. Circa 1910s. Military, Board Game. 200

1204. Which, What or Where. © 1907. Q & A, Card Game. 50

1205. Which, What or Where? A Geography Game. © 1907. Geography, Card Game. 50

1206. Who Knows? Circa 1890s. Q & A, Card Game. 65

1207. Who-Did? Circa 1910-15. Miscellaneous, Card Game. 50

1208. Wild Flowers. Circa 1895. Plants, Card Game. 60

1209. Wild West Game. Circa 1910s. Western, Board Game. 250

1210. Words and Sentences, Game of, Regular Edition. Circa 1890. Word, Card Game. 50

1211. Words and Sentences, Game of, Wooden Box. Circa 1890. Word, Card Game. 75

1212. Words and Sentences, Game of. Circa 1877. Word, Card Game. 125

1213. Wyhoo! © 1897. Strategy, Card Game. 75

1214. Yacht Race, The Pennant. © 1905. Sports, Boating, Board Game. $250

1215. Yacht Race. Circa 1895. Sports, Boating, Board Game. 150

1216. Zoo Game, The. © 1905. Animals, Card Game. 65

1217. Zum. Circa 1900s. Social, Card Game. 40

Brewster & Co., Printers

1218. Brewster's Educational Game Cards. Series No. 1 - Geographical. © 1882. Geography, Card Game. 50

A. M. Brown

1219. Geographics. © 1880. Geography, Card Game. 75

Clark Brown

1220. Young America's Home and School History Cards. © 1884. History, Card Game. 125

F. H. Brown & Co.

1221. States, Hosford's Game of. © 1894. Geography; History, Card Game. 125

G. P. Brown & Co.

1222. Wild Birds, Game of. © 1914. Animals, Birds, Card Game. 75

W. T. Buckner

1223. National Finance. © 1895. Economics, Card Game. 125

Buehi Book Co.

1224. Wiggs. © 1903. Social, Card Game. 65

Burdette Co.

1225. Anarchist (author J. W. Burdette). © 1886. Political, Card Game. 200

M. C. Burkel

1226. Johnny, Pipe the Whistle Out, Fortune. Circa 1900. Mystic, Card Game. 100

Butler & Goldey

1227. Synthesis (© Charles P. Goldey). © 1881. Miscellaneous, Card Game. 150

C & O'B Co.

1228. California - The Great Educator. © 1913. Geography, Card Game. 125

California Educational Games Co.
1229. Pirate and Traveler. © 1906. Travel,
　Board Game. $250

Mrs. C. L. Camp
1230. Mountain Building (author Mrs. C. L. Camp).
　© 1891. Architecture, Card Game. 200

Carber Card Co.
1231. Business Men's Series, The. Circa 1900.
　Economic, Card Game. 150

J. Carr
1232. Arithmomachy (J. Carr, author). © 1890.
　Numbers, Card Game. 50

S. W. Carr
1233. Presidential Electoral Game. © 1892. Political,
　Card Game. 200

N. F. Carryl
1234. Colors. © 1884. Education, Card Game. 75

Centaphrase Society
1235. Lingo. © 1916. Words, Card Game. 35

H. B. Chaffee Manufacturing Co.
1236. Battle for the Flag. © 1887. Military,
　Board Game. 500

Chaffee & Selchow
1237. A B C Darien. © 1899. Word, Card Game. 75
1238. Basketball. © 1898. Sports, Basketball,
　Board Game. 1800
1239. Battle for the Flag, The Game of. © 1887.
　Military, Board Game. 500
1240. Bell Boy Game, The. © 1898. Social,
　Board Game. 300
1241. Ben Hur. © 1899. Military, Board Game. 2250
1242. Bicycle Race, The. © 1898. Sports,
　Miscellaneous, Board Game. 1000
1243. Birds of North America. © 1879. Animals,
　Birds, Card Game. 75
1244. Blow Foot Ball. © 1898. Sports, Football,
　Board Game. 100
1245. Cowboy Game, The. © 1898. Western,
　Cowboys, Board Game. 800
1246. Dewey at Manila. © 1899. Military, Card Game. ... 200
1247. Donkey Party Game. © 1902. Animal,
　Board Game. 125
1248. Fascination. © 1890. Miscellaneous,
　Board Game. 200
1249. Geschalft or The Game of Business. © 1897.
　Economic, Board Game. 1200
1250. Lee at Havana. © 1899. Military, Spanish
　American War, Card Game. 200

1251. Lilliput Golf. © 1900. Sports, golf, Board Game. $500
1252. Little Corporal, The. © 1899. Military,
　Board Game. 500
1253. Merry Go-Round, The. © 1898. Circus,
　Board Game. 1500
1254. Miles at Puerto Rico. © 1899. Military,
　Card Game. 200
1255. Moose-Hunt. © 1896. Animal, Adventure,
　Board Game. 1500
1256. Old King Cole, Game of. Circa 1890s. Nursery
　Rhyme, Board Game. 250
1257. Old Maid, Game of. © 1898. Social,
　Card Game. 150
1258. Old Mother Goose, Game of. Circa 1890.
　Nursery Rhyme, Board Game. 350
1259. Old Woman Who Lived in a Shoe, The. Circa
　1890. Nursery Rhyme, Board Game. 300
1260. Oorlog, The Game of. © 1898. Miscellaneous,
　Board Game. 250
1261. Parlor Golf. 1897. Sports, golf, Board Game. 1000
1262. Pool, Game of. © 1898. Sports, Miscellaneous,
　Board Game. 1500
1263. Roosevelt at San Juan. © 1899. Military,
　Card Game. 350

1264. Schley at Santiago Bay. © 1899. Military,
　Spanish American War, Card Game. 200
1265. Seal Hunting in Alaska. Circa 1890s. Animal,
　Adventure, Board Game. 1500
1266. Shafter at Santiago. © 1899. Military, Spanish
　American War, Card Game. 200
1267. Silverlocks and the Three Bears. © 1898.
　Nursery Rhymes, Board Game. 1000
1268. Skating Race Game, The. ©1898. Sports,
　Skating, Board Game. 1800
1269. Tiger Hunt, Game of. © 1899. Animal,
　Board Game. 1200
1270. Vassar Board Race, The. © 1899. Sports,
　Boating, Board Game. 2000
1271. War and Diplomacy, Game of. © 1899. Military,
　Spanish American War, Card Game. 200
1272. Young Athlete, The. © 1898. Sport,
　Board Game. 2200

Cheyenne Game Co.
1273. Cheyenne. 1907. Western, Indian, Card Game. 150

Chicago Game Co.
1274. Blind Auction. © 1913. Economics,
　Board Game. $200
1275. Cross Country Race, The. Circa 1913. Travel,
　Board Game. 1500
1276. Diamond Ball. Circa 1913. Skill, Board Game. 300
1277. Marveldex Game Board. Circa 1913.
　Combination, Board Game. 150
1278. Pana Kanal. © 1913. Travel, Board Game. 250
1279. Rush Punt Football. Circa 1915. Sports,
　Football, Board Game. 400
1280. Spider & the Bee, The. ©1912. Animal, Insects,
　Board Game. 200
1281. States and Cities. Circa 1913. Travel,
　Board Game. 250
1282. Whirl Wheel. Circa 1913. Miscellaneous,
　Board Game. 200
1283. Win-a-Peg. Circa 1913. Skill, Board Game. 150
1284. World to World Airship Race, The New. Circa
　1915. Travel, Board Game. 2500

Chicago, Burlington & Q R.R.
1285. Through Train (author Joseph Vail). © 1894.
　Travel, Rail, and Board Game. 200

Child Welfare Publishers, Inc.
1286. Flower Game, The. © 1912. Plants, Card Game. 65
1287. Funnyface Game. © 1912. Social, Card Game. 50
1288. Garden Speller. © 1912. Words, Card Game. 65
1289. Jolly Faces Game, The. © 1912. Social,
　Card Game. 50
1290. Playtime Speller. © 1912. Words, Card Game. 50
1291. Wonder Speller, The. © 1912. Words,
　Card Game. 50
1292. Wonderland Zoo. © 1912. Animals,
　Card Game. 65

George A. Childs
1293. Football, The Game of. © 1895. Sports, Football,
　Board Game. 250

Cincinnati Game Co.
1294. Addition and Subtraction. © 1902. Numbers,
　Card Game. 50
1295. Astronomy. © 1905. Space, Card Game. 755
1296. Authors. © 1897. Literary, Card Game. 50
1297. Birds. © 1899. Animal, Card Game. 65
1298. Constructive Geometry. © 1903. Numbers,
　Card Game. 75
1299. Domestic Animals. © 1903. Animal,
　Card Game. 65
1300. Famous Paintings. © 1897. Art, Card Game. 80
1301. Flags. © 1896. Geography, Card Game. 65
1302. Fortunes, Game of. © 1902. Economics,
　Card Game. 75
1303. Fractions. © 1902. Numbers, Card Game. 75

1304. Illustrated Mythology. © 1901. Fantasy-
　Mythology, Card Game. $100
1305. In Dixieland, Game of. © 1897. Ethnic,
　Card Game. 250
1306. In the White House. © 1896. Political,
　Card Game. 75
1307. Individual and Progressive Nile. © 1896.
　Miscellaneous, Card Game. 60
1308. Multiplication and Division. © 1903. Numbers,
　Card Game. 65
1309. Mythology. © 1900. History, Card Game. 60
1310. New Testament Game. © 1899. Religious,
　Card Game. 60
1311. Our National Life. © 1903. History, Card Game. 75
1312. Quotes of Authors. Circa 1900. Literary,
　Card Game. 50
1313. Shakespeare, Game of. © 1901. Literary,
　Card Game. 65
1314. Wild Animals (Normal Size). © 1903. Animal,
　Card Game. 50
1315. Words, Game of. © 1903. Word, Card Game. 35

C. M. Clark Pub. Co.
1316. Stage. © 1904. Theatrical, Card Game. 125
1317. Stage. Purple box Edition. ©1904. Theatrical,
　Card Game. 125

Edgar O. Clark
1318. Fish Pond. Circa 1890s. Animal, Fish,
　Board Game. 150
1319. Golf, The Game of. © 1900. Sports, Golf,
　Board Game. 600
1320. Hippodrome, The. Circa 1900. Circus,
　Board Game. 400
1321. Owl and the Pussy Cat, The. Circa 1900.
　Animal, Board Game. 500
1322. Postal Delivery Boys. Circa 1900.
　Communications, Board Game. 400
1323. Robinson Crusoe for Little Boys, Game of.
　Circa 1900. Adventure, Board Game. 250
1324. Rough Riders, The Game of. © 1890. Military,
　Spanish American War, Board Game. 750
1325. Steeple Chase. © 1900. Sports, Racing,
　Board Game. 450

Clark & Sowden

1326. Anagrams & Lotto, Tokalon Series. © 1893.
Word, Card Game. $45

1327. Authors Illustrated, Tokalon Series. 1893.
Literary, Card Game. 100

1328. Authors, Hidden. © 1892. Literary, Card Game. 50

1329. Authors, Vignette (210). © 1895. Literary,
Card Game. 50

1330. Brownies, Game of. © 1895. Comic,
Card Game. 200

1331. Butterfly Stop. © 1893. Card Game. 75

1332. Charge, The., Tokalon Series. © 1899. Teddy
Roosevelt leading the charge, Military, Spanish
American War, Board Game. 1000

1333. Chessindia. © 1895. Classic, Board Game. 85

1334. Coonies (101). © 1895. Ethnic, Board Game. 500

1335. Fish Pond, Game of. © 1895. Animal, Fish,
Board Game. 150

1336. Five in a Row, Cats on a Fence, Tokalon Series.
© 1895. Animal, Cat, Board Game. 250

1337. Fox & Hounds. © 1902. Animal, Board Game. 150

1338. Gipsy Fortune Teller (102). © 1902. Mystic,
Card Game. 100

1339. Golf, The Game of. © 1905. Sports, Golf,
Board Game. 350

1340. Hunting the Rabbit. Circa 1890s. Animal,
Board Game. 225

1341. Nimble Spider, Tokalon Series. Circa 1890s.
Animal, Card Game. 150

**1342. Old Maids as played by Mother Goose, The
Game of.** © 1892. Nursery Rhyme, Card Game. 75

1343. Peter Coddles Dinner Party, Tokalon Series. ©
1890. Social, Card Game. 65

1344. Rip Van Winkle, Tokalon Series. © 1900.
Literary, Board Game. 300

1345. Wang, The Game of. © 1892. Miscellaneous,
Card Game. 65

1346. Who Can Mount the Donkey. Circa 1890s.
Animal, Board Game. 125

1347. Yacht Race. Circa 1895. Sports, Boating,
Board Game. 300

Mary E. Clarke

1348. Missionary Pioneers. © 1885. Religious, Cards. 75

S. L. Clemens

1349. Mark Twain's Memory Builder. © 1891. Mental
Activity, Cards. 225

Clinton Hall

1350. Robber, Game of. Circa 1900. Law & Order,
Card Game. $150

Clintonville Novelty Works

1351. Authors, Improved Game of Oriental. Circa
1900. Literary, Card Game. 50

Coin Card Co.

1352. Coin Cards. Circa 1910s. Economic,
Card Game. 75

C. S. Colby

**1353. Winning Game, The (author a W.C.T.U. Lady
of Boston).** © 1891. Miscellaneous, Card Game. 65

College Game Co.

1354. College, The Greatest Game on Earth. © 1908.
Education, Card Game. 75

Combination Card Game Co.

1355. Parlor Card Game. © 1904. Miscellaneous,
Card Game. 50

1356. Trail, Parlor Card Game. © 1904. Social, Card
Game. 100

**1357. Trail, Chase, Dogon, Red Heads, Numbers,
Word Building, and Finding His Sweetheart.** ©
1904. Combination, Card Game. 100

Combination Publishing Co.

**1358. Harmony, The Game of (by Rev. James W.
Shearer).** © 1892. Musical, Card Game. 100

Morton E. Converse Co.

1359. Faba Baga, or Parlor Quoits. © 1883. Skill,
Skill Game. 75

Laura Gerould Craig

1360. Progressive Game of Biography. © 1893.
History, Card Game. 100

1361. Progressive Game of Geography, The. 1893.
Geography, Card Game. 65

David C. Cook Publishing Co.
1362. Bible Game Occupations. © 1900. Religious,
    Card Game. $35
1363. Bible Game Occupations. Variant cover. ©
    1900. Religious, Card Game. 35
1364. New Testament Books, Bible Game of. © 1900.
    Religious, Card Game. 35

Co-operative Game & Novelty Co.
1365. Black Sheep, The, with The Scape Goat. ©
    1909. Animal, Card Game. 75
1366. Scape Goat, The. © 1909. Animal, Card Game. 75

Jesse A. Crandall
1367. Teddy's Ride from Oyster Bay to Albany. ®
    1899. Political, Board Game. 4000

C. R. Crow
1368. Our Friends in Fur. © 1890. Animal,
    Card Game. 125

Cushman & Denison Mfg. Co.
1369. Finding the Pole. © 1908. Travel, Board Game. 250

Cutler & Saleeby Co.
1370. India Bombay. Circa 1920s. Classic,
    Board Game. 75

L. R. Damon
1371. Guess Again. Circa 1880s. Q & A, Card Game. 50
1372. Pilgrims Progress, The Game of. © 1890.
    Religious, Card Game. 65

W. O. Dapping
1373. Great American Game Base Ball, The. © 1906.
    Sports, Baseball, Board Game. 250

H. H. Dargin
1374. Base Ball Game, Clark & Martin's New. ©
    1885. Sport, Baseball, Board Game. 300

Decker & Decker, Colby
1375. American Characters, Game of. © 1908.
    History, Card Game. 65
1376. Bible Characters. © 1889. Religious,
    Card Game. 35
1377. Characters Foreign, Game of. © 1916. History,
    Card Game. 50
1378. Characters, Foreign, Game of. © 1889.
    Geography, Card Game. 65

1379. Cities, A Game of. © 1887. Geography,
    Card Game. $65
1380. States, The. © 1890. Geography, Card Game. 55
1381. States, The. Later edition. © 1912. Geography,
    Card Game. 50
1382. World, A Game of the. © 1889. History,
    Card Game. 60

Dewey Game & Novelty Co.
1383. Dewey Game, The. Circa 1898. Military,
    Card Game. 150

Wm. H. Dietz
1384. Bible Links. © 1896. Religious, Card Game. 40

Domino Sugar
1385. Crystal Domino Sugar Cards, Premium. Circa
    1900. Premium, Card Game. 75

Geo. B. Doan Co.
1385a.Amerst, The American Star. © 1905,
    Theatrical Board Game. 200

L. L. Doud
1386. Albion Business Authors (Albion, MI). © 1895.
    Literary, Card Game. 100

S. H. Dudley
1387. Our Bird Friends. © 1901. Animal, Card Game. 65

Economic Game Co.
1388. Landlord's Game, The. © 1904. Economic,
    Board Game, First Monopoly Game invented by
    Elizabeth Magie Philips. 6000

Educational Game Co.
1389. Bible Authors, Game of. © 1895. Religious,
    Card Game. 40
1390. Trip Through Europe, A. Circa 1890s. Travel,
    Board Game. 200

Elliot Mfg.
**1391. Old Homestead, Games at the - Popular Race
    Game.** © 1881. Travel, Board Game. 250

Eurika Study System
1392. Tess Mads. © 1911. Religious, Card Game. 60

Evangelical Pub Co.
1393. Bible Authors. © 1895. Religious, Card Game. 40
1393a.Bible Girls. © 1905. Religious Card Game. 50

Fairbanks, Palmer & Co.
1394. Chautauqua Game of Astronomy. © 1882.
Space, Card Game. $125

Fireside Game Co.
1395. Arithmetic- Play, Game of. © 1899. Numbers,
Card Game. 50
1396. Artists, Game of. © 1896. Art, Card Game. 75
1397. Bible Game. © 1899. Religious, Card Game. 50
1398. Birds, Game of. © 1899. Animal, Card Game. 75
1399. Chestnut Burrs. © 1896. Plant, Card Game. 150
1400. Flags of the World, Game of. © 1896.
Geography, Card Game. 65
**1401. Flags of the World, Game of, Pan-Am Expo
Edition.** © 1896. Geography, Card Game. 125
1402. Flowers, Game of. © 1899. Plant, Card Game. 75
1403. Fraction Play. © 1896. Numbers, Card Game. 75
1404. In Castleland, Game of. © 1896. History,
Geography, Card Game. 50
1405. Mayflower, The. © 1897. History, Card Game. 85
1406. Nationalities, Game of. © 1897. Geography,
Card Game. 50
1407. Our Union, Game of. © 1896. History,
Card Game. 75
1408. Pines, The. © 1898. Plant, Card Game. 125
1409. Poem Illustrated, Game of. © 1898. Literary,
Card Game. 65
1410. Poems, Game of. © 1898. Literary, Card Game. 65
1411. Population, Game of. © 1896. Geography, Card
Game. 60
1412. Strange People, Game of. © 1895. Ethnic, Card
Game. 75
1413. White Squadron, U. S. Navy Vessels. © 1898.
Military, Spanish American War, Card Game. 125
1414. Wild Animals, Game of, Small Edition. © 1895.
Animal, Card Game. 50
1415. Yellowstone, Game of. © 1900. Geography,
Card Game. 75
1416. Young Folks Favorite Authors. © 1897.
Literary, Card Game. 50

A. M. Fitch & Co.
1417. Fitch's Game of Natural History. © 1897. Plant,
Animal, Card Game. 75

A. Flanagan, Lack & Fey
1418. Presidents & Historical Events, Game of. Circa
1910. Political, History, Card Game. $150

Flanagan Pub.
**1419. Mother Earth's Produce Game, by
C. B. Sheldon.** © 1897. Plant, Card Game. 100

Flinch Card Co.
1420. Bourse or Stock Exchange. © 1903.
Stock Market, Card Game. 100

1421. Competition or Department Store. © 1904.
Economic, Card Game. 125
1422. Flinch. © 1913. Number, Card Game. 25
1423. Roodles. © 1912. Number, Card Game. 35

A. B. Floyd
1424. War, or American Generals and their Battles.
© 1890. Military, Card Game. 150

A. F. Foll
1425. Our Country. © 1884. History, Board Game. 125

Forbes Co.
1426. Politics. © 1889. Political, Card Game. 150

W. M. Ford
1427. Progressive Chautaqua Cards. © 1899. Social,
Card Game. 35

Forker Manufacturing Co.
1428. Geography, Game of (© by Wm. Forker). ©
1888. Geography, Card Game. 75

E. W. Frick
1429. Famous Scripture People. © 1892. Religious,
Card Game. 50

F. B. Frye
1430. National Temperance Game, The. © 1890.
Political, Card Game. $75

Margaret A. Gardner
1431. Musical-Biography (author Margaret A.
Gardner). © 1891. Musical, Card Game. 75

A. C. Garrott
1432. Lone Star Game, or Texas History Made Easy
(author Garrott). © 1890. History, Card Game. 125

Gavitt Printing & Pub. Co.
1433. Gavitt's Stock Exchange. © 1904. Stock Market,
Card Game. 75
1434. Gavitt's Stock Exchange. Black & Grey. ©
1903. Stock Market, Card Game. 75

Geographic Educator
1435. Game of Know Your Vegetables, The. Circa
1900. Plant, Card Game. 100

Gibson Game Co.
1436. Little Shoppers. © 1915. Economic,
Board Game. 250

Glenleven
1437. Glenleven's New Boat Race, The. Circa 1900s.
Sports, Sea, Board Game. 300

Gloucester Novelty Co.
1438. Council. © 1910. Indians, Card Game. 150

Goss Bros.
1439. Uncle Sam's Cabinets, Part 1. © 1901. Political,
Card Game. 200
1440. Uncle Sam's Cabinets. Part 2. © 1901. Political,
Card Game. 200

Gray's Portland Business College
1441. Driver, or Parlor Golf (© J. W. Keller). Circa
1910. Sports, Golf, Board Game. 150

Grebnelle Game Co.
1442. Champion Base Ball Parlor Game. 1914. Sport,
Baseball, Board Game. 1250

Greenfield Novelty Co.
1443. States, Hosford's Game of. © 1894. Geography,
History, Card Game. 75

Grow & Co.
1444. Rivers. © 1890. Geography, Card Game. 85

Halma Co.
1445. Basilinda. © 1890. Strategy, Board Game. $300
1446. Halma, 1st Edition. © 1885. Classic,
Board Game. 50
1447. Halma, 2nd Edition. © 1889. Classic,
Board Game. 50

A. M. Heston, Publisher
1448. Paola. © 1893. Economic, Board Game. 200

Leroy Hill
1449. America. © 1895. History, Board Game. 300

A. J. F. Hoffmann Novelty Co.
1450. Educational Music Game. © 1914. Musical,
Card Game. 75

Mary S. Holmes
1451. Philadelphia Buildings, The Game of, © 1899.
Architecture, History, Card Game. 100

Holt & Folger
1452. New Parlor Game, Capture of Mr. Raffles. ©
1905. Social, Card Game. 150

Home Game Co.
1453. Bird Center Etiquette, A Card Game. © 1904.
Animal, Card Game. 75
1454. Bunco. © 1904. Numbers, Card Game. 35

C. I. Hood & Co.
1455. Auto Race, The. Circa 1910. Travel, Card Game. 150
1456. Hood's Spelling School, Premium Hood's
Sarsparilla. © 1897. Word, Card Game. 7
1457. Hood's War Game, U.S. vs. Spain. © 1898.
Military, Spanish American War, Card Game. 150

L. E. Hooker & Co.
1458. American History. © 1890. History, Card Game. 75

E. I. Horsmann
1459. Klondike, Game of. © 1897. Adventure,
Board Game. 350
1460. Magnetic Jack Straws. © 1891. Classic,
Skill Game. 50
1460a.Portrait Authors. Circa 1890s, Literary Card Game. 100
1460b.Prize Birds, Popular Edition. Circa 1890s.
Animal, Card Game. 65
1460c.Ring A Peg, The New Game. Pat 1898. Action
Skill Game. 70
1461. Snap, The Game of. © 1883. Classic,
Card Game. 55

W. J. Hosmer
1462. Book of Books (author W. J. Hosmer). © 1887.
  Religious, Card Game. $50

Household Words Game Co.
1463. Household Words, Game of. © 1916. Words,
  Card Game. 60

Alfred F. Howe
1464. Cities of Our Country. © 1892. Geography,
  Card Game. 75

J. W. Howell
1465. Pronouncit, The Game of. © 1894. Words,
  Card Game. 65

Ideal Book Builders
1466. Funny Face Game. © 1912. Miscellaneous,
  Board Game. 75
1467. Jolly Faces Game, The. © 1912. Clown, Circus,
  Board Game. 85
1468. Wonder Garden Game. © 1912. Plant,
  Board Game. 100

Indianapolis News
1469. Indiana Authors, Game of. © 1900. Literary,
  Card Game. 100

J. W. S.& S., New York
1470. National Football Match, The. Circa 1890s.
  Sports, Soccer, Board Game. 75

H. N. Jenkins
1471. Negro Characterism Game of. © 1890. Ethnic,
  Card Game. 150

Walter Johnson Game Co.
1472. Walter Johnson Baseball Game. Circa 1910s.
  Sports, Baseball, Board Game. 450

J. W. Keller
1473. Hounds & Hares. Circa 1890s. Animal,
  Board Game. 125

J. W. Kelly
1474. Touchdown or Parlor Foot Ball, The Game of.
  © 1897. Sport, Football, Premium, Card Game. 200

L. I. W. Kent
1475. Musical Logomachy (author L. I. W. Kent). ©
  1891. Musical, Card Game. 75

Lackner & Feyren
1476. Presidents & Historical Events, Game of. ©
  1894. Political, History, Card Game. 100

Ladies' Home Journal (Curtis Pub.)
**1477. Night Before Christmas (by Esperanza
  Gabay).** © 1910. Holiday, Card Game. $250

Lafferty and Smith
**1478. Battle of Gettysburg, A Parlor Game. Table
  top Wooden board.** Circa 1900. Military, CW,
  Board Game. 650

Dr. Walter Lamb
1479. Checker Game of Classics, The. © 1887.
  Literary, Board Game. 150

R. H. Lathrop
1480. Grant's National Victory. Circa 1884. Military,
  Board Game. 300

Lawson Card Co.
1481. Lawson's Baseball Card Game. © 1884. Sports,
  Baseball, Card Game. 500

Leonard Mfg. Co.
1482. Combinola, Combination Board, Large Wood.
  © 1905. Combination, Board Game. 350

Lion Coffee Co.
1483. Animals. © 1900. Animal, Advertising,
  Card Game. 50
1484. Astronomy. Circa 1900s. Space, Card Game. 100
1485. Authors. Circa 1900s. Literary, Card Game. 50
1486. Birds, Game of, Premium. © 1900. Animal,
  Premium, Card Game. 50
1487. Buy and Sell, Game of. Circa 1900s. Economic,
  Card Game. 60
1488. Chance, Game of. © 1900. Premium,
  Card Game. 50
1489. Chinese Game. Circa 1900. Ethnic, Card Game. 50
1490. Chink, Game of. © 1908. Ethnic, Premium,
  Card Game. 50
1491. Circus, Game of. © 1903. Circus, Card Game. 65
1492. Color Casino, Game of. © 1903. Miscellaneous,
  Advertising, Card Game. 50
1493. Countries. © 1903. Geography, Advertising,
  Card Game. 60
1494. Donkey. © 1894. Animal, Card Game. 50
1495. Eureka, Game of. © 1900. Premium,
  Card Game. 50
1496. Fairies' Palace, The. © 1894. Fantasy,
  Card Game. 65
1497. Familiary Quotations, A New Game. Circa
  1900s. Literary, Card Game. 50
1498. Famous People. Circa 1900. History, Premium,
  Card Game. 60
1499. From Log Cabin to the White House. © 1895.
  Political, Card Game. 75
1500. Inventions. © 1908. History, Card Game. 75
1501. Jack Straws. Circa 1900. Premium, Skill Game. 50
1502. Jeremiah Judkin's Trip to the Fair. Circa 1900s.
  Fair, Card Game. 50

Lion Coffee Co. continued

1503. Knowledge, Game of Premium. © 1900.
Premium, Card Game. $50
1504. Lion and Tiger. Circa 1900s. Animal, Card
Game. 50
1505. Lion Authors, Game of. © 1894. Literary,
Adventure, Card Game. 50
1506. Literature, Game of. Circa 1900s. Literary, Card
Game. 50
1507. Maypole. © 1895. Miscellaneous, Card Game. 50
1508. Monkey. © 1900. Animal, Premium, Card Game. 50
1509. Months. Circa 1900. Premium, Time,
Card Game. 50
1510. Mother Goose. Circa 1900. Nursery Rhyme,
Card Game. 50
1511. National Rulers. © 1900. History, Premium,
Card Game. 60

1512. Nations, Game of, Premium. © 1903. History,
Premium, Card Game. 50
1513. Nursery Rhymes. Circa 1910. Nursery Rhymes,
Card Game. 50
1514. Old Maid Premium. Circa 1900. Classic,
Card Game. 50
1515. Our Country, Premium. © 1894. History,
Premium, Card Game. 60
1516. Our Navy. © 1898. Military, Card Game. 65
1517. Our Union, Premium. Circa 1900. Premium,
Card Game. 65
1518. Pachesi. Circa 1900s. Miscellaneous,
Card Game. 50

1519. Patent Medicine, Premium. © 1903. Premium,
Card Game. 85
1520. Pig, Game of. Circa 1900s. Animal, Card Game. 50
1521. Politics, Premium. © 1900. Politics, Premium,
Card Game. 75
1522. Polly Wants a Cracker. © 1903. Nursery
Rhymes, Card Game. 50

1523. Queen's Guards. Circa 1892. Royal,
Card Game. $50
1524. Rueben Rubberneck's Visit to Chicago. Circa
1900s. Social, Card Game. 50
1525. Samuel Goodall's Vacation. Circa 1900s. Social,
Card Game. 50
1526. Sir Kinkum Funny Duster. Circa 1900s. Social,
Card Game. 50
1527. Snap. Circa 1900s. Classic, Card Game. 50
1528. Spelling, Premium. © 1900. Word, Premium,
Card Game. 50
1529. Spy, The, Premium. Circa 1900. Literary,
Card Game. 100
1530. States, Game of, Premium. © 1900. Geography.
Premium, Card Game. 60
1531. Stop, New Game of, Premium. © 1903.
Premium, Card Game. 50
1532. Uncle Tom's Cabin. Circa 1900s. Literary -
Ethnic, Card Game. 100
1533. Wars, Game of. Circa 1900. Military, Adventure,
Card Game. 65
1534. Wars of the World, Premium. © 1900. Military,
Premium, Card Game. 50
1535. Words, Game of. Circa 1900s. Words,
Card Game. 50

Littlefield Mfg. Co.
1536. Quarterback. © 1914. Sports, Football,
Board Game. 250

Loizeaux Brothers
1537. Illustrated Game of Bible Names. Circa 1910s.
Religious, Card Game. 35
**1538. Bible Names for Old & Young, Illustrated
Game of.** Circa 1890. Religious, Card Game. 35

D. Lothrop & Co.
**1539. Analyzer Alphabets (by Mrs. A.D.T.
Whitneys).** © 1881. Words, Card Game. 35

L. H. Mace & Co.
1540. Red, White and Blue, The New Game of. ©
1891. Political, Card Game. 75

Carl Mack Mfg. Co.
1541. Custer's Last Fight. © 1911. Military,
Board Game. 350
1542. War, The Game of. © 1911. Military,
Board Game. 250

Mrs. Nellie T. Magee
1543. Bible ABC's & Bible Promises. Circa 1900.
Religious, Card Game. 40
1544. Bible Books. Circa 1890s. Religious,
Card Game. 35
1545. Bible Cities. Circa 1890s. Religious, Card Game. 45
1546. Bible Characters. Circa 1890s. Religious,
Card Game. 45

C. W. Marsh

1547. Fan-I-Tis, Fan's Baseball Fun. © 1913. Sports,
Baseball, Board Game. $2000

Albert M. Martin, General Secretary

1548. Art History (Albert M. Martin, author). ©
1882. Art, Card Game. 75

The Martin Co.

1549. Spillikins. Circa 1890s. Action, Board Game. 100

Mather Game Co.

1550. Parlor Base Ball. Circa 1907. Sports, Baseball,
Board Game. 250

McGill & Delany

1551. Our National Ball Game. © 1886. Sports,
Baseball, Board Game. 600

E. M. McLean

**1552. Chicago and the World's Columbian
Exposition.** Circa 1892. Fair, Card Game. 250

McLoughlin Bros.

1553. 100 Soldiers on Parade. © 1890. Military,
Soldier Game. 750
1554. 25 Soldiers on Parade. Circa 1900s. Military,
Soldier Game. 225
1555. Across the Sea or Trip to Europe. © 1896.
Travel, World, Board Game. 1200
1556. Advance & Retreat. Quail & rabbit cover, ©
1901. Strategy, Board Game. 300
1557. Aesop's Fables. © 1888. Literary, Card Game. 150
1558. Air Ship Game, The. © 1904. Travel, Air, and
Board Game. 1000
1559. Aladdin, or The Wonderful Lamp. © 1911.
Adventure, Card Game. 150
1560. All Around the World, Game of, Pearl Series.
© 1898. Travel, Board Game. 500
1561. Ambuscade, Bounce, and Constellation. ©
1877. Combination, Board Game. 300
1562. America's Yacht Race Game, The. Circa 1900s.
Sports, Boating, Board Game. Two children
cover. 1000
1563. American Battles. Circa 1890s. Military, Spanish
American War, Card Game. 150
1564. American Boys Company D. Circa 1915.
Organizations, Board Game. 250
1565. Anagrams Double Eagle. Circa 1890s. Word,
Card Game. 125
1566. Around the World with Nellie Bly. © 1890.
Travel, Board Game. Red background cover. 200
1567. Authors, Improved, Popular Edition. Circa
1890s. Literary, Card Game. 50
1568. Authors, Game of, Red Box. Circa 1880s.
Literary, Card Game. 75
1569. Authors, Game of. Circa 1880s. Literary,
Card Game. 75

1570. Authors, Game of. Circa 1900. Literary,
Card Game. $75
1571. Automobile Race Game. Circa 1904. Sports,
Cars, Board Game, Standard series, Santa in car. 1500
1572. Baa Baa Black Sheep, Game of. © 1886.
Animal, Card Game. 175
1573. Ba-A Ba-A Black Sheep, Game of. © 1888.
Animal, Card Game. 175
1574. Base-ball, Game of. © 1886. Sports, Baseball,
Board Game. Horizontal board. 1800
1575. Basketball, Game of. Circa 1910s. Sports,
Basketball, Board Game. Young men and women
playing cover. 1250
1576. Battles, or Fun for Boys, Game of. © 1889.
Military, Board Game. 1800
1577. Bible Information, Game of. © 1888. Religious,
Card Game. 75
1578. Bicycle Race, Game of. © 1891. Sports, Bikes,
Board Game. Vertical cover. 1000
1579. Bicycle Racing. © 1900. Sport, Bikes,
Board Game. 1000
1580. Big Game Hunting. © 1911. Animals,
Board Game. 800
1581. Bo Peep Game. © 1895. Nursery Rhymes,
Board Game. 500
**1582. Bobbing-Tribang-Robbing the Miller, Games
of.** Circa 1880s. Combination, Board Game. 300
1583. Bombardment, The Game of. © 1895. Military,
Spanish American War, Board Game. 350
1584. Boy's Own Football Game. Circa 1895. Sports,
Football, Board Game. 1250
1585. Boys and Girls. © 1900. Social, Card Game. 150
1586. Boy's in Blue, The. © 1891. Military,
Card Game. 500
1587. Bulls and Bears, The Great Wall Street Game.
© 1885. Stock Market, Board Game. 15000
1588. Captive Princess, Game of. Circa 1890s.
Adventure, Board Game. 450
1589. Catching Mice, Game of. © 1888. Animal, Cat,
Board Game. 400
**1590. Centennial Game of Columbia's Presidents,
The.** 1889. Political, Card Game. 500
1591. Christmas Goose. © 1890. Holiday,
Board Game. 1500
1592. Christmas Jewel, Game of the. © 1899. Holiday,
Board Game. 800
1593. Christmas Stocking, The. © 1889. Holiday,
Board Game. 1000
1594. Circus Clown, Game of. © 1905. Circus,
Board Game. 500
1595. City Life, The Game of. © 1889. Occupations,
Card Game. 250
1596. Cock Robin, Game of. © 1885. Animal,
Card Game. 250
1597. College Boat Race, Game of. © 1896. Sports,
Boating, Board Game. 1800
1598. Colors, The Game of. © 1888. Kiddie, Board
Game. 250
1599. Comical Chit Chat Game. Circa 1882. Social,
Card Game. 175

McLoughlin Bros. continued

1600. Commercial Traveler, The Game of. © 1890. Economic, Board Game. $500

1601. Cousin Peter's Trip to New York, Game of. Circa 1898. Social, Card Game. 100

1602. Crossing the African Desert. Circa 1911. Travel, Board Game. 600

1603. Crusaders, Game of the. © 1888. History, Board Game. 400

1604. Day at the Circus. © 1898. Circus, Board Game. 500

1605. Department Store Game, The. Circa 1911. Economics, Board Game. 700

1606. Derby Steeple Chase, The. © 1899. Sports, Horseracing, Board Game. 300

1607. Derby Steeple Chase, The. © 1890. Sports, Horseracing, Board Game. 300

1608. Diamond Game of Base Ball, The. Circa 1885. Sports, Baseball, Board Game. 750

1609. Diamond Heart, Game of. © 1902. Romance, Board Game. 300

1610. Discovering the North Pole, Game of. © 1909. Travel, Board Game. 1000

1611. District Messenger Boy, Game of. © 1899. Communications, Board Game. 500

1612. District Messenger Boy or Merit Rewarded, Game. © 1886. Communications, Board Game. 450

1613. District Telegraph Boy. © 1895. Communications, Board Game. 650

1614. Domino Rex, Game of. Circa 1880s. Strategy, Board Game. 150

1615. Donkey Party Game, The. © 1901. Classic, Skill Game. 150

1616. Eastern Fortune Telling Game. © 1897. Mystic, Card Game. 150

1617. Elite Conversation Cards, Social & sentimental. © 1890. Social, Card Game. 150

1618. Elite Conversation Cards, The, Loves & Likes. © 1890. Social, Card Game. 150

1619. Elite Conversational Cards, Comical, The. © 1890. Social, Card Game. 150

1620. Errand Boy, The. © 1891. Communications, Board Game. 500

1621. Familiar Quotations, Game of. © 1887. Literary, Card Game. 100

1622. Familiar Quotations, The New Game of. © 1890. Literary, Card Game. 100

1623. Familiar Quotations from Popular Authors, Game. © 1890. Literary, Card Game. 75

1624. Farmer Jones' Pigs. Circa 1890s. Animal, Board Game. 250

1625. Filch, The Game of. © 1904. Miscellaneous, Card Game. 75

1626. Fish Pond, Game of. Circa 1890s. Animal, Board Game, one angular. 150

1627. Fish Pond, Game of. © 1890. Animal, Board Game, boy & girl in boat. 250

1628. Fish Pond, Game of. © 1890. Animal, Sea, Board Game, Goldfish cover. 150

1628a.Fish Pond, Game of. Circa 1890s. Two sturgeon cover, Animal Board Game. $150

1628b.Fish Pond, Game of. Circa 1890s, 28 colorful fish cover, animal board Game. 175

1629. Fish Pond, The Improved Game of. © 1890. Animal, Sea, Board Game, large four sail boats. 350

1629a.Fish Pond, The Improved Game of. Circa 1890s. Four children fishing cover, Board Game. 125

1630. Fish Pond. Eight fish cover. Circa 1900s. Animal, Sea, Board Game. 150

1630a. Fish Pond. Circa 1910s. Two children standing with yellow background, large size, Board Game. 250

1631. Flag Game, The. © 1887. Geography, Card Game. Horizontal box with Washington. 150

1632. Flag Game, The. © 1898. Geography, Card Game. 125

1633. Fly Away Jack & Jill. © 1894. Nursery Rhymes, Board Game. 350

1634. Football, Game of. © 1895. Sports, Football, Board Game. 1200

1635. Four and Twenty Black Birds. Circa 1890s. Nursery Rhymes, Board Game. 1500

1636. Fox & Geese, The New. Circa 1888. Animal, Board Game. 250

1637. Fox and Geese, Game of, Pearl Series. © 1903. Animal, Board Game. Both dressed in human dress. 450

1638. Frog He would a Wooing Go, Game of a. © 1902. Animal, Card Game. 400

1639. From Log Cabin to White House. Circa 1895. Political, Card Game. 300

1640. Fun at the Circus, Game of. © 1897. Circus, Board Game. 1200

1641. Geographical Cards. © 1883. Geography, Cards. 150

1642. Geographical Game, Grandma's. © 1904. Geography, Card Game. 125

1643. Get There, Game of. © 1898. Patriotic, Board Game. 750

1644. Going to the Klondike, The Game of. © 1898. Adventure, Board Game. 1500

1645. Golden Eagle Anagrams. Circa 1890s. Word, Card Game. 125

1646. Good Old Aunt, The. © 1892. Social, Card Game. 150

1647. Goosy Goosy Gander. Circa 1895. Nursery Rhyme, Board Game. 900

1648. Grandmama's Sunday Game, Old Testament. © 1887. Religious, Card Game. 125

1649. Grandmama's Sunday Game (New Testament). © 1897. Religious, Card Game. 125

1650. Grandmama's Sunday New Testament Game. © 1887. Religious, Card Game. 125

1651. Grandma's Arithmetical Game. © 1900. Numbers, Card Game. 125

1652. Grandma's Game of Mince Pie. © 1880. Food, Board Game. 150

1653. Grandma's Improved Game of Riddles. © 1890. Reading, Card Game. 125

McLoughlin Bros. continued

1654. Guess Again, The Game of. © 1910. Q & A,
Card Game. $125

1655. Gypsy Fortune Telling Game, The. © 1905.
Mystic, Board Game. 900

1656. Hand of Fate. © 1901. Mystic, Board Game. 3000

1657. Harlequin, The Game of the. © 1895. Clowns,
Board. 1200

1657a. Harlequinade Game. Circa 1900. Clowns
Board Game. 200

1658. Heraldry, A New Society Game. © 1893. Social,
Card Game. 250

1659. Hide and Seek, Game of. Circa 1895. Kiddie,
Board Game, five children as clowns cover. 1500

1660. Historical Cards, Improved. © 1884. History,
Card Game. 200

1661. Home Base Ball Game. © 1887. Sports,
Baseball, Board Game, square box with batter
and catcher. 2500

1662. Home Fish Pond, The. © 1900. Animal, Sea,
Board Game. 150

1663. Horseless Carriage Race, The. Circa 1911.
Sports, Cars, Board Game. 1200

1664. House that Jack Built, The. Circa 1890s.
Nursery Rhymes, Card Game. 150

1665. Humpty-Dumpty. Circa 1911. Nursery Rhymes,
Board Game. 250

1666. Hunt the Hare, Game of. © 1891. Animal,
Board Game. 350

1666a. Hunting, New Game of. © 1904. Animal,
Board Game. 1000

1667. Hunting the Tiger. © 1897. Animal,
Board Game. 1000

1668. Hunting Wild Animals. Circa 1911. Animals,
Board Game. 900

1669. Illustrated Authors, Game of. © 1900. Literary,
Card Game. 100

1669a. Illustrated Authors, Game of. Circa 1900,
Literary card Game. 75

1670. Improved Game of Fish Pond, The. © 1890.
Animal, Sea, Board Game, long narrow box, four
children cover. 150

1671. Improved Historical Cards. © 1884. History,
Card Game. 200

1672. Improved Star Authors, The. Circa 1900.
Literary, Card Game. 125

1672a. Improved Game of Star Authors. Longfellow
portrait cover, circa 1890s, Card Game. 75

1673. India, Game of. Circa 1910s. Classic,
Board Game. 150

1674. Intercollegiate Football. Circa 1909. Sports,
Football, Board Game. 750

1675. Jack of All Trades, The Game of. © 1890.
Careers, Card Game. 300

1676. Jack Sprat, The Game of. © 1888. Nursery
Rhyme, Card Game. 150

1677. Jack the Giant Killer. © 1890. Literary,
Adventure, Board Game. 1000

1678. Jerome Park Steeple-Chase. Circa 1880s.
Sports, Horseracing, Board Game. 800

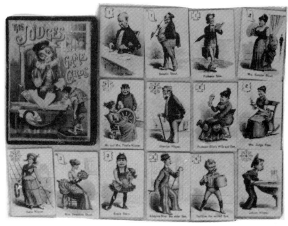

1679. Judges Game Cards, The. © 1889. Law &
Order, Card Game. $150

1680. Just Like Me, Game of. © 1888. Social,
Card Game. 150

1681. King's Quoits, New Game of. © 1893. Skill,
Skill Game. 600

1682. Kings and Queens, New & Popular. © 1890.
History, Board Game. 500

1683. Klymo, Game of. © 1892. Miscellaneous,
Board Game. 125

1684. Kriss Kringle's Visits, The Game of. Circa
1911. Holiday, Board Game. 1200

1685. Leap Frog, Game of. © 1900. Animal,
Board Game. 350

1686. Letter Carrier, The. © 1890. Communications,
Board Game. 350

1687. Letters, Game of. Circa 1911. Words, Card
Game. 75

1688. Little Jack Horner, The Game of. © 1888.
Nursery Rhyme, Card Game. 300

1688a. Little Red Riding Hood Game. Circa 1890s,
Literary board Game. 1000

1689. Logomachy, the Premium Game. © 1889.
Word, Card Game. 150

1690. Lost Diamond, The Game of. Circa 1880s.
Strategy, Board Game. 250

1691. Lost Heir, Game of. Circa 1890s. Social,
Card Game. 175

1692. Lost Heir, Game of. Two Boy Cover. © 1893.
Social, Card Game. 175

1693. Lost in the Woods. Circa 1895. Kiddie,
Board Game. 2000

1694. Magnetic Fish Pond, The Game of. © 1891.
Animal, Sea, Board Game. 400

1695. Man in the Moon, Game of the. © 1901. Space,
Board Game. Man holding moon facing. 5000

1696. Mansion of Happiness. Circa 1895. Social,
Board Game. 750

1697. Matrimony or Old Maid, Game of. Circa 1890s.
Social, Board Game. 300

1698. McAllister and the 150. Circa 1895. History,
Board Game. 750

McLoughlin Bros. continued

1699. Merry Christmas Games, The. Circa 1891.
Holiday, Board Game. $1500

1700. Merry Christmas Goose Chase, The Game of.
© 1901. Holiday, Christmas, Board Game. 1700

1701. Merry Fishing Game. Circa 1895. Animal, Fish,
Board Game. 200

1702. Merry Game of Old Maid, The, Elite Edition.
© 1892. Classic, Card Game. 250

1703. Messenger Boy and Checkers. Circa 1890.
Combination, Board Game. 150

1704. Migration, New Game of. Circa 1891. Animal,
Card Game. 300

1705. Mill & Checkers. Circa 1910s. Combination,
Board Game. 125

1706. Mother Goose and Her Friends. © 1892.
Nursery Rhymes, Board Game. 350

1707. Mother Goose's Christmas Party. © 1899.
Holidays, Board Game. 1200

**1708. Mother Goose's Party or the Game of Old
Maid.** © 1892. Nursery Rhyme, Card Game. 200

1709. Mystic, Cards of Knowledge. © 1887. Mystic,
Card Game. 150

1710. Nations or Quaker Whist, Game of. © 1898.
Geography, Card Game. 300

1711. Naval War, Game of. © 1898. Military,
Board Game. 1000

1712. New and Improved Fish Pond. © 1890. Animal,
Sea, Board Game. 150

1713. New Pilgrim's Progress, The. © 1893.
Religious, Board Game. 350

1714. Newport Yacht Race. © 1891. Sports, Boating,
Board Game. 800

1715. North Pole by Air Ship, Game of, To the. ©
1897. Travel, Air, and Board Game. 1000

1716. Nosey. © 1905. Ethnic, Board Game. 650

1717. Old Bachelor, Merry Game of. Circa 1870s.
Social, Card Game. 300

1718. Old Fashioned Jack Straws. © 1888. Classic,
Skill Game. 125

1719. Old Father Goose. Circa 1895. Nursery Rhymes,
Board Game. 350

1720. Old King Cole, Game of. © 1888. Nursery
Rhyme, Card Game. 200

1721. Old Maid, The Game of. Circa 1890s. Classic,
Card Game. 200

1722. Old Maid, Game of. © 1900. Classic,
Card Game. 75

1723. Old Maid and Old Bachelor, The Game of. ©
1904. Social, Board Game. 350

1724. Old Time Comic Conversation Cards. © 1887.
Social, Card Game. 125

1725. Over Land and Sea. Circa 1911. Travel,
Board Game. 750

1726. [Parcheesi] in Arabic. Circa 1890s. Classic,
Board Game. 200

1727. Parlor Foot-Ball. © 1891. Sports, Football,
Board Game. 750

1728. Peter Coddle, The Improved Game of. Circa
1890s. Social, Card Game. 125

1729. Peter Coddle and His Trip to N. Y. Circa 1890s.
Reading, Card Game. $125

1730. Philippine, Game of. © 1900. History,
Card Game. 250

1731. Phoebe Snow, Game of. © 1899. Personality,
Board Game. 200

1732. Pinafore Game. Circa 1895. Musical,
Card Game. 300

1733. Playing Department Store, Game of. © 1898.
Economics, Card Game. 1200

1734. Pug and Poodle. Circa 1910. Comic,
Card Game. 200

1735. Puss in the Corner, The Game of. © 1888.
Animal, Board Game. 350

1736. Pussy and the Three Mice, Game of. © 1890.
Animal, Board Game. 1200

1737. Queens of Literature. Circa 1886. Literary,
Card Game. 150

1738. Red Riding Hood and the Wolf. © 1887.
Nursery Rhymes, Board Game. 500

1739. Rhymes & Chimes. Circa 1910. Comic,
Card Game. 125

1740. Rival Armies, The Game of, Pastime Series. ©
1903. Military, Board Game. 600

1741. Rival Doctors, The. © 1893. Occupations, Board
Game. 500

1742. Rival Policemen. © 1896. Law & Order, Board
Game. 2500

1743. Robbing the Miller, Game of. © 1897. Law &
Order, Board Game. 500

1744. Robinson Crusoe. Circa 1900s. Literary,
Adventure, Board Game. 300

1745. Round the World with Nellie Bly. Nellie with
two telephone poles. © 1890. Travel, World,
Board Game. 300

1746. Royal Game of Kings and Queens, The. ©
1892. Royal, Board Game. 800

1747. Santa Claus or Game of Presents. © 1895.
Holidays, Board Game. 1200

1748. Skirmish at Harper's Ferry, A New Game. ©
1891. Military, Board Game. 1500

1749. Snake Game. © 1888. Animal, Reptile,
Board Game. 600

McLoughlin Bros. continued

1750. Snap, Game of, Punch & Judy Series. © 1892.
Classic, Card Game. $150

1751. Snip, Snap, Snorum, Game of. © 1898. Social,
Card Game. 200

1752. Spider's Web, Game of. © 1898. Animal,
Insects, Board Game. 150

1753. Standard Authors, Game of. Circa 1890s.
Literary, Card Game. 75

**1754. Star Authors, Game of. Red & Gold Box
Edition.** © 1887. Literary, Card Game. 125

1755. Stars and Stripes, or Red, White and Blue. ©
1900. Patriotic, Board Game. 3000

1755a.Store Keepers Game. © 1889. Economic
Card Game. 250

1756. Strategy, Game of. © 1891. Military,
Board Game. 650

1757. Susceptibles, The. © 1891. Social, Board Game. 900

1758. Telegraph Boy, Game of the. © 1888.
Communication, Board Game. 800

1759. To The North Pole by Airship, Game of. ©
1904. Travel, Air, and Board Game. 1000

1760. Tobogganing at Christmas, Game of. © 1899.
Holidays, Board Game. 1200

1761. Toll Gate, Game of. © 1894. Animal, Travel,
Board Game. 400

1762. Trip Around the World, Game of. © 1897.
Travel, Board Game. 1500

1763. Troublesome Pigs, Game of. Circa 1900s.
Animal, Board Game. 250

1764. Two Game Combination, India & Checkers.
Arab on camel cover, circa 1900s. Combination,
Board Game. 150

1764a.Two Game Combination, Mill & Checkers,
Mill with sail cover, 1900, Combo Board Game. 175

1765. Uncle Josh's Trip. © 1906. Reading,
Card Game. 150

1766. Uncle Sam's Mail, Game of. Circa 1890s.
Communications, Mail, Board Game. 450

1767. Ups and Downs. © 1899. Social, Board Game. 2800

1768. Visit of Santa Claus, Game of the. © 1899.
Holiday, Board Game. 3500

1769. Visit to the Old Homestead. © 1903. Social,
Board Game. 1500

1770. Walking the Tight Rope, Game of. © 1897.
Circus, Board Game. 350

1771. War at Sea or Don't Give Up the Ship. © 1898.
Military, Board Game. 1500

1772. What D'ye Buy, The Game of, Banner Series.
© 1898. Economic, Card Game. 175

1773. Where's Johnny, A Pleasing Game. Circa
1890s. Reading, Card Game. 125

1774. Where's Johnny. © 1887. Reading, Card Game. 125

1775. Whirlpool, The Game of. © 1899. Travel, Sea,
Board Game. 200

1776. Who's Who, The Game of. © 1890.
Miscellaneous, Card Game. 150

1777. Wild Animals, Game of. © 1900. Animal, Card
Game. 150

1778. Wild West Game, The. © 1896. Western,
Board Game. $3000

1779. Wonderful Joe. © 1905. Reading, Card Game. 150

1780. Yacht Race at Sandy Hook. © 1888. Sports,
Boating, Board Game. 600

1781. Yacht Race. © 1888. Sports, Boating,
Board Game. 600

1781a.Yacht Race Game, The. Pat 1887, Sports,
Boating, Board Game. 300

1782. Yacht Racing Game, The. © 1887. Sports,
Boating, Board Game. 600

1783. Yale Princeton Foot Ball Game. Circa 1895.
Sports, Football, Board Game. 900

1784. Young Folk's Geographical Game. © 1895.
Geography, Card Game. 125

1785. Young Folks Historical Game. © 1890. History,
Card Game. 150

1786. Young Folks Scriptural Cards. © 1902.
Religious, Card Game. 125

1787. Zimmer's Base Ball Game. Circa 1895. Sports,
Baseball, Board Game. 20000

E. E. Miles
1788. Eureka Bible Game. © 1896. Religious,
Card Game. 50

Miller & Gould
1789. Politix. © 1907. Political, Board Game. 150

Esmond Mills
1790. Bunny Esmond Games, Premium. Circa 1910s.
Animal, Card Game. 125

W. H. Moore & Co.
1791. Administrations. © 1894. Political, Card Game. 150

Morehouse Mfg. Co.
1792. Wizard Base Ball Game. Circa 1912. Sports,
Baseball, Board Game. 350

V. E. Morrill
1793. Neutral. © 1914. Military, History, Card Game. 150

Moth and Flame Pub Co.
1794. Moth and the Flame, The. © 1906. Theatrical,
Card Game. 200

A. W. Mumford
1795. Industries, Game of. Circa 1890s. Economic,
Card Game. 125

1796. Literature Game. © 1897. Literary, Card Game. 75

National Games Co., Inc.
1797. Play Ball. Circa 1912. Sports, Baseball,
Board Game. 250

Nature Study Publishing Co.
1798. Birds. © 1897. Animals, Birds, Card Game. $75

L. H. Nelson Co.
1799. Traffic. © 1908. Travel, Board Game. 125

Nemo Card Co.
1800. Gammut. 1904. Miscellaneous, Card Game. 50

New Century Game Co.
1801. New Century Game of Proverbs. © 1900.
Religious, Card Game. 40

New Century Educational Co.
1802. New Century Busy Work-Wild Animals. Circa
1900. Animals, Card Game. 75

New Haven Toy, Game & Novelty Co.
1803. Hub-Checkers. © 1894. Strategy, Board Game. 250

New York Game Co.
1804. Champion Base Ball Game, The. © 1913.
Sports, Baseball, Board Game. 200

Newspaper Premium
1805. Snip-Snap. Circa 1900. Comics, Advertising,
Card Game. 500

Wm. R. Norris
1806. Zylo-Karta Games, Folding wooden board. ©
1886. Travel, Board Game. 300

Noyes, Snow & Co.
1807. Portrait Authors. Circa 1880s. Literary,
Card Game. 75

The Numerica Co.
1808. Numerica, Game of. © 1894. Number,
Card Game. 35

NY American Journal Exam
1809. Maud or "Hee Haw", The. Game of. 12/2/1906.
Comics, Advertising, Card Game. 750

Olympia Games
1810. Quarterback. © 1914. Sports, Football,
Board Game. 250

Optimus Printing Co.
1811. Trusts and Busts, or Frenzied Finance. © 1904.
Economics, Card Game. 125

Orotech Co.
1812. Chateau Thierry. Circa 1915-9. Military,
Board Game. $250

J. Ottmann Lithograph Co.
1813. Christmas Mail. Circa 1900s. Holiday,
Christmas, Board Game. 800
1814. Commerce. © 1900. Economic, Card Game. 125
1815. Daisy Fox & Geese. Circa 1900. Animal, Board
Game. 150
1816. Foxy Grandpa at the World's Fair. Circa 1910.
Fair - Comic, Card Game. 500
1817. Gypsy Queen. Circa 1890s. Mystic, Card Game. 100
1818. Little Drummer, The. Circa 1900. Military,
Board Game. 400
1819. Merry Steeple Chase, The. Circa 1890s. Sports,
Horseracing, Board Game. 250
1820. Pantaloon Target. Circa 1890s. Circus, Action
Game. 250
1821. Peter Coddles, Game of. Circa 1890s. Reading,
Card Game. 100
1822. Pin the Tail on the Donkey, Black cover. Circa
1900. Classic, Skill Game. 65
1823. Rex, Game of. Circa 1900. Number, Card Game. 75
1824. Sailor, The Game of. Circa 1900. Military,
Board Game. 250
1825. Success, Game of. Circa 1900. Social,
Card Game. 400

1826. West Point. © 1902. Military, Board Game. 400

Pacific Coast Borax Co.

1827. Whiz, 20-Mule-Team Borax. Circa 1900.
Western, Card Game. $200

Page Woven Wire Fence

1828. Page Fence, Advertising Premium. © 1894.
Advertising, Card Game. 150

Pan Am. Expo. Ed. M-N. Co.

1829. Buffalo, The Game of. Circa 1901. Geography,
Card Game. 150

Panic Game Co.

1830. Panic-The Great Wall Street Game. © 1903.
Stock Market, Card Game. 85

George S. Parker & Co.

1831. Amusing Game of the Corner Grocery, The.
Circa 1880s. Economic, Board Game. 150
1832. Baker's Dozen. © 1884. Miscellaneous,
Card Game. 125
1833. Banking, Game of. © 1883. Economics, Card
Game. Parker's First Game. 750
1834. Baseball. © 1886. Sports, Baseball,
Board Game. 1000
1835. Billy Bumps Visit to Boston. © 1890. Reading,
Card Game. 125
1836. Dickens Game. © 1885. Literary, Card Game. 125
1837. Garrison. © 1886. Military, Board Game. 350
1838. Ivanhoe. © 1890. Literary, Card Game. 150
1839. Johnny's Historical Game. © 1890. History,
Card Game. 125
1840. Literary Salad. © 1888. Literary, Card Game. ... 125
1841. Merry Game of the Country Auction, The. ©
1888. Economic, Board Game. 150
1842. Oliver Twist. © 1888. Literary, Card Game. 175
1843. Peculiar Game of Yankee Peddler, The. Circa
1880s. Economic, Card Game. 150
1844. Tadpole Pool, The. © 1888. Animal,
Card Game. 200
1845. War, The Game of. © 1888. Military,
Card Game. 200
1846. When My Ship Comes In. © 1888. Reading,
Card Game. 150

Parker Brothers

1847. A B C, The Game of. Circa 1890s. Word,
Card Game. 35
1848. Across the Continent. © 1899. Travel,
Board Game. 250
1849. Actors, The Game of Popular. © 1893. Theatre,
Card Game. 200
1850. Advance Guard. Circa 1912. Strategy,
Board Game. 250
1851. Airship Game, The. © 1903. Travel, Air,
Board Game. 1000
1852. Alphabet. © 1892. Words, Card Game. 35
1853. American Cities. © 1893. Geography,
Card Game. 125

1854. American Derby. © 1893. Sports, Horseracing,
Board Game. $300
1855. American Eagle Geography. © 1890.
Geography, Card Game. 100
1856. American History, The Game of. Circa 1890s.
History, Card Game. 125
1857. Amusing Game of Innocence Abroad, The. ©
1888. Travel, World, Board Game. 400
1858. Apple Pie. © 1895. Miscellaneous, Card Game. .. 150
1859. Artists, Life's Game of. © 1912. Art,
Card Game. 100
1860. Artists. 1900. Art, Card Game. 125
1861. Auction Letters. © 1900. Word, Card Game. 50
1862. Auction, The Game of. © 1893. Economic,
Card Game. 135
1863. Authors Illustrated, The Game of. Circa 1890s.
Literary, Card Game. 50
1864. Authors Petite Deluxe, Game of. © 1893.
Literary, Card Game. 35
1865. Authors, The Game of, New Edition. © 1907.
Literary, Card Game. 50
1866. Authors, The Game of. © 1890. Literary, Card
Game. 50
1867. Authors, The Game of. © 1896. Literary, Card
Game, five children cover. 75
1868. Babes in the Woods. Circa 1900s. Kiddie,
Board Game. 150
1869. Barnum's Greatest Show on Earth. © 1894.
Circus, Board Game. 2000
1870. Base Ball Game, The Major League. © 1890.
Sports, Baseball, Board Game. 600
1871. Base Ball Game, The Professional Game of. ©
1890. Sports, Baseball, Board Game. 900
1872. Base Ball. © 1894. Sports, Baseball,
Board Game. 400
1873. Baseball Game. © 1913. Sports, Baseball,
Board Game. 400
1874. Battle of Manila, The. © 1898. Military, Spanish
American War, Board Game. 700
1875. Battle of Santiago. © 1898. Military,
Board Game. 400
1876. Battles, The Game of. Circa 1900s. Military,
Card Game. 150
1877. Bible Game. Circa 1890s. Religious,
Card Game. 35
1878. Bicycle Cards, A Game. © 1897. Sports,
Miscellaneous, Card Game. 150
1879. Bicycle Game, Century Run. © 1897. Sports,
Miscellaneous, Board Game. 750
1880. Bicycle Game, Junior. © 1897. Sports,
Miscellaneous, Board Game. 350
1881. Bicycle Game, The New. © 1894. Sports,
Miscellaneous, Board Game. 800
1882. Bicycling. © 1900. Sports, Miscellaneous,
Board Game. 750
1883. Block. © 1904. Numbers, Card Game. 50
1884. Boer and Briton. © 1900. Military,
Board Game. 400
1885. Bombardment of the Fort. Circa 1890s.
Military, Board Game. 400
1886. Boston Baked Beans. Circa 1910s. Skill Game,
Action Game. 125

Parker Bros. continued

1887. Boy Scouts, The Game of. © 1912.
Organizations, Card Game. $350
1888. Brownies and Other Queer Folk, The. © 1894.
Comics, Card Game. 350
1889. Buffalo Bill, The Game of. © 1898. Adventure,
Western, Board Game. 650
1890. Buffalo Hunt. © 1898. Animal, Board Game. 350
1891. Buffalo Hunt. © 1900. Animal, Board Game. 175
1892. Business or Going to Work, Game of. © 1895.
Economic, Board Game. 400
1893. Buster Bump's Automobile Trip. Circa 1923.
Travel, Card Game. 65
1894. Cake Walk. 1899. Ethnic, Board Game. 1500
1895. Captain Kid and His Treasure. 1895.
Adventure, Board Game. 650
1896. Charles Dickens Game, The. © 1912. Literary,
Card Game. 150
1897. Chivalry. © 1888. Military, Board Game. 500
1898. Christian Endeavor, Game of. © 1890.
Religious, Board Game. 350
1899. Christmas Dinner, A. © 1897. Holiday,
Christmas, Board Game. 650
1900. Christmas Tree. © 1893. Holiday, Board Game. 700
1901. Cinderella, A Game. © 1895. Literary,
Card Game. 125
1902. Circus. © 1900. Circus, Board Game. 400
1903. Cities Game of. © 1898. Geography,
Card Game. 150
1904. Cock Robin. © 1895. Nursery Rhymes,
Card Game. 125
1905. Comic Game of Sir Hinkle Funny-Duster, The.
Circa 1900. Reading, Card Game. 75
1906. Comical Farm Yard Game, The. © 1895.
Animal, Card Game. 125
1907. Comical Game of Who. Circa 1890s. Reading,
Card Game. 50
1908. Coon Hunt Game, The. © 1903. Ethnic,
Board Game. 1500
1908a.Country Auction, The Merry Game of. Circa
1890s, Economic Card Game. 175
1909. Country Fair, The. © 1895. Economic,
Card Game. 150
1910. Crazy Traveler. Pat. 1908. Miscellaneous,
Board Game. 150
1911. Crossing the Ocean. © 1893. Travel, World,
Board Game. 300
1912. Cycling, The Game of. © 1910. Sports,
Board Game. 750
1913. Department Store, Game of Playing. © 1898.
Economic, Card Game. 150
1914. Detective Game. © 1900. Law & Order,
Board Game. 350
1915. Dewey's Victory. © 1900. Military, Board Game. 500
1916. Dinner. Circa 1900. Food, Board Game. 125
1917. Domestic Animals. © 1900. Animal,
Card Game. 50
1918. Dreamland, Wonder Resort Game. © 1903.
Circus, Board Game. 850
1919. Drummer Boy, The. Circa 1890s. Military,
Spanish American War, Board Game. 450

1920. East is East and West is West. © 1900.
Geography, Board Game. $400
1921. Election. © 1892. Political, Card Game. 100
1922. English History. © 1895. History, Card Game. 125
1923. Fame, The Game of. Circa 1890s. History,
Card Game. 125
1924. Famous Men, The Game of. Circa 1890s.
History, Card Game. 125
1925. Famous, The Game of. © 1890. History,
Card Game. 100
1926. Favorite Art, Game of. © 1897. Art,
Card Game. 125
1927. Fighting in the Soudan. © 1899. Military,
Board Game. 600
1928. Fighting with the Boers. © 1899. Military,
Board Game. 500
1929. Fish Pond, Boy on sturgeon cover. Circa 1890.
Animal, Sea, Board Game. 150
1930. Flag, Improved Game of. © 1915. Geography,
Card Game. 35
1931. Flowers, Game of. Circa 1910s. Plant,
Card Game. 35
1932. Football, The Game of. Circa 1890s. Sports,
Football, Board Game. 500
1933. Frenzied Finance. © 1905. Economic,
Card Game. 75
1934. Fun at the Zoo: A Game. © 1902. Animal,
Card Game. 150
1934a.Funny Crooked Man, The Game of. © 1898.
Nursery Rhymes, Board Game. 125
1935. Garrison Game. © 1891. Military, Board Game. 300
1936. Geography Up to Date. Circa 1890s. Geography,
Card Game. 50
1937. George Washingtons's Dream. © 1899. Social,
Card Game. 75
1938. Going to the Picnic. © 1902. Social,
Board Game. 200
1939. Gold Hunters, The. © 1902. Adventure,
Board Game. 250
1940. Golf. © 1896. Sports, Golf, Board Game. 350
1941. Golf. © 1907. Sports, Golf, Board Game. 250
1942. Good Old Game of Corner Grocery, The. ©
1903. Economic, Card Game. 175
1943. Good Old Game of Innocence Abroad, The. ©
1888. Travel, Board Game. 350
1944. Great Authors. © 1910. Literary, Card Game. 50
1945. Great Cities. © 1898. Travel, Card Game. 100
1946. Grocery Store, Game of, Improved Edition. ©
1889. Economic, Card Game. 200
1947. Halma, 3rd Edition. © 1916. Classic,
Board Game. 75
1948. Happy Families. © 1901. Social, Card Game. 100
1949. Happy-Hoppers. © 1899. Comics, Board Game. 250
1949a.Hare and Hounds. © 1895. Sports,
Board Game. 150
1950. Heads and Tails, The Game of Nickel Edition.
© 1900. Miscellaneous, Card Game. 75
1951. Hickery Dickery Dock. Circa 1900s. Kiddie,
Nursery Rhyme, Board Game. 125
1952. History Up to Date. Circa 1890s. History,
Card Game. 125

Parker Bros. continued

1953. Hold the Fort. © 1895. Military, Spanish American War, Board Game. $400

1954. House that Jack Built, The. © 1895. Nursery Rhymes, Board Game. 250

1955. How Silas Popped the Question. © 1915. Social, Card Game. 50

1956. I Doubt It. Circa 1910. Social, Card Game. 50

1957. I'm a Millionaire. © 1907. Economic, Card Game. 60

1958. Improved Geographical Game. Circa 1890s. Geography, Card Game. 60

1959. Innocence Abroad, The Amusing Game of. © 1888. Travel, Board Game. 500

1960. International Authors, The Game of. © 1893. Literary, Card Game. 65

1961. International Automobile Race. Circa 1912. Sports Cars, Board Game. 1200

1962. Italian History. © 1896. History, Card Game. 200

1963. Jack and the Beanstalk. © 1895. Nursery Rhyme, Board Game. 250

1964. Jack Sprat, The Game of. © 1900. Nursery Rhyme, Board Game. 250

1965. Jack Straws, New Edition. Circa 1900s. Classic, Skill Game. 40

1966. Jack Straws, The Game of, (Brownies cover). Circa 1890s. Comics, Classic, Skill Game. 150

1966a. Jack the Giant Killer, The Game of. Circa 1900s. Literary, Board Game. 200

1967. Jolly Game of Quack, The. Circa 1900. Animal, Card Game. 125

1968. Jolly Tars, The Game of. Circa 1890s. Military, Board Game. 700

1969. Jumping Frog Game (718). Circa 1912. Animal, Card Game. 250

1970. Jungle Animals. © 1900. Animals, Card Game. 60

1971. Kan Yu Du It. © 1890. Miscellaneous, Card Game. 75

1972. Kilkenny Cats, The Amusing Game of. © 1890. Animals - Cat, Card Game. 200

1973. King's Castle. © 1902. History, Board Game. 300

1974. Klondike. © 1895. Adventure, Board Game. 850

1975. Komical Konversation Kards. © 1893. Reading, Card Game. 35

1976. Kwiz, Series A. Circa 1910s. Q & A, Card Game. $50

1977. Letters & Anagrams. Circa 1890s. Word, Card Game. 35

1978. Letters, Game of, Salem Edition. Circa 1890s. Word, Card Game. 45

1979. Life Boat Game. © 1899. Adventure, Board Game. 750

1980. Limited Mail and Express, The. © 1892. Travel, Rail, Co, Board Game. 600

1981. Literary Salad, A Feast of Reason. © 1890. Literary, Card Game. 75

1982. Literary Salad, A Game of Quotations. © 1890. Literary, Card Game. 75

1983. Literary Women. © 1891. Literary, Card Game. 125

1984. Little Bo-Peep. © 1895. Nursery Rhymes, Board Game. 250

1985. Little Boy Blue. © 1898. Nursery Rhymes, Board Game. 250

1986. Little Golden Locks, A Game. Circa 1900s. Nursery Rhyme, Board Game. 250

1987. Little Grocer, The. © 1895. Economic, Board Game. 300

1988. Little Mother Goose. © 1890. Nursery Rhyme, Card Game. 125

1989. Little Red Riding Hood. © 1895. Nursery Rhymes, Board Game. 250

1990. London Game, The. © 1898. Geography, Board Game. 1500

1991. Maxfield Parish Soldier. Circa 1910. Military, Board Game. 900

1992. Menagerie. © 1895. Circus, Card Game. 150

1993. Merry Christmas, The Game of. © 1898. Holiday, Christmas, Board Game. 1600

1994. Merry-Go-Round. © 1912. Circus, Board Game. 400

1995. Mock Trial. © 1910. Law & Order, Card Game by M. Phillips. 150

1996. Motor Carriage Game, The. © 1899. Travel, Car, Board Game. 1200

1997. Mrs. Casey Wants to Know. Circa 1910. Social, Card Game. 75

1998. My Mother Sent Me to the Grocery Store. © 1902. Economic, Card Game. 100

1999. Napoleon, Game of. © 1895. Military, Napoleonic, Board Game. 1200

2000. National Flower Game, The. © 1895. Plant, Card Game. 150

Parker Bros. continued

2001. National-American Base Ball Game, The. Circa
1900s. Sports, Baseball, Card Game. $250

2002. Nations, Game of. © 1910. Geography,
Card Game. 100

2003. New Bicycle Game, The. © 1894. Sports, Bike,
Board Game. 700

2004. New Testament. © 1900. Religious, Card Game. 35

2005. New York, Game of. © 1898. Geography,
Board Game. 800

2006. Night Before Christmas. © 1896. Holiday,
Board Game. 1000

2007. Noah's Ark, The Game of. Circa 1890s. Animal,
Religion, Card Game. 125

2008. Old Bachelor, The Game of. © 1898. Social,
Card Game. 125

2009. Old Fashioned Spelling Bee. © 1910. Word,
Card Game. 50

2010. Old King Cole. © 1901. Nursery Rhyme,
Board Game. 250

2011. Old Maid, The Board Game. © 1910. Classic,
Board Game. 250

2012. Old Testament, The. Circa 1910s. Religious,
Card Game. 35

2013. Old Woman in the Shoe, The. © 1900. Nursery
Rhyme, Board Game. 250

2014. Our Country. Circa 1910. History, Card Game. 50

2015. Our Navy. © 1899. Military, Spanish American
War, Card Game. 150

2016. Panama Canal Game. Circa 1910. Geography,
Board Game. 400

2017. Parker Bros. War Game. © 1915. Military,
World War I, Board Game. 250

2018. Pat and His Pigs, The Game of. © 1896.
Animal, Mammal, Board Game. 200

2019. Peculiar Game of My Wife and I, The. © 1888.
Reading, Card Game. 125

2020. Peggity. © 1892. Strategy, Board Game. 50

2021. Penny Post, The Game of. © 1892.
Communications, Board Game. 800

2022. Peter Coddle's Trip to N. Y., Nickel Edition.
Circa 1890s. Reading, Card Game. 50

2023. Peter Coddle's Trip to N. Y., The Game of.
Circa 1890s. Social, Card Game. 75

2024. Peter, Peter Pumpkin Eater. © 1901. Nursery
Rhyme, Board Game. 250

2025. Peter Coddle Tells of His Trip to Chicago. Circa
1900s. Reading, Card Game. 75

2026. Philippine War. © 1898. Military, Board Game. 400

2027. Picture Reading Game. Circa 1890s. Reading,
Card Game. 50

2028. Pike's Peak or Bust, Model #1. © 1895. Travel,
Board Game. 125

2029. Pike's Peak or Bust, Model #2. © 1895. Travel,
Board Game. 100

2030. Pike's Peak or Bust, Model #3. © 1895. Travel,
Board Game. 100

2031. Pillow-Dex. © 1896. Miscellaneous, Card Game. 35

2032. Pit. © 1903. Stock Market, Card Game. 10

2033. Pitch, The Game of. © 1910. Skill,
Action Game. $75

2034. Poems, Game of. © 1898. Literary, Card Game. 50

**2035. Pollyanna, Red & Gold letters board &
implement box.** © 1915. Classic, Board Game. 75

2036. Pollyanna, The Glad Game. ® 1915. Classic,
Board Game. 100

2037. Popular Game of Tiddley Winks, The. Circa
1900s. Classic, Action Game. 45

2038. Popular Jack-Straws. Circa 1890s. Classic,
Skill Game. 50

2039. Ports and Commerce, Game of. © 1899.
Economic, Geography, Card Game. 150

2040. Princess in the Tower. © 1892. Adventure,
Board Game. 350

2041. Prisoner of Zenda. © 1896. Adventure,
Board Game. 750

2042. Prisoner's Base. © 1896. Military, Board Game. 450

2043. Puss in the Corner. © 1895. Animal, Cat,
Board Game. 300

2044. Quien Sabe. © 1906. Western, Card Game. 65

2045. Quit. © 1905. Social, Card Game. 35

2046. Race for the Cup. © 1896. Sports, Boating,
Board Game. 500

2047. Railroad Game, The. Circa 1900s. Travel, Rail,
Board Game. 1000

2048. Red Riding Hood, Game of. © 1895. Nursery
Rhyme, Board Game. 200

2049. Rembrandt's Playing Cards. Circa 1900. Art,
Card Game. 100

2050. Ring the Pin. Circa 1900. Classic, Skill Game. 65

2051. Robin Hood, The Game of. © 1893. Literary,
Adventure, Board Game. 250

2052. Robinson Crusoe, Game of. © 1895. Literary,
Card Game. 150

2053. Roly Poly Game, The. Circa 1910s. Skill,
Action Game. 100

2054. Rook. © 1910. Numbers, Card Game. 10

2055. Roosevelt's Charge. Circa 1900s. Military,
Board Game. 1000

**2056a.Rough Riders, A Game, The Teddy Roosevelt
on cover.** Circa 1900s. Military, Board Game. 900

2056. 'Round the World Joe. © 1891. Reading,
Card Game. 75

2057. Santa Claus, The Game of. © 1899. Holiday,
Board Game. 1000

Parker Bros. continued

2058. Scouts, The Game of, Variant box. © 1912.
Organization, Card Game. $85

2059. Sherlock Homes. © 1904. Detective,
Card Game. 65

2060. Sherlock Homes., Variant box cover. © 1904.
Detective, Card Game. 65

2061. Sherlock Homes., Variant box cover. © 1904.
Detective, Card Game. 65

2062. Shopping, The Game of. Circa 1890s.
Economic, Card Game. 175

2063. Siege of Havana, The. © 1898. Military,
Board Game. 500

2064. Sir Hinkle Funny-Duster, Comical Game. ©
1903. Social, Card Game. 50

2065. Snap, Game of., (Blue on white cover). Circa
1890s. Classic, Card Game. 50

2067. Snap, The Game of. Nickel Edition. Circa
1890s. Classic, Card Game. 50

2068. Spanish Main. © 1890. Military, Board Game. 750

2069. Speculation, The Game of. Circa 1890s. Stock
Market, Card Game. 125

2070. Steeple Chase, Game of. © 1891. Sports, Horse
Racing, Board Game. 400

2071. Strange Game of Forbidden Fruit, The. ©
1887. Social, Card Game. 150

2072. Street Car Game, The. Circa 1890s. Travel, Rail,
Board Game. 450

2073. Sweet William and Marigold. © 1899. Plant,
Card Game. 125

2074. Taking the Fort. Circa 1900s. Military,
Board Game. 400

2075. Telka, Ancient Romans cover. © 1891. History,
Board Game. 500

2076. Ten Little Niggers, The Game of. © 1895.
Ethnic, Board Game. 1500

2077. Tiddledy Winks. Circa 1900s. Classic, Skill
Game. 40

2078. Tom, Tom the Pipers Son. Circa 1900s. Nursery
Rhyme, Board Game. 250

2079. Toot. © 1905. Travel, Road, Card Game. 50

2080. Toy-Town Telegraph Office. © 1910.
Communications, Board Game. 250

2081. Trades, The Game of. © 1889. Economic,
Card Game. 200

2082. Trafalgar. © 1899. Military, Board Game. 1500

2083. Train for Boston. © 1890. Travel, Rail,
Board Game. 1500

2084. Travel, The Game of. © 1894. Travel,
Board Game. 750

2085. Trolley. © 1904. Travel, Rail, Card Game. 125

2086. Twentieth Century Limited. © 1904. Travel,
Rail, Board Game. $250

2087. U.S. Army Game. Circa 1917. Military, World
War I, Card Game. 75

2088. Uncle Sam's Farm, Game of. © 1895. Animal,
Card Game. 125

**2089. United States History Illustrated, The Game
of.** © 1903. History, Card Game. 250

2090. United States History. © 1900. History,
Card Game. 125

2091. War in Cuba. © 1897. Military, Board Game. 800

2092. War in South Africa, The. © 1900. Military,
Board Game. 800

2093. War of 1812. © 1892. Military, Board Game. 800

2094. Waterloo. © 1895. Military, Napoleonic,
Board Game. 1000

2095. Watermelon. © 1896. Ethnic, Food,
Board Game. 500

2096. West Point Cadet Game, The. © 1901. Military,
Board Game. 400

2097. What Color is Your Car? Circa 1910s. Travel,
Car, Board Game. 125

2098. Who? The Comical Game of. © 1899. Social,
Card Game. 75

2099. Wide World & A Journey Round it, The. ©
1896. Geography, Board Game. 500

2100. Wild Animals. © 1903. Animal, Card Game. 125

2101. World History, The Game of the. © 1894.
History, Card Game. 150

2102. World's Fair Game (Chicago). © 1891. Fair,
Board Game. 1500

2103. Yachting. © 1895. Sports, Boating, Board Game. 350

**2104. Yachts The International Race, Columbia vs
Shamrock.** © 1910. Sports, Sea, Board Game. 350

2105. Yale-Harvard Game. © 1894. Sports, Football,
Board Game. 1000

2106. Yankee Doodle. © 1895. History, Board Game. 750

2107. Ye Witchcraft Game. © 1889. Mystic,
Card Game. 200

2108. Yes or No. © 1910. Social, Card Game. 65

2109. Young People's Bible Game. Circa 1890s.
Religious, Card Game. 75

2110. Young People's Geographical Game. Circa
1890s. Geographical, Card Game. 75

2111. Zoo, Game of Animals. © 1895. Animal,
Card Game. 125

Parlor Golf Co.

2112. Parlor Golf. Circa 1913. Sports, Golf,
Board Game. 250

E. M. Patrick

2113. From NY to San Francisco. © 1881. Travel,
Board Game. 200

Harry Pearl

**2114. Pearl's Historical Authors (author Harry
Pearl).** © 1889. History, Card Game. 75

Henry Peck
2115. Great American Game Baseball, The. Circa
1910s. Sports, Baseball, Board Game. $200
2116. National Base Ball Game. Circa 1900-10.
Sports, Baseball, Board Game. 200

Arba Perry
2117. Kard Kelly: Kelly Pool with Cards. © 1915.
Miscellaneous, Board Game. 75

J. Phaneuf
2118. Patriotic Game (author Emile Pingault). ©
1887. History, Card Game. 125

Philadelphia Game Mfg.
**2119. Major League Baseball Game, Wood side,
Green.** Circa 1910s. Sports, Baseball,
Board Game. 500

D. S. Pillsbury
2120. Geographical Game of the Old World. © 1875.
History, Card Game. 75

Pittsburgh Game & Novelty
2121. Let Us Have Peace. © 1916. Political,
Card Game. 150

Mrs. Charles Fremont Pond
2122. Constitution, Game of. © 1913. History,
Card Game. 125

Popular Games Co.
2123. Inside Baseball. © 1911. Sports, Baseball,
Board Game. 450

L. Prang & Co.
2124. Courtship of Jonathan Peas, The. Circa 1890.
Social, Card Game. 100

Theo. Presser Pat.
2125. Allegrando, Musical Game. © 1884. Musical,
Card Game. 100
2126. Elementaire Musical Game. © 1896. Musical,
Card Game. 100
2127. Great Composers, The. Circa 1900s. Musical,
Card Game. 100
2128. Musical Authors. Circa 1890s. Musical,
Card Game. 100
2129. Triads or Chords, Game of. © 1898. Musical,
Card Game. 100

Procter Amusement Co.
2130. Champion Game of Baseball, The. Circa 1900s.
Sports, Baseball, Board Game. $2000

Providence Rhode Island Game Co.
**2130a.Great Game, Uncle Sam at War with Spain,
The.** Pat 1898, Military Board Game. 200

Read & White Game Co.
2131. Trix. © 1904. Social, Card Game. 50

W. S. Reed Toy Co.

**2132. Politics, or Race for the Presidency, The Game
of.** © 1888. Political, Board Game. 450
2133. Wild Birds, Game of. © 1914. Animal, Card
Game. 100
2134. World's Educator, The. Wooden box. Circa
1890s. Q & A, Board Game. 250

Miss I. H. Richeson
2135. Botanical Game (author Miss I. H. Richeson).
© 1896. Plants, Card Game. 100

C. R. Romain & Co.
**2136. Geographical Games: Cities; Countries;
Mountains and Lakes; Rivers (author Clara R.
Grow).** © 1890. Geography, Cards. 100

Saalfield Publishing Co.
2137. Halloween Party Game. Circa 1908. Holiday,
Card Game. 125

A. Schoenhut Co.
2138. Naval War Game (© 1912 by Munn & Co.) ©
1915. Military, Board Game. $350

Selchow & Righter Co.
2139. Anagrams or Word's Alive. © 1880. Word,
Card Game. 45
2140. Buster Brown Necktie Party, Circa 1900.
Comics, Action Game. 250
2141. Chessindia. © 1915. Classic, Board Game. 150
2142. Dinner Party. Circa 1900. Social, Card Game. 150
2143. Exchange. © 1904. Economic, Card Game. 150
2144. Foxy Grandpa an Up to Date Game. Circa
1910s. Comics, Card Game. 250
2145. Foxy Grandpa Hat Party. Circa 1910s. Comics,
Skill Game. 3250
**2146. Gems of Art, with Art Sale; Display Solitaire;
Word Making.** © 1880. Art, Card Game. 125
2147. Ge-O-Graph-O. © 1882. Geography,
Board Game. 75
2148. Hare and Hounds, or Cross-Country Race (©
R. Cogan). © 1890. Animal/Travel, Board Game. 250
2149. Komical Konversation Kards. © 1893. Social,
Card Game. 75
2150. Lasso, The Jumping Rag. © 1912. Western,
Board Game. 125
2151. Mixed Pickles. Circa 1880s. Miscellaneous,
Card Game. 75
2152. Old Maid, Game of. Circa 1890. Classic,
Card Game. 75
2153. Peter Coddle's Trip to N. Y. © 1900. Reading,
Card Game. 75
2154. Sliced Objects. Frog cover. Circa 1890s. Animal,
Board Game. 300
2155. Spelling Muddle, Game of. Circa 1890s. Word,
Card Game. 75

Sharp Co.
2156. Sharp's Shooter. © 1895. Skill, Board Game. 200

C. C. Shepherd
2157. House that Jack Built, A New Picture Game. ®
1881. Social, Card Game. 250
**2158. Who Killed Cock Robin? A New Play in Ten
Parts.** © 1882. Social, Card Game. 250

Wm. Shepherd & Co.
2159. Shepherd's National Game of Finance. Circa
1890. Economic, Card Game. 150

J. E. Sherrill
**2160. Events and Dates of United States History
(author J. E. Sherrill).** © 1886. History,
Card Game. 100
2161. Geography. © 1886. Geography, Card Game. 100
2162. Mythology. © 1886. History, Card Game. 125

J. H. Singer
2163. Authors, Game of, No. 2. Circa 1890s. Literary,
Card Game. $65
2164. Base Ball, Game of. Circa 1887. Sports,
Baseball, Board Game. 300
2165. Billow X, The Improved Game. Circa 1890s.
Miscellaneous, Board Game. 125
2166. Blue Beard, Game of. Circa 1890s. History,
Adventure, Card Game. 200
2167. Bopeep, Game of. Circa 1890s. Nursery Rhyme,
Board Game. 400
2168. Cash. Circa 1900. Economic, Board Game. 350
2169. Country Fish Pond. Circa 1900's. Animal, Sea,
Board Game. 150

2170. Crossing the Alps. © 1890. Geography,
Board Game. 150
2171. Cuckoo. © 1891. Animal, Board Game. 100
2172. Dog Show, The. Circa 1890s. Animal,
Board Game. 350
2173. Dr. Busby, Game of. © 1890. Literary, Social,
Card Game. 65
2174. Drummer Boy, Game of. Circa 1890. Military,
Board Game. 250
2175. Ducks and Drakes, Game of. © 1887. Animal,
Board Game. 150
2176. Fox and Geese, Game of. Circa 1890s. Animal,
Card Game. 75
2177. Fox and Geese, Game of. No. 2. Circa 1890s.
Animal, Card Game. 150
2178. Funny Game Toboggan Slide, A. © 1890.
Sports, Board Game. 200
2179. Go-Bang, Game of. Circa 1910s. Miscellaneous,
Board Game. 125
2180. Golf, The Game of. Circa 1898. Sports, Golf,
Board Game. 300
**2181. Goosy Gander, or Who Finds the Golden Egg,
Game of.** © 1890. Animal, Board Game. 250
2182. Jumping Frog, Game of. © 1890. Animal,
Board Game. 350
2183. Keeping Store, Game of. Circa 1890. Economic,
Card Game. 150
2184. Marriage, Game of. Circa 1890s. Romance,
Card Game. 300
2185. Menagerie, Game of. © 1890. Animal,
Card Game. 250
2186. Messenger Boy, Game of. Circa 1890s.
Communication, Occupation, Board Game. 200

J. H. Singer (continued.)

2187. Nellie Bly. Circa 1900s. Person, Travel,
Board Game. $250
2188. Peter Coddle & His Trip to New York. Circa
1890s. Reading, Card Game. 50
2189. Pocahontas. © 1890. Indians, Board Game. 400
2190. Politics, Game of. © 1890. Political, Card Game. 150
2191. Road to Washington, The. © 1884. Politics,
Board Game. 250
2192. Saratoga Steeple Chase. © 1900. Sports,
Horseracing, Board Game. 300
2193. Shop Boy, The. © 1900. Economic,
Board Game. 300

2194. Singer's Snake Game. Circa 1910s. Animal,
Board Game. 250
2195. Snap, Game of. Circa 1890s. Classic,
Card Game. 50
2195a.Steeple Chase. Circa 1890s, Sport board Game. 150
2196. Store, Game of. Circa 1890s. Economic,
Card Game. 150
2196a.Tossem, Game of. Frog Cover. Circa 1900.
Animal, Board Game. 80
2197. Yachting, Game of. © 1900. Sports, Sea,
Board Game. 125
2198. Yachting. © 1890. Sports, Sea, Board Game. 250

C. L. Sirrene

2199. Social Brownies, The Game Of. © 1894.
Comics, Board Game. 750

Frank J. Smith

2200. North Pole. © 1909. Travel, Board Game. 350

G. Henderson Smith

2201. Board of Trade Game. © 1895. Economic,
Card Game. 125

L. U. Snead

2202. New Bible Cards. Circa 1887. Religious,
Card Game. 50

E. H. Snow

2203. Life, The Game of. © 1883. Social, Card Game. $125
2204. Lost Heir. © 1883. Social, Card Game. 125
2205. Quotations & Characters from Shakespeare. ©
1883. Literary, Card Game. 150

Snow, Woodman & Co.

2206. Tally Ho!, The Royal Game of. Circa 1880.
Royal, Card Game. 125

Snyder Bros.

2207. Trolley. © 1904. Travel, Rail, Card Game. 125
2208. Trolley. Gold Edge Box. © 1904. Travel, Rail,
Card Game. 135

Some 'R' Set Card Co.

2209. Some ' R' Set. © 1903. Numbers, Card Game. 50

A. G. Spalding & Bros.

2210. Our National Ball Game. Circa 1887. Sports,
Baseball, Board Game. 300

Ezra M. Sparlin

2211. Historical Queries. © 1895. History,
Card Game. 100

Sparta, Wisc. Mfg.

2212. Business Men's Series, The. © 1904. Economic,
Card Game. 125

Spear's Games, US Market

2213. Comical Tivoli Game. Circa 1910s. Circus,
Skill Game. 150
2214. Red, White & Blue, Spear's Game of. Circa
1910s. Miscellaneous, Board Game. 100

Spelling Bee Game Co.

2215. Spell. © 1912. Word, Card Game. 65

Sprague Wholesale Co.

2216. Makers of History, The. © 1904. History,
Card Game. 100

M. V. Staley
2217. **Geo-Histo.** © 1886. Geography/History,
    Card Game. $100

Standard Playing Card Co.
2218. **Chantecler.** © 1910. Miscellaneous, Card Game. 50

Star Publishing Co.
2219. **World's Fair, Game of; with Rivalry.** © 1892.
    Fair, Card Game. 250

Statler Mfg. Co.
2220. **United States Geographical Lotto.** Circa 1900.
    Geography, Card Game. 75

Hetty L. Staveley
2221. **Sleeping Beauty Game, The (author H. L.
    Staveley).** Circa 1882. Literary, Card Game. 125

C. J. Stein
2222. **Geography Game.** Circa 1890s. Geography,
    Card Game. 100

Steins
2223. **Household Words.** © 1916. Word, Card Game. 75

Sterling Co., Ltd.
2224. **Politics, Game of.** © 1900. Political, Card Game. 150

Strat Game Co., Inc.
2225. **Strat: The Great War Game.** © 1915. Military,
    Board Game. 150

Sweethearts Co.
2226. **Sweet Hearts, The Game of.** Circa 1900. Social,
    Card Game. 125

System Thrift Book Co.
2227. **Saving Game, The (by Albert H. Lewis).** ©
    1917. Economic, Card Game. 150

Teddy's Multi-Card Game

2228. **Teddy's Multiplication Cards.** © 1905.
    Numbers, Card Game. 500

Peter G. Thompson & Co.
2229. **Election.** Circa 1900. Political, Card Game. $125
2230. **Geographical Cards, Improved.** © 1883.
    Geography, Card Game. 75
2231. **Historical Cards, Improved.** © 1884. History,
    Card Game. 100
2232. **Musical Authors, Game of.** Circa 1880s.
    Musical, Card Game. 100
2233. **Mythology, Game of.** © 1884. Religious,
    Card Game. 100

Wilkins Thompson Co.
2234. **China.** Pat. 1905. Strategy, Board Game. 250
2234a.**White House.** © 1904. Political, Card Game. 75

Frank G. Thomson
2235. **National Game of Presidents (author Frank G.
    Thomson).** © 1881. Political, Card Game. 150

Trips Card Co.
2236. **Trips.** Circa 1880s. Travel, Card Game. 125

Two Bee's, (Baker/Bennet)
2237. **Foxy Grandpa's Christmas Tree.** Circa
    1905-15. Comics, Christmas, Board Game. 600

U. S. Playing Card Co.
2238. **Birds.** © 1899. Animal, Card Game. 50
2239. **U. S. Card Dominoes.** Circa 1895-9. Classic,
    Card Game. 50

U. S. Publishing
2240. **Gaskell's Popular Historical Game.** © 1884.
    History, Card Game. 125

United Games Co.
2241. **Frog Who Would A-Wooing Go, The.** © 1914.
    Animal, Board Game. 200
2242. **Sailor Boy, The.** © 1910. Military, Board Game. 150
2243. **World Series Base Ball Game.** © 1915. Sports,
    Baseball, Board Game. 250

United Presbyterian Board
2244. **66, The Game of Games.** © 1916. Religious,
    Card Game. 75

United States Soldier Co.
2245. **World War Games (G. D. Hartlett, inventor).** ©
    1914. Military World War I, Board Game. 600

Valley Novelty Works
2246. **Capture the Fort.** Circa 1914. Military,
    Board Game. 300

John R. Van Wormer
2247. Political Bluff (author John R. Van Wormer).
© 1892. Political, Card Game. $150

J. B. Wade
2248. Books of the Bible (author J. B. Wade). © 1889.
Religious, Card Game. 50

Warsaw Paper Box Co.
2249. President Game (© J. G. Bauer). © 1914.
Political, Card Game. 150

J. W. Wheeler
2250. Musical Hits. © 1893. Musical, Card Game. 125

Bettie C. Williams
2251. Pleasant Geography of the United States. ©
1893. Geography, Card Game. 75

Warner Williams
2252. Music, Noel's Game of. Circa 1890. Music,
Card Game. 125

Willys Overland Co.
2253. Going to Market. © 1915. Economic,
Card Game. 200

H. S. Windie Mfg. Co.
2254. Great Allied War Game, The. Circa 1914.
Military, World War I, Board Game. 350

Louis Wolf & Co.
2255. World's War Winner. © 1915. Military, World
War I, Board Game. 350

F. A. Wright
2256. Moneta, Game of. © 1880. Economics,
Card Game. $125
2257. Options, The Game of. © 1883. Stock Market,
Card Game. 175

Yale-Harvard W.O. Dapping
2258. Great American Game Baseball, The. © 1906.
Sports, Baseball, Board Game. 250

Yankee Navy Card Co.

2259. Yankee Navy Game, The. © 1910. Military,
Card Game. 125

Willis G. Young
2260. Chocolate-Splash. © 1916. Social, Board Game. 200
2261. Fig Mill. © 1916. Miscellaneous, Board Game. 150
2262. Peg at My Heart. © 1914. Skill, Action Game. 150

C. L. Zimmer Co.
2263. Game of Base-Ball, A. Circa 1892. Sports,
Baseball, Board Game. 20000

SILVER AGE GAMES

A & P Cereal
Price

2265. A & P Coast to Coast Relay Race, Leg #5, Trains. Circa 1930s. Travel, Rail, Board Game. $85

2266. A & P Coast to Coast Relay Race, Leg #3, Airplanes. Circa 1930s. Travel, Air, Board Game. 100

2267. A & P Coast to Coast Relay Race, Leg #2, Boats. Circa 1930s. Travel, Sea, Board Game. 85

2268. A & P Coast to Coast Relay Race, Leg #4, Motor Cars. Circa 1930s. Travel, Road, Board Game. 85

2269. A & P Coast to Coast Relay Race, Leg #1. Trucks and Busses Circa 1930s. Travel, Board Game. 85

2269a. A & P Coast to Coast Relay Race, Leg #6. Trolley cars. Circa 1930s. Travel, Board Game. 85

Abgate

2270. Quest, The Game Of Knowledge. 1938. Q & A, Board Game. 35

Abingdon Press
2271. Bible Game of Facts, Places and Events. 1922. Religious, Card Game. 35

Ace Leather Goods Co.
2272. American Football Game. 1930. Sports, Football, Board Game. 125

Advance Games, Inc.
2273. 3 Point Landing. 1942. Travel, Air, Board Game. 125

2274. Be a Wiz-Play Radio Quiz. Circa 1940. Q & A, Board Game. 50

2275. Bengalee, The Game of the East. 1945. Adventure, Board Game. 125

2276. Bomber Attack. 1942. Military, World War II, Board Game. 150

2277. Crazy Alley. Circa 1940s. Miscellaneous, Board Game. 75

2278. Let'em Have It. Our Fighting Rangers. Circa 1944. Military, World War II, Board Game. 150

2279. Looping the Loop. 1940s. Travel, Air, Board Game. $125

2280. Lucky Nine, Word Bingo, Radio Quiz, Spinning Bingo. Circa 1940s. Combination, Numbers, Board Game. 35

Advance Manufacturing
2281. Hit and Run. Circa 1922. Sports, Baseball, Card Game. 150

Advertising Service Co.
2282. Tripoley © Fireside Games. © 1832. Classic, Board Game. 50

Affinity Card Co.
2283. Affinity. 1913. Miscellaneous, Card Game. 50

Alfred Day Co.
2284. Adaco. Circa 1920. Numbers, Card Game. 25

All American Football
2285. Football Game. Circa 1933. Sports, Football, Board Game. 250

All Metal Products Co.
2286. Coast Defense. 1930s. Military, Board Game. 300

All-American Games Co.
2287. Lucky 7th Baseball Game. 1937. Sports, Baseball, Board Game. 100

All-Fair
2288. Add-Too. 1940. Mathematics, Board Game. 35

2288a. All-Fair Combination Games, Tennis & Baseball. 1930. Sports, Board Game. 75

2289. Army Checkers. 1943. Military, World War II, Board Game. 125

2290. Authors. Circa 1935-40. Literary, Card Game. 35

2291. Battle of Ballots. 1931. Political, Board Game. 300

2292. Battle. 1943. Military, World War II, Board Game. 125

2293. Bean-Em. 1931. Ethnic, Skill Game. 500

2294. Blinky Blinx (411). 1928. Miscellaneous, Board Game. 250

2295. Bomber Raid. 1943. Military, World War II, Board Game. 150

2296. Buck Rogers in the 25th Century. 1936. Space, Comics, Card Game. 600

2297. Bunker Golf. 1928. Sports, Golf, Board Game. 250

2298. Capital Cities Air Derby, The. 1929. Travel, Air, Board Game. 350

2299. Captain Hop Across Jr. 1928. Travel, Air, Board Game. 200

2300. Cargo For Victory. 1943. Military, World War II, Economic, Board Game. 125

2301. Challenger Cup Race. 1940. Sports, Boating, Board Game. 300

2302. Cities. 1932. Geography, Card Game. 50

All-Fair continued

2303. Cities, Variant cover. 1932. Geography, Card Game. $50

2304. Dickory-Dock. 1935. Kiddie, Board Game. 100

2305. Dim Those Lights. 1932. Travel, Law & Order, Board Game. 500

2306. Emmett Kelly's Circus Game. Circa 1940s. Personality, Circus, Board Game. 150

2307. Flap Jacks. 1931. Ethnic, Skill Game. 200

2308. Fortune Teller Cards. Circa 1940s. Mystic, Card Game. 100

2309. Frank Bucks Bring 'Em Back Alive. 1937. Personality, Animal, Card Game. 150

2310. G. H. Q. 1943. Military, World War II, Board Game. 125

2311. Glydor. 1931. Travel, Air, Board Game. 250

2312. Goin' to Town. Circa 1940s. Travel, Board Game. 125

2313. Hi! Neighbor, The Trade Game of Pan-American Bingo. © 1943. Economics, Board Game. 100

2314. Hi-Ho Rolo. 1930. Miscellaneous, Board Game. 100

2315. Hi-Way Henry. 1928. Comics, Board Game. 2000

2316. Horses. 1927. Sports, Horseracing, Board Game. 125

2317. International Game of Spy. Circa 1939. Law & Order, Board Game. 125

2318. Jaunty Butler Bowl Over. 1931. Ethnic, Skill Game. 350

2319. Jav-Lin. 1931. Ethnic, Skill Game. 250

2320. Jolly Cop Ring Toss. 1929. Occupations, Law & Order, Skill Game. 250

2321. Ko-Ko the Clown. 1930s. Circus, Board Game. 250

2322. Liberty Flag Game. Circa 1940s. Military, World War II, Card Game. 75

2323. Lingo, The New Cross Word Game. 1938. Word, Card Game. 40

2324. Noah's Ark Fishing Game. 1930. Animal, Fish, Board Game. 125

2325. Old Maid, by Vernon Grant. Circa 1930s. Classic, Art, Card Game. $100

2326. Old Maid, Nursery Rhymes & Fairy Tales. Circa1935-40. Classic, Nursery, Card Game. 75

2327. Our Gang Tipple-Topple Game. 1930. Movie, Skill Game. 600

2328. Paratroops. Circa 1940s. Military, World War II, Soldier Game. 125

2329. Pipers 3. 1932. Miscellaneous, Skill Game. 125

2330. Pirates Gold. Circa 1940s. Adventure, Board Game. 125

2331. Play Boy Tiddley Winks. Circa 1932. Skill, Action Game. 50

2332. Poor Jenny, The Game of. 1927. Ethnic, Board Game. 200

2333. Pop and Plop. 1928. Ethnic, Skill Game. 300

2334. Prowl Car. Circa 1940s. Law & Order, Board Game. 150

2335. Race to the Moon. Circa 1932. Space, Board Game. 850

2336. Radio Game for Little Folks. 1926. Communications, Board Game. 150

2337. Simba. Circa 1930s. Ethnic, Board Game. 250

2338. Skippy. Circa 1930s. Comics, Card Game. 150

2339. Sky-Hawks. Circa 1932. Travel, Air, Board Game. 250

2340. Spedem Auto. 1922. Sports, Car, Board Game. 150

2341. Spedem, Junior Auto Race Game. 1927. Sports, Car Racing, Board Game. 100

2342. Squadron Insignia. Circa 1940s. Military, World War II, Card Game. 150

2343. Stand Up Soldiers in Action. 1942. Military, World War II, Soldier Game. 125

2344. Stop and Go. 1927. Travel, Law, Board Game. 200

2345. Stop and Shop. 1930. Economic, Board Game. 100

2346. Tick Tock. Circa 1932. Time, Board Game. 125

2347. Tiddley Winks, latter edition. Circa 1940s. Classic, Skill Game. 35

2348. Tiddley Winks. Circa 1930s. Classic, Skill Game. 60

2349. Tiddley Winks. Circa 1940s. Classic, Skill Game. 35

2350. Tip the Bell Boy. 1929. Ethnic, Skill Game. 250

2351. Toonin Radio Game. Circa 1920s. Communications, Board Game. 200

2352. Totuum. 1923. Historic, Board Game. 300

2353. Traffic, The Game of. Circa 1940s. Travel, Road, Board Game. 125

All-Fair continued

2354. Treasure Hunt. Circa 1930s. Kiddie, Board
Game. $250

2355. U. S. Rummy. Circa 1935-40. Classic, Card Game. 65

2356. W P A, Work-Progress-Action. Circa 1935.
Social Action, Board Game. 150

2357. Watch on the Rind. 1931. Ethnic, Board Game. 600

2358. Way to the White House, The. 1927. Political,
Board Game. 300

2359. Witzi-Wits. 1926. Q. & A, Card Game. 65

2360. Word Bank. 1945. Word, Board Game. 35

**2361. World Flyers Around the World Flight, Game
of.** 1927. Travel, Air, Board Game. 350

2362. Wyntre Golf. 1922. Sports, Golf, Board Game. 400

2363. X-Plor US, Large box with no planes. 1922.
Geography, Board Game. 300

2364. X-Plor US, Small box with planes on cover.
1922. Geography, Board Game. 150

2365. Yatteau. Circa 1920s. Sports, Sea, Board Game. 250

2366. Zippy Zepps, Air Game. Circa 1920s. Travel,
Air, Board Game. 1000

2367. Zoom, Original Game of. Circa 1940s. Travel,
Air, Board Game. 100

Allie-Patriot Games

2368. Liberty, Enlightening the World. 1917. History,
Card Game. 350

Allstate Engineering Serv

2369. Torpedo Attack. Circa 1940. Military, World
War II, Board Game. 200

Alphadice Co.

2370. Alphadice. Circa 1933. Words, Card Game. 35

America War Games Co.

2371. America in the War. 1917. Military, World War I,
Card Game. 400

America, Inc.

2372. Alphabet Rummy (© N. V. Christensen). ©
1933. Words, Card Game. 35

American Games Co., Inc.

2373. Five Star Final. Circa 1932. Communications,
Board Game. 200

2374. Golph, Gamiest of Games (© J. H. Keating). ©
1928. Miscellaneous, Board Game. 150

American Indoor Baseball

2375. American Indoor Baseball Game. 1920s.
Sports, Baseball, Board Game. 250

American News Co., Inc.

2376. American Football Game. 1935. Sports,
Football, Board Game. $100

American Screen Co.

2377. Amos & Sandy Acrobats. 1930. Skill, Board
Game. 100

American Soldier Co.

2378. Audubon Bird Game, The. Circa 1924. Animals,
Birds, Card Game. 75

American Speech Game Co.

2379. Better Speech, Better Americans. 1922. Words,
Card Game. 50

American Toy Airship Co.

2380. Mumbly Peg, Game of. Circa 1920s
Miscellaneous, Board Game. 50

American Toy Mfg. Co.

2381. Exciting Motor Boat Race, An. Circa 1932.
Sports, Boating, Board Game. 200

2382. Lids Off, The (by Arthur Dritz). Circa 1937.
Action, Board Game. 125

2383. Modern Warfare. Circa 1915. Military, Board
Game. 250

2384. Opportunity Hour for Amateurs. Circa 1937.
Q & A, Board Game. 755

2385. Surrender of the Fort. Circa 1915. Military,
Board Game. 250

2386. War of the Allies. Circa 1915. Military, Board
Game. 250

2387. War of the Nations. Circa 1915. Military, Board
Game. 250

American Toy Works

2388. Action Rolling Circus. 1930s. Circus, Board
Game. 200

2389. Aero-Chute Target Game. Circa 1935-9. Travel,
Air, Skill Game. 225

2390. Baggy Beans 'Goes to Town'. Circa 1938-40.
Action, Skill Game. 125

2391. Checkers Avion. Circa1938-40. Classic, Board
Game. 50

2392. Circus Lotto. Circa 1930s. Circus, Board Game. 125

2393. Dave Dawson Pacific Battle Game. 1942.
Military, World War II, Board Game. 500

2394. Dave Dawson Victory Game. 1942. Military,
World War II, Board Game. 500

2395. Flip It, Auto Race & Transcontinental Tour.
Circa1938-40. Travel, Combination, Board Game. 150

2396. Jungle Skittles. Circa 1940-4. Ethnic, Board
Game. 150

American Toy Works continued

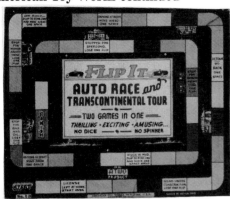

2397. **Kastle Kwoits.** Circa1939-40. Architecture, Skill Game. $125
2398. **Lets Play Games, Golf, Polo, Boots & Saddles.** 1939. Combination, Sports, Golf, Political, Board Game. 75
2399. **Mumbly-Darts.** Circa 1930s. Miscellaneous, Skill Game. 65
2400. **My Word, Horserace.** Circa 1930s. Combination, Word, Board Game. 125
2401. **Opportunity Hour for Amateurs.** 1937. Social, Board Game. 75
2402. **Quoits Ahoy.** Circa 1941-2. Military, World War II, Board Game. 250
2403. **Rocket Darts.** 1939. Space, Skill Game. 400
2403a.**Rollo Circus.** Circa 1940s. Circus Board Game. 75
2404. **Skit Skat.** 1939. Animal, Cat, Board Game. 200
2405. **Tip-Cat.** Circa 1940s. Animal, Cat, Board Game. 150
2406. **Walt Disney Snow White and the Seven Dwarfs.** 1938. Disney, Board Game. 400
2407. **Walt Disney's Game Parade Academy Award Winners.** 1938. Disney, Board Game. 400
2408. **Wampum, Bub, Chen-Check.** Circa 1938-9. Ethnic, Board Game. 150
2409. **Yumph.** 1939. Miscellaneous, Board Game. 75

H. H. Anchor
2410. **Whoopee, Combination Game Board.** Circa 1930. Combination, Board Game. 75

G. H. Anderson
2411. **Major League Baseball Game.** 1943. Sports, Baseball, Board Game. 150
2412. **Pocket Edition Major League Baseball Game.** 1943. Sports, Baseball, Board Game. 125

Anderson & Sons
2413. **Flagship.** 1944. Military, Card Game. 125
2414. **Sabotage.** 1943. Military, World War II, Card Game. 150

Anderson Press
2415. **Questo.** 1936. History? Board Game. $75

O. B. Andrews
2416. **Campaign.** Circa 1935. Military, Board Game. 150
2417. **Fox and Cheese.** Circa 1935. Animal, Board Game. 125
2418. **Midway Ring-Over.** Circa 1935. Circus, Board Game. 125

Angelus Press
2419. **Words, The Fascinating Game of.** © 1935. Words, Card Game. 50

Anonymous
2420. **Authors, Game of.** Circa 1930s. Literary, Card Game. 35
2421. **Big League Baseball Game.** Circa 1920s. Sports, Baseball, Board Game. 100
2422. **Little Jack Horner Golf Course.** Circa 1920s. Sports, Golf, Board Game. 250
2423. **Monkey Face.** Circa 1940s. Animal, Card Game. 125
2424. **Peg and Midget.** Circa 1915-20. Comics, Card Game. 150
2425. **Play Radio Game.** Circa 1920s. Communications, Board Game. 100
2426. **Tourex, The Game of.** Circa 1920s. Travel, Car, Board Game. 250

Anonymous, (Russell)
2427. **Snap, The Game of.** Circa 1930s. Classic, Card Game. 50

Arcade Mfg. Co.
2428. **Baseball Game.** Circa 1932. Sports, Baseball, Board Game. 200

Archer Toy Co.
2429. **Air Mail, The.** 1930s. Travel, Air, Board Game. 200

Armchair Games
2430. **Armchair Golf.** Circa 1940s. Sports, Golf, Board Game. 100

Arnold Specialty Co.
2431. **Pass 'N' Punt.** 1940. Sports, Football, Board Game. 150

Arrco Playing Card Co.
2432. **Hold Your Horses.** 1924. Animal, Card Game. 125

Arrow Mfg. Co.
2433. **Kick-off Football Game.** Circa 1932. Sports, Football, Board Game. 200

Artists and Writers Guild
2434. **Damp Deck.** Circa 1932. Art, Card Game. 100

Atkins & Co., Inc.
2435. Grande Auto Race. 1920. Sports, Cars, Board
    Game. $150

Atlanta Game Co.
2436. Shanghai. 1937. Military, World War II, Paper &
    Pencil. 100

Atlas Game Co.
2437. Pigglie Wiggle, Premium. 1921. Premium,
    Board Game. 150

B & M Mfg. Co.
2438. Jungle Race. Circa 1943. Ethnic, Board Game. 125
2439. Tell-A Plane. Circa 1943. Travel, Air, Board
    Game. 200

B & S. Inc.
2440. Spinning Traveler. Circa 1920s. Geography,
    Board Game. 150

Baldwin Mfg. Co., Inc.
2441. Aerial Bomber. 1942. Military, Board Game. 150
2442. Air Defense. 1939. Military, Board Game. 200
2443. Basketball Game. Circa 1948. Sports,
    Basketball, Board Game. 150
2444. Coast Defense. 1942. Military, Board Game. 150
2445. Coast Guard in Action. 1942. Military, Board
    Game. 150
2446. Man-Dar-In. Circa 1940s. Ethnic, Board Game. 125
2447. Par-A-Shoot. Circa 1940. Military, World War II,
    Board Game. 200
2448. Sink the Invader. Circa 1941. Military, World
    War II, Board Game. 200

L. G. Ballard Mfg. Co.
2449. Star Checkers, The Original. © 1938. Classic,
    Board Game. 50

Bambino Products Co.
2450. Bambino. 1934. Sports, Baseball, Board Game. 200

Bar-Zim Mfg. Co.
2451. New York to Paris Aerorace. Circa 1928.
    Travel, Air, Board Game. 200

W. Bartholomre
2452. Roulette Baseball Game. 1929. Sports, Baseball,
    Board Game. 150

C. M. Bartrug
2453. Speeding. 1937. Travel, Road, Card Game. 150

Frederich H. Beach (Beachcraft Games)
2454. After Dinner, 1st Series. 1936. Mental Activity,
    Paper & Pencil. $60
2455. After Dinner, 2nd Series. 1936. Mental Activity,
    Paper & Pencil. 50
2456. After Dinner, 3rd Series. 1936. Mental Activity,
    Paper & Pencil. 50
2457. After Dinner, 4th Series. 1936. Mental Activity,
    Paper & Pencil. 50
2458. Are You a Sacred Cow, 5th Series. 1937.
    Mental Activity, Paper & Pencil. 50
2459. Are You a Sacred Cow, 6th Series. 1938.
    Mental Activity, Paper & Pencil. 50
2460. Crime and Mystery. Circa 1935. Law & Order,
    Pen & Paper. 65
2461. Crime and Mystery, by J.H. Wallis. 1937. Law
    & Order, Paper & Pencil. 65
2462. Four Little Mysteries. 1930s. Law & Order, Pen
    & Paper. 65
2463. Lowell Thomas Questionnaire. 1930s.
    Personality, Board Game. 65
2464. Peanut Party Game, inc.: Feeding the
    Elephant; Hit the Prize and Win It; Peanut
    Blowing Game; Peanut Chop Stick Race;
    Peanut Golf; Peanut Partners; Peanut Pushers;
    Spoon Relay; Two Finger Spoon Race; William
    Tell. © 1939. Kiddie, Pen & Paper. 50
2465. Pictorial Mysteries. 1930s. Q & A, Paper &
    Pencil. 50
2466. Puzzlems. 1935. Puzzle, Paper & Pencil. 50
2467. Question Box, The, 1st Series. 1937. Q & A,
    Paper & Pencil. 50
2468. Sippa Fish. 1936. Animal, Sea, Board Game. 50

2469. Take It and Double, 1st Series. 1943. Numbers,
    Board Game. 40
2470. Take It and Double, 2nd Series. 1943. Numbers,
    Board Game. 40

Beachcraft Games
2471. Bug, The Old Army Game. © 1939. Animal, Pencil & Paper. $65
2472. Flash!-News. 1937. Communication, Board Game. 250
2473. Libel. 1938. Law & Order, Paper & Pencil. 65
2474. Map-Peeno. 1943. Geography, Board Game. 50
2475. Question Box, The, 2nd Series. 1938. Q & A, Paper & Pencil. 50

Beacon Hudson Co.
Open Championship Gold Game. Circa 1925. Sports, Golf, Board Game. 150

Bee-Jay Products Co., Inc.
2476. Snapit! Circa 1925. Miscellaneous, Card Game. 40
2477. Spellette. Circa 1925. Words, Card Game. 40

Beistle
2478. Hallowe'en Spot Game. Circa 1930s. Holiday, Hallowe'en, Board Game. 100
2479. Halloween Kitty Card Game. Circa 1930s. Holiday, Hallowe'en, Card Game. 125

Belasco Mechanics Corp.
2480. Ponygo. Circa 1922. Miscellaneous, Card Game. 59

Chas. H. Belknap Co.
2481. Basket Ball. Circa 1918. Sports, Basketball, Board Game. 200
2482. Snappy Foot Ball. Circa 1918. Sports, Football, Board Game. 200
2483. Visual Geography, Belknaps. Circa 1918. Geography, Board Game. 125

Bell Speciality Co.
2484. Radio, The Game of. Circa 1920s. Communications, Board Game. 75

B. B. Bellows
2485. Pronunciation. 1944. Word, Card Game. 50

Ben-Hur Products Inc.
2486. Polly Woggle. Circa 1932. Miscellaneous, Board Game. 125

Carl F. Benner
2487. Cootie, The Game of. 1925. Skill, Skill Game. 125

Benson Games
2488. Recovery. Circa 1939. Miscellaneous, Card Game. 150

Beruth Co.
2489. Slide Kelly! 1936. Sports, Baseball, Board Game. $150

Edwin E. Besser Co.
2490. Radio Ball. Circa 1924. Communications, Board Game. 125

Best Manufacturing Co.
2491. SportMaster, include: Backgammon; Baseball; Bestbet. © 1933. Sports, Combination, Board Game. 125

Biddle Corp.
2492. Neutral Game of War, Peace and Indemnity. 1916. Military, Board Game. 150

Henri Blum & Co., Inc.
2493. Deck-O-Cards Roulette. © 1938. Chance, Card Game. 50

"Bookie" Games Co.
2494. Bookie. 1931. Sports, Horseracing, Board Game. 150

Bortan Products
2495. Ask and Answer. 1938. Q & A, Board Game. 75

Joseph Borzellino & Son
2496. Soldier on the Fort, The. 1931. Military, Board Game. 150

Bowlett Co.
2497. Bowlett. 1931. Sports, Bowling, Board Game. 150

Bowlline Game Co.
2498. Parlor-Bowl Baseball. 1940. Sports, Baseball, Board Game. 125

C. E. Bradley
2499. Diving Fish. Circa 1920. Animal, Fish, Board Game. 150

Milton Bradley
2500. 12 Game Combination Board. 1937. Combination, Board Game. 50
2501. 3 Men on a Horse, A Movie Hit. 1936. Movie, Board Game. 125
2502. Abbie An' Slatts, The Game of. 1944. Comics, Board Game. 125
2503. Above the Clouds. 1938. Travel, Air, Board Game. 200

Milton Bradley continued

2504. Acey Deucy. Circa 1935. Skill, Board Game. $75

2505. Adventures of Robin Hood. 1938. Adventure, Board Game. 200

2506. Adventures of Superman, The. 1938. Super Heroes, Board Game. 300

2507. Adventures of the Nebbs. Circa 1920s. Comics, Board Game. 300

2508. Air Mail, Game of. Circa 1920s. Com., Travel, Air, Board Game. 150

2508a.Air Mail, Game of. Horizontal red biplane cover, Travel, Air, Board Game. 150

2509. Air Raid Warden. 1943. Military, World War II, Board Game. 175

2510. Airmail, The Game of. Circa 1926-8. Travel, Air, Board Game. 150

2511. Airmail. 1938. Travel, Air, Co, Board Game. 150

2512. Airplane Trip. Circa 1943. Travel, Air, Board Game. 125

2513. Anagrams. Circa 1940s. Word, Card Game. 25

2514. Ancient Game of China. 1923. Classic, Board Game. 50

2515. Andy Gump, His Game. Circa 1930s. Comics, Board Game. 150

2516. Animal Ball Game. 1939. Animals, Board Game. 40

2517. Animal Grab. Circa 1938. Animals, Board Game. 50

2518. Around the World with Nellie Bly. 1920. Geography, Board Game. 200

2519. Around the World. 1936. Travel, Air, Board Game. 300

2520. At the Circus. 1938. Circus, Board Game. 150

2521. Auctioneer. 1938. Economic, Board Game. 100

2522. Auto Game, The. Circa 1910s. Travel, Car, Board Game. 250

2523. Auto Race Game. 1925. Sports, Car, Board Game. 300

2524. Auto Race Game. Circa 1930s. Travel, Car, Board Game. $200

2525. Auto Race. Circa 1930s. Sports, Car, Board Game. 200

2526. Aviation Game. 1920s. Travel, Air, Board Game. 250

2527. Babe Ruth's Baseball Game. 1926. Sports, Baseball, Board Game. 750

2528. Balaroo. 1936. Miscellaneous, Skill Game. 125

2529. Bank Roll. 1938. Economic, Board Game. 125

2530. Barney Google and Spark Plug Game. 1926. Comics, Board Game. 200

2531. Baseball & Checkers. Circa 1920s. Sports, Baseball, Cm, Board Game. 200

2532. Baseball. 1941. Sports, Baseball, Board Game. 150

2533. Bataan, The Battle of the Philippines. 1943. Military, World War II, Board Game. 250

2534. Battle of the Tanks. 1942. Military, World War II, Board Game. 200

2535. Battle Winks. Circa 1943. Military, Board Game. 150

2536. Bear Hunt for the Honey Pot. 1945. Animal, Board Game. 125

2537. Behind the Eight Ball. 1940. Miscellaneous, Board Game. 100

2538. Big Board, The. 1937. Stock Market, Board Game. 150

2539. Big Chief. 1938. Western, India, Board Game. 125

2540. Bingo, 25 Card Set. 1936. Classic, Board Game. 10

2541. Bizerte Gertie. 1944. Military, World War II, Board Game. 250

2542. Blackout, Large Format. 1939. Military, World War II, Board Game. 150

2543. Blackout. 1939. Military, World War II, Board Game. 175

2544. Bombs Aloft. 1941. Military, World War II, Board Game. 250

2545. Boy Scouts, A Game. Circa 1910s. Organizations, Board Game. 150

2546. Bradleys Big Top Game. 1931. Circus, Board Game. 150

2547. Brewsters Millions. 1937. Movie, Economic, Board Game. 200

2548. Carnival. 1937. Circus, Board Game. 150

2549. Chameleon (4176). © 1938. Miscellaneous, Board Game. 125

2550. Chester Gump Game, In The City of Gold. Circa 1930s. Comics, Board Game. 250

2551. Chester Gump Game. 1938. Comics, Board Game. 200

2552. Chinamen. Circa 1943. Classic, Board Game. 125

2553. Chinese Star Checkers. 1938. Classic, Board Game. 35

2554. Chinese Star Checkers. 1938. Classic, Board Game. 35

2555. College Football. Circa 1944-8. Sports, Football, Board Game. 125

Milton Bradley continued

2556. Cops and Robbers. 1939. Law & Order, Board Game. $150

2557. Country Fair, The. 1937. Economic, Board Game. 125

2558. Cowboy. 1922. Western Cow, Board Game. 150

2559. Cross Country Marathon. 1926. Sports, Board Game. 150

2560. Crusader Horse Race Game. Circa 1943. Sports, Horseracing, Board Game. 125

2561. Dog Chase (4689). Circa 1938. Sport, Board Game. 125

2562. Down and Out. Circa 1929. Miscellaneous, Action Game. 75

2563. Down the Pike with Mrs. Wiggs at the St. Louis Exposition. 1904. Reading, Card Game. 65

2564. Dr. Busby. 1936. Social, Card Game. 40

2565. Duck on the Rock. Circa 1940s. Animal, Bird, Board Game. 50

2566. Easy Money, 4th Edition. 1937. Economic, Board Game. 100

2567. Easy Money, 3rd Edition. 1936. Economic, Board Game. 125

2568. Easy Money, 1st Edition. 1935. Economic, Board Game. 150

2569. Easy Money, 2nd Edition. 1936. Economic, Board Game. 135

2570. Ella Cinders. 1944. Comics, Board Game. 125

2571. Endurance Run. Circa 1930. Sports, Board Game. 200

2572. Facts Worth Knowing Games - Science. Circa 1943. Q & A, Card Game. 35

2573. Facts Worth Knowing Games - Fine Arts. Circa 1943. Q & A, Card Game. 35

2574. Facts Worth Knowing Games - Government. Circa 1943. Q & A, Card Game. 35

2575. Feed the Monk. Circa 1943. Miscellaneous, Board Game. 125

2576. Fibber Mcgee and the Wistful Vista Mystery. 1940. Personality, Card Game. 50

2577. Fighting Marines (4031). © 1943. Military, Board Game. 200

2578. Fine Arts. 1939. Art, Card Game. 50

2579. Fire Department, Game of. Circa 1920s Occupation, Board Game. 225

2580. Fire Department. Circa 1938. Occupations, Board Game. 150

2581. Fish Pond, 10 Fish cover. Circa 1920s. Animal, Sea, Board Game. 125

2582. Fish Pond. Circa 1920s. Animal, Sea, Board Game. 125

2583. Five Star Final. 1937. Communications, Board Game. 225

2584. Flight to Paris, The. 1927. Travel, Air, Board Game. 275

2585. Fliver Game. 1930. Travel, Road, Board Game. $300

2586. Game Combination, U. S. Mail & Checkers. Circa 1920s. Combination, Communications, Board Game. 150

2587. Gasoline Alley, A Game of Walt & Skeezix. Circa 1930s. Comics, Card Game. 150

2588. Get In the Scrap. 1944. Military, World War II, Board Game. 275

2589. Gingerbread Boy, The Game of the. 1938. Nursery Rhymes, Board Game. 125

2590. Gliding, Game of. 1926. Travel, Air, Board Game. 300

2591. Glyder Racing Game. Circa 1930s. Travel, Air, Board Game. 250

2592. G-Men. 1935. Law & Order, Card Game. 250

2593. Go to the Head of the Class, 2nd Series. 1938. Q & A, Board Game. 150

2594. Go to the Head of the Class, 3rd Series. 1938. Q & A, Board Game. 125

2595. Going to the Worlds Fair Game. 1939. Fairs, Board Game. 300

2596. Golden State Limited. 1935. Travel, Rail, Board Game. 125

2597. Government. 1939. Politics, History, World War II, Board Game. 150

2597a. Gracie Allen Murder Case, A Game. 1939. Personality, Movie, Law & Order. 650

2598. Grandmas Game of Bible Questions. 1926. Religious, Card Game. 35

2599. Great Charlie Chan Detective Mystery Game, The. 1937. Personality, Law & Order, Board Game. 400

2600. Gullivers Travels. 1939. Literary, Adventure, Board Game. 250

2601. Gumps at the Seashore, The. Circa 1930s. Comics, Board Game. 250

2602. Hand of Fate. Circa 1943. Mystic, Board Game. 125

2603. Happy Hooligan Game. 1925. Comics, Board Game. 300

2604. Harlem, Game of. 1934. Miscellaneous, Board Game. 125

Milton Bradley continued

2605. Harold Teen Game, Up the Ladder. 1935.
Comics, Board Game. $200

2606. Harold Teen, A Game, Smaller box. Circa
1920s. Comics, Board Game. 150

2607. Harold Teen, A Game. Circa 1920s. Comics,
Board Game. 200

**2608. Hazards Bowling on the Green, Bradleys
(4573).** 1931. Sports, Golf, Board Game. 125

2609. Hialeah Horse Racing Game. 1940. Sports,
Horseracing, Board Game. 150

2610. Hippety Hop, Game of. Circa 1940s. Kiddie,
Board Game. 75

2611. Hook. Circa 1943. Miscellaneous, Board Game. 75

2612. Horse Racing. 1935. Sports, Horseracing, Board
Game. 125

2613. Ice Hockey. 1941. Sports, Hockey, Board Game. 150

2614. Jack and Jill, or Who Brought the Water. 1938.
Nursery Rhyme, Board Game by Howard R.
Garis. 100

2615. Jack and Jill. Circa 1920s. Nursery Rhyme,
Board Game. 125

2616. Jack Straws, Magnetic. 1920. Classic, Skill
Game. 25

2617. Jack Straws, Royal (4095). 1936. Classic, Skill
Game. 25

2618. Jack Straws, Senior (4418). 1930s. Classic, Skill
Game. 30

2619. Jack Straws. Circa 1920s. Classic, Skill Game. 25

2620. Jolly Animal Picnic Game. Circa 1943. Animal,
Board Game. 125

2621. Jolly Clown Whoopee Game (4001). Circa
1938. Circus, Board Game. 125

2622. Joyland. 1940. Kiddie, Board Game. 100

2623. King of the Turf. Circa 1930s. Sport,
Horseracing, Board Game. 150

2624. Kop the Kaiser. Circa 1917. Military, World
War I, Board Game. 250

2625. Leap for Life Game. Circa 1920s. Travel, Air,
Board Game. 250

2626. Lettergrams (4141). © 1938. Word, Card Game. 30

2627. Lightning Express, A Railroad Game. Circa
1930s. Travel, Rail, Board Game. 150

2628. Li'l Abner, Game of. 1944. Comics, Board
Game. 125

2629. Liners and Transports (4667). 1936. Travel,
Sea, Board Game. 200

2630. Little Orphan Annie Game. 1927. Comics,
Board Game. 250

2631. Little Orphan Annie Game. Circa 1930s.
Comics, Board Game. 250

2632. Little Orphan Annie Travel Game. Circa 1930s.
Comics, Board Game. 175

2633. Long Green, The. 1936. Sports, Horseracing,
Board Game. 100

2634. Lost Heir, Game of the. Circa 1920s. Social,
Card Game. $50

2635. Lotto, Dressed Animal Cover. 1939. Animal,
Board Game, Clasic childrens artist cover. 85

2636. Mandarins (4206). Circa 1938. Ethnic, Board
Game. 75

2637. Men of Destiny. 1942. History, Board Game. 125

2638. Merry Game of Fibber Magee, The. 1940.
Personality, Board Game. 50

2639. Merry Game of Spinaroo, The. Circa 1930s.
Action, Board Game. 60

2640. Mister Wiskers. 1938. Animal, Card Game. 50

2641. Moon Man. Circa 1943. Space, Board Game. 350

2642. Moon Mullens Game, The. Circa 1920s.
Comics, Board Game. 300

2643. Moon Mullins Automobile Race. Circa 1920s.
Comics, Car Racing, Board Game. 250

2644. Moon Mullins Game. 1927. Comics, Board
Game, Dinner off table cover. 300

2645. Moon Mullins Game. 1938. Comics, Board
Game. 200

2646. Moon Mullins Gets the Run-A-Round. Circa
1930s. Comics, Board Game. 200

2647. Mother Goose. Circa 1920s. Nursery Rhyme,
Board Game. 125

2648. Moving Picture Game, The. 1932. Movie, Board
Game. 150

2649. Movie-Land Lotto. Circa 1920s. Movie, Board
Game. 150

2650. Nancy & Sluggo Game. 1944. Comics, Board
Game. 150

2651. Nebbs, Game of the. 1915. Comics, Card Game. 125

2652. Nebbs, Game of the. Deluxe larger edition.
1915. Comics, Card Game. 150

2653. Nobby Sticks. 1937. Miscellaneous, Action
Game. 50

2654. Oasis, Game of. 1937. Travel, Board Game. 200

2655. Okay, A Snappy Card Game (4855). Circa
1938. Miscellaneous, Card Game. 50

2656. Old Mother Hubbard. Later Edition. 1910.
Nursery Rhyme, Card Game. 125

2657. On the Midway. Circa 1925. Circus, Board
Game. 350

2658. Orphan Annie to the Rescue. Circa 1930s
Comics, Board Game. 200

2659. Outboard Motor Boat, The. Circa 1935. Travel,
Sea, Board Game. 250

2660. Overland Limited, The. Circa 1930s. Travel,
Rail, Board Game. 200

2660a. Over the Garden Wall. Circa 1920s, Action
board Game. 125

Milton Bradley continued

2661. Parachute Jump Game. 1936. Travel, Air, Board Game. $150

2662. Parachute Jump, The Game of. Circa 1920s. Travel, Air, Board Game. 300

2663. Parlay. 1941. Sports, Horseracing, Board Game. 150

2664. Paul Wings Spelling Bee Game. 1938. Word, Board Game. 65

2665. Pecks Bad Boy with the Circus. 1939. Movie, Circus, Board Game. 200

2665a. Pirate and Traveler. © 1936, Adventure Board Game. 150

2666. Play Safe, Blue and Red Label. 1936. Economic, Board Game. 250

2667. Play Safe. 1936. Economic, Board Game. 250

2668. Plunder. 1939. Adventure, Board Game. 150

2669. Presidents, The Game of. 1934. Political, Card Game. 150

2670. Put a Hat on Uncle Wiggly (by Howard R. Garis). © 1919. Literary, Board Game. 150

2671. Quiz Me, Game of Useful Knowledge. 1939. Q & A, Card Game. 25

2672. Quiz-Me, Game of Geography (4930). © 1938. Q & A, Card Game. 25

2673. Quiz-Me, Game of Numbers (4289). © 1939. Q & A, Card Game. 25

2674. Quiz-Me, Game of Numbers (4929). © 1938 Q & A, Card Game. 25

2675. Quiz-Me, Game of Riddles (4774). © 1940. Q & A, Card Game. 25

2676. Quiz-Me, Game of Riddles. 1942. Q & A, Card Game. 25

2677. Quiz-Me, Game of Riddles. Variant box. 1938. Q & A, Card Game. 25

2678. Quiz-Me, Game of Riddles. Variant box. 1940. Q & A, Card Game. 25

2679. Quiz-Me, Game of Useful Knowledge (4931). © 1938. Q & A, Card Game. 25

2680. Radio Game, Radio & knobs cover. Circa 1930s. Communications, Board Game. 175

2681. Radio Game. Circa 1920s. Communications, Board Game. $150

2682. Radio. 1944. Communications, Board Game. 125

2683. Raggedy Ann, Game of. 1940. Comics, Board Game. 250

2684. Raggedy Ann's Magic Pebble Game. 1941. Literary, Board Game. 200

2685. Railroad Game. 1940. Travel, Rail, Board Game. 125

2686. Reg'lar Fellers. 1926. Comics, Board Game. 250

2687. Ring My Nose. Circa 1920s. Miscellaneous, Skill Game. 125

2688. Rip-Van-Winkle. 1929. Literary, Adventure, Board Game. 150

2689. Royal-Purple, The Game of. 1937. Miscellaneous, Board Game. 150

2690. Santa Claus Game. Circa 1920s. Holiday, Xmas, Board Game. 400

2691. Saratoga. 1943. Sports, Horseracing, Board Game. 150

2692. Scavenger Hunt. Circa 1933. Social, Card Game. 100

2693. Scouting, Game of. 1926. Organizations, Board Game. 150

2694. Scram, Game of. Circa 1930s. Miscellaneous, Board Game. 150

2695. Senior Combination Board. Circa 1920s. Combination, Board Game. 65

2696. Shag. © 1937. Miscellaneous, Card Game. 100

2697. Skeezix and the Airmail. Circa 1930s. Comics, Board Game. 250

2698. Skeezix Game, The. Circa 1930s. Comics, Board Game. 250

2699. Skeezix Visits Nina. Circa 1937-9. Comics, Board Game. 200

2700. Skeezix. Circa 1930s. Comics, Card Game. 125

2700a. Skillets and Cakes. Circa 1930s, Food Board Game. 100

2701. Skippy, Game of. 1932. Comics, Board Game. 250

2702. Smitty Game. Circa 1930s. Comics, Board Game. 250

2703. Smitty Speed Boat Race Game. Circa 1930s. Comics, Sport, Sea, Board Game. 250

2704. Snow White and the Seven Dwarfs, The Game of. 1937. Disney, Board Game. 250

2705. Snug Harbor, Submarine Game. Circa 1920s. Military, Board Game. 200

2706. Speed Boat Race. Circa 1930s. Sports, Sea, Board Game. 200

2707. Spider and Fly Game. Circa 1940s. Animal, Board Game. 75

2708. Spoof, The Cheer -Up Game. 1918. Social, Card Game. 45

2709. Spot, Game of. 1925. Animal, Mammal, Board Game. 150

2710. Spotta. 1942. Animal, Board Game. 200

2711. Stop Look and Listen, Game of. 1935. Travel, Board Game. 175

Milton Bradley continued

2712. Storming the Castle. 1932. Military, Board
Game. $150

2713. Streamline Express Game, The. 1936. Travel,
Rail, Board Game. 200

2714. Submarine Chaser. 1939. Military, World War II,
Board Game. 200

2715. Sunset Limited. Circa 1930s. Travel, Rail, Board
Game. 150

2716. Superman Speed Game. 1941. Super Heroes,
Board Game. 200

2717. Three Blind Mice, Game of (4737). 1925.
Nursery Rhyme, Board Game. 125

2718. Three Little Pigs. Circa 1943. Animal, Board
Game. 75

2718a. Three Little Kittens, The. Circa 1920s,
Animal, Cat Board Game. 125

2719. Three Men in a Tub. 1932. Movie, Board Game. 150

2720. Three Musketeers, The. Three facing busts.
Circa 1930s. Adventure, Board Game. 250

2721. Three Musketeers, The. Deluxe Edition. Circa
1930s. Adventure, Board Game. 200

2722. Tiddley Winks. 1939. Miscellaneous, Skill
Game. 30

2723. Tiddley Winks. 1932. Classic, Skill Game. 30

2724. Tiger Tom, Game of. Circa 1920. Animal, Board
Game. 125

2725. Time. 1938. Social, Board Game. 150

2726. Tip Top Fish Pond. 1937. Animal, Fish, Board
Game. 75

2727. Tom Sawyer, The Game of. 1937. Literary,
Adventure, Board Game. 200

2728. Toonerville Trolley Game. 1927. Comics, Board
Game. 225

2729. Toy Town Target. Circa 1920s. Miscellaneous,
Skill Game. 125

2730. Trade Winds. 1943. Travel, Adventure, Board
Game. 150

2731. Traffic, Game of. 1935. Travel, Road, Board
Game. $150

2731a.Transatlantic Flight, The Game Of. Circa
1930s, Travel, Air, Board Game. 250

2732. Traps and Bunkers, Game of Golf. Circa
1926-8. Sports, Golf, Board Game. 200

2733. Treasure Island. 1943. Adventure, Literary,
Board Game. 125

2734. Trocadero (4856). © 1940. Miscellaneous,
Board. 100

2735. Twentieth Century Limited, The. Circa 1930s.
Travel, Rail, Board Game. 150

2736. Uncle Sams Mail. Circa 1930s. Communications,
Board Game. 150

2737. Uncle Wiggily Game. 1918. Literary, Board
Game. 125

2738. Uncle Wiggily's New Airplane Game. Circa
1920s. Travel, Air, Literary, Card Game. 200

2739. Values, The Money Management Game. Circa
1920s. Economic, Board Game. 250

2740. Vita Lee. 1941. Self-Improvement, Board Game. 275

2741. Vox Pop. Circa 1938-9. Q & A; Board Game. 65

2742. Voyage Around the World, Game of. Circa
1920s. Geography, Board Game. 400

2743. Voyage Round the World, Game of. Circa
1930s. Travel, Air, Board Game. 300

2744. Wall Street The Game of Speculation. 1933.
Stock Market, Board Game. 150

2745. Walt & Skeezix. Circa 1920s. Comics, Board
Game. 250

2746. Walt Disney's Pinocchio. 1939. Disney, Board
Game. 250

2747. Wheel of Fortune. 1940. Mystic, Board Game. 150

2748. Whoopee. 1929. Social, Card Game. 45

2749. Wild West (4683). Circa 1943. Western, Board
Game. 125

2750. Winnie Winkle, Game of. Circa 1920s. Comics,
Board Game. 250

2751. Winnie Winkle, Glider Race Game. Circa
1920s. Comics, Air, Board Game. 200

2752. Wise Cracks. Circa 1920s. Social, Card Game. 125

2753. Wise Old Goose (4654). Circa 1938. Animal,
Board Game. 125

Brinkman Engineering Co.
2754. Baseball. Circa 1932. Sports, Baseball, Board
Game. 250

2755. Shoot the Moon. Circa 1929. Space, Board Game. 300

Brooks Co.
2756. Bunnies Circus. Circa 1935. Circus, Board Game. 150

Broughton Specialty Co.
2757. **Bomb Tokyo (Poph-It Cereal Co.).** 1942.
   Military, Board Game. $125

Paul Bunyan Inc.
2757a. **Paul Bunyan.** References to CCC camps, 1938.
   Hunting and fishing, Board Game. 150

Buzza Co.
2758. **Tally Tale-Teller (A Fortune Telling Game).**
   1924. Mystic, Card Game. 100

Byrne Novelty Co.
2759. **Original Radio Game, The.** Circa 1930s.
   Communications, Board Game. 75

C. & P. Products Co.
2760. **Kennel-Club Card Game.** 1939. Animal, Card
   Game. 125

Cadaco Ltd.
2761. **Adventures of Pinocchio, The.** 1939. Literary,
   Board Game. 150
2762. **Bas-Ket.** 1935. Sports, Basketball, Board Game. 150
2763. **Down the Hatch.** 1943. Military, World War II,
   Board Game. 150
2764. **Elmer Laydens Scientific Football Game.** 1940.
   Sports, Football, Board Game. 100
2765. **Eric Laydens Scientific Football, 1st edition.**
   1936. Sports, Football, Board Game. 200
2766. **Foto World.** 1935. Travel, World, Board Game. 150
2767. **Jingo.** 1942. Miscellaneous, Board Game. 75
2768. **Lection.** Circa 1936. Political, Board Game. 200
2769. **Movie Mart.** Circa 1935. Movie, Board Game. 200
2770. **Party Package.** 1939. Social, Board Game. 75

2771. **Top of the Town.** 1937. Movie, Board Game.
   Early Movie Game. 250

2772. **Touchdown.** Circa 1935. Sports, Football, Board
   Game. $150
2773. **Transport Pilot.** Circa 1938. Travel, Air, Board
   Game. 150
2774. **Treasure Hunt.** 1942. Adventure, Board Game. 125
2775. **Twenty Grand.** Circa 1936. Economics, Board
   Game. 150
2776. **Varsity Football Game.** 1942. Sports, Football,
   Board Game. 125

Capital Card Co.
2777. **Matrimony Card Game.** 1927. Romance, Card
   Game. 100

Capitol Game Co.
2778. **Va-Lo, The Football Card Game.** 1925. Sport,
   Football, Card & Board Game. 200

M. Carlton Dank Toy
2779. **Obstacle Golf.** Circa 1931. Sports, Golf, Board
   Game. 150

Geo. S. Carrington Co.
2780. **Jeep Board, The.** 1943. Military, World War II,
   Board Game. 225

Carrom Industries
2781. **Fox Hunt.** Circa 1946. Sports, Board Game. 150
2782. **Traffic** 1938. Travel, Road, Board Game. 150

Castle Films
2783. **Broadway Handicap, Movies of Races &
   betting.** 1944. Sports, Horseracing, Visual Game.
   With 8mm movies of races. 300

Champion Spark Plug
2784. **Champion Road Race, Premium.** 1934. Sports,
   Car Racing, Board Game. 125

Chase & Sandborn
2785. **Charlie McCarthys Radio Party, Premium.**
   1938. Personality, Premium, Board Game. 125

Checards Co.
2786. **Checards (inv. by Allan C. Bussey).** Circa 1935.
   Miscellaneous, Card Game. 65

Chicago Printing & Pub.
2787. **Combat.** 1942. Military, World War II, Board
   Game. 300

Child Welfare Pub.

2788. Building Fun, #416, Pat 1929. Architecture,
Board Game. $75

2789. Garden Speller, #416, Pat 1918. Word, Board
Game. 50

2790. Ideal Speller, #414, Pat 1929. Word, Board
Game. 50

2791. Playland Reader, #408, Pat 1929. Word, Board
Game. 50

2792. Playtime Game, #406, Pat 1929. Word, Board
Game. 50

2793. Wonder Speller, #402, Pat 1929. Word, Board
Game. 50

N. V. Christensen

2794. America. 1933. Geographical, Card Game. 150

Clover Games, Inc.

2795. Big Chief Apache. Circa 1941. Western, Board
Game. 125

2796. Destroyer. Circa 1941. Military, World War II
Board Game. 200

2797. Fish Quick. Circa 1941. Animal, Board Game. 75

2798. Kangaroo Race. Circa 1941. Animal, Board
Game. 125

2799. Postmaster. Circa 1941. Communication, Board
Game. 125

2800. Ups & Downs. 1940. Miscellaneous, Board
Game. 75

Club Aluminum Products

2801. Whirling Words. © 1942. Words, Card Game. 50

Clyan Hall, Sturditoy

2802. Hollywood Derby. 1930s. Sports, Horseracing,
Board Game. 150

Coleman, Kerns & Williams

2803. High Command. 1942. Military, World War II,
Board Game. 350

Columbia Broadcasting Co.

2804. Trip through Columbia Network Studios, A.
1934. Premium, Board Game. 125

Combat Card Co.

2804a. Combat. © 1941. Military, World War II, Card
Game. 100

Commerce Game Sales Co.

2805. Commerce, Game of. © 1925. Economic, Board
Game. $150

Concord Toy Co.

2806. Ring-Toss, Animal cover. Circa 1940s. Animal,
Skill Game. 50

Connecticut Tele & Elec.

2807. Radio Mike. Circa 1932. Communications,
Board Game. 75

Continental Sales

2808. Ward Cuffs Football Game. 1938. Sports,
Football, Board Game. 300

Continental Toys

2809. Bombardier Bombsight. 1944. Military, Board
Game. 200

Cooper & Bros.

**2810. Sigs-The Game of United States Forces,
Insignia.** 1943. Military, World War II, Card
Game. 125

Corey Game Co.

2811. A.B. Name Rhyming Game. 1942. Word, Board
Game. 40

2812. Air-Attack. 1943. Military, World War II, Board
Game. 250

2813. Al Djemma. 1944. Adventure, Board Game. 150

2814. All American Basketball. 1941. Sports,
Basketball, Board Game. 150

2815. All Star Football Game. Circa 1945. Sports,
Football, Board Game. 150

2816. All-American Basketball Game. 1940. Sports,
Basketball, Board Game. 150

2817. Barage. 1941. Military World War II, Board
Game. 150

2818. Baseball Game. 1943. Sports, Baseball, Board
Game. 150

2819. Blockade, A Game for Armchair Admirals.
1941. Military, World War II, Board Game. 200

2820. Captive Princess, The. 1942. Adventure, Board
Game. 150

Corey Game Co. continued

2821. Cat' 'n' Mouse. 1945. Animal, Board Game. $75

2821a. Cock-A-Doodle-Doo. 1940, Farm, Board

Game. 125

2821b. Funny Fellows. 1943. Kiddie, Action Game. 50

2822. Hippity-Hop. 1940. Kiddie, Board Game. 125

2823. I've Got It. 1940. Action, Board Game. 50

2824. Jig-A-Roo. 1945. Kiddie, Board Game. 100

2825. Jungle Shooting. 1947. Animal, Board Game. 100

2826. Kick-Off. 1941. Sports, Football, Board Game. 150

2827. Man About Town. 1941. Social, Board Game. 250

2828. Pirate and Traveler. 1941. Travel, Board Game. 125

2829. Pirates Island. 1942. Adventure, Board Game. 165

2830. Pixie. 1940. Fantasy, Board Game. 100

2831. Pop-In. 1942. Kiddie, Board Game. 60

2832. Raffles. 1939. Economic, Board Game. 125

2833. Shah-Shah. 1941. Animal, Board Game. 75

2834. Spin-A-Quiz. 1941. Q & A, Board Game. 50

2835. Spin-O. 1940s. Miscellaneous, Skill Game. 50

2836. Strategy. 1938. Military, World War II, Board

Game. 200

2837. Strategy. 1944. Military, World War II, Board

Game. 150

2838. Suffolk Downs-Club Edition. Circa 1930s.

Sports, Horseracing, Board Game. 125

2839. Tiddley Winks Barrage Game. 1941. Military,

World War II, Skill Game. 125

2840. Top Hockey. 1943. Sports, Hockey, Board Game. 150

2841. Wild West Shooting Game. 1942. Western, Skill

Game. 150

2842. Yankee Trader. 1941. Economic, Board Game. 125

2843. You're Out Baseball Game. 1941. Sports,

Baseball, Board Game. $150

Coroom Games
2844. Hang the Tyrants. 1944. Military, World War II,

Board Game. $200

Cracker Jack Co.
2845. Gold Rush, The. Circa 1930. Adventure, Card

Game. 75

2846. Midget Auto Race. Circa 1930. Sports, Cars,

Card Game. 75

Craig-Hopkins & Co.
2847. Electric Quiz Game. 1945. Q & A, Board

Game. 35

2848. Lets Fish. Circa 1945. Animal, Fish, Board

Game. 65

2849. Round-Up. Circa 1946. Western, Board Game. 75

2850. Stadium Football. Circa 1946. Sports, Football,

Board Game. 150

G. F. Cran
2851. Follow the Flag to Victory. 1942. Military, World

War II, Board Game. 200

Thomas Carroll Co.
2852. National Game of Baseball. Circa 1925. Sports,

Baseball, Board Game. 200

Cronston Co.

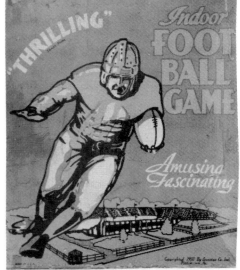

2853. Thrilling Indoor Football Game. 1933. Sports,

Football, Board Game. 250

Cross Word Games, Inc.
2854. Puzz, The Cross Word Game. Circa 1925.
Words, Card Game. $50

Crosticon Co., Inc.
2855. Crosticon. © 1924. Words, Card Game. 50

Cutler & Saleeby Co., Inc.
2856. Fish Pond. Circa 1920s. Animal, Sea, Board
Game. 75
2857. India Bombay. Circa 1920-5. Classic, Board
Game. 75
2858. Long Flight. 1930s. Travel, Air, Board Game. 200
2859. Ski-Hi, Flight to Paris. Circa 1929. Travel, Air,
Board Game. 250
2860. Turtle Race. 1920s. Animal, Board Game. 150

D. & H. Games
2861. Racing Stable, The Game of. 1936. Sports,
Horseracing, Board Game. 250

Laurence D'Orsay
2862. Plot Cards. © 1935. Movies, Card Game. 125

Dalton Playing Card Co.
2863. Politics - The National Card Game. Circa 1930.
Political, Card Game. 150

Charles B. Darrow
2864. Monopoly, Large white box. 1935. Economic,
Board Game. 2500
2865. Monopoly, Original large white box edition.
1934. Economic, Board Game. 4000
**2866. Monopoly, Separate red on black implement
box.** 1935. Economic, Board Game. 1500

John J. Davala
2867. Aero Sham Battle, The Game of. © 1941.
Military, World War II, Board Game. 200

Davies & Health
2868. Battleship Chess. Circa 1935. Military, Board
Game. 150

Derby Games Co.
2869. Donkey Derby. © 1937. Sports, Board Game. 125

Diamond Game Co.
2870. Diamond baseball dart game. Circa 1933.
Sports, Baseball, Skill Game. $150

Diamond Toy Co., Inc.
2871. America First, The National Election Game. ©
1939. Political, Board Game. 250

Domogame Co., Inc
2872. Whippet Race. ©. 1937. Sports, Dog Racing,
Board Game. 150

Domogof
2873. Tee Off! 1935. Sports, Golf, Board Game. 200

M. A. Donahue & Co.
2874. Donkey Party. Circa 1920s. Classic, Skill Game. 50

Wallie Dorr
2875. Foolish Questions by Rube Goldberg. Circa
1924-26. Q & A, Personality, Card Game. 125
2876. Touring. Circa 1924. Travel, Road, Card Game. 75

O. A. Drewgwitz Co.
2877. Ot-O-Win Horseshoe Game. Circa 1920s. Sport,
Misc., Board Game. 100

Durable Toy & Novelty
2878. Home Run. Circa 1935. Sports, Baseball, Board
Game. 150
2879. Hunters Shot. Circa 1935. Animal, Board Game. 75
2880. Radio Questionnaire. 1928. Communications,
Board Game. 75
2881. Stay Off Street, SOS Safety Game. Circa 1930s.
Travel, Car, Board Game. 150

Earl Novelty Mfg. Co.
2882. Total Victory. Circa 1939-44. Military, World
War II, Board Game. 300

Educational Card & Game
2883. Heroes of America. 1920s. Historical, Card
Game. 65

Educational Game Co.
2884. Bild-A-Word Game. 1929. Word, Card Game. 35

Edwards Manufacturing Co.
2885. Monte Cristo. Circa 1932. Chance, Board Game. 125
2886. Whippet Derby. Circa 1932. Sports, Board Game. 150

Eichorn, Virchow & Yates
2887. Hit-the-Deck. Circa 1932. Military, Board Game. 150

Einson-Freeman Pub. Co.

2888. Basketball Tiddley Winks. 1935. Sports, Basketball, Board Game. $150

2889. Bring 'Em Back Alive. 1934. Adventure, Board Game. 250

2890. Count of Monte Cristo. Circa 1935. Literary, Board Game. 200

2891. Department Store. Circa 1935. Economics, Board Game. 200

2892. Dick Tracy Detective Game. 1933. Comics, Law, Board Game. 250

2893. Five Races of Mankind. Circa 1935. Travel, Board Game. 200

2894. Hot Dog Race. Circa 1935. Animal, Board Game. 150

2895. Indian Ambush. Circa 1935. Western, Board Game. 150

2896. Jim Hawkins on Treasure Island, The Game of. 1934. Adventure, Board Game. 200

2897. Little Black Sambo, Game. 1934. Ethnic, Literary, Board Game. 300

2898. Merry Merry Go Round. 1935. Circus, Board Game. 150

2899. Nineteenth Hole Golf Game. Circa 1930s. Sports, Golf, Board Game. 200

2900. Pioneers of the Santa Fe Trail. 1934. Western, Board Game. 250

2901. Popeye in Plunderland. Circa 1935. Comics, Board Game. 250

2902. Popeye the Sailor Shipwreck Game. 1933. Comics, Board Game. 200

2903. Popeye to the Rescue. 1934. Comics, Board Game. 150

2904. Pre-Flight Trainer. 1942. Military, World War II, Board Game. 275

2905. Rip Van Winkles Nine Pins. Circa 1935. Literary, Board Game. 150

2906. Seaside Shooting Gallery. Circa 1935. Skill, Board Game. 150

2907. Star Ride. 1934. Space, Board Game. 600

2908. Stop Thief. 1934. Law & Order, Board Game. 150

2909. Tarzan Rescue. Circa 1935. Comics, Board Game. 350

2910. Tarzan Treasure Island. 1934. Comics, Board Game. 300

2911. Tom Sawyer on the Mississippi. 1935. Adventure, Board Game. 250

2912. Walt Disney's Three Little Pigs Game. 1933. Disney, Board Game. 200

Can the Thief Outwit the Police?

2913. Wild West, Wild East! Bring 'em Back Alive Maverick Jims. 1935. Adventure, Western, Board Game. $250

Electra Co.
2914. Ask Electra, The Game of Mystery. 1929. Mystic, Board Game. 125

Electric Game Co., Inc
2915. Air-Base Checkers. 1942. Military, Board Game. 150

2916. Electric Basketball (64-X). © 1949. Sports, Basketball, Board Game. 125

2917. Electric Bunny Run. 1940s. Animal, Board Game. 75

2918. Electric Fire Fighters. 1940s. Occupations, Board Game. 100

2919. Electric Football. Circa 1930s. Sports, Football, Board Game. 125

2920. Electric Golf. 1939. Sports, Golf, Board Game. 150

2921. Electric Hockey. Circa 1941. Sports, Hockey, Board Game. 150

2922. Electric Patrol. 1940. Law & Order, Board Game. 125

2923. Jim Prentice Electric Baseball. Circa 1930s. Sports, Baseball, Board Game. 125

2924. Jim Prentice Electric Basketball. Circa 1930s. Sports, Basketball, Board Game. 125

2925. Jim Prentice Electric Football. Circa 1930s. Sports, Football, Board Game. 125

2926. Let's Go to College. 1944. Q & A, Board Game. 150

2927. Whiz Football. 1945. Sports, Football, Board Game. 125

Eloise Novelties

2928. Trip to the Beaches, A. Circa 1929. Travel,
Board Game. $150

2929. Uncle Ben in Hollywood. Circa 1929. Movies,
Board Game. 150

Elten Game Corp.

2930. Balance the Budget. 1938. Economic, Political,
Card Game. 125

Embee Dist. Co.

2931. Bringing Up Father Game. 1920. Comics,
Board Game. 200

The Embossing Co.

**2932. Frisko "The Roaring Game of the Barbary
Coast".** 1937. Miscellaneous, Board Game. 50

2933. Jack-Be-Nimble. Circa 1930s. Nursery Rhyme,
Board Game. 100

2934. Sniff. Circa 1930s. Miscellaneous, Board Game. 50

2935. Toss Word Rainbow Game. Circa 1920s. Word,
Board Game. 50

2936. Symbolo. Circa 1930s. Miscellaneous, Board
Game. 50

Empire Plastic Co.

2937. Dr. I. Q. Jump. 1940s. Q & A, Board Game. 50

Fair Lady Co.

2938. Season (© Paul Lee). © 1936. Time, Card Game. 75

J. M. Farmer

2939. Farmers Electric Maps. 1938. Geography,
Board Game. 100

M. H. Fenkel

2939a. Learn the Morse Code. 1944. Educational,
Board Game. 35

The Finance Game Co.

2940. Finance (1st edition). 1936. Economic, Board
Game. 350

2941. Finance, this edition is licensed by Parker Bros.
1936. Economic, Board Game. 250

Fitzpatrick Bros. Inc.

2942. Who is Guilty? Premium American Advertising.
1937. Premium, Law & Order, Board Game. 150

**2943. Meet the Missus, Premium American
Advertising.** 1937. Premium, Social, Board Game. $150

Fort Wayne Paper Box Co.

2944. Hollands Indoor Golf Game. Circa 1926.
Sports, Golf, Board Game. 150

Maurice L. Freedman Co.

2945. Warfare Naval Combat. 1940s. Military, World
War II, Board Game. 200

French & Co.

2946. Benson Football Game, The. Circa 1930s.
Sports, Football, Board Game. 300

J. F. Friedel Co.

2947. Seige. Circa 1930s. Military, Board Game. 150

J. H. Frome

2948. Frome Sentence Builder, The. 1928. Word,
Board Game. 50

B. L. Fry Prod. Co.

2949. Baby Barn Yard. 1943. Animal, Board Game. 35
2950. Barn Yard. 1943. Animal, Board Game. 35
2951. Jackpot. 1943. Chance, Board Game. 35

Full-O-Fun, Co.

2952. Let's Go Golfun. Circa 1930. Sports, Golf, Board
Game. 125

Fulton Specialty Co.

2953. Wizard, The. 1921. Mystic, Board Game. 125

Fun Education Co.
2954. Funedco Whiz. 1928. Miscellaneous, Card Game. $50
2955. Funedco. 1928. Miscellaneous, Card Game. 50

Funhouse, Inc.
2956. Spotter School. © 1943. Military, World War II,
Card Game. 125

Funnies
2957. Funnies. 1924. Comics, Card Game. 150

Furniture Stylists Inc.
2958. Seeing Nellie Home. 1932. Romance, Board
Game. 250

The Fut-Bal Co.
2959. Fut-Bal. Circa 1940s. Sports, Football, Board
Game. 150

G H Q Inc.
2960. Military Strategy. 1939. Military, Board Game. 200

F. Gable Co.
2961. Buckaroo. 1936. Western, Board Game. 150

Samuel Gabriel Sons & Co.
2962. Around the Clock. Circa 1930s. Learning, Card
Game. 75
2963. Ballyhoo. 1931. Word, Card Game. 100
2964. Black Sambo, Game of. 1939. Literary, Ethnic,
Board Game. 300
2965. Chee Chow, Game of. 1939. Miscellaneous,
Board Game. 125
2966. Ching Cong. 1939. Ethnic, Board Game. 50
2967. Clipper Race. Circa 1930s. Travel, Air, Board
Game. 200
2968. Clock Lotto (T-239). 1921. Time, Board Game. 50
2969. Clown Twins. Circa 1935-9. Circus, Board Game. 75
2970. Clown Winks. Circa 1935. Skill, Board Game. 75
2971. Fighting the Flames (T-246). 1931. Occupation,
Board Game. 350
2972. Frog Frolics. 1921. Animal, Board Game. 125
2973. Indian Arrow-Heads. Circa 1930s. Ethnic,
Board Game. 150
2974. Jim Duffer Golf Game. 1934. Sports, Golf,
Board Game. 150
2975. Jumping Jupiter. Circa 1930s. Space, Board
Game. 350
2976. Kuppit. Circa 1940s. Miscellaneous, Board
Game. 50
2977. Let's Auto-Tour (T-290). Circa 1942. Travel,
Cars, Board Game. 200
2978. Let's Go Shopping. 1937. Animal, Board Game. 150
2979. Peter Rabbit Game (T-249). Circa 1935.
Literary, Board Game. 100

2980. Play Post Office. Circa 1942. Communications,
Board Game. $125
2980a.Spoon and Egg Game. Circa 1930s. Skill
Game. 35
2981. Top Hat. Circa 1930s. Miscellaneous, Board
Game. 125
2982. Traffic Jam. 1936. Travel, Car, Board Game. 125
2983. We Play Store (T-231). Circa 1940. Economics,
Board Game. 125

Gamble Hinged Music Co.
2984. Maestro, The Musical Bingo. 1939. Music, Card
Game. 125

Game Makers Inc.
2985. Bomber Ball. Circa 1942-4. Military, World
War II, Board Game. 200
2986. Dickory Dock Bowling Game. Circa 1938-40.
Nursery Rhymes, Skill Game. 75
2987. Hens a Hoppin. Circa 1930s. Animal, Board
Game. 75
2988. Jig Race by Arthur Dritz. Circa 1940s.
Miscellaneous, Board Game. 100
2989. Pursuit. Circa 1940-45. Military, World War II,
Board Game. 175
2990. U Bang It. Circa 1938-42. Ethnic, Board Game. 125

Game of Knowledge Pub.
2991. Kwiz. Pat 1927. Q & A, Card Game. 50

Games Co.
2992. Cross Country (mfg. for The Higbee Co.).
1935. Travel, Board Game. 150
2993. Stock Market, The. Circa 1936. Stock Market,
Board Game. 150

Games Makers Inc.
2994. Aero-Ball. Circa 1940s. Miscellaneous, Board
Game. 150

Games of Fame
2995. Flagship. 1944. Military, World War II, Board
Game. 150
2996. Jeepers. 1943. Skill, Board Game. 175

Gano Game Co.
2997. Irons and Woods. 1941. Sports, Golf, Board
Game. 200
2998. Invasion. 1941. Military, World War II, Board
Game. 350

Geauga Publishers Inc.
2999. Barnyard Swap (© H. C. Parsons). © 1941.
Animal, Board Game. 75

Gem Publishing Co.
3000. Treasure Island, Game of. 1923. Adventure,
    Literary, Board Game. $250

General Mills
3001. Cheerios Bird Hunt. 1930s. Premium, Animal,
    Board Game. 75
3002. Cheerios Hook the Fish. 1930s. Premium,
    Animal, Board Game. 75

General Printing Co.
3003. Hi-Seas. 1942. Military, World War II, Board
    Game. 350

C. Gilbert Co.
3004. Gilbert Meteor Game. Circa 1930s. Skill, Board
    Game. 75

Girl Scouts
3005. Trupe, A Girl Scout Game. 1939. Organizations,
    Card Game. 75

Glevum Games,
3006. White Wings. Circa 1930s. Animal, Board Game. 100

Glob-Astral Co.
**3007. Glob-Astral, A Social Game - Advice and
    Fortune.** © 1937. Mystic, Card Game. 75

Glow Prod. Co.
3008. Ticker, The Wall Street Game. 1929. Stock
    Market, Board Game. 150

Gluck Manufacturing Co.
3009. Bunny Hunt, The. Circa 1926. Animal, Board
    Game. $75
3010. Jungle Game. Circa 1926. Animal, Board Game. 75
3011. World Flyers. Circa 1926. Travel, Air, Board
    Game. 150

Gnirol Game Co.
3012. Gnirol and the Pilgrims Party. 1920. Historical,
    Card Game. 50

Gong Bell Mfg. Co.
3013. Tumble Golf. Circa 1931. Sports, Golf, Board
    Game. 150

Goodennough & Woglom
3014. Acme Bible Book Game, The. Circa 1930s.
    Religious, Card Game. 25
3015. Bible Lotto, The Game of. Circa 1920s.
    Religious, Card Game. 25
3016. Bible Rhymes, The Game of. Circa 1930s.
    Religious, Board Game. 25
3017. Historical Lotto, The Game of. Circa 1930s.
    Historical, Board Game. 35
3018. Hymn Quartettes. Circa 1933. Religion, Music,
    Card Game. 50
3019. Traits, The Game of. 1933. Religion, Card
    Game. 65

Goody Mfg. Co.
3020. Safety City Game. Circa 1935. Travel, Board
    Game. 125

Goosman Mfg. Co.
3021. Junior Hockey. Circa 1938. Sports, Hockey,
    Board Game. 150

Gorham Press
3022. Navy Game, The. Circa 1940. Military, World
    War II, Board Game. 150

Gossage Music Co.
3023. Swing It, Record Game. 1942. Music, Board
    Game. 125

Gotham Sales Co.
3024. War Bingo. Circa 1940s. Military, World War II,
    Board Game. 100

Graphicut Corp.
3025. Eureko! © 1942. Miscellaneous, Card Game. 100

Albert A. Gregg
3026. Gregg Football Game, The. 1924. Sports,
Football, Board Game. $300

William J. Gregory
3027. Word Squares. 1934. Words, Card Game. 35

Griebel Games Co.
3028. Know Your Own United States. 1919.
Geography, Card Game. 50
**3029. Know Your Own United States (© Emma M.
Griebel).** © 1920. Geography, USA, Card Game. 50

Carl W. Grimm
3030. Musical Casino. 1927. Music, Card Game. 125

Gropper
3031. Hunting in the Jungle. 1920s. Animal, Board
Game. 100

Gruhn & Melton
3032. Razz-O-Dazz-O Six-Man Football. 1938.
Sports, Football, Board Game. 150

H-Bar-O Ranch
3033. H-Bar-O, Mail Premium. Circa 1930s.
Western, Card Game. 125

Habob Co.
3034. Magic-Race (Horse Race). 1942. Sports,
Horseracing, Paper & Pencil. 100

Hagen and Thompson
3035. Rum-E-Golf. Sports, Golf, Card Game. 100

Haras Mfg. Co.
3036. Sweepstakes. Circa 1930s. Sports, Horseracing,
Board Game. 150

W. H. Harper
3037. Tic Tac Toe. © 1943. Classic, Paper & Pencil. 25

J. De Hart
3038. Monday Morning Coach. 1934. Sports,
Football, Board Game. 250

Hartford Mfg. Co.
3039. Touchdown, The New Game. Circa 1920s.
Sports, Football, Board Game. 150

Paul Heath
3040. California Mine A Million. Circa 1936.
Adventure, Board Game. $150

The Henriksen Mfg. Co.
3041. Funny Fellers. 1920. Comics, Board Game. 250
3042. Mamas Darlings. 1920. Comics, Board Game. 300
3043. Pick or Pickle. © 1920. Miscellaneous, Board
Game. 100

3044. Oh Min. 1920. Comics, Board Game. 250
3045. Ring A Ring. 1920. Miscellaneous, Board Game. 100
3046. Scout Trail. 1920. Organizations, Board Game. 150

Henschel & Co./Whitman
3047. America Derby, The. Circa 1930s. Sports,
Horseracing, Board Game. 150

Herbert Specialty Mfg. Co.
3048. Coo Coo (Series D Children). C. 1925.
Miscellaneous, Card Game. 75
3049. Peg-Way Coo Coo, Series # 1. 1921.
Miscellaneous, Board Game. 75

Higbee Co.
3050. Cross Country. 1935. Travel, Board Game. 125

Hollywood Game Co.
3051. Going Hollywood. 1943. Movie, Board Game. 150
3052. Hollywood Burlesque. 1928. Movies, Board
Game. 200

Hood Rubber Co.
3053. We V Nap Horse Race Game. Circa 1920.
Sports, Horseracing, Board Game. 150

Household Words Game

3054. Household Words, Game of. © 1916. Words,
Card Game. $50

Mrs. Alice W. Hunt

3055. Woodard Biblical Game. Circa 1920. Religious,
Card Game. 45

Huschle Bros., Inc.

3056. Fireside Baseball. Circa 1925. Sports, Baseball,
Board Game. 200

Hustler Toy Corp.

3057. Aero Race. Circa 1929. Travel, Air, Board
Game. 150

3058. Country Club Golf. 1920s. Sports, Golf, Board
Game. 159

**3059. Great American Game, Baseball, The, Wood
side.** 1923. Sports, Baseball, Board Game. 200

Hustler/Frantz

3060. Inter Collegiate Football. 1923. Sports, Football,
Board Game. 250

Illinois Game & Toy Co.

3061. Battlefield. 1943. Military, Board Game. 200

Illinois Valley Mfg. Co.

3062. Whiffle Circus. Circa 1932. Circus, Board Game. 150

Imperial Methods Co.

3063. Derby Winner. Circa 1936. Sports, Horseracing,
Board Game. 150

3064. Ten Grand. Circa 1932. Sports, Horseracing,
Board Game. 150

3065. Twenty Grand. Circa 1932. Sports, Horseracing,
Board Game. 150

Indiana Game Co.

3066. Bo McMillins Indoor Football Game. 1939.
Sports, Football, Board Game. 250

Indoor Games Co.

3067. Forest Ranger Game, The. 1930s. Occupations,
Board Game. Connection with CCC Camps. 200

Inter Paper Goods

3068. Radio. 1926. Communications, Board Game. $75

Intercollegiate Football Inc.

3069. American Football Game. 1935. Sports,
Football, Board Game. 200

Interstate News Service

3070. I.N.S. History Cards, Series D. 1926. History,
Card Game. 50

Interstate School Service

**3071. A1, A2: Discovery of American and Period of
Colonization (Interstate History Cards - sold in
sets of 15 cards each).** © 1926. Historical, Card
Game. 50

**3072. B1, B2: Inter colonial Wars, French and
Indian War and American Revolution
(Interstate History Cards).** © 1926. Historical,
Card Game. 50

**3073. C1, C2: From Adoption of the Constitution to
the Civil War (Interstate History Cards - sold
in sets of 15 cards each).** © 1926. History, Card
Game. 50

**3074. D1, D2: Beginning of the Civil War to the
Present Time (Interstate History Cards - sold
in sets of 15 cards each).** © 1926. Historical,
Card Game. 50

**3075. Interstate History Cards (sold in sets of 15
cards each).** © 1926. History, Card Game. 50

Interstate Patent Enterprises

3076. Stock Market Game. Circa 1933. Stock Market,
Board Game. 250

James R. Irvin & Co., Inc.

3077. Cats Meow. Circa 1932. Animal, Cat, Card Game. 125

3078. Gypsy Fortune Teller. Circa 1932. Mystic, Card
Game. 100

3079. Quintuplets Game. 1935. Personality, Card
Game. 100

3080. Scream. Circa 1932. Holiday, Card Game. 125

Jacmar Mfg. Co.
3081. Electric Quiz. Circa 1930s. Q & A, Board Game. $50

Jay Co.
3082. Stick the Dictator. 1944. Military, World War II,
Board Game. 350

Jaynar Speciality Co.
3082a. Dunninger's Telepathascore. Circa 1930s.
Mystic, Board Game. 125

Jayline
3083. Ration Board. 1943. History, World War II,
Board Game. 300

Jenion Co.
3084. Honk-Honk-Honk. 1929. Travel, Road, Card
Game. 150

Johnson Store Equipment.
3085. Lou Gehrig's Game. Circa 1935. Sports,
Baseball, Board Game. 500

S. A. Joseph
3086. Staff Frolics. Circa 1930s. Social, Board Game. 125

Judson Press
3087. Bible A B C & Promises. 1930. Religious, Card
Game. 25

Junior Games Co., Inc.
3088. Golf Junior. 1921. Sports, Golf, Board Game. 125

Kamms Games
3089. Casey at the Mound, Kamms Baseball. Circa
1945. Sports, Baseball, Board Game. 300

Kam-Ra Card Co.
3090. Kam-ra, Motion Picture Card Game. 1928.
Theatrical, Card Game. 100
3091. Kam-Ra! (© Josephine Q. Miranda). © 1928.
Movies, Card Game. 100

Kaywood
3092. Sea Battle. Circa 1940s. Military, World War II,
Board Game. 125

Kellogg's Cereals
3093. Kellogg's Baseball Game, Premium. 1936.
Sports, Baseball, Board Game. 125
3094. Kellogg's Boxing Game, Premium. 1936.
Sports, Boxing, Board Game. 125

3095. Kellogg's Football Game, Premium. 1936.
Sports, Football, Board Game. $125
3096. Kellogg's Golf Game, Premium. 1936. Sports,
Golf, Board Game. 125
3097. Kellogg's Racing Game, Premium. 1936.
Sports, Car Racing, Board Game. 125
3098. Kellogg's Story Book Of Games # 1. 1931.
Nursery Rhyme, Board Game. 50
3099. Kellogg's Story Book Of Games # 2. 1931.
Nursery Rhyme, Board Game. 50
3100. Kellogg's Story Book Of Games # 3. 1931.
Nursery Rhyme, Board Game. 50
3101. Kellogg's Story Book Of Games # 4. 1931.
Nursery Rhyme, Board Game. 50

Kenilworth Press
3102. Three Little Pigs, The Game of The. Circa
1930s. Disney, Board Game. 300

Kerger Co.
3103. Varsitee Football Playing Cards. 1938. Sports,
Football, Card Game. 200

Kerk Guild
**3104. Van Loon Story of Mankind, The, Large cloth
board.** 1931. History, Personality, Board Game. 250

Kernal
3104a. Pass, Game of. 1924. Strategy, Board Game. 40

E. D. Kerr Co.
3105. Election, Game of. 1936. Political, Card Game. 200

Kindred, MacLean & Co.
3106. Bo-Lem-Ova. Circa 1944. Sports, Bowling,
Board Game. 75

King Larson McMahon
3107. Battle Checkers. 1942. Military, World War II,
Board Game. 100

King Mfg. Co.

3108. All American Game of Ballots. 1940. Political,
Board Game. $200

Klak Co.

3109. Victory. Circa 1920. Military, Board Game. 150

Knapp Electric Inc.

3110. Ges-It. 1929. Q & A, Board Game. 50

3111. Knapp Electro Game Set, Auto Race. 1929.
Sports, Car Racing, Board Game. 75

3112. Knapp Electro Game Set, Air Race. 1929.
Travel, Air, Board Game. 75

3113. Knapp Electro Game Set, Baseball. 1929.
Sports, Baseball, Board Game. 75

3114. Knapp Electro Game Set, Football. 1929.
Sports, Football, Board Game. 75

Koboco Games Co.

3114a. 5th Column Spy Hunters, Game of. 1940. Spy,
Law & Order, Board Game. 400

Krieger Novelty Co.

3115. Play Ball Baseball Game. Circa 1928. Sports,
Baseball, Board Game. 150

M. J. Harding

3115a. Life of the Party, The. © 1930. Social, Board
Game. 50

Herman C. Kupper

3116. Speed Up. Circa 1918. Sports, Car, Board Game. $125

La Rue Sales Inc.

3117. Hit That Line Football Game. Circa 1930s.
Sports, Football, Board Game. 150

LaSalle Games Co.

3118. Little Red Bushy-Tail. Circa 1920. Animal,
Board Game. 600

Le Velle Mfg. Co.

3119. Tip-Top Boxing, Dempsey-Wills. 1922. Sports,
Boxing, Skill Game. 300

3120. Yale-Harvard Football Game. 1922. Sports,
Football, Board Game. 350

Wingert Leefers

3121. Napoleon, The Popular Advertising Game.
Circa 1920. History, Board Game. 125

The Leister Game Co.

3122. At Ease. 1943. Miscellaneous, Card Game. 50

3123. Autographs. 1945. History, Card Game. 150

3124. To the Aid of Your Party. © 1946. Political,
Card Game. 35

Lemor Novelty Co.

3125. Tit for Tat Indoor Hockey. 1920s. Sports,
Hockey, Board Game. 200

Lever Bros.

3126. Whoopo-Lifebuoy Premium Game. 1934.
Premium, Board Game. 150

Levi & Gade

3127. Skyways. 1937. Travel, Air, Board Game. 200

3128. Stock Market, The. 1936. Stock Market, Board
Game. 250

Lewis Instructor Games

3129. Air Combat Trainer. 1942. Military, World
War II, Board Game. 200

Liberty League

3130. Baseball Game. 1917. Sport, Baseball, Card
Game. 125

Liberty Show Printing Co.

3131. Four Horsemen Football Game. Circa 1932.
Sports, Football, Board Game. 200

Lido Toy
3132. Sea Battle. Circa 1942-3. Military, World War II, Board Game. $75

Wayne W. Light Co.
3133. Football As-You-Like-It. 1940. Sports, Football, Board Game. 150

Lindstrom Tool & Toy Co.
3134. Lindstroms Klik. Circa 1930s. Miscellaneous, Board Game. 150
3135. Lucky Strike & Horse Race Game. 1933. Sports, Horseracing, Board Game. 125
3136. Six Day Bike Race. 1930s. Sports, Bike, Board Game. 150

Littlefield Mfg. Co.
3137. Big League. Circa 1932. Sports, Baseball, Board Game. 150
3138. Covered Wagon, Game of. Circa 1928. Western, Board Game. 150
3139. Machine Gun Nest, Game of. Circa 1928. Military, Board Game. 200

Oswald Lord
3140. Politics. 1935. Politics, Board Game. 150

E. S. Lowe Co.
3141. Big League Game of Baseball. © 1943. Sports, Baseball, Board Game. 100

3142. Fox Hunt. 1930s. Sports, Board Game. 100
3143. Horse Race. 1943. Sports, Horseracing, Board Game. 75
3144. Jeep Board, The. 1944. Military, World War II, Board Game. 50
3145. Radio Amateur Hour, The. Circa 1930s. Communications, Board Game. 75

Samuel Lowe Co.
3146. 32 Games. Circa 1930s. Combination, Board Games. 25

3147. Airplane Speedway (581-11). © 1941. Sports, Air, Board Game. $50
3148. Cross Country. 1941. Sports, Board Game. 40
3149. Game of the Three Bears. Circa 1940s. Nursery Rhyme, Board Game. 35
3150. Hornet Airplane Games. 1941. Military, World War II, Board Game. 150
3151. Land and Sea, War Games. 1941. Military, World War II, Board Game. 150
3152. Little Red Hen (581-7). 1941. Animal, Board Game. 35
3153. Midget Auto Race. 1941. Sports, Car, Board Game. 60
3154. Mother Goose Game. 1941. Nursery Rhyme, Board Game. 35
3155. Pirate Ship Game. 1941. Adventure, Board Game. 50
3156. Sparks-Code Game. 1943. Communications, Board Game. 50
3157. Three Little Pigs, The Game of. 1941. Nursery Rhyme, Board Game. 35
3158. Treasure Chest of Games. Circa 1930s. Combination, Board Game. 25

Lubbers & Bell Mfg. Co.
3159. Blox-O. 1923. Miscellaneous, Board Game. 35

Lubbers-Peg.
3160. Puzzle-Peg. 1929. Miscellaneous, Puzzle Game. 35

Lucas Co.
3161. Conquest. 1936. Military, AR, Board Game. 150

Lutz & Sheinkman
3162. Buck Rogers Game of 25th Century. 1934. Space, Super Heroes, Board Game. 450
3163. Capt. Ashley McKinley W/ Bird at the South Pole. 1935. Personality, Historical, Board Game. 350
3164. Tarzan of the Apes. Circa 1935. Comics, Board Game. 450
3165. Buck Rogers, 3 Game Combo. 1934. Space, Superhero, Board Game. 750

Lynco Inc.
3166. Philips H. Lords Gang Busters. Circa 1930s. Personality, Law & Order, Board Game. 250

MacClatchie Mfg. Co.
3167. Ticker Tape. Circa 1932. Stock Market, Board Game. 150

Madmar Quality Co.
3168. Foot-Race Game. Circa 1925. Sports, Board Game. $100
3169. Happy Hunting Ground, The. 1919. Western, Board Game. 125
3170. Wolf & Sheep Game. Circa 1920. Animal, Board Game. 100
3171. Wolf Card Game. Circa 1925. Animal, Card Game. 75

Man O'War
3172. Indoor Horse Racing. 1924. Sports, Horseracing, Board Game. 150

Mandarin Mfg. Corp.
3173. Nineteenth Hole, The. Circa 1924. Sports, Golf, Board Game. 200

H. M. Mannheimer
3174. Pay as You Enter, 20th Century Game. 1918. Travel Rail, Board Game. 125

Mar
3175. Quizical Questions by Professor Quiz. Circa 1930s. Q & A, Board Game. 50

Marhelie Co.
3176. Zingari Fortune Telling Dice. Circa 1929. Mystic, Card Game. 50

Marietta Games

3177. Scarlett O'Harra. Circa 1930s. Literary, Board Game. 125

Marks Brothers Co.
3178. Baseball Game & G-Man Target. 1940. Baseball, Law & Order, Board, Action. 250
3179. Belmont Park. 1920. Sports, Horseracing, Board Game. 175
3180. Mickey Mouse Bean Bag Game. 1930s. Disney, Board Game. 150
3181. Mickey Mouse Circus Game. 1930s. Disney, Board Game. 175
3182. Mickey Mouse Coming Home Game. 1930s. Disney, Board Game. 150

3183. Mickey Mouse Hoop-La Game. 1930s. Disney, Board Game. $150
3184. Mickey Mouse Rollem Bowling Game. 1930s. Disney, Board Game. 175
3185. Mickey Mouse Scatterball Game. 1930s. Disney, Board Game. 150
3186. Mickey Mouse Soldier Set Bowling Game. 1930s. Disney, Board Game. 175
3187. Obstacle Golf. Circa 1931. Sports, Golf, Board Game. 150
3188. Slugger Baseball Game (511). 1930s. Sports, Baseball, Board Game. 175
3189. Who's Afraid of the Big Wolf, Game of. 1933. Disney, Board Game. 250

Howard Mason
3190. Astronomy. 1922. Space, Card Game. 150

Master Toy Co.
3191. Bike Race Game, The. 1940s. Sports, Bicycling, Board Game. 100
3192. Coast to Coast. Circa 1940s. Travel, U.S., Board Game. 100
3193. Hallowe'en. Circa 1935. Holiday, Card Game. 150
3194. Kissing Game. Circa 1943. Romance, Card Game. 150

3195. Our Defenders. Circa 1940. Military, World War II, Board Game. 150
3196. U. S. A. Game of. Circa 1942. Geography, Board Game. 100

Ralph Mayhew
3197. Whirl-A-Word. Circa 1930. Word, Card Game. 50

McDowell Game Co.
3198. Allie-Patriot Game (© Elizabeth M. McDowell & Frederick Mellor). © 1917. Military, World War I, Board Game. 350

James McGowan Assoc.
3199. Guilty, The Funny Money Game. © 1937.
Economy, Card Game. $100

McKay
3200. Who's Who in Missions. 1922. Religious, Card
Game. 75

McLoughlin Bros.
3201. New U. S. Merchant Marine, The. 1918.
History, World War I, Board Game. 350

Melhado
3202. Veuisee. Circa 1930s. Strategy, Board Game. 150

Merchandisers Inc.
3203. Admirals, The Naval War Game. 1939.
Military, World War II, Board Game. 350

Metaleotric Corp.
3204. Frontier. 1937. Miscellaneous, Board Game. 125

Walter Meyner
3205. Battle, The Game of. Circa 1920. Military, Board
Game. 150

Midwest Book & Game
3206. Categories. Circa 1932. Q & A, Card Game. 35

David M. Miller
3207. Victory Game. Circa 1919. Military, World
War I, Board Game. 150

M. H. Miller
3208. Motor Race. Circa 1920s. Sports, Car, Board
Game. 125

Mills Games Mfg. Co.
3209. Exports and Transportation, Game of. ©.
1936. Economic, Board Game. 150

Minature Game Co.
3210. Minature Golf. Circa 1930s. Sports, Golf, Board
Game. 125

Missouri Store Co.
3211. Missouri Cards. © 1919. Geography, Card Game. 75

Modern Games Co.
3212. Four Musketeers, The. Circa 1925. Adventure,
Board Game. 125

Modern Makers Inc.
3213. Horses. 1927. Sports, Horseracing, Board Game. $150

Modern Novelties
3214. Put the Yanks in Berlin. Circa 1942. Military,
World War II, Board Game. 200
3215. Trap the Jap in Tokyo. Circa 1943. Military,
World War II, Board Game. 200

Monday Morning Coach
3216. Monday Morning Coach. Circa 1935. Sports,
Football, Board Game. 150

Montour Novelty Co.
3217. Take Your Profit. Circa 1936. Economics, Board
Game. 125
3218. Middleman, The Game of. 1937. Economic,
Board Game. 150
3218a.Abdigation, The Game of. 1937. Historical,
Board Game. 225

Robert Morey

3219. Privilege. 1938. Social, Art, Card Game. 200

F. L. Morgan Co.
3220. Chi-Chi Chinese Daily Fortune Teller. Circa
1926. Mystic, Card Game. 50

Morris-Systems Pub. Co.
3221. 400. The. 1933. Miscellaneous, Board Game. 125

T. J. Morrison
3222. Home Run-With Bases Loaded! Johnny Evers.
1938. Sports, Baseball, Board Game. 250

Municipal Service
3223. Howard H. Jones College Football Game, The New. 1932. Sports, Football, Personality, Board Game. $300

Murray-Way
3224. Murray-Way States Game, The. 1929. Geographical, Card Game. 35

Mutuels, Inc.
3225. Mutuels. 1938. Stock Market, Board Game. 125

Myart Mfg. Co.
3226. Carnival, The. 1936. Circus, Board Game. 125

N. Mfg. Co.
3227. National Radio Game, The. Circa 1920s. Communications, Board Game. 75

Nat. Card Baseball
3228. National Card Baseball Game. 1923. Sports, Baseball, Card Game. 100

National Advertising Games
3229. Shopping Game. Circa 1930s. Economic, Board Game. 125

National Assoc. Service
3230. Gimme, Gimme. 1942. Miscellaneous, Board Game. 100

National Bindery & Game
3231. Radio Flash. © 1922. Communications, Board Game. 75

National Biscuit Co.
3232. Traveling to Wheatsworth Castle. 1936. Travel, Adventure, Board Game. 75

National Game Co.
3233. Play Ball. Circa 1920s. Sports, Baseball, Board Game. 150

National Games
3234. All-American Football Game. 1935. Sports, Football, Board Game. 150
3235. National Football Game. 1938. Sports, Football, Board Game. 150
3236. Toy Town Target Game. Circa 1940s. Kiddie, Skill Game. 100

National Playthings
3237. Rodeo Toy Game. Circa 1940s. Western, Board Game. $100

National Refining Co.
3238. En-Ar-Co Automobile Game. 1919. Travel, Car, Premium, Board Game. 100
3239. En-Ar-Co Automobile Tour. 1919. Travel, Car, Board Game. 100

Nature Games
3239a.Chipmunk, Animal Game. Circa 1930s, Animal, Card Game. 40
3239b.Cinnabar, Rocks & Minerals. Circa 1930s, Card Game. 40
3240. Gold Finch, Bird Game. Circa 1930s. Animal, Card Game. 40
3240a.Goldenrod, Wild Flower Game. Circa 1930s, Plant, Card Game. 40
3240b.Juniper, Trees Game. Circa 1930s, Plant, Card Game. 40
3241. Larkspur, Flower Game. Circa 1930s. Plant, Card Game. 40
3242. Monarch. Circa 1930s. Animal, Card Game. 40
3243. Monarch. Later Edition. Circa 1940s. Animal, Card Game. 30

Nauman Games
3244. World Air Derby, The. Circa 1930s. Travel, Air, Board Game. 125

New "Arts" Sales Co.
3245. Gas Rashun. 1943. History, World War II, Board Game. 200

New York Toy & Game Co.
3246. Jimmy Durante Schnozzola Game. Circa 1935. Personalities, Board Game. 175
3247. Torpedo Action Game. Circa 1942-45. Military, World War II, Board Game. 200

Newspaper Specialties Inc.
3248. Hi-Ho (© Wallach & Messier; Manufactured by American Record Corp.). © 1932. Music, Card Game. 125

Noble & Noble
3249. Alice in Wonderland. 1923. Literary, Adventure, Board Game. 150
3250. Animal Fair. 1922. Animal, Card Game. 100
3251. Rules of the Road, Seamanship Cards. 1943. Travel, Sea, Card Game. 65

Nok-Out Co.
3252. Dizzy and Daffy Dean Nok-Out Baseball Game.
Circa 1935. Sports, Baseball, Board Game. $350

Northwest Prod. Co.
3253. Direct Hit. 1945. Military, World War II, Board
Game. 250
3254. Push-Em-Up-Victory Bomber. 1940s. Military,
World War II, Board Game. 200
3255. San Loo, Chinese Checkers. Circa 1930s.
Classic, Board Game. 75
3256. Tactics. 1940. Military, World War II, Board
Game. 250
3257. Te-Ho Hockey. Circa 1936. Sports, Hockey,
Board Game. 200

Novelty Games Co.
3258. Wishing Well, The (© L.F.G.). © 1944. Mystic,
Card Game. 50

Nucraft Toys

3259. Crash, The New Airplane Game. 1928. Travel,
Air, Board Game. 125
3260. Flying Fun. 1928. Travel, Air, Card Game. 75
3261. New Lindy Flying Game, The. 1927. Travel,
Air, Card Game. 100

Nussbaum Novelty Co.
3262. K. D. Basketball Game. Circa 1935. Sports,
Basketball, Board Game. 150

Offset-Gravure Corp.
3263. Merchant Prince. 1937. Economic, Card Game. 75
**3264. Trailer Trails with Terry the Terrible Speed
Cop.** 1937. Travel, Card Game. 75

Olympia Games Co.
3265. Golflet. Circa 1917. Sports, Golf, Board Game. 125

Oriental Gaming Card Co.
3266. War, The Game of. Circa 1930s. Military, Card
Game. $100

Oriole Toy Co.
3267. Chateau Thierry. Circa 1919. Military, World
War I, Board Game. 150

Orotech Co.
3268. Auto Race, Game of. Circa 1920s. Sports, Car,
Board Game. 150
3269. Chase-U-Game. Circa 1920. Travel, Board Game. 125
3270. Financial Flurry Game. Circa 1920. Economic,
Board Game. 125
3271. Mystic Maze Game. Circa 1920. Mystic, Board
Game. 100

Otis-Lawson Co.
3272. Junior Bombsight Game. 1942. Military, World
War II, Board Game. 100

Ovaltine
**3273. Little Orphan Annie's Treasure Hunt,
Premium.** 1933. Comics, Premium, Board Game. 125
**3274. Orphan Annie, Treasure Isle of Health &
Happiness.** 1933. Comic, Premium, Board
Game. 125

Warren D. Ownby
3275. Histro (© Warren D. Ownby). © 1939. Historical,
Card Game. 50

Palace Toy Co., Inc.
3276. Indoor Sports Base Ball. 1920s. Sports,
Baseball, Board Game. 150

Palley Mfg. Co.
3277. Palley Golf Game. 1927. Sports, Golf, Board
Game. 100

Pan American Toy Co.
3278. Peter Rabbit's Egg-Rolling Game. Circa 1921.
Animal, Board Game. 75
3279. Quaddy Golf. Circa 1921. Sports, Golf, Board
Game. 125

Parker Brothers
3280. Ace of Aces. 1938. Travel, Air, Board Game. 125
3281. Across the Continent. 1935. Geography, Board
Game. 150
3282. Across the Continent, The United States Game.
1922. Travel, US, Board Game. 200

Parker Brothers continued

3283. Admiral Byrds South Pole Game-"Little America". 1934. Personality, Travel, Board Game. $500

3284. Alice in Wonderland Game. Circa 1930s. Literary, Adventure, Board Game. 150

3285. All American Football Game. 1925. Sports, Football, Board Game. 125

3286. Americana. 1937. Historical, Board Game. 125

3287. Amusing Game of Shell Out. 1940. Miscellaneous, Board Game. 150

3288. Anagrams, Crossword. 1938. Words, Card Game. 25

3289. Animal Top Game. 1929. Animals, Board Game. 50

3290. Army Air Corps Game, Variant cover. Circa 1942-4. Military, World War II, Board Game. 250

3291. Army Air Corps Game. Circa 1942-4. Military, World War II, Board Game. 250

3292. Authors, Best Edition. © 1943. Literary, Card Game. 30

3293. Authors, Great. 1920. Literary, Card Game. 30

3294. Auto Race. 1925. Sports, Car, Board Game. 150

3295. Aviation, The Air Mail Game. © 1928. Travel, Air, Card Game. 100

3296. Bailing Out. Circa 1930s. Travel, Air, Board Game. 200

3297. Bargain Day. 1937. Economic, Board Game. 350

3298. Baron Munchausen Game, The. 1933. Social, Card Game. 75

3299. Baseball, Game of. © 1926. Sports, Baseball, Board Game. 150

3300. Bell Merry Go Round. Circa 1941. Circus, Board Game. 50

3301. Bingo or Beano. 1933. Classic, Board Game. 12

3301a. Big Trail, The. Circa 1930s. Based on the Raoul Walshs Fox Movietone picture staring John Wayne, Adventure western board game. One of the first movie related games. 500

3302. Birds, Game of. Circa 1910s. Animal, Card Game. 30

3303. Boake Carters Game Star Reporter. 1937. Personality, Communication, Board Game. 250

3304. Bobby & Betty's Trip to the N. Y. World's Fair. 1939. Fairs, Board Game. 200

3305. Bowlem. 1941. Sports, Bowling, Board Game. 40

3306. Bowlem. Circa 1930s. Sports, Bowling, Skill Game. 50

3307. Boy Hunter, The. Circa 1925. Adventure, Board Game. 125

3308. Boy Scouts' Progress Game, The. 1926. Organizations, Board Game. 250

3309. Boy Scouts, The Game of. 1912. Organization, Card Game. 75

3310. Broadway, The Popular Game of. Parcheese type. 1917. Classic, Board Game. 150

3311. Buccaneers. 1930. Adventure, Board Game. $125

3312. Bulls and Bears, A Stock Exchange Game. 1936. Stock Market, Board Game. 200

3313. Bunny Rabbit Game. © 1942. Animal, Board Game. 75

3314. Buster Bumps Automobile Trip. Circa 1920s. Travel, Road, Card Game. 50

3315. Calling All Cars. Circa 1938. Travel, Car, Board Game. 150

3316. Camelot, Brown Box. 1931. Military, Strategy, Board Game. 75

3317. Camelot, Two Knights on box cover. 1931. Military, Strategy, Board Game. 125

3318. Camelot. 1930. Military, Strategy, Board Game. 75

3319. Camelot. 1931. Military, Strategy, Board Game. 65

3320. Camouflage, Game of. 1918. Military, World War I, Card Game. 75

3321. Camp Fire Girls. 1926. Organizations, Card Game. 125

3322. Captain Kidd and His Pirate Crew. Circa 1941. Adventure, Board Game. 75

3323. Captain Kidd Junior, Walking the Plank. 1926. Adventure, Board Game. 100

3324. Cats and Dogs. 1929. Animals, Board Game. 65

3325. Chinese Checkers, Wooden board. Circa 1930s. Classic, Board Game. 35

3326. Citadel. 1940. Military, Medieval, Board Game. 125

3327. Comical History of America. © 1924. History, Card Game. 60

3328. Commandos. 1942. Military, World War II, Board Game. 125

3329. Conflict, Board and box, Pressed wood implements 1940. Military, World War II, Board Game. 150

3330. Conflict, Board and implement box. 1940. Military, Board Game. 125

3331. Conflict, Long box. 1940. Military, Board Game. 150

3332. Contack. © 1939. Miscellaneous, Card Game. 35

3333. Cottontail and Peter. 1922. Animal, Board Game. 65

3334. Crossword Lexicon. 1937. Word, Card Game. 10

3335. Crow Hunt. 1930. Animal, Board Game. 75

3336. Crows in the Corn. 1930. Animal, Skill Game. 125

3337. Derby Day. 1930. Sports. Horseracing, Board Game. 125

3338. Devil to Pay, The. 1939. Miscellaneous, Board Game. 75

3339. Dig. 1940. Miscellaneous, Skill Game. 30

3340. District Attorney. 1936. Law & Order, Board Game. 150

3341. Dodging Donkey, The. Circa 1924. Animal, Board Game. 65

Parker Brothers continued

3342. Dog Fight. 1940. Military, World War II, Board
Game. $250

**3343. Donald Duck's Party for Young Kinds, Walt
Disney's.** 1938. Disney, Board Game. 200

3344. Dopey Bean Bag. Circa 1941. Disney, Skill
Game. 150

3345. Double Somerset. Circa 1941. Miscellaneous,
Card Game. 30

3346. Duck Shooting. Circa 1920s. Animal, Skill
Game. 35

3347. Eddie Cantors "Tell it to the Judge". 1936.
Personality, Board Game. 75

3348. El Dorado. 1941. Adventure, Board Game. 250

3349. Excuse Me! 1933. Social, Card Game. 50

3350. Ferdinands Chinese Checkers with the Bee.
1939. Disney, Board Game. 125

3351. Finance. 1936. Economic, Board Game. 150

3351a.Finance and Fortune. Circa 1930s, Economic Board
Game 125

3352. Fire Alarm Game. 1938. Occupation, Board
Game. 125

3353. Five Wise Birds, The. Circa 1920s. Animal,
Board Game. 75

3354. Flags, New Game of. 1933. Geography, Card
Game. 35

3355. Flinch. © 1938. Miscellaneous, Card Game. 10

3356. Flying Four, The. Circa 1920s. Travel, Air,
Board Game. 250

3357. Flying the Beam, Large Transport on cover.
1941. Travel, Air, Board Game. 165

3358. Flying the Beam. 1941. Travel, Air, Board
Game. 150

3359. Flying the United States Airmail. 1929. Travel,
Air, Board Game. 250

3360. Football, the Game of. © 1926. Sports, Football,
Board Game. 150

3361. Golf, Amateur. 1928. Sports, Golf, Board Game. 150

3362. Great European War Game, The. Circa 1917-
20. Military, World War I, Board Game. $150

3363. Hendrik Van Loons Wide World Game. Circa
1930s. Personality, Geography, Board Game. 150

3364. Hickety Pickety. 1924. Animal, Board Game. 45

3365. Highway Patrol. 1936. Law & Order, Board
Game. 150

3366. Hokum. 1927. Miscellaneous, Card Game. 35

3367. Hop Off. Circa 1930s. Travel, Air, Card Game. 350

3368. Humpty Dumpty. 1924. Nursery Rhymes, Board
Game. 75

3369. In the Soup. 1928. Miscellaneous, Board Game. 75

3370. Japanola. 1928. Classic, Board Game. 50

3371. Journey to Bethlehem, The. 1923. Religious,
Board Game. 150

3372. Jury Box, The. Series #1. 1936. Law & Order,
Paper & Pencil Game. 35

3373. Jury Box, The. Series #2. 1936. Law & Order,
Paper & Pencil Game. 35

3374. Jury Box, The. Series #3. 1936. Law & Order,
Paper & Pencil Game. 35

3375. Jury Box, The. Series #4. 1936. Law & Order,
Paper & Pencil Game. 35

3376. Jury Box, The. Series #5. 1936. Law & Order,
Paper & Pencil Game. 35

3377. No Game

3378. Keno. Circa 1932. Miscellaneous, Card Game. 25

3379. Kings Men. 1937. Strategy, Board Game. 250

3380. Kismet, The Game of. 1943. Adventure, Board
Game. 100

3381. Knights Journey, The. 1928. Historical, Board
Game, With painted knight soldier pawns. 500

3382. Knockout Andy. 1926. Miscellaneous, Skill
Game. 75

3383. Lame Duck. 1928. Animal, Board Game. 65

3384. Landlords Game (by E. M. Philips). Circa 1941.
Economic, Board Game. 300

3385. Leapin Lena. 1920. Travel, Car, Board Game. 100

3386. Lexicon. © 1935. Words, Card Game. 15

3387. Lincoln Highway and Checkers. 1926. Travel,
Land, Board Game. 150

3388. Lindy - The New Flying Game, Wide yellow
box. 1928. Travel, Air, Card Game. 65

3389. Lindy - The New Flying Game. 1928. Travel,
Air, Card Game. 75

3390. Lindy, Improved Edition. 1927. Travel, Air,
Card Game. 65

3391. Little Red Bushy-Tail. 1923. Animal, Mammals,
Board Game. 75

**3392. Little Red Riding Hood, The Three Little Pigs,
& The Big Bad Wolf (Disney).** 1934. Disney,
Board Game. 200

Parker Brothers continued

3393. Lone Ranger Game. 1939. Western, Board Game. $125

3394. Lowell Thomas' Travel Game "World Cruise". 1937. Personality, Geography, Board Game. 150

3395. Lucky Strike. 1933. Miscellaneous, Skill Game. 125

3396. Make a Million. 1934. Economic, Card Game. 35

3397. Make-a-Million, New Edition. © 1945. Economic, Card Game. 30

3398. Make-a-Million, Pocket Edition. 1934. Economic, Card Game. 30

3399. Man Hunt. 1937. Law & Order, Board Game. 250

3400. Melvin Purvis' "G" Men. Circa 1930s. Law & Order, Board Game. 200

3401. Mexican Pete (I-Got-It). 1937. Ethnic, Board Game. 50

3402. Mill, The Game of. 1939. Miscellaneous, Board Game. 50

3403. Monopoly, 1st Deluxe Edition. 1935. Economic, Board Game Wooden box. 1500

3404. Monopoly, 1st Parker, Trade Mark only. 1935. Economic, Board Game. 750

3405. Monopoly, 2nd Printing, U.S. Patent 1509312. 1935. Economic, Board Game. 350

3406. Monopoly, Deluxe. 1935. Economic, Board Game, brown leatherette paper with gold lettering. 800

3407. Monopoly, Green box, & board. 1946. Economic, Board Game. 65

3406a. Monopoly, red border box, like 3406 50

3408. Monopoly, No patent on board, Darrows name at Jail's end. 1935. Economic, Board Game. **Transitional from Darrow to Parker.** 1100

3409. Monopoly, With metal playing pieces. $ in center. 1936. Economic, Board Game. 50

3410. Monopoly. New Edition. Like 3409. 1937. Economic, Board Game. 35

3411. Monopoly. Two patent #s. 1946. Economic, Board Game. Large white box. 50

3412. Monte Carlo. Circa 1932. Chance, Board Game. 65

3413. Mrs. Casey Wants to Know. Circa 1930s. Reading, Card Game. 50

3414. National Game of Peace for Our Nation, The. 1939. History, World War II, Board Game. 175

3415. Navy Weftup. 1942. Military, World War II, Card Game. 125

3416. Nip and Tuck, Hockey. 1928. Sports, Hockey, Board Game. $150

3417. Oil, The Game of. 1939. Economic, Board Game. 250

3418. Oz, The Wonderful Game of. 1921. Literary, Board Game. Metal playing pieces. 1000

3419. Parlor Bedlam. 1936. Social, Board Game. 100

3420. Peg Baseball. 1924. Sports, Baseball, Board Game. 125

3421. Peg Top. 1929. Strategy, Board Game. 60

3422. Pegity, The Game of. 1939. Strategy, Board Game. 35

3423. Peg'ity. Circa 1925. Strategy, Board Game. 45

3424. Peter Coddle at the New World's Fair. 1932. Fairs, Card Game. 100

3425. Peter Coddles Trip to the World's Fair. 1939. Fairs, Board Game. 75

3426. Picture Reading Game for Little Ones. Circa 1920s. Reading, Card Game. 50

3427. Pieces of Eight. Circa 1930s. Adventure, Board Game. 150

3428. Pigskin, Tom Hamilton's Football Game. 1934. Sports, Football, Board Game. 150

3429. Pirate and Traveler. 1936. Adventure, Board Game. 100

3430. Pirates' Treasure, The. Circa 1920s. Adventure, Board Game. 125

3431. Pit, Art cover by John Held Jr. Circa 1930s. Stock Market, Card Game. 50

3432. Playing the Ponies. Circa 1932. Sports, Horseracing, Board Game. 125

3433. Politics. 1936. Politics, Board Game. 150

3434. Polly Pickles. 1921. Movie, Board Game. 150

3435. Polly Put the Kettle On. 1923. Skill, Board Game. 75

3436. Pollyanna, Blue board & implement box. Circa 1920s. Classic, Board Game. 35

3437. Pollyanna. Circa 1920s. Classic, Board Game. 65

3438. Presidents, Game of. Circa 1930-2. Political, Card Game. 50

3439. Prisoner of Zenda, The. 1937. Movie, Adventure, Board Game. 200

3440. Psychic Base ball Game. 1935. Sports, Baseball, Board Game. 150

3441. Quick Wit. 1938. Social, Card Game. 30

3442. Quick Wit. Glyvas Williams Edition. 1938. Social, Card Game. 65

3443. Quiz Kids, Own Game Box. 1940. Q & A, Board Game. 35

3444. Raceway. Circa 1941. Sports, Board Game. 100

3445. Radio Game. Circa 1920s. Communications, Card Game. 75

3446. Ranger Commandos, World War II. 1942. Military, World War II, Board Game. 125

3447. Real Radio Game. 1926. Communications, Board Game. 75

Parker Brothers continued

3448. Rocket. Circa 1930s. Space, Board Game. $250

3449. Royal Game of India. © 1940. Classic, Board Game. 50

3450. S. S. Van Dines Great Detective Game, Philo Vance. 1937. Law & Order, Board Game. 150

3451. Scoop, The Game of. 1937, Board Game. This is a different Game from the later Scoop. 200

3452. Sea Rider. Circa 1940. Travel, Sea, Board Game. 125

3453. Shell Out. Circa 1941. Skill, Board Game. 150

3454. Sky Riders, Game of. 1940. Space, Board Game. 600

3455. Sky Shoot. Circa 1941. Skill, Board Game. 150

3456. SkyScraper Game. 1937. Architecture, Board Game. 500

3457. Society or High Hat. 1937. Economic, Board Game. 600

3458. Sorry! 1935. Miscellaneous, Board Game. 65

3459. South America Game. 1942. Geography, Board Game. 125

3460. South American Blow Gun Game. 1941. Skill, Board Game. 125

3461. Speed Boat. Circa 1920s. Travel, Sea, Board Game. 150

3462. States & Cities, Game of. © 1945. Geography, Board Game. 65

3463. Stock Exchange. 1936. Stock Market, Board Game, Supplement with Monopoly. 600

3464. Stratosphere. Circa 1930s. Space, Board Game. 250

3465. Sunk. 1939. Military, World War II, Board Game. 200

3466. Tarzan. 1941. Comics, Board Game. 500

3467. That's Me. 1937. Miscellaneous, Board Game. 100

3468. Thumbs Up, The Victory Game. © 1941. Military, Board Game. 150

3469. Tiddly Winks Game, Fairies Cauldron. Circa 1925. Classic, Skill Game. 50

3470. Tiddly Winks, Bowling, Ten Pins. Circa 1920. Classic, Skill Game. 50

3471. Tit Tat Toe, Game of. Circa 1930s. Classic, Board Game. 35

3472. Tom Hamilton's Pigskin. 1935. Sports, Football, Personality, Board Game. $125

3473. Tom Mix Circus Game. 1935. Personality, Western, Circus, Board Game. 275

3474. Tom Mix's Game Wildcat. 1935. Western, Personality, Card Game. 125

3475. Touring - Famous Automobile Game, 1st Issue. 1926. Travel, Car, Card Game. 100

3476. Touring - Famous Automobile Game, New Box. 1926. Travel, Car, Card Game. 75

3476a. Touring. as above, red deluxe box gold printing 60

3477. Touring - Famous Automobile Game. 1937. Travel, Car, Card Game. 50

3477a. Touring. © 1947, Red car and trailer cover, ... 45

3478. Touring - Famous Automobile Game. 1954. Travel, Car, Card Game. 35

3479. Touring - Famous Automobile Game. 1955. Travel, Car, Card Game. 35

3480. Touring - Famous Automobile Game. 1957. Travel, Car, Card Game. 35

3481. Touring - Famous Automobile Game. 1958. Travel, Car, Card Game. 35

3482. Touring - Famous Automobile Game. 1965. Travel, Car, Card Game. 30

3483. United States Air Mail, The. 1929. Travel, Air, Co, Board Game. 300

3484. Walt Disney's Own 3 Little Pigs-"Who's Afraid of the Big Bad" 1933. Disney, Board Game. 250

3485. Walt Disney's Own Game Donald Duck's Party. 1938. Disney, Board Game. 200

3486. Walt Disney's Own Game Ferdinand the Bull. 1938. Disney, Board Game. 150

3487. Walt Disney's Own Game Red Riding Hood. Circa 1930s. Disney, Board Game. 150

3488. Walt Disney's Own Game Snow White. 1938. Disney, Board Game. 250

3489. Walt Disney's Pinocchio Game. 1939. Disney, Board Game. 250

3490. We, The Magnetic Flying Game. Circa 1928-9. Travel, Air, Board Game. 150

3491. What Color is Your Car? © 1923. Social, Card Game. 50

3492. What's the Time. 1920. Educational, Board Game. 65

3493. Who's Who, Variant edition. 1929. Q & A, Board Game. 50

3494. Who's Who. 1929. Q & A, Board Game. 50

3495. Wild Goose Hunting. 1929. Animal, Board Game. 65

3496. Wings, The Air Mail Game. 1928. Travel, Air, Card Game. 65

3497. Winnie-The-Pooh Game. 1933. Literary, Board Game. 200

3498. World's Fair Card Game. 1939. Fairs, Card Game. 75

Paul Educational Games
3499. Heroes of America. 1929. History, Card Game. $50
3500. Nations, Games of the. © 1929. History, Card Game. 50

H. A. Peck
3501. Great American Game of Baseball, The. Circa 1930-5. Sports, Baseball, Board Game. 150

Personal Appearance Products
3501a. Gene and Glenn's Personal Appearance. Circa 1930s, Theatrical, Board Game. 125

H. J. Phillips Co.

3502. Chop Suey Game. Circa 1930s. Skill, Board Game. 125
3503. Quiz of the Whiz, The, by J. N. Ding. 1921. Q & A, Card Game. 50

Piroxloid Products Corp.
3504. Ancient Game of the Mandarins. 1923. Classic, Board Game. 65
3505. Big Six: Christy Mathewson Indoor Baseball Game. 1922. Sports, Baseball, Board Game. 500

Pittsburgh Game & Novelty
3506. Let U.S. Have Peace. 1916. Political, World War I, Board Game. 150

Pla-Golf Co.
3507. Pla-Golf. 1938. Sports, Golf, Board Game. 100

Plane Facts Co.
3508. Plane Packet. 1943. Military, World War II, Card Game. 125

3509. Smiling Jacks Victory Bombers. 1944. Comics, Card Game. $150

Pla-Rite, Selchow & Righter
3510. Tidley Winks. Circa 1920s. Classic, Skill Game. 30

PlayGames, Inc.
3511. American Varsity Football. 1934. Sports, Football, Board Game. 175

Playthings Corp.
3512. Climbing Mt. Zip. Circa 1918. Adventure, Board Game. 125
3513. Land and Water Battle Game. Circa 1918. Military, World War I, Board Game. 150
3514. Peanut Race, The. Circa 1918. Travel, Board Game. 50

Playtime Products Co.
3515. Word Rummy Game. Circa 1935. Word, Card Game. 30

Plaza Mfg. Co.
3516. Fiddle Stix. Circa 1930s. Miscellaneous, Skill Game. 50

Polaris Co.
3517. Polaris, by Charles Muir, Book, Board & box. 1926. Space, Literary, Board Game. 300

Polygon Corp.
3517a. Helios, The Game of the Gods. 1938. Mythology, Strategy, Board Game. 85

R. L. Polk & Co.
3518. Pontiac Safety Drive Game, The. Premium. 1937. Travel, Road, Board Game. 125

George Vincent Post
3519. Monte Carlo Whippet Derby. 1927. Sports, Dog Racing, Board Game. 100

Post Cereal
3520. Mickey Mouse Horseshoes. 1935. Disney, Board Game. 100

Jack Pressman & Co., Inc.
3521. Bomb! The Navy. Circa 1942. Military, World War II, Board Game. 125
3522. Derby Day. Circa 1936. Sports, Horseracing, Board Game. 100
3523. Electric Speed Classic. Circa 1932. Sports, Cars, Board Game. 125
3524. Fish Pond. Circa 1935. Animal, Fish, Board Game. 65

Jack Pressman & Co. continued
3525. Foto-Finish Horse Race. ©. 1940. Sports, Horseracing, Board Game. $100
3526. Hop Ching Checker Game. Circa 1940s. Classic, Board Game. 35
3527. Jungle Hunt. Circa 1928. Animal, Board Game. 75
3528. Tiddledy Winks, Jumbo. 1920s. Classic, Skill Game. 35
3529. Treasure Hunt. Circa 1928. Adventure, Board Game. 75
3530. Whippet Race. 1920s. Sports, Dog Racing, Board Game. 125
3531. Yacht Race (930). 1930s. Sports, Boating, Board Game. 100
3532. Yacht Race. Circa 1930s. Sports, Sea, Board Game. 100

Procter & Gamble
3533. Original Professor Quiz Radio Game, The. 1939. Premium, Communications, Board Game. 50
3534. Original Professor Quiz, The. 1939. Q & A, Board Game. 50

Proctor Amusement Co.
3535. "Baseball", The Champion Game of. 1940s. Sports, Baseball, Board Game. 150
3536. Champion European War Game, The. Circa 1917. Military, World War I, Board Game. 150
3537. "Champion" European War Game. 1940s. Military, World War II, Board Game. 125

Psychic Baseball Corp.
3538. Psychic Baseball. 1927. Sports, Baseball, Card Game. 100

R. T. A. Co.
3539. NRA, Game of Prosperity. 1933. Social Action, Board Game. 175

Radio Game Co.
3540. Radio, Game of. 1924. Communications, Card Game. 75

Radio Questionnaire Corp.
3541. Radio Questionnaire. 1928. Communications, Board Game. 65

Radio Quiz Corp.
3542. Radio Quiz, The. Circa 1928. Communications, Board Game. 65

Radio Sports
3543. Knute Rockne Football & World Series Baseball. Circa 1940s. Sports, BB-Football, Board Game. $350

Rainshine Game Co.
3544. Military Checkers. 1935. Military, Board Game. 75

Ram-Fair Co.
3545. Dice Ball, Baseball Game. 1937. Sports, Baseball, Board Game. 100

Realistic Game & Toy
3546. Bowling Bozo. Circa 1929. Circus, Board Game. 75

3547. Realistic Baseball. 1925. Sports, Baseball, Board Game. 150

Redlich Mfg. Co.
3548. Double Header, Wooden Sides. Circa 1930s. Sports, Baseball, Board Game. 200

Reed Game
3549. Spot 'Em. Circa 1940s. Military, World War II, Board Game. 150

Reeves Co.
3550. Ocean Flyer. Circa 1929. Travel, Board Game. 150

Regensteiner Corp.
3551. Kuti-Kuts (Cutie cuts): A Comic Cartoon Game (inv. by Charles Lederer). © 1922. Comics, Card Game. 75

Reinmuth
3552. Melodio. 1939. Musical, Card Game. $125

Remedial Education Center
3553. Go Fish. 1943. Animal, Board Game. 35

Remotrol Co.
3554. Coast Defense. Circa 1941. Military, World War II, Board Game. 150

3555. Merchant Marine. Circa 1941. Travel, Sea, Board Game. 150

3556. Yacht Club. Circa 1941. Sports, Boating, Board Game. 125

Rex Manufacturing Co.
3557. Greyhound Racing Game. © 1938. Sports, Dog racing, Board Game. 125

Rexall
3558. Streamlined Train Game, Premium. Circa 1930s. Travel, Rail, Premium, Board Game. 200

Riecks Ice Cream
3559. Mickey Mouse Cones Card Game. 1934. Disney, Adventure, Card Game. 150

Rigby-Grey
3560. Robin Hood's Strong Bowman. Circa 1930s. Adventure, Board Game. 125

Rippon Co. Inc.
3561. Rippon Magic Fishing Game. © 1935. Animal, Fish, Board Game. 50

Rodale
3562. Animals, Game of (Learn Spanish). 1944. Animal, Word, Card Game. 65

3563. Comparisons, Game of (Learn Spanish). 1944. Word, Card Game. 65

3564. Occupations, Game of (Learn Spanish). 1944. Word, Occupations, Card Game. 65

3565. Opposites, Game of (Learn Spanish). 1944. Word, Card Game. 65

3566. Synonyms, Game of (Learn Spanish). 1944. Word, Card Game. 65

Rogarsons Assoc.
3567. Gypsy-Doodle. 1939. Mystic, Board Game. 75

Roller Derby
3568. Roller Derby. Circa 1940. Sports, Board Game. 125

Rosana Co.
3569. Real Football. Circa 1922. Sports, Football, Board Game. 200

Rosebud Art Co.
3570. Bag of Fun, A. 1932. Combination, Skill Game. $40

3571. Beat the Drum. 1942. Miscellaneous, Board Game. 75

3572. Big Apple. 1938. Strategy, Board Game. 100

3573. Bingo. Circa 1930s. Classic, Board Game. 20

3574. Catchem. Circa 1930s. Miscellaneous, Skill Game. 75

3575. Chucklers Game, The. 1931. Strategy, Board Game. 50

3576. Dwarfs Twirling Game, The. Circa 1930s. Miscellaneous, Skill Game. 65

3577. Giggles. Circa 1930s. Social, Board Game. 50

3577a.Hare and the Tortoise, The. Circa 1930s, Animal board Game. 100

3578. Hickory Dickary Dock, Game of. Circa 1930s. Learning, Board Game. 50

3579. Home Baseball Game. 1936. Sports, Baseball, Board Game. 125

3580. Hunting Game, The. Circa 1930s. Animal, Board Game. 60

3581. Jumbo Ring Toss Game. 1940. Animal, Action Game. 25

3582. Junior Basketball Game. Circa 1930s. Sports, Basketball, Board Game. 100

3583. Kick Ball. Circa 1930s. Action, Board Game. 75

3584. King High "The Game of Supreme". Circa 1930s. Miscellaneous, Board Game. 75

3585. Kitty Kat Cup Ball. Circa 1930s. Animal, Skill Game. 125

3586. Life of the Party. Circa 1930s. Social, Board Game. 125

3587. Life of the Party. Variant. Circa 1930s. Social, Board Game. 125

3588. Lucky Planet, The Game of the Stars. 1939. Space, Board Game. 250

3589. Manchu Checkerettes. Circa 1930s. Ethnic, Board Game. 35

3590. Play Ball. Circa 1935-9. Sports, Baseball, Board Game. 100

3591. Popeye Pipe Toss Game. 1935. Comics, Skill Game. 150

3592. Popeye Ring Toss. 1937. Comics, Skill Game. 100

3593. Puns, The Game of. 1937. Word, Board Game. 125

3594. Rolaweel. 1926. Miscellaneous, Board Game. 35

3595. Roll-O Card Game. Circa 1940s. Miscellaneous, Card Game. 30

3596. Sixty Six, The Game of. Circa 1930s. Numbers, Board Game. 45

3597. Soli-Peg. Circa 1930s. Miscellaneous, Board Game. 35

3598. Spin-O-Peg. Circa 1930s. Miscellaneous, Board Game. 30

Rosensteel-Pub. Printing
3599. Big Ten Football Game. Circa 1929. Sports,
Football, Board Game. $150

Rosenwald-Milios Co.
3600. Radio Flash, The Game of. 1922.
Communications, Board Game. 250

Walter L. Rothschild
3601. Zimba. 1919. Miscellaneous, Board Game. 75

Royal Toy
3602. Alley Oop, Can Edition. 1937. Comics, Board
Game. 50

Ruckelshaus Game Corp.
3603. Black Falcon of the Flying G-Men, The. 1939.
Movie, Law & Order, Board Game. 650

Russell Manufacturing Co.
3604. Authors & Spin-A-Top. Circa 1940s.
Combination, Card Game. 35
3605. Authors, #51. 1935. Literary, Card Game. 25
3606. Bachelor Girl Game. © 1945. Romance, Card
Game. 100
3607. Basketball. Circa 1930s. Sports, Basketball, Card
Game. 125
3608. Beano, The Popular Game of. Circa 1930s.
Social, Card Game. 30
3609. Bull Frog. © 1939. Animal, Card Game. 75
3610. Buried Treasure, The Game of. 1922.
Adventure, Board Game. 75
3611. Dr. Quack, #52. 1935. Animal, Card Game. 30
3612. Dr. Quack, The Game of. 1922. Animal, Card
Game. 35
3613. Famous White House Game. 1928. Political,
Board Game. 100
3614. Funny Frolics or 10,000 Smiles. Circa 1930s.
Social, Board Game. 35
3615. Goof Race and Ten Pins. Circa 1930. Ethnic,
Board Game. 250
3616. Indian Backgammon. Circa 1930s. Classic,
Board Game. 50
3617. Mystic and Airplane Race. Circa 1935. Mystic,
Air, Board Game. 150
3618. Old Maid & Spin-A-Top. Circa 1930s.
Combination, Card & Skill. 35
3619. Old Maid Thrift Game. Circa 1930s. Classic,
Card Game. 35
3620. Old Maid. #50. 1935. Classic, Card Game. 25
3621. Old Maid-Authors-Dr. Quack, Games of. Circa
1930s. Combination, Card Game. 35
3622. Pan-Cake Tiddly Winks. Circa 1930s. Ethnic,
Skill Game. 50

3623. Par The New Golf Game. 1926. Sports, Golf,
Card Game. $75
3624. Patriotic Picture Quiz Game. Circa 1941.
History, Card Game. 100
3625. Radio Ball. Circa 1928. Skill, Board Game. 50
3626. Ring Toss. Circa 1930s. Classic, Skill Game. 25
3627. Sky Trails. (Small Book Shelf Vol. II). Circa
1940s. Travel, Air, Card Game. 65
3628. Slap Jack. 1930. Classic, Card Game. 50
3629. Slap Jack. #54. 1935. Misc., Card Game. 50

3630. Speed King, Game of. 1922. Sports, Car, Board
Game. 175
3631. Sufficient. Circa 1930s. Social, Card Game. 75
3632. Take-Off. 1930. Travel, Air, Card Game. 125
3633. Thrift Game. #55. 1935. Economic, Card
Game. 40
3634. Tortoise and the Hare, Game of. 1922. Animal,
Board Game. 165
3635. Tumbledown Race. Circa 1928. Miscellaneous,
Board Game. 100
3636. Whirley-Goof Game. Circa 1928.
Miscellaneous, Board Game. 125
3637. Wow, Game of. 1932. Miscellaneous, Board
Game. 75
3638. Yankee Doodle Baseball. Circa 1928. Sports,
Baseball, Board Game. 125

P. Rust (Sole Agent)
3639. New States Game, The. Circa 1925. Geography,
Card Game. 50

S & S Games Co.
3640. National Game, A Base-Ball Card Game. ©
1936. Sports, Baseball, Card Game, Photo cards. 800

S & W Fine Foods
3641. Happy Marriage Game. 1938. Romance, Board
Game. 100

Saalfield
3642. Billy Whiskers. Circa 1923-6. Animal, Board
Game. 125
3643. Greatest Show on Earth, The. 1924. Circus,
Board Game. 150

Thomas Sales Co.
3644. Inflation, The New Game. 1936. Economics, Board Game. $125

Walter H. Schaefer
3645. Pals Kartoon Cards. © 1939. Comics, Card Game. 125

Jos. Scheider Inc.
3646. Poppin' Popeye. Circa 1930s. Comics, Skill Game. 250

Schode Manufacturing
3647. Rotary Golf. Circa 1930. Sports, Golf, Board Game. 150

Scholastic Pub. Co.
3648. Arbo. 1927. Miscellaneous, Card Game. 50
3649. Match It, Game of Trees. 1927. Plant, Card Game. 50

Schultz-Illinois-Star Co.
3650. U-Bat-It. Circa 1920s. Sports, Baseball, Board Game. 125

George E. Schweig & Sons
3651. Unscramble Animals (Series B). 1930s. Animals, Card Game. 50

Scott, Foresman & Co.
3652. Say the Word. Circa 1940s. Word, Card Game. 35

Scripture Memory System
3653. Scripture Memory Cards (by Mrs. Robert A. Hadden). 1932. Religion, Card Game. 35

Sears-Sackett Co.
3654. Coast Defense Game. Circa 1921. Military, Board Game. 150

Seibel Publishing Co., Inc.
3655. Stadium/Big League Combination. Circa 1925. Sports, Baseball, Board Game. 150

Selchow & Richter
3656. Ali Baba. Circa 1929-32. Adventure, Board Game. 275
3657. Cabby! 1938. Travel, Car, Board Game. 125
3657a. Cabby! As above with deluxe gold on blue box. 125
3658. Cabby! Circa early 1930s. Travel, Car, Board Game. 150
3659. Cavalcade, Deluxe Edition. Circa 1930s. Sports, Horseracing, Board Game. 150

3660. Cavalcade, Separate board & box. Circa 1940s. Sports, Horseracing, Board Game. $75
3661. Cavalcade. Circa 1940s. Sports, Horseracing, Board Game. 100
3662. Champs: Land of Brauno. 1940. Military, Board Game. 75
3663. Dale Carnegie Game, The. 1938. Personality, Board Game. 175
3664. Doodle-Bug Race. Circa 1930s. Animal, Insect, Board Game. 300
3665. Ed Wynn, The Fire Chief. 1937. Personality, Occupation, Board Game. 150
3666. Elsie and Her Family, Jr. Edition. 1941. Comics, Board Game. 100
3667. Elsie and Her Family. 1941. Comics, Board Game. 125
3668. Empires. Circa 1942-4. Military, Economic, World War II, Board Game. 325
3669. Feed'n the Kitty. 1937. Animal, Board Game. 75
3670. Fishing, For Compliments, by Art Dritz. Circa 1930s. Animal, Board Game. 75
3671. Flying Aces. 1934. Military, World War II, Board Game. 125
3672. Have-You-It. 1928. Social, Card Game. 50
3673. Have-You-It. Yellow It. cover Variation. 1928. Social, Card Game. 50
3674. Home Team Baseball Game. 1918. Sports, Baseball, Board Game. 200
3675. Hot Numbers. Circa 1940s. Number, Board Game. 35
3676. Indian Trail. Circa 1930s. Western, India, Board Game. 300
3677. Jamboree. 1936. Economic, Board Game. 150
3678. Jump. Circa 1930s. Strategy, Board Game. 50
3678a. Lasso, The Jumping Ring. Clown cover. Circa 1930s, Circus action game. 200
3679. Little Bo-Peep. Circa 1920s. Nursery Rhyme, Board Game. 200
3680. Little Boy Blue. Circa 1930s. Nursery Rhyme, Board Game. 200
3681. Little Colonel. Circa 1920s. Movie, Board Game. 200
3682. Luck-A-Chuck. Circa 1930s. Miscellaneous, Board Game. 55
3683. Mr. Doodles Dog, Junior Edition. Circa 1930s. Animal, Board Game. 75
3684. Mr. Doodles Dog. Circa 1930s. Animal, Board Game. 100
3685. Nuggets The Rush to the Klondike. 1936. Adventure, Board Game. 150
3686. Parcheesi. Circa 1930s. Classic, Board Game. 35
3687. Peter Pan. 1927. Nursery Rhyme, Board Game. 200
3688. Radio Ramble. 1927. Communications, Board Game. 100
3689. Rainy Day Golf. Circa 1930s. Sports, Golf, Board Game. 150

Selchow & Richter continued

3690. Reg 'Lar Fellers Bowling Game. Circa 1920s.
Comics, Skill Game. $350

3691. Rock-A-By Birdies. Circa 1920s. Animals,
Board Game. 75

3692. Salute. 1942. History, II, Board Game. 150

3693. Shoot*A*Cak. Circa 1930s. Western, Skill
Game. 300

3694. Snake Eyes. Circa 1930s. Amimal, Board Game. 65

3695. Speed. Circa 1940s. Travel, Board Game. 150

3696. Stepping Stones. Circa 1920s. Occupations,
Board Game. 300

3697. Sumrun, The Great Racing Game. 1925.
Sports, Horseracing, Board Game. 150

3698. Sweep. 1930s, Board Game. Witch on cover. 200

3699. Thief of Bagdad, Jr. Edition, The. Circa 1930s.
Adventure, Board Game. 100

3700. Thief of Bagdad. Circa 1940s. Adventure, Board
Game. 125

3701. Tidley Winks. Circa 1930s. Classic, Skill Game. 30

3702. We Wow Wang. 1940. Social, Card Game. 50

3703. Wood Anagrams. Circa 1930s. Word, Card
Game. 50

Nelville C. Seymour

3704. Wicket Golf. 1930s. Sports, Golf, Board Game. 125

Shackman

3705. Leaning Tower of Piza Game. Circa 1930s.
Miscellaneous, Skill Game. 50

The Shaw Co.

**3706. Indianapolis 500 Mile Race Game, with Wilbur
Shaw.** 1938. Sports, Car, Board Game, Cards with
photos of early car racing greats. 600

Sheboygan Coaster & Wagon

3707. Wee-Tee Indoor Golf. 1931. Sport, Golf, Board
Game. 125

Shell Oil

3708. Stop and Go. Premium. 1936. Travel, Premium,
Board Game. 85

G. A. Simon Novelty Co.

3709. Skirmish (© Geo. A. Simon). © 1933. Military,
Board Game. 125

Simon & Schuster

3709a. Guggenheim. © 1927. Q & A, Paper & Pencil
Game. In book form. 50

3709b. Mental Whoopee, 1st Edition. © 1932. Q & A,
Paper & Pencil Game. $50

3709b. Mental Whoopee, 2nd Edition. 1932 Fall.
Q & A, Paper & Pencil Game. 50

3710. Mental Whoopee, 3rd Edition. 1933. Q & A,
Paper & Pencil Game. 50

3711. Mental Whoopee, 4th Edition. 1934. Q & A,
Paper & Pencil Game. 50

3712. Mental Whoopee, 5th Edition. 1935. Q & A,
Paper & Pencil Game. 50

3713. Mental Whoopee, 6th Edition. 1936. Q & A,
Paper & Pencil Game. 50

3714. Mental Whoopee, 7th Edition. 1936. Q & A,
Paper & Pencil Game. 50

3715. Mental Whoopee, 8th Edition. 1937. Q & A,
Paper & Pencil Game. 50

3716. Reward. 1937. Mental Activity, Paper & Pencil
Game. 60

**3717. Snap Judgement (by Herbert E. Marks &
Jerome S. Meyer).** 1933. Mental Activity, Paper
& Pencil Game. 50

Stephen Slesingere

3718. Alley Oop, Boxed Set. 1937. Comics, Board
Game. 600

3719. Winnie-The-Pooh Game. 1931. Literary, Board
Game. 350

John Smarkola

3720. Speedway Motor Race. Circa 1925. Sports, Cars,
Board Game. 125

3721.

Edward Smith Mfg. Co.

3722. After-Dinner. 1935. Mental Activity, Paper &
Pencil. Game. 50

3721a.Life of the Party. 1938. Mental Activity, Paper
& Pencil. 40

Karl Smith
3723. Skyscraper. 1937. Architecture, Board Game. $250

Norman C. Smith
3724. I-Got-It. 1936. Miscellaneous, Card Game. 50

Smith Kline & French Co.
3725. Battle of the Marne, The. 1920. Military, Board Game. 150
3726. Chasing Villa. 1920. Military, Board Game. 150
3727. Escape of the Boeben. 1920. Military, Board Game. 150
3728. Forward Pass. 1920s. Sports, Football, Board Game. 200
3729. Over the Hurdles. 1920s. Sports, Racing, Board Game. 150
3730. Pat Morgan's Own Ball Game. 1930s. Sports, Baseball, Board Game. 850
3731. Redskins & Cowboys. Circa 1920s. Western, Board Game. 150
3732. Speedway Motor Race. Circa 1920s. Sports, Car, Board Game. 125

Socko Insect Spray
3732a. Socko the Monk, The Game of, Premium. 1935. Animal, Premium, Board Game. 100

Spare-Time Corp.
3733. Going to the Fair. 1943. Economic, Board Game. 150
3734. Spare-Time Bowling. © 1945. Sports, Bowling, Board Game. 125
3735. Victo. © 1942. Military, Board Game. 200
3736. Victo. 1943. Military, World War II, Board Game. 200

Spear, N. Y.
3737. Around the World with the "Graf Zeppelin". C. 1932-38. Travel, Air, Card Game. 300

Springfield Photo Mt. Co.
3738. Spelling and Anagrams. 1930. Word, Card Game. 30

Standar Industries
3739. Air Mail Race. 1927. Travel, Air, Board Game. 125

Standard Oil Co.
3740. Bully Time in Spain with Gene and Glenn and Jake and Lena. 1933. Travel, Board Game. 125
3741. Red Crown Game, The, Premium. 1937. Travel, Car, Premium, Board Game. 125
3742. Red Crown Game, The. 1937. Premium, Car, Board Game. 125

Starex Novelty Co.
3743. Salvo. 1931. Military, Paper & Pencil. $100

Stars & Stripes Game Co.
3744. Stars and Stripes, Football Game. 1941. Sports, Football, Board Game. 135

Stoll & Edwards
3745. Adventures of Tom Sawyer and Huck Finn, The. 1921. Literary, Adventure, Board Game. 250
3746. Alice in Wonderland, Game of. 1923. Literary, Adventure, Board Game. 200
3747. Authors of To-day, Game of. 1929. Literary, Card Game. 50
3748. Black Beauty. 1921. Literary, Animal, Board Game. 150
3749. Blue Birds Game, The. Circa 1922. Animals, Birds, Board Game. 125
3750. Boxing Game, The. 1928. Sports, Boxing, Board Game. 150
3751. Chess & Checkers. Circa 1927-9. Classic, Board Game. 35
3751a. Cinderella, Game of. Circa 1920s, Literary Board Game. 200
3752. Coo Coo-Numdrums, Game of. Circa 1920s. Miscellaneous, Board Game. 125
3753. Defenders of the Flag. ©. 1922. Military, Card Game. 125
3754. Grand Slam. Circa 1930. Sport, Baseball, Board Game. 150
3755. Lion Hunt, The. 1926. Animal, Mammal, Board Game. 150
3756. Little Black Sambo, Game of. 1921. Ethnic, Literary, Board Game. 300
3757. Nursery Rhymes. 1921. Nursery Rhyme, Board Game. 125
3758. Peg Pen, Game of. 1929. Miscellaneous, Board Game. 50
3759. Pony Express, The. 1926. Communications, Board Game. 150
3760. Quizzer, The Game of. 1927. Q & A, Board Game. 50
3761. Scouting. 1926. Western, Board Game. 175
3762. Tom Sawyer and Huck Finn, Adventures of. 1925. Adventure, Literary, Board Game. 200

Stoll & Einson (Playjoy)
3763. Cinderella. 1934. Literary, Adventure, Board Game. 150
3764. Dog Sweepstakes. 1935. Animal, Board Game. 150
3765. Down the Rabbit's Hole with Alice in Wonderland. 1934. Literary, Adventure, Board Game. 150

Stoll & Einson (Playjoy) continued
3766. Marooned in the South Seas. 1934. Adventure,
Literary, Board Game. $150
3767. Pirates' Raid. 1934. Adventure, Board Game. 150
3768. Santa Fe Trail. 1934. Western, Board Game. 150
**3768a. Tom Sawyer and Huck Finn, The Adventures
of.** 1934, Literary board Game. 150
3769. Treasure Island Game. 1934. Literary,
Adventure, Board Game. 150
3770. Waterloo Game, The. 1935. Military,
Napoleonic, Board Game. 200

Nathan Stone
3771. Paris to Berlin, The Latest War Game. 1918.
Military, World War I, Board Game. 165

T. H. Stough
3772. Sto-Auto Race. Circa 1920. Sports, Cars, Board
Game. 125

Stox, Inc.
3773. Stock Exchange, The Game of. 1929. Stock
Market, Board Game. 150

Strathmore Games Co.
3774. Sea Battle. 1944. Military, World War II, Board
Game. 125

L. E. Sultzer
3775. Hear and See Football. 1935. Sports, Football,
Board Game. 125

Sunshine Biscuit Co.
3776. Sunshine Funmaker Game Cards. 1932. Mental
Activity, Paper & Pencil. 30

Sunshine Shredded Wheat
3777. Sunshine Maze Games, Premium. Circa 1930s.
Premium, Board Game. 25
3778. Sunshine Target Practice Game, Premium.
Circa 1930s. Premium, Skill Game. 25

Supply Sales Co.
3779. Traveling Salesman, The. Circa 1923.
Economics, Board Game. 125

Syntactic Book Co.
3780. Ultimate Literary, Game of. 1925. Literary,
Card Game. 50

System Thrift Book Co.
3781. Saving Game, The (by Albert H. Lewis). 1917.
Economics, Card Game. 75

Tackle Game Co.
3782. Tackle. 1933. Sports, Football, Board Game. $125

Tactical Game Co.
3783. Tactical Baseball. Circa 1933. Sports, Baseball,
Board Game. 125
3784. Tactical Football. Circa 1933. Sports, Football,
Board Game. 125

Ted Toy-Lers
3785. All American Base Ball Game. Circa 1924.
Sports, Baseball, Board Game. 125
3786. All American Football. Circa 1924. Sports,
Football, Board Game. 125

Teddys Multi-Card Game
3787. Teddy's Multiplication Cards. Later Edition.
1921. Numbers, Card Game. 350

Tek Toothbrush
3788. Snow White Game, Premium. 1937. Premium,
Board Game. 125

Robert Teller Sons
3789. Outlaw Rummy. 1939. Law & Order, Card
Game. 75

Thwaites
3790. Patience. Circa 1932. Miscellaneous, Card
Game. 50

L. E. Tilley
3791. Are You a Sacred Cow? 1st Edition. Circa
1930s. Q & A, Board Game. 50
3792. Are You a Sacred Cow? 2nd Edition. Circa
1930s. Q & A, Board Game. 50
3793. Are You a Sacred Cow? 3rd Edition. Circa
1930s. Q & A, Board Game. 50

Tilley & Sherman
**3794. Colonial Stoopnagle & Budds Are You A
Sacred Cow, 1st Series.** 1933. Mental Activity,
Paper & Pencil. 50
**3795. Colonial Stoopnagle & Budds Are You a
Sacred Cow, 2nd Series.** 1934. Mental Activity,
Paper & Pencil Game. 50
**3796. Colonial Stoopnagle & Budds Are You a
Sacred Cow, 3rd Series.** 1935. Mental Activity,
Paper & Pencil Game. 50
**3797. Colonial Stoopnagle & Budds Are You a
Sacred Cow, 4th Series.** 1936. Mental Activity,
Paper & Pencil Game. 50

Toddy Inc.
3798. African Hunt. © 1933. Animal, Board Game. 100
3799. America's Cup Yacht Race. © 1933. Sports,
Boating, Board Game. 125

Toddy Inc. continued
3800. Calcutta Sweepstakes. © 1933. Board Game. $125
3801. Coast to Coast Air Race. © 1933. Travel, Air, Board Game. 125
3802. Pirate Treasure Hunt. © 1933. Adventure, Board Game. 100
3803. Tour of the World. © 1933. Travel, Board Game. 125

Tone Products Corp of A.
3804. Strike Three by Carl Hubble. Circa 1940s. Sports, Baseball, Board Game. 250

Toto Sales Co.
3805. Toto the New Game (BaseBall). 1925. Sports, Baseball, Board Game. 75
3806. Toto The New Game. 1925. Miscellaneous, Board Game. 50

Toy Creations, Inc.
3807. Benny Goodman, A Game of Musical Information. Circa 1930s. Musical, Board Game. 150
3808. Bombs Away! 1943. Military, World War II, Board Game. 150
3808a. Court of Missing Heirs, The. ©. 1940, Board Game. ... 125
3809. Democracy. 1940. Political, Board Game. 175
3810. Kate Smith's Own Game, America. Circa 1930s. Personality, History, Board Game. 125
3811. Lester Patrick's Official Hockey Game. 1939. Sports, Hockey, Board Game. 200
3812. Official Basketball Game. 1940. Sports, Basketball, Board Game. 150
3813. Official Radio Football Game. 1939. Sports, Football, Board Game. 150
3814. Official Radio Baseball Game. 1939. Sports, Baseball, Board Game. 150
3815. Phililip Lord's Gang Buster Action Games. Circa 1938. Law & Order, Board Game. 200
3816. Pile 'Em High. Circa 1938. Miscellaneous, Board Game. 75
3817. Pocket Baseball. 1940. Sports, Baseball, Board Game. 50
3818. Pocket Football. 1940. Sports, Football, Board Game. 50
3819. Pot O'Gold. 1940. Miscellaneous, Board Game. 75
3820. Professor Wiz Party Games. Circa 1938. Q & A, Board Game. 50
3821. Shadow Game, The. 1940. Comics, Super Hero Board Game. 1000
3822. Soldiers and Sailors Game. Circa 1941-2. Military, World War II, Board Game. 200
3823. Spot-A-Plane Game. 1942. Military, World War II, Board Game. 200
3824. Uncle Jim's Question Bee, Jr. Series. Circa 1930s. Q & A, Board Game. 65

3825. Uncle Jim's Question Bee. 1940. Q & A, Board Game. $65
3826. V for Victory Game. Circa 1941. Military, World War II, Board Game. 150

Toyad Corp.
3827. Blaze Away. 1940s. Military, World War II, Board Game. 150
3828. Bomb Sight Target Game. 1944. Military, World War II, Board Game. 150

T-P Card Co.
3829. Silver Strike. 1939. Miscellaneous, Card Game. 50

Transogram Co.
3830. Airdrome. Circa 1935. Travel, Air, Board Game. 75
3831. Airway. Circa 1934. Travel, Air, Board Game. 100
3832. Big Business. 1936. Economic, Board Game. 75
3833. Black Birds (255). Circa 1935. Animals, Board Game. 65
3834. Bucking Broncos. 1935. Western, Board Game. 100
3835. Dog Race, Smaller box. 1937. Animal, Mammals, Board Game. 50
3836. Dog Race. 1937. Animal, Mammals, Board Game. 75
3837. Duck Shooting Game. Circa 1935. Animal, Board Game. 75
3838. Flying High. 1931. Travel, Air, Board Game. 125
3839. Happy Landing. 1938. Travel, Air, Board Game. 75
3840. Hats Off Bowling Game. © 1944. Skill, Action Game. 50
3841. Hungry Willie. Circa 1939-40. Food, Board Game. 65
3842. Krokay. 1937. Classic, Skill Game. 50
3843. Movie Millions. 1936. Movie, Board Game. 200
3844. Orje, The Mystic Prophet. 1929. Mystic, Board Game. 50
3845. Prince Valiant. Circa 1940s. Comics, Board Game. 75
3846. Ride 'Em Cowboy & Knuckle Down. 1931. Western, Board Game. 65
3847. Save the Sailor. Circa 1935. Travel, Sea, Board Game. 100
3848. Sidewalks of New York. Circa 1935. Geography, Board Game. 100
3849. Sink the Ship. 1942. Military, World War II, Board Game. 100
3850. Sugar Bowl. 1939. Miscellaneous, Board Game. 50

Traydac
3851. Scrambles. © 1935. Miscellaneous, Card Game. 50

Trend Game Co.
3852. H.V. Kaltenborn Game of Diplomacy, The. 1939. Military, World War II, History, Board Game. Black cover. 200
3852a. H.V. Kaltenborn. As above Orange cover. 200

Triumph Specialities Mfg.
3853. **Tumbling Twins, The.** Circa 1920s. Animal,
   Skill Game. $150

Trojan Games
3854. **America's Football.** Circa 1939. Sports,
   Football, Board Game. 150
3855. **Light Horse H. Cooper Golf Game.** 1943.
   Sports, Golf, Board Game. 250

Tudor Toys
3856. **Musical Lotto.** 1936. Music, Board Game. 75

Tur-Boy Co.
3857. **Base Ball Card Game.** Circa 1920. Sports,
   Baseball, Card Game. 75

W. P. Ulrich
3858. **Star Baseball Game.** 1941. Sports, Baseball,
   Card Game. 150

United Games Co.
3859. **Mother Hubbard.** Circa 1910s. Nursery Rhyme,
   Board Game. 100
3860. **Peter Coddles Trip to New York.** Circa 1920s.
   Reading, Card Game. 50

Universal Baseball
3861. **Universal Baseball Playing Cards.** 1929. Sports,
   Baseball, Card Game. 125

Universal Playing Card
3862. **Universal Baseball.** © 1929. Sports, Baseball,
   Board Game. 125

Universal School of Music
3863. **Modern Orchestra Game, The.** Circa 1920.
   Music, Card Game. 75

University Feature
3864. **Doo Dad Circus Game.** © 1921. Circus, Board
   Game. 100

Van Wagenen
3865. **Defense, Game of, (Atlantic Theater).** 1941.
   Military, World War II, Board Game. 300
3866. **Defense, Game of, (Pacific Theater).** 1941.
   Military, World War II, Board Game. 300
3866a. **Attack,** 1941, Military WWII Board Game. 400
3866b. **Pursuit!** 1941, Military WWII Board Game. 250

The Veep Co.

3867. **Du-Ration.** Circa 1942-4. Historical, World
   War II, Board Game, Home front Game. $250

Victory Game Co.
3868. **Victory Rummy.** 1942. Military, World War II,
   Card Game. 100

Vitaplay Toy Co.
3869. **Coney Island Playland Park.** Circa 1940.
   Circus, Board Game. 125
3870. **Fishing Game (by Arthur Dritz) (621).** 1940s.
   Animal, Board Game. 75
3871. **Jumping Monkeys.** Circa 1945. Animal, Board
   Game. 65

Volume Sprayer Mfg. Co.
3872. **Hurry Home.** 1942. Premium, Board Game. 75

W & L Game Co.
3873. **Bomb A Jap.** 1940s. Military, World War II,
   Board Game. 150
3874. **Set the Sun.** 1940s. Military, World War II, Board
   Game. 150

J. M. Waggaman
3875. **Greens Highroad to Health & Happiness.**
   1930s. Physical Fitness, Board Game. 100

Waltham Industries
3876. **Dictator.** 1939. Military, World War II, Board
   Game. 400

Waners Baseball Game
3877. **Waners Baseball Game.** 1937. Sports, Baseball,
   Personality, Board Game. 450

Wannatoy Co.
3878. **Direct Hit.** 1943. Military, World War II, Board
   Game. 200

Frederick Warne & Co.
3879. Peter Rabbit's Race Game. 1921. Animal,
Board Game. $75

Warner Mfg. Co.
3880. Major Bowes Amateur Hour Game. Circa
1930s. Personality, Board Game. 75
3881. Targo. Circa 1935. Skill, Board Game. 100

Wealth Unlimited
3882. Wealth. 1936. Economic, Board Game. 150

Westinghouse
3883. Blondie Goes to Leisureland, Premium. 1940.
Comics, Premium, Board Game. 100

Wheaties, J. Armstrong
3884. Big Ten Football Game, The, Premium. 1936.
Sports, Football, Board Game. 75

White & Williams Game
3885. Test Your Gridiron Skill. 1943. Sports, Football,
Board Game. 100

White King
3886. White King Game, The. Premium. 1922.
Premium, Board Game. 75

Chief Whitetree
3886a. Brokerage Game. By Chief Whitetree from
Seneca Indian tribe in Oklahoma. 1940. Ethnic,
Wall Street. Board Game. 150

Whitman Pub. Co.
3887. 16 Ready to Play Games. 1931. Combination,
Board Game. 25
3888. 44 Games. Circa 1938-40. Combination,
Board Game. 35
3889. 72 Party Stunts. 1935. Social, Card Game. 40
3890. 72 Party Stunts. Variant cover. 1935. Social,
Card Game. 40
3891. 72 Party Stunts. Variant with woman on cover.
1935. Social, Card Game. 40
3892. 8 Games in One, (Racing Themes). 1936.
Combination, Sport, Racing, Board Game. 35
3893. All Star Basketball Game. 1935. Sports,
Baseball, Board Game. 125
3894. All Star Comics. 1934. Comics, Card Game. 150
3895. Authors, The Game of. Circa 1935-9. Literary,
Card Game. 30
3896. Authors. Circa 1940s. Literary, Card Game. 30
3897. Basketball Game. 1941. Sports, Basketball,
Board Game. 125

3898. Battle Stations, The Game of. 1942. Military,
World War II, Board Game. $150
3899. Battleship Game, The. 1940. Military, World
War II, Board Game. 125
3900. Big League Baseball. © 1938. Sports, Baseball,
Card Game. 125
3901. Big League Baseball Game, by A. E. Gustafson.
1938. Sports, Baseball, Board Game. 150
3902. Big League Baseball Game. 1935. Sports,
Baseball, Board Game. 125
3903. Blondie Playing Card Game. 1941. Comics,
Card Game. 75
3904. Bridge Dice. Circa 1930s. Miscellaneous, Board
Game. 25
3905. Cap the Hat, The Game of. 1938.
Miscellaneous, Board Game. 50
3906. Cat & Witch. Circa 1930s. Animal, Holiday,
Board Game. 125
3907. Charlie Chan. 1939. Theatrical, Card Game. 75
3908. Charlie McCarthy Put and Take Bingo. 1938.
Personality, Board Game. 100
3909. Charlie McCarthy Rummy Card Game. 1938.
Personality, Card Game. 65

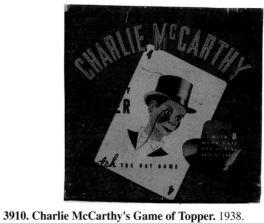

3910. Charlie McCarthy's Game of Topper. 1938.
Personality, Card Game. 125
3911. Chinese Marble Checkers. 1938. Classic, Board
Game. 35
3912. Corner the Market. 1938. Economic, Board
Game. 150
3913. Cowboys & Indians Also Junior Golf. 1935.
Western, Golf, Board Game. 125
3914. Dick Tracy Card Game. 1934. Comics, Card
Game, Red background cover. 75
3915. Dick Tracy Card Game. Variant cover. 1934.
Comics, Black shadow background cover. 75
3916. Dick Tracy Detective Game. 1937. Comics,
Law, Board Game. 150
3917. Dick Tracy, Super Detective. Variant cover.
1937. Comics, Card Game. 85
3918. Dive Bomber, The Game of. 1942. Military,
World War II, Board Game. 125

Whitman Pub. Co. continued

3919. Donkey Party. Circa 1930s. Classic, Animal,
Skill Game. $30

3920. Donkey Ring Toss Game. 1941. Animal, Skill
Game. 30

3921. Double Trouble, The Game of. 1941.
Miscellaneous, Board Game. 50

**3922. Edgar Bergen's Charlie McCarthy Q & A
Game.** 1938. Q & A, Personality, Card Game. 75

3923. F. B. I. Agent, The Games of. ©. 1942. Spy,
Board Game. 125

3924. Ferdinand the Bull in the Arena, The Game of.
1938. Disney, Board Game. 150

3925. Ferdinand the Bull. 1938. Disney, Card Game. 75

3926. Flying Jack. Circa 1935-9. Travel, Air, Board
Game. 125

3927. Football, Horizontal green box. 1941. Sports,
Football, Board Game. 250

3928. Fortune Telling Game. 1934. Mystic, Board
Game. 75

3929. Fortune Telling Playing Cards. 1938. Mystic,
Card Game. 75

3930. Gang Busters Game (Philips H. Lord). 1939.
Law & Order, Board Game. 200

3931. G-Men Clue Games. 1938. Law & Order, Board
Game. 200

3932. Good Neighbor Game. 1942. Social, Board
Game. 75

**3933. Grand National, A Sweepstakes Game of
Chance.** 1937. Sports, Horseracing, Board Game. 100

3934. Grand Slam, The Game of. Circa 1930-2.
Miscellaneous, Card Game. 100

3935. Here Comes Jumbo. Circa 1935. Animal, Card
Game. 50

3936. Hitch Hicker, The Game of. 1937. Ethnic,
Travel, Board Game. 200

3937. Hollywood Movie Bingo, Female in Star cover.
1939. Movie, Board Game. 75

3938. Hollywood Movie Bingo, Green & Yellow box.
1937. Movie, Board Game. 75

3939. Hollywood Movie Bingo, Red & Yellow box.
1937. Movie, Board Game. 75

3940. How Good Are You? 1937. Q & A, Board
Game. 50

3941. India, The Game of. Circa 1930s. Classic, Board
Game. 50

3942. India, The Game of. Circa 1930s. Classic, Board
Game. 50

3943. Inspector Wade of Scotland Yard. 1937. Law &
Order, Card Game. 125

3944. Jingle Quiz, #3 Catch Questions. 1940. Q & A,
Card Game. 35

3945. Kentucky Derby. 1938. Sports, Horseracing,
Board Game. 35

3946. Landing Force, The Game of. 1942. Military,
World War II, Board Game. $150

3947. Library of Games, (Bookshelf of 6 Card
Games). 1939. Combination, Card Game. 80

3948. Little America, Antarctic Game. Circa 1930s.
History, Geography, Board Game. 250

3949. Little Orphan Annie Rummy Cards. Circa
1930s. Comics, Card Game. 75

3950. Lucky Duck. 1941. Animal, Board Game. 40

3951. Mail Coach Game. 1939. Communication,
Board Game. 100

3952. Mail Must Fly, Round Up, The. 1935.
Communication, Board Game. 125

3953. Mickey Mouse Old Maid Cards, Variant cover.
1937. Disney, Card Game. Red balloon cover. 75

3954. Mickey Mouse Old Maid Cards. 1937. Disney,
Card Game, Blue square cover. 75

3955. Midget Speedway, The Game of. 1942. Sports,
Car, Board Game. 125

3956. Monkey Shines. Circa 1930s. Animal, Card
Game. 35

3957. Mother Goose Game (3952). 1940. Nursery
Rhyme, Card Game. 50

**3958. Navigator-A Boat Race Game W/ a Deck of
Cards.** 1938. Sports, Yacht, Board Game. 100

3959. Night Before Christmas, The. 1939. Holiday,
Xmas, Board Game. 150

3960. Og, Son of Fire. Circa 1930s. Comics, Board
Game. 150

3961. Oh Blondie. 1940. Comics, Board Game. 75

3962. Old Hogans Goat. 1939. Animal, Board Game. 50

3963. Old Maid, The Game of. Circa 1930s. Classic,
Card Game. 40

3964. Old Maid. Circa 1930s. Classic, Card Game. 40

3965. One Thousand Conundrums. 1939. Word,
Board Game. 35

3966. Over the Top. 1939. Miscellaneous, Action
Game. 35

3967. Party Fun. 1935. Social, Card Game. 35

3968. Party Games and Puzzles. 1934. Combination,
Board Game. 25

3969. Peg Pen, Game of. 1929. Strategy, Board Game. 50

3970. Pirate Gold, The Game of. 1938. Adventure,
Board Game. 125

3971. Pirates Cave & Wild West Rodeo 1931.
Western, Board Game. 100

3972. Pirates Cove & Wild West Rodeo, The. 1931.
Adventure, Western, Board Game. 100

**3973. Pitfalls, A Pinocchio Marble Game, Walt
Disney's.** © 1939. Disney, Board Game. 100

3974. Play Football, Dark blue cover. 1939. Sports,
Football, Board Game. 125

3975. Play Football. 1934. Sports, Football, Board
Game. Halfback running left. 125

Whitman Pub. Co. continued

3976. Play Football. 1934. Sports, Football, Board Game. Facing running halfback. $125

3977. Play Football. 1934. Sports, Football, Board Game. Halfback running right. 100

3978. Popeye, Party Game. 1937. Comics, Board Game. 100

3979. Popeye, Red Box Edition. 1937. Comics, Card Game. 75

3980. Pop-eye, Variant cover. 1934. Comics, Card Game. 75

3981. Pop-eye, Variant cover. 1934. Comics, Card Game. 75

3982. Pop-eye, Variant cover. 1934. Comics, Card Game. 75

3983. Pop-eye. 1934. Comics, Card Game. 75

3984. Put the Tail on Ferdinand the Bull. 1938. Disney, Skill Game. 125

3985. Quiz 4 Party Game. 1937. Q & A, Board Game. 40

3986. Quiz Kids, Radio Question Bee. 1941. Q & A, Card Game. 40

3987. Rainbow Cards. 1932. Miscellaneous, Card Game. 35

3988. Red Ryder Target Game, The. 1939. Comics, Board Game. 150

3989. Royal Mounted Games, The. 1938. Adventure, Board Game. 125

3990. Rummy Card Game. Circa 1935-40. Classic, Card Game. 30

3991. Rummy Royal, Smaller box. 1937. Miscellaneous, Card Game. 30

3992. Rummy Royal. 1937. Miscellaneous, Card Game. 30

3993. Scarlet Ranger, The Game of. Circa 1930s. Western, Board Game. 100

3994. Snap, Game of. 1940. Classic, Card Game. 35

3995. Snap, The Game of. 1930. Classic, Card Game. 35

3996. Squadron Scramble. 1941. Military, World War II, Card Game. 75

3997. Stamps. 1937. Collecting, Card Game. 150

3998. Stop and Go. 1939. Travel, Law & Order, Board Game. 125

3999. Stratosphere, Almond shaped Spaceship. 1936. Space, Board Game. 250

4000. Stratosphere. 1936. Space, Board Game. $250

4001. Swing Game, The. Circa 1935. Music, Board Game. 50

4002. Target Ball. Circa 1938-9. Miscellaneous, Skill Game. 50

4003. Telegrams, Game of. 1941. Communications, Board Game. 75

4004. Telling Tommy Card Game. 1935. Social, Card Game. 50

4005. Ten Playing Card Games. 1940. Combination, Card Game. 35

4006. Terry and the Pirates, The Game of. 1937. Comics, Board Game. 200

4007. Three Ring Circus/ Steeplechase. 1931. Circus, Horseracing, Board Game. 100

4007a. Tidley Winks, Circa 1930s, Skill Game. 50

4008. Tiger Hunt. Circa 1930s. Animal, Board Game. 75

4009. Tumble Tom. 1941. Miscellaneous, Board Game. 50

4010. Victory Bomber, A Target Game. Circa 1943-5. Military, World War II, Board Game. 150

4011. Walt Disney's Donald Duck. 1941. Disney, Card Game. 75

4012. Walt Disney's Pinocchio. 1939. Disney, Card Game. 75

4013. What's the Answer. Circa 1930s. Q & A, Card Game. 50

4014. Whip. Circa 1930s. Western, Card Game. 50

4015. Whirlpool. Circa 1930s. Miscellaneous, Board Game. 50

4016. Who is the Thief. 1933. Law & Order, Card Game. 65

4016a. Wings of America. 1940. Military, World War II, Board Game. 150

4017. Wizard of Oz, The Game of the. 1939. Literary, Board Game. 400

4018. Wolf Hunt and Race to Saturn. 1935. Animal, Space, Board Game. 125

4019. Words, Game of. 1938. Word, Card Game. 35

4020. Zoom, The Airplane Card Game. 1941. Travel, Air, Card Game. 75

4021. Zoom, The Airplane Game. 1941. Travel, Air, Card Game. 75

4022. Zoom, The Airplane Game. Red & Black cover. 1941. Travel, Air, Card Game. 75

Wilder Manufacturing Co.

4023. Al-Nav. 1932. Travel, Sea, Board Game. 250

4024. Arc Dominoes, Variant cover. Circa 1930s. Animal, Board Game. 50

Wilder continued

4025. Arc Dominoes. Circa 1930s. Animal, Board
Game. $50

4026. Backgammon and Checkers. Circa 1930s.
Combination, Class, Board Game. 35

4027. Balloon Game. Circa 1930s. Miscellaneous,
Board Game. 65

4028. Big Game Hunt, The. Circa 1930s. Animal,
Board Game. 125

4029. Boxing. Circa 1922. Sports, Boxing, Board
Game. 125

4030. Bungalow Building Game. Circa 1930s.
Architecture, Board Game. 200

4031. Bunny Ring. Circa 1922. Animal, Board Game. 75

4032. Buried Treasure Game. Circa 1930s. Adventure,
Board Game. 200

4033. Chancit (1011). Circa 1918. Miscellaneous,
Board Game. 50

4034. Clown Toss Game. Circa 1930s. Circus, Skill
Game. 65

4035. Combination Board Air & Road Races. Circa
1920s. Combination, Board Game. 100

**4035a.Combination Board Games, Auto Race &
Game Hunt.** Circa 1920s, Combination board
Game. 125

4036. Combination Board Game, Eagle, Bear &
Spider cover. Circa 1930s. Combination, Animal,
Board Game. 125

4037. Combination Board Games, Indian Home.
Circa 1930s. Combination, Board Game. 75

**4038. Combo Games, Auto, Army & Navy, Game
Hunt.** Circa 1920s. Combination, Board Game. 100

4039. Construction Game. Circa 1922. Architecture,
Board Game. 150

4040. Devil Dog Marine (57). 1921. Miscellaneous,
Board Game. 125

4041. Factory Assembly. 1922. Economic, Board
Game. 125

4042. Fighting the Wolf Pack. Circa 1931.
Adventure,   Board Game. 125

4043. Fire Fighters Game. Circa 1930s. Occupation,
Board Game. 200

4044. Fish Pond. Circa 1920s. Animal, Sea, Board
Game. 75

4045. Fore Country Club. 1929. Sports, Golf, Board
Game. 250

4046. Fore, Game of Golf. 1929. Sports, Golf, Board
Game. 250

4047. Gawara Hunters Game. Circa 1918. Animal,
Board Game. 125

4048. Hi-Fly Baseball Game. Circa 1927. Sports,
Baseball, Board Game. 150

4049. India Home and Checkers. Circa 1930s.
Combination, Board Game. $75

4050. Indoor Horse Shoe. Circa 1930s. Classic, Skill
Game. 50

4051. Indoor Horseshoe. Circa 1925-9. Sports, Skill
Game. 50

4052. Jack and the Beanstalk, Bean Bag Game. Circa
1930s. Nursery Rhyme, Skill Game. 200

4053. Jack Straws. Circa 1930s. Classic, Skill Game. 35

4054. Jig-A-Roomp Frog Shooting Game. Circa 1931.
Animal, Board Game. 125

4055. Jolly Robbers. 1930. Adventure, Board Game. 125

4056. Liberty War Game. Circa 1918. Military, Board
Game. 150

4057. Loop the Loop. 1921. Travel, Air, Board Game. 150

4058. Mother Carey's Ducks. Circa 1930s. Animal,
Board Game. 75

4059. Movie-Land Keeno. 1929. Movie, Board Game. 85

4060. Mystic Writing. Circa 1930s. Mystic, Board
Game. 150

4061. Obstacle Race. Circa 1930s. Travel, Road,
Board Game. 100

4062. Ocean to Ocean Flight Game, Blue Box, wings
logo. Circa 1930s. Travel, Air, Board Game. 125

4063. Ocean to Ocean Flight Game, Red Box.
Diamond logo Circa 1920s. Travel, Air, Board
Game. 125

4064. Old Maid. Circa 1930s. Classic, Card Game. 50

4065. Palm Beach Auto Race. Circa 1927. Sports,
Cars, Board Game. 125

4066. Pop the Question. Circa 1920s. Social, Card
Game. 75

4067. Post Office Game. Circa 1930s. Communication,
Board Game. 100

4068. Punt Football Game (69). 1930s. Sports,
Football, Board Game. 150

4069. Radio Game. Circa 1930s. Communications,
Board Game. Diamond logo. 125

4070. Radio Game. Circa 1930s. Communications,
Board Game, three people at radio. 125

4071. Ride a Cock Horse and Go Bang. Circa 1931.
Classic, Board Game. 100

4072. Ring Toss. Circa 1930s. Classic, Skill Game. 35

4073. Robin Hood. Circa 1930s. Adventure, Board
Game. 200

4073a.Shoot the Crow. Circa 1930s. Animal, Action Game. 100

**4074. Star Flight, Combo, Marketing &
Housekeeping.** Circa 1930s. Space, Combination,
Board Game. 750

4075. Stop Thief. Circa 1920s. Law & Order, Card
Game. 100

4076. Store Management Game. Circa 1930s.
Economic, Board Game. 400

4077. Throwing the Bull. 1930s. Animal, Board
Game. 75

Wilder continued

4078. Tiddledy Winks. Circa 1930s. Classic, Skill
Game. $35

4079. Tiddley Winks. Circa 1930s. Classic, Skill
Game. 35

4080. Touchdown Football Game. Circa 1930s. Sports,
Football, Board Game. 200

4081. Toyland Railway Game. Circa 1920s. Travel,
Rail, Board Game. 100

4082. Wilders Baseball Game. Circa 1930s. Sports,
Baseball, Board Game. 250

4083. Wilders Football Game. Circa 1930s. Sports,
Football, Board Game. 200

4083a. Wilders Football Game, as above but smaller
size box. 100

4084. William Tell Shooting Game. Circa 1931. Skill,
Board Game. 150

Wilkinson

4085. Radar-Salvo. 1945. Military, World War II,
Board Game. 75

Williams Games

4086. Navigator. Circa 1930s. Travel, Sea, Board
Game. 125

Roger Q. Williams Inc.

4087. Famous Flyers Race Around the World. 1931.
Travel, Air, Board Game. 150

The Wits Co.

4088. Wits. 1922. Social, Card Game. 35

Wiz Novelty Co.

4089. Attack. 1941. Military, World War II, Board
Game. 150

4090. Veda the Magic Answer Man. Circa 1941.
Mystic, Board Game. 50

Wolverine Sup. Co.

4091. Pitch Em Indoor Horseshoes. Circa 1930s.
Sport, Skill Game. 65

Woolsey Manufacturing

4092. Woolsey's Football Game. Circa 1930. Sports,
Football, Board Game. 150

WPA Museum Extension

4093. Map Game: Pennsylvania County Seats. Circa
1935. Geography, Board Game. 100

Henery O. Wurth Co.

4094. Star Basket-Ball Game. 1926. Sports,
Basketball, Board Game. 125

Paul Yejoff

4095. Sea Scouts. Circa 1930. Organizations, Board
Game. $100

Willis G. Young

4096. Pin-Nock'l. 1917. Classic, Skill Game. 100

4097. Spear-Em. © 1916. Skill, Action Game. 100

4098. Submarine Drag. 1917. Military, World War I,
Board Game. 150

Youngstown Games

4099a. Footballer, The. Circa 1930s. Sport, Football,
Board Game. 100

4099b. Baseballer, The. Circa 1930s. Sport, Baseball,
Board Game. 100

4099c. Bert Wheelers' Game of Taxi. Circa 1930s.
Personality, Travel, Board Game. 75

Zondervan Pub. Co.

4099. Bible Authors. Circa 1920s. Religious Game. 35

4100. Bible Boys. Circa 1920s. Religious, Card Game. 40

4101. Lemons Bible Game. 1929. Religious Game. 35

4102. Who am I? Quizzes and Bible Characters.
1942. Religious, Card Game. 35

Zondine Game Co.

4103. Hollywood Producer. 1940s. Movies, Board
Game. 200

4104. Red Skeltons "I Dood It". 1943. Personality,
Board Game. 150

4105. Take It or Leave It. 1942. Board Game. 65

Zulu Toy Mfg. Co., Inc.

4106. Animal Bowling Game. Circa 1927. Animals,
Board Game. 75

4107. Animal Hunting Game. 1927. Animals, Board
Game. 100

4108. City of Gold. 1926. Adventure, Board Game. ... 300

4109. Covered Wagon, The Game of. 1927. Western,
Board Game. 250

4110. David Goes to Greenland, The Game of. 1928.
Literary, Board Game. 600

4111. Matchit, The Game of Trees. 1920s. Plants,
Board Game. 75

4112. Tiddledy Winks. Circa 1927. Classic,
Skill Game. 35

4113. Zulu Blowing Game. 1927. Ethnic, Skill Game. 150

Grover C. Zweifel

4114. Zweifel Card Golf. 1932. Sports, Golf, Card
Game. 100

MODERN AGE GAMES

3M Corp.   Price

4116. Acquire. Later Edition, Plastic tiles. Circa 1960s. Economic, Board game. $25

4117. Acquire. © 1963. Economic, Board game, 1st edition, wood tiles. 35

4117a.Backgammon. © 1973, Classic board game. 25

4118. Bazaar, Trading Game. © 1968. Economic, Board game. 30

4119. Big League Baseball. © 1966. Sports, Baseball, Board game. 25

4120. Blue Line Hockey. © 1968. Sports, Hockey, Board game. 35

4121. Break Thru. © 1965. Military, Board game, wheel version, stamped on gold pieces. 35

4121a.Break Thru. As above later edition. 25

4122. Challenge Bridge, flat box edition. © 1972. Classic, Card game. 12

4122a.Challenge Football. © 1975. Sports, Football Board game. 22

4123. Challenge Golf at Pebble Beach. © 1972. Sports, Golf, Board game. 20

4124. Choir, The. Circa 1960s. Miscellaneous, Board game. 15

4125. Contigo. © 1974. Strategy, Board game. 28

4125a.Evade. © 1971, Gamette, strategy board game. 25

4126. Events. © 1974. Historical, Board game. 22

4127. Executive Decision. © 1971. Economic, Board game. 25

4128. Facts in Five. © 1967. Q & A, Board game. 22

4129. Feudal. © 1967. Strategy, Military, Board game. 30

4130. Foil. © 1969. Strategy, Board game. 35

4130a.Foil. © 1971, Strategy, Board game. 15

4130b.Foil. © 1970, as above but gamette. 18

4131. High Bid. © 1965. Economic, Card game, bookshelf edition. 25

4132. High Bid. © 1970. Economic, Card game. 18

4133. High Bid. © 1976. Economic, Card game. 15

4134. High Bid, 1st edition, larger bookshelf box, very rare. © 1963. Economic, Card game. 125

4135. Image. © 1972. Miscellaneous, Board game. 25

4135. Jumpin. © 1964. Metal pawns, Board game. 30

4136. Jumpin. © 1964. Strategy, Board game. 25

4137. Mr. President, 1st edition. © 1961. Political, Board game. 35

4138. Mr. President. © 1965. Political, Board game. ... 25

4139. Mr. President. © 1967. Political, Board game. ... 20

4140. Octrix. © 1970. Strategy, Board game. 15

4141. Oh Wah Ree. © 1962. Strategy, Board game. ... 25

4141a.Oh Wah Ree. © 1966. As above. 20

4142. Phlounder. © 1962. Strategy, Board game, wooden tiles. 45

4142a.Phlounder. As above but plastic tiles. 25

4143. Ploy. Circa 1960s. Strategy, Board game. 25

4144. Point of Law. © 1972. Law & Order, Board game. 22

4145. Pro Football. © 1966. Sports, Football, Board game. 20

4146. Quinto. © 1964. Strategy, Board game. 25

4147. Regatta. © 1966. Sports, Sea, Board game. 20

4148. Sleuth. © 1971. Mystery, Board game. 20

4149. Speed Circuit. © 1971. Sports, Car, Board game. 20

4150. Stocks and Bonds. © 1965. Stock Market, Board game. 25

4151. Thinking Man's Football. © 1969. Sports, Football, Board game. 20

4152. Thinking Man's Golf. © 1966. Sports, Golf, Board game. $30

4153. Twixt. © 1962. Strategy, Board game. 22

4154. Venture. © 1970. Economic, Card game. 20

4155. Venture. Variant Packaging. © 1970. Economic, Card game. 30

4156. Win, Place & Show. © 1966. Sports, Horseracing, Board game. 20

7-Up
4157. We Dunit, New Black History, Premium. © 1965. Ethnic, Card game. 30

20th Century All American Enterprises
4157a. All American Handicap. Circa 1950s. Sports, Horseracing, Record game. 35

A Couple Cowboys
4158. Nightmare, The Video Board Game. © 1990. Monster, Board game. 22

A. P. A. Transport Corp.
4159. Fast Freight Game (A.P.A.), Ad game for transporting. © 1977. Travel, Advertising, Board game. 35

AAA Thought Co. Inc.
4160. Photo-Finish. © 1972. Sports, Horseracing, Board game. 20

ABC Promotions
4161. Dating Game, The, Party Pack, with 45-rpm record. © 1967. TV, Romance, Board game. 30

4162. WABC-TV's Media Careers, Ad Game for TV. © 1977. Advertising, Comics, Board game. 20

A-Be-Co
4163. Music # 1. © 1984. Music, Board game. 15

Abracadabra Games
4164. Word Pyramid. © 1986. Word, Board game. 10

Accu-Stat Game Co.
4165. Pennant Drive. © 1980. Sports, Baseball, Board game. 20

Ace Playing Card Co.
4166. Jet Aircraft. Circa 1970s. Travel, Air, Card game. 12

4167. Racing Cars. Circa 1970s. Travel, Road, Card game. 12

4168. Rockets. Circa 1970s. Space, Card game. 12

4169. Ships. Circa 1970s. Travel, Sea, Card game. 10

4170. Sports Cars. Circa 1970s. Travel, Road, Card game. 12

Acorn Industries
4171. Ben Hur, Chariot Race Game. © 1959. Movie, Board game. $150

Advance Games Co.
4172. 3 Point Landing. Circa 1940s. Travel, Air, Board game. 65
4172a.Bengalee, Game of the East. Circa 1940s, Adventure, Board game. 65
4172b.Happy Horse. Circa 1940s, Animal, Board game. 35

Aid Association for Lutherans
4173. Happy Highway Game, The. © 1989. Religious, Board game. 18

Air-O-Games
4174. Airderby. © 1950. Travel, Air, Board game. 20

Alcazar Games, Inc.
4175. Seige. © 1976. Military, Board game. 22

Aldon
4176. Mighty Mouse Spin Targets Game. © 1958. Cartoon, Action game. 100

A-List Production
4177. Political Influence, An American Tradition. © 1994. Political, Board game. 25
4178. Questionable Integrity. © 1992. Q & A, Board game. 20

All About Town, Inc.
4179. All About (Cities) different city issues. Circa 1980s. Cities & Towns, Board game. 20
4180. All About Cumberland, Maryland. © 1981. Cities & Town, Board game. 20
4181. All About Minneapolis. © 1982. Cities & Towns, Board game. 20

All-Fair
4182. Baseball. © 1946. Sports, Baseball, Board game. 65
4183. Big Chief. Circa 1950s. Western, Board game. 50
4184. Captain Kangaroo/ Mr. Green Jeans. © 1950. TV, Card game. 20
4185. Emit Kelly's Circus Game. © 1953. Circus, Board game. 150
4186. Football. © 1946. Sports, Football, Board game. 75
4187. Jace Pearson's Tales of the Texas Rangers. © 1956. TV, Board game. 100
4188. Pachisi. Circa 1940s. Classic, Board game. 20
4189. Peter Rabbit Rummy. © 1950. Nursery Rhyme, Card game. 15
4190. Pirate's Gold. © 1946. Adventure, Board game. 75
4191. Pot O'Gold. © 1945. Economic, Board game. 50
4192. Pro Locker Basketball. © 1960. Sports, Basketball, Board game. 50
4193. Round Up. © 1946. Western, Board game. 50
4194. Space Mouse. © 1964. Space, Animal, Card game. 25
4195. Spaceship. Circa 1940s. Space, Board game. 200

4196. Spot-A-Plate. Circa 1950s. Miscellaneous, Board game. $50
4197. Sweeps. Hand with money cover. © 1945. Sports, Horseracing, Board game. 50
4198. Sweeps. Man in polka dot suit cover. © 1945. Sports, Horseracing, Board game. 50
4199. Sweeps. Three players with money cover. © 1945. Sports, Horseracing, Board game. 50
4200. No game.
4201. Treasure Hunt. Circa 1950s. Adventure, Board game. 50
4202. Ups and Downs. Circa 1950s. Action, Board game. 35
4203. Wonderful Wizard of Oz, The. Circa 1960s. Literary, Board game. 45
4204. Woody Woodpecker. © 1968. Cartoon, Card game. 22

Layman Allen
4205. Wiff N' Proof. © 1966. Strategy, Board game. 25

Allis-Chalmers
4117a.Hi Lo, The Lift Truck Game. © 1968. Advertizing, Travel, Board game. 90

Allison
4206. Car 54, Where are You? © 1961. TV, Law, Board game. 125
4206a.Highway Traffic Game. © 1957. Travel, Board game. 45

Alpha Games International
4207. Inquizitive. © 1984. Q & A, Board game. 12

Alphxis and Omecyn Enter.
4208. Ords, The Odessey into the 21st Century. © 1993. Space, Board game. 22

Alpsco
4209. Games People Play Game, The, Based on book by E. Berne. © 1967. Literary, Social Concern, Board game. 35

Alucard Ltd.
4210. Chap Acquitted. © 1979. Social Concern, Board game. 20

Amacom
4210a.C. E. O. © 1984. Economic, Board game. 18

Amay
4211. Sniggle. © 1980. Kiddie, Board game. 12

Ambac Inc.
4212. Insure! © 1986. Economic, Board game. 18

America Airlines
4213. Astro World Game, Ad game for Airline. © 1971. Travel, Advertising, Board game. 18

American
4214. Gong Show, The. © 1977. TV, Game, Board game. 15
4215. Treasure Island. © 1954. Adventure, Board game. 20
4216. Wall Street Game, The. © 1986. Stock Market, Board game. 18

American Board Games Inc.
4217. **Popularity Lottery.** Circa 1990s. Gambling,
Board game. $20

American Greetings
4218. **Conrolling Interest.** © 1972. Economic, Board
game. 20
4219. **Linkup.** © 1972. Strategy, Board game. 15

American Iguana Inc.
4219a.**Class.** © 1970. Social, Board game. 30

American Management Associations
4219b.**CEO.** © 1984. Economic, Board game. 22

American Publishing Corp.
4219a.**Maloney's Pub.** © 1978. Drinking, Board game. 30
4220. **Monster Madness.** © 1990. Monster, Board
game. 20
4221. **Credibility Gap.** © 1967. Social Concern, Board
game. 25
4222. **Thrift, A Banking Game, Premium, Lincoln
Bank.** © 1963. Economic, Board game. 25
4223. **Hobbit Game, The.** © 1977. Fantasy, Board
game. 20
4223a.**Police Surgeon Game.** For Colgate-
Palmolive Co. © 1972. TV, Premium,
Board game. 45
4224. **Ski Gammon.** © 1962. Sports, Ski, Board game. 35
4225. **White Cover Girl, A Manpower Game.** ©
1966. Career, Board game. 35

American Radar Corp.
4226. **Radaronics.** © 1946. Military, Board game. 50

American Symboug Corp.
4227. **Watergate Scandal, The.** © 1973. History,
Political, Card game. 25

American Toy and Furniture
4227a.**Time Machine, The.** © 1963. Board game. 100

American Toys
4228. **Rocket Patrol Magnet Target Game.** Circa
1950s. Space, Action game. 20
4229. **Stadium Checkers.** © 1952. Strategy, Board
game. 30

Ampersand Press
4230. **AC/DC.** Circa 1990s. Educational, Board game. 8
4231. **Bug Game, The.** © 1994. Animal, Card game. 8
4232. **Garden Game, The.** © 1996. Plant, Board
game. 8
4233. **Good Heavens.** Circa 1990s. Space, Board
game. 8
4234. **Humming Bird Game, The.** Circa 1990s.
Animal, Card game. 8
4235. **Into the Forest.** Circa 1990s. Plant, Board
game. 8
4236. **Krill, A Whale of a Game.** © 1981. Animal,
Card game. 12
4237. **Oh Wilderness.** Circa 1990s. Adventure, Board
game. 8
4238. **Onto the Desert.** © 1995. Animal, Card game. 8
4239. **Pollination Game, The.** Circa 1990s. Plant,
Board game. 8
4240. **Predator - The Food Chain Card Game.** ©
1973. Animal, Card game. 15

Amsco Toys
4241. **Amsco Chaos.** © 1965. Economic, Board game. $22
4242. **Grand Prix.** © 1966. Sports, Car, Board game. 25
4243. **Marble Raceway.** © 1964. Miscellaneous,
Action game. 25
4244. **Rocket Satellite Action Game.** © 1952. Space,
Action game. 60
4245. **Roy Rogers Magic Play-Around Game.** ©
1955. Western, Personal, Board game. 125

AMV Publications
4246. **Pocket Football.** © 1992. Sports, Football, Board
game. 12

Amway
4247. **Sly.** © 1975. Strategy, Board game. 15

Animal Town Game Co.
4248. **Chicken in Every Pot, A.** Circa 1980s. Animal,
Board game. 15
4249. **Peter Principle Game, The.** © 1976. Social Concern, Board game. 22
4250. **Save the Whales.** © 1978. Animal, Board game. 25

Ralph Anspach
4251. **Anti.** © 1973. Economic, Board game. 25
4252. **Anti-Monopoly.** Circa 1960s. Economic, Board
game. 25
4253. **Anti-Monopoly, green box.** © 1968. Economic,
Board game. 25
4254. **Anti-Monopoly III, Star Peace.** © 1987.
Economic, Board game. 35

Ansudon
4255. **Baseball Action.** Miscellaneous, Sports,
Baseball, Board game. 20

Antfamco
4255a.**Oil Power.** © 1980. Oil, Board game. 50

Anti-Monopoly Inc.
4256. **Anti-Monopoly.** © 1973. Economic, Board
game. 25

APBA
4244a.**APBA,** team envelopes sell for $ 7-10 each
4257. **APBA Baseball Master Game, each year 1960s.**
Circa 1960s. Sports, Baseball, Board game. 100
4258. **APBA Baseball Master Game, each year 1970s.**
Circa 1970s. Sports, Baseball, Board game. 75
4259. **APBA Baseball Master Game, each year 1980s.**
Circa 1980s. Sports, Baseball, Board game. 50

APBA continued

4260. APBA Baseball Master Game, each year 1990s. Circa 1990s. Sports, Baseball, Board game. $25

4261. APBA Major League Baseball Game, 1st edition. © 1951. Sports, Baseball, Board game. 150

4262. APBA Major League Baseball Game, each year 1950s. Circa 1950s. Sports, Baseball, Board game. 125

4263. APBA Pro Basketball, 1st edition. © 1965. Sports, Basketball, Board game. 150

4264. APBA Pro Basketball, last edition. © 1991. Sports, Basketball, Board game. 25

4265. APBA Pro Basketball, later editions each year 1960s. Circa 1960s. Sports, Basketball, Board game. 75

4266. APBA Pro Basketball, later editions each year 1970s. Circa 1970s. Sports, Basketball, Board game. 50

4267. APBA Pro Basketball, later editions each year 1980s. Circa 1980s. Sports, Basketball, Board game. 35

4268. APBA Pro Bowling, 1st edition. © 1979. Sports, Bowling, Board game. 65

4269. APBA Pro Bowling, later editions each year 1990s. Circa 1990s. Sports, Bowling, Board game. 25

4270. APBA Pro Bowling, later editions each year 1980s. Circa 1980s. Sports, Bowling, Board game. 30

4271. APBA Pro Golf, issued intermittently. Circa 1970-90s. Sports, Golf, Board game. 25

4272. APBA Pro Golf, 1st Edition. © 1963. Sports, Golf, Board game. 75

4273. APBA Pro Hockey, 1st edition. © 1993. Sports, Hockey, Board game. 35

4274. APBA Pro Hockey, later editions each year 1990s. Circa 1990s. Sports, Hockey, Board game. 25

4275. APBA Pro League Football, 1st edition. © 1958. Sports, Football, Board game. 125

4276. APBA Pro League Football, 2nd edition. © 1959. Sports, Football, Board game. 75

4277. APBA Pro League Football, later editions each year 1960s. Circa 1960s. Sports, Football, Board game. 60

4278. APBA Pro League Football, later editions each year 1970s. Circa 1970s. Sports, Football, Board game. 50

4279. APBA Pro League Football, later editions each year 1980s. Circa 1980s. Sports, Football, Board game. 35

4280. APBA Pro League Football, later editions each year 1990s. Circa 1990s. Sports, Football, Board game. 25

4281. APBA Saddle Racing Game, 1st Edition. © 1971. Sports, Horseracing, Board game. 50

4282. APBA Saddle Racing Game, later edition year 1970s. Circa 1970s. Sports, Horseracing, Board game. 35

4283. APBA Saddle Racing Game, later edition each year 1990s. Circa 1990s. Sports, Horseracing, Board game. 20

4284. APBA Saddle Racing Game, later editions each year 1980s. Circa 1980s. Sports, Horseracing, Board game. 25

Apjac

4285. Doctor Dolittle's Magic Answer Machine. © 1967. Movie, Board game. $20

Apple Street

4286. Family Ties Game. © 1986. TV, Board game. 18

ARC

4287. Superstar TV Sports. © 1980. Sports, Miscellaneous, Board game. 25

Archie

4288. Advertizement Game, The. Miscellaneous, Advertising, Board game. 25

Arco Ind. Ltd.

4289. Flintstone Quick Score Target Game, The. © 1977. TV, Cartoon, Skill game. 50

Ariel

4290. Taxi! Circa 1980s. TV, Board game. 20

Ari-Hi Co.

4291. I-Qubes. © 1948. Word, Dice game. 10

Aristoplay Inc.

4292. A Time for Native Americans. © 1993. Indians, Card game. 8

4293. Alpha Animals Game. © 1992. Animal, Board game. 15

4294. By Jove. Circa 1980s. History, Board game. 18

4295. Constellation Station. © 1993. Space, Board game. 18

4296. Dinosaurs and Things. Circa 1990s. Animal, Board game. 15

4297. Friends Around the World, A Game of World Peace. Circa 1990s. Social, Board game. 18

4298. Herd Your Horses! © 1993. Animals, Board game. 15

4299. Knights and Castles. © 1990. Military, Board game. 18

4300. Land Ho/ Terra Terra. © 1990. Travel, History, Board game. 18

4301. Ludi at the Circus Maximus. Circa 1990s. History, Word, Board game. 15

4302. Made for Trade. Circa 1980s. Economic, Board game. 18

4303. Music Maestro II. Circa 1982-88. Music, Board game. 18

4304. Nova True Science. © 1994. TV, Science, Board game. 15

4305. Play's the Thing, The, Introduction to Shakespeare. © 1994. Literary, History, Board game. ... 18

4306. Pollution Solution, The Game of. © 1989. Social Concern, Board game. 20

4307. Pyramids and Mummies. Circa 1990s. History, Puzzle game. 18

4308. Stelescope Constellation Station, The. © 1990. Space, Board game. 18

4309. Time for Native Americans, The. Circa 1990s. Ethnic, Card game. 18

4310. Where in the World. © 1986. Geography, Board game. 15

Arkco

4311. Party - Movies & TV. © 1985. Movies & TV, Card game. 12

Arkco continued

4312. Trivia Party - Literature & Arts. © 1985. Literary, Q & A D, D, Trivia Party - Movies & TV, Card game. $12

4313. Trivia Party - Movies and TV. © 1985. Movie, TV, Card game. 12

4314. Trivia Party - Music. © 1985. Music, Q & A, Card game. 12

4315. Trivia Party - People. © 1985. History, Q & A, Card game. 12

4316. Trivia Party - Pot Luck. © 1985. Q & A, Card game. 12

4317. Trivia Party - Sports. © 1985. Sports, Q & A, Card game. 12

Armadillo Games

4318. Toxins. © 1983. Social Concern, Board game. 20

Arrco Playing Card Co.

4319. Skeeter. Circa 1970s. Miscellaneous, Card game. 15

4320. Space-O. Circa 1960s. Space, Card game. 20

Artcraft Paper Prod.

4321. Fore. © 1954. Sports, Golf, Board game. 25

Ashburn Industries Inc.

4322. Baseball's Greatest Moments. © 1979. Sports, Baseball, Board game. 20

4323. Longball. © 1975. Sports, Baseball, Board game. 25

Athletic Products Inc.

4324. Dave Garroway's Game of Possesion. © 1955. TV, Personality, Board game. 75

4325. Today with Dave Garroway. Circa 1950s. TV, Board game. 125

Athol-Research

4326. Creature Features. © 1975. Monster, Board game. 22

Aulic Council

4327. Jack the Ripper. © 1983. Law & Order, Board game. 18

Aurora

4328. ABC Monday Night Football. © 1972. Sports, Football, Board game. 75

4329. Aurora Derby. © 1970. Sports, Horseracing, Board game. 35

4330. Can-Doo. Circa 1970s. Skill, Action game. 15

4331. Flip-It Jackpot. © 1973. Gambling, Action game. 15

4332. Jimmy the Greek Odds Maker Poker-Dice. © 1974. Personality, Gambling, Dice game. 10

4333. Jimmy the Greek Oddsmaker Football. © 1974. Sports, Football, Board game. 25

4334. Karate Men Fighting Action Game. © 1970. Military, Action game. 40

4335. Monday Night Baseball. © 1973. Sports, Baseball, Board game. 35

4336. No game

4337. Pursuit! © 1973. Military, WWI, Board game. 25

4338. Roger Staubach ABC Monday Night Football. © 1973. Sports, Football, Board game. 85

4339. Skittle Baseball. © 1973. Sports, Baseball, Board game. $18

4340. Skittle-Bowl. © 1969. Classic, Action game. 15

Avalon Hill

4341. Acquire. © 1976. Economic, Board game. 30

4342. Air Empire. © 1961. Economic, Tr, Board game. 75

4343. Bali. © 1980. Miscellaneous, Card game. 15

4344. Baseball Strategy. © 1973. Sports, Baseball, Board game. 22

4345. Basketball Strategy. © 1974. Sports, Basketball, Board game. 20

4346. Beat Inflation Strategy Game, The. © 1975. Social Concern, Board game. 20

4347. Black Magic Valor Kit. © 1974. Fantasy, Board game. 18

4348. Blind Justice, The Game of Lawsuits. Circa 1990s. Law & Order, Board game. 18

4349. Book of Lists, The. © 1979. Q & A, Board game. 15

4350. Bureaucracy. © 1981. Social Concern, Board game. 22

4351. Business Strategy. Circa 1980s. Economic, Board game. 28

4352. Candidate. Circa 1990s. Political, Board game. 20

4353. Challange Football. Circa 1980s. Sports, Football, Board game. 20

4354. Challenge Basketball All-Stars. Circa 1980s. Sports, Basketball, Board game. 20

4355. Civilization. © 1982. History, Board game. 22

4356. Collector, The. © 1977. Economic, Board game. 20

4357. Decathlon. Circa 1990s. Sports, Board game. 18

4358. Dinosaurs of the Lost World. © 1989. Animal, Board game. 15

4359. Diplomacy. © 1976. International, Board game. 25

4360. Dispatcher. © 1958. Travel, Rail, Board game. 85

4361. Dragonhunt. © 1982. Fantasy, Board game. 18

4362. Dune. © 1979. Science Fiction, Board game. 18

4363. Elric. © 1984. Fantasy, Board game. 15

4364. Feudal. © 1976. Strategy, Military, Board game. 15

4365. Foreign Exchange. © 1979. Economic, Board game. 20

4366. Gold! © 1981. Economic, Board game. 20

4367. Gunslingers. © 1982. Western, Board game. 20

4368. Image. © 1977. History, Board game. 15

4369. Journey's of St. Paul. © 1968. Religious, Board game. 30

4370. Le Mans. © 1961. Sports, Cars, Board game. 50

4371. Magic Realm. © 1978. Mystic, Board game. 15

4372. Management. © 1961. Economic, Board game. 55

4373. Nieuchess. © 1961. Strategy, Board game. 65

4374. Origins of World War II. © 1971. Military, Board game. 20

4375. Outdoor Survival, 2nd Printing. © 1973. Social Concern, Board game. 20

Avalon Hill continued

4376. Paydirt! Circa 1980s. Sports, Football, Board game. $20

4377. Peter Principle Game, The. © 1981. Social Concern, Board game. 18

4378. Rail Baron. ©1977. Travel, Rail, Board game. 20

4379. Shakespeare, The Game of. © 1966. Literary, Board game. 30

4380. Showbiz, The Entertainment Game. Circa 1990s. Entertain, Board game. 20

4381. Slapshot. © 1982. Sports, Hockey, Board game. 25

4382. Smokers Wild. © 1981. Social Concern, Board game. 20

4383. Source of the Nile. © 1979. Adventure, Board game. 18

4384. Squander. © 1965. Social Concern, Board game. 20

4385. Statis Pro Baseball. © 1978. Sports, Baseball, Board game. 20

4386. Statis Pro Major League Game of Pro-Baseball. © 1979. Sports, Baseball, Board game. ... 18

4387. Stock Market Game, The. Circa 1970s. Stock Market, Board game. 20

4388. Stocks and Bonds. Circa 1970s. Stock Market, Board game. 20

4389. Superstar Baseball. Circa 1960s. Sports, Baseball, Board game. 18

4390. Trivia, Game of, Set 1. © 1981. Q & A, Board game. 15

4391. Tuf, A Game of Math. Circa 1970s. Numbers, Board game. 12

4392. Tuf-Abet. Circa 1970s. Word, Board game. 12

4393. TV Wars. Circa 1990s. Communications, Board game. 20

4394. UFO. © 1978. Science Fiction, Board game. 18

4395. Up Front. © 1983. Miscellaneous, Card game. 12

4396. Verdict II. © 1961. Law, Board game. 35

4397. We the People. © 1993. Political, Board game. 20

4398. Win, Place and Show. © 1977. Sports, Golf, Board game. 18

4399. Wizard's Quest. © 1979. Mystic, Board game. 15

4400. Yellowstone. Circa 1990s. Plant, Board game. 20

Avalon Hill, McCormick

4401. Good Cooking, The Game of. Circa 1990s. Food, Board game. 25

4402. Spices of the World, Ad Game with Spice Company. Circa 1990s. Food, Board game. 30

Avalon Hill-Sports Illustrated

4403. Bowl Bound. © 1978. Sports, Football, Board game. 18

4404. Football Strategy. Circa 1980s. Sports, Football, Board game. 18

4405. Pro Golf. © 1982. Sports, Golf, Board game. 18

4406. Pro Tennis. Circa 1980s. Sports, Tennis, Board game. 25

4407. Title Bout. Circa 1980s. Sports, Boxing, Board game. 20

Avcoin Management, Inc.

4408. Kiss. © 1978. Music, Board game. 35

Avon

4409. Moon Flight. © 1970. Space, Board game. 35

B & B

4410. Race Trap. Circa 1950s. Sports, Car, Board game. $25

B & F Marketing Inc.

4410a. Challenge the I. R. S. © 1975. Political, Economic, Board game. 25

B. Dazzle Inc.

4411. Scrambled Squares. © 1994. Skill, Board game. 8

4412. Scrambled Squares Ferocious Felines. © 1994. Animal, Card game. 8

4413. Scrambled Squares Soccer. © 1944. Sports, Soccer, Card game. 8

Bakers Chocolate

4414. Pantomine Quiz, Chocolate premium. © 1953. Q & A, Board game. 30

Baldemar Sanchez

4415. Escalation. © 1990. Military, Board game. 20

Baldwin Mfg. Co.

4416. King Pin Deluxe Bowling Alley. © 1947. Sports, Bowling, Board game. 60

4417. Par-A-Shoot Game. © 1947. Sports, Golf, Action game. 100

Rigely Banada

4418. Tournament Golf. © 1969. Sports, Golf, Board game. 25

F. J. Bandholtz

4419. Give. © 1949. Economic, Board game. 40

Banlee

4420. Billy Blastoff Space Game. © 1969. Space, Board game. 45

J. Banning

4421. Jack Bannings Putt-Pins (Bowling-Golf). Circa 1950s. Sports, Bowling, Golf, Board game. 20

BAOA, Inc.

4138a. Black Americans Of Achievement, The Game. © 1993. Ethnic, Board game. 20

Bardell

4422. Huckleberry Hound Spin-O Game. © 1959. TV, cartoon, Board game. 60

Bare Brothers

4423. World Class Liar. Circa 1990s. Strategy, Card game. 8

Baron/Scott Ent. Inc.

4424. Fart the Game. © 1990. Social, Board game. 12

4425. Lifestyles of the Poor and Disgusting. Circa 1980s. Social Concern, Board game. 20

4426. Sexual Trivia. Circa 1980s. Romance, Board game. 20

Barris Corp.

4427. Birdie Golf. © 1964. Sports, Golf, Board game. 45

Bancroft Barrow
4428. Art Game, The. © 1981. Art, Board game. $20

Barton-Cotton, Inc.
4429. Smokey. Circa 1950s. Social Concern, Board
game. 200

Bar-Zim
4429a.Haul the Freight. © 1962. Trucking,
Board game. 75
4430. Romper Room Magic Teacher. Circa 1960s. TV,
Board game. 50

Beck Design
4431. Watergate. © 1973. Political, History,
Board game. 25

Belith Enterprises
4432. Bileth Baseball. Miscellaneous, Sports, Baseball,
Board game. 20

Bell Telephone of PA.
4433. Diablo, The Safe-Driving Game. © 1957.
Education, Car, Board game. 30

Benchmark, Inc.
4433a.Bulls and Bears. © 1992. Wall Street, Board
game. 20

Donald E. Benge

4434. Conquest. © 1972. Military, Board game. 50

Berkshire Game Co.
4435. Divorce, of Course. © 1983. Social Concern,
Board game. 20

Better Games Inc.
4436. Dollars and Sense. © 1980. Economic, Board
game. 20

Bettye-B Pro.
4437. Adventures of Robin Hood, The. © 1956.
Adventure, Board game. 75
4438. B. T. O., Big Time Operator. © 1956. Economic,
Board game. 100
4439. Break the Bank, Photo of Bert Parks. © 1955.
TV, Game, Board game. 50
4440. High Dice. © 1956. Miscellaneous, Dice game. 15
4441. Masquerade Party. © 1955. TV, Board game. 75
4442. Trapped. © 1956. Mystery, Board game. 125

Betzold Games, Inc.
4443. Revelation. © 1984. Religious, Board game. $18

Bible Games Inc.
4444. Bible Challenge. © 1984. Religious, Board
game. 15

Bicycle Games
4445. Garfield Card Game. © 1978. Comics, Card
game. 15

Big Apple Game Co.
4446. Big Apple. © 1976. Cities & Towns, Board
game. 20

Big Fun A Go Go, Inc.
4447. TriBond. © 1989. Q & A, Board game. 15

Big League Game Co.
4448. Dan Kerateter's Classic Football. © 1971.
Sports, Football, Board game. 25

Big League Promotions
4449. NFL Playoff, Various teams. © 1991. Sports,
Football, Board game. 15

Big Top Games
4449a.Crazy Horse. © 1957. Board game. 22
4449b.Farm Management Game. © 1961. Farm,
Board game. 65
4450. Par, 73. © 1961. Sports, Golf, Board game. 22

Billy and Ruth Promotion
4451. Billy and Ruth, premium. © 1954. Premium,
Board game. 30

Marceil G. Bishop
4451a.Symphony Lotto. © 1956. Music, Card game. 35

BLM
4452. Big League Manager Basketball. © 1965.
Sports, Basketball, Board game. 30
4453. Big League Manager Football. © 1965. Sports,
Football, Board game. 30

Blossom Design
4454. Sailor's Game, The. © 1986. Sports, Sea, Board
game. 25

Bobron Brothers
4455. Auto Dealership. © 1982. Economic, Board
game. 20

J. L. Boler
4456. Nuclear Escape. © 1985. Military, Board game. 20

Bond Sports Enterprises
4457. Replay Series Baseball. © 1983. Sports,
Baseball, Board game. 15

Fred Bonner Corp.
4458. Matchbox, Traffic Game. © 1968. Toy, Car,
Board game. 50

Boyce & Elggren Inc.
4459. Double Talk 2nd Edition. © 1992. Social, Board
game. $17

Boynton Games
4460. USA Trivia. © 1989. Q & A, Board game. 15

Milton Bradley
4461. $10,000 Pyramid Game, The. © 1974. TV,
Game, Board game. 25

4462. $20,000 Pyramid. © 1975. TV, Game, Board
game. 20

4463. 12 O'Clock High. © 1965. TV, Military II, Card
game. 35

4464. 13 Dead End Drive. © 1993. Mystery, Board
game. 25

4465. 4 Alarm. © 1963. Adventure, Board game. 20

4466. 4 Cyte, The Championship Word Game. ©
1967. Word, Board game. 15

4468. Acme Checkout Game. © 1959. Economic,
Board game. 50

4469. Addams Family Card Game, The. © 1965. TV,
Monster, Card game. 50

4470. Addams Family, The. © 1974. Monster, Board
game. 18

4471. Air Combat. © 1968. Military, Board game. 25

4472. Air Trix, The Airstream Game. © 1976. Skill,
Action game. 15

4473. All in the Family Game, The. © 1972. TV,
Board game. 18

4474. Allan Sherman's Camp Granada Game. ©
1965. Personality, Board game. 50

4475. Allowance Game. © 1979. Economic, Board
game. 18

4476. Alumni Fun. © 1964. TV, Board game. 18

**4477. Amazing Spider-Man Game with the Fantastic
Four, The.** © 1977. Super Heroes, Board game. 22

4478. Amazing Spiderman Game, The. © 1967.
Super Heroes, Board game. 50

4479. America Heritage Game of Civil War. © 1961.
Military, Civil War, Board game. 30

4480. American Airlines Travel Game. © 1955.
Travel, Board game. 30

4481. American Airlines Travel Games, Premium. ©
1955. Premium, Travel, Board game. 30

4482. American Dream, The. © 1979. Economic,
Board game. 20

4483. Animal Crackers Game. © 1979.
Miscellaneous, Board game. $18

4484. Animal Fun Game. © 1953. Animal, Board
game. 18

4485. Animal Twister. © 1967. Animal, Board game. 15

4486. Annie Oakley Game. Circa 1960s. TV, Western,
Board game. 45

4487. Annie Oakley Game. Variant Cover. Circa
1960s. TV, Western, Board game. 45

4488. Apple's Way. © 1974. TV, Board game. 18

4489. Archie Bunker's Card Game. © 1972. TV, Card
game. 20

4490. Around the World. © 1962. Q & A, Board
game. 25

4491. Autofun. © 1963. Travel, Board game. 15

4492. Axis and Allies. © 1986. Military, WWII, Board
game. 35

4493. Babar and His Friends, See-Saw. © 1960.
Literary, Board game. 35

4494. Back off Buzzard. © 1991. Skill, Action game. 12

4495. Balaroo. © 1967. Skill, Action game. 15

4496. Bamboozle. © 1962. TV, Board game. 20

4497. Baretta, The Street Detective Game. © 1976.
TV, Detective, Board game. 18

4498. Bargain Hunter. © 1981. Economic, Board
game. 15

4499. Barnabas Collins Game Dark Shadows. ©
1969. TV, Monster, Board game. 35

4500. Bash! © 1965. Skill, Action game. 15

4501. Batman Jigsaw Puzzle Game. © 1966. Super
Heroes, Puzzle game. 45

4502. Batman Mini Board Card game. © 1964. Super
Hero, Card game. 45

4503. Batman, The Game of. © 1966. Super Heroes,
Board game. 40

4504. Battle Cry. © 1975. Military, WWII, Board
game. 25

4505. Battle of the Planets. © 1979. TV, Science
Fiction, Board game. 18

4506. Battle-Cry, American Heritage Series. © 1961.
Military, Civil War, Board game. 45

4507. Battleship, Photo cover. © 1967. Military, Board
game. 12

4508. Beat the Clock Game. © 1969. TV, Game, Board
game. 25

4509. Beatles, Flip Your Wig Game, The. © 1964.
Music, Board game. 100

4510. Beetle Bailey, The Old Army Game. © 1963.
Comics, Board game. 65

4511. Bermuda Triangle Game. © 1976. Adventure,
Board game. 22

4512. Beverly Hillbillies Card Game, The. © 1963.
TV, Card game. 25

4513. Beverly Hills, 90210. © 1991. TV, Card game. 12

4514. Bid it Right, The Price is Right. © 1964. TV,
Game, Card game. 15

4515. Big Foot. © 1977. Monster, Board game. 15

4516. Big Town. © 1962. Travel, Land, Board game. 35

4517. Bird Barn. © 1966. Animal, Board game. 20

4518. Blop. © 1966. Skill, Board game. 15

4519. Bobbin Noggin. © 1964. Skill, Action game. 115

4520. Bobbsey Twins, The. © 1957. Literary, TV,
Board game. 20

4521. Bockaroo. Circa 1950s. Western, Board game. 15

4522. Body English. © 1967. Skill, Action game. 15

4523. Body Language with Lucille Ball. © 1975. TV,
Personality, Board game. 20

Milton Bradley continued

4524. Boob Tube. © 1962. Skill, Board game. $15

4525. Brainwaves. © 1977. Strategy, Board game. 12

4526. Branded Game. © 1966. TV, Western, Board
game. 40

4527. Broadside, American Heritage Series. © 1962.
Military, Board game. 125

4528. Broadside. © 1975. Military, Board game. 35

4529. Broadsides & Boarding Parties. © 1984.
Military, Board game. 22

4530. Buck Rogers Game. © 1979. Super Hero, Space,
TV, Board game. 35

4531. Bucket of Fun. © 1968. Skill, Action game. 15

4531a. Bugs Bunny Adventure Game. Bugs in hole
cover, Circa 1950s, Cartoons, Board game. 40

**4532. Bugs Bunny Adventure Game, Blue Bugs
cover.** © 1961. Cartoons, Board game. 40

4533. Bullwinkle Hide 'N Seek. © 1961. Cartoon, TV,
Board game. 75

4534. By the Numbers. © 1962. TV, Game, Board
game. 22

4535. Call My Bluff. © 1965. TV, Game, Board game. 20

4536. Camouflage. © 1961. TV, Board game. 18

4537. Candyland Game. © 1962. Kiddie, Board
game. 45

4538. Candyland. © 1955. Kiddie, Board game. 45

4539. Captain Kangaroo Tic Tagaroo. © 1956. TV,
Board game. 32

4540. Captain America Game. © 1966. Super Hero,
Board game. 60

4541. Captain America Game. © 1977. Super Heroes,
Board game. 20

4542. Captain and the Kids. © 1947. Comics, Board
game. 125

4543. Captain Caveman and the Teen Angels Game.
© 1980. Cartoon, TV, Board game. 15

4544. Captain Video. © 1954. TV, Space, Board
game. 125

4545. Car Travel Game. © 1958. Travel, Car, Board
game. 25

4546. Carol Burnett's Card Game. © 1964.
Personality, Card game. 22

4547. Carrier Strike! © 1977. Military, Board game. 35

**4548. Cartoon Cards, with Flintstones, Pink Panther,
Yogi Etc.** © 1979. Cartoon, Card game. 22

4548a. Casper the Friendly Ghost Game. Small red
box, Circa 1950s, Cartoons, Board game. 60

4549. Casper the Friendly Ghost Game. Blue box, ©
1959. Comics, Cartoon, Board game. 25

4550. Cenepede. © 1983. Game, Board game. 18

4551. Championship Baseball. © 1984. Sports,
Baseball, Board game. 20

4552. Charles Goren's Advanced Bridge for One. ©
1967. Classic, Card game. 15

4553. Charles Goren's Beginner's Bridge. © 1965.
Classic, Card game. 15

4554. Charles Goren's Bridge for One. © 1967.
Classic, Card game. 15

4555. Charles Goren's Bridge for Two. © 1964.
Classic, Card game. 15

4556. Charlie's Angles Game, Cheryl on cover. ©
1978. TV, Detective, Board game. 25

4557. Charlie's Angles Game, Farrah on cover. ©
1977. TV, Detective, Board game. 25

4558. Chaseback. © 1962. Skill, Board game. 10

4559. Cherry Street. © 1966. TV, Mystery, Board
game. 15

4560. Chevyland Sweepstakes, Ad game for car. ©
1968. Advertising, Board game. 30

4561. Cheyenne Game, Clint Walker with pistol. ©
1957. TV, Western, Board game. $60

4562. Cheyenne Game, Picture of Ty Hardin. ©
1958. TV, Western, Board game. 50

4563. Chicken Out. © 1966. Animal, Board game. 15

4564. Chips Game. © 1977. TV, Law & Order, Board
game. 18

4565. Chit Chat. © 1963. Words, Card game. 15

4566. Chitty Chitty Bang Bang. © 1968. Movie,
Board game. 30

4567. Choo Choo Charlie Game. © 1969. Travel, Rail,
Board game. 30

4568. Chopper Strike. © 1976. Military, Board game. 18

**4569. Chuggedy Chug, Paul Winchell & Jerry
Mahoney.** © 1955. TV, Personality, Board game. 50

4570. Chutes and Ladders, Children at slide box. ©
1956. Classic, Board game. 20

4571. Chutes and Ladders, Red box. Circa 1950s.
Classic, Board game. 22

**4572. Civil War, Game of the, American Heritage
Series.** © 1961. Military, Civil War, Board game. 55

4573. Clickety-Clak. © 1953. Kiddie, Board game. 20

4574. Columbo Detective Game. © 1973. TV,
Detective, Board game. 18

4575. Combat. © 1965. TV, Card game. 20

4576. Comic Card Game. © 1972. Comics, Card
game. 30

**4577. Concentration, 3rd Edition, Lower blue band
cover.** © 1960. TV, Game, Board game. 20

**4578. Concentration, 9th Edition, Upper red band
cover.** © 1964. TV, Game, Board game. 15

4579. Concentration, 1st Edition. © 1958. TV, Game,
Board game. 22

4580. Connect Four. © 1974. Strategy, Board game. 10

4581. Conquest of the Empire. © 1984. Military,
Board game. 45

4582. Conspiracy. © 1982. Law & Order, Board
game. 12

4583. Cracker Jack Game, Ad game for candy. ©
1976. Advertising, Board game. 18

4584. Crocodile Dentist. © 1991. Kiddie, Board
game. 10

4585. Cross Up, Lucille Ball photo on cover. © 1974.
Word, Card game. 15

4586. Cut Up Shopping Spree Game. © 1968.
Economic, Board game. 18

4587. Dark Shadows. © 1969. TV, Monster, Board
game. 35

4588. Dastardly and Muttley. © 1969. TV, Cartoon,
Board game. 30

4589. Day with Ziggy, A. © 1977. TV, Cartoon, Board
game. 15

4590. Dead Stop! Game. © 1979. Strategy, Board
game. 10

4591. Deputy Dawg Game. © 1960. TV, Cartoon,
Board game. 45

4592. Deputy Game, The. © 1960. TV, Western, Board
game. 55

Milton Bradley continued

4593. Disney Presents Follow that Mouse Game. ©
1986. Disney, Board game. $15

4594. Disney's All Aboard Game. © 1986. Disney,
Board game. 15

4595. Disney's Chip & Dale Rescue Rangers. © 1992.
Disney, Board game. 15

4596. Disney's Darkwing Duck Game. © 1993.
Disney, Board game. 15

4597. Disney's Duck Tales Game. © 1990. Disney,
Board game. 15

4598. Disney's Tale Spin Game. © 1992. Disney,
Board game. 15

4599. Disney's The Hunchback of Notre Dame. Circa
1990s. Disney, Board game. 15

4600. Diver Dan, Tug-O-War Game. © 1961. TV,
Board game. 45

4601. Dogfight, American Heritage Series. © 1963.
Military, WWI, Board game. 50

4602. Dolly and Daniel Whale Game. © 1963. TV,
Animal, Board game. 40

4603. Domination. © 1982. Strategy, Board game. 10

4604. Donkey Kong. © 1981. Game, Board game. 12

4605. Doubletrack. © 1981. Skill, Board game. 10

4606. Drag Strip! © 1965. Sports, Car, Board game. 35

4607. Dream House TV Home Game. © 1968. TV,
Game, Board game. 18

4608. Drop in the Bucket. Circa 1960s. Skill, Action
game. 12

4609. Duran Duran Game, In the Arena. © 1985.
Music, Board game. 75

4610. Dynamite Shack Game. © 1968. Skill, Action
game. 15

4611. Dyno Mutt, The. © 1977. TV, Board game. 20

4612. Easy Money, The Game of. Circa 1950s.
Economic, Board game. 30

4613. Easy Money. © 1974. Economic, Board game. 22

4614. Electronic Battleship. © 1977. Military, Board
game. 18

4615. Electronic Battleship. © 1979. Military, Board
game. 15

4616. Electronic Mall Madness. © 1990. Social
Concern, Board game. 15

4617. Electronic Stratego. Circa 1980s. Strategy,
Military, Board game. 15

4618. Emergency Game. © 1974, Miscellaneous, TV,
Board game. 25

4619. Enemy Agent, The game of foreign intrigue. ©
1976. Spy, Board game. 18

**4620. Enter the Dangerous World of James Bond
007.** © 1965. Spy, Board game. 22

4621. Exit. © 1983. Miscellaneous, Board game. $12

4622. Expanse. © 1950. Travel, Board game. 40

4623. Eye Guess. © 1966. TV, Game, Board game. 15

4624. Eye Witness, What Do You Remember? Game.
© 1971. Memory, Board game. 18

4625. F Troop Mini-Board Card game. © 1965. TV,
Military, Card game. 45

4626. Fact Finder Fun. © 1964. Q & A, Board game. 15

4627. Family Feud. © 1977. TV, Game, Board game. 15

4628. Fang Bang. © 1967. Skill, Action game. 20

4629. Fantastic Four Featuring Herbie the Rocket. ©
1978. Super Heroes, Board game. 20

4630. Fantastic Voyage Game. © 1968. Cartoon, TV,
Board game. 25

4631. Fastest Gun. © 1974. Western, Board game. 20

4632. Fat Albert and The Cosby Kids. © 1973. TV,
Cartoon, Board game. 18

4633. FBI Crime Resistance Game. © 1976. Law &
Order, Board game. 35

4634. Feeley Meeley. © 1967. Skill, Action game. 15

4635. Felix the Cat Game. © 1960. Cartoon, TV, Board
game. 40

4636. Felix the Cat. © 1968. Comics, Board game. 30

4637. Fess Parker Trail Blazers Game. © 1964. TV,
Western, Board game. 35

4638. Finders Keepers. © 1968. Strategy, Board
game. 15

4639. Fireball XL5. © 1964. TV, Science Fiction,
Board game. 125

4640. Flagship Airfreight, The Airline Cargo Game.
© 1946. Travel, Air, Board game. 75

4641. Flintstones Game, The. © 1971. TV, Cartoon,
Board game. 25

4642. Flintstones Game, The. © 1980. TV, Cartoon,
Board game. 18

4643. Flying Nun, The. © 1968. TV, Board game. 25

4644. Fonz, Hang Out At Arnolds, The. © 1976. TV,
Board game. 20

4645. Foresight. © 1962. Miscellaneous, Board game. 15

4646. Forest Friends. © 1962. Animal, Board game. 18

4647. Forest Friends. © 1956. Animal, Board game. 20

4648. Fortress America. © 1986. Military, Board
game. 35

4649. Frantic Frogs Game, Windup frogs. © 1965.
Animal, Board game. 30

4650. Fun on the Farm. © 1947. Economic, Board
game. 40

4651. Fun on the Farm. © 1957. Animal, Board
game. 30

4652. Funky Phantom Game. © 1971. TV, Cartoon,
Board game. 20

4653. G.I. Joe. © 1987. Toy, Military, Board game. 15

4654. Geography Lotto. © 1956. Geography, Board
game. 15

4655. Get the Message. © 1964. TV, Game, Board
game. 18

4656. Ghosts. © 1985. Monster, Board game. 15

4657. Gidget Fortune Teller Game. © 1966. TV,
Board game. 30

4658. Gilligan, The New Adventures of. © 1974. TV,
Board game. 25

4659. Go Back. © 1967. Skill, Action game. 15

4660. Go to the Head of the Class, 10th Series. ©
1957. Q & A, Board game. 15

4661. Go to the Head of the Class, 11th Series. ©
1959. Q & A, Board game. 15

**4662. Go to the Head of the Class, 17th Series, green
slate.** © 1967. Q & A, Board game. 15

Milton Bradley continued

4663. Go to the Head of the Class, 5th Series. © 1949.
Q & A, Board game. $25

4664. Go to the Head of the Class, 6th Series. © 1950.
Q & A, Board game. 25

4665. Go to the Head of the Class, 7th Series. © 1951.
Q & A, Board game. 20

4666. Go to the Head of the Class, 8th Series. © 1953.
Q & A, Board game. 20

4667. Go to the Head of the Class, 9th Series. © 1955.
Q & A, Board game. 20

**4668. Going! Going! Gone! The Flea Market Auction
Game.** © 1974. Economic, Board game. 18

4669. Good Ol' Charlie Brown Game. © 1971.
Comics, Board game. 25

4670. Gordo and Pepito. © 1947. Comics, Board
game. 100

4671. Grab a Loop. © 1968. Skill, Action game. 15

4672. Grease. © 1978. Movie, Board game. 20

4673. Great Grape Ape Game, The. © 1975. Cartoon,
TV, Board game. 15

4674. Green Hornet Quick Switch Game. © 1966.
Super Hero, Action game. 225

4675. **Guess Again.** © 1967. Q & A, Board game. 15

4676. Guided Missile Navy Game. © 1964. Military,
Board game. 35

4677. Gumby Game, The. © 1988. Cartoon, TV, Board
game. 15

4678. H.R. Pufnstuf Game. © 1971. TV, Board game. 35

4679. Hair Bear Bunch, The. © 1971. TV, Cartoon,
Board game. 15

4680. Hangman, Vincent Price on cover. © 1976.
Skill, Action game. 15

4681. Happiness, Game of. © 1972. Travel, Board
game. 20

4682. Happy Face Game. © 1968. Kiddie, Board
game. 15

4683. Happy Little Train Game, The. © 1957. Travel,
Rail, Board game. 18

**4684. Hardy Boys Game, The, Based on the TV
Cartoon.** © 1978. Cartoon, TV, Board game. 18

4685. Harlem Globe Trotters Game, The. © 1971.
Sports, Basketball, Board game. 35

4686. Hero Quest Game System. © 1990. Fantasy,
Board game. 20

**4687. High Spirits with Calvin & the Colonel, Game
of.** © 1960. TV, Board game. 40

**4688. Hit the Beach, World War II Game, American
Heritage.** © 1965. Military, WWII, Board game. 50

4689. Hobbit Game, The. © 1978. Fantasy, Board
game. 25

4690. Homestretch. © 1974. Kiddie, Board game. 15

4691. Hopalong Cassidy Chinese Checkers. © 1951.
TV, Western, Board game. 75

4692. Hopalong Cassidy. © 1950. TV, Western, Board
game. 110

4693. Hoppity Hopper Game. © 1965. TV, Cartoon,
Board game. 75

4694. Hotels. © 1987. Architecture, Board game. 50

4695. Houndcats Game. © 1973. TV, Cartoons, Board
game. 18

**4696. How to Succeed in Business without Really
Trying.** © 1963. Music, Broadway, Board game. 35

4697. Howdy Doody's T.V. Game. © 1953. TV, Board
game. 85

4698. Howdy-Doody's Adventure Game. © 1956. TV,
Board game. 75

4699. Huckleberry Hound Tiddly Winks Tennis. ©
1959. TV, Cartoon, Action game. $25

4700. Huckleberry Hound Western Game. © 1959.
TV, Cartoon, Board game. 28

4701. Huckleberry Hound. © 1981. TV, Cartoon,
Board game. 18

4702. I Dream of Jeannie Game. © 1965. TV, Board
game. 75

4703. Illya Kuryakin. © 1966. TV, Law & Order, Card
game. 28

4704. Incredible Hulk Game with the Fantastic Four.
© 1978. Super Heroes, Board game. 20

4705. Inspector Gadget Game. © 1983. Cartoon, TV,
Board game. 18

4706. Intrigue, Liner & Tugboat cover. © 1950. Spy,
Board game. 40

4707. Intrigue, Liner, Key & Briefcase cover. © 1950.
Spy, Board game. 35

4708. Ipcress File, The. © 1966. Movie, Board game. 40

4709. Jackpot! © 1974. TV, Game, Board game. 15

4710. James Bond 007 Card Game. © 1964. Spy, Card
game. 30

4711. James Bond 007 Goldfinger Game. © 1966.
Movie, Law, Board game. 75

4712. James Bond 007 Thunderball Game. © 1965.
Movie, Spies, Board game. 75

4713. James Bond Secret Agent 007 Game. © 1964.
Movie, Law, Board game. 30

4714. Jeanne Dixon's Game of Destiny. © 1968.
Mystic, Board game. 18

4715. Jeopardy! © 1964. TV, Game, Board game. 15

4716. Jet World. © 1975. Travel, Air, Board game. 15

4717. Jetsons Fun Pad Game, The. © 1963. TV,
Cartoons, Board game. 85

4718. Jetsons Game, The. © 1985. TV, Cartoon, Board
game. 15

4719. Joker, Joker, Joker. © 1979. TV, Game Show,
Board game. 12

4720. Joker's Wild. © 1973. TV, Game Show, Board
game. 12

4721. John Drake, Secret Agent. © 1966. TV, Spy,
Board game. 50

4722. Jonny Quest Card Game. © 1965. TV, Cartoon,
Card game. 75

4723. Jumanji, The Game. © 1995. Movie, Board
game. 12

4724. Kermit the Frog. © 1980. TV, Card game. 12

4725. Kigmy Game by Al Capp. © 1950. Comics,
Skill game. 150

4726. King Kong Game. © 1966. Monster, Board
game. 250

4727. King Leonardo and His Subjects. © 1960.
Cartoon, TV, Board game. 50

4728. King Oil. © 1974. Economic, Board game. 50

4729. Knock, Knock. © 1982. Q & A, Board game. 15

Milton Bradley continued

4730. Know the Stars and Planets. © 1960. Space, Board game. $45

4731. Kojak, The Stake Out Detective Game. © 1975. TV, Detective, Board game. 18

4732. Kookie Chicks. © 1964. Kiddie, Board game. 15

4733. Kooky Carnival Game. © 1969. Skill, Action game. 15

4734. Korg: 70,000 B.C., The. © 1974. TV, Science Fiction, Board game. 20

4735. Kreskin's ESP, Advanced Fine Edition, four eyes on cover. © 1967. Mystic, Board game. 20

4736. Kreskin's ESP. © 1966. Mystic, Board game. 18

4737. Land of the Lost. © 1975. TV, Science Fiction, Board game. 35

4738. Laser Attack Game. © 1978. Military, Board game. 18

4739. Legend of Jessie James Game. © 1966. TV, Western, Board game. 75

4740. Legend of the Lone Ranger, The. © 1980. Western, TV, Board game. 15

4741. Let's Drive, Road Safety Fun Game. © 1967. Travel, Car, Board game. 25

4742. Let's Make a Deal. © 1964. TV, Game, Board game. 25

4743. Let's Play Tag. © 1958. Kiddie, Board game. 20

4744. Let's Take A Trip. © 1962. Travel, Board game. 20

4745. Leverage. © 1983. Economic, Board game. 12

4746. Life, The Game of. Mid 1960s. Economic, Board game. 20

4747. Life, The Game of, 100th Anniversary Issue. © 1960. Economic, Board game. 25

4748. Li'l Abner His Game. © 1946. Comics, Board game. 125

4749. Limbo Legs. © 1969. Skill, Action game. 15

4750. Little Lulu Adventure Game. © 1946. Comics, Board game. 175

4751. Little Mermaid. © 1990. Disney, Board game. 18

4752. Lobby, A Capital Game. © 1949. Political, Board game. 60

4753. Lobby, A Capital Game. © 1952. Political, Board game. 50

4754. Lobby, A Capital Game. © 1961. Political, Board game. 40

4755. Lolli Plop, Skill Game. © 1962. Skill, Action game. 15

4756. Lone Ranger. © 1966. TV, Western, Board game. 28

4757. Looney Tunes Game. © 1968. Cartoons, Board game. 45

4758. Lord of the Rings, Adventure Game. © 1979. Fantasy, Board game. $20

4759. Lost in Space Game. © 1965. TV, Science Fiction, Board game. 75

4760. Lost World Jurassic Park Game, The. © 1996. Science Fiction, Movie, Board game. 20

4761. Lucan Game. © 1977. TV, Board game. 20

4762. Lucky Town. © 1946. Architecture, Board game. 40

4763. Lucy's Tea Party Game. © 1971. TV, Personality, Board game. 45

4764. Mad's Spy vs Spy. © 1986. Comics, Spy, Board game. 15

4765. Make a Face. © 1962. TV, Game, Board game. 20

4766. Man from U.N.C.L.E. Card Game. © 1965. TV, Spy, Card game. 25

4767. Man from U.N.C.L.E. Shoot Out! © 1965. TV, Spy, Board game. 50

4768. Man Hunt. © 1972. Detective, Board game. 20

4769. Margie, The Game of Woopee! © 1961. TV, Board game. 22

4770. Marvel Comics Super-Hero. © 1978. Super Hero, Card game. 15

4771. Marvel Comics Super-Hero. © 1978. Super Hero, Board game. 20

4772. M*A*S*H Game. © 1981. TV, Board game. 30

4773. Match Game, The, 1st. Edition. © 1963. TV, Game, Board game. 35

4774. Match Game. © 1974. TV, Game, Board game. 30

4775. McDonald's Game, The. © 1975. Food, Advertising, Board game. 25

4776. Melvin. © 1990. Kiddie, Board game. 12

4777. Men into Space, Bill Lundigan Picture. © 1960. Space, Board game. 125

4778. Men into Space. © 1960. Space, Board game. 65

4779. Men of Destiny. © 1956. History, Board game. 25

4780. Merry Circus Game. © 1960. Circus, Board game. 25

4781. Mickey Mouse, Follow the Leader Game. © 1971. Disney, Board game. 20

4782. Mighty Mouse Game with Heckle and Jeckle. © 1957. Cartoons, Board game. 40

4783. Mighty Mouse Target Game. © 1958. Cartoon, Board game. 45

4784. Milton the Monster Game. © 1966. Monster, Board game. 35

4785. Missing Links. © 1964. TV, Game, Board game. 15

4786. Mister Bug Goes to Town. © 1955. Animal, Board game. 45

4787. Monster Mansion. © 1981. Monster, Board game. 20

4788. Monster Old Maid. © 1964. Monsters, Card game. 30

4789. Monster Squad, The. © 1977. Monster, Board game. 30

4790. Mork & Mindy Card Game. © 1978. TV, Card game. 18

4791. Mosquito. © 1966. Skill, Action game. 15

4792. Mother's Helper. © 1969. Home Economics, Board game. 20

4793. Mr. Bug Goes to Town. © 1955. Animal, Board game. 25

4794. Mr. T Card Game. © 1983. TV, Card game. 12

4795. Mr. T Game. © 1983. TV, Board game. 15

Milton Bradley continued

4796. Munsters Card Game, The. © 1964. TV,
Monsters, Card game. $50

4797. Mystery Date Game. © 1965. Romance, Board
game. 175

4798. Mystery Date Game. © 1972. Dating, Board
game. 125

4799. Mystery Mansion. © 1981. Mystery, Board
game. 18

4800. Name that Tune, with record, Red box. © 1959.
TV, Music, Game, Board game. 25

4801. Name that Tune, with record, White box. ©
1957. TV, Music, Game, Board game. 30

4802. NASCAR Daytona 500. © 1990. Sports, Car,
Board game. 20

4803. New Kids on the Block. © 1990. Music,
Personality, Board game. 15

4804. Nosey Neighbor Card Game. © 1981. Social,
Card game. 12

4805. Now You See It. © 1975. TV, Game, Board
game. 15

4806. Off to See the Wizard Game. © 1968. Cartoon,
TV, Board game. 20

4807. Offical Baseball Game. © 1969. Sports,
Baseball, Board game. 100

4808. Offical New York World'a Fair Game, The. ©
1963. Fairs, Board game. 75

**4809. Offical New York World's Fair Panorama
Game, The.** © 1964. Fairs, Board game. 85

4810. Official Baseball Card Game, 1st edition. ©
1953. Sports, Baseball, Card game. 225

4811. Official Baseball Card Game. © 1970. Sports,
Baseball, Card game. 65

4812. Oh No! © 1966. Skill, Action game. 18

4813. Oh What a Mountain. © 1980. Kiddie, Board
game. 12

4814. On the Ball. © 1964. Skill, Action game. 15

4815. Operation Skill Game. © 1965. Skill, Action
game. 20

4816. Outer Limits, The. © 1964. Science Fiction,
Board game. 150

4817. P D Q. © 1965. TV, Game, Board game. 15

4818. P.T. Boat 109. © 1963. History, Military, Board
game. 35

4819. Pac-Man Card Game. © 1982. Game, Card
game. 10

4820. Pac-Man Game. © 1982. Game, Board game. ... 15

4821. Paddle Pool. © 1974. Skill, Board game. 12

4822. Park and Shop, Picture of shopping center. ©
1960. Economic, Board game. 65

4823. Park and Shop. © 1970. Economic, Board
game. 65

4824. Partridge Family. © 1971. TV, Board game. 35

4825. Pass the Pigs. Circa 1990s. Animal, Board
game. 10

**4826. Pass Word, 2nd Edition, Blue cloth back-
ground cover.** © 1962. Word, TV, Board game. ... $10

4827. Pass Word, 3rd edition, Large cartoon cover. ©
1963. Word, TV, Board game. 8

4828. Pass Word, 5th. edition, red & blue MB. ©
1964. Word, TV, Board game. 6

**4829. Pass Word, Collectors Edition, Wood paper
box.** © 1963. Word, TV, Board game. 8

4830. Pass Word, Fine Edition, Square box. © 1963.
Word, TV, Board game. 7

4831. Pass Word, Original edition, CBS Logo. ©
1962. Word, TV, Board game. 12

4832. Pass Word, Red & white box. Circa 1960s.
Word, TV, Board game. 5

4833. Pass Word, Red, white & blue box. Circa 1960s.
Word, TV, Board game. 5

4834. Pathfinder, Photo of game cover. © 1977.
Strategy, Board game. 12

4835. Pathfinder, White & Green cover. © 1954.
Strategy, Board game. 18

4836. Patty Duke Game. © 1963. TV, Personality,
Board game. 35

4837. PD Cue Bumper Pool. © 1973. Sports, Pool,
Board game. 12

4838. Personality Game. © 1968. TV, Board game. ... 22

**4839. Peter Rabbit in the Cabbage Patch, The Game
of.** © 1946. Nursery Rhyme, Board game. 35

4840. Peter Rabbit. © 1948. Nursery Rhyme, Board
game. 30

4841. Pink Panther Game, The. © 1970. Movie,
Cartoon, Board game. 28

4842. Pirate & Traveler. © 1953. Adventure, Board
game. 30

4843. Pirate & Traveler. © 1960. Adventure, Board
game. 25

4844. Pitfall! © 1983. Miscellaneous, Board game. ... 12

4845. Pivot Golf. © 1973. Sports, Golf, Board game. ... 65

4846. Pivot Pool. © 1972. Sports, Pool, Board game. ... 75

4847. Pivot. © 1960. Miscellaneous, Board game. 8

4848. Planet of the Apes. © 1974. Movie, Science
Fiction, Board game. 35

4849. Plus One Electric Board Game. © 1980.
Numbers, Board game. 12

4850. Pop Yer Top! © 1968. Skill, Action game. 20

4851. Popeye. © 1980. Movie Comic, Board game. 18

4852. Pop-Up Store Game. Circa 1950s. Economic,
Board game. 75

4853. Pow Cannon Game. © 1964. Military, Action
game. 35

4854. Power Barons. © 1986. Economic, Board
game. 25

Milton Bradley continued

4855. **Prize Property, 1st edition.** © 1959.
Architecture, Board game. $25

4856. **Prize Property.** © 1974. Architecture, Board
game. 20

4857. **Pro Bowling.** © 1962. Sports, Bowling, Board
game. 35

4858. **Pro Football.** © 1964. Sports, Football, Board
game. 35

4859. **Quick Draw McGraw Game.** © 1981. TV,
Cartoon, Board game. 20

4860. **Quick Draw McGraw.** © 1960. TV, Cartoons,
Board game. 32

4861. **Quizmo.** © 1953. Numbers, Board game. 15

4862. **Quotations, The Game of.** © 1987. Literary,
Q & A, Board game. 10

4863. **Rack-O.** © 1961. Miscellaneous, Card game. 5

4864. **Raggedy Ann.** © 1954. Comics, Literary, Board
game. 35

4865. **Raggedy Ann.** © 1974. Literary, Board game. ... 18

4866. **Rainbow Game.** Circa 1940s. Kiddie, Board
game. 30

4867. **Real Ghostbusters Game, The.** © 1984. TV,
Monster, Board game. 18

4868. **Recall, The Game of Observation.** © 1967.
Memory, Board game. 18

4869. **Restless Gun Game, The.** © 1959. TV, Western,
Board game. 45

4870. **Richie Rich.** © 1982. Comics, Board game. 12

4871. **Rickenbacker Ace Game "Keep Em Flying".**
© 1946. Military, Board game. 150

4872. **Rifleman Game, The.** © 1959. TV, Western,
Board game. 50

4873. **Ripley's Believe It or Not!** © 1984. Personality,
Board game. 15

4874. **Road Runner Game.** © 1968. Cartoons, Board
game. 32

4875. **Rocky and His Friends Game.** © 1960. TV,
Cartoons, Board game. 60

4876. **Rodney Dangerfield's No Respect.** © 1985.
Personality, Board game. 15

4877. **Roller Coaster.** © 1973. Skill, Action game. 18

4878. **Roller Derby.** © 1974. Sports, Skating, Board
game. 18

4879. **Roundabout.** © 1987. Strategy, Board game. $12

4880. **S.W.A.T. Game, The.** © 1976. TV, Board game. 15

4881. **Saban's VR Troopers Game.** © 1994. Science
Fiction, Board game. 15

4882. **Sale of the Century.** © 1969. TV, Game, Board
game. 12

4883. **Sammy, the White House Mouse.** © 1977.
Comic, Literary, Board game. 18

4884. **Sandlot Slugger.** © 1968. Sports, Baseball,
Action game. 28

4885. **Santa's Workshop.** © 1959. Holiday, Xmas,
Board game. 50

4886. **Scatter Gories.** © 1988. Q & A, Board game. 12

4887. **Scavenger Hunt.** © 1983. Economic, Board
game. 12

4888. **Scooby Doo Game.** © 1971. TV, Board game. 35

4889. **Scooby-Doo & Scrappy-Doo Game.** © 1983.
TV, Cartoons, Board game. 15

4890. **Scooby-Doo, Where are You?** © 1973. Cartoon,
TV, Board game. 22

4891. **Scotland Yard.** © 1985. Law & Order, Board
game. 15

4892. **Screaming Eagles.** © 1987. Military, Board
game. 15

4893. **Scruples.** © 1986. Social, Board game. 12

4894. **Sealab 2020 Game.** © 1973. TV, Science Fiction,
Board game. 25

4895. **Séance.** © 1972. Mystic, Board game. 65

4896. **Secrets Game, The.** © 1987. Miscellaneous,
Board game. 15

4897. **Seige Game.** © 1966. Military, Board game. 22

4898. **Sergeant Preston Game.** © 1956. TV, Board
game. 45

4899. **Shenanigans, Carnival of Fun Game.** © 1966.
Circus, Board game. 40

4900. **Shogun.** © 1986. Military, Board game. 35

4901. **Shotgun Slade.** © 1960. TV, Western, Board
game. 45

4902. **Showdown Yahtzee.** © 1991. Miscellaneous,
Dice game. 12

4903. **Sigmund and the Sea Monsters Game.** © 1974.
TV, Monsters, Board game. 35

4904. **Simpsons Don't Have a Cow, The.** © 1990. TV,
Cartoon, Dice game. 15

4905. **Skatebirds Game.** © 1978. TV, Board game. 15

4906. **Skillets and Cakes.** © 1946. Ethnic, Food, Board
game. 30

4907. **Skill-It.** © 1966. Skill, Action game. 12

4908. **Skirmish, American Heritage Series.** © 1975.
Military, Board game. 30

4909. **Slam Back.** © 1974. Skill, Action game. 10

4910. **Slap Stick.** © 1966. Skill, Board game. 20

4911. **Slide 5.** © 1980. Strategy, Board game. 12

4912. **Smurf Game, The.** © 1981. Cartoon, TV, Board
game. 15

4913. **Snap Judgement.** © 1968. TV, Game, Board
game. 10

4914. **Snoopy Vs. the Red Baron.** © 1970. Comics,
Action game. 35

4915. **Snoopy Card Game.** © 1965. TV, Card game. 20

4916. **Snoopy Come Home Game.** © 1966. Comics,
Board game. 28

4917. **Snoopy's Doghouse Game.** © 1977. Comic,
Board game. 22

4918. **Snuffy Smith Time's a Wastin' Game.** © 1963.
Comics, Board game. 35

Milton Bradley continued

4919. Solitaire, with Lucille Ball on cover. © 1971. Personality, Board game. $18

4920. Sonny Fox Fact Finder. © 1962. Q & A, Board game. 15

4921. Sons of Hercules Game, The. © 1966. Movie, Board game. 85

4922. Soupy Sez Go-Go-Go! © 1961. TV, Board game. 75

4923. Space:1999. © 1976. TV, Science Fiction, Board game. 18

4924. Speed Buggy Game. © 1973. TV, Board game. 20

4925. Splat! The Bug. © 1991. Kiddie, Board game. 12

4926. Sports Arena. © 1962. Sports, Board game. 60

4927. Spot Cash. © 1959. Economic, Board game. 12

4928. Spots. © 1959. Memory, Board game. 25

4929. Spots. Circa 1940s. Animal, Board game. 35

4930. Square Mile. © 1962. Architect, Economic, Board game. 45

4931. Squirt. © 1955. Animal, Board game. 25

4932. Stage II. © 1985. Theatrical, Board game. 18

4933. Star Trek Game. © 1979. TV, Science Fiction, Board game. 30

4934. Starsky and Hutch Detective Game. © 1977. TV, Detective, Board game. 15

4935. States, Game of the, Horozontal red, white and blue cover. © 1960. Economic, Board game. 15

4936. States, Game of the, Vertical red, white and blue cover. © 1954. Economic, Board game. 18

4937. Stay Alive Game. © 1971. Strategy, Board game. 10

4938. Steady Eddie. © 1962. Skill, Action game. 20

4939. Stop Thief, Electronic Cops and Robbers. © 1979. Law & Order, Board game. 15

4940. Strata 5. © 1984. Strategy, Board game. 12

4941. Stratego, cameo of four at play. © 1962. Military, Board game. 15

4942. Stratego, Man and boy at play. © 1970s. Military, Board game. 10

4943. Stratego, Two horseman one footsoldier cover, 1st edition. © 1961. Military, Board game. 22

4944. Stratego. © 1964. Military, Board game. 12

4945. Stretch-Out Sam. © 1990. Skill, Action game. 12

4946. Stump Card Game. © 1968. Miscellaneous, Card game. 10

4947. Stump. © 1968. Strategy, Board game. 10

4948. Stymie Card Game, Bewitched. © 1964. TV, Card game. 35

4949. Sub Attack Game. © 1965. Military, Board game. 35

4950. Sub Search Game. © 1973. Military, Board game. 25

4951. Summit. © 1961. Miscellaneous, Board game. 40

4952. Sunken Treasure. © 1976. Adventure, Board game. 22

4953. Super Heroes Strategy Game. © 1980. Super Heroes, Board game. 15

4954. Super Spy. © 1971. Spy, Board game. 25

4955. Supercar to the Rescue Game. © 1962. TV, Board game. 100

4956. Superheroes Card Game. © 1978. Super Hero, Card game. 18

4957. Superman - Fantastic Four. © 1977. Super Hero, Board game. 25

4958. Superman and Superboy. © 1967. Super Hero, Board game. 75

4959. Superman II Game. © 1980. Super Heroes, Board game. 18

4960. Supermarket Sweep. © 1966. TV, Game, Board game. $30

4961. Superstition. © 1977. Monster, Board game. 20

4962. Swahili Game. © 1968. Strategy, Board game. 15

4963. Swat Baseball. © 1948. Sports, Baseball, Board game. 35

4964. Swat. Miscellaneous, TV, Board game. 15

4965. Swayze. Circa 1954. Personality, Board game. 20

4966. Sweet Valley High Game, by Francine Pascal. © 1988. Literary, Romance, Board game. 15

4967. Swivel. © 1972. Skill, Board game. 12

4968. Swords and Shields. © 1970. Military, Board game. 25

4969. Tales of Wells Fargo Game. © 1959. TV, Western, Board game. 65

4970. Tank Battle. © 1975. Military, Board game. 22

4971. Tarzan to the Rescue Game. © 1977. Literary, Board game. 15

4972. Tarzan. © 1984. Literary, Board game. 12

4973. Tee Party. © 1968. Sports, Golf, Board game. 10

4974. Tee'd off. © 1966. Skill, Board game. 25

4975. Tell it to the Judge, The Club Game. © 1952. Travel, Law, Board game. 45

4976. Terminator 2, Judgement Day. Circa 1990s. Movie, Space, Board game. 18

4977. Terrytoons Mighty Mouse Game. © 1978. Cartoons, Board game. 20

4978. Test Driver Game, The. © 1956. Travel, Car, Board game. 75

4979. Think-Thunk. © 1973. Skill, Action game. 12

4980. Three Musketeers. © 1950. Adventure, Board game. 45

4981. Three on a Match. © 1973. TV, Game, Board game. 15

4982. Thundarr The Barbarian. © 1982. Fantasy, Board game. 15

4983. Thunder Road. © 1986. Sports, Cars, Board game. 12

4984. Tic-Tac-Aroo with Captain Kangaroo. © 1956. TV, Personality, Board game. 35

4985. Tilt 'N Roll, Obstacle Puzzle. © 1964. Skill, Action game. 18

4986. Time Bomb. © 1964. Skill, Action game. 40

4987. Times to Remember. © 1991. Q & A, Board game. 15

4987a.Tom and Jerry. © 1948, Cartoons, Board game. ... 100

4988. Tom and Jerry Game. © 1968. Cartoons, Board game. 25

4989. Tom and Jerry. © 1977. Cartoon, TV, Board game. 20

4990. Torpedo Run. © 1986. Military, Board game. 15

4991. Trip Hammer. © 1974. Skill, Action game. 12

4992. Trump, The Game. © 1989. Economic, Board game. 10

4993. Turbo. © 1981. Sports, Car, Game, Board game. ... 15

4994. Tussle. Circa 1960s. Skill, Action game. 15

4995. TV Jackpot Game. © 1975. TV, Game, Board game. 8

4996. Twiggy. © 1967. Personality, Board game. 35

4997. Twinkles, His Trip to the Star Factory Game. © 1961. Cartoon, TV, Board game. 65

4998. Twister. © 1966. Skill, Board game. 18

4999. Uncle Wiggily. © 1954. Literary, Animal, Board game. 20

5000. Uncle Wiggly Game. © 1949. Literary, Board game. 30

Milton Bradley continued

5001. Uncle Wiggly Game. © 1988. Literary, Board
game. $12

5002. Underdog. © 1964. TV, Cartoon, Board game. 50

5003. Universal Monster Mansion. © 1981. Monster,
Board game. 20

5004. UpWords. © 1983. Word, Board game. 8

5005. Vegas, The Family Game of Skill & Luck. ©
1973. Gambling, Board game. 10

5006. Video Village. © 1960. TV, Game, Board game. 40

5007. Visit to Walt Disney World, The. © 1972.
Disney, Board game. 20

5008. Voice of the Mummy. © 1971. Monster, Board
game. 75

5009. Volley, A Volleyball game. © 1976. Sports,
Board game. 10

5010. Voyage to the Bottom of the Sea. © 1964. TV,
Card game. 30

5011. Voyage to the Bottom of the Sea. © 1964. TV,
Adventure, Board game. 35

5012. Wacky Races Game, The. © 1968. TV, Board
game. 45

5013. Wagon Train. © 1960. TV, Western, Board
game. 50

5014. Walk Along Sesame Street. © 1975. TV, Board
game. 12

5015. Walt Disney's Mary Poppins. © 1964. Disney,
Board game. 40

5016. Waltons Game, The. © 1974. TV, Board game. 30

5017. Welcome Back Kotter Card Game. © 1976. TV,
Card game. 15

5018. Wells Fargo Game. © 1959. TV, Western, Board
game. 75

5019. Wendy the Good Little Witch Game. © 1966.
TV, Cartoon, Board game. 175

5020. Whatzit? © 1987. Strategy, Board game. 121

5021. Wheel of Fortune TV Game. © 1975. TV,
Game, Board game. 15

**5022. Where's the Beef?, Ad game for Wendy's Fast
Food.** © 1984. Advertising, Board game. 12

5023. Where's Willie? © 1966. TV, Board game. 30

5024. Which Witch? Circa 1970s. Monster, Board
game. 75

5025. Whirl Out Game. © 1971. Skill, Action game. 18

5026. Whirligig. © 1963. Social, Board game. 18

5027. Who Framed Roger Rabbit Game. © 1987.
Disney, Board game. 45

5028. Who What or Where Game, The. © 1970. TV,
Game, Board game. 10

5029. Whoopee! Margie, The Game of. © 1961. TV,
Board game. 22

5030. Why, Alfred Hitchcock Presents. © 1958.
Personality, Mystery, Board game. 25

5031. Why, Mystery Game, Alfred Hitchcock. ©
1967. Personality, Mystery, Board game. 25

5032. Why, Presented by Alfred Hitchcock. © 1961.
Personality, Mystery, Board game. 18

5033. Wide World of Sports-Auto Racing. © 1974.
Sports, Car, Board game. 18

5034. Wide World of Sports-Golf. © 1974. Sports,
Golf, Board game. 18

5035. Wide World of Sports-Tennis. © 1974. Sports,
Tennis, Board game. 22

5036. Wild Life. © 1974. Animal, Board game. 15

5037. Win, Place and Show. Circa 1945-9. Sports,
Horseracing, Board game. 45

5038. Wipe Off Target Game. © 1959. Strategy, Board
game. $20

5039. Woody Woodpecker. © 1958. Cartoon, Board
game. 30

5040. World of Micronauts, The. © 1978. Adventure,
Board game. 15

5041. Wow Pillow Fight Game for Girls. © 1964.
Skill, Action game. 35

5042. Wrestling Superstars. © 1985. Sports,
Wrestling, Board game. 15

5043. Wuzzles, by Walt Disney. © 1985. Disney, Board
game. 15

5044. WWF Wrestling. © 1991. Sports, Wrestling,
Board game. 15

5045. Yogi Bear Game. © 1971. TV, Cartoon, Board
game. 25

5046. Yogi Bear Game. © 1980. TV, Cartoon, Board
game. 15

5047. You Don't Say Game. © 1969. TV, Game, Board
game. 10

5048. Zaxxon. © 1982. Game, Board game. 12

5049. Zero Zap. © 1987. Strategy, Board game. 12

5050. Zillionare. © 1987. Economic, Board game. 10

David Bremson

5051. Arnold Palmer's Inside Golf. © 1961. Sports,
Golf, Board game. 85

Bright Ideas

5052. Go to Texas. © 1979. Travel, USA, Board
game. 25

Broadman Supplies

5053. Bible Match-A-Verse. © 1959. Religious, Card
game. 20

Broman-Percepta Corp.

5054. 99, Game of. © 1963. Strategy, Board game. 45

Brownair Co.

4469a.Aerospace Trading Game. © 1977. Economic,
Board game. 30

Brown Game Inc.

5055. Lot the Calf. © 1964. Western, Board game. 30

Lide Brunhoff

5056. Babar 7 Families Card Game, The. Circa
1980s. Literary, Card game. 18

Brunner Game Co.
5056a.FAD: The Farm Game. © 1956. Farm, Board
game. $45

Bryad
5057. Rainy Day Golf. © 1980. Sports, Golf, Board
game. 20

Buckeye Pipe Line Co.
5058. Retirement Planning System. © 1981. Social
Concern, Board game. 40

Budweiser
5059. Bud Vs Bud Light Checkers, Ad game for beer.
Circa 1990s. Advertising, Board game. 15

Built-Rite (also see Warren)
5060. 300 Mile Race. © 1955. Sports, Car, Board
game. 20
5061. 4 Quarter Basketball Game. Circa 1960s.
Sports, Basketball, Board game. 18
5062. Basketball Game. Circa 1950s. Sports,
Basketball, Board game. 20
5063. Beachhead Invasion Game. Circa 1950s.
Military, Board game. 45
5064. Bowling, Pocket Size. Circa 1950s. Sports,
Bowling, Card game. 10
5065. Buffalo Bill Jr. Cattle Round Up Game. ©
1956. TV, Western, Board game. 40
5066. Casper's Picture Lotto. © 1959. Comics, Board
game. 30
5067. Cattle Round-Up Game. © 1956. Western,
Board game. 22
5067a. Dude Ranch. Circa 1950s, Western, Board
game. 25
5068. Felix the Cat Down on the Farm Game. ©
1956. Comics, Board game. 65
**5069. Funday Cartoons Card Game, Harvey
Cartoons.** Circa 1950s. Cartoons, Card game. 35

5070. Gene Autry's Dude Ranch Game. © 1956.
Personal, Western, Board game. 65
5071. Greeny Grasshoppers. Circa 1950s. Animal,
Card game. 22
5072. Jet Race Game. Circa 1960s. Travel, Air, Board
game. 28
5073. Jr. Quarterback Football Game. © 1960.
Sports, Football, Board game. 25
5074. Little Beaver's 3 Game Set. © 1956. TV,
Western, Board game. 65
5075. Little Leaguer Baseball Game. Circa 1950s.
Sports, Baseball, Board game. 45
5076. Lucky "9" Race Game. © 1956. Sports, Car,
Board game. 32
5077. Old Maid. © 1964. Classic, Card game. 10

5078. Ozark Ike's Complete 3 Game Set. © 1956.
Comics, Board game. $75
5079. Popeye Games. © 1958. Comics, Board game. .. 75
5080. Popeye Sliding Board & Ladders. © 1958.
Comics, Board game. 50
5081. Popeye's 3 Game Set. © 1956. Comics, Board
game. 50
5082. Popeye's Good Time & "Blow Me Down".
Circa 1950s. Comics, Board game. 55
5083. Race-O-Rama, 4 Race Games. Circa 1960s.
Sports, Car, Board game. 20
5084. Red Ryder's 3 Game Set. © 1955. Comics,
Board game. 85
5085. Senior Prom. © 1966. Romance, Board game. .. 35
5086. Swish Basketball Game. © 1955. Sports,
Basketball, Board game. 25
**5087. Wild Bill Hickock and Jingles Pony Express
Game.** © 1956. TV, Western, Board game. 65
5088. Wild Bill Hickock, Calvary & Indians Game.
Circa 1950s. TV, Western, Board game. 65

Burger King
5089. Burger King Championship Checkers. © 1988.
Advertising, Board game. 15

John E. Burleson
5090. Battle Stations. © 1952. Military, Board game. .. 35

Burlu Enterprises
5091. Let's Play Golf. © 1968. Sports, Golf, Board
game. 20
5092. Let's Play Golf, The Hawaiian Open. © 1968.
Sports, Golf, Board game. 35

Business Week
5092a.Business Week Game, The. © 1977. Economic,
Board game. 25

C.N.N. Inc.
5093. CNN, The Game. © 1994. History, Q & A,
Board game. 15

Cadaco Inc.
**5094. All Star Baseball, Ethen Allen's Managers
Supplement.** © 1957. Sports, Baseball, Board
game. 75
**5095. All Star Baseball, Green background No. 8
batter.** © 1960. Sports, Baseball, Board game. 65
**5096. All Star Baseball, Green background, two
Players & Ump.** © 1962. Sports, Baseball, Board
game. 65
5097. All Star Baseball. © 1966. Sports, Baseball,
Board game. 75
5098. All Star Baseball. © 1967. Sports, Baseball,
Board game. 65
5099. All Star Baseball. © 1968. Sports, Baseball,
Board game. 35
5100. All Star Baseball. © 1969. Sports, Baseball,
Board game. 35
5101. All-American Football Game, Photo cover. ©
1969. Sports, Football, Board game. 25
**5102. All-American Football Game, single red shirt
player cover.** © 1960. Sports, Football, Board
game. 45

Cadaco continued

5103. All-American Football Game. © 1958. Sports, Football, Board game. $50

5104. All-American Football Game. © 1965. Sports, Football, Board game. 45

5105. All-Star Baseball. © 1957. Sports, Baseball, Board game. 50

5106. All-Star Baseball. © 1989. Sports, Baseball, Board game. 15

5107. American Derby, The. © 1951. Sports, Horseracing, Board game. 125

5108. Amoco's the Mileage Game, Ad game for Gasoline Co. © 1976. Travel, Board game. 30

5109. Bas-ket, Photo cover. © 1969. Sports, Basketball, Board game. 30

5110. Bas-ket, Red Cover. © 1960. Sports, Basketball, Board game. 40

5111. Butterflies. © 1967. Animal, Board game. 15

5112. Cannonball Run, The. © 1981. Movie, Board game. 25

5113. Chase, A Nature Study Game, The. © 1966. Animal, Board game. 40

5114. Chutzpah. © 1967. Ethnic, Board game. 30

5115. Cinderella Game, The. © 1975. Literary, Board game. 15

5116. College Basketball. © 1954. Sports, Basketball, Board game. 50

5117. Confetti the Clown. © 1968. Circus, Board game. 20

5117a.Cub Scouting, The Game of. © 1980. Organizations, Board game. 15

5118. Egg-Citement! © 1973. Strategy, Board game. 15

5119. Ethan Allen's All-Star Baseball Game. © 1946. Sports, Baseball, Board game. 95

5120. Feed the Elephant. © 1952. Animal, Mammal, Board game. 22

5121. Fighter-Bomber. © 1977. Military, Board game. 25

5122. Five Famous Favorites. © 1946. Combo, Board game. 20

5123. Foto-Electric Baseball. © 1950. Sports, Baseball, Board game. 35

5124. Foto-Electric Bowling. © 1978. Sports, Bowling, Board game. 20

5125. Foto-Electric Football, Blue sky white stripes background. © 1956. Sports, Football, Board game. 35

5126. Foto-Electric Football, Football photo cover. © 1971. Sports, Football, Board game. 20

5127. Foto-Electric Football, Three players blue background. © 1965. Sports, Football, Board game. 25

5128. Foto-Electric Football. © 1950. Sports, Football, Board game. 45

5129. Geo-Graphy World Wide. © 1954. Travel, World, Board game. 22

5130. Goldilocks. © 1955. Nursery Rhyme, Board game. 20

5131. Good Guys 'n' Bad Guys. © 1973. Western, Board game. 18

5132. Grandmother's House We Go, To. © 1974. Nursery Rhyme, Board game. 15

5133. Happy Birthday Game Party Pak. © 1974. Social, Board game. 22

5134. Hockey. © 1958. Sports, Hockey, Board game. 50

5135. Hookey. © 1946. Animal, Sea, Board game. 35

5136. International Grand Prix. © 1975. Sports, Car, Board game. 20

5137. Jack and Jill. © 1948. Nursery Rhyme, Board game. $30

5138. Jack and the Beanstalk Memory Game. © 1976. Nursery Rhyme, Board game. 18

5139. Jubilee. © 1954. Miscellaneous, Board game. 35

5140. King Tut's Game. © 1977. Classic, Board game. 20

5141. Little Black Sambo. © 1953. Ethnic, Literary, Board game. 125

5142. Little Boy Blue. © 1955. Nursery Rhyme, Board game. 35

5143. Little Prince. © 1974. Kiddie, Board game. 15

5144. Magic Midway. © 1962. TV, Board game. 35

5145. Mammoth Hunt. © 1962. Animal, Board game. 35

5146. Maneuver. © 1967. Military, Board game. 22

5147. Marlin Perkins' Zoo Park. © 1955. Personality, Animal, Board game. 40

5148. Martin Luther King Jr. © 1980. Personality, Ethnic, Board game. 125

5149. Match Point Tennis. © 1971. Sports, Tennis, Board game. 35

5150. Merry-Go-Round. © 1971. Circus, Board game. 15

5151. Moon Shot. © 1967. Space, Board game. 45

5152. Mostly Ghosts! © 1975. Monster, Board game. 20

5153. Mother Goose Game. © 1971. Nursery Rhyme, Board game. 15

5154. Mug Shots. © 1975. Miscellaneous, Board game. 15

5155. National Pro Football, Hall of Fame. © 1965. Sports, Football, Board game. 25

5156. NBA Bas-ket. © 1983. Sports, Basketball, Board game. 20

5157. Noah's Ark, Pre-School. © 1971. Kiddie, Board game. 20

5158. Noah's Ark. © 1951. Animal, Board game. 30

5159. Offical Drivers Ed Game. © 1973. Travel, Education, Board game. 25

5160. Oh Hell. © 1973. Strategy, Card game. 15

5161. Old Mother Hubbard. Red box. © 1954. Nursery Rhyme, Board game. 25

5162. Old Mother Hubbard. Blue box. © 1955. Nursery Rhyme, Board game. 25

5163. One Arm Bandit. © 1966. Gambling, Action game. 25

5163a.Oreo Cookie Factory. © 1977. Board game. 18

5164. Photo-Electric Football. © 1951. Sports, Football, Board game. 40

5165. Pink Panther. © 1981. Cartoon, Board game. 35

5166. Pitchin' Pal. © 1953. Skill, Action game. 25

5167. Pro Foto-Football. © 1977. Sports, Football, Board game. 25

5168. Pro Foto-Football. © 1986. Sports, Football, Board game. 15

5169. Quiz Panel. © 1954. Q & A, Board game. 15

5170. Red Herring. © 1945. Animal, Sea, Board game. 40

5171. Red Rover Game, The. © 1963. Animal, Board game. 30

5172. Ring Master. © 1947. Circus, Career, Board game. 45

5173. Rudolph, the Red-Nosed Raindeer. © 1977. Holiday, Xmas, Board game. 30

5174. Rules of the Road, Driver Education Game. © 1977. Travel, Car, Ed, Board game. 25

5175. Scat. © 1967. Miscellaneous, Board game. 20

5176. Screen Challenge. © 1991. Movie, Q & A, Board game. 22

5177. See the USA Game. © 1968. Travel, US, Board game. 25

5178. Seven Seas. © 1960. Travel, Board game. 35

Cadaco continued

5179. Sharpshooter. © 1951. Skill, Action game. $35
5180. Sherlock Holmes Game, The. © 1974. Literary, Detective, Board game. 20
5181. Sinbad. © 1978. Movie, Board game. 18
5182. Skedaddle, Game of Hurdles. © 1965. Kiddie, Board game. 20
5183. Skip-A-Cross. © 1953. Skill, Action game. 15
5184. Skipper. © 1949. Travel, Sea, Board game. 45
5185. Snow White and the Seven Dwarfs. © 1977. Literary, Board game. 20
5186. Space Pilot. © 1951. Space, Board game. 85
5187. Spell It. © 1951. Word, Number, Board game. 15
5188. Squaresville. © 1968. Skill, Board game. 20
5189. S-S-S-Scat. © 1967. Skill, Action game. 22
5189a. Stampede! The Cowboy Marble Game. Circa 1950s, Western, Board marble game. 55
5190. Tag You're It!, The Game of. © 1963. Kiddie, Board game. 18
5191. Telephone Game, The. © 1982. Communications, Board game. 20
5192. Ten Commandments Bible Game. © 1988. Religious, Board game. 15
5193. Thirteen. © 1959. Strategy, Board game. 15
5194. Ticker Tape. © 1963. Stock Market, Board game. 35
5195. Ting-A-Ling Bingo. © 1974. Holiday, Board game. 12
5196. Top Cop. © 1961. Cops, Board game. 45
5197. Top Scholar. © 1957. Q & A, Board game. 25
5198. TOP-ography. © 1958. Geography, Board game. 25
5199. Travel with Woody Woodpecker. © 1956. Cartoon, Board game. 65
5200. Treasure Hunt. © 1951. Adventure, Board game. 25
5201. Tripoley, The Game of, Green molded plastic board. © 1968. Gambling, Board game. 8
5202. Tripoley, The Game of, Overhead photo. © 1969. Gambling, Board game. 8
5203. Tripoley, The Game of, Red box. © 1965. Gambling, Board game. 8
5204. Undercover. © 1960. Detective, Board game. 35
5205. Undersea World Game, The. © 1971. Animal, Fish, Board game. 25
5206. Varsity. © 1955. Sports, Football, Board game. 35
5207. White Shadows. © 1980. TV, Board game. 12
5208. Who Dunit? © 1954. Mystery, Board game. 25
5209. Wing Ding. © 1951. Skill, Action game. 20
5210. Wizard of Oz Game, The. © 1974. Literary, Fantasy, Board game. 18
5211. Woody Woodpecker. © 1956. Cartoon, Movie, Board game. 35
5212. Yoo Doo. © 1982. Strategy, Board game. 15
5213. Your America. © 1974. Q & A, History, Board game. 20

Campbell's Soup Co.

5213a. Campbell's Alphabet Soup Game. Game in can container. Circa 1940s, Advertising, Word game. 40

Camden Products Inc.

5213b. Kick-Off Soccer. © 1978. Sports, Soccer, Board game. 32

Cameo-Milton Bradley

5214. Psych-Out. © 1971. Social Concern, Board game. 30

5214a. Summit, The Game of International Power Politics. © 1961. Military, Board game. $75

Campaign Game Co.

5215. Campaign. A Game of American Politics. © 1966. Political, Board game. 40

Campfire Outfitting Co.

5216. Honors. Circa 1950. Organizations, Card game. 75

Don Candall

5217. Victory Over Communism. © 1964. International, Board game. 125

Candidates Inc.

5218. Running for President. © 1982. Political, Board game. 25

Capex Co.

5219. Egg and I, The. © 1947. Movie, Board game. 25
5220. Galloping Golf. Circa 1940s. Sports, Golf, Board game. 22

Capital Airlines

5221. Capital Air Race, Premium. © 1955. Premium, Travel, Board game. 25

Cap'n Crunch Cereal

5222. Cap'n Crunch's Crunch Power Game. © 1988. Premium, Board game. 6
5223. Cap'n Crunch's Hot Air Race. © 1991. Travel, Premium, Board game. 6
5224. Cap'n Crunch's Jungle Safari. © 1991. Travel, Premium, Board game. 6
5225. Cap'n Crunch's Undersea Adventure. © 1991. Travel, Premium, Board game. 6

Captoys

5226. Baseball Card All Star Game. © 1987. Sports, Baseball, Card game. 10

Cardinal Industries

5227. $1,000,000 Chance of a Lifetime. © 1986. TV, Quiz, Board game. 8
5228. $25,000 Pyramid. Circa 1980s. TV, Quiz, Board game. 40
5229. General Hospital, The Game of. © 1982. TV, Doctors, Board game. 15
5230. Jumble. © 1975. Skill, Action game. 8

Cardinal Industries continued
5231. Labyrinth, Wooden. Circa 1980s. Skill, Board
game. $20
5232. Loudmouth, Morton Downey Jr. © 1988. TV,
Personality, Board game. 12
5233. National Lampoon Game of Sell Out. Circa
1980s. Social Concern, Board game. 15
**5234. Nightmare on Elm Street, A, The Freddy
Game.** © 1989. Movie, Monster, Board game. 30

Career Explorers
5235. Career Explorers. © 1994. Career, Board
game. 10

Carievale Productions Ltd.
5235a.Gourmet Challenge. © 1964. Food Board
game. 35

Carrom Industries
5236. Big Game Hunt. © 1947. Animal, Action game. 35
5237. Gusher, Win a Million. © 1946. Economic,
Board game. 60
5238. Kikit Skittles. © 1966. Skill, Action game. 15
5239. Nok Hockey. © 1949. Sports, Hockey, Board
game. 65

Phil Carter
5240. Changing Society. © 1981. Social Concern,
Board game. 25

Case & McGrath, Inc.
5240a.New Product Development Game, The. ©
1975. Economic, Board game. 25

Cavanaugh Assoc.
5241. Frank Cavanaugh's American Football. ©
1955. Sports, Football, Board game. 50

Cayla Games Inc.
5242. Speculation. © 1989. Stock Market, Board
game. 15

CE-Hanna-Barbera
5243. Flintstones 3-D Chess, The. © 1993. TV,
Classic, Board game. 30

Celebrity Challenge Games
5244. Celebrity Challenge. © 1992. Q & A, Board
game. 18

Center for the Gifted Child
5244a.Gold Rush. © 1963. Adventure, Board game. 50

Cereal Give Away
**5245. Nickelodeon, The Ren & Stimpy Show Target
Toss.** © 1994. TV, Premium, Skill game. 8

Championship Games
5246. Championship Baseball. © 1966. Sports,
Baseball, Board game. 25
5247. Championship Basketball. © 1966. Sports,
Basketball, Board game. 30
5248. Championship Golf. © 1966. Sports, Golf,
Board game. 45
5249. Pro Quarterback. © 1965. Sports, Football,
Board game. 30

Chaosium
5250. Elric, ziplock game, 1st edition. © 1977.
Fantasy, Board game. $22

Char-Down
5251. New York City's Great Blizzard. © 1977. Cities
& Towns, Board game. 22

Chariot Victor Publishing
5252. Exiled - It's Dangerous in the Desert. © 1998.
Religious, Travel, Board game. 20

Chaswell Co.
5253. Snafu. © 1952. Miscellaneous, Card game. 15

Chatham Hill Games
5254. 1876 Baseball. © 1976. Sports, Baseball, Board
game. 18
**5255. Catchpenny, The Game of 18th-century
"Mon-o-poly".** © 1996. History, Economics,
Board game. 18
5256. Erie Canal Game & Songs, The. Circa 1990s.
Historical, Board game. 18
5257. Gettysburg, The Battlefield Game. Circa 1990s.
Military, Civil War, Board game. 22
5258. Piqadilly. © 1996. Word, Board game. 20
5259. Underground Railroad Game & Songs, The.
Circa 1990s. Ethnic, History, Board game. 20

Cheerios
5260. Bird Hunt, [Cheerios Box Game]. Circa 1950s.
Animal, Board game. 18
5261. Brazil, [Cheerios Box Game]. Circa 1950s.
Travel, World, Board game. 20
5262. Hook the Fish, [Cheerios Box Game]. Circa
1950s. Animal, Board game. 18
5263. Number Tag, [Cheerios Box Game]. Circa
1950s. Numbers, Board game. 15
5264. Spell Down, [Cheerios Box Game]. Circa 1950s.
Word, Board game. 15

Chesapeake Bay Trading Co.
5265. Pax. © 1955. Military Post WWII, Card game. 125

Chessex
5265a.Stock Exchange Option, Monopoly addition,
© 1992 . Stock Market, Board game. 40

Cheston Industries
5266. Nemo. © 1969. Mystic, Board game. 20

Chex Ches Games
5267. Chex Ches Football. © 1971. Sports, Football,
Board game. 20

Citation Prod.
5268. Operation Rescue. © 1963. Space, Board game. 75
5269. Space Pilot. © 1963. Space, Board game. 75

The City Enterprise
5270. I Survived New York. © 1981. Miscellaneous,
Card game. 22

Civic Fundraising Henco
5271. Millionare, Danbury Ct. © 1984. Cities &
Towns, Board game. 20
5271a.Millionare, various cities and towns. © 1984.
As above, Cities and towns, Board game. 20

Class Struggle Inc.
5272. Class Struggle. © 1978. Social Concern, Board game. $28

Classic Games
5273. Cheers. © 1992. TV, Board game. 20
5274. Classic Major League Baseball. © 1990. Sports, Baseball, Board game. 20
5275. Claymania. © 1993. Skill, Board game. 17
5276. Gone with the Wind. © 1993. Movie, Board game. 25
5277. Gone With the Wind, The Game. Circa 1990s. Movie, Board game. 25
5278. Star Trek: The Game. © 1992. Science Fiction, Board game. 30

Vida Fox Clawson
5278a.Emigration, The Game of. The Mormon Trek. © 1947. Religious, Adventure, Board game. 25

Earl L. Clay
5278a.Super Hi-ways: Chicago-New York. © 1963. Travel, Board game. 55

Clever Games Co.
5279. Beat the Market. © 1968. Stock Market, Board game. 35

CO-5 Company
5280. Aggravation. Circa 1960s. Miscellaneous, Board game. 6
5281. Aggravation, The Original. © 1962. Miscellaneous, Board game. 5
5282. Gooses Wild. © 1966. Gambling, Board game. 5
5283. Gumby and Pokey Playfull Trails. © 1968. TV, Cartoon, Board game. 65

Coach House
5284. Bicentennial Games, The. © 1975. Military, Board game. 50

Cobus Enterprises
5285. Occupation. © 1955. Careers, Board game. 30

Coleco Games
5286. Alf Game, The. © 1987. TV, Board game. 15

Colonial Williamsburg Foundation

5287. Great Game of Visiting Williamsburg. © 1958. History, Geography, Board game. 45

Colorforms
5288. Drip Dragster, Race a Drop of Water. © 1971. Sports, Board game. 28

Colorful Products Inc.
5289. New Frontier, The Game of Nobody can Win. © 1962. Political, Board game. $50

Columbia Games Inc.
5290. Dixie, 1st Bull Run. © 1994. Military, Civil War, Card game. 15
5291. Dixie, Gettysburg. © 1996. Military, Civil War, Card game. 15
5292. Dixie, Shilo. © 1996. Military, Civil War, Card game. 15

Columbyss Game & Puzzle
5293. Interstate. © 1984. Travel, Land, Board game. 15

Comedy Central
5293a.In Decision 96. © 1996. Political, Board game. 22

Communications Research
5294. Blacks and Whites. © 1970. Social Concern, Board game. 18
5295. Body Talk. © 1970. Action, Board game. 18
5296. Woman and Man. © 1971. Social Concern, Board game. 20

Companion Games
5296a.Trial of the Century. 1996. Political, Board game. 22

Compete Games
5296a.Beat the Competition! © 1989. Economic, Board game. 22

Conglomerate Board Games
5296a.Conglomerate. © 1986. Economic, Board game. 22

Con-Fro Game Co.
5297. Face-Off. Circa 1989. Sports, Hockey, Board game. 15

Contemporary Jewish Learning Materials, Inc.
5298. Aliyah. © 1977. Religious, Board game. 25

David Cook Pub. Co.
5299. Lion and the White Witch, The. © 1983. Fantasy, Board game. 20
5300. Prince Caspian. © 1983. Fantasy, Board game. 20
5301. Voyage of Dawn Trader. © 1983. Fantasy, Board game. 20

Cooper-Ated Products
5301a.Play Safe. ©1951.Travel, Car, Board game...................50

Corey Game Co.
5302. Cock-A-Doodle-Doo. © 1946. Animal, Board game. 35
5303. Magnetic Fish Pond. © 1946. Animal, Board game. 25
5304. Suffolk Downs Racing Game. © 1947. Sports, Horseracing, Board game. 75

Corx Inc.
5305. Corx. © 1993. Strategy, Board game. $15

J. Cossman & Co.
5306. Military Chess. © 1959. Military, Board game. 20

Courtland Playthings
5307. Stick the I.R.S. © 1981. Social Concern, Board
game. 18

CPM Associates Inc.
5308. Encounter at Hanover. © 1983. Cities & Towns,
Board game. 18

Craig-Hopkins & Co.
5309. Ali Baba and the Forty Thieves. © 1945.
Literary, Adventure, Board game. 65
5310. Pennant Chasers Baseball Game. © 1946.
Sports, Baseball, Board game. 60

Cram
**5311. Pla-O-Map Game, made by Indiana globe
company.** © 1968. Geography, Board game. 20

Donald L. Cranmer
5312. Hot-Rod. © 1954. Travel, Car, Board game. 25

Crea-tek
5313. Ad•dic'tion. © 1968. Word, Board game. 15
5314. Info-Mania. © 1968. Q & A, Board game. 15
5315. Seduction. © 1966. Social, Board game. 30
5316. Splurge. © 1968. Gambling, Board game. 15

Creates
5317. Election '68. © 1967. Political, Board game. 40

Creative Ideas
5318. Mystery Checkers. Circa 1950s. Strategy, Board
game. 20

Creative Merchandisers
**5319. Money Matters, Manhattan Savings Bank
Westchester Offices.** © 1975. Economic,
Advertising, Premium, Board game. 15

Creative Playthings
5320. Black Cat. © 1973. Animal, Card game. 20

Creative Teaching Assoc.
5321. Grocery Cart. © 1986. Economic, Board game. 15

Crestline Mfg.
5322. Playoff Football. Circa 1970s. Sports, Football,
Board game. 18

Crisloid Plastics
5323. Jackpot, The Las Vegas Game. © 1969. Classic,
Card game. 15

Croquet, Ltd.
5324. Houston Astros, Baseball Challenge Game. ©
1980. Sports, Baseball, Board game. 20

Cross-Country Games
5324a.Cross-Country Trucking Game. © 1980.
Trucking, Board game. $35

Cross Challange Corp.
5325. BMX "Cross Challange" Action Game. ©
1988. Sports, Board game. 25

Crowley Conceptions
4469a.Is The Pope Catholic!?! © 1985. Religious,
Board game. 22

Crown & Andrews
5326. Save the World. © 1990. Social Concern, Board
game. 15

F & C Cruz
5327. Ords. © 1987. Miscellaneous, Board game. 15

John Culnane
5327a.Inside Golf, Sam Snead picture on cover. ©
1961. Sports, Golf, Board game. 75

John J. Culbertson
5327b.Spirit Champions of Tae Kwon Do. © 1987.
Sports, Board game. 30

Cuna Mutual Insurance Society
5328. Managing Your Money. © 1969. Economic,
Board game. 32

Curry Games
5329. I.N.I.T.I.A.L Response. © 1993. Social, Board
game. 15

Cynthia & Jerome Rubin
5330. Boston Game, The. © 1973. Cities & Towns,
Board game. 22

D. A. G. Corp.
5331. Trade the Market. © 1969. Stock Market, Board
game. 35

Dadan, Inc.
5332. Big Board, For Juniors, The. © 1962. Stock
Market, Board game. 15
Big Board, The. © 1958. Stock Market, Board
game, yellow box. 35
5333a.Big Board. As above, yellow box with black
stripe name, later edition. 25
5334. NBC-TV News Game w/ Chet Huntley. © 1962.
Personality, Communication, Board game. 30

Danboo Games
5335. Dalmania. Circa 1990s. Animal, Board game. 15

Dark Lore Inc.
5336. Dark Lore. © 1993. Mystic, Board game. 22
5337. Dark Lore, The Original Horror Trivia Game!
Circa 1990s. Q & A, Monster, Board game. 25

Dashound
5338. Lazy Pool. © 1965. Sports, Pool, Board game. 15

Daven

5339. Rich Man, Poor Man, Beggarman, Thief. ©
1984. Law & Order, Board game. $15

Daws & Plah Games Inc.

5340. Red Baron Stearman. © 1994. Miscellaneous,
Board game. 15

Day

5341. Plymouth Drag Race Game. © 1967. Sports,
Car, Board game. 30

Dearborn Industries

5342. 20 to 2. © 1949. Strategy, Board game. 15

Decipher Inc.

5343. Brain Game, The. © 1987. Mind, Board game. 12
5344. Ink Blotz. © 1989. Mind, Board game. 15
5345. No Dice. © 1987. Miscellaneous, Board game. 10
5346. Number Quest. © 1987. Numbers, Board game. 10
5347. Tip the Cows. © 1989. Miscellaneous, Board
game. 12

Decor Note Co.

**5348. Drivers Training Game, Let's Drive, Old
Scratch.** © 1959. Education, Car, Board game. 30
5349. Mr. President, U.S.A. © 1960. Political, Card
game. 25

Delight

5349a.Prep Game, The. © 1981. Social, Board game. 20

Richard DeLuccie

5349b.Real Baseball. Circa 1980s, Sports, Baseball,
Board game. 25

Design Origin

5350. Original Home Jai-Alai Game, The. © 1984.
Sports, Board game. 30

Destiny Books

5350a. Leela, The Game of Self-Knowledge. By
Harish Johari. © 1980, Self help, Board game. 35

Development Games Inc.

5350b.Wall Street Raiders. © 1988. Stock Market,
Board game. 18

Dewl Plasti-Toy Corp.

5351. Rock and Roll. © 1957. Music, Board game. 35

James A. Dhein

5352. Jurisprudence. © 1974. Law & Order, Board
game. 30
5353. Trial Lawyer. © 1977. Law, Career, Board
game. 25

Dinozoo Inc.

5354. Dinozoo. © 1993. Animal, Board game. 15

Diplomat Games

5354a.Chippendales After Hours Game. © 1983.
Board game. $35

Diplomat Sales Co.

5355. Office Party. © 1969. Social, Board game. 20
5356. Strip Tac Toe. © 1969. Social, Board game. 20

Direct Broadcast Programs Inc.

5357. Director's Choice. © 1984. Movie, Board
game. 18

Discovery Games

5358. Source of the Nile. © 1978. Adventure, Board
game. 20

Discere, Ltd.

5358a.Ludi At The Circus Maximus. © 1989.
Historical, Sports, Board game. 25

DMC Productions

5359. Tax and Spend. © 1993. Political, Board game. 20

DMR

5360. Let's Bowl a Game. © 1960. Sports, Bowling,
Board game. 15
5361. Let's Play Baseball. © 1965. Sports, Baseball,
Board game. 20
5362. Let's Play Basketball. Circa 1950s. Sports,
Basketball, Card game. 12

Dolphin Games

5362a.Kyle Rote's Pro-Ball. © 1962. Sports, Football
Board game. 125

Dooley-Fant Inc.

5363. Hee Haw. © 1975. TV, Board game. 25

Dot Records

**5364. Cinderfella Road Race Game, With Jerry
Lewis.** © 1960. Movie, Personality, Record
game. 65

Double Quarterback

5365. Double Quarterback. © 1949. Sports, Football,
Board game. 40

Douglas Malewicki

5366. Nuclear War. © 1965. Military, Board game. 100

Barbara Doyle-Carlton

5367. Ax Your Tax. © 1979. Social Concern, Board
game. 25

Dreiling
5368. Praise the Loot? © 1987. Economic, Board game. $12

Dubarry International, Inc.
5369. Intellectual Quests, The New Age Board Game. Circa 1990s. Q & A, Board game. 17

Ducked Wing
5370. Mad, Spy Vs Spy Card Game. © 1994. Comics, Law & Order, Card game. 12

Duff Sisters, Inc.
5371. Elvis Welcomes You to His World. © 1978. Music, Personality, Board game. 50

Edmond Dujardin
5372. Mille Bornes, America Model. © 1960. Travel, Card game. 15

E. W. Dulch
5373. Know Your States Game. © 1955. Geography, Card game. 15

Dwarfstar
5374. Barbarian Prince. © 1981. Fantasy, Board game. 15

Dynamic Design
5375. Airport. © 1972. Travel, Air, Board game. 22
5376. Beat Detroit. © 1972. Social Concern, Board game. 15
5377. Blitz. © 1972. Dice, Board game. 10
5378. Chug-A-Lug Drinking Party Game. © 1969. Social, Board game. 20
5379. Diet, The Cheating Man's Game. © 1972. Social Concern, Board game. 25
5379a.Drug Attack. © 1971. Social Concern, Board game. 28
5380. Family Game, The. © 1971. Social Concern, Board game. 22
5381. Feel Wheel, The. © 1972. Social Help, Board game. 20
5382. Lie, Cheat and Steal, The Game of Political Power. © 1971. Political, Board game. 20
5382a.Outlaw Trail. © 1972. Western, Board game. 25
5383. Society Today. © 1971. Social Concern, Board game. 25
5384. Who Can Beat Nixon. © 1970. Political, Board game. 38

E&M Games
5385. Dream On. © 1992. Q & A, Board game. 15

EDS Games
5386. Mega Nation. © 1989. Military, Board game. 15

Ed-U-Card Co.
5387. Animal Bird Fish Card Game. © 1947. Animal, Card game. 10
5388. Batter Up, Baseball Card Game. © 1948. Sports, Baseball, Card game. 15
5389. Bullwinkle Card game. © 1963. TV, Cartoon, Card game. 15

5390. Busy Bee. © 1958. Animal, Card game. $10
5391. Card Magic. Circa 1950s. Miscellaneous, Card game. 10
5392. Catchphrase. © 1975. Word, Card game. 6
5393. Cowboys & Indians. © 1949. Cowboys & Indians, Card game. 15
5394. Daniel Boone. © 1965. Westerns, Card game. 15
5395. Davy Crockett. © 1955. TV, Card game. 15
5396. Donald Duck. © 1960. Disney, Card game. 18
5397. Flintstones Animal Rummy. © 1961. Cartoon, TV, Card game. 15
5398. Go Fish, King Size. © 1973. Animal, Card game. 6
5399. Green Hornet. © 1966. Super Heroes, Card game. 20
5400. Howdy Doody Dominos. © 1951. TV, Board game. 20
5401. Huckleberry Hound. © 1961. TV, Card game. 18
5402. Johnny Can Read. © 1956. Word, Card game. 8
5403. Jungle Book Card Game. © 1966. Disney, Card game. 15
5404. Larry Harmons Laurel & Hardy. © 1972. Movie, Card game. 12
5405. Los Angeles Dodgers Game. © 1964. Sports, Baseball, Card game. 20
5406. Man from U.N.C.L.E. Playing Cards. © 1965. TV, Spy, Card game. 20
5407. Mets Baseball Game. © 1961. Sports, Baseball, Card game. 22
5408. Mickey Mouse. Circa 1970s. Disney, Card game. 15
5409. Mixies. © 1965. Miscellaneous, Card game. 10
5410. New York World's Fair Children Card Game. © 1963. Fairs, Card game. 22
5411. Pinky Lee's Who am I? © 1954. TV, Personality, Board game. 15
5412. Popeye Card Game. Circa 1960s. Comics, Card game. 15
5413. Quick Draw McGraw. © 1961. TV, Card game. 18
5414. Rootie Kazootie Word Game. Circa 1950s. TV, Card game. 20
5415. Satellite Space Race. © 1957. Space, Card game. 20
5416. Space Race, White box red letters. Circa 1970s. Space, Card game. 12
5417. Space Race. © 1969. Space, Card game. 12
5418. St. Louis Cardinals Baseball Game. © 1964. Sports, Baseball, Card game. 20
5419. Story Card Game. © 1947. Nursery Rhyme, Card game. 15
5420. Terrytoon Edition Old Maid. Circa 1960s. Cartoons, Card game. 15
5421. Top Pro Football Quiz Game. © 1970. Sports, Football, Board game. 12
5422. Tracks. Circa 1950s. Travel, Rail, Board game. 18
5423. Tree Spotter Cards. Circa 1950s. Plant, Card game. 12
5424. Walt Disney Presents Jungle Book. © 1966. Disney, Card game. 15
5425. World's Fair Children's Game. © 1964. Fairs, Card game. 20
5426. Yogi Bear Card Game. © 1961. TV, Cartoon, Card game. 15

Educational Design, Inc.
5426a.Fortran, Input: Reason, Output: Pleasure. Circa 1980s. Computer, Board game. 35

Educational Insights
5427. Worldwide Pen Pals World Geography Game. © 1989. Geography, Board game. $20
5428. Input/Output Game. © 1982. Strategy, Board game. 20
5429. Name that Country. Circa 1990s. Travel, World, Board game. 20
5430. Name That State. Circa 1990s. Travel USA, Board game. 20
5431. Presidential Card Game. Circa 1990s. Political, Card game. 20

Educational Materials
5432. Civil War Map Game. Circa 1988. Historical, Board game. 15

Educational Products Inc.
5433. Greek Myths and Legends. © 1977. Fantasy, Card game. 15
5434. Productivity Management Game. © 1974. Educational, Board game. 25

Educational Research Corp.
5435. Merit, The Catholic Game. © 1962. Religious, Board game. 30

Edutainment
5436. Geografacts, The Game of the World. © 1993. Geography, Board game. 15
5437. Passtimes, The Game of History. © 1993. History, Board game. 18

Elder Interprises
5438. Dualing. © 1977. Strategy, Board game. 15

Eldon
5439. Bowl-A-Matic. © 1963. Sports, Bowling, Action game. 18

Electric Game Co.
5440. Electric Baseball, 3 color cover. Circa 1940s. Sports, Baseball, Board game. 22
5441. Electric Basketball, 3 color cover. Circa 1940s. Sports, Basketball, Board game. 25
5442. Electric Commin' Round the Mountain. © 1954. Comics, Board game. 30
5443. Electric Football, 3 color cover. Circa 1940s. Sports, Football, Board game. 22
5444. Electric Hockey. Circa 1950s. Sports, Hockey, Board game. 30
5445. Electric Hot Potato. © 1960. Skill, Board game. 15
5446. Electric Jack Straws. Circa 1950s. Skill, Board game. 15
5447. Electric Speedway. Circa 1950s. Sports, Car, Board game. 20
5448. Electric Whiz Checkers. © 1961. Strategy, Board game. 12
5449. Electric Whiz Farm Roundup. © 1961. Farm, Board game. 50
5450. Electric Whiz Raceway. © 1961. Sports, Car, Board game. 45
5451. Electronic Classroom Game. © 1957. Q & A, Board game. 25
5452. Electric Whiz Fire Fighters. © 1961. Careers, Board game. 35

5453. Jim Prentice Electric Farmer's Round Up. Circa 1950s. Food, Board game. $50
5454. Jim Prentice-Electric Comin' Round The Mountain. Circa 1850s. Comics, Board game. 50
5455. Plinkety Plunk. © 1957. Skill, Board game. 30
5456. Whiz Baseball. © 1945. Sports, Baseball, Board game. 35

Electronic Design Concepts
5457. Greatest Baseball Teams of the Century. Miscellaneous, Sports, Baseball, Board game. 30

EMAR Co.
5457a.Sink-Em. Circa 1950s, Military, Board game. 40

EMD Enterprises
5458. Jerry Kramer's Instant Replay. © 1970. Sports, Football, Board game. 20

Empak Pub. Co.
5459. African-History Discovery. © 1991. Ethnic, History, Board game. 25

Empire Plastics
5460. Chubby Checker Twister. © 1961. Music, Personality, Board game. 85
5461. Empire Auto Race. Circa 1950s. Sports, Car, Board game. 50
5462. Zingo. Circa 1950s. Skill, Action game. 30

Endgame Entertainment
5463. Movie Mania. © 1992. Movie, Board game. 22
5464. Music Mania. © 1996. Music, Board game. 18
5465. Movie Mania (Trivia Edition). © 1996. Movie, Card game. 15

Enterprises of America
5466. Hopalong Cassidy Target Practice & Hold-Up Game. © 1950. TV, Western, Action Game. 125

Entex Industries
5467. Defender. © 1982. Miscellaneous, Board game. 30
5468. Turtles. © 1982. Animal, Board game. 15

Entrepreneurial Games
5469. Entre's Fun & Games in Accounting. © 1988. Numbers, Board game. 20

Eon Products
5470. Darkover. © 1979. Fantasy, Board game. 25

Epoch
5471. Pom Pom Game. © 1968. Skill, Action game. 25

Errobert Inventions Inc.
5472. War on Drugs. © 1989. Social Concern, Board game. 22

Eskay Co.
5473. Big Board. © 1975. Stock Market, Board game. 35

Esquire Magazine
5474. Blind Date, Magazine premium. Circa 1950s. Romance, Board game. 30

ESR
5475. Amazing Mr. Nim. © 1965. Q & A,
    Board game. $40

Eugenia Doughtie
5476. Target: The Moon Space Game. © 1962. Space,
    Board game. 60

Ewing
5477. Coast to Coast. © 1955. Travel, Board game. 25
5478. Motorace. © 1955. Sports, Car, Board game. 25
**5479. Walt Disney's Davy Crockett Radar Action
    Game.** © 1955. Disney, Action game. 50

Excalibre Games
5480. Heavy-Weight Boxing. © 1979. Sports, Boxing,
    Board game. 25

Exclusive Playing Card Co.
5481. Fun with Numbers, Deck # 9, Multipication. ©
    1951. Numbers, Card game. 12
5482. Ruff and Ready TV Favorite Spelling Game. ©
    1959. TV, Cartoon, Card game. 32
5483. Spellbound. © 1954. Word, Card game. 12

Executive Playthings
5483a.Executive Venture. © 1986. Economic,
    Board game. 20

Explorations Inc.

5484. Big Wig, The Great Game of Politics. © 1973.
    Political, Board game. 30

Extreme Enterprises
5485. Kave Keepers. © 1981. Adventure, Board
    game. 25

F & W Publishing
5486. First Class Farmer. © 1965. Economic, Board
    game. 30

F D Enterprises
5487. Capital Edition. © 1993. Town & Cities, Board
    game. 15
5488. Facts-A-Nation. © 1991. Q & A, History, Board
    game. 15

Family Games
5489. Godfather Game, The. © 1971. Law & Order,
    Board game. 35
5490. Godfather Game, The (Black Violin Case Box).
    © 1971. Law & Order, Board game. 50

5491. Howard Hughes. © 1972. Personality, Board
    game. $40

Family Pastimes
5492. New America. © 1980. Travel, Board game. 65
5492a.Explorer. © 1982. Adventure, Board game. 25

Fantasy Games Unlimited
5493. Citadel, ziplock bag. © 1976. Fantasy, Board
    game. 22

Calvin Harry Farley
5493a.Farley Football. Circa 1970s. Sports, Football
    Board & Card game. 35

Feature Games
5494. Bowlo. © 1957. Sports, Bowling, Card game. 20

Len Feder
5495. LF Baseball. © 1980. Sports, Baseball, Board
    game. 15

Fernbrooke Enterprises
5496. Weigh-Out. © 1971. Social Concern, Physical,
    Board game. 22

Carl Fisher, Inc.
5496a.Allegro. © 1980. Music, Board game. 30

H. Fishlove & Co.
5497. Crosby Derby, The, Bing Crosby Photo. ©
    1947. Sports, Horseracing, Board game. 85

Flying Buffalo
5498. Nuclear Escalation. © 1983. International,
    Board game. 50
5498a.Nuclear Proliferation. 1980s. Military, Card
    game. 40

Fontanelle

5499. Ticker Tape. © 1960. Economic, Board game. 35

Foster Enterprises
5499a.Profit Farming. © 1979. Farm, Board game. 25

Four Star
5500. America, The Great Board Game. © 1992.
    Travel USA, Board game. 20

Four-One-One
5501. Volunteers! The Name of the Game Today. ©
    1983. Economic, Board game. 20

Helene Fox, Inc.
5502. Snob, A Fantasy Shopping Spree. © 1983. Economic, Board game. $50

Frandzel & Share
5503. Daze of our Loans. © 1988. Social Concern, Board game. 20

Franes
5504. Avanté. © 1967. Military, Board game. 20

Frank Sacks
5505. Movie Game, The. © 1981. Movie, Board game. 18

Franklin Merchandise
5505a.Great Downhill Ski Game. © Sports, Ski, Board game. 20

Franklin Mint
5506. Monopoly, Deluxe Edition, Hardwood box board-Table. © 1991. Economic, Board game. 250

Frontwoods
5506a.Dog Show Game, The. © 1990. Animal, Board game. 25

Fun & James, Inc.
5507. Screenplay. © 1992. Movie, Board game. 20

Funtastic, Inc.
5508. Psyche-Paths. © 1969. Self Help, Board game. 25
5509. Score Four. © 1968. Miscellaneous, Board game. 10

Fun-Time Products
5510. GammonBall. © 1980. Sports, Miscellaneous, Board game. 20

Saml. Gabriel Sons & Co.
5511. Bent Outta Shape. © 1981. Skill, Action game. 15
5512. British Square. © 1978. Classic, Board game. 12
5513. Chutes Away. © 1977. Skill, Action game. 12
5514. Deep Sea Diving Game. © 1956. Adventure, Board game. 35
5515. Earth Satellite Game. © 1956. Space, Board game. 60
5516. Frontier Fort Rescue Race. © 1956. Western, Board game. 22
5517. Harpoon, The Real Whale Hunt Game. © 1955. Animal, Board game. 65
5518. It. Game of Tag. © 1956. Kiddie, Board game. 12
5519. J. Fred Muggs 'Around the World' Game. © 1955. TV, Travel, Board game. 65
5520. Lion Hunt. © 1956. Animal, Board game. 30
5521. Mt. Everest. Circa 1950s. Adventure, Board game. 35
5522. Original Little Rascals Clubhouse Bingo, The. © 1958. Movie, Board game. 55
5523. Peter Rabbit. © 1946. Animal, Board game. 25
5524. Pirate's Cove. © 1956. Adventure, Board game. 30
5525. Poucho Checkers. © 1977. Classic, Board game. 15

5526. Ramar of the Jungle Blow Gun Game Target Game. © 1955. TV, Adventure, Action game. $100
5527. Spiro T. Agnew, American History Challenge Game. © 1971. History, Politics, Board game. 75
5528. Stampede. © 1956. Western, Board game. 35
5529. Stock Car Road Race. © 1956. Sports, Car, Board game. 30
5530. Stock Market Game, The. © 1955. Stock Market, Board game. 30
5531. Sudden Death. © 1978. Skill, Board game. 15
5532. Truth or Consequences. © 1955. Q & A, Board game. 45
5533. Walt Disney Character, My First Game. © 1955. Disney, Board game. 50
5534. Walt Disney's Mickey Mouse Stand-Up Lotto. © 1956. Disney, Board game. 50
5535. Walt Disney's My First Game. © 1955. Disney, Board game. 50
5536. Walt Disney's Official Davy Crockett Rescue Game. © 1955. Disney, TV, Western, Board game. 50

Gaffney
5537. Lone Ranger & The Silver Bullets Game. © 1959. TV, Western, Board game. 125
5538. No Game

Galoob
5538a.L. A. Law. © 1988. TV Board game. 18

Galt & Co.
5539. Connect. © 1969. Strategy, Board game. 15

Gambol Entertainment Inc.
5540. Celebrity Challenge. © 1993. Q & A, Board game. 17

Game Creations
5541. Eloping. © 1946. Romance, Board game. 150

Game Gems
5542. Annie Oakley Game. © 1965. TV, Western, Board game. 100
5543. Bewitched. © 1965. TV, Board game. 125
5544. Boris Karloff Monster Game. © 1965. Monster, Board game. 400
5545. Flash Gordon. © 1965. Super Hero, Science Fiction, Board game. 100
5546. Gilligan's Island Game. © 1964. TV, Board game. 500
5547. Kentucky Jones Horse Auction Game. © 1965. TV, Animal, Board game. 100
5548. Lassie Game. © 1965. TV, Board game. 75

Game Geste, Inc.
5549. Reel Schpeel. © 1994. Movie, Board game. 17

Game Keepers
5550. W. C. Fields. © 1972. Personality, Card game. 30

Game Makers
5551. Notable Quotables. Circa 1990s. Word, Board game. 15

Game Masters

5552. Student Survival. © 1968. Educational,
Board game. $40

Gamofiles Unlimited

5552a.Front Page. © 1974. Communications,
Board game. 45

Game Partners

5553. Beyond the Stars. © 1964. Stars, Board game. 50

Game Plan

5554. Election. © 1972. Political, Card game. 25

Game Room Productions

5555. Sqwurm. © 1979. Strategy, Board game. 10

Game Shop Inc.

5556. Goal Line Stand. © 1980. Sports, Football,
Board game. 22

Game Time Games

5557. Classic Major League Baseball Travel Edition.
© 1987. Sports, Baseball, Board game. 15
5557a.Classic Major League Baseball Game. ©
1987. 1st edition. Sports, Baseball, Board game. 50
5558. Grand Imperialism. © 1978. Military,
Board game. 25

Game Venings

5559. King Hamlet. © 1980. Literary, Board game. 22

Game Works Inc.

5560. Middle Age Crazy. © 1985. Social Concern,
Board game. 20
5561. Mid-Life Crisis. © 1982. Social Concern,
Board game. 15
5562. Over the Hill. © 1986. Skill, Action game. 15
5563. Romantic Journey, The. © 1987. Romance,
Board game. 20

Gamecraft

5564. Real-Life Basketball. © 1974. Sports,
Basketball, Board game. 25

Gameophiles Ltd.

5565. Great City Game of Rome, The. © 1974.
Travel, World, Board game. 25

Games & Gadgets Inc.

5566. Sight Four. Circa 1990s. Numbers, Board game. 10

Games & Names

5567. Treffles. © 1976. Word, Card game. $8

Games, ETC.

5567a.LDS Church History Game. © 1973. Religious,
Board game. 25

Games for Industry

5568. Crusade, Lawerence Welk's All Star ACS Kit.
© 1967. TV, Personality, Board game. 40
5569. Call Kelly. © 1966. Careers, Board game. 35

Games Galore

5569a.Condomania 2000. © 1979. Board game. 25

Games of Fame

5570. Bluff. © 1945. Social, Card game. 25

Games of Games

5571. Cartel. © 1974. Economic, Board game. 25

Games Research Inc.

5572. Diplomacy, Brown box, 1st edition. © 1961.
International, Board game. 75
5573. Diplomacy, Red box, picture of board on cover.
© 1961. International, Board game. 35
5574.Presidential Convention! © 1960. Political,
Board game. 65

Games Workshop

5574. Doctor Who. © 1980. TV, Super Hero,
Board game. 18
5575. Judge Dredd. © 1983. Super Hero,
Board game. 18

Gamescience Corp.

5576. Confrontation. Circa 1950s. Military,
Board game. 25

Gamewright

5577. Honor of the Samurai. © 1996. Oriental,
Board game. 15
5578. Quests of the Round Table. © 1995. History,
Card game. 12

Gamma Two

5579. Klondike. © 1975. Adventure, Board game. 20

Gammon Games

5580. Gamblers Golf. © 1975. Sports, Golf, Board
game. 15

Gamut of Games

5581. 6 Pack of Paper & Pencil Games, The. © 1974.
Q & A, Paper & Pencil. 10
5582. Cartel, 2nd Edition. © 1974. Economic, Board
game. 20
5583. Diamondhead Game. © 1975. TV, Board
game. 10
5584. Infinity. © 1974. Space, Board game. 10
5585. My Word. © 1974. Word, Board game. 10
5586. Realm. © 1974. Strategy, Board game. 10

Gardner & Co.

5587. 20,000 Leagues Under the Sea. Circa 1960s. Disney, Board game. $75

5588. All-Star Football. Circa 1950s. Sports, Football, Board game. 35

5589. Boots & Saddles. © 1958. Western, Board game. 25

5590. Captain Kangaroo Let's Build a House. © 1956. TV, Board game. 50

5591. Championship Golf. Circa 1950s. Sports, Golf, Board game. 30

5592. Donald Duck Beanbag Game. Circa 1950s. Disney, Board game. 65

5593. Jan Murray's Treasure Hunt. Circa 1950s. TV, Game, Board game. 25

5594. Mickey Mouse Basketball. Circa 1950s. Disney, Basketball, Board game. 65

5595. Mickey Mantle's Big League Baseball. © 1955. Sports, Baseball, Board game. 175

5596. Phil Silvers Sgt. Bilko. Circa 1950s. TV, Board game. 60

5597. Stock Car Race. Circa 1950s. Sports, Car, Board game. 35

5598. Travel. Circa 1960s. Travel, Board game. 25

5599. Uranium Rush. © 1955. Scientific, Board game. 125

5600. Verne Gagne World Champion Wrestling. Circa 1950s. Sports, Wrestling, Board game. 150

5601. Walt Disney Character Quick or Be Caught Game. Circa 1960s. Disney, Board game. 40

5602. Walt Disney's Davy Crockett. Circa 1950s. Disney, Board game. 45

5603. Walt Disney's Donald Duck Flips His Lid. Circa 1960s. Disney, Board game. 50

5604. Walt Disney's Zorro Beanbag-Darts. © 1960. Disney, Action game. 70

Gavin & Brackenridge

5605. Your Money. © 1988. Economic, Board game. 18

GDW

5606. Brotherhood, The. © 1983. Law & Order, Board game. 22

5607. Campaign Trail. © 1983. Political, Board game. 25

5608. Dark Nebula. © 1980. Space, Board game. 20

5609. Traveller. © 1981. Science Fiction, Board game. 25

Gelles-widmer Co.

5610. Pay the Cashier. © 1957. Economic, Board game. 25

General Foods

5611. Post Doctor Dolittle Card Game, Premium cereal. © 1967. Movie, Card game. $20

5611a.Kool-Aid Kid's Trivia Game. © 1985. Advertising, Food, Board game. 25

General Mills

5612. Bullwinkle's Electronic Quiz Game. © 1962. TV, Cartoon, Board game. 50

5613. Going for Toy Story Toy Glory. © 1996. Movie, Board game. 6

5613a.War Battle Game, Kix premium. 1945, Premium, Military, Board game. 65

5614. Tiddly-Winks Game. Trix Cereal. © 1967. Action game. 25

General Sportcraft Co.

5615. Orient, patterned after Go. © 1959. Classic, Board game. 15

Genesis Enterprises

5616. Rrib-Bit, Plastic frogs tokens. © 1973. Animal, Board game. 15

Geografacts

5617. Geografacts. © 1991. Geography, Board game. 15

Gerney Games

5618. ASG Major League Baseball. © 1973. Sports, Baseball, Board game. 25

5619. Official NBA Basketball Game. Circa 1970s. Sports, Basketball, Board game. 35

Gestion Group

5620. Big Bucks, The World of Business. © 1987. Economic, Board game. 18

Giambrone Ent.

5621. Mega Gammon. Circa 1990s. Strategy, Board game. 15

Gibby Games, Inc.

5621a.Corporate Ladder. © 1986. Economic, Board game. 25

Gibco Inc.

5622. Civil War Wit. © 1986. Military, Civil War, Card game. 15

A. C. Gilbert

5623. Tuggy. Circa 1960s. Skill, Action game. 15

Glenn Industries

5624. Tee Off by Sam Snead. © 1973. Sports, Golf, Board game. 50

Global Godmother, Inc.

5625. Eco Game. Circa 1990s. Plant, Board game. 17

Gloria Game Co.

5626. Taxology. © 1957. Political, Board game. 30

Go For It, Ltd.
5626a.Hilton Head Island Fever. © 1982.
City & States, Board game. $22

Golden (see also Whitman and Western)
5627. Barbie, Queen of the Prom Game. © 1991.
Doll, Dating, Board game. 15
5628. Go Bots. © 1985. Toy, Board game. 12
5629. Great Shakes, Charlie Brown. Circa 1980s.
Comics, Dice game. 18
5630. Gremlins Game. © 1984. Movie, Monster,
Board game. 15
5631. Race to Riches. © 1989. Economic,
Board game. 15
5632. Return to Oz Game. © 1985. Movie,
Board game. 15

Golden Capitol
5633. Golden Quizziac, The. © 1960. Q & A, Board
game. 15

Golden Rock Co.
5634. Around the World Travel Game. © 1975.
Travel, Air, Board game. 25

Golden, Western Pub.
5635. Solarquest. © 1988. Space, Board game. 25

Goodenough & Woglom
5636. Bible Lotto, Game of. Circa 1940s. Religious,
Board game. 12

F. Goodman
5637. Championship Fight Game. Circa 1950s.
Sports, Boxing, Board game. 55

Gotham Pressed Steel
5638. All-Star Basketball Bagatelle. © 1950. Sports,
Basketball, Board game. 45
5639. All-Star Bowling. © 1961. Sports, Bowling,
Board game. 35
5640. Carl Hubbel Mechanical Baseball. © 1948.
Sports, Baseball, Board game. 200
5641. Gotham All Star Bowling, Metal components.
Circa 1960s. Sports, Bowling, Board game. 35
5642. Jackie Robinson Baseball Game. Circa 1950s.
Sports, Baseball, Board game. 1000
5643. Johnny Bench Magnetic Baseball Game. ©
1971. Sports, Baseball, Board game. 85

Goyham
5644. Pro League Basketball. © 1958. Sports,
Basketball, Board game. 45

Grace Games
5644a.Self-Concept Game, The. © 1981. Religious,
Self help, Board game. 20

Grand Products
5644a.Grand Star. © 1978. Sports, Football Board
game. 20

Granete St. Novelty Co.
5645. We Want Freedom, Elect Yourself President.
Circa 1950s. Political, Card game. 45

Ernst C. Grant Ltd.
5646. Penn-State-O-Poly. © 1987. Cities & Town,
Board game. $18

Great Games Inc.
5647. Derby Downs. © 1973. Sports, Horseracing,
Board game. 22
5648. Kangaroo. Circa 1970s. Animal, Board game. ... 15
5648a.Scrambler, The. © 1973. Sports, Football Board
game. 20

Great Pennant Races
5649. Great Pennant Races. © 1980. Sports, Baseball,
Board game. 15

Great White North Game Co.
5650. Corporate Circles. © 1985. Economic, Board
game. 18

Green Giant
5651. Jolly Green Giant Card Game. © 1970. Food,
Comic, Card game. 15

W. M. Grimes
5652. Par Golf. © 1959. Sports, Golf, Board game. ... 25

Groovy Games Inc.
5653. Boston Scene. © 1977. Cities & Towns, Board
game. 20
5654. Chicago Scene. © 1977. Cities & Towns, Board
game. 20
5655. New York Scene. © 1977. Cities and Towns,
Board game. 20

Gulf Oil
5656. Go-Gulf Game, Gasoline oil premium. Circa
1960s. Premium, Board game. 28

H & K Publishing
5656a.San Francisco, The Tour Game. © 1979. City
& State, Board game. 20

H. D.& K. Products
5657. Majority Rules. Circa 1980s. Political,
Board game. 20

Haecker Industries
**5658. Gabby Hays Champion Shooting Target
Game.** © 1950. Western, Personal, Action game. 200

John M. Hall Enterprises
5659. In-Side Golf. © 1967. Sports, Golf, Board
game. 22

Hall of Fame Games
5659a.Handicap Harness Racing. © 1978. Sports,
Horseracing Board game. 18

Hammerhead Enterprises
5660. Capital Punishment. © 1981. Social Concern,
Board game. 35
5661. Public Assistance. © 1980. Social Concern,
Board game. 30

Hanlon-Red Reparee
5662. Counter Ploy. © 1975. Strategy, Board game. $12

John Hansen
5663. 221-B Baker Street-The Master Detective Game. © 1977. Detective, Board game. 15
5664. Glastnost. © 1988. Political, Board game. 20
5664a. New York Scene. © 1981. Cities & Towns 18
5664b. Los Angeles Scene. © 1981. Cities & Towns 18
5664c. Cincinnati Scene. © 1981. Cities & Towns 18
5664d. Chicago Scene. © 1981. Cities & Towns......................... 18
5664e. San Francisco Scene. © 1981. Cities & Towns 18
5664f. Washington Scene. © 1981. Cities & Towns 18
5664g. Houston Scene. © 1981. Cities & Towns.......................... 18
5664h. Boston Scene. © 1981. Cities & Towns 18
5664i. Hawaii Scene. © 1981. Cities & Towns 18
5664j. Dallas Scene. © 1980. Cities & Towns 18
5664k. Phoenix Scene. © 1980. Cities & Towns 18
5664l. Denver Scene. © 1980. Cities & Towns............................ 18
5664m. New Orleans Scene. © 1980. Cities & Towns.................. 18
5664n. Milwaukee Scene. © 1980. Cities & Towns..................... 18
5664o. San Antonio/Austin Scene. © 1980. Cities & Towns 18
5664p. Kansas City Scene. © 1980. Cities & Towns 18
5664q. Salt Lake City Scene. © 1980. Cities & Towns 18
5664r. Wichita Scene. © 1980. Cities & Towns 18
5664s. Oklahoma Scene. © 1980. Cities & Towns 18
5664t. Ft. Worth Scene. © 1980. Cities & Towns 18
5664u. Philadelphia Scene. © 1980. Cities & Towns 18
5665. Minneapolis-St. Paul Scene. © 1981. Cities & Towns, Board game. 18
5665a. Various Cities and Town Games , As above 1- 15 18
5665b. Stock Market Specialist. © 1983. Stock Market, Board game. 25
5666. Trivial Detective Game. © 1985. Q & A, Detective, Board game. 18

John Hansen-Amex
5667. Stock Market Specialist. © 1983. Stock Market, Board game. 20

Happy Hour Inc.
5668. Hunch. © 1956. Strategy, Board game. 15
5669. Ticky the Clown Clock. © 1956. Time, Board game. 18
5670. Billionare, You Can be a, Uranium Hunting Game. © 1956. Economic, Board game. 65

Hardswell Press
5671. So You Think You Know Maine. © 1985. Cities & Town, Board game. 18

Harett-Gilmar
5672. Adventures of Davy Crockett, The. Circa 1950s. Adventure, Board game. 65
5673. All-Star Electric Baseball & Football. © 1955. Sports, Baseball, Football, Board game. 35
5674. Billboard. Circa 1950s. Advertising, Board game. 150
5675. Circus Boy. © 1956. TV, Board game. 75
5676. Hot Rod. © 1953. Travel, Car, Board game. 40
5677. Howdy Doody's Electric Doodles. Circa 1950s. TV, Board game. 65
5678. Howdy Doody's 3-Ring Circus. © 1955. TV, Circus, Board game. 65

5679. Howdy Doody's Electric Carnival Game. Circa 1950s. TV, Board game. $65
5680. Mighty Mouse Rescue Game. © 1956. Cartoons, Board game. 75
5681. Plane Parade. Circa 1950s. Travel, Air, Board game. 40
5682. Play U.S.A. Circa 1950s. Travel, Board game. 25
5683. Playland. Circa 1950s. Miscellaneous, Board game. 30
5684. Robin Hood and His Merry Men. © 1955. Adventure, Board game. 40
5685. Table Top Bowling. Circa 1950s. Sports, Bowling, Board game. 25
5686. Traffic Jam. © 1954. Travel, Car, Board game. 50
5687. Travel America. Circa 1950s. Travel, Board game. 30
5688. Treasure Island. Circa 1950s. Adventure, Board game. 40
5689. Wiry Dan, Adventure of Pinocchio. Circa 1950s. Literary, Board game. 30

5690. Wiry Dan's Electric Baseball Game. © 1953. Sports, Baseball, Board game. 35
5691. Wiry Dan's Electric Football Game. Circa 1950s. Sports, Football, Board game. 35

Harmony Toy Ltd.
5692. Adventures with Clifford the Big Red Dog. © 1993. Literary, Animal, Board game. 15
5693. Berenstein Bears, Hidden Honey Pot, The. © 1993. Literary, Animal, Board game. 15
5694. Berenstein Bears, Hide and Seek, The. © 1993. Literary, Animal, Board game. 15
5695. Berenstein Bears, So Much To Do, The. © 1993. Literary, Animal, Board game. 15
5696. Clues with Clifford the Big Red Dog. © 1993. Q & A, Animal, Card game. 12
5697. Thomas the Tank Engines's, All Aboard Alphabet. © 1993. Literary, Rail, Board game. 12
5698. Thomas the Tank Engines's, B-I-N-G-O-Train. © 1993. Literary, Rail, Board game. 12
5699. Thomas the Tank Engines's, Hats Off. © 1993. Literary, Rail, Board game. 12
5700. Thomas the Tank Engines's, Railroad Rescue. © 1993. Literary, Rail, Board game. 12
5701. Thomas the Tank Engines's, Tricky Track Dominoes. © 1993. Literary, Rail, Board game. 10
5702. Thomas the Tank Engines's, Whistle Stop Surprise. © 1993. Literary, Rail, Board game. 12

Harwell Assoc.
5703. Newtown. © 1971. Cities Board game. 20
5704. Newtown. © 1975. Cities Board game. 20

Hasbro

5705. 2 for the Money. © 1955. TV, Game, Board game. $25

5706. Across the USA. © 1966. Geography, Board game. 20

5707. Airplane Game. © 1966. Travel, Air, Board game. 25

5708. Amazing Dunninger Mind Reading Game, The. © 1967. Mystic, Board game. 50

5709. Aquaman, Justice League of America. © 1967. Super Hero, Board game. 140

5710. Archie's Fun Game. © 1963. Comics, Board game. 200

5711. Banana Splits Game, The. © 1969. TV, Music, Board game. 75

5712. Batman and Robin Game, Marble Maze Game. © 1966. Super Heroes, Board game. 85

5713. Batman and Robin Game. © 1965. Super Heroes, Board game. 75

5714. Batman Game. © 1973. Super Heroes, Board game. 60

5715. Batman Game. © 1978. Super Heroes, Board game. 50

5716. Catch a Chicken Torie. © 1968. Animal, Board game. 15

5717. Challenge the Yankees. © 1964. Sports, Baseball, Board game. 300

5718. Chiclets Gum Village Game, Ad for gum. © 1959. Advertising, Board game. 35

5719. Clobbler and the Elves, The. © 1964. Nursery Rhyme, Board game. 20

5720. Cowboys and Indians. © 1966. Western, Board game. 20

5721. Creature from the Black Lagoon Mystery Game, The. © 1963. Monster, Board game. 375

5722. Dancing Princess, The. © 1964. Miscellaneous, Board game. 35

5723. Dating Game, The. © 1967. TV, Romance, Board game. 35

5724. Dick Tracy Marble Maze. © 1966. Comics, Board game. 100

5725. Doctor Dolittle, Marble Maze. © 1967. Movie, Board game. 75

5726. Dodge Ball. © 1973. Skill, Action game. 15

5727. Dondi Finders Keepers Game. © 1960. TV, Board game. 40

5728. Dondi, Potatoe Race Game. Circa 1960s. TV, Board game. 40

5729. Dondi, Prairie Race Game. Circa 1960s. TV, Board game. 40

5730. Don't Bug Me. © 1967. Skill, Action game. 15

5731. Double Dealer, Jerry Lewis on Cover. © 1973. Personality, Gambling, Board game. 25

5732. Down on the Farm. © 1966. Animal, Board game. 20

5733. Dracula Mystery Game. © 1963. Monster, Board game. 300

5734. Dracula's I Vant to Bite Your Finger Game. © 1981. Monster, Board game. 20

5735. Ensign O'Toole, U.S.S. Appleby Game. © 1963. TV, Board game. 35

5736. Family Game. © 1967. TV, Game, Board game. 20

5737. Fearless Fireman Thrilling Game and Toy. © 1955. Occupations, Board game. 75

5738. Flash, Justice League of America. © 1967. Super Heroes, Board game. 200

5739. Flying Nun Flying Maze Game. © 1967. TV, Action game. $65

5740. Frankenstein Horror Target Game. © 1964. Monster, Action game. 250

5741. Frankenstein Mystery Game. © 1963. Monster, Board game. 300

5742. Freefall. © 1968. Skill, Action game. 15

5743. G.I. Joe Adventure Board Game. © 1982. Toy, Military, Board game. 15

5744. G.I. Joe Combat Infantry Game. © 1967. Toy, Military, Board game. 75

5745. G.I. Joe Commando Attack Game. © 1985. Toy, Military, Board game. 17

5746. G.I. Joe Marine Paratroop Game. Circa 1960s. Toy, Military, Board game. 45

5747. G.I. Joe Navy Frogman Game. © 1967. Toy, Military, Board game. 75

5748. G.I. Joe, Capture Hill 79. © 1966. Toy, Military, Board game. 65

5749. G.I. Joe. © 1982. Toy, Card game. 22

5750. Game of the Week. © 1969. Sports, Baseball, Board game. 50

5751. Gold Trail. © 1966. Skill, Action game. 40

5752. Great Estate, The, with Jerry Lewis on cover. © 1973. Personality, Board game. 50

5753. Haunted House. © 1962. Monster, Board game. 150

5754. Hillbillies Feudin' Time. © 1964. Miscellaneous, Board game. 35

5755. Hillbillies Hoedown. © 1964. Miscellaneous, Board game. 35

5755a.Home Game. Circa 1950s, Arlene Frances and Hugh Downs on cover, TV Home building board game. 100

5756. Home Stretch, The. © 1970. Sports, Horseracing, Board game. 30

5757. How to Succeed. Circa 1950s. Careers, Board game. 45

5758. Humpty Dumpty Marble Game. © 1966. Nursery Rhyme, Board game. 40

5759. Interpretation of Dreams. © 1969. Mystic, Board game. 40

5760. It Takes Two. © 1970. Social, Board game. 20

5761. Jack and Jill Jacks Game. © 1966. Nursery Rhyme, Board game. 15

5762. Knock Your Block Off. © 1969. Skill, Action game. 22

5763. Knuckle Busters. © 1967. Sports, Boxing, Board game. 40

Hasbro continued

5764. Laughin, Squeeze Your Bippy Game. © 1968. TV, Board game. $65
5765. Leave it to Beaver Ambush Game. © 1959. TV, Western, Board game. 65
5766. Leave it to Beaver Money Maker Game. © 1959. TV, Economic, Board game. 65
5767. Leave it to Beaver Rocket to the Moon. © 1959. TV, Space, Board game. 75
5768. Let's Face it. © 1955. Social, Board game. 20
5769. Loli Pop Lane. © 1964. Food, Board game. 20
5770. Love, The Game of. © 1968. Romance, Board game. 25
5771. Magic Miles. © 1956. Travel, Board game. 25
5772. Marble Maze. © 1966. Skill, Board game. 20
5773. Mentor. Circa 1960s. Q & A, Board game. 75
5774. Merry Milkman Exciting Game and Toy. © 1965. Occupations, Board game. 85
5775. Mighty Hercules Game, The. © 1963. Cartoon, Board game. 500
5776. Mob Strategy. © 1969. Law & Order, Board game. 65
5777. Mummy. © 1965. Monster, Board game. 250
5778. Munsters Drag Race Game. © 1965. Monster, Board game. 1100
5779. Munsters Masquerade Game. © 1964. Monster, Board game. 1300
5780. Munsters Picnic Game. © 1965. Monster, Board game. 800
5781. NBC Game of the Week. © 1969. Sports, Football, Board game. 40
5782. NBC Pro Playoff. © 1969. Sports, Football, Board game. 30
5783. NBC World of Wall Street. © 1969. Stock Market, Board game. 30
5784. Newlywed Game, The, Wedding cake cover. © 1979. TV, Board game. 15
5785. Newlywed Game, The, 3rd edition, yellow stripes box. © 1969. TV, Board game. 20
5786. Newlywed Game, The, Original Edition, red, pink & white. © 1967. TV, Board game. 25
5787. Olive Oyl-I'll Catch My Popeye Game. © 1965. Comics, Board game. 65
5788. Penguin Polo. © 1968. Skill, Board game. 25
5789. Phantom of the Opera Mystery Game. © 1963. Monster, Movie, Board game. 400
5790. Pie in Your Eye Game. Circa 1960s. Skill, Action game. 25
5791. Police Patrol Action Game and Toy. © 1955. Occupations, Board game. 30
5792. Pooch. © 1954. Strategy, Board game. 20
5793. Popeye is the Strongest Man in the World. © 1965. Comics, Board game. 65
5794. Post Office Game. © 1968. Communication, Board game. 25
5795. Simple Simon Balloon Game. © 1966. Nursery Rhyme, Board game. 30
5796. Singing Bone, The. © 1962. Movie, Board game. 40
5797. Spin the Bottle Game. © 1968. Romance, Board game. 20
5798. Spot a Car Bingo. Circa 1950s. Travel, Car, Board game. 25
5799. Square-It. © 1961. Skill, Board game. 15
5800. Star Trek Game. © 1974. Science Fiction, TV, Board game. 125
5801. Star Trek Marble Maze Game. © 1967. Space, Board game. 150

5802. Star Wars, Destroy Death Star. © 1977. Movie, Science Fiction, Board game. $25
5803. Strike Bowling. © 1958. Sports, Bowling, Board game. 20
5804. Super Heroes Bingo. © 1965. Super Hero, Board game. 65
5805. Super Sunday Football. © 1973. Sports, Football, Board game. 20
5806. Superboy Game. © 1965. Super Heroes, Board game. 100
5807. Superman Game, Search for Superman's Deadliest Enemy. © 1965. Super Heroes, Board game. 135
5808. Superman Game. © 1973. Super Heroes, Board game. 50
5809. Superman Game. © 1978. Super Heroes, Board game. 40
5810. Superman Marble Maze. © 1966. Super Hero, Board game. 40
5811. Thimble Theatre Game Starring Wimpy. © 1965. Comics, Board game. 65
5812. Thimble Theatre Game, Olive Oil. © 1965. Comics, Board game. 65
5813. Think-A-Tron. © 1961. Q & A, Board game. 65
5814. Three Chipmunks Acorn Hunt. © 1960. TV, Board game. 35
5815. Three Chipmunks Big Record. © 1960. TV, Board game. 35
5816. Three Chipmunks, Cross Country Game, The. © 1960. Music, Animal, Board game. 35
5817. Tie 'N Tangle. © 1967. Skill, Action game. 12
5818. Tootsie Roll Train Game. Circa 1950s. Advertising, Travel, Board game. 40
5819. Trap the Rat. © 1964. Strategy, Board game. 15
5820. Two for the Money. © 1955. TV, Q & A, Board game. 25
5821. Vegas. © 1969. Gambling, Board game. 20
5822. War of the Networks. © 1979. Communications, Board game. 20
5823. Whodunit. © 1968. Mystery, Board game. 25
5824. Wimpy, Where are My Hamburgers? © 1965. Comics, TV, Board game. 65
5825. Wolfman Mystery Game. © 1963. Monster, Board game. 200
5826. Wonder Woman Game. © 1978. Super Heroes, Board game. 60
5827. Wonder Woman, Justice League of America. © 1967. Super Hero, Board game. 150
5828. World of Wall Street, The. © 1969. Stock Market, Board game. 22
5829. Zok. © 1967. Action, Board game. 15

Hasbro-Bradley Co.

5830. Transformers Card Game. © 1985. Toy, Card game. 12

Jay Hawker Games, Inc.
5831. Swish. © 1948. Sports, Basketball, Board game. 35

Headgames
5832. Final Strategy. Circa 1980s. Strategy, Board game. 20

Henard Industries, Inc.
5833. Airport. © 1988. Air, Board game. 18

Henry-Gingold
5833a.Artist, The. Game. © 1982. Art, Board game. $35

Herald Toy Prod. Co.
5834. Arthur Godfrey's Par-Tee Golf. © 1954.
Personal, Sports, Golf, Board game. 65

Heritage
5835. Demonlord. © 1982. Fantasy, Board game. 18

Hersch & Co.
5836. Song Burst. © 1990. Music, Board game. 17

Hesse Ltd.
5837. Discover Iowa. © 1979. Cities & Towns,
Board game. 20

Daallah Heyari
5838. Vari. © 1989. Miscellaneous, Board game. 15

High Game Enterprises
5839. Question of Scruples, A. © 1984. Q & A,
Board game. 15

G & E Hill
5840. Roots, The Game of. © 1978. History,
Board game. 35

James R. Hock
5841. F/11 Armchair Quarterback. © 1964.
Sports, Football, Board game. 30

Margaret S. Hoffecher
5842. Horseshow. © 1965. Sports, Horse,
Board game. 50

Lenape Hoking
5843. Pow-Wow the Game. © 1993. Ethnic,
Board game. 22

Holiday's Games
5844. Hal Holiday's Football Strategy. © 1953.
Sports, Football, Board game. 75

Hollywood Games
5845. Real Estate, Game of. © 1946. Economic,
Board game. 100

Holyoke Game Co.
5846. Dragon's Teeth. © 1948. Strategy, Board game. 30

Home Court
5847. Home Court Basketball (Charlie Eckman).
© 1954. Sports, Basketball, Board game. 125

Bruce Honig
5848. Create. © 1985. Miscellaneous, Board game. 15

Hoosier Basketball Co.
5849. Dribbling Around Basketball. Circa 1950s.
Sports, Basketball, Card game. 15

M. Hopper
5850. Batter Up. © 1946. Sports, Baseball, Board
game. 25

Horatio
5851. Baseball Game, The. © 1988. Sports, Baseball,
Board game. $25

Horn Abbot
5852. UBI. © 1986. Geography, Board game. 25

House of Curmudgeon
5852a.Mr. Murl Game, The. © 1984. Board game. 25

House of Games
5853. 4000 A. Intersteller Conflict Game. © 1972.
Space, Board game. 40
5854. Flash Gordon Game. © 1977. Science Fiction,
Comics, Board game. 40
5855. Project CIA, A Spy Training Game. © 1973.
Spy, Board game. 40
5856. Ulcers. © 1969. Social Concern, Board game. 35

Hoyle
5857. 50s & 60s Trivia Game-#9. © 1984. History,
Q & A, Card game. 12
5858. Bible, Trivia Game-#10. © 1984. Religious,
Q & A, Card game. 12
5859. End of the Line. © 1984. Strategy, Board game. 15
5860. Grand Master of the Martial Arts. © 1986.
Sports, Card game. 15
5861. Kids Trivia Game-#7. © 1984. Kiddie, Q & A,
Card game. 12
5862. Legend of Camelot. © 1987. Adventure, Board
game. 12
5863. Movie Trivia Game-#1. © 1984. Movie, Q & A,
Card game. 12
5864. Music Trivia Game-#3. © 1984. Music, Q & A,
Card game. 12
5865. People's Court, The. © 1986. TV, Board game. 20
5866. Political Trivia Game-#6. © 1984. Political,
Q & A, Card game. 12
5867. Potpourri Trivia Game-#12. © 1984. Q & A,
Card game. 12
5868. Raise the Titanic. © 1987. Adventure, Board
game. Rare, Pulled off the market due to survivors
protests. 125
5869. Rand McNally Destination, Vacation. © 1986.
Geography, Board game. 18
5870. Smarts. © 1984. Strategy, Board game. 15
5871. Sports Trivia Game-#5. © 1984. Sports, Q & A,
Card game. 12
5872. Streetwise. © 1984. Social Concern, Board
game. 20
5873. Teen's Trivia Game-#8. © 1984. Q & A, Card
game. 12
5874. Television Trivia Game-#2. © 1984. TV, Q & A,
Card game. 12
5875. Travel Trivia Game-#11. © 1984. Travel, Q &
A, Card game. 12
5876. World Trivia Game-#4. © 1984. History, Q & A,
Card game. 12

Hubbard & Co.
5877. One Armed Bandit, Hardware Premium. ©
1949. Premium, Numbers, Dice game. 65

Hubley
5878. Golferino. © 1963. Sports, Golf, Board game. 18
5879. Jungle Hunt. © 1964. Skill, Action game. 15

Huckleberry Group
5880. New Canaan. © 1975. Cities and Towns, Board game. $22

Hunt-Wesson Foods
5881. Walt Disney's Peter Pan Games, Food Premium. © 1969. Disney, Premium, Board game. 75

Ideal Toy Corp.
5882. 12 O'Clock High (Paul Burke picture). © 1965. TV, Military, Board game. 65
5883. 12 O'Clock High (Robert Lansing picture). © 1965. TV, Military, Board game. 65
5884. 4 Little Pigs. © **1961.** Animal, Board game. 18
5885. Addams Family, The. © 1964. TV, Monster, Board game. 95
5886. All Pro Baseball. Miscellaneous, Sports, Baseball, Board game. 40
5887. All-Pro Baseball. © 1967. Sports, Baseball, Board game. 40
5888. All-Pro Basketball. © 1969. Sports, Basketball, Board game. 35
5889. All-Pro Football. © 1967. Sports, Football, Board game. 35
5890. All-Pro Hockey. © 1969. Sports, Hockey, Board game. 65
5891. Amazing Spider-Man Web Spinning Action Game. © 1979. Super Heroes, Board game. 40
5892. And Then There Were None. © 1967. Mystery, Board game. 40
5893. Auctioneer. © 1972. Economic, Board game. 30
5894. Baby Sitter. © 1966. Home Economics, Board game. 25
5895. Bang Box Game. © 1969. Skill, Action game. 20
5896. Batman Card Game. © 1966. Super Heroes, Card game. 40
5897. Battleboard. © 1972. Military, Board game. 22
5898. Battleline Game. © 1964. TV, Military, Board game. 50
5899. Battling Tops Game. © 1968. Action, Board game. 65
5900. Bee Bopper Game. © 1968. Social, Action game. 20
5901. Big Sneeze Game, The. © 1968. Skill, Action game. 15
5902. Blast, The Game of. © 1973. Military, Board game. 15
5903. Block the Clock. © 1981. Skill, Action game. 12
5904. Blondie, Sunday Funnies Board Game. © 1972. Comics, Board game. 50
5905. Blowout Game. © 1978. Skill, Action game. 10
5906. Bop the Beetle. © 1962. Skill, Action game. 25
5907. Boss, The. © 1972. Economic, Board game. 15
5908. Bozo Pop-Outs Game. © 1961. Circus, Board game. 25
5909. Bozo the TV Lotto. © 1961. Circus, Board game. 25
5910. Breaking Point. © 1976. Skill, Action game. 15
5911. Bruce Force, Lost in Outer Space. © 1963. Adventure, Board game. 65
5912. Bruce Force, and the Treasure of Shark Island. © 1963. Adventure, Board game. 50
5913. Buck-A-Roo! Game. © 1970. Skill, Action game. 12
5914. Bullwinkle and Rocky. © 1963. TV, Cartoon, Board game. 75
5915. Camp Runamuck Game. © 1965. Miscellaneous, Board game. 60

5916. Can You Catch It Charlie Brown? © 1976. Comics, Board game. $25
5917. Captain Kangaroo TV Lotto. © 1961. TV, Board game. 25
5918. Careful The Toppling Tower. © 1967. Skill, Action game. 20
5919. Careful. © **1967.** Skill, Action game. 15
5920. Cars N' Trucks, Build-A-Game. © 1961. Economic, Board game. 20
5921. Cars N' Trucks. © **1961.** Travel, Land, Board game. 25
5922. Case of the Elusive Assassin, The. © 1967. Mystery, Board game. 60
5923. Catch a Crook Game. © 1970. Law & Order, Board game. 35
5924. Chicken Lotto. © 1966. Animal, Board game. 15
5925. Chips are Down Game. © 1970. Skill, Action game. 12
5926. Chips Game. © 1981. TV, Law & Order, Board game. 15
5927. Chop Suey Game. © 1967. Ethnic, Skill game. 15

5928. Cimarron Strip Game. © 1967. TV, Western, Board game. 75
5929. Cloak and Dagger. © 1984. Law & Order, Board game. 15
5930. Cold Feet. © 1967. Skill, Action game. 12
5931. Combat at Anzio Beachead. © 1963. Military, Board game. 55
5932. Combat, The Fighting Infantry Game, Vic Morrow photo. © 1963. TV, Military, Board game. 60
5934. Crazy Clock Game. © 1964. Skill, Board game. 45
5935. Criss Cross. © 1971. Skill, Board game. 15
5936. Curse of the Cobras Game. © 1982. Monster, Board game. 35
5937. Dear Abby Game. © 1972. Personality, Card game. 25
5938. Deduction. © 1976. Strategy, Board game. 12
5939. Deputy Dawg TV Lotto. © 1961. TV, Cartoon, Board game. 30
5940. Dick Tracy Crime Stopper. © 1963. Comics, Board game. 65
5941. Dick Tracy, A Sunday Funnies Game. © 1972. Comics, Board game. 55
5942. Diner's Club, Credit Card Game. © 1961. Economic, Board game. 35
5943. Disney Score Around Game. © 1964. Disney, Board game. 40
5944. Doctor, Doctor! © 1978. Careers, Board game. 15
5945. Double Exposure. © 1961. TV, Game, Board game. 25

Ideal continued

5946. Dr. Kildare. © 1962. TV, Medical, Board game. $18

5947. Dukes of Hazzard Game, The. © 1981. TV, Board game. 15

5948. Egg Race Game. © 1968. Skill, Action game. 15

5949. Electra Woman and Dynagirl. © 1977. Super Heroes, Board game. 65

5950. Electronic Detective. © 1979. Law & Order, Board game. 15

5951. Electronic Radar Search Game. © 1969. Military, Board game. 25

5952. F Troop Game. © 1965. TV, Board game. 100

5953. Fantasy Island Game. © 1978. TV, Board game. 25

5954. Fish Bait Game. © 1965. Skill, Board game. 25

5955. Fu Manchu's Hidden Hoard. © 1967. Ethnic, Board game. 45

5956. Fugitive Game, The, Image of David Jansen. © 1964. TV, Board game. 125

5957. Fugitive Game, The. © 1964. TV, Board game. 100

5958. Funny Finger. © 1968. Skill, Action game. 15

5959. Garrison's Gorillas. © 1967. Military, Board game. 75

5960. General, The. © 1980. Military, Board game. 15

5961. Get Smart Mini-Board Card Game. © 1966. TV, Spy, Card game. 35

5962. Get Smart, Time Bomb Game. © 1965. TV, Spy, Board game. 75

5963. Go Gin Card Game. © 1968. Strategy, Card game. 10

5964. Godzilla Game. © 1964. Monster, Board game. 250

5965. Grand Slam Game. © 1969. Skill, Action game. 15

5966. Great Escape, The. © 1967. Strategy, Board game. 35

5967. Gunfight at O.K. Corral. © 1973. Western, Board game. 45

5968. Hands Down. © 1964. Skill, Action game. 15

5969. Hang on Harvey! Game. © 1969. Skill, Board game. 35

5970. Hide & Seek. © 1967. Skill, Board game. 15

5971. Hollywood Squares, The. © 1974. TV, Game, Board game. 20

5972. Honey West. © **1965**. TV, Board game. 90

5973. Hoopla, The Game of. © 1966. Skill, Action game. 15

5974. Hungry Henry Game. © 1969. Skill, Action game. 25

5975. I Spy Game. © 1965. TV, Detective, Board game. 60

5976. I Spy Mini Board Card Game. © 1966. TV, Mystery, Card game. 30

5977. Incredible Hulk Smash-Up Action Game, The. © 1979. Super Heroes, Skill Game. 40

5978. Ironside Game. © 1967. TV, Law & Order, Board game. 125

5979. It's About Time. © 1965. TV, Board game. 100

5980. James Bond, Message from M Game. © 1966. Spy, Board game. 250

5981. Jaws, The Game of. © 1975. Movie, Action game. 20

5982. Junk Yard Game, The. © 1966. Skill, Action game. 15

5983. Kaboom Balloon Busting Game. © 1965. Skill, Action game. 15

5984. Karate Tops. © 1971. Skill, Action game. 18

5985. Ker Plunk. © 1967. Skill, Action game. 15

5986. King Kong Game. © 1963. Monster, Board game. $225

5987. King Kong. © 1976. Movie, Monster, Board game. 18

5988. King of the Sea. © 1975. Travel, Sea, Board game. 15

5989. King Zor The Dinosaur Game. © 1962. Toy, Monster, Board game. 100

5990. Knock the Clock. © 1971. Skill, Action game. 12

5991. Land of the Giants. © 1968. TV, Board game. 150

5992. Leapin' Lizard. © 1971. Skill, Action game. 12

5993. Let's Make a Deal. © 1974. TV, Game, Board game. 15

5994. Liz Tyler, and the Mystery of the Crown Jewels. © 1963. Adventure, Board game. 35

5995. Liz Tyler, Hollywood Starlet. © 1963. Adventure, Board game. 35

5996. Look Out Below Game. © 1968. Skill, Action game. 35

5997. Lucky Star Gum Ball Game. © 1961. Action, Board game. 15

5998. Magilla Gorilla Bowl and Toss Game. © 1964. Monster, Action game. 15

5999. Magilla Gorilla Game. © 1964. Monster, Board game. 135

6000. Magilla Gorilla Target Barrel. © 1964. Monster, Action game. 150

6001. Man from U.N.C.L.E. Game, The. © 1965. TV, Spy, Board game. 35

6002. Man from U.N.C.L.E. Thrush Ray Gun Affair. © 1965. TV, Spy, Board game. 125

6003. Maniac Electronic Game. © 1979. Miscellaneous, Board game. 15

6004. Marble-Head Game. © 1969. Action, Marble game. 20

6005. Mind over Matter, The Great Julian Presents. © 1967. Mystic, Board game. 25

6006. Mission Impossible. © 1966. TV, Board game. 75

6007. Mouse Trap Game. © 1963. Skill, Board game. 35

6008. Mouse Trap Game. © 1975. Skill, Board game. 15

6009. Mr. Machine Game. © 1961. Toy, Board game. 35

6010. Mr. Mad. © 1970. Miscellaneous, Board game. 15

6011. Mr. Rembrandt. © 1970. Art, Board game. 12

6012. Murder on the Orient Express. © 1967. Mystery, Literary, Board game. 50

6013. Mushmouse & Punkin Puss Feudin' Hillbillies Target Game. © 1964. TV, Cartoon, Action game. 100

6014. MVP Baseball, The Sports Card Game. © 1989. Sports, Baseball, Card game. 15

6015. Mystic Skull, The Game of VooDoo. © 1964. Monster, Board game. 50

6016. NBA All-Pro Basketball. © 1969. Sports, Basketball, Board game. 25

6017. NHL All-Pro Hockey. © 1969. Sports, Hockey, Board game. 50

6018. Nirtz, The Game is. © 1961. Strategy, Board game. 15

6019. No Time for Sergeants Game. © 1964. TV, Board game. 35

6020. Nurses Game, The. © 1963. TV, Board game. 50

6021. Offical NFL Football Game. © 1968. Sports, Football, Board game. 30

6022. Oh, Nuts! Game. © 1969. Skill, Action game. 15

6023. P.T. Boat 109 Game. © 1963. Military, Board game. 50

6024. No game

6025. Pattie Playpal. © 1961. Toy, Home Economics, Card game. 15

Ideal continued

6026. Peter Potamus Target Barrel. © 1964. TV, Cartoon, Action game. $95

6027. Pie Face. © 1966. Skill, Action game. 15

6028. Poison Ivy Game. © 1969. Miscellaneous, Board game. 20

6029. Popeye and His Pals. © 1963. Comics, Board game. 60

6030. Popeye Skooz-It Game. © 1963. Comics, Board game. 50

6031. Poppin Hoppies Game. © 1968. Skill, Action game. 15

6032. Quick Shot Game. © 1970. Action, Marble game. 20

6033. Quickflip Volleyball Game. © 1973. Sports, Board game. 25

6034. Radar Search. © 1969. Military, Board game. 25

6035. Ransom. © 1961. Strategy, Board game. 15

6036. Rebel The. © 1961. TV, Western, Board game. 75

6037. Rebound. © 1971. Skill, Action game. 15

6038. Rebound. © 1980. Skill, Action game. 12

6039. Reese's Pieces Game, Ad for candy game. © 1983. Food, Board game. 20

6040. Remember. Circa 1960s. Memory, Board game. 12

6041. Rex Morgan M. D., Sunday Funnies Game. © 1972. Comics, Board game. 50

6042. Ricochet Rabbit & Droop-A-Long Coyote Game. © 1965. TV, Cartoon, Board game. 75

6043. Roboforce Card Game. © 1984. Science Fiction, Card game. 10

6044. Rock, Paper, Scissors. © 1968. Classic, Action game. 12

6045. Rubik's Cube Card Game. © 1982. Miscellaneous, Card game. 10

6046. Rubik's Race. © 1982. Strategy, Board game. 12

6047. Salvo, The Game of Naval Strategy. © 1961. Military, Board game. 22

6048. Seven Keys. © 1961. TV, Game, Board game. 15

6049. Sha-EE, Game of Destiny. © 1963. Strategy, Board game. 18

6050. Sinking of the Titanic Game, The. © 1976. Historical, Board game. 35

6051. Skin Divers. © 1961. Sports, Swim, Board game. 20

6052. Skully. © 1961. Skill, Action game. 15

6053. Slap Happy. © 1971. Skill, Action game. 10

6054. Slap Trap Game. © 1967. Skill, Action game. 15

6055. Smokey the Forest Fire Preventin' Bear. © 1961. Animal, Board game. 45

6056. Snake's Alive! The Game of. © 1966. Skill, Action game. 15

6057. Snap Bowling. © 1973. Sports, Bowling, Board game. 12

6058. Solid Gold Music Trivia. © 1984. Music, Board game. 18

6059. Soupy Sales Game, The. © 1965. TV, Board game. 90

6060. Soupy Sales Mini-Board Card Game. © 1965. TV, Card game. 40

6061. Speedway. © 1961. Sports, Car, Board game. 25

6062. Star Trek Game. © 1967. TV, Space, Board game. 80

6063. Sting Game, The. © 1976. Movie, Board game. 22

6064. Stump the Stars. © 1962. TV, Movie, Board game. 25

6065. Superman Card Game. © 1966. Super Heroes, Card game. 50

6066. Superman Match II. © 1979. Super Heroes, Board game. $50

6067. Sure Shot Baseball. © 1970. Sports, Baseball, Board game. 25

6068. Sure Shot Basketball. © 1970. Sports, BKB, Board game. 25

6069. Sure Shot Hockey. © 1969. Sports, Hockey, Board game. 45

6070. Surprise Package. © 1961. TV, Game, Board game. 15

6071. Swacki Game. © 1968. Skill, Action game. 18

6072. Swap, The Wheeler-Dealer Game. © 1965. Economic, Board game. 25

6073. T. H. E. Cat Game, Card game. © 1966. TV, Card game. 50

6074. T. H. E. Cat Game. © 1966. TV, Board game. 125

6075. Tammy Game, The. © 1963. TV, Board game. 35

6076. Terry and the Pirates. © 1972. Comics, Board game. 60

6077. Terrytoons Pop-outs Game. © 1961. Cartoon, TV, Board game. 35

6078. Terrytoons TV Lotto. © 1961. Cartoon, TV, Board game. 35

6079. Tiger Island, The Game of. © 1966. Animal, Board game. 60

6080. Tiltin' Milton Game. © 1968. Skill, Action game. 30

6081. Time Tunnel Card Game, The. © 1966. TV, Science Fiction, Card game. 85

6082. Time Tunnel Game, The. © 1966. TV, Science Fiction, Board game. 125

6083. Tin Can Alley. © 1977. Skill, Action game. 35

6084. Tiny Thumbelina. © 1963. Toy, Board game. 25

6085. Tip It. © 1965. Skill, Action game. 20

6086. Top Across Game. © 1969. Skill, Action Game. 15

6087. Top It. © 1972. Skill, Action game. 15

6088. Top the Top. © 1971. Skill, Action game. 15

6089. Tornado Bowl Game. © 1971. Action, Board game. 15

6090. Toss Across. © 1969. Skill, Action game. 15

6091. Trap Tennis. © 1975. Sports, Tennis, Board game. 20

6092. Trap. © 1972. Strategy, Board game. 15

6093. Travels of Jaimie McPheeters Game. © 1963. TV, Western, Board game. 75

6094. Tumble Bumble. © 1970. Skill, Action game. 15

6095. Twilight Zone Game, The. © 1964. TV, Science Fiction, Board game. 150

6096. Up 'N Over. © 1971. Skill, Action game. 15

Ideal continued

**6097. Walt Disney's Official Mouseketeer Whizzer
Wheel.** © 1964. Disney, Board game. $45

**6098. Walt Disney's Winnie the Pooh Honey Tree
Game.** © 1966. Disney, Board game. 50

6099. Weird-Ohs Game, Toy Characters. © 1964.
Monster, Board game. 175

6100. Welcome Back, Kotter. © 1976. TV, Board
game. 20

6101. Winning Ticket. Circa 1960s. Economic, Board
game. 15

6102. Wonderbug Game. © 1977. TV, Board game. 25

6103. Wrestle Around Game. © 1969. Marble, Board
game. 20

6104. Yipes. © 1976. Monster, Board game. 15

6105. Your Surprise Package. © 1961. TV, Game,
Board game. 25

6106. Zig Zag Zoom. © 1970. Skill, Action game. 15

Ideal Factory

6106a.Race Across Texas Board Game. © 1985
Travel, Car, Board game. 20

Ideal Spellbinder Games

6107. Space Flight. Circa 1960s. Space, Board game. 35

Imagination Plus

6108. Ha Choo. © 1992. Miscellaneous, Board game. 18

Impact Communications

6109. Northwest Passage. © 1969. Travel, Board
game. 25

Incredible Game Co.

6110. In You Face. © 1993. Social, Board game. 17

6111. Extinction, The Last Game They Ever Played.
© 1996. Animal, Card game. 18

Intellectual Technologies,Inc.

6112. Travel Buff. Circa 1990s. Travel, Board game. 15

Intelligames

6112a.World Traveler. © 1980. Travel, World, Board
game. 25

Intempo Toys

6113. In the Picture. © 1991. Art, Board game. 22

6113a.Piccolo Park. © 1989. Music, Board game. 22

International Games Inc.

6114. Dukes of Hazzard. © 1981. TV, Card game. 18

6115. Gremlins Card game. © 1984. Movie, Science
Fiction, Card game. 12

6116. Land Race Card Game. © 1983. Travel, Road,
Card game. 10

6117. O'No 99. © 1982. Numbers, Card game. 8

6118 Sea World Treasure Key. © 1983. Animal,
Board game., based on the Theme Park. 18

6119. Sea World, Fish Card Game. © 1983. Animal,
Card game. 12

6120. Skip-Bo. © 1986. Miscellaneous, Card game. 10

6121. Sting. © 1984. Movie, Card game. 10

6122. Stun. © 1986. Miscellaneous, Card game. 8

6123. Top That! © 1987. Miscellaneous, Card game. 8

6124. Toxic Crusaders Battle for Tromaville Game.
© 1991. Comics, Board game. 15

6125. Toxic Crusaders Card Game. © 1991. TV, Card
game. $8

Interpretive Marking Pro.

6126. National Parks Wit. © 1985. History, Card
game. 10

Intromark Inc.

6127. Evolution Game, The. © 1989. Science, Board
game. 22

6128. Satellite. © 1991. Communications, Board
game. 22

Intuitive ZMarketing

6129. How to Host a Murder, Grapes of Rath. ©
1986. Mystery, Board game. 20

Invicta Games

6130. Ergo. © 1977. Strategy, Board game. 10

6131. Mastermind. © 1972. Miscellaneous, Board
game. 10

6131a.Opportunity, endorsed by Ronald Reagan. ©
1983. Political, Strategy, Board game. 35

Invicto

6132. Space Lines 3-D Game. © 1969. Space, Board
game. 12

Iron Crown Enterprises

6133. Fellowship of the Ring. © 1983. Fantasy, Board
game. 18

Island Paradox

6134. Gallivant Games. © 1991. Travel, Board game. 15

I-Soltd. Inc.

6135. Bali. © 1954. Miscellaneous, Card game. 12

Itemation Inc.

6136. Energy Crisis Game. © 1973. Social Concern,
2Board game. 30

6137. Stamp Collectors Game. © 1973. Collecting,
Board game. 20

6138. Super Group. © 1973. Music, Board game. 20

ITOS Enterprises

6139. Mad Dash. © 1994. Social, Board game. 15

6140. Mad Dash, Three Minutes Across America.
Circa 1990s. Travel, USA, Board game. 15

Its About Time, Inc.

6140a. L. A. Game, © 1988. City & State, Board
game. 20

J & J Co.

6141. Zip-Zingo-The Travel Game. © 1954. Travel,
Board game. 30

Jacmar Mfg. Co.

6142. 20,000 Leagues Under the Sea. © 1954. Disney,
Board game. 75

6143. Adventure in Science, An. © 1950. Q & A,
Board game. 25

6144. Jacmar Big League Electric Baseball. Circa
1950s. Sports, Baseball, Board game. 65

6145. Mr. Brain. © 1959. Q & A, Action Game. 18

Jacmar Mfg. Co. continued

6146. Robot Sam the Answer Man. © 1950. Q & A, Board game. $25

6147. Speed-O-Rama. Circa 1950s. Sports, Car, Board game. 39

6148. Walt Disney's Disneyland Tours. Circa 1950s. Disney, Board game. 55

6149. Walt Disney's Electric Disneyland Tours Quiz. © 1959. Disney, Board game. 60

6150. Walt Disney's Mickey Mouse Lotto. © 1950. Disney, Board game. 30

6151. Walt Disney's Mickey Mouse. © 1950. Disney, Board game. 30

Jack Jaffe

6152. Save the President. © 1979. Political, Board game. 28

Jac Productions

6152a. Vanity Chase. © 1988. Licence plate game. 20

Jambam

6153. Medical Madness. © 1982. Social Concern, Board game. 25

Jamotta

6154. Chicanery. © 1979. Social, Board game. 20

Jax Ltd.

6155. Beverly Hills. © 1982. Cities & Towns, Board game. 22

Jaymar Specialty Co.

6156. Beetle Bailey's Hilarious New Army Game. Circa 1950s. Comics, Board game. 85

6157. Beetle Bailey's Furlough. Circa 1950s. Comics, Board game. 85

6158. Blondie and Dagwood's Race for the Office. © 1950. Comics, Board game. 50

6159. Donald Duck Tiddley Winx. Circa 1950s. Disney, Skill Game. 40

6160. Popeye's Old Maid. Circa 1970s. Comics, Card game. 18

6161. Snuffy Smith's Hootin Holler Bug Derby. Circa 1950s. Comics, Board game. 35

6162. Soupy Sales, Funny Rummy. Circa, 1970s. TV, Card game. 20

6163. Soupy Sales, Hearts. Circa 1970s. TV, Card game. 20

6164. Soupy Sales, Old Maid. Circa 1970s. TV, Card game. 20

6165. Super Crow Shoot. © 1958. Skill, Action game. $15

6166. Toy Parade. Circa 1950s. Kiddie, Board game. 15

JDK Baseball

6167. JDK Baseball. © 1983. Sports, Baseball, Board game. 22

Jedco

6168. Welfare Game, The. © 1978. Social Concern, Board game. 25

Jessup Paper Box Co.

6169. Jet Race Game. Circa 1980s. Travel, Air, Board game. 15

Jewish Educational Toys

6170. Kosherland. Circa 1990s. Ethnic, Board game. 17

6171. Let My People Go! © 1994. Ethnic, Board game. 20

6172. Magical Mitzvah Park. © 1995. Ethnic, Board game. 15

6173. Torah, Slides and Ladders. Circa 1990s. Ethnic, Board game. 17

6174. Tradition. Circa 1990s. Ethnic, Board game, ... 17

Jockette Co.

6175. Jockette. Circa 1950s. Miscellaneous, Board game. 22

H. C. Jocoby Inc.

6176. Arbitrace. © 1986. Stock Market, Board game. 18

J. Johnstone

6177. Stock Car Speedway, Game of. © 1965. Sports, Car, Board game. 35

Johnston Games Inc.

6177a. Blue Light Special. K-Mart Shopping game. © 1986, Advertizing, Economic, Board game. 35

W. Bowdoin Jones

6177b. Real Action Quarterback Football, with Mean Joe Green. © 1985. Sports, Football, Board game. 65

C. Joseph-Carenter Game Pro

6178. Inflation. © 1974. Economic, Board game. 28

JRA Fun Group

6179. High-Politix. © 1976. Political, Board game. 30

Judson Press

6180. Bible Cities. Circa 1950s. Religious, Card game. 15

Jumbo

6181. Jumbo Jet. © 1963. Travel, Air, Board game. 20

Just Games

6182. Orient Express. © 1985. Travel, Rail, Board game. 15

6183. Pro, Baseball, Card Game. Circa 1980s. Sports, Baseball, Card game. 15

Kamm's games
6184. Casey at the Mound, Kamm's Baseball. Circa 1946. Sports, Baseball, Board game. $250

Kapcar Prod.
6185. Pot Luck. © 1979. Miscellaneous, Board game. 20

Kavanaugh
6186. Extra Innings. © 1975. Sports, Baseball, Board game. 25

KDN Enterprises
6187. Big Wheel. © 1983. Economic, Board game. 18

Keck Enterprises
6187a. Rose Bowl. © 1949. Sports, Football Board game. 125

Kellogg's
6188. Big Otis - Catapult Game. © 1960. Premium, Action Game. 25
6189. Kellogg's Soccer Slam, Kellogg's Raisin Bran. © 1997. Sports, Soccer, Premium, Skill game. 8
6190. Mini Clue Jr.Game. © 1992. Mystery, Board game. 10
6191. Mini Outta Control Game. © 1992. Miscellaneous, Board game. 6
6192. Mini Sorry! © 1992. Classic, Board game. 10
6193. Nintendo Board game. © 1992. Combo, Board game. 8
6194. Tony the Tiger Astronaut Space Game, Premium cereal. Circa 1960s. Space, Board game. 25

Kellogg's Cocoa Krispies
6195. Super Mario Kart Choco Island Challenge. © 1994. Animal, Board game. 8

Kellogg's Corn Pops
6196. Table Top Soccer. © 1984. Sports, Soccer, Board game. 10

Kelloggs Pop-Tarts Crunch
6197. Mini Express Monopoly, Premium. © 1996. Economic, Board game. 12

Kellogg's Smacks
6198. Spooky Scary House Call with Dig'em Game. © 1993. Monster, Board game. 10

R. O. Keltner
6199. Brett Ball. © 1981. Sports, Baseball, Board game. 50
6200. George Brett's 9th Inning Baseball Game, Brett Ball. © 1981. Sports, Baseball, Board game. 50

Kenner
6201. Alien Game. © 1979. Movie, Science Fiction, Board game. 35
6202. Beat the Buzz. © 1958. Q & A, Board game. 15
6203. Hop and Stomp. © 1969. Skill, Action game. 15
6204. Knock Off. © 1969. Skill, Action game. 15
6205. Orbiting Spaceway. © 1970. Space, Board game. 20
6206. Raiders of the Lost Ark Game. © 1981. Movie, Adventure, Board game. 25

6207. See-Action Football Game, O.J. Simpson cameo Photo. © 1974. Sports, Football, Board game. $150
6208. Sleep Walker. © 1976. Skill, Action game. 15
6209. Star Wars Adventures of R2D2 Game. © 1977. Movie, Science Fiction, Board game. 30
6210. Star Wars Game, Escape from Death Star. © 1977. Movie, Science Fiction, Board game. 30
6211. Star Wars, Hoth Ice Planet Adventure Game. © 1980. Movie, Science Fiction, Board game. 30

Kenton Hardware Co.
6212. Bandit Trail Game, Featuring Gene Autry. Circa 1950s. Western, Personality, Board game. 250

Kentucky Fried Chicken
6212a. Scrambled Squares Dominoes. © 1997. Dinasaur Domino game. 3

Kenworthy Educational Serv.
6213. Dog House Game. © 1946. Animal, Board game. 25

Kessler
6214. Wildcatter. © 1981. Adventure, Career, Board game. 22

Key Games (Saalfield)
6215. Scrambled Headlines. © 1961. Communications, Board game. 30

King-Seeley
6216. Campus Queen. © 1967. Romance, Board game. 35

Kiplinger Washington Editors
6217. Hat in the Ring, Presidental Nominating Gamer. © 1971. Political, Board game. 28

Klipspringer Editions Inc.
6218. Litter Bug. Circa 1980s. Social Concern, Board game. 25

Knickerbocker Plastic
6219. Badge 714 Dragnet. © 1955. TV, Detective, Board game. 150
6220. Dragnet Radar Action Game. © 1955. TV, Law & Order, Board game. 100
6221. Dragnet Target Game. © 1955. TV, Law & Order, Action game. 125
6222. Mr. Magoo at the Circus Target Game. © 1956. Cartoon, Action game. 125
6223. Quick Draw McGraw Moving Target. © 1960. Cartoon, TV, Action game. 125
6224. Siren Sparkle Space Game. Circa 1950s. Space, Action game. 75
6225. Walt Disney's Zorro Target Game. © 1959. Disney, Action game. 100

Koch Sports Products
6226. KSP Baseball. © 1983. Sports, Baseball, Board game. 20
6227. KSP Basketball. © 1983. Sports, Basketball, Board game. 20

Kohner Bros.
6228. Building Boom. © 1950. Architecture, Economics, Board game. 25

Kohner Bros.
6229. Cross Over the Bridge. © 1970. Travel, Board game. $15
6230. Ginasta. © 1954. Classic, Card game. 8
6231. Hat's Off. © 1967. Skill, Board game. 15
6232. Headache. © 1968. Skill, Board game. 15
6233. Hi-Q. © 1964. Q & A, Board game. 10
6234. Sky's the Limit, The. © 1955. TV, Game, Board game. 25
6235. Snakes in the Grass. © 1960. Skill, Action game. 18
6236. Trouble. © 1965. Skill, Board game. 12

Kontrell
6237. Peter Max Chess Game. Circa 1960s. Art, Classic, Board game. 200

Kool Pops
6238. Captain Action Card Game, Premium. © 1967. Toy, Comics, Card game. 35

Koplow Games
6239. Organized Crime. © 1974. Law & Order, Board game. 35

Kozco Inc.
6240. Atlantic City Tycoon. © 1985. Chance, Board game. 20

Kreig-Brand
6241. Cross Country. © 1969. Travel, Board game. 35

Krummacher
6242. Economy Game, The. © 1975. Economic, Board game. 28

K-Tel International
6243. K-Tel Superstar Game, with 45 record, Ad for records game. © 1973. Music, Board game. 35

Kuz Inc.
6244. Mack Four. © 1993. Miscellaneous, Board game. 20

L. & D. Robtoy Ent.
6245. Buck Fever. © 1984. Animal, Board game. 25

L. A. Producers
6246. Comrades, Russian Monopoly. © 1988. Political, Board game. 25

John Ladell
6247. Shopping. © 1973. Economic, Board game. 25

Laff'n Learn
6248. Walt Disney's Ludwig Von Drake Card game. © 1960. Disney, Card game. 30

Lakeshore
6249. Allowance Game, The. © 1984. Economic, Board game. 20

Lakeside
6250. 20,000 Leagues Under the Sea. © 1975. TV, Board game. 25
6251. 25 Ghosts. © 1969. Mystic, Board game. 20

6252. Aggravation, Black box, Standard edition. © 1970. Miscellaneous, Board game. $15
6253. Aggravation, Split-Level. © 1971. Miscellaneous, Board game. 15
6254. Barrel of Monkeys. © 1969. Animal, Action Game. 15
6255. Beanbag Buccaneers. Circa 1960s. Skill, Action game. 15
6256. Big Deal. © 1977. Economic, Board game. 12
6257. Blockade. © 1979. Strategy, Board game. 10
6258. Bug House. © 1964. Animal, Board game. 15
6259. Chaos. © 1971. Strategy, Board game. 12
6260. Easy on the Ketchup Game. © 1975. Skill, Action game. 12
6261. Entertainment Tonight. © 1984. TV, Board game. 18
6262. Giant Barrel of Monkeys. © 1969. Skill, Action game. 15
6263. Haunted Mansion Game. Circa 1970s. Monster, Board game. 75
6264. Intercept. © 1978. Military, Board game. 12
6265. Isolation. © 1978. Strategy, Board game. 12
6266. Kismet. © 1971. Strategy, Board game. 15
6267. Lunch Bunch Easy on the Ketchup. © 1975. Kiddie, Board game. 12
6268. Perfection. © 1973. Skill, Action game. 15
6269. Perquackey. © 1967. Word, Dice game. 15
6270. Play it Cool. © 1962. Animal, Board game. 15
6271. Playful Trails Game, Gumby and Gumby's Pal Pokey. © 1968. Cartoon, TV, Board game. 65
6272. Score Four. © 1978. Strategy, Board game. 12
6273. Spare-Time Bowling. © 1974. Sports, Bowling, Dice game. 15
6274. Three Blind Mice. © 1967. Animal, Board game. 15
6275. Topper. © 1962. Skill, Action game. 15
6276. Walt Disney World 20,000 Leagues Under the Sea Game. Circa 1980s. Disney, Board game. 20
6277. Walt Disney World Haunted Mansion Game. Circa 1980s. Disney, Board game. 22

Paul Lamond Games
6278. Pass Out Travel Game. © 1974. Social, Drink, Board game. 22
6278a. Complete Bastard Game, How to be a. © 1987. Board game. 18

Lancer Products
6278b. Standard NFL All-American Football. © 1963. Standard Oil premium, Sports and premium game. 25

Lansing
6279. Pro Quarterback. © 1964. Sports, Football, Board game. 35

Laramie
6280. Bullwinkle Electronic Quiz Game. © 1971. TV, Cartoon, Board game. 25
6281. Bullwinkle Magnetic Travel Game. © 1971. TV, Cartoon, Board game. 50
6282. Dick Tracy Target Set. © 1969. Comics, Action game. 50
6283. Land of the Lost Bagatelle. © 1975. TV, Board game. 25

Las Vegas West Inc.
6284. **Las Vegas Junket.** © 1979. Classic, Card game. $15

Last Gasp
6285. **Offical Dealer McDope Dealing Game.** © 1975.
Social Concern, Board game. 35

Late for the Sky Prod. Co.
6286. **America in a Box.** © 1996. Travel, USA, Board
game. 17
6287. **Boome's.** © 1996. Miscellaneous, Board game. 17

6288. **Coloradoopoly.** © 1990. Schools, Board game. 16
6288a. **Various University Opopoly's** Circa 1990...................... 16.

H. Law Inc.
6289. **North to Alaska.** © 1984. Geography, Board
game. 25

Lay's Packing
6290. **Lunar Landing Game, Premium for Lay's
Potato Chips.** © 1969. Space, Premium, Board
game. 35

Lee/Raymond
6291 **Elvis Presley, 'King of Rock' Game.** © 1978.
Music, Personality, Board game. 55

Lehigh County Assoc for the Blind
6291a. **Everybody Wants to be President.** © 1975.
Political, Board game. 65

LEI
6292. **Escapades.** Circa 1990s. Q & A, Card game. 10
6293. **Wisdom.** © 1995. Social, Board game. 10

Leister
6294. **Bride Bingo.** © 1957. Romance, Board game. 15
6295. **Stork Bingo.** © 1970. Home Economics, Board
game. 12

Philip Levine
6296. **Say No Now, Game.** © 1989. Social Concern,
Board game. 15

Marvin Levy Inc.
6297. **Exodus Out of Egypt.** © 1992. Religious, Board
game. 20

Lido Toy Corp.
6298. **Air Race Around the World.** Circa 1950s.
Travel, Air, Board game. $22
6299. **Felix the Cat Target Game.** © 1960. Comics,
Action game. 60
6300. **Flintstones Target Set.** © 1962. TV, Cartoon,
Action game. 75
6301. **Jeep Patrol.** Circa 1950s. Military, Board game. ... 25
6302. **Rocket Race to Saturn.** © 1950. Space, Board
game. 35
6303. **Sea Battle.** Circa 1950s. Military, Board game. 30

Lilco Enterprises
6304. **Brand Image.** © 1958. Advertising, Board
game. 60

W. E. Lindsley
6305. **Generals.** Circa 1940s. Military, Board game. 150

Lindstrom Tool & Toy Co.
6306. **Airways.** © 1950. Travel, Air, Board game. 65

Lindenwood Jerseys
6306a. **Tanbark Trail.** © 1966. Farm, Board game. 25

Lionel
6307. **Double Crossing.** © 1988. Travel, Rail, Board
game. 25

Lith-O-Word
6308. **Las Vegas Wild.** © 1954. Numbers, Board
game. 15

Little Caesars
6309. **Little Caesars Football! Football!, Premium.**
Circa 1990s. Sports, Football, Board game. 12

Lord & Freber, Inc.
6310. **Line Drive.** © 1953. Sports, Baseball, Board
game. 75

Lorentzen-Fillmer
6311. **Law School Game, The.** © 1984. Careers, Board
game. 25

Lorimar
6312. **Dallas, A Game of the Ewing Family.** © 1980.
TV, Board game. 20

Lost Horizons
6313. **Lose, The Game of.** © 1991. Economic, Board
game. 17

E. S. Lowe
6314. **Ad-Lib.** © 1970. Social, Board game. 10
6315. **Bet a Million.** Circa 1950s. Gambling, Board
game. 15
6316. **Big Numbers.** © 1975. TV, Game, Board game. 12
6317. **Bowl A Score.** © 1962. Sports, Bowling, Board
game. 15
6318. **Bowl-A-Strike.** © 1962. Sports, Bowling, Board
game. 15
6319. **Brain Storm.** © 1972. Q & A, Board game. 12
6320. **Chute-5.** © 1973. Strategy, Dice game. 12
6321. **Countdown.** © 1967. Space, Board game. 65

E. S. Lowe, continued

6322. Dollar Bill Poker, with TV's Odd Couple on cover. © 1974. TV, Gambling, Board game. $12
6323. Dragonmaster. © 1981. Fantasy, Board game. 10
6324. Flight Captain. © 1972. Travel, Air, Board game. 15
6325. Fox Hunt. Circa 1940s. Sports, Board game. 35
6326. Go, 1st. Lowe Edition. © 1951. Classic, Board game. 20
6327. Go. © 1974. Classic, Board game. 15
6327a.Guru, © 1968. Flower power art, Strategy, Board game. 30
6328. Heads Up. © 1968. Skill, Action game. 15
6329. Home Stretch Harness Racing. © 1967. Sports, Horseracing, Board game. 40
6330. Mandinka. © 1978. Strategy, Board game. 12
6331. Mikado, Game of Go. © 1951. Classic, Board game. 15
6332. Nile. © 1967. Strategy, Board game. 20
6333. Rose Bowl, Photo cover. © 1966. Sports, Football, Board game. 40
6334. Rose Bowl. Circa 1940s. Sports, Football, Board game. 60
6335. Scribbage. © 1967. Word, Board game. 10
6336. Showdown Poker. © 1971. Gambling, Board game. 12
6337. Society Scandals. © 1978. Social Concern, Board game. 25
6338. Thoroughbred. Circa 1940s. Sports, Horseracing, Board game. 50
6339. Traffic. © 1968. Travel, Road, Board game. 35
6340. World Series. © 1947. Sports, Baseball, Board game. 60
6341. Yahtzee, Challenge. © 1971. Word, Dice game. 12
6342. Yahtzee, Challenge. © 1974. Word, Dice game. 12
6343. Yahtzee, Deluxe Edition. © 1961. Word, Dice game. 15
6344. Yahtzee. © 1956. Word, Dice game. 18

E. S. Lowe (Milton Bradley)
6345. High Hand. © 1964. Miscellaneous, Board game. 12

Lowell Toy Mfg Co.
6346. $64,000 Question Quiz Game. © 1955. TV, Game, Board game. 40

6347. 77 Sunset Strip. © 1960. TV, Detective, Board game. 75
6348. Bat Masterson. © 1958. TV, Board game. 60
6349. Beat the Clock. © 1954. TV, Action, Board game. 35
6350. Ben-Hur. © 1959. Movie, Board game. 85
6351. Big Town. Circa 1950s. TV, Board game. 95
6352. Bozo in Circus-Land. © 1965. Circus, Board game. 40

6353. Candid Camera Games. © 1963. TV, Board game. $65
6354. Captain Kid. Circa 1950s. Adventure, Board game. 25
6355. College Bowl. © 1962. TV, Game, Board game. 50
6356. Discovery, Home Game. Circa 1954-5. TV, Board game. 25
6357. Dollar a Second. © 1955. TV, Game, Board game. 35
6358. Dough-Re-Mi. © 1960. TV, Game, Board game. 40
6359. Face the Facts. © 1961. TV, Game, Board game. 25
6360. Groucho's You Bet Your Life. © 1955. TV, Game, Personality, Board game. 85
6361. Gunsmoke. © 1958. TV, Western, Board game. 55
6362. Hansel and Gretel. © 1963. Nursery Rhyme, Board game. 25
6363. Hawaiian Eye. © 1963. TV, Board game. 75
6364. Herman Hickman's All American Action Football Game. Circa 1950s. Sports, Football, Board game. 95
6365. Humpty Dumpty. © 1960. Nursery Rhyme, Board game. 25
6366. I've Got a Secret, I'm Garry Moore...and. © 1956. TV, Game, Board game. 40
6367. Jack the Giant Killer. Circa 1950s. Nursery Rhyme, Board game. 25
6368. Jan Murray's Charge Account. © 1961. TV, Economic, Board game. 25
6369. Jingle Dingle's Weather Game. © 1954. TV, Board game. 25
6370. Joe Palooka Boxing Game. © 1952. Comics, Board game. 125
6371. Justice. © 1955. Law, Board game. 125
6372. Laramie. © 1960. TV, Western, Board game. 70
6373. Mr. Magoo Visits the Zoo Game. © 1961. Cartoon, Board game. 50
6374. No game
6375. Navy Log, TV Game. © 1957. TV, Military, Board game. 85
6376. Person-alysis. © 1957. Social Concern, Board game. 35
6377. Peter Gunn Detective Game. © 1960. TV, Detective, Board game. 75
6378. Pinocchio, New Adventures of. © 1960. Literary, Board game. 25
6379. Price is Right, The. © 1958. TV, Q & A, Board game. 30
6380. Ralph Edwards' This is Your life. Circa 1950s. TV, Personal, Board game. 35
6381. Rawhide Game. © 1960. TV, Western, Board game. 100
6382. Red Riding Hood. © 1963. Nursery Rhyme, Board game. 15
6383. Revlon's $64,000 Question Junior Quiz Game, The. © 1955. TV, Game, Board game. 35
6384. Revlon's $64,000 Question Quiz Game, The. © 1955. TV, Game, Board game. 35
6385. Robinson Crusoe. © 1961. Adventure, Board game. 45
6386. Sea Hunt. © 1961. TV, Board game. 85
6387. Show-Biz, The Game of the Stars. © 1956. Movie, Board game. 75
6388. Steve Canyon. © 1959. Comics, Board game. 75
6389. Strike It Rich. © 1955. TV, Game, Board game. 30
6390. Surfside 6. © 1962. TV, Detective, Board game. 85
6391. Three Stooges Fun House Game. © 1959. TV, Board game. 275

Lowell Toy Mfg Co. continued

6392. Tic-Tac-Toe Q & A Game. © 1957. Q & A, Board game. $25

6393. To Tell the Truth. © 1957. TV, Game, Board game. 40

6394. Twenty One, TV Quiz Game. Circa 1950s. TV, Q & A, Board game. 45

6395. Wanted Dead Or Alive. © 1959. TV, Western, Board game. 135

6396. What's My Line? © 1955. TV, Game, Board game. 65

6397. Window Shopping. © 1962. TV, Game, Board game. 40

6398. Wizard of Oz. © 1962. Literary, Board game. 25

6399. Your First Impression. © 1962. TV, Game, Board game. 30

6400. Yours for a Song. © 1961. TV, Game, Board game. 40

6401. Zip Code. © 1964. Career, Card game. 60

Lucky Ten Co.

6402. Lucky Ten, The Money Game. © 1974. Gambling, Card game. 15

Lykable Games

6403. Gone Bananas! © 1984. Skill, Action game. 10

J. R. Mackey

6404. I Wanna Be President. © 1983. Political, Board game. 30

Macmilan

6405. Gas Crisis. © 1979. Social Concern, Board game. 28

The Maestre Company

6405a.Take-a-Tour To Puerto Rico. © 1965. Travel, Board game. 25

Mad Magazine

6406. Mad's Spy vs. Spy Combat Card Game. Circa 1990s. Spy, Comics, Card game. 15

Magic Wand Corp.

6407. Combat Tank Game. © 1964. Military, Action game. 35

6408. Fireball XL5, Magnetic Dart Game. © 1963. TV, Science Fiction, Action game. 125

6409. International Airport Game. © 1964. Travel, Board game. 35

6410. No listing

6411. International Grand Prix. © 1964. Sports, Car, Board game. 30

6412. Supercar Target Game. © 1962. TV, Action game. 250

D. Magiera Co.

6412a.Mail Order. © 1973. Economic, Board game. 25

Magnus Co.

6412a. George Blanda's Monday Night Touchdown. © 1972. Sports, Football Board game. 55

H. C. Manley

6413. Lucky Strike. © 1972. Miscellaneous, Board game. $15

Mansfield-Zesiger Mfg.

6414. Bambino Baseball Game. © 1946. Sports, Baseball, Board game. 75

Marina Enterprises

6415. Wine Celler. © 1971. Food, Board game. 25

C. P. Marino

6416. Blizzard of '77. © 1977. Historical, Board game. 22

Marino Group Inc.

6417. Dinosaur Survival. © 1987. Animal, Board game. 18

6418. Travel America. © 1986. Travel, Land, Board game. 15

Mario Fishel Toy&Game

6419. Bull and Bears. © 1989. Stock Market, Board game. 18

Marken

6420. Penta. © 1971. Strategy, Board game. 12

Marlan

6421. Funtastic Fitness Game, The, Christain Version. © 1982. Fitness, Board game. 25

6422. Funtastic Fitness Game, The. © 1982. Fitness, Board game. 25

Maruca Inc.

6422a.Bottom Line, The. © 1986. Economic, Board game. 18

Marx Toys

6423. Arnold Palmer's Indoor Golf Game. © 1968. Sports, Golf, Board Game. 75

6424. Barnstormer. © 1970. Skill, Action game. 15

6425. Batman Pinball Game. © 1966. Super Heroes, Board game. 100

6426. Batman Shooting Arcade. © 1966. Super Heroes, Action game. 250

6427. Bops and Robbers. © 1972. Skill, Action game. 35

6428. Bucket Ball. © 1972. Skill, Action game. 25

6429. Bust 'Em Target Game. Circa 1950s. Skill, Action game. 25

6430. Flintstones Mechanical Shooting Gallery. © 1962. TV, Cartoon, Action game. 200

6431. Knock It Off. © 1978. Skill, Action game. 25

6432. Magic Shot Shooting Gallery. © 1961. Skill, Action game. 30

6433. Man from U.N.C.L.E. Pinball Affair. © 1966. TV, Spy, Board game. 250

6434. Man from U.N.C.L.E. Secret Code Wheel pinball Game. © 1966. TV, Spy, Board game. 300

6435. Man from U.N.C.L.E. Target Game. © 1965. TV, Spy, Action game. 250

6436. Man from U.N.C.L.E. Target Game. © 1966. TV, Spy, Action game. 250

6437. Perils of Pauline. © 1964. Cartoon, TV, Board game. 75

6438. Popcorn. © 1976. Skill, Action game. 20

Marx Toys, continued

6439. Rex Mars Space Target Game. Circa 1950s.
Space, Action game. $125
6440. Untouchables Target Game. © 1960. TV, Law
& Order, Board game. 175
6441. Wanted Dead or Alive Target Game. © 1959.
TV, Western, Action game. 250
6442. Yogi Bear Circus Bagatelle. © 1960. TV,
Cartoon, Board game. 75

Gayle Mason

6443. Never Alone, Bible Cards. © 1989. Religious,
Card game. 15

Mass Marketing

6444. They're at the Post, Record plays the results.
© 1976. Sports, Horseracing, Board game. 30

Mastermind Sports

6445. Pro Coach Football. Miscellaneous, Sports,
Football, Board game. 20

Matchbox

6446. Bing-It. Circa 1960s, Sport, Board game. 20
6447. Cascade. © 1972. Skill, Action game. 20

Mattel, Inc.

6448. Animal Talk Game. © 1963. Animal, Board
game. 18
6449. Archies Card Game. © 1970. Comics, Card
game. 30
6450. Bandersnath. © 1968. Kiddie, Card game. 8
6451. Barbie Charms the World Game. © 1986.
Romance, Toy, Board game. 18
6452. Barbie Game, The. © 1960. Toy, Romance,
Board game. 50
6453. Barbie World of Fashion. © 1967. Toy, Board
game. 55
6454. Barbie's Keys to Fame Game. © 1963. Career,
Board game. 40
6455. No game
6456. Bats in Your Belfry. © 1964. Monster, Action
game. 75
6457. Beany and Cecil Match-It Tile Game. © 1961.
TV, Cartoon, Board game. 25
6458. Big Thumb. © 1970. Skill, Action game. 12
6459. Blarney. © 1970. Q & A, Action game. 12
6460. Boundary. © 1970. Skill, Board game. 12
**6461. Bug's Life, A, Bug Collector King-Size Card
Game.** © 1998. Movie, Animal, Card game. 12
6462. Cathedral, Plastic Buildings. © 1986. Strategy,
Architecture, Board game. 25
6463. Chatty Cathy Game. © 1962. Toy, Board game. 40
6464. Doctor Dolittle. © 1967. Movie, Board game. 45
6465. Donny & Marie Osmond TV Show. © 1976.
TV, Personality, Board game. 20
6466. Fast Eddie Game. © 1970. Skill, Marble game. 12
6467. Flea Circus. © 1964. Skill, Action game. 15
6468. Flip Flop Go. © 1962. Strategy, Board game. 15
6469. Flipper Flips. © 1965. TV, Animal, Board game. ... 40
6470. Gentle Ben Animal Hunt. © 1967. TV, Board
game. 35
6471. Godzilla Game. © 1978. Monster, Board game. 18
6472. Happy Happy Birthday. © 1964. Kiddie, Board
game. 15

**6473. Hawaiian Punch Game, Ad game for fruit
drink.** © 1978. Advertising, Board game. $18
6474. High Gear Game. © 1962. Skill, Board game. 15
6475. Hot Wheels Wipe Out Game. © 1968. Toy, Car,
Board game. 40
6476. Jonathan Livingston Seagull. © 1973. Literary,
Board game. 22
**6477. Jumping DJ Surprise Action Game, Beany
& Cecil.** © 1962. Cartoon, TV, Action game. 32
6478. Larry Hagman Presents Flip Out. © 1985.
Personality, Dice game. 15
6479. Lie Detector. © 1960. Law & Order, Board
game. 50
6480. Magnatel. © 1961. Skill, Action game. 15
6481. Major Matt Mason Space Exploration Game.
© 1967. Science Fiction, Toy, Board game. 90
**6482. Masters of the Universe, Battle for Eternia
Game.** © 1986. TV, Board game. 15
**6483. Masters of the Universe, Snake Mountain
Rescue Game.** © 1986. TV, Board game. 15
6484. No game
6485. Merv Griffin's Word for Word Game. © 1963.
TV, Game, Personality, Board game. 22
6486. Musingo. © 1962. Music, Board game. 15
6487. Pop-Za-Ball Target Game. © 1961. Skill,
Action game. 15
6488. Predicaments, Hosted by Joan Rivers. © 1986.
Personality, VCR game. 18
6489. Scr-unch. © 1967. Skill, Action game. 15
6490. Skipper Game, Barbie's Little Sister. © 1964.
Toy, Board game. 30
6491. Slick Shooter Penny Arcade Game. © 1974.
Skill, Action game. 20
6492. Slip Disc. © 1971. Skill, Action game. 15
6493. Smack-A-Roo. © 1964. Skill, Action game. 15
6494. Sonar Sub Hunt. © 1961. Military, Board game. ... 65
6495. Splat. © 1968. Skill, Board game. 15
6496. Spring Chicken. © 1968. Animal, Board game. 15
6497. Sprint Drag Race Game. © 1965. Sports, Car,
Board game. 35
6498. Spy Detector Game. © 1977. Spy, Board game. ... 40
6499. Superman Comic Game. © 1971. Super Heroes,
Board game. 25
6500. Talk to Cecil. © 1961. TV, Board game. 75
6501. Talking Football. © 1971. Sports, Football,
Board game. 20
6502. Talking Monday Night Football. © 1977.
Sports, Football, Board game. 20
6503. Tarzan Comic Game. © 1971. Comics, Board
game. 25
6504. Tight Squeeze. © 1967. Skill, Action game. 25
6505. Wayne's World VCR Board Game. © 1992.
Movie, Board game. 20
6506. Where's Waldo? Memory Game. © 1991.
Literary, Board game. 20
6507. Word War. © 1978. Word, Board game. 10

Maturity Corp.

6508. Make-Out Game, The. © 1984. Romance,
Board game. 20

Maxim Games Co.

6509. Tally It. © 1945. Numbers, Card game. 15

Mayfair Games Inc.

6510. 1835. © 1991. Military, Board game. 20

Mayfair Games Inc. continued
6511. British Rails. © 1984. Travel, Rail, Board game. $20
6512. Demo Derby. Circa 1980's Sports, Car, Board game. 18
6513. Dragonriders of Pern. © 1983. Science Fiction, Board game. 18
6514. ElfQuest Board game, The. Circa 1980s. Comic, Fantasy, C, Board game. 18
6515. Elric, Battle at the End of Time. © 1982. Fantasy, Board game. 18
6516. Empire Builder. © 1982. Travel, Rail, Board game, 1st Edition, metal tokens. 30
6516a. Empire Builder. © 1988, as above later edition. 20
6517. Eurorails. © 1991. Travel, Rail, Board game. 20
6518. Express. © 1991. Travel, Rail, Card game. 20
6519. Family Business. © 1989. Law & Order, Card game. 18
6520. Fantasy Adventures. © 1995. Fantasy, Card game. 18
6521. Lone Wolf & Cub Game. Circa 1980s. Comic, Board game. 22
6522. Road to the White House. © 1992. Political, Board game. 18
6523. Sim City, The Card Game. © 1995. Science Fiction, Card game. 17
6524. Star Trek II, The Wrath of Khan. © 1982. Space, Card game. 15
6525. Thieves' World, Sanctuary. © 1982. Fantasy, Board game. 15
6526. Xanth. © 1991. Fantasy, Board game. 17

McDaniel Brothers
6526a. Sue and Counter-Sue. © 1981. Law Board game. 32

McGraw Hill Book Co.
6527. 4 Cyte, The Championship Word Game. © 1963. Word, Board game. 15

McGuffin-Ramsey
6528. Strategy Manager Baseball. © 1967. Sport, Baseball, Board game. 35

McJay Game Co.
6529. Rich-Farmer Poor-Farmer. © 1978. Social Concern, Board game. 25

McKell Games
6529a.Recyclomania. © 1991. Social Concern, Board game. 20

Meant to Be Ltd.
6529b.Last Call! © 1989. Q & A Board game. 18

Media Games
6530. Space Shuttle 101. © 1978. Space, Board game. 35

Mego Corp.
6531. Dallas. © 1980. TV, Card game. 15
6532. Obsession. © 1978. Skill, Board game. 12

Don Meier Publications
6533. Marlin Perkins' Wild Kingdom Game. © 1977. Personality, Animal, Board game. 20

Meljak Games

6534. Offical Globetrotter Basketball, The. Circa 1950s. Sports, Basketball, Board game. $75

Mendocino Game Co.
6535. Pirateer. © 1994. Adventure, Board game. 16

Memphis Plastic Enterprises
6535a. Fooba-Rou Football Game. © 1955. Sports, Football, Board game. 30

Merdel
6536. Box Hockey. © 1971. Sports, Hockey, Board game. 22

Merit
6537. Junior Table Top Bowling Alley. © 1961. Sports, Bowling, Board game. 25
6538. Table Top Bowling Alley. © 1958. Sports, Bowling, Board game. 25

Clifton K. Merriam
6539. Pursuing Pursuit. © 1994. Miscellaneous, Board game. 15

Merry Manufacturing
6540. Superman. © 1966. Super Hero, Board game. 55

Mesa Games
6540a.Marathon. © 1979. Sports, Track, Board game. 15

Mettoy
6541. Cheyenne Target Game. © 1962. TV, Western, Action game. 235

Mickey Games
6542. Fastbreak Basketball. Miscellaneous, Sports, Basketball, Board game. 20

Mike², Inc.
6543. Earth Alert. © 1990. Plant, Board game. 18

Mikrofun, Inc.
6544. Doonsbury Game, The. © 1993. Comics, Board game. $20

Milco
6545. Arabian Horse Game, The. © 1984. Animal, Horse, Board game. 28

Chris Miller
6545a. Network Negotiator. © 1988, Turner Broadcasting promo game, Communication Board game. 35

Randy Miller
6546. Celtic Realm. © 1979. Ethnic, Board game. 25

Miller's Outpost
6547. Miller's Outpost Game, The, Clothing store Ad game. © 1976. Advertising, Board game. 25

Mind Games Inc.
6548. Clever Endeavor. © 1989. Q & A, Board game. 18
6549. I Q Game, The. © 1992. Q & A, Board game. 17

Mind Over Matter Games
6549a. Such a Deal. © 1990. Economic, Board game. 20

Mindscape
6550. ABC Sports Winter Olympics. © 1987. Sports, Olympics, VCR game. 25

Monarch Publishers
6550a. Risquè. © 1985. Sexual, Paper & Pencil. 20

Monkey Business Group
6550b. Kenny Rogers, The Record Game. © 1984. Music, Board game. 30

Monmouth Games, Inc.
6551. Box Office. © 1991. Movie, Board game. 18

Morey & Neely
6552. Karter Peanut Shell Game. © 1978. Strategy, Board game. 25

M. J. Morgan Co.
6553. Daring Passages. © 1993. Travel, Board game. 18

Morning Star Creations
6554. NBA Opoly. © 1994. Sports, Basketball, Board game. 18

Geo. E. Mousley
6555. Count of Monte Cristo, The. © 1956. TV, Adventure, Board game. 100
6556. Fury, Western Bingo Game. © 1956. TV, Western, Board game. 100

MPH Co.
6557. Across the Board Horse Racing Game. © 1975. Sports, Horseracing, Board game. 25
6557a. Airline: The Jet Age Game. © 1977. Travel, Air, Board game. 22

Mr. B.
6558. Mystic Eye. © 1964. Mystic, Board game. $15

Muckler Enterprises
6559. Munich Decathlon. © 1971. Sports, Board game. 32

Mulgara Products
6560. Airline. © 1985. Travel, Air, Board game. 20

Howard Mullen
6561. Sail Away. A Racing Game. © 1962. Sports, Sea, Board game. 50

Muller-Game Master, Inc.
6562. Jesus Deck, The. 1972. Religious, Card game. 20

Werner Muller
5935a. Dutch Blitz Game. © 1960. Amish Lotto game. 65

Multiple Plastics
6563. Spider's Web. © 1969. Animal, Board game. 15

Multiple Prod. Corp.
6564. Animal Trap Game. Circa 1950s. Animal, Board game. 30

Multiple Toy Makers
6565. Love Computer, The. © 1970. Romance, Board game. 25

Murphy's Automotive Games
6566. Conservation. © 1980. Social Concern, Board game. 18

Muscle Mass Inc.
6567. Warrior Quest. © 1988. Fantasy, Board game. 15

Musicraft Industries
6568. Plays the Beats. © 1963. Music, Board game. 35

N/N Game Co.
6569. Greyhound Pursuit. © 1985. Sports, Dog Race, Board game. 20

Nabisco
6570. Nabisco Chewza Cookie Game, Magazine Premium. © 1964. Food, Premium, Board game. 22

Nasta Ind. Inc.
6571. Superfriends Magnetic Pa'cheesie Game. © 1980. Super Heroes, Board game. 22

"National"
6572. Falls, Wrestling Game. Circa 1950s. Sports, Wrestling, Card game. 135

National Games
6573. Anti. © 1977. Economic, Board game. 20
6574. Anti-Monopoly II. © 1977. Economic, Board game. 18

National Games, Inc.

6575. 49ers, The, Large stage coach on vertical box. Circa 1950s. Western, Board game. $45

6576. 49ers, The, Small stage coach on horizontal box. Circa 1950s. Western, Board game. 45

6577. 49ers-Round Up-Odds & Ends. Circa 1950s. Combo, Board game. 35

6578. 7 Peg Games. Circa 1940s. Strategy, Board game. 18

6579. Arabian Nights, Game of. Circa 1950s. Adventure, Board game. 40

6580. Arabian Nights-Triple Play-7-in One. Circa 1950s. Combo, Baseball, Board game. 35

6581. Big Game. Circa 1950s. Animal, Board game. 35

6582. Chinese Checkers. Circa 1940s. Classic, Board game. 15

6583. Crosswords, Deluxe Edition. Circa 1940s. Word, Board game. 15

6584. Fish Pond. Circa 1950s. Animal, Board game. 35

6585. Frog He Would A-Wooing Go, A. Circa 1950s. Animal, Nursery Rhyme, Board game. 50

6586. India, Game of. Circa 1950s. Classic, Board game. 20

6587. Jack and the Beanstalk, Game of. Circa 1950s. Nursery Rhyme, Board game. 50

6588. Jack Sprat, Game of. Circa 1950s. Nursery Rhyme, Board game. 50

6589. Jack Sprat-Puzzle Solitare-Merelles. Circa 1950s. Combo, Board game. 35

6590. Little Bo Peep. Circa 1950s. Nursery Rhyme, Board game. 50

6591. Marble Bowl. Circa 1950s. Marble, Board game. 25

6592. Old Maid. Circa 1950s. Classic, Card game. 15

6593. Par Golf. Circa 1950s. Sports, Golf, Board game. 45

6594. Play Basketball with Bob Cousey. Circa 1950s. Sports, Basketball, Board game. 150

6594a. Play Teacher. Circa 1950s. Board game. 20

6595. Race of the Turtles and Hares, The. Circa 1950s. Animal, Board game. 45

6596. Raceway. © 1954. Sports, Horseracing, Board game. 40

6597. Ring Toss. Circa 1940s. Classic, Skill game. 15

6598. Robin Hood. Circa 1950s. Literary, Adventure, Board game. 55

6599. Sherlock Holmes, The Game of Great Detective. © 1956. Detective, Board game. 65

6600. Squad Car. Circa 1950s. Travel, Car, Board game. 85

6601. Three Little Pigs, The. Circa 1950s. Nursery Rhyme, Board game. 35

6602. Top Secret. © 1956. Spy, Board game. 100

National Geographic Society

6603. National Geographic, Global Pursuit. © 1987. Geography, Board game. $20

6604. On Assignment with National Geographic. © 1990. Geography, Board game. 18

National Novelty Corp.

6605. Television. © 1953. TV, Board game. 100

National Wildlife Fed.

6606. Ranger Rick and the Great Forest Fire. © 1960. Comics, Board game. 125

Nationopoly Sales Corp.

6606a. Honoluluopoly. © 1989. Cities, Board game. 22

Nature Graph

6607. Star Games. © 1955. Space, Card game. 20

NBC

6608. Mating Game. © 1969. TV, Romance, Board game. 15

Ne Gamco

6609. Pro Golf Game. © 1962. Sports, Golf, Board game. 25

Nedmadji Game Co.

6610. Negamo Pro Golf. Circa 1980s. Sports, Golf, Board game. 20

6611. Negamo Basketball. Miscellaneous, Sports, Basketball, Board game. 20

Ness Adventures, Inc.

6612. Wagon Wheels to Oregon. © 1993. Travel, History, Board game. 17

New Earth Games

6613. Nuke. Circa 1980s. Social Concern, Board game. 22

New Jersey Bell

6614. Uniquely New Jersey, Ad Game for Telephone. © 1986. Communications, Board game. 22

Thomas Newton

6614a. 18 Wheeler. © 1978. Trucking, Board game. 20

New York Worlds Fair

6615. New York World's Fair Game. © 1963. Fairs, Board game. 35

Newsweek

6616. Ultimate Trivia Game, The. © 1984. Q & A, Board game. 15

Nonsense Factory

6617. Nonsense. © 1980. Miscellaneous, Board game. 15

Northern Signal Co.

6618. Speculation. © 1948. Stock Market, Board game. 45

6619. Tantalizer. Circa 1950s. Action, Puzzle game. 25

Northwest Corner
6620. **Senet Game.** © 1987. Classic, Board game. $20
6621. **Ur Game.** © 1987. Classic, Board game. 20

Norton Games, Inc.
6622. **Octopus.** © 1954. Animal, Sea, Board game. 75
6623. **On Stage.** © 1954. Theatrical, Board game. 65

Novel Toy
6624. **Coney Island Penny Pitch.** © 1950. Circus,
    Action game. 25
6625. **Mystic Wheel Of Knowledge.** © 1950. Q & A,
    Board game. 18
6626. **Wise Old Owl.** Circa 1950s. Q & A, Board game. 18

Novelty Mfg. Co.
6627. **Arm Chair Quarterback.** © 1955. Sport,
    Football, Board game. 35

Nu Age
6628. **Animalysis.** © 1949. Self Help, Board game. 25

O'Connor/Hall
6629. **Official Skins Golf Game, The.** © 1985. Sports,
    Golf, Board game. 30

Octogo Games
6630. **Green Game, The.** Circa 1980s. Economic,
    Board game. 15
6631. **Tugs.** © 1990. Literary, Board game. 15

Ohio Art
6632. **Astro Launch.** © 1963. Space, Board game. 100
6633. **Koo Koo Choo Choo!** © 1967. Kiddie, Board
    game. 18

Omar Bread
6634. **Lucky 3 Game, Bread premium.** Circa 1950s.
    Premium, Board game. 20

Omni House
6635. **Salvation.** © 1980. Religious, Board game. 20

Onoma Productions, Inc
6635a.**Dynasty.** © 1969. Historical, Oriental Strategy,
    Board game, in metal canister. 100

Opoly Games 'N Things
6636. **Clintonoploy.** © 1995. Political, Board game. 18

Orc Production Corp.
6637. **Total Depth.** © 1984. Miscellaneous, Board
    game. 40

Omni Magazine
6638. **Planit, The Omni Evolution Board Game,**
    magazine premium. © 1991. Premium, Social
    Concern, Board game. 15

Osobo
6638a.**Tryology, Denver Edition.** © 1979. Cities Board
    game. 15

6638b.**Tryology, New York Edition.** © 1979, As
    above. $15
6638c.**Tryology, Richmond Edition.** © 1979. As
    above. 15
6638d.**Tryology, Various cities,** As above. 15

Pacific Game Co.
6639. **Canoga.** © 1972. Military, Board game. 12
6640. **Space Checkers.** © 1971. Strategy, Board game. 12
6641. **Teed Off.** © 1972. Sports, Golf, Dice game. 18

Pango Inc.
6642. **L.A.P.I.S.** © 1990. Miscellaneous, Board game. 15

Panther Games
6643. **Shanghai Trader.** © 1986. Economic,
    Adventure, Board game. 18

Paperback Games
6644. **Subway Vigilante Game, The.** Circa 1980s. Law
    & Order, Board game. 22

Par It
6645. **Par It.** Circa 1950s. Sports, Golf, Card game. 20

Paraclete Press.
6646. **Saints Alive! Card Game.** © 1985. Religious,
    Card game. 22

Paraphase Inc.
6646a.**Derail.** © 1991. Travel rail Board game. 20

Pari Sales Co.
6647. **Pari, Horse Race Card Game.** © 1959. Sports,
    Horseracing, Card game. 25

Park Plastics Co.
6648. **Gunsmoke Target Game.** © 1958. TV, Western,
    Action game. 100

Parker Brothers
6649. **10-Four, Good Buddy, CB Radio Game.**
    © 1976. Travel, Communication, Board game. 20
6650. **1-2-3 Game Hot Spot!** © 1961. Action, Board
    game. 15
6651. **A Team, The, Mr. T On cover.** © 1984. TV,
    Board game. 12
6652. **Across the Continent, Train scene cover.**
    © 1952. Travel, US, Board game. 45
6653. **Across the Continent, U.S. map cover.** © 1960.
    Travel, US, Board game. 35
6654. **Advance to Boardwalk.** © 1985. Economic,
    Board game. 15
6655. **All the Kings Men.** © 1979. Military, Board
    game. 20
6656. **Annette's Secret Passage Game.** © 1958.
    Adventure, Board game. 60
6657. **Annie.** © 1981. Comics, Board game. 15
6658. **Arkansas Bluff.** © 1975. Classic, Card game. 15
6659. **As the World Turns.** © 1966. TV, Board game. 25
6660. **Astron, The Game that Moves as You Play.**
    © 1955. Travel, Board game. 75
6661. **Avalanche.** © 1966. Marble, Board game. 15

Parker Bros. continued

6662. Aviation. Circa 1950s. Travel, air, Card game. $25

BABAR

THE KING OF THE ELEPHANTS GAME BY PARKER BROTHERS
NO READING REQUIRED

6663. Babar. © 1978. Literary, Board game. 22
6664. Bantu. © 1955. Strategy, Board game. 20
6665. Barney Miller. © 1977. TV, Board game. 18
6666. Baseball Game. © 1949. Sports, Baseball, Card game. 45
6667. Baseball Game. © 1950. Sports, Baseball, Board game. 35
6668. Baseball, Black Background and Red stripe. © 1959. Sports, Football, Board game. 30
6669. Baseball, Football & Checkers. © 1957. Sports, Combo, Board game. 25
6670. Baseball, Green with Red Strip cover. © 1959. Sports, Baseball, Board game. 30
6671. Baseball. © 1967. Sports, Baseball, Board game. .... 25.
6672. Batman Forever. © 1995. Super Heroes, Board game. 20
6673. Batman Returns. © 1992. Movie, Super Hero, Card game. 15
6673a. Batman Returns, 3-D Board Game. © 1992, Super-Hero Board game. 20
6674. Batman, The Animated. © 1992. Super Heroes, Board game. 20
6675. Battlestar Galactica. © 1978. Space, Board game. 18
6676. Beggars and Thieves. © 1984. Law & Order, Card game. 15
6677. Billionaire. © 1973. Economic, Board game. 20
6678. Bing Crosby's Game Call Me Lucky. © 1954. Sports, Horseracing, Board game. 45
6679. Bionic Crisis, Six Million Dollar Man. © 1975. TV, Science Fiction, Board game. 15
6680. Bionic Woman, The. © 1976. TV, Science Fiction, Board game. 15
6681. Bird Watcher. © 1958. Animal, Board game. 20
6682. Black Cat Game, The. Circa 1940s. Animal, Card game. 45
6683. Blondie Game, The. © 1969. Comics, Board game. 20
6684. Boggle. © 1976. Word, Board game. 10
6685. Bonanza, Michigan Rummy Game. © 1970. TV, Board game. 45
6686. Bonkers. © 1978. Miscellaneous, Board game. 20
6687. Booby-Trap, Horizontal box. © 1965. Skill, Board game. 15
6688. Booby-Trap, Vertical box. © 1965. Skill, Board game. 15
6689. Boom or Bust, Game of, Square box, 1st Edition. © 1951. Economic, Board game. 150

6690. Boom or Bust, Game of, Red box, 2nd Edition. © 1951. Economic, Board game. $110
6691. Bowl-Em. Circa 1950s. Sports, Bowling, Board game. 20
6692. Bozo The World's Most Famous Clown. © 1960. Circus, Board game. 45
6693. Bruce Jenner Decathlon Game. © 1979. Sports, Board game. 22
6694. Buckshot! © 1970. Skill, Action game. 15
6695. Bug Out. © 1971. Skill, Action game. 15
6696. Bunny Rabbit Game. © 1961. Animal, Board game. 18
6697. Burr Tillstrom's Kukla and Ollie. © 1962. TV, Personality, Board game. 40
6698. Calling All Cards. Circa 1940s. Travel, Car, Board game. 40
6699. Cam, The Great Game of, shorter version of Camelot. © 1949. Strategy, Board game. 40
6700. Camelot, Two knights on beige cover. © 1961. Strategy, Board game. 30
6701. Camelot. © 1955. Strategy, Board game. 40
6702. Camelot. © 1958. Strategy, Board game. 40
6703. Caper. © 1970. Law & Order, Board game. 35
6704. Care Bears, Card Game, Which Bears Where? © 1983. Animals, Card game. 15
6705. Careers, Revised edition. © 1979. Careers, Board game. 18
6706. Careers, The Game, Red box. © 1958. Occupations, Board game. 25
6707. Careers, The Game, 1st edition. © 1955. Occupations, Board game. 35
6708. Careers, The Game, Green, red and blue stripe box. © 1958. Occupations, Board game. 25
6709. Careers, The Game, Orange box. © 1965. Occupations, Board game. 25
6710. Castle Risk. © 1986. Military, Board game. 22
6711. Cat and Mouse. © 1964. Animal, Board game. 16
6712. Centurions. © 1986. Science Fiction, Board game. 10
6713. Charlie Brown's All-Star Baseball Game. © 1965. Comics, Sp, Baseball, Board game. 65
6714. Cherry Ames, Nursing Game. © 1959. TV, Medical, Board game. 75
6715. Children's Hour, The. © 1946. Kiddie, Board game. 25
6716. Civil War Game, 1863. © 1961. Military, Board game. 35
6717. Claim to Fame. © 1990. Adventure, Board game. ... 15
6718. Climb the Mountain. © 1951. Adventure, Board game. 35
6719. Close Encounters of the Third Kind. © 1978. Movie, Space, Board game. 20
6720. Clue, The Great Detective Game, Green implement box. © 1949. Mystery, Board game. 55
6721. Clue, The Great Detective Game, Gold box. © 1963. Mystery, Board game. 45
6722. Clue, The Great Detective Game, Green box. © 1950. Mystery, Board game. 35
6723. Clue, The Great Detective Game, Orange box. © 1956. Mystery, Board game. 30
6724. Clue, The Great Museum Caper Game. © 1991. Mystery, Board game. 18
6725. Code Name: Sector. © 1977. Military, Board game. 18
6726. Conflict, Arrow cover. © 1960. Military, Board game. 65

Parker Bros. continued

6727. Conflict, Black tank cover. © 1964. Military, Board game. $50

6728. Coup D'Etat. © 1966. Military, Nepo, Card game. 20

6729. Cowboy Roundup Game. © 1952. Western, Board game. 20

6730. Crow Hunt. Circa 1950s. Animal, Action game. 45

6731. Curious George Game, The. © 1977. Comics, Board game. 20

6732. Dealer's Choice. © 1972. Economic, Board game. 25

6733. Dig, Blue Box. © 1959. Word, Action game. 5

6734. Dig, Red box. © 1968. Letters, Action game. 5

6735. Dig, Red letters. Circa 1950s. Letters, Action game. 5

6736. Dig, White letters. Circa 1950s. Letters, Action game. 5

6737. Dinosaur Island. © 1980. Animal, Board game. 18

6738. Disneyland, It's a Small World Game. © 1965. Disney, Board game. 35

6739. Disneyland Monorail Game, Blue box. © 1960. Disney, Board game. 50

6740. Disneyland Monorail Game. © 1960. Disney, Board game. 50

6741. Disneyland Pirates of the Caribbean Game. © 1965. Disney, Board game. 50

6742. Disneyland Riverboat Game. © 1960. Disney, Board game. 50

6743. Dixie, The Game of. © 1954. Miscellaneous, Card game. 25

6744. Domain. © 1983. Strategy, Board game. 15

6745. Donald Duck's Party Game. © 1955. Disney, Board game. 55

6746. Don't Go to Jail, Monopoly Dice Game. © 1991. Law & Order, Dice Game. 12

6747. Double Some 'R' Set, 2ⁿᵈ Edition. © 1947. Numbers, Card game. 12

6748. Dune. © 1984. Movie, Space, Board game. 30

6749. Dungeon Dice. © 1977. Dice, Board game. 15

6750. E.T. The Extra-Terrestrial. © 1982. Movie, Science Fiction, Board game. 22

6751. Eddie Cantor's Tell it to the Judge, Yellow box. Circa 1950s. Personal, Travel, Board game. 35

6752. Elmer Wheelers Fat Boy Game. © 1951. Literary, Physic, Board game. 55

6753. Encore. © 1989. Economic, Board game. 18

6754. Escape from Colditz. Circa 1960s. Military, Board game. 35

6755. Escort, Game of Guys & Gals. © 1955. Romance, Board game. 50

6756. Ewok, Favorite Five. © 1984. Movie, Science Fiction, Card game. 18

6757. Ewok, Paw Pals. © 1984. Movie, Science Fiction, Card game. 18

6758. Ewok, Say "Cheese!" © 1984. Movie, Science Fiction, Card game. 18

6759. Express Monopoly Card Game, Blue Box. © 1993. Economic, Card game. 15

6760. Fangface. © 1979. Cartoon, TV, Board game. 18

6761. Fast 111's. © 1981. Sport, Car, Board game. 25

6762. Finance and Fortune, The Game of. © 1955. Economic, Board game. 35

6763. Finance, Blue cover with four houses & a bank. © 1956. Economic, Board game. 32

6764. Five Wise Birds, The. © 1954. Skill, Action game. 25

6765. Flinch, Three player cartoon cover. © 1963. Number, Card game. $5

6766. Flinch., Variant cover. © 1954. Number, Card game. 6

6767. Flinch., Variant cover. © 1954. Number, Card game. 6

6768. Flinch. © 1954. Number, Card game. 6

6769. Flip for Fun. © 1966. Travel, Board game. 15

6770. Fomula-1, Bold Photo cover. © 1964. Sports, Car, Board game. 50

6771. Fomula-1. © 1963. Sports, Car, Board game. 45

6772. Football, Baseball, & Checkers. © 1948. Sports, Miscellaneous, Board game. 40

6773. Fox and Hounds, Game of. © 1948. Animal, Board game. 35

6774. Free Parking. © 1988. Travel, Road, Card game. 15

6775. Fun City. © 1965. Economic, Board game. 22

6776. Fun City. © 1987. Economic, Board game. 12

6777. Funny Bones. © 1968. Social, Card game. 15

6778. Gambler. © 1977. Economic, Ch, Board game. 15

6779. Garfield. © 1978. Comics, Board game. 18

6780. George of the Jungle. © 1968. TV, Cartoon, Board game. 75

6781. Gnip Gnop. © 1971. Skill, Action game. 15

6782. Go for It! © 1985. Strategy, Board game. 15

6782a. Going to Jerusalem. © 1955, Religious Board game. 55

6783. Goodbye, Mr. Chips Game. © 1969. Movie, Board game. 35

6784. Goosebumps, Shrieks and Spiders Game. © 1995. Monsters, Board game. 15

6785. Grape Escape. © 1997. Miscellaneous, Board game. 15

6786. Grapple. © 1973. Strategy, Board game. 15

6787. Great American Flag Game. Circa 1950s. Flag, Geography, Board game. 25

6788. Great Game Cam, The. © 1949. Strategy, Board game. 45

6789. Guiness Book of World Records Game, The. © 1979. History, Board game. 20

6790. Guinness Game of World Records. © 1975. Q & A, Board game. 25

6791. Happy Days. © 1975. TV, Board game. 18

6792. Hardy Boys Mystery Game, The. © 1978. Mystery, Literary, Board game. 18

6793. Have Gun Will Travel. © 1959. TV, Western, Board game. 75

6794. Hex, The Zig-Zag Game. © 1950. Strategy, Board game. 18

6795. Hey Pa, There's a Goat on the Roof. © 1965. Animal, Board game. 40

6796. Hip Flip. © 1968. Skill, Action game. 15

Parker Bros. continued

6797. Holly Hobbie Wishing Well Game. © 1976.
Literary, Board game. $18

6798. Hollywood "Go". © 1954. Movie, Board game. 20

6799. Hot Spot! The 1-2-3 Game. © 1961. Numbers,
Board game. 15

6800. Howdy Doody's Own Game. Circa 1950s. TV,
Board game. 75

6801. Howdy-Doody Beanbag Game. © 1951. TV,
Action game. 55

6802. Hurry Up. © 1971. Skill, Action game. 15

**6803. Indiana Jones from the Raiders of the Lost
Ark.** © 1982. Movie, Board game. 18

6804. Inside Moves. © 1985. Strategy, Board game. 15

6805. Instant Replay. © 1980. Sports, Football, Board
game. 15

6806. Inventors. © 1974. Occupation, Board game. 20

6807. Jack Straws. Circa 1950s. Skill, Action game. 12

6808. Kewpie Doll Game. © 1963. Toy, Board game. 18

6809. Keyword. © 1953. Word, Board game. 18

6810. Kimbo. © 1960. Strategy, Board game. 15

6811. Knight Rider. © 1983. TV, Board game. 18

6812. Krull. © 1983. Fantasy, Card game. 15

6813. Krull. © 1983. Movie, Fantasy, Board game. 20

6814. No game

6815. Landside. © 1971. Political, Board game. 35

6816. Larry Harmon's Bozo. © 1967. Circus, Board
game. 85

6817. Lavern & Shirley. © 1977. TV, Board game. 20

6818. Let's Furnish a House. © 1947. Architecture,
Board game. 120

6819. Li'l Abner Game, The. © 1969. Comics, Board
game. 20

6820. Little House on the Prairie. © 1978. TV, Board
game. 30

6821. Little Noddy's Taxi Game. © 1956. Literary,
Board game. 75

6822. Little Red School House Game. © 1952. Kiddie,
Board game. 35

6823. Lone Ranger. © 1956. TV, Western, Board
game. 40

6824. Long Shot. © 1962. Sports, Horseracing, Board
game. 35

6825. Lost Gold, Hidden Treasure Game. © 1975.
Adventure, Board game. 20

6826. Lost Treasure. © 1982. Adventure, Board game. 15

6827. Mad Magazine Card Game. © 1980. Literary,
Card game. 10

6828. Mad Magazine Game, The. © 1979. Literary,
Board game. 10

6829. Magnificent Race, The. © 1975. Travel, Car,
Board game. 22

6830. Make a Million. © 1954. Economic, Card game. 15

6831. Marine World. © 1968. Travel, Sea, Board
game. 25

6832. Mask, The. © 1995. Comics, Board game. 20

6833. Mask. © 1985. Military, Board game. 15

6834. Masterpiece, The Art Auction Game. © 1970.
Art, Board game. 20

6835. Miami Vice. © 1984. TV, Board game. 15

6836. Mickey Mouse Game Box. © 1953. Disney,
Board game. 35

6837. Mickey Mouse Picture Matching Game.
© 1953. Disney, Board game. 30

6838. Mille Bornes, French card game. © 1962.
Travel, Card game. 20

6839. Mille Bornes, Photo cover. © 1971. Travel, Card
game. $5

6840. Mindmaze. © 1970. Strategy, Board game. 12

6841. Miss America Pageant Game, The. © 1974.
Career, Board game. 25

6842. Monopoly, (Deluxe), 2 color plastic houses.
© 1956. Economic, Board game. 40

6843. Monopoly, Braille Edition. Circa 1980s.
Economic, Board game. 65

6843a.Monopoly, Centennial Olympic Games. ©
1996. Sport, Economic, Board game. 35

**6844. Monopoly, Deluxe Edition, 50th Anniversary,
Metal Box.** © 1985. Economic, Board game. 50

6845. Monopoly, Deluxe Edition, 50th Anniversary.
© 1985. Economic, Board game. 35

**6846. Monopoly, Deluxe Edition, 60th Anniversary
Edition.** © 1995. Economic, Board game. 22

**6847. Monopoly, Deluxe Edition, Photo of game
cover.** © 1978. Economic, Board game. 20

**6848. Monopoly, Deluxe Edition, Red & brown
cover.** Circa 1960s. Economic, Board game. 35

6849. Monopoly, Deluxe Edition, Train cover. ©
1957. Economic, Board game. 85

**6850. Monopoly, Deluxe Edition, white box with
General Mills.** Late 1960s. Economic, Board
game. 15

**6851. Monopoly, Impliment box with Rich Uncle,
green edge.** © 1954. Economic, Board game. 35

**6852. Monopoly, Impliment box with Rich Uncle, red
edge.** © 1954. Economic, Board game. 35

6852a.Monopoly, Mustang Edition. © 1999.
Economic, Car, Board game. 30

6853. Monopoly, NASCAR. © 1997. Economic, Board
game. 30

6854. Monopoly, NFL. © 1998. Economic, Board
game. 30

6855. Monopoly, Star Wars Edition. © 1997. Science
Fiction, Economic, Board game. 30

6855a. Monopoly, United States Navy. © 1998.
Economic, Board game. 40

6856. Monopoly. © 1975. Economic, Board game. 20

6857. Moon Tag. © 1957. Space, Board game. 175

6858. Mork & Mindy Game. © 1979. TV, Board
game. 20

6859. Mother Goose Rhymes Games. © 1954.
Nursery Rhyme, Card game. 15

6860. Mr. Ed. © 1962. TV, Animal, Board game. 35

6861. Muppet Show, The. © 1977. TV, Board Game. 18

6862. My Lucky Stars. © 1992. Girl, Board game. 15

**6863. Nancy Drew Mystery Game, The, Nancy in red
cover.** © 1957. Literary, Detective, Board game. ... 75

6864. Nancy Drew Mystery Game, The. © 1959.
Mystery, TV, Literary, Board game. 65

6865. Never Say Die. © 1959. Action, Dice game. 10

6866. Nicktoons Doug. © 1992. TV, Board game. 15

6867. Nicktoons Rugrats. © 1992. TV, Board game. 15

6868. Number Please. © 1961. TV, Game, Board
game. 12

6869. On Guard. © 1967. Strategy, Board game. 10

6870. Option. © 1983. Economic, Board game. 8

6871. Orbit. © 1966. Space, Board game. 30

6872. Outwit. © 1978. Strategy, Board game. 10

6873. Pay Day. © 1976. Economic, Board game. 15

6874. Pegity. © 1953. Strategy, Board game. 10

6875. People Weekly. © 1984. Q & A, Board game. 15

Parker Bros. continued

6876. Perfict Match Game. © 1992. Romance, Board game. $15

6877. Phil & Tony Esposito's Action Hockey. © 1973. Sports, Hockey, Board game. 45

6878. Pigskin. © 1946. Sports, Football, Board game. 40

6879. Pigskin. © 1956. Sports, Football, Board game. 35

6880. Pigskin. © 1960. Sports, Football, Board game. 25

6881. Pit, Photo cover. © 1973. Stock Market, Card game. 5

6882. Pit, Red Vertical box. © 1947. Stock Market, Card game. 8

6883. Pit, Red & Blue Color Pit. Circa 1950s. Stock Market, Card game. 6

6884. Pit, Red horizontal box. © 1947. Stock Market, Card game. 8

6885. Plotz! © 1971. Strategy, Board game. 12

6886. Pole Position. © 1983. Sports, Car, Board game. 15

6887. Police Academy, The Series. © 1989. TV, Board game. 15

6888. Politics, Election Game. © 1960. Political, Board game. 25

6889. Politics, The Game, Election Game. © 1952. Political, Board game. 40

6890. Pollyanna, Multi colored letters. Circa 1950s. Classic, Board game. 15

6891. Pollyanna, Dixie. © 1952. Classic, Board game. 25

6892. Popeye Card game, based on the Arcade Game. © 1983. Comics, Card game. 10

6893. Popeye. © 1983. Game, Comic, Board game. 15

6894. Pow Wow. © 1973. Skill, Action game. 10

6895. Prediction Rod. © 1970. Mystic, Board game. 10

6896. Pro Draft, Topps cards included. © 1974. Sports, Football, Board game. 15

6897. No game

6898. Probe, Three cameos of players atop Probe. © 1974. Word, Board game. 8

6899. Probe, 1st edition. © 1964. Word, Board game. 10

6900. Punch Line. © 1978. Word, Card game. 10

6901. Push Over. © 1981. Skill, Action game. 10

6902. Quibic. © 1965. Miscellaneous, Board game. 10

6903. Rattle Battle. © 1970. Strategy, Board game. 12

6904. Reddy-Clown 3-ring Circus Game. © 1952. Circus, Board game. 35

6905. Rescuers, The. © 1977. Disney, Board game. 18

6906. Rich Uncle, Blue & Grey background cover. © 1955. Stock Market, Board game. 45

6907. Rich Uncle, Deluxe Edition, Grey cover. © 1946. Stock Market, Board game. 60

6908. Rich Uncle, Orange background cover. © 1946. Stock Market, Board game. 50

6909. Rich Uncle, Yellow background cover. © 1959. Stock Market, Board game. 40

6910. Rio, The Game of. © 1956. Travel, Board game. 35

6911. Risk and Castle Risk. © 1990. Military, Board game. .... CRP

6912. Risk, with plastic playing pieces. © 1959. Military, Board game. 35

6913. Risk, with plastic playing pieces. © 1965. Military, Board game. 25

6914. Risk, with soldier playing pieces. © 1990. Military, Board game. .... CRP

6915. Risk, with wooden playing pieces. 1st edition. © 1959. Military, Board game. 100

6916. Roll-It. © 1954. Word, Dice game. 10

6917. Ropes and Ladders. © 1954. Miscellaneous, Board game. $15

6918. Ruffhouse. © 1980. Strategy, Board game. 10

6919. Saban's VR Troopers. © 1994. Science Fiction, Card game. 20

6920. Saddle Up. © 1980. Animal, Horse, Board game. 25

6921. Say When! © 1961. TV, Game, Board game. 18

6922. Scan. © 1970. Miscellaneous, Card game. 12

6923. Scoop!, The Game, Publish Your Own Newspaper. © 1956. Communications, Board game. 75

6924. Screech. © 1972. Miscellaneous, Board game. 15

6925. Senet. © 1946. Classic, Board game. 30

6926. Shadowlord! © 1983. Fantasy, Board game. 15

6927. Sheriff of Dodge City. © 1966. Western, Board game. 15

6928. Situation 4. © 1968. Economic, Board game. 18

6929. Situation 7, Space Puzzle Game. © 1969. Puzzle, Board game. 18

6930. Six Million Dollar Man. © 1975. TV, Science Fiction, Board game. 15

6931. Skatterbug, The Game of. © 1951. Action, Board game. 18

6932. Skudo. © 1949. Strategy, Board game. 12

6933. Sky Lanes. © 1958. Travel, Air, Board game. 75

6934. Sleeping Beauty Game, Walt Disney. © 1958. Disney, Board game. 25

6935. Sleeping Beauty Game, Walt Disney. Circa 1970s. Disney, Board game. 15

6936. Smess the Ninny's Chess. © 1970. Strategy, Board game. 12

6937. Snap Card Game. © 1954. Classic, Card game. 12

6938. Snapshot. © 1972. Miscellaneous, Card game. 15

6939. Sorry, The Great Game, three-quarter photo of board cover. © 1970. Classic, Board game. 12

6940. Sorry, The Great Game, Dark green box. © 1958. Classic, Board game. 20

6941. Sorry, The Great Game, Overhead photo of board cover. © 1964. Classic, Board game. 18

6942. Sorry, The Great Game, 1st edition. © 1950. Classic, Board game. 25

6943. Sorry, The Great Game, 1st edition, Board & implement box. © 1950. Classic, Board game. 15

6944. Space Age Game. © 1953. Space, Board game. 75

6945. Space Game. © 1953. Space, Board game. 65

6946. Square Off. © 1972. Strategy, Board game. 15

6947. Star Reporter, Blue-grey background, 4-color. © 1960. Communications, Board game. 75

6948. Star Reporter, Red and Grey box. © 1952. Communications, Board game. 100

6949. Star Reporter, Three red star cover. © 1952. Communications, Board game. 100

6950. Star Wars, Empire Strikes Back, Yoda, The Jedi Master. © 1981. Movie, Science Fiction, Board game. 20

Parker Bros. continued

6951. Star Wars, Return of the Jedi, Battle at Sarlacc's Pit Game. © 1983. Movie, Science Fiction, Board game. $20

6952. Star Wars, Return of the Jedi, Wicket the Ewok. © 1983. Movie, Science Fiction, Board game. 20

6953. Star Wars. © 1982. Movie, Science Fiction, Board game. 18

6954. State Capitals, Game of. © 1952. Q & A, Geography, Board game. 22

6955. States and Cities, The Game of. © 1947. Geography, Card game. 25

6956. Steps to Toyland. © 1955. Kiddie, Board game. 25

6957. Strawberry Shortcake Card Game, Win a Wisker. © 1981. TV, Card game. 8

6958. Sunken Treasure. © 1948. Adventure, Board game. 20

6959. Super Powers. © 1984. Super Heroes, Board game. 20

6960. Superman III. © 1983. Super Heroes, Card game. 15

6961. Survive! © 1982. Adventure, Board game. 15

6962. Tattler Quiz Game. © 1947. Q & A, Card game. 12

6963. Tennis. © 1975. Sports, Tennis, Board game. 15

6964. They're Off, Horse Race Game. Circa 1950s. Sports, Horseracing, Board game. 35

6965. Thistle. © 1966. Miscellaneous, Card game. 15

6966. Thunderbirds. © 1967. TV, Board game. 60

6967. Tiny Tim Game of Beautiful Things, The. © 1970. Personality, Board game. 55

6968. Tit Tat Toe. Circa 1950s. Classic, Board game. 15

6969. Tom and Jerry. © 1948. Cartoon, Board game. 40

6970. Tom Swift. © 1966. Literary, Science Fiction, Board game. 275

6971. Top Ten Bowling. © 1963. Sports, Bowling, Board game. 15

6972. Touch. © 1970. Mystic, Board game. 15

6973. Touring, Map box. © 1955. Travel, Car, Card game. 30

6974. Touring, Map Letters Cover. © 1958. Travel, Car, Card game. 25

6975. Touring, Red Car and Trailer. © 1947. Travel, Car, Card game. 35

6976. Touring, Scene with speed limit 45. © 1954. Travel, Car, Card game. 25

6977. Touring, Scenes with line drawing of car. © 1958. Travel, Car, Card game. 25

6978. Touring, Yellow box Model T Ford. © 1965. Travel, Car, Card game. 8

6979. Trade Winds, Caribbean Sea Game. © 1960. Pirate, Adventure, Board game. 50

6980. Treasure Trail, Game of. © 1950. Kiddie, Board game. 30

6981. Trivial Pursuit, The Vintage Years. © 1989. Q & A, Board game. 18

6982. Trust Me. © 1981. Social, Board game. 15

6983. Tugboat. © 1974. Travel, Sea, Board game. 12

6984. Tycoon. © 1966. Economic, Board game. 18

6985. Uncle Wiggily Game, The. © 1971. Literary, Board game. 20

6986. Undersea World of Jacques Cousteau. © 1968. TV, An, Sea, Per, Board game. 35

6987. Universe. © 1967. Strategy, Board game. 22

6988. Voltron. © 1984. Science Fiction, Board game. 12

6989. Walt Disney Presents Peter Pan Game. Circa 1970s. Disney, Board game. 15

6990. Walt Disney Presents Pinocchio Game. Circa 1980s. Disney, Board game. $15

6991. Walt Disney, Babes in Toyland. © 1961. Disney, Board game. 20

6992. Walt Disney's Adventureland Game. © 1956. Disney, Board game. 45

6993. Walt Disney's Babes in Toyland. © 1961. Disney, Board game. 20

6994. Walt Disney's Cinderella. © 1950. Disney, Board game. 35

6995. Walt Disney's Fantasyland Game. © 1956. Disney, Board game. 45

6996. Walt Disney's Hardy Boys Treasure Game. © 1957. Literary, Board game. 50

6997. Walt Disney's Jungle Book Game. © 1966. Disney, Board game. 30

6998. Walt Disney's Mary Poppins Carousel Game. © 1964. Disney, Movie, Board game. 25

6999. Walt Disney's Mickey Mouse Game. © 1976. Disney, Board game. 22

7000. Walt Disney's Mouseketeer Game. © 1963. Disney, Board game. 30

7002. Walt Disney's Official Frontierland Game. © 1955. Disney, Board game. 55

7002a. Walt Disney's Peter Pan Game. Circa 1950s, Disney Board game. 35

7003. Walt Disney's Presents Pinocchio Game. © 1971. Disney, Board game. 15

7004. Walt Disney's Robin Hood Circa 1970s. Disney, Board game. 15

7005. Walt Disney's Swamp Fox. © 1960. Disney, Board game. 35

7006. Walt Disney's Sword in the Stone. © 1963. Disney, Movie, Board game. 35

7007. Walt Disney's Tomorrowland. © 1956. Disney, Board game. 45

7008. Walt Disney's Uncle Remus Game. © 1947. Disney, Board game. 75

7009. Walt Disney's Winnie the Pooh, Blue sky cover. © 1979. Disney, Board game. 45

7010. Walt Disney's Winnie the Pooh. © 1964. Disney, Board game. 60

7011. Walt Disney's Wonderful World of Disney. © 1962. Disney, Board game. 40

7012. Walt Disney's Zorro Game. © 1966. Disney, Board game. 30

7013. Waterworks. © 1972. Miscellaneous, Card game. 18

7014. Who? Game of Hidden Identity. © 1951. Social, Board game. 25

7015. Who's It. © 1976. Miscellaneous, Board game. 15

7016. Wicket the Ewok. © 1983. Science Fiction, Movie, Board game. 18

Parker Bros. continued

7017. Wide World Travel Game, Six picture discs cover. © 1962. Travel, World, Board game. $25

7018. Wide World Travel Game, Yellow letters. © 1957. Travel, World, Board game. 30

7019. Willow. © 1988. Fantasy, Board game. 15

7020. Winnie the Pooh. © 1954. Literary, Board game. 75

7021. Wit's End, Game of. ©1948. Strategy, Board game. 22

7022. Yacht Race, Saturday Housed. © 1961. Sports, Sea, Board game. 50

Park Plastic Co.

7023. Bullwinkle Motorized Target Game. © 1961. TV, Cartoon, Action game. 150

7024. Bullwinkle Target and Ring Toss Game. © 1961. TV, Cartoon, Action game. 75

7025. Bullwinkle, Fli-Hi Target Game. © 1961. TV, Cartoon, Action game. 175

7026. Group Therapy. © 1969. Social Concern, Board game. 25

Parva

7027. Prince Valiant Cross Bow Pistol Game. © 1948. Comics, Skill game. 135

Joseph Pascal

7028. Defend Your Capital. © 1976. Economic, Board game. 25

Pass Out Games Inc.

7029. Pass Out, The Drinking Game. © 1962. Sexual, Drink, Board game. 25

7030. Sip and Go Naked. © 1978. Sexual, Drink, Board game. 18

7031. Sip and Strip. © 1978. Sexual, Drink, Board game. 18

Pastime Games

7032. Doctors Game, The. © 1992. Careers, Card game. 20

7033. Lawers Game, The. © 1992. Careers, Card game. 20

7034. Politicians Game, The. © 1992. Careers, Card game. 20

Patrotic Novelty Corp.

7035. Option Game Board, The. © 1976. Stock Market, Board game. 25

Payton Prod.

7036. United Nations, Game About the. © 1961. Q & A, Board game. 25

Peace Works Inc.

7037. Give Peace a Chance. © 1987. Social Concern, Board game. 20

Peerless Playthings Co.

7038. Swingin' Sam. Circa 1960s. Skill, Action game. 15

Pente Games

7039. Pente. © 1982. Strategy, Board game. 5

Pepper Lane Industries

7040. Miami Vice. © 1984. TV, Detective, Board game. $15

Pepsi Co.

7041. Pepsi-Cola Across the U.S.A.! © 1984. Advertising, Board game. 20

Percision Sports Game Co.

7042. PSG Baseball. Miscellaneous, Sports, Baseball, Board game. 15

Perfect Game Co.

7043. Jose Canseco's Perfect Baseball Game. © 1991. Sports' Baseball, Board game. 15

Peerless Playthings

7043a.Bottles Up. ©1962. Skill, Bottle game. 25

Perl Products

7044. Official Boston Marathon Game. © 1978. Sports, Horseracing, Board game. 28

Perrani Prod.

7045. Liberation of Kuwait. © 1991. Military, Board game. 25

Persue the Pennant

7046. Pursue the Pennant. © 1984. Sports, Baseball, Board game. 20

Phillips

7047. Spill & Spell. © 1959. Word, Dice game. 10

Phon-o-Game Co.

6421a.Race A Plane. © 1947. Travel, Air, Phonograph Board game. 30

Plan B. Corp.

7048. Caveat Emptor. © 1971. Economic, Board game. 28

Planet-3 Games Co.

7049. Moscow! Auction! Circa 1990. Economic, Board game. 30

Play Ed (Russell)

7050. Sequencers. Circa 1980s. Miscellaneous, Card game. 15

Play Rite, Inc.

7051. Johnny Unitas Football Game, The. © 1960. Sports, Football, Board game. 125

Pofo Inc.

7052. Play Baseball. © 1979. Sports, Baseball, Board game. 25

Points Westward

7053. Columbus! The Game of Exploration, Conquest and Trade. © 1991. Travel, Economic, Board game. 22

Polaroid
7054. Polaroid's Party Pack, Ad game for camera.
© 1969. Advertising, Board game. $30

Polygon Corp.
7055. Pony Express, The Game of. © 1947. Western,
Communications, Board game. 35

Positive Products
7055a. Hurricane Hugo Game. © 1989. Board game. 20

Post Cereal
7056. Bugs Bunny Head Start Game. © 1961.
Cartoon, Premium, Board Game. 25
7057. Bugs Bunny Space Race. © 1961. Cartoon,
Premium, Board Game. 25
7058. Bugs Bunny Trapped. © 1961. Cartoon,
Premium, Board Game. 25
7059. Central Bedrock U*S*A Race Game. © 1987.
Travel, TV, Premium, Board game. 8
**7060. Critter Cards Card Game, Linus The
Lionhearted Premium.** © 1965. TV, Cartoon,
Card game. 25
7061. Doctor Dolittle, Card Game, Cereal Premium.
© 1967. Movie, Card game. 25
7062. Eastern Bedrock U*S*A Race Game. © 1987.
Travel, TV, Premium, Board game. 18
7063. Linus Critter Cards. © 1964. Cartoon, Card
Game. 25
7064. Western Bedrock U*S*A Race Game. © 1987.
Travel, TV, Premium, Board game. 18

Power Games Inc.
7065. Power, The Game. © 1994. Military, Board
game. 25

James C. Powers
7066. Regatta. © 1946. Sports, Sea, Board game. 75

PowerTechnics Game Corp.
7067. Power Technics, The Game of. © 1991.
Economic, Board game. 18

Predators & Prey Inc.

7068. Predators & Prey. © 1996. Animal, Board
game. 15

Pressman Toy Corp.
7069. Action Baseball for Mickey Mantle. © 1967.
Sports, Baseball, Board game. $100
7070. Action Baseball for Roger Maris. © 1967.
Sports, Baseball, Board game. 75
7071. Action Baseball for Tom Seaver. © 1967.
Sports, Baseball, Board game. 75
7072. Action Baseball. © 1964. Sports, Baseball,
Board game. 30
7073. Action Golf. Circa 1960s. Sports, Golf, Board
game. 35
7074. Addams Family, The. © 1991. Monster, Board
game. 18
7075. American Pachinko. © 1970. Skill, Action
game. 15
7076. Batman Batarang Toss. © 1966. Super Heroes,
Action game. 35
7077. Beany and Cecil Ring Toss. © 1961. TV,
Cartoon, Action game. 40
7078. Beany and Cecil Skill Ball. © 1961. TV,
Cartoon, Action game. 50
7079. Bomb the Navy. Circa 1940s. Military, Board
game. 50
7080. Broadcast Baseball. Circa 1938-41. Sports,
Baseball, Board game. 75
7081. Doorways to Adventure. © 1986. Adventure,
Board game. 15
7082. Football. Circa 1940s. Sports, Football, Board
Game. 60
7083. Fortune 500 Business Game. © 1976.
Economic, Board game. 22
7084. Groucho TV Quiz. © 1954. TV, Q & A, Board
game. 65
7085. Home Game. © 1950. Miscellaneous, Board
game. 35
7086. Jeopardy. © 1986. Q & A, Board game. 15
7087. Lone Ranger & Tonto Spin to Win Game.
© 1967. TV, Western, Board game. 40
7088. Magnetic Flying Saucers. © 1951. Space, Board
game. 25
7089. Marvel Super Heroes Game. © 1982. Super
Heroes, Board game. 15
7090. Mighty Mouse Skill-Roll Game. © 1958.
Cartoon, Action game. 45
7091. Mr. Peepers School Bag & Game Kit. © 1955.
TV, Board game. 50
7092. Offical Roger Maris Baseball Game. Circa
1950s. Sports, Baseball, Board game. 75
7093. Petropolis. © 1976. Economic, Board game. 25
7094. Pinky Lee Game Time. © 1955. TV, Board
game. 45
7095. Race to Riches. © 1989. Economic, Board
game. 15
7096. Rat Patrol Spin to Win Game. © 1967. Military,
Board game. 50
7097. Richie Rich Big Money Game. © 1977. Comics,
Board game. 15
7098. Skill Ball. © 1950. Skill, Action game. 15
7099. Superman Spin Game. © 1967. Super Heroes,
Board game. 30
7099a. Tabloid Teasers. © 1991. Communications,
Board game. 20
7100. Temple of Fu Manchu. © 1967. Skill, Action
game. 35
7101. Things and Places. © 1960. Q & A, Board
game. 15
7102. Tick, The. © 1995. Comics, Board game. 15
7103. Tigo. Circa 1980s. Strategy, Board game. 12

Pressman Toy Corp. continued

7104. Time Tunnel Spin-To-Win, The. © 1967. TV,
Science Fiction, Board game. $125

7105. Treasure Trolls. © 1994. Fantasy, Board game. 15

7106. Uncanny X-Men Alert, The. © 1992. Super
Heroes, Board game. 18

7107. Veda Magnetic Quiz Game. Circa 1950s.
Q & A, Board game. 20

7108. Wheel of Fortune, Deluxe. © 1986. TV, Game,
Board game. 15

7109. Winky Dink TV Game. © 1955. TV, Board
game. 40

Presto Prod. Co.

7110. Air Mail. Circa 1950s. Travel, Air, Board game. 25

Pride Distributors

7111. Brightonopoly. © 1989. Cities & Towns, Board
game. 20

Pro Group Inc.

7111a. Golf: The Game. © 1985. Sports, Golf, Board
game. 25

Pro Replay

7112. Pro Replay Football. Circa 1980s. Sports,
Football, Board game. 20

Professional Games Inc.

7113. Attorney Power. © 1982. Law, Careers, Board
game. 25

7114. Medical Monopoly. © 1979. Careers, Board
game. 25

Progressive Research Co.

7115. Look All-Star Baseball Game. Circa 1960s.
Sports, Baseball, Board game. 40

Pro-Mentor Enterprises

7116. Johnny Unitas Football. © 1970. Sports,
Football, Board game. 125

PSI Journeys

7117. PSI Kick. Circa 1990s. Mystic, Board game. 20

Psychology Today

7118. Cities Game, The, Urban Blight. © 1970. Social
Concern, Board game. 25

Pug-I-Loo Game Co.

7119. Pug-I-Lo. © 1960. Sports, Boxing, Board game. 35

Pursue the Pennant

7120. Pursue the Pennant. © 1989. Sports, Baseball,
Board game. 20

Quaker Puffed Wheat

**7121. Sergeant Preston Gets His Man! Cereal
premium.** Circa 1950s. Radio, Premium, Board
game. 25

**7122. Sergeant Preston"Great Yukon River Canoe
Race".** Circa 1950s. Radio, Premium, Board
game. 25

Quaker Wheat Cereal

**7123. Sgt. Preston Gets His Man, Premium from
cereal.** © 1949. Premium, Radio, Board game. $30

Quaker Oats - Life Cereal

7124. Bewitched Hunt Game. © 1949. TV, Premium,
Board game. 30

Quality Games

7125. Dave Garroway's Today Game. © 1960. TV,
Personality, Board game. 65

7126. Mail Run, TV's Pony Express. © 1960. TV,
Western, Board game. 65

R. J. V. Enterprises

7127. American Gold. © 1988. Economic, Board
game. 22

R. P. Productions

7128. Crash! The Stock Market Game. © 1988. Stock
Market, Board game. 18

Race Car Gaming, Inc.

7128a.Richard Petty, Super Speedway Strategies.
1980s. Sports, Car racing, Board game. 35

Rachat, Inc.

7128b.Corporate Pursuit. ©1986. Stock Market,
Board game. 25

Radio Printing Co.

7129. Accent. © 1955. Miscellaneous, Board game. 20

Rally Round Games

7130. Allegiance "The Constitution Game". © 1964.
Political, Board game. 65

RAM Games

7131. Ultimate Sports Trivia. © 1992. Sports, Q & A,
Board game. 15

RAM Innovations

7132. Tycoon, The Real Estate Game. © 1986.
Economic, Board game. 20

Ramcar Family Ent.

7133. Bottle Hunt. © 1974. Hobby, Board game. 30

Ranco Games

7133a.Wheeler Dealer. © 1977. World Trade Board
game. 30

J & L Randall

7134. Oil. Circa 1960s. Economic, Board game. 65

Random House

**7135. Teenage Mutant Ninja Turtles Pizza Power
Game.** © 1987. Comics, Board game. 15

Ranger Steel Prod. Corp.

7136. Town and Country Traffic. Circa 1950s. Travel,
Board game. 100

7136a.Western Lasso. Circa 1950s Western Board
game. 50

RCA
7137. Mel Allen's Baseball Game. © 1959. Sports, Baseball, Record game. $75

Real-Action Games
7138. Real-Action Baseball Game. © 1966. Sports, Baseball, Board game. 45

Real Games Inc.
7138a.Real Fishing. © 1988. Sports, Fishing, Board game. 25

Realitic Games Mfg.
7139. Bobby Shanz Baseball Game. © 1954. Sports, Baseball, Board game. 75

Reco Toy & Game Co.
7140. Garroway's Game of Possessions. © 1955. Personality, Board game. 75
7141. Today. © 1960. TV, Board game. 60

Record Games Inc.
7141a.Speedway. © 1963. Includes record of racing sounds, Sport car racing Board game. 75

Recreational Games Inc.
7142. Philadelphia Lawer. Circa 1950s. Law, Board game. 45

Red Bar Game Co.
7143. Red Bar. © 1954. Miscellaneous, Card game. 20

Redlich Mfg. Co.
7144. Alpha Football Game. Circa 1940s. Sports, Football, Board game. 85
7144a.Alpha Baseball Game. Circa 1940s Sports, Baseball, Board game. 85

Reed & Associates, Inc.
7145. Shazam. Circa 1940s. Super Heroes, Board game. 50

Regal Mfg. Co.
7146. Auto Bingo. © 1966. Travel, Board game. 15
7147. Find-A-Car Bingo. © 1966. Travel, Car, Board game. 15
7148. License Number Bingo. © 1966. Travel, Board game. 15

7149. Regal Finger-Tip Baseball Game. Circa 1950s. Sports, Baseball, Board game. $20
7150. Traffic Safety Bingo. © 1966. Travel, Board game. 20

Reilly O' Company
5150a. Luck O' the Irish. © 1985. Ethnic, Board game. 22

Reingell Industries, Inc.
7151. States and Statesman. © 1959. Political, Board game. 45

Reiss
7152. Compatibility. © 1974. Social Concern, Board game. 22
7152a. Harry Lorayne Memory Game, The. © 1976. Board game. 22
7153. Lie, Cheat and Steal, The Game of Political Power. © 1976. Political, Board game. 25
7154. Mary Hartman, Mary Hartman. © 1977. TV, Board game. 25
7154a. Naughty Game, Happy Hooker, Xaviera Hollander. © 1974. Board game. 20
7154b. Next President, The. © 1971. Political, Board game. 50

Remco
7155. Chitty Chitty Bang Bang, Electric Movie Quiz Game. © 1968. Movie, Board game. 35
7156. Double or Nothin'. © 1958. Skill, Action game. 15
7157. Family Affair, Where's Mrs. Beasley? © 1968. TV, Board game. 22
7158. Fascination Checkers. Circa 1960s. Skill, Board game. 25
7159. Fascination Pool. © 1962. Skill, Board game. 10
7160. Fascination, The Electric Maze Game, 1st edition. © 1961. Skill, Board game. 18
7161. Fascination, The Electric Maze Game, Photo cover. © 1968. Skill, Board game. 12
7162. Fascination, The Electric Maze Game, Two children cover. © 1961. Skill, Board game. 15
7163. Flap Jack. Circa 1960s. Skill, Action game. 12
7164. Gentle Ben Electric Quiz Game. © 1967. TV, Board game. 35
7165. Giant Wheel Cowboys 'N Indians. © 1958. Western, Board game. 25
7166. Giant Wheel Speed Boat Game. © 1960. Sport, Boat, Board game. 25
7167. Giant Wheel Thrills & Spills Horse Race Game. © 1958. Sport, Horseracing, Board game. 25
7168. Hawaii Five-O. © 1968. TV, Law & Order, Board game. 65
7169. Heidi Elevator Game. © 1965. TV, Toy, Board game. 22
7170. Hippopotamus Electronic Puzzle Game. © 1961. Strategy, Board game. 40
7171. Hot Potato. © 1959. Skill, Action game. 15
7172. Hulla Baloo. © 1965. TV, Music, Board game. 75
7173. Johnny on the Pony. © 1959. Animal, Board game. 25
7174. Journey to the Unknown Game. © 1968. Monster, Board game. 200
7175. Lancer Game. © 1968. TV, Western, Board game. 75
7176. Land of the Giants Shoot & Stick. © 1968. TV, Science Fiction, Action game. 100

Remco continued

7177. Lost in Space 3-D Game. © 1966. Space, Board game. $65

7178. Magic! Magic! Magic! Game. © 1975. Magic, Board game. 25

7179. Melvin the Moon Man. Circa 1960s. Space, Dice game. 35

7180. Mod Squad Game, The. © 1968. TV, Detective, Board game. 100

7181. Notch. Circa 1960s. Western, Dice game. 15

7182. Pinhead, Game of Hide and Seek. © 1959. Kiddie, Board game. 30

7183. Shindig Teen Game. © 1961. TV, Music, Board game. 65

7184. Shmo. © 1959. Kiddie, Dice game. 25

7185. That Girl. © 1969. TV, Board game. 35

7186. Trip Trap. © 1969. Skill, Action game. 15

Rennoc Games & Toys

7187. Sports Arena No. 1. © 1954. Sports, Board game. 125

Replay Games

7188. Replay Baseball. Miscellaneous, Sports, Baseball, Board game. 20

7189. Replay Pro Football. Miscellaneous, Sports, Football, Board game. 20

Replogle Globes Inc.

7190. Global Air Race, with round globe as Board. © 1952. Travel, Air, Board game. 35

7191. Holiday. © 1958. Geography, Board game. 45

Research Games Inc.

7192. Fran Tarkenton's Pro Football. © 1967. Sports, Football, Board game. 75

7193. Gil Hodges' Pennant Fever. © 1970. Sports, Baseball, Board game. 125

7194. Movie Moguls. © 1970. Movie, Board game. 100

7195. Oscar Robertson's Pro Basketball Strategy. © 1969. Sports, Basketball, Board game. 85

7196. Rocky Gratziano, A Century of Great Fights. © 1969. Sports, Boxing, Board game. 150

7197. Vince Lombardi's Game. © 1970. Sports, Football, Board game. 75

Research Games Inc./Athol Game Co.

7198. Weekend in Vegas. © 1974. Travel, Board game. 18

Resolutions Concepts, Inc.

7199. Resolution? The Game of Savings & Loan Crisis. © 1992. Economic, Board game. 22

Revall

7200. Yertle. The Game of. © 1960. Literary, Board game. 100

Review & Herald Pub. A.

7201. Bible Characters Game. Circa 1950s. Religious, Card game. 15

7201a.Bible Journeys, No. 2, Life of Christ. © 1964. Religious, Board game. 30

Ribbit Toy Co.

7202. Stock Car Racing Game with R. Petty & C. Yarborough, The. © 1981. Sports, Car, Board game. $50

Richard Industries

7203. Parlor Ponies. © 1945. Sports, Race, Card game. 25

Rich-Mar Sco-Dar Inc.

7204. Rollacolor Family Game. © 1965. Social, Board game. 25

Right in Boulder, Inc.

7204a. Slick Willie's Sacrifice. © 1993. Political, Board game. 20

Rigley Banada

7204b. Tournament Golf. © 1969. Sports, Golf Board game. 18

Rimkeit-Walker Enterprises

7204c. Mount St. Helens Volcano Game! © 1980. Travel Board game. 20

Ritt Bros. & Co.

7205. Skrimage. Circa 1950s. Sports, Football, Board game. 45

RJRTC

7206. Camel The Game, Ad game for cigarette. © 1992. Advertising, Dice game. 15

R-Mark Games Co.

7206a.Regular Golf. © 1978. Sport, Golf, Board game. 25

Robor Games

7207. Starchase. © 1989. Science Fiction, Board game. 22

Rock Harbor Creations

7208. Bold Adventure. © 1982. Religious, Board game. 25

Rodgers and Cauthen, Inc.

7208a.Agri-Venture. © 1974. Farming, Board game. 25

N. D. Roemer

7209. Play Pace Racing Game. © 1949. Sports, Horseracing, Board game. 50

Rogde Co.

7210. Roy Rogers Rodeo Game. © 1949. Western, Personal, Board game. 75

Rohrwood
7211. NFL Franchise. © 1982. Sports, Football, Board game. $18

Rojo Enterprises
7212. Boating Trivia. © 1986. Q & A, Board game. 20

Roll for the Gold Record, Inc.
7213. Roll for the Gold Record. © 1992. Music, Board game. 17

Romac Ind.
7214. Power Play. © 1970. Sports, Hockey, Board game. 45

Alpa Romeo Inc.
7215. Driving Spirit Safety Game, The. © 1987. Educational, Car advertising Board game. 60

Romart
7216. Laugh-In Knock Knock Jokes Game. © 1969. TV, Board game. 35

Roniwood Inc.
7217. Pro Football Franchise. © 1987. Sports, Football, Board game. 20

Roulette Records, Inc.
7217a. Co*Star, The Record Action Game, With Sir Cedric Hardwicke. Circa 1950s, Theater, Record game. 25
7217b. Co*Star, as above, **with Cesar Romero.** 25
7217c. Co*Star, as above, **with Fernando Lamas.** 25
7217d. Co*Star, as above, **with Arlene Dahl.** 25
7217e. Co*Star, as above, **with George Raft.** 25
7217f. Co*Star, as above, **with June Havoc.** 25
7217g. Co*Star, as above, **with Basil Rathbone.** 30
7217h. Co*Star, as above, **with Virgina Mayo.** 25
7217i. Co*Star, as above, **with Tallulah Bankhead.** 25
7217j. Co*Star, as above, **with Vincent Price.** 35
7217k. Co*Star, as above, **with Paulette Goddard.** 25
7217l. Co*Star, as above, **with Don Ameche.** 25
7217m. Co*Star, as above, **with Jimmie Rodgers.** 25
7217n. Co*Star, as above, **with Pearl Bailey.** 25
7217o. Co*Star, as above, **with "Slapsy" Maxie Rosenbloom.** 25

Royal Palm Int.
7218. Gold Medal World Olympian Game, The. © 1978. Sports, Board game. 30

Royal Tot Mfg. Co.
7219. Bomb Target Game. Circa 1950s. Military, Board game. 45

C. & J. Rubin
7220. New York Game. © 1977. Cities & Town, Board game. 25

Russell Mfg. Co.
7221. Bambi, Vol. 4, Bookcase. © 1946. Disney, Card game. 20
7222. Bambi. © 1965. Disney, Card game. 25
7223. Believe it or Not, Famous People. © 1964. Personality, Hi, Card game. 15

7224. Disneyland Monorail Card Game. © 1960. Disney, Card game. $15
7225. Donald Duck, Vol. 1, Bookcase. © 1946. Disney, Card game. 20
7226. Flags of the United Nations, Game of. Circa 1950s. Geography, Card game. 12
7227. Flash, The. © 1977. Super Heroes, Card game. 20
7228. Howdy-Doody. © 1954. TV, Card game. 25
7229. Ludwig Von Drake. © 1960. Disney, Card game. 25
7230. Mickey Mouse Funny Rummy. Circa 1950s. Disney, Card game. 25
7231. Mickey Mouse, Vol. 3, Bookcase. © 1946. Disney, Card game. 20
7232. Mickey Mouse. © 1946. Disney, Card game. 25
7233. Mickey Mouse. © 1965. Disney, Card game. 20
7234. Monster Flip Cards. Circa 1970s. Monster, Card game. 20
7235. Old Maid. Circa 1960s. Classic, Card game. 8
7236. Pinocchio, Vol. 2, Bookcase. © 1946. Disney, Card game. 20
7237. Ripley's Believe it or Not, Animals. © 1964. Personality, An, Card game. 12
7238. Ripley's Believe it or Not, Science. © 1964. Personality, Ss, Card game. 12
7239. Ripley's Believe it or Not, Ships. © 1964. Personality, Tr, Card game. 12
7240. Ripley's Believe it or Not, Sports. © 1964. Personality, Sp, Card game. 12
7241. Ripley's Believe it or Not, War. © 1964. Personality, Mi, Card game. 12
7242. Santa Clause Game. © 1964. Holiday, Card game. 25
7243. Shazam! Card Game. © 1977. Super Hero, Card game. 25
7244. Sky Trails. © 1951. Travel, Air, Card game. 30
7245. Snow White and the Seven Dwarfs, Vol. 6. © 1946. Disney, Card game. 20
7246. Super Hero, Batman. © 1977. Super Heroes, Card game. 25
7247. Super Hero, Robin. © 1977. Super Heroes, Card game. 25
7248. Super Hero, Shazam. © 1977. Super Heroes, Card game. 25
7249. Super Hero, Superman. © 1977. Super Heroes, Card game. 25
7250. Super Hero, Wonder Woman. © 1977. Super Heroes, Card game. 25
7251. Tail, The Donkey Game. Circa 1950s. Animal, Card game. 8
7252. Three Little Pigs, The, Vol. 5, Bookcase. © 1946. Disney, Card game. 20
7253. Three Little Pigs, The. © 1965. Disney, Card game. 20
7254. Walt Disney, Catch the Mouse. Circa 1970s. Disney, Card game. 15
7255. Walt Disney, Catch the Mouse. Circa 1970s. Disney, Card game. 15
7256. Walt Disney's Mary Poppins Card Game. © 1964. Disney, Card game. 18
7257. Walt Disney's Mary Poppins. Circa 1960s. Disney, Card game. 18

Rykodisc, Inc.
7258. Play it by Ear. © 1991. Q & A, Board game. 22
7259. Play it by Ear. Volume 2. © 1992. Q & A, Board game. 22

S & T Enterprises, Inc
7260. Triology. © 1994. Miscellaneous, Board game. $12

Saalfield Artcraft
7261. Bob Feller Big league Baseball. Circa 1949.
Sports, Baseball, Board game. 85

Saalfield Pub. Co.
7262. Blockhead! © 1954. Skill, Action game. 15
7263. Bluff. © 1963. Political, Dice game. 15
7264. Bob Feller's Big League. Circa 1950s. Sports,
Baseball, Board game. 100
7265. Bricko. © 1953. Board game. 15
7266. Bunny Ho. © 1954. Animal, Board game. 15
7267. Campaign, The American "Go" Game.
© 1961. Military, Board game. 18
7268. Campaign. © 1961. Military, Board game. 22
7269. Casey Jones Game Box. © 1959. TV, Board
game. 45
7270. David and Goliath. © 1957. Religious, Board
game. 25
7271. Donkey Party Game. © 1950. Animal, Action
Game. 35
7272. Fire Fighters. © 1957. Careers, Board game. 25
7273. Frontier Marshall & Star of India. © 1959.
Western, Comb, Board game. 20
7274. Get Smart, Sorry About That Game. © 1966.
TV, Spy, Board game. 60
7275. Get Smart, Would You Believe Game. © 1966.
TV, Spy, Board game. 60
7276. Herman and Katnip Game Box. © 1960.
Cartoon, Board game. 25
7277. King of the Mountain. © 1957. Miscellaneous,
Board game. 20
7278. Special Detective and Speedwat. © 1959. Dete,
Sports, Car, Board game. 25
7279. Super 3 Space Games. © 1959. Space, Board
game. 60

7280. Third Man. © 1969. Strategy, Board game. 25
7281. Uranium. © 1955. Economic, Board game. 100
7282. Walter Lanz Picture Dominoes. © 1963.
Cartoon, Board game. 40
7283. Woody Woodpecker's Game Box. © 1964.
Cartoon, Board game. 35

Safari Ltd.
7284. American Art Quiz Card Game. © 1989. Art,
Q & A, Card game. 10
7285. American History Rummy. © 1989. History,
Card game. 10

7286. Dinosaurs. Circa 1980s. Animal, Card game. $12
7287. Presidental Rummy. © 1989. Political, Card
game. 10

Salesmarketing Inc.
7288. Fourhanded Checkers. © 1975. Classic, Board
game. 10

Samar Enterprises
7289. Las Vegas Baseball. © 1987. Sports, Baseball,
Board game. 18

Sampson
7290. Travel Buff. © 1993. Travel, Board game. 20

Samsonite
7291. Mission Space Game. © 1970. Space, Board
game. 65
7292. Samsonite Basketball. © 1969. Sports,
Basketball, Board game. 50
7293. Samsonite Football. © 1969. Sports, Football,
Board game. 45
7294. Samsonite Pro Football Game. © 1970. Sports,
Football, Board game. 45

Val Samuelson
**7294a.Cocky Compass Game, Through Palm
Springs.** © 1955. Travel, Early City Game. 65

San Fernando Valley Game Co.
7295. Mulligans, Pinehurst Championship Edition.
© 1947. Sports, Golf, Board game. 65

Sanborn Educational Research
7296. Search. © 1958. Educational, Occupation, Board
game. 45

D. Santee
7297. Sod Buster. © 1980. Farming, Board game. 18

Saunders Game Corp.
7297a. Space Shuttle: The Game. © 1985. Space,
Board game. 20

SBM Enterprises
7298. Profit. © 1976. Economic, Board game. 25

John Scarne Games Inc.
7299. I-Q Solitare. © 1956. Q & A, Board game. 10
7300. Teeko. © 1952. Strategy, Board game. 20

Scarne's Challenge
7301. Scarne's Challenge. © 1949. Miscellaneous,
Board game. 20

W. H. Schaper
7302. Air Traffic Controller Game. © 1974. Travel,
Air, Board game. 22
7303. Ants in the Pants, Photo cover. © 1976. Animal,
Action game. 10
7304. Ants in the Pants. © 1970. Animal, Action
game. 12
7305. Bango! Bango! Circa 1960s. Skill, Action
game. 10
7306. Black Ball Express. © 1957. Travel, Rail, Board
game. 25

W. H. Schaper continued

7307. Casper, The Friendly Ghost, Glow in the Dark. © 1974. Comics, Board game. $30

7308. Chicken, The Game of. © 1957. Animal, Board game. 15

7309. Clean Sweep Game. © 1967. Skill, Board game. 15

7310. Cootie, Deluxe 6, Contains 6 Cooties. Circa 1950s. Animal, Dice game. 45

7311. Cootie, Photo cover. Circa 1960s. Animal, Dice game. 15

7312. Cootie, The Game of, Pictures 4 Cooties. Circa 1950s. Animal, Dice game. 25

7313. Cootie, The Game of. ©1949. Animal, Dice game. 25

7314. Don't Cook Your Goose. © 1971. Skill, Action game. 15

7315. No game

7316. Don't Go Overboard. © 1971. Skill, Action game. 15

7317. Dunce. © 1955. Miscellaneous, Dice game. 18

7318. Hop Pop Game. © 1968. Animal, Board game. 15

7319. Huff 'N Puff Game. © 1968. Skill, Action game. 15

7320. I'm George Gobel. © 1955. TV, Personality, Board game. 75

7321. Kick Back. © 1965. Skill, Action game. 15

7322. King of the Hill. © 1964. Skill, Board game. 35

7323. Last Straw, The. © 1966. Skill, Action game. 15

7324. Little Stinker Game, Cards as tiles. © 1956. Animal, Card game. 12

7325. Money Card. © 1972. Economic, Board game. 20

7326. Monkeys and Coconuts. © 1965. Animal, Board game. 30

7327. Moon Blast off. © 1970. Space, Action game. 30

7328. Pull the Rug Out Game. © 1968. Skill, Action game. 15

7329. Put & Take Game. © 1965. Gambling, Action game. 15

7330. Put and Take. © 1956. Miscellaneous, Skill game. 18

7331. Puzzling Pyramid, The. © 1959. Skill, Action game. 18

7332. Shake Bingo. Circa 1960s. Classic, Board game. 15

7333. Skunk. © 1968. Animal, Dice game. 15

7334. Stadium Checkers, Photo cover. Circa 1960s. Marble, Board game. 18

7335. Stadium Checkers, The Game of. © 1952. Marble, Board game. 25

7336. Stagecoach. © 1958. Western, Board game. $20

7337. Thing Ding. Circa 1960s. Skill, Action game. 15

7338. Tilt Score. © 1964. Skill, Action game. 15

7339. Tumble Bug. Circa 1950s. Skill, Action game. 18

7340. Twizzle Game, The. Circa 1950s. Skill, Action game. 18

7341. Voodoo Doll Game. © 1967. Monster, Action game. 25

7342. Whirly Bird. © 1958. Skill, Action game. 20

7343. Who You? Game. © 1968. Animal, Action game. 15

Schluf

7344. Chameleon. © 1988. Animal, Card game. 15

Schmid Games Co.

7345. Boomers, Fighters & Bombers. Circa 1970s. Military, Board game. 25

7346. Stock Market. © 1959. Stock Market, Board game. 40

Joseph Schneder, Inc.

7347. Tarzan in the Jungle Target Game. © 1935. Comics, Action game. 350

Scientific Games Deve. Co.

7348. Consensus. © 1967. Miscellaneous, Board game. 75

Scott's Baseball Cards

7349. Scott's Baseball Card Game. © 1983. Sports, Baseball, Board game. 15

Scrimmage Inc.

7349a. Scrimmage. © 1978. Sports, Football, Board game. 25

Scripture Press Pub.

7350. Becoming One. © 1977. Religious, Board game. 25

Sears

7351. Flintstone Game Alley. © 1978. TV, Combo, Board game. 100

7352. What's What. © 1964. Q & A, Board game. 15

Second Avenue Creations

7353. Discover America. © 1993. Travel USA, Board game. 17

G. L. Seibel

7353a. Boxing Game, The Winner. © 1956. Sports, Boxing game. 40

Selchow & Righter

7354. Abbot & Costello, "Who's on First?" © 1978. Movie, Personality, Board game. 25

7355. Alfred's Other Game. © 1985. Comic, Board game. 15

7356. Allstate Travel Games (Sears). © 1964. Travel, Car, Board game. 35

7357. Alphabet Game. © 1972. Word, Board game. 35

7358. Animal land. © 1974. Animal, Board game. 20

7359. Arabian Knights Flying Carpet Game. © 1972. Adventure, Board game. 15

Selchow & Righter continued

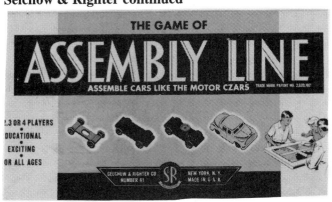

7360. Assembly Line, The Game of, 4 car cover. Circa 1960s. Economic, Board game. $50
7361. Assembly Line, The Game of, 1st edition. © 1953. Economic, Board game. 65
7362. Bang. The Game of the Old West. © 1956. Western, Board game. 45
7363. Barbara Takes a Trip. © 1977. Travel, Board game. 25
7364. Behind the "8" Ball Game. © 1969. Mystic, Card game. 25
7365. Bewitch. © 1964. Mystic, Board game. 25
7366. Blast Off! © 1953. Space, Board game. 100
7367. Bride Game. © 1971. Romance, Board game. 30
7368. Bulldog. © 1974. Animal, Board game. 20
7369. Buzz. © 1955. Miscellaneous, Board game. 20
7369a. Cabby! Circa 1950s. Travel, Car, Board game. 65
7370. Cap-It. © 1957. Cartoon, Board game. 15
7371. Cargoes by William Longyear, Box & Board. Circa 1950s. Economic, Board game. 30
7372. Cargoes by William Longyear, Deluxe Edition. Circa 1950s. Economic, Board game. 65
7373. Cargoes by William Longyear. Circa 1950s. Economic, Board game. 60
7374. Cattleman, The. © 1977. Western, Board game. 20
7375. Charades for Juniors. © 1968. Social, Action game. 12
7376. Charades. © 1968. Social, Action game. 15
7377. Chess for Juniors. © 1965. Classic, Board game. 10
7378. Coney Island, The Game of. © 1956. Circus, Board game. 55
7379. Consetta. © 1946. Strategy, Board game. 40
7380. Cook's Tours-European Travel Game. © 1972. Travel, World, Board game. 25
7381. Crazy Threes. © 1948. Numbers, Board game. 15
7382. Cross Roads. © 1972. Architecture, Buildings, Board game. 25
7383. Dead Pan. © 1956. Skill, Marble game. 20
7384. Decoy. © 1956. Animal, Board game. 40
7385. Dick Tracy. © 1961. Comics, Board game. 45
7386. Doctor Quack. © 1961. Animal, Board game. 18
7387. Doondogggle, The Game of Comic Elections. © 1952. Political, Board game. 40
7388. Down You Go. © 1954. TV, Game, Board game. 15
7389. Dr. Tangle. © 1987. Skill, Action game. 12
7390. Drive-In. © 1949. Movie, Board game. 150
7391. Ellsworth Elephant. © 1960. Animal, Board game. 20
7392. Elsie Game, The. Circa 1940s. Comics, Board game. 75
7393. Emily Post Popularity Game. © 1970. Romance, Board game. 32

7394. Engineer. Circa 1950s. Careers, Board game. $25
7395. Escape to the Casbah. © 1975. Adventure, Board game. 22
7396. Fire Chief. © 1957. Careers, Board game. 30
7397. Flash, The Press Photographer Game. © 1956. Communications, Board game. 100
7398. Freddy the Fireman. © 1966. Careers, Board game. 22
7399. Game Galore. Circa 1950s. Combo, Board game. 15
7400. Game Inventor's Kit. © 1968. Miscellaneous, Board game. 22
7401. Get That License. © 1955. Travel, Board game. 40
7402. Gingerbread Man. © 1961. Food, Board game. 25
7403. Globe Trotter. Circa 1950. Geography, Board game. 35
7404. Go for Broke. © 1965. Economic, Board game. 20
7405. Goldilocks and the Three Bears. © 1974. Nursery Rhyme, Board game. 20
7406. Heroes and Events, Game of. © 1962. Q & A, Board game. 25
7407. Home Baseball Game. © 1957. Sports, Baseball, Board game. 45
7408. Home Team Baseball. © 1957. Sports, Baseball, Board game. 45
7409. Home Team Baseball. © 1964. Sports, Baseball, Board game. 30
7410. Hopskip and Jump. © 1965. Skill, Action game. 15
7411. Hot Numbers. © 1948. Kiddie, Board game. 18
7412. Huggin' the Rail. © 1948. Sports, Car, Board game. 65
7413. Interstate Highway. © 1963. Travel, Land, Board game. 40
7414. Ipswich. © 1983. Strategy, Board game. 15
7415. Jotto. © 1973. Q & A, Board game. 15
7416. Karate, The Game of. © 1964. Sports, Martial Arts, Board game. 40
7417. Kommissar. © 1966. Cold War, Board game. 35
7418. La Riga. © 1957. Strategy, Board game. 15
7419. Landmarks, The Game of. © 1962. History, Board game. 30
7420. Life Magazine Remembers. © 1985. Historical, Board game. 20
7421. Little Benny. © 1957. Animal, Board game. 15
7422. Little Orphan Annie. © 1978. Movie, Comics, Board game. 20
7423. Lottery Game. © 1972. Economic, Board game. 25
7424. MacDonald's Farm Game. © 1948. Animal, Board game. 20
7425. MacDonald's Farm Game. © 1965. Animal, Board game. 15
7426. Madame Planchette Horoscope Game. © 1967. Mystic, Board game. 20
7427. McDonald's Farm. © 1948. Animal, Board game. 20
7428. Mechanic Mac. © 1961. Careers, Board game. 25
7429. Meet the Presidents. © 1950. Political, Board game. 20
7430. Mr. Ree, blue-purple box. © 1957. Mystery, Board game. 50
7431. Mr. Ree, Green box. © 1946. Mystery, Board game. 50
7432. Mr. Ree, Purple and Gold cover. Circa 1950s. Mystery, Board game. 75
7433. Mr. Ree, purple box. © 1957. Mystery, Board game. 40
7434. NBC Peacock Game. © 1966. TV, Board game. 25

Selchow & Righter continued

7435. Numberland Counting Game. © 1972.
Numbers, Board game. $12

7436. Numble. © 1968. Word, Board game. 15

7437. Old Shell Game, The. © 1974. Skill, Board
game. 15

7438. Opinion Poll. © 1970. Social, Board game. 25

7439. Parcheesi Jr. Edition. Circa 1950s. Classic,
Board game. 8

7440. Parcheesi, Brown Board and Implement box.
Circa 1940s. Classic, Board game. 18

7441. Parcheesi, Gold on blue implement box. Circa
1950s. Classic, Board game. 15

7442. Parcheesi, Gold Seal Edition. Circa 1950s.
Classic, Board game. 15

7443. Parcheesi, Popular edition, blue box. Circa
1950s. Classic, Board game. 10

7444. Parollette. © 1948. Miscellaneous, Board game. 20

7445. Pass it On. © 1978. Strategy, Board game. 15

7446. Peanuts. © 1959. Comics, Board game. 50

7447. Policeman. © 1957. Law, Occupation, Board
game. 25

7448. Possibility Thinkers Game. © 1977. Religious,
Board game. 25

7449. Postman. © 1957. Careers, Board game. 25

7450. Pow, the Frontier Game. © 1955. Western,
Board game. 20

7451. Products and Resourses, The Game of. © 1962.
Economic, Board game. 30

7452. Prospecting. © 1953. Adventure, Career, Board
game. 45

7453. Qwink. © 1985. Strategy, Board game. 10

7454. R.S.V.P. © 1967. Q & A, Board game. 25

7455. Roman X, The Game of the Caesars. © 1964.
Historical, Board game. 30

7456. RPM. © 1971. Word, Board game. 20

7457. Runaway Zoo. © 1965. Animal, Board game. 20

7458. Russian Roulette. © 1976. Strategy, Board
game. 25

7459. Safari. © 1950. Animal, Board game. 25

7460. Scrabble for Juniors. © 1968. Word, Board
game. 15

7461. Scrabble, Crossword Game, Plastic tiles. Circa
1950s. Word, Board game. 15

**7462. Scrabble, Crossword Game, 1st edition, wood
tiles.** © 1953. Word, Board game. 50

**7463. Scrabble, Crossword Game, Deluxe, Revolving
board.** © 1953. Word, Board game. 65

7464. Scrabble, Crossword Game, Blanket board.
Circa 1970s. Word, Board game. 35

7465. Scrabble, Sentence Cube Game. © 1971. Word,
Dice game. 15

7466. Snoopy. © 1960. Comics, Board game. 65

7467. Spacewalk, The 21st Century Labyrinth.
© 1970. Skill, Space, Board game. $35

7468. Straight Arrow. © 1950. Comics, Board game. 65

7469. Straightaway. © 1961. Sports, Cars, Board
game. 45

7470. Super Market. © 1953. Economic, Board game. 30

7471. Tangle. © 1964. Skill, Board game. 15

7472. Taxi! © 1960. Travel, Car, Board game. 45

7473. Tic Tac Toe Times 10. © 1977. Classic, Board
game. 15

7474. Tic Tac Tower. © 1969. Strategy, Board game. 15

7475. Tom & Jerry Game, The. © 1962. Cartoons,
Board game. 50

7476. Toot! Toot! © 1864. Travel, Rail, Board game. 20

7477. Trap-Em. © 1957. Animal, Board game. 30

7478. Troke, Castle Checkers. © 1962. Strategy,
Board game. 5

7479. Tune-In TV Bingo. © 1970. TV, Board game. 12

7480. UBI. © 1986. Geography, Board game. 18

7481. United States Map Game. © 1962. Geography,
Board game. 20

7482. Ur. © 1977. Classic, Board game. 20

7483. Wash Out. © 1955. Home Economics, Board
game. 20

7484. What Shall I Be? (Boys). © 1968. Careers,
Board game. 15

7485. What Shall I Be? (Girls). © 1966. Careers,
Board game. 15

7486. What Shall I Wear? © 1969. Careers, Board
game. 15

7487. What's Up? © 1970. Q & A, Board game. 15

7488. Whodunit. © 1972. Mystery, Board game. 20

7489. Wuffle Tree. © 1955. Plant, Board game. 25

Set Ent.

7490. Set. © 1991. Miscellaneous, Card game. 10

Shaw Games

7491. Candidate. © 1979. Political, Board game. 30

Sheinwold

7492. Autobridge. © 1946. Miscellaneous, Board
game. 20

Shell Oil Co.

7493. Rasputin's Revenge, (Anastasia). © 1997.
Premium, Movie, Board game. 5

Sher-Co.

7494. Booth's Pro Conference Football. © 1977.
Sports, Football, Board game. 22

Sherman Games

7495. Money Power, The Investment Strategy Game.
© 1980. Economic, Board game. 22

Shindana

7496. Jackson Five. © 1972. Music, Personal, Board
game. 25

Shipps, Ltd.

7497. James Clavell's Shogun. © 1983. Literary, Card
game. 20

Showker Inc.
7497a.That's Truckin'. © 1976. Trucking, Board
game. $25

Shoenhut
7498. 4-5-6 Pick Up Sticks. © 1947. Skill, Action
game. 15

Simsco
7499. Magnetic Cowboy Roundup. © 1950. Western,
Board game. 30

Siritama Co.
7500. Skill Games, Baseball, Tennis, Football. Circa
1950s. Sports, Baseball, Football, T, Board game. 35

Skip-Bo Co.
7501. Skip-Bo. © 1967. Strategy, Board game. 15

Skor-Mor
7502. Dr. Livingstone I Presume. Circa 1970s.
Miscellaneous, Historical, Board game. 25
7502a.Peter Principle Game, The. © 1973. Board
game. 20
7502b.Prime Time. © 1973. TV Game Board game. 30
7502c.Secret Telegram. 1970s. Mystery, Board game. 25
7503. Sports Yesteryear. © 1977. Sports,
Miscellaneous, Board game. 20
7504. Yesterday. © 1973. Strategy, Board game. 25

Skye Marketing
7505. Hideaway. Circa 1970s. Strategy, Board game. 18

Smethport Speciality
7506. Inspector Gadget, Spin N' Match Game.
© 1984. TV, Law & Order, Card game. 20

Sming Game Co.
7507. Grand Slam. © 1979. Sports, Baseball, Board
game. 22

Bill Smith
7508. Coin-Walk Coin Game. © 1988. Hobby, Board
game. 20

Michael Smith
7509. Newspaper Game, The. © 1977.
Communications, Board game. 25

Smithsonian Inst.
7510. Treasures of the Smithsonian. © 1992. Art,
Board game. 22

Snafoo Games
7511. Snafooey. © 1982. Strategy, Board game. 15

Solar Wind Toys, Inc.
7511a.Space Shuttle Adventure. © 1989. Space,
Board game. 35

Sonny Co. Ltd.
7512. Cutthroat. © 1978. Adventure, Board game. 15

Southfork Dallas Collection
7513. Dallas, Empire Building Strategy. © 1985. TV,
Economic, Board game. 18

Southwest Investments
7514. Skaters Only. © 1988. Sports, Board game. $30

Spear's Game
7515. Travel Scrabble. © 1948. Word, Board game. 20

Spectrum Games
7516. Robert Ludlum's Counter-Espionage. © 1988.
Spy, Board game. 15

Speculation
7517. Speculation, The Stock Market Game. © 1969.
Stock Market, Board game. 35

Speerit Games Co.
7518. Fourth and Goal Football Game. © 1993.
Sports, Football, Board game. 17
7519. Pennant Quest. Circa 1990s. Sports, Baseball,
Board game. 17

Spencer-Murray Corp.
7520. Broker. © 1961. Stock Market, Board game. 40

SPI
7521. Scrimmage. © 1973. Sports, Football, Board
game. 20
7522. Spies. © 1981. Spy, Board game. 18

Spiegel-Reid
7523. Make or Break. © 1961. Miscellaneous, Board
game. 15

Sports Action
7524. National Pro Hockey. © 1985. Sports, Hockey,
Board game. 20

Sports Dynasty, Inc.
7525. Sports Dynasty, The Game for Champions.
Circa 1990s. Sports, Board game. 17

Sports Games Inc.
7526. Authentic Major League Baseball Game.
© 1962. Sports, Baseball, Board game. 35
7526a. Football Game. © 1962. Sports, Football Board
game. 30

Sports Illustrated
7527. Bowl Bound. © 1973. Sports, Football, Board
game. 20
7528. Decathlon. © 1972. Sports, Board game. 25
7529. Go for the Green! © 1973. Sports, Golf, Board
game. 20
7530. Paydirt. © 1973. Sports, Football, Board game. 20
7531. Sports Illustrated Baseball. © 1972. Sports,
Baseball, Board game. 25
7532. Sports Illustrated College Football. © 1971.
Sports, Football, Board game. 20
7533. Sports Illustrated Handicap Golf. © 1971.
Sports, Golf, Board game. 25
7534. Sports Illustrated, All Time, All Star Baseball.
© 1973. Sports, Baseball, Board game. 20

Sports Illustrated continued
7535. Super Star Baseball. © 1974. Sports, Baseball,
   Board game. $20
7536. Superstar Baseball. © 1966. Sports, Baseball,
   Board game. 25
7537. Track Meet. © 1972. Sports, Track, Board
   game. 28

Sports Illustrated-Avalon Hill
7538. U.S.A.C. Auto Racing. Circa 1980. Sports, Car,
   Board game. 100

Sportsbet
7539. Sportsbet. © 1986. Sports, Board game. 15

Sportswise Inc.
7540. Sooperbowl Pro-Football Game. © 1967.
   Sports, Football, Board game. 35

Spring
7541. Exploration, The World of Language. © 1967.
   Word, Board game. 20

SRK Creations Ltd.
7542. Gambler's Paradise. © 1995. Gambling, Board
   game. 15

St. Croit, Inc.
7543. Welfare Game, The. © 1971. Social Concern,
   Board game. 25

Standard Games
7544. Promised Land. © 1977. Religious, Board game. 25

Standard Oil
**7545. Standard Oil Travel Road Game, Premium gas
   station.** Circa 1950s. Travel, Road, Board game. 42

Standard Pub. Co.
7546. Bible Baseball. © 1945. Sports, Baseball, Board
   game. 18

Standard Toykraft
7547. Approved Little League Baseball Game, The.
   © 1954. Sports, Baseball, Board game. 50
7548. Beverly Hillbillies Game, The. © 1963. TV,
   Board game. 50
7549. Dennis the Menace Game. © 1960. TV, Comics,
   Board game. 60
7550. Dick Van Dyke Game, The. © 1962. TV, Board
   game. 225
7551. Gidget Game. © 1965. TV, Board game. 75
7552. Green Acres Game, The. © 1965. TV, Board
   game. 125
7553. Little League Baseball. Circa 1950s. Sports,
   Baseball, Board game. 50
**7554. Mr. Magoo Maddining Adventures Game, The
   Nearsighted.** © 1964. Cartoon, Board game. 50
7555. My Fair Lady Game, The. Circa 1960s. Music,
   Board game. 35
7556. Offical National Football League Quarterback.
   © 1965. Sports, Football, Board game. 45
7557. Petticoat Junction Game, The. Circa 1950s. TV,
   Board game. 85
7558. Picture This. © 1963. TV, Game, Board game. 25

7559. Supercar Road Race Game. © 1962. TV, Board
   game. $75
7560. Top Me. © 1957. Skill, Action game. 20
7561. Wackiest Ship in the Navy, The. © 1964. TV,
   Board game. 55

Michael Stanfield
7562. Jolly Postman, The. © 1968. Careers, Board
   game. 30

Starpoint Inc.
7562a.Spacer, The Space Game. © 1982. Space,
   Board game. 50

Starr Bros. Service
7563. Tollroad Turnpike. © 1964. Travel, Road, Board
   game. 50

State College Game Lab.
7564. Big League Baseball Card Game. © 1949.
   Sports, Baseball, Card game. 40

Statis-Pro
7565. Midwest Research ML Baseball.
   Miscellaneous, Sports, Baseball, Board game. 25
7566. Statis-Pro Football. Circa 1970s. Sports,
   Football, Board game. 22

Steven Mfg.
7567. Crazy Car Race. © 1972. Skill, Action game. 20

Paul Stone
7568. Rocket Race. © 1958. Space, Board game. 150

Storeplay Inc.
**7569. Meltdown, The Nuclear Energy Conflict
   Game.** © 1980. Military, Board game. 30

Stratagame, Inc.
7570. Espionage. © 1973. Spies, Board game. 25

Strategy House, Inc.
7570a. International Ski Team Race. With Ski
   Magazine. © 1971. Sports, Ski, Board game. 35

Strathmore
7571. Walt Disney's Zorro Slate Game. © 1960.
   Disney, Board game. 65

Strat-O-Matic Game Co.
7572. Strat-O-Matic Baseball. © 1980. Sports,
   Baseball, Board game. 35
7573. Strat-O-Matic Baseball. © 1976. Sports,
   Baseball, Board game. 45
7574. Strat-O-Matic Hockey. © 1978. Sports, Hockey,
   Board game. 45
7575. Strat-O-Matic Pro Football. © 1976. Sports,
   Football, Board game. 40
7576. Strat-O-Matic Pro Football. © 1980. Sports,
   Football, Board game. 30
7577. Strat-O-Matic Pro Football. © 1981. Sports,
   Football, Board game. 28
7578. Strat-O-Matic Pro Football. © 1984. Sports,
   Football, Board game. 25

Strat-O-Matic Game Co. continued
7579. Strat-O-Matic Sports "Know-How". © 1984.
Sports, Miscellaneous, Board game. $20

Strauss
7580. Call It Golf. © 1966. Sport, Golf, Board game. 25

Sudbury Mfg. Co.
7581. Span It, Climb the Mountain. Circa 1940s.
Adventure, Board game. 40

Sue You Co.
7582. Sue You. © 1994. Law, Board game. 20

Sunmarc
7582a. Beat the Cat. © 1970. Sports, Snowmobile
Racing Board game. 40

Super Star Game Co.
7583. Superstar Pro Wrestling Game. © 1984. Sports,
Wrestling, Board game. 25

Superior
7584. Super Target Dart Game. Circa 1950s. Space,
Action game. 40

Superior-T.Cohn
7585. Walt Disney's Zorro Target Game. © 1960.
Disney, Action game. 75

Supremacy Games
7585a. Rollout. © 1987. Economic, Board game. 25

Surfing Magazine
7586. Ride the Surf. © 1963. Sports, Surf, Board game. 35

Swan Designs
7587. Presidential Fever. © 1979. Political, Board
game. 40

E. T. Swindle
**7588. Country Music "Stars on Tour" Celebrity
Game.** © 1974. Music, Board game. 40

Symmetry Games Inc.
7589. Rock & Roll, The Music Biz Game. © 1988.
Music, Board game. 25

T.H.E. Game Co.
7590. T.H.E. Pro Football. Miscellaneous, Sports,
Football, Board game. 20

T.T. Products Co.
7591. Bulls "N" Bears. © 1955. Stock Market, Board
game. 35

Taeco
7592. Road Race Skill Drive Game. © 1963. Sports,
Car, Board game. 22

Take One Gamea
7593. Hot Property! The Board Game. © 1985.
Movie, Board game. 18

B. J. Tall
7594. Big Time Colorado Football. © 1983. Sports,
Football, Board game. $25

Gary Tallman
7595. S.O.B.-Save our Bureaucrats. © 1980. Social
Concern, Board game. 25

Tarco
7596. Casper Electronic Adventure Game. © 1962.
Comic, Board game. 35

Sidney Tarrson Co.
7596a. Rocket Satellite. Circa 1950s. Space, Board
game. 60
7596b. Skill Drive. Circa 1950s, Travel, Board game. 25
7596c.Wild West Roundup. Circa 1950s, Western,
Board game. 35

TDC Games
7597. Couch Potato Game, The. © 1987. Social
Concern, Board game. 15
7598. Dirty Minds, The Game of Naughty Clues.
© 1990. Sexual, Card game. 15
**7599. Dirty Minds, Volume Two, The Game of
Naughty Clues.** © 1992. Sexual, Card game. 15
7600. Falsies, The Game of Sexual Fibs. © 1990.
Sexual, Card game. 15
7601. Family the Game. © 1990. Social, Card game. ... 15
7602. Harassment. © 1992. Social, Board game. 25
**7603. Reminiscing, The Game for People Over
Thirty.** © 1989. Q & A, Board game. 15
7604. Sexual Secrets. © 1990. Sexual, Card game. 15
7605. Stupid Game, The. © 1990. Social, Board game. 12

Teachers
7606. Endangered Species. © 1976. Animal, Board
game. 25

Teaching Concepts Inc.
7607. Circulation. © 1973. Education, Board game. 35
7608. Space Hop. © 1973. Space, Board game. 45
7608a. Star Hop. © 1981. Space, Board game. 65

Tech Enterprises

7609. Solar Conquest. © 1966. Space, Science Fiction,
Board game. 50

Tech Ventures
7610. Blue Chip Stock Market Game. © 1958. Stock Market, Board game. $45

Tee Off Games Inc.
7611. Tee Off on Golf. © 1994. Sports, Golf, Board game. 17

Tee Pee Toys
7612. Fun Places of the USA. © 1978. Travel, Board game. 15

Teenage Games
7613. Elvis Presley. © 1957. Music, Personal, Board game. 150

Tega-Rand
7614. Dotto. © 1981. Strategy, Board game. 12
7615. In the Chips, New York. © 1981. Economic, Board game. 20
7615a. In the Chips, San Francisco. © 1980. As above. 20
7616. In the Chips, Silicon Valley investment game. © 1980. Economic, Board game. 25
7616a. Runner's World, Marathon Game. © 1981 Sports, Board game. 50

Tenore Games
7617. Movie Memory. © 1990. Movie, Board game. 18

Texall Corp.
7618. Gab, Gracie Allen's Rummy Game. © 1950. Personality, Card game. 75

Texantics Unlimited
7619. Razzle Dazzle Football Game. © 1954. Sports, Football, Board game. 75
7620. Texas Millionaire, Neiman-Marcus'. © 1953. Economic, Board game. 35

TGD Games
7621. First Down. © 1970. Sports, Football, Board game. 20

Theme Products
7622. Black Experience, The. © 1971. Ethnic, History, Board game. 40
7622a. Captain Soul Adventure Game. © 1971. Ethnic, Super Hero, Board game. 40

Thibault
7623. Beat the Draft. Circa 1960s. Social Concern, Board game. 35
7624. Big Funeral. © 1964. Social Concern, Board game. 32

Thurston Games Ltd.
7625. Moonshine. © 1979. Travel, Law and Order Board game. 30

Thyne Sales Inc.
7626. Think. © 1955. Q & A, Board game. 30

Tiger Electronics-Games
7627. Electronic Battle Cry. © 1989. Military, Board game. 15

7627a. M.C. Hammer, Rap A Round. With music tape. © 1991. Ethnic, Music, Board game. $35
7628. Motor Mouth. © 1990. Personality, Board game. 15
7628a. Chauvainist Pigs. © 1991. Social, Board game. 20

Tiger Toys
7629. Land of the Lost Board game. © 1992. Science Fiction, Board game. 17

Time Inc.
7630. Sports Illustrated Pro Football. © 1970. Sports, Football, Board game. 22
7631. Time. © 1979. Q & A, Board game. 18

Time Inc.-Parker Bros.
7632. SI, The Sporting Word Game. © 1961. Sports, Miscellaneous, Board game. 22

Time Travel
7633. Time Travel Baseball. © 1979. Sports, Baseball, Board game. 18

Tod Lansing
7634. Championship Baseball. © 1966. Sports, Baseball, Board game. 25

Tom McAn Shoe Co.
7635. Store. Ad game for shoes. © 1970. Advertising, Economic, Board game. 30

Tomy
7636. Nuttsy Tennis. © 1974. Sports, Tennis, Board game. 25

Tongue-N-Chic
7637. Beverly Hills. © 1979. Cities & Towns, Board game. 22

Top Ten Game Co.
7638. Top Ten College Basketball. © 1980. Sports, Basketball, Board game. 18

Topper
7639. Charley 'N Me Robot Game. © 1967. Kiddie, Board game. 25
7640. Clock-A-Game. © 1966. Word, Board game. 20
7641. Clock-A-Word. © 1966. Word, Action game. 15
7642. Silly Safari. © 1966. Animal, Board game. 22

Toy Development Co.
7643. Airlift. © 1954. Travel, Air, Board game. 60

Toy Factory
7644. Little Creepies Monster Game. © 1974. Monster, Board game. 22

Toy Town
7645. Official Babe Ruth's Baseball Game. Circa 1940s. Sports, Baseball, Board game. 100

Toymasters
7646. Play Ball Hockey. © 1960. Sports, Hockey, Board game. 35
7647. Popeye Carnival. © 1960. Comics, Action game. 50

Tracianne

7648. Apollo, A Voyage to the Moon. © 1969. Space,
Board game. $55

Trade Wind Inc.

7649. NFL Armchair Quaterback. © 1986. Sports,
Football, Board game. 20

Trademark Century Games

7650. Real Estate the Game. © 1985. Economic,
Board game. 22

Traditional Games

**7651. Paths & Burrows, World of Beatrix Potter,
painted figures.** © 1988. Literary, Board game. 40

Tran Enterprises

7652. Animal Kingdom, The. © 1992. Animal, Board
game. 17
7653. International Soccer The Game. © 1992.
Sports, Board game. 17

Transogram

7654. 3 In-A-Row Bible Quiz. © 1960. Religious,
Board game. 20
7655. 3 In-A-Row Home Quiz. © 1960. Q & A, Board
game. 15
7656. Adventures of Popeye Game. © 1957. Comics,
Board game. 70
7657. Adventures of Rin Tin Tin, The. © 1955. TV,
Board game. 50
7658. Alligaroo. © 1964. Animal, Board game. 20
7659. Analysis. © 1968. Self Help, Board game. 20
7660. Angela Cartwright's Buttons & Bows Game. ©
1960. Home Economics, Board game. 55
7661. Aquanauts Game, The. © 1961. TV, Board
game. 65
7662. Arrest And Trial. © 1963. TV, Law & Order,
Board game. 65
7663. Atom Ant Saves the Day. © 1966. Cartoon, TV,
Board game. 80
7664. Bamm-Bamm Game, Color Me Happy. ©
1961. TV, Cartoon, Board game. 85
7665. Baseball. © 1969. Sport, Baseball, Board game. 30
7666. Basketball. © 1969. Sport, Basketball, Board
game. 30
7667. Bears and Bees. © 1962. Animal, Board game. 20
7668. Ben Casey M. Game. © 1961. TV, Medical,
Board game. 35
7669. Betsy Ross and the Flag Game. © 1961.
Historical, Board game. 35
7670. Big Blast. © 1967. Skill, Action game. 30
**7671. Big Business, National Money Game, The
Famous.** Circa 1960s. Economic, Board game. 25
7672. Big Business, Popular edition. © 1954.
Economic, Board game. 28
7673. Big Business, Quality edition, Yellow letters.
© 1959. Economic, Board game. 25
7674. Bingo-Matic, The Original. © 1960. Word,
Board game. 15
7675. Birthday Cake. © 1962. Kiddie, Board game. 20
7676. Black Beauty, The Game of. © 1958. Animal,
Horse, Board game. 35
7677. Blondie, The Hurry Scurry Game. © 1966.
Comics, Board game. 40

7678. Book of Knowledge Electromatic Dial Quiz.
© 1961. Q & A, Board game. $15
7679. Bottle Buster Target Game. © 1962. Skill,
Action game. 15
7680. Bozo Ring Toss. © 1961. Circus, Action game. 25
7681. Bozo Sling Dart Game. © 1961. Circus, Action
game. 25
7682. Bozo the Clown Circus Game. © 1960. Circus,
Board game. 35
**7683. Break-A-Plate Carnival Pitch Game,
Huckleberry Etc.** © 1961. TV, Cartoon, Action
Game. 75
7684. Buccaneers, A Sea-Faring Game, The. © 1957.
Adventure, Board game. 45
7685. Buck Rogers. Circa 1905s. Super Hero, Science
Fiction, Board game. 70
7686. Bullwinkle Travel Adventure Game. Circa
1970s. TV, Cartoon, Board game. 45
7687. Burke's Law Target Game. © 1964. TV, Law &
Order, Action game. 60
7688. Burke's Law. © 1962. TV, Board game. 50
7689. Buttons and Bows. © 1960. Home Economics,
Board game. 25
7690. Calling Superman. © 1954. Super Heroes,
Board game. 85
7691. Candy Capers. © 1968. Kiddie, Board game. 20
7692. Captain Gallant. © 1955. TV, Adventure, Board
game. 50
**7693. Captain Kangaroo Parade Around the
Treasure House Game.** © 1969. TV, Kiddie,
Board game. 25
7694. Champion 6 in 1 Sports Combination. © 1959.
Sports, Board game. 15
7695. Cherry Pie Fun Game. © 1966. Food, Board
game. 15
7696. Convoy The Naval War Game. Circa 1960s.
Military, Board game. 28
7697. Count Down Space Game. © 1960. Space,
Board game. 40
7698. Daniel Boone Card Game. © 1964. Western,
Card game. 20
7699. Detectives Game, The. © 1961. TV, Detective,
Board game. 40
7700. Dino the Dinosaur Game. © 1961. TV, Board
game. 50

7701. Doc Holliday Wild West Game. © 1960. TV,
Western, Board game. 50
7702. Dog Race. © 1951. Sports, Board game. 30
7703. Dragnet Maze. © 1955. TV, Law & Order, Board
game. 75

Transogram continued

7704. Dragnet, The Game of. © 1955. TV, Detective, Board game. $45

7705. Dream Date. © 1963. Romance, Board game. 45

7706. Eddie Arcaro Blue Grass Handicap Horse Race Game. © 1961. Sports, Horseracing, Board game. 75

7707. Egg Heads. © 1962. Miscellaneous, Board game. 15

7708. Eliot Ness The Untouchables Game. Circa 1950s. TV, Law & Order, Board game. 60

7709. Espionage. © 1963. Spy, Board game. 50

7710. FBI Game, The. © 1961. Law & Order, Board game. 75

7711. Fess Parker Wilderness Trail Card Game. © 1964. Western, Board game. 45

7712. Firehouse Mouse Game. © 1971. Animal, Action game. 35

7713. Flintstones Magnetic Fish Pond Game. © 1962. TV, Cartoon, Board game. 40

7714. Flintstones Pitch 'N Bowl. © 1961. TV, Cartoon, Action game. 50

7715. Flintstones Sling Dart Game. © 1962. TV, Cartoon, Action game. 35

7716. Flintstones Smash-A-Roo Game. © 1963. TV, Cartoon, Action game. 50

7717. Flintstones Stoneage Game. © 1961. TV, Cartoon, Board game. 50

7718. Flintstones Stoneage Tiddley Winks. © 1962. TV, Cartoon, Skill game. 30

7719. Flintstones Tumble Race. © 1961. TV, Cartoon, Board game. 30

7720. Flintstones Window Whacker Game. © 1962. TV, Cartoon, Action game. 55

7721. Four Lane Road Racing Game. © 1964. Sports, Car, Board game. 20

7722. Fred Flintstones Just for Kids Target Game. © 1962. Cartoon, TV, Action game. 50

7723. Frisky Frog. © 1962. Skill, Action game. 35

7724. Gang Way for Fun Game (Broadside TV). © 1964. TV, Board game. 35

7725. Gingerbread Man Game. © 1962. Food, Board game. 15

7726. Gomer Pyle Game. Circa 1960s. TV, Board game. 55

7727. Gray Ghost, The. © 1958. TV, Board game. 50

7728. Green Ghost Game. © 1965. Monster, Board game. 100

7729. Hands Up Harry. © 1964. Western, Action game. 25

7730. Hanna-Barbera Break-A-Plate. © 1961. Cartoon, TV, Action game. 50

7731. Hanna-Barbera Ruff and Reddy Circus Game. © 1962. TV, Cartoon, Board game. 40

7732. Hashimoto-Sam Game. © 1963. TV, Board game. 50

7733. Hector Heathcote Game. © 1963. TV, Board game. 75

7734. Hey, Hey, The Monkees. © 1967. Music, Board game. 100

7735. Hocus Pocus. © 1968. Magic, Action game. 65

7736. Hogan's Heroes Bluff Out Game. © 1966. TV, Board game. 65

7737. Home Quiz. © 1960. Q & A, Board game. 15

7738. Hop N' Pop. © 1964. Skill, Action game. 15

7739. Hopalong Cassidy Lasso Game, The Official. © 1950. TV, Western, Board game. 75

7740. Hopalong Cassidy Pony Express Toss. © 1950. TV, Western, Action game. $100

7741. Hoppy the Hopparoo. © 1965. TV, Cartoon, Board game. 125

7742. Hot Diggity Dog. © 1967. Circus, Board game. 20

7743. Huck Finn Game. © 1969. TV, Cartoon, Board game. 30

7744. Huckleberry Hound "Bumps" Game. © 1961. TV, Cartoon, Board game. 40

7745. Huckelberry Hound & Yogi Bear Break-A-Plate Game. © 1961. Cartoon, TV, Action game. 60

7746. Huckle Chuck. © 1961. TV, Cartoon, Action game. 75

7747. Huckleberry Hound Juggle Roll. © 1960. TV, Cartoon, Board game. 60

7748. Huckleberry Hound Lids Off Bowling Game. © 1960. TV, Cartoon, Action game. 50

7749. Huckleberry Hound Tumble Race. © 1961. TV, Cartoon, Board game. 35

7750. Jack and the Beanstalk, Adventure Game. © 1957. Adventure, Board game. 22

7751. Jackie Gleason's, And Awa-a-a-a-y We Go! TV Fun Game. © 1956. TV, Personality, Board game. 100

7752. Jetson's Fun Pad Game. © 1963. Cartoon, TV, Board game. 75

7753. Jetsons Game, Out of This World, The. ©1962. TV, Cartoon, Board game. 100

7754. Jetson's Rosey the Robot Game, The. © 1962. TV, Cartoon, Board game. 125

7755. Johnny Quest Game. © 1964. Space, TV, Board game. 500

7756. Johnny Ringo Game. © 1960. TV, Western, Board game. 75

7757. Jungle Fun. © 1968. Skill, Action game. 25

7758. Junior Bingo-Matic. © 1968. Classic, Board game. 12

7759. Ka-Bala, Glows in the Dark. © 1967. Mystic, Board game. 75

7760. Kennedy's, The. © 1962. Personality, Political, Board game. 65

7761. Krokay. © 1955. Sports, Croquet, Board game. 25

7762. Laurel and Hardy Ring Toss. © 1962. TV, Cartoon, Action game. 35

7763. Laurel and Hardy. © 1962. TV, Cartoon, Board game. 50

7764. Liar's Poker. © 1968. Gambling, Board game. 20

7765. Lieutenant, The. © 1962. TV, Board game. 75

7766. Life and Legend of Wyatt Earp Game, The. © 1958. TV, Board game. 50

7767. Linus the Lionhearted Uproarious Game. © 1965. Cartoon, TV, Board game. 85

7768. Lone Ranger Target Game. © 1967. TV, Western, Action game. 50

7769. Lucky Louie. © 1968. Skill, Action game. 25

7770. Lucy Show Game, The. © 1962. TV, Personality, Board game. 150

7771. Mandrake the Magician. © 1966. Super Heroes, Board game. 45

7772. Master Spy Target Game. © 1965. Spy, Action game. 35

7773. McHale's Navy Game. © 1962. TV, Military, Board game. 45

7774. Meatball the Hungry Lion Ball Toss Game. © 1964. Animal, Action game. 35

7775. Michael Todd's Around the World in 80 Days. © 1957. Movie, Board game. 30

Transogram continued

7776. Mighty Comics Super Heroes Game. © 1966.
Super Heroes, Board game. $125

**7777. Mighty Mouse Presents the Game of Hide 'N
Seek.** © 1962. Cartoon, Board game. 50

7778. Miss Popularity Game. © 1961. Social, Board
game. 45

7779. No game

7780. Monkey Tree. © 1962. Animal, Board game. 25

7781. Monkey's Uncle. © 1967. Animal, Action game. 20

7782. Mr. Magoo's Maddening Misadventures.
© 1970. Cartoon, Board game. 25

7783. Mr. Novak Game. © 1963. TV, Board game. 40

7784. My Favorite Martian Game. © 1963. TV,
Science Fiction, Board game. 60

7785. National Velvet Game. © 1961. TV, Horse,
Board game. 35

7786. Nine Men's Morris. © 1956. Classic, Board
game. 15

7787. Oop Stix. © 1966. Skill, Action game. 15

7788. Operation Orbit. © 1962. Space, Action game. 125

7789. Outlaws Exciting Western Game. © 1961. TV,
Western, Board game. 85

7790. Overland Trail. © 1960. TV, Western, Board
game. 75

7791. Paul Winchell & Jerry Mahoney's TV Fun Kit.
© 1958. TV, Personality, Board game. 85

7792. Pebbles Flintstone Game. © 1962. TV, Cartoon,
Board game. 50

7793. Pebbles Flintstone Magnetic Fish Pond Game.
© 1963. TV, Cartoon, Board game. 60

7794. Pebbles Live Wire Game. © 1963. Cartoon, TV,
Board game. 65

7795. Perry Mason Game. © 1959. TV, Lawyer, Board
game. 35

7796. Phantom Game, The. © 1966. Super Heroes,
Board game. 135

7797. Philip Marlowe Detective Game. © 1960. TV,
Detective, Board game. 40

7798. Pigs in a Poke. © 1962. Animal, Board game. 15

7799. Play Your Hunch. © 1961. TV, Game, Board
game. 25

7800. Popeye Ball Toss. © 1966. Comics, Action game. 65

7801. Popeye Magnetic Fishing Game. © 1958.
Comics, Board game. 35

7802. Popeye Ring Toss. © 1961. Comics, Action
game. 35

7803. Popeye Sling Dart Game. © 1961. Comics,
Action game. 30

7804. Pot O' Gold. © 1962. Skill, Action game. 20

7805. Quarterback Football Game. © 1969. Sports,
Football, Board game. 25

7806. Qwik Quiz Game. © 1958. Q & A, Board game. 20

7807. Race A Car. © 1961. Sports, Car, Board game. 35

7808. Rat Patrol, The. © 1966. TV, Military, Board
game. 75

7809. Rip Cord. © 1962. TV, Board game. 60

**7810. Rocky Colavito Baseball, Bowling Ball Dart
Game.** © 1960. Sports, Baseball, Board game. 75

7811. Rosey the Robot. © 1962. TV, Cartoon, Board
game. 125

7812. Route 66 Travel Game. © 1962. TV, Travel,
Board game. 175

7813. Ruff and Ready at the Circus. © 1962. TV,
Cartoon, Board game. 45

7814. Scoot. © 1955. Miscellaneous, Board game. 25

7815. Scoreaword. © 1953. Word, Board game. 20

**7816. Screwball, The Mad Mad Mad Game. Newman
with mike.** © 1960. Literary, Board game. $45

7817. Screwball, The Mad Mad Mad Game. © 1960.
Literary, Board game. 65

7818. See New York "Round the Town Game".
© 1964. City & Town, Board game. 100

7819. Seven-Up Game. © 1961. Skill, Action game. 20

7820. Sheri Lewis in.. Sheriland Game. © 1959. TV,
Personality, Board game. 60

7821. Shuttle Game. © 1962. Kiddie, Board game. 20

7822. Silly Sidney Count Shoot Target Game.
© 1963. TV, Cartoon, Action Game. 75

7823. Silly Sidney. © 1963. TV, Board game. 45

7824. Snaggle Puss Fun at the Picnic. © 1961. TV,
Cartoon, Board game. 45

7825. Space Angel. © 1965. TV, Board game. 100

7826. Spider's Maze. © 1966. Skill, Action game. 25

7827. Spy's-A-Poppin. © 1965. Spy, Action game. 35

7828. Stagecoach West Game. © 1961. TV, Western,
Board game. 60

7829. Stampin'. © 1989. Hobby, Board game. 15

7830. Steve Scott Space Scout. © 1952. Science
Fiction, Board game. 100

7831. Stingray Target Game. © 1966. TV, Action
game. 150

7832. Stingray, The Underwater Maze Game.
© 1966. TV, Board game. 150

7833. Stoney Burke Game. © 1963. TV, Western,
Board game. 55

7834. Story of the U.S. Air Force, The. © 1962.
History, Literary, Board game. 35

7835. Strategic Command Game. © 1962. Military,
Board game. 50

7836. Sugar Bowl. © 1950. Food, Board game. 30

7837. Syncron-8. © 1963. Skill, Board game. 20

7838. Taffiy's Baubles & Bangles Game. © 1966.
Home Ec, Board game. 50

7839. Taffy's Party Game. © 1966. Romance, Board
game. 50

7840. Taffy's Shopping Spree Game. © 1964. Toy,
Doll, Board game. 50

7841. Tennessee Tuxedo Game. © 1963. Cartoon, TV,
Board game. 150

7842. Terry Tell Time Game. Circa 1950s. Time,
Board game. 20

7843. Terrytoons Hide N' Seek Game. © 1960.
Comics, Board game. 65

7844. Tic-Tac-Dough, TV Game. © 1957. TV, Q & A,
Board game. 20

7845. Tigrrrr Score-A-Matic Ball Toss. © 1966. Skill,
Action game. 35

7846. Tom and Jerry Bowling Set. © 1966. Cartoon,
Board game. 50

Transogram continued

7847. Tom and Jerry Magnetic Fishing Game.
© 1966. Cartoon, Board game. $45

7848. Tom and Jerry Platter Splatter. © 1966.
Cartoon, Action game. 50

7849. Tom and Jerry Target Game. © 1966. Cartoon,
Action game. 50

7850. Tom and Jerry, Adventures in Blunderland.
© 1965. Cartoon, Board game. 50

7851. Top Cat Shoe Toss Game. © 1962. Cartoon,
Action game. 150

7852. Totem. © 1962. Ethnic, Card game. 25

7853. Touche' Turtle Game, The. © 1962. Cartoon,
TV, Board game. 135

7854. U.S. Air Force, The Story of the. © 1961.
Military, Board game. 35

7855. Virginian Game, The. © 1962. TV, Western,
Board game. 100

7856. Wally Gator Game. © 1962. TV, Cartoon, Board
game. 80

7857. Walt Disney's Cinderella Card Game. © 1965.
Disney, Card game. 15

7858. Walt Disney's Disneyland Game. Circa 1950s.
Disney, Board game. 50

7859. Walt Disney's Donald Duck Ring Toss. © 1961.
Disney, Action Game. 35

7860. Walt Disney's Game of Step 'N Slides. Circa
1950s. Disney, Board game. 65

7861. Walt Disney's Ludwig Von Drake Cannoneers.
© 1962. Disney, Action game. 55

7862. Walt Disney's Ludwig Von Drake Ring Toss.
© 1962. Disney, Action game. 30

**7863. Walt Disney's Ludwig Von Drake Score-A-
Matic Ball Toss.** © 1960. Disney, Action game. 75

**7864. Walt Disney's Ludwig Von Drake Wiggle-
Waggle Game.** © 1962. Disney, Board game. 60

**7865. Walt Disney's Mickey Mouse Top Hat Target
Game.** © 1963. Disney, Action game. 60

7866. Walt Disney's Micky Mouse Club Rummy.
© 1966. Disney, Card game. 22

7867. Walt Disney's Peter Pan Game. © 1953. Disney,
Board game. 40

7868. Walt Disney's Steps and Chutes. © 1963.
Disney, Board game. 40

7869. West Point Story, The. © 1961. Literary,
History, Board game. 65

7870. Wild Wild West. © 1966. TV, Western, Board
game. 325

7871. Word Fun. © 1955. Word, Board game. 20

7872. Wyatt Earp Game. © 1958. TV, Western, Board
game. 50

**7873. Yogi Bear and Huckleberry Hound Bowling
Set.** © 1961. TV, Cartoon, Board game. 60

7874. Yogi Bear Game, Go Fly a Kite. © 1961. TV,
Cartoon, Board game. 50

7875. Yogi Bear Score-A-Matic Ball Toss Game.
© 1960. TV, Cartoon, Action game. 60

7876. Yogi Bear Sling Ring Toss Game. © 1962. TV,
Cartoon, Action game. 35

Traps Mfg.

7877. Traps, The Game of, Golf Game. Circa 1950s.
Sports, Golf, Board game. 60

Travel Products

7878. Turnpike. © 1955. Travel, Road, Board game. 45

J. C. Treacle

7879. Original Preppie Board Game, The. Circa
1980s. Social Concern, Board game. $25

Tri-Ang

7880. High Finance. Circa 1980s. Economic, Board
game. 22

Triangle Pub. Inc.

7881. TV Guides' TV Game. © 1984. TV, Q & A,
Board game. 18

W. Roy Tribble

7882. Courtroom, America Game of Law. Circa
1970s. Law, Board game. 28

A. H. Trice

7883. Business Cycles. © 1979. Economic, Board
game. 28

Tri-Game Creations

7884. Treasure Resort. Circa 1990s. Travel, USA,
Board game. 15

Trikilis

7885. Paul Brown's Football Game. © 1947. Sports,
Football, Board game. 175

Trio Games Co.

7886. Fairway Golf, Photo of Billy Maxwell. © 1954.
Sports, Golf, Board game. 150

Tri-Valley Games

7887. Baseball Challenge. © 1980. Sports, Baseball,
Board game. 20

Trivial War History Games

7888. Civil War Trivia Board Game. © 1989. Q & A,
Military, Board game. 15

Troutman
7889. Buck Skin Sam's Pennsylvania Black Bear / Big Buck Game. Circa 1960s. Animal, Card game. $25

Tru-Craft
7890. Noggin, The Game that Spells Backward. © 1955. Word, Board game. 15

TSG
7891. TSG I, Pro Football. © 1971. Sports, Football, Board game. 25

TSR
7892. All My Children. © 1985. TV, Board game. 20
7893. Battle of the Five Armies, boxed game. © 1975. Fantasy, Board game. 30
7894. Battle of the Five Armies, ziplock game. © 1975. Fantasy, Board game. 25
7895. Boot Hill. © 1984. Western, Board game. 20
7896. Buck Rogers Martian War. © 1990. Science Fiction, Board game. 20
7897. Buck Rogers, Battle for 25th Century. © 1988. Science Fiction, Board game. 20
7898. Bullwinkle and Rocky. © 1988. Cartoon, TV, Board game. 18
7899. Cheers. © 1987. TV, Board game. 22
7900. Escape from New York The Game. © 1980. Movie, Board game. 20
7901. Fantasy Forest. © 1980. Fantasy, Board game. 18
7902. Gang Busters. © 1980. Law & Order, Board game. 15
7903. Honeymooners Game, The. © 1986. TV, Board game. 25
7904. Hunt for Red October, The. © 1988. Literary, Military, Board game. 22
7905. Marvel Super Heroes, Basic Set. © 1991. Super Heroes, Role Playing game. 22
7906. New Dungeon, The. © 1989. Fantasy, Board game. 15
7907. Star Frontiers, Night Hawks. © 1983. Science Fiction, Board game. 18
7908. Top Secret. © 1980. Spy, Board game. 18
7909. Vampyre. © 1980. Monster, Board game. 20

Tudor Games
7910. NFL Play Action. © 1979. Sports, Football, Board game. 40
7911. NFL Strategy. © 1979. Sports, Football, Board game. 40
7912. NFL Strategy. © 1986. Sports, Football, Board game. 25
7913. Tru-Action Electric Baseball. Circa 1960s. Sports, Baseball, Board game. 35
7914. Tru-Action Electric Football. Circa 1960s. Sports, Football, Board game. 50
7915. Tru-Action Electric Horserace. Circa 1960s. Sports, Horseracing, Board game. 40
7916. Tru-Action Electric Sports Car Race. Circa 1960s. Sports, Car, Board game. 45
7917. Tudor Electric Horse Racing Game. © 1959. Sports, Horseracing, Board game. 50
7918. Tudor Electric Sports Car Race. © 1959. Sports, Cars, Board game. 50
7919. Walt Disney's Mickey Mouse Electric Treasure Hunt. © 1960. Disney, Board game. 75

Brenda Turner
7920. Monotony. © 1984. Economic, Board game. $22

J. R. Tusson
7921. Transaction. © 1962. Economic, Board game. 35

TV Film Sales
7922. Heckle & Jeckle 3-D Target Game. © 1958. Cartoon, Action game. 65

Tyco Games
7923. National Enquirer Game. © 1990. Social Concern, Board game. 18

Tyndale House Publoshing Co.
7923a. Generosity. © 1985. Religious, Board game. 22

Tyne Games
7924. Crusader Rabbit Game. Circa 1950s. TV, Cartoon, Board game. 150
7925. Hexed. © 1960. Monster, Puzzle game. 15

U.S. Games Systems Inc.
7926. Wyvern. © 1995. Miscellaneous, Card game. 12

Ultimate Game Co.
7927. Ultimate College Basketball. Circa 1980s. Sports, Basketball, Board game. 20

Ultimate Golf Inc.
7928. Ultimate Golf. © 1985. Sports, Golf, Board game. 22

Uncle Milton
7929. Ant Farm Game. © 1969. Q & A, Board game. 25
7930. Mix 'N Spell. © 1968. Word, Card game. 15
7931. Uncle Milton's Exciting Ant Farm Game. © 1969. Toy, Board game. 25

Ungame Co.
7932. Credit Ability. © 1980. Economic, Board game. 22
7933. Do What is Right. © 1983. Social, Board game. 20
7934. Love Boat, The. © 1980. TV, Board game. ... 20
7935. New Zoo Revue, The. © 1981. TV, Board game. ... 18
7936. Roll-A-Role. Circa 1980s. Social, Psychology, Board game. 12
7937. Social Security. © 1976. Social Concern, Board game. 22
7938. Space Shuttle 101. © 1981. Space, Board game. 30

Unique Promotions
7939. Lewisboro, N.Y., The Game of. © 1990. Cities & Town, Board game. 20

United Nations Constructors
7940. Space Chase. © 1967. Space, Board game. 60

United States Playing Card
7941. Euchre. Circa 1970s. Miscellaneous, Card game. 15

Universal Games Inc.
7942. Apollo 13 (Solar Quest). © 1995. Space, Board game. $22
7943. Intrigue-International Game of World Conquest. © 1965. Military, Board game. 30
7944. Merger. © 1965. Economic, Board game. 30
7945. Secrecy. © 1965. Spy, Board game. 35

University Creations
7946. Invest. Miscellaneous, Stock Market, Board game. $20

University Games
7947. ASAP, The Quick-Think Game. © 1986. Word, Board game. 17
7948. Batman Game, The. © 1989. Super Heroes, Board game. 22
7949. Dick Tracy Game, The. © 1990. Movie, Comics, Board game. 20
7950. Dinomite, The Dinosaur Adventure Game. © 1994. Animal, Board game. 17
7951. Dinosaur World. © 1993. Animal, Board game. 20
7952. Flintstones Memory Card Game, The. © 1994. TV, Cartoon, Card game. 15
7953. Funtastic World of Hanna-Barbera Game. © 1994. TV, Cartoon, Board game. 12
7954. Inspector Gadget Detective Kit Game. © 1994. TV, Cartoon, Board game. 17
7955. Peter Pan Game, The. © 1990. Literary, Board game. 12
7956. Sierra Club Game, The. © 1994. Plant, Animal, Board game. .... 17.
7957. Sleeping Beauty Game, The. © 1990. Literary, Board game. 12
7958. Where in the USA is Carmen San Diego? © 1994. Travel, USA, Board game. 17
7959. Where in the World is Carmen San Diego? © 1994. Travel, World, Board game. 17
7960. Yo Yogi Card Game. © 1994. TV, Cartoon, Card game. 12

Unknown
7961. Afro-American History Mystery Game. © 1971. Ethnic, Q & A, Puzzle game. 40
7962. Muppet Show. © 1978. TV, Card game. 25

UPA Cartoon Show
7963. Gay Puree Board Game. © 1962. Cartoon, TV, Board game. 50

Urban Systems Inc.
7964. Dirty Water Game. © 1970. Social Concern, Board game. 30
7965. Ecology. © 1970. Social Concern, Board game. 30
7966. Population Game, The. © 1970. Social Concern, Board game. 25
7967. Smog, The Air Pollution Game. © 1970. Social Concern, Board game. 30
7968. Water Pollution Game, The. © 1970. Social Concern, Board game. 30

James Vail

7969. Jurisprudence. © 1975. Law & Order, Board game. $28

Valley Games Inc.
7970. Hi Jacked. © 1973. Law & Order, Board game. 32

Valley Isle Association
7970a. Power Play. © 1985. Economic, Board game. 25

Victory Games
7971. 007 James Bond, The Man with the Golden Gun. © 1985. Movie, Spy, Board game. 25
7972. Nightmare on Elm Street Game, A. © 1987. Monster, Board game. 25
7973. Scramble, Air Battle Game. Circa 1970s. Military, Board game. 18

Sevedeo A. Vigil
7974. Stretch Call. © 1986. Sports, Horseracing, Board game. 15

Vision Quest Enterprises, Inc.
7975. Global Survival. © 1992. Social Concern, Board game. 17

Vista Inc.
7976. Duck Hunter. © 1980. Animal, Bird, Board game. 25

Visual Dynamics
7977. Driver-Ed. © 1969. Education, Travel, Board game. 30

Voyagers Inc.
7978. Voyagers. © 1996. Travel, Board game. 17

Wales Games Systems
7979. Montezuma. © 1952. Western, Board game. 75
7980. Roundup, 64-32 Ranch. © 1952. Western, Board game. 75
7981. Stampede, 64-32 Ranch. © 1952. Western, Board game. 80
7982. Tagalong Cowboy Joe. © 1950. Western, Board game. 80
7983. Vamoose, 64-32 Ranch. © 1952. Western, Board game. 75
7984. Vaquero, 64-32 Ranch. © 1952. Western, Board game. 75

J. C. Walk & Co.
7985. **Investment Club, The.** © 1962. Stock Market,
        Board game. $40

The Warden, Inc.
7986. **Warden, The.** Circa 1990. Law & Order, Board
        game. 20

Warren (also see Built-Rite)
7987. **Basketball Card Game.** Circa 1940s. Sports,
        Basketball, Card game. 20
7988. **Break Par Golf Game.** Circa 1950s. Sports,
        Golf, Board game. 25
7989. **Cap'n Crunch Island Adventure Game.** Circa
        1980s. Comic, Cereal, Board game. 20
7990. **Cartoon Capers Game.** Circa 1970s. Cartoon,
        Board game. 35
7991. **Felix the Cat Rummy.** Circa 1950s. Comics,
        Card game. 45
7992. **Football Card Game.** Circa, Sports, Football,
        Card game. 20
7993. **Heathcliff, Munch Out.** © 1982. Comics, Board
        game. 20
7994. **Manage Your Own Baseball Team.** Circa
        1950s. Sports, Baseball, Board game. 30
7995. **Monster Maze Crazy Eights.** Circa 1980s.
        Monster, Board game. 20
7996. **Murder She Wrote.** © 1985. TV, Mystery, Board
        game. 20
7997. **Oh Magoo.** © 1978. Cartoons, Board game. 35
7998. **Pink Panther Game.** © 1978. Cartoons, Board
        game. 35
7999. **Power Lords Board Game.** © 1983. TV, Board
        game. 15
8000. **Simon Says.** Circa 1970s. Social, Board game. ... 15
8001. **Spooky Marble Maze Game, The.** © 1971.
        Monster, Board game. 20

Watkins-Strathmore Co.
8002. **Everybody's Talking.** © 1967. TV, Game, Board
        game. 22
8003. **Hollywood Squares, The.** © 1966. TV, Game,
        Board game. 20
8004. **MGM Tom & Jerry Merry-Go-Round.** © 1959.
        Cartoons, Board game. 30
8005. **Peeko.** © 1964. Word, Board game. 15

Wattson Games.
8006. **Tycoon, Rag to Riches Game.** © 1976.
        Economic, Board game. 25

D. Wayne
8007. **Ramar of the Jungle, The New Jungle Game.**
        Circa 1950s. TV, Adventure, Board game. 100

Ways Unlimited, Inc.
8007a. **Big Smile, The Dental Health Game.** © 1986.
        Health, Board game. 25

Jon Weber
8008. **B-B Ball Players Baseball Game.** Circa 1960s.
        Sports, Baseball, Board game. 35

Weatherford & Harber Enterprises
8008a. **Outta-Space Game.** © 1965. Space, Board
        game. 75

Weekend Farmer Co.
8009. **Farming Game, The.** © 1979. Occupation,
        Board game. $420

Weidon Productions
8010. **Energy Quest.** © 1977. Social Concern, Board
        game. 25

Wei-Gill Inc.
8011. **Earl Gillespie, Baseball Game.** © 1961. Sports,
        Baseball, Card game. 55

Wella Corp.
8011a. **Merchandiser, Sally Store Manager Success
        Game, The.** © 1992. Economic, Board game. ... 30

Wendy's Int.
8012. **Go Fish Dinos, Premium.** © 1992. Premium,
        Card game. 5

Wesley Industries
8012a. **Trek, The Road Map Game.** © 1954. Travel,
        US, Board game. 30

West End Games
8013. **Tales of Arabian Nights.** © 1985. Adventure,
        Board game. 15

Western Pub. Co. (See also Whitman and Golden)
8014. **Democracy.** © 1969. Political, Board game. 35
8015. **Golden Trivia Game.** © 1984. Q & A, Board
        game. 15
8016. **Masters of the Universe.** © 1983. TV, Fantasy,
        Card game. 15
8017. **Race to Riches.** © 1989. Economic, Board
        game. 18
8018. **Solarquest.** © 1988. Science Fiction, Board
        game. 20

Westland Physics
8019. **Prospectors Pete's Game of Gold Rush.**
        © 1973. Adventure, Board game. 28

West Shore Games
7419a. **Willie's White House.** © 1998. Political Board
        game. 22

Wff'N Proof
8020. **Configurations.** © 1972. Strategy, Board game. ... 20
8021. **Configurations, cardboard Hexagonal box.**
        © 1972. Strategy, Board game. 20
8022. **Configurations, Later editions.** © 1972.
        Strategy, Board game. 20
8022a. **On-Sets.** © 1967. Dice game. 12

Wham-O
8023. **Chubby Checker's Limbo.** © 1961. Music,
        Personality, Board game. 100

Whatchamacallit
8024. **Chutzpah.** © 1975. Social, Board game. 35
8025. **My Son the Doctor.** © 1969. Careers, Board
        game. 30
8026. **Take It Off.** © 1969. Social, Board game. 18

Wine Diversions, Ltd.
8026a. **Wine Game, The.** © 1978. Food, Board game. $25

Whitehall Games
8027. **Desperado.** © 1985. Western, Board game. 15
8028. **Pilgrimage.** © 1984. Religious, Board game. 18

Lisbeth Whiting Co.
8029. **Adventures of Lassie.** © 1955. TV, Animal,
Board game. 90
8030. **Adventures of Sir Lancelot.** © 1957. Adventure,
Board game. 75
8031. **Get Smart, Quiz Machine.** © 1966. TV, Spy,
Board game. 45
8032. **Lone Ranger Silver Bullets Game.** © 1956. TV,
Western, Board game. 100
8033. **Pinky Lee and the Runaway Frankfurters.**
© 1954. TV, Personality, Board game. 75
8034. **Spanky and His Rascals.** © 1956. Movie, Board
game. 125

Whitman Pub. Co. (See also Golden and Western)
8035. **Amazing Chan and the Chan Clan, The.**
© 1973. TV, Board game. 18
8036. **Archie Game, The.** © 1969. Comics, TV, Board
game. 45
8037. **Art Linkletter's Game of "People are Funny".**
© 1954. Personality, Card game. 30
8038. **Art Linkletter's House Party.** © 1968. TV,
Personality, Board game. 30
8039. **Black Hole, Space Alert Game, The.** © 1979.
Science Fiction, Movie, Board game. 20
8040. **Black Hole, Voyage of Fear Game, The.**
© 1982. Science Fiction, Movie, Board game. 20
8041. **Brady Bunch Game, The.** © 1973. TV, Board
game. 85
8042. **Bug-A-Boo Game.** © 1968. Skill, Action game. 15
8043. **Bugs Bunny's "Under the Cawit" Game.**
© 1972. Cartoon, Board game. 20

8044. **Bullwinkle Ring Toss Game.** © 1972. TV,
Cartoon, Skill game. 22
8045. **Bullwinkle's Supermarket Game.** © 1976. TV,
Cartoon, Board game. 35
8046. **Buy and Sell.** © 1953. Economic, Board game. 25
8047. **Cabbages and Kings.** © 1955. Miscellaneous,
Card game. 22
8048. **Cap the Hat.** © 1965. Skill, Action game. 15
8049. **Catchword.** © 1954. Q & A, Board game. 15
8050. **Charge It!** © 1972. Economic, Board game. 20
8051. **Chitty Chitty Bang Bang- "Ask For".** © 1968.
Movie, Card game. 15

8052. **Chitty Chitty Bang Bang-Switcheroo.** © 1968.
Movie, Card game. $15
8053. **Clash of the Titans Game.** © 1981. Movie,
Fantasy, Board game. 20
8054. **Clown Capers.** Circa 1950s. Circus, Board
game. 18
8055. **Clown Checkers.** Circa 1960s. Circus, Board
game. 15
8056. **Collision!** © 1969. Cars, Board game. 25
8057. **Corner the Market, Two color cover, 1950s.**
© 1938. Economic, Board game. 25
8058. **Counterpoint.** Circa 1960s. Strategy, Board
game. 12
8059. **Creature Castle Game.** © 1979. Monster, Board
game. 18
8060. **Dark Shadows Game.** © 1968. TV, Monster,
Board game. 35
8061. **Davy Crockett Indian Scouting Game.** © 1955.
Disney, Board game. 75
8062. **Dennis the Menace Tiddley Winks.** © 1961. TV,
Skill game. 35
8063. **Disney Checkers.** © 1977. Disney, Board game. 30
8064. **Donald Duck.** © 1949. Disney, Card game. 25
8065. **Dudley Do-Right's Find Snidely Game.**
© 1976. Cartoon, Board game. 20
8066. **Fame and Fortune Game.** © 1962. Economic,
Board game. 15
8067. **Family Affair.** © 1971. TV, Board game. 20
8068. **Fast Golf.** © 1977. Sports, Golf, Board game. 18
8069. **Flintstones Big Game Hunt Game.** © 1962. TV,
Cartoon, Board game. 75
8070. **Flintstones Break Ball, The.** © 1962. TV,
Cartoon, Action game. 50
8071. **Flintstones Cut-Ups Car Game,** © 1962. TV,
Cartoon, Card game. 30
8072. **Flintstones Mit-Full.** © 1962. TV, Cartoon,
Action game. 50
8073. **Four Complete Games.** Circa 1950s.
Combination, Card game. 15
8074. **Fox and Hound Game, The.** © 1981. Sports,
Animal, Board game. 15
8075. **Hearts.** Circa 1960s. Classic, Card game. 6
8076. **Heckle and Jeckle's Ski Trail Game.** © 1971.
Cartoons, Board game. 22
8077. **Hide 'N' Thief.** © 1965. Law & Order, Board
game. 18
8078. **Hi-Ho Cherry-O Game.** © 1960. Kiddie, Board
game. 18
8079. **Hi-Ho Santa Claus Game.** © 1962. Holiday,
Board game. 35
8079a. **Hock Shop Game.** © 1975. Economic, Board
game. 20
8080. **Hollywood Squares, The.** © 1967. TV, Game,
Board game. 30
8081. **Hollywood Stars, The Game of.** © 1955. Movie,
Board game. 40
8082. **Hot Wheels Game.** © 1982. Sports, Cars, Board
game. 20
8083. **Huey, Dewey, & Louie, Ice Cream Cone Game.**
© 1977. Disney, Board game. 25
8084. **Jr. Executive.** © 1963. Economic, Board game. 20
8085. **Kentucky Derby Horse Racing Game.** © 1969.
Sports, Horseracing, Board game. 20
8086. **Little Lulu Game, The.** © 1973. Comics, Board
game. 22
8087. **Looney Toons Balloon Game.** © 1977.
Cartoons, Board game. 22

Whitman continued

8088. Lucky Fisherman Game. © 1959. Animal, Sea, Board game. $15

8089. Mary Poppins Game. © 1964. Disney, Board game. 40

8090. Masters of the Universe Pop-Up Game. © 1982. TV, Board game. 22

8091. Merry-Go-Round Game. © 1965. Skill, Board game. 18

8092. Mickey Mouse Club Game in Disneyland. © 1955. Disney, Board game. 65

8093. Money Game of Junior Executive, The, House with Children. © 1960. Economic, Board game. 25

8094. Money Game of Junior Executive, The, Two children. © 1963. Economic, Board game. 18

8095. Money! Money! Money! © 1957. Economic, Board game. 25

8096. Monkey Shines. Circa 1940s. Animal, Card game. 20

8097. Mousey. © 1969. Animal, Board game. 15

8098. Peter Potamus and Yo-Yo Card Game. © 1965. TV, Cartoon, Card game. 22

8099. Phalanx. © 1964. Military, Board game. 35

8100. Play Cards! © 1969. TV, Game, Board game. 12

8101. Popeyes Ship Ahoy! Game. © 1975. Comics, Board game. 22

8102. Popeye's Spinach Hunt Game. © 1976. Comics, Board game. 22

8103. Popeye's Treasure Map Game. © 1977. Comics, Board game. 22

8104. Porky Pig's Donut Factory Game. © 1976. Cartoons, Board game. 25

8105. Regatta. © 1958. Sports, Sea, Board game. 35

8106. Relate. © 1972. Miscellaneous, Board game. 18

8107. Ripley's Beleve it or Not! Game. © 1979. Educational, Board game. 18

8108. Road Runner Game, The. © 1969. Cartoons, Board game. 30

8109. Road Runner Pop-Up-Game, The. © 1982. Cartoons, Board game. 30

8110. Rocky and Bullwinkle Magic Dot Game. © 1962. TV, Cartoon, Board game. 25

8111. Rodeo, The Wild West Game. © 1957. Circus, Western, Board game. 20

8112. Ropes and Ladders. © 1957. Classic, Board game. 15

8113. Rummy Card Game. Circa 1950s. Classic, Card game. 8

8114. Sad Sam The Target-Ball Man. © 1966. Skill, Action game. 10

8115. Safari. © 1959. Animal, Board game. 18

8116. Secret of Nimh Game, The. © 1982. TV, Board game. 18

8117. Shopping Center Game. © 1957. Economic, Board game. 25

8118. Silly Carnival. © 1969. Circus, Board game. 12

8119. Snap Card Game, #2995. Circa 1960s. Classic, Card game. 8

8120. Snap Card Game, #4904. Circa 1970s. Classic, Card game. 6

8121. Snare. © 1954. Skill, Action game. 15

8122. Spider and the Fly. © 1962. Animal, Board game. 15

8123. Stock Car Racing Game. © 1956. Sport, Car, Board game. 25

8124. Stock Market Game Deluxe edition. © 1968. Stock Market, Board game. $28

8125. Superman Flying Bingo. © 1966. Super Heroes, Board game. 35

8126. Switchboard. © 1976. Strategy, Board game. 10

8127. Swoop. © 1969. Kiddie, Board game. 12

8128. Tally Ho! © 1961. Animal, Board game. 22

8129. Tammy Card Game. © 1964. Toy, Card game. 18

8130. Tilty. © 1967. Skill, Action game. 12

8131. Top Cat Game. © 1962. TV, Cartoon, Board game. 135

8132. Track & Trap. © 1969. Animal, Board game. 15

8133. Treasure Kit Of Card Games. Circa 1950s. Combination, Card game. 25

8134. Tribulation, The Game of. © 1981. Miscellaneous, Board game. 10

8135. Tweety and Sylvester's "I Tawt I Taw a Puddy Tat" Game. © 1972. Cartoon, Board game. 25

8136. Underdog to the Rescue. © 1975. TV, Cartoon, Board game. 25

8137. Underdog's Save Sweet Polly Game. © 1972. TV, Cartoon, Board game. 35

8138. Walt Disney One Hundred and One Dalmatians. © 1960. Disney, Board game. 35

8139. Walt Disney Tiddledy Winks. © 1963. Disney, Board game. 50

8140. Walt Disney World Game. © 1977. Disney, Board game. 25

8141. Walt Disney's 101 Dalmatians Game. © 1960. Disney, Board game. 35

8142. Walt Disney's Babes in Toyland Game. © 1961. Disney, Board game. 25

8143. Walt Disney's Disneyland. © 1964. Disney, Card Game. 50

8144. Walt Disney's Donald Duck Big Game Box. © 1979. Disney, Board game. 22

8145. Walt Disney's Donald Duck Money Bag Game. © 1970. Disney, Board game. 30

8146. Walt Disney's Goofy Finds His Marbles, Variant. © 1972. Disney, Board game. 25

8147. Walt Disney's Goofy Finds His Marbles. Circa 1970s. Disney, Board game. Orange box 25

8148. Walt Disney's Goofy Goes to the Sea Game. © 1972. Disney, Board game. 25

8149. Walt Disney's Goofy's Mad Maze. © 1970. Disney, Board game. 25

8150. Walt Disney's Ludwig Von Drake Tiddledy Winks. © 1961. Disney, Skill game. 50

8151. Walt Disney's Mickey Mouse Castle Escape. © 1977. Disney, Board game. 25

8151a. Walt Disney's Mickey Mouse Don't Wake the Dragon Game. © 1977. Disney, Board game. 25

Whitman continued

8152. Walt Disney's Mickey Mouse Pop-Up Game.
© 1981. Disney, Board game. $30

8153. Walt Disney's Mickey Mouse's Pizza Party Game. © 1974. Disney, Board game. 25

8154. Walt Disney's Mickey Mouse's Tree House Game. © 1976. Disney, Board game. 25

8155. Walt Disney's Pinocchio Game. © 1962. Disney, Board game. 25

8156. Walt Disney's Pluto's Big Bike Race Game.
© 1974. Disney, Board game. 25

8156a. Walt Disney's Pluto's Lost Bone Game.
© 1976. Disney, Board game. 22

8157. Walt Disney's Snow White Game. © 1980.
Disney, Board game. 20

8158. Walt Disney's Sword in the Stone. © 1963.
Disney, Board game. 30

8158a. Walt Disney's Uncle Scrooge's Gold Race.
© 1973. Disney, Board game. 22

8159. Walt Disney's Zorro Game. © 1965. TV,
Disney, Board game. 65

8160. Walt Disny's Wonderful World of Color.
© 1961. Disney, Board game. 50

8161. What's Cooking. © 1967. Food, Board game. 22

8162. Whats My Line? © 1969. TV, Game, Board game. 55

8163. What's Up Doc?, Bugs Bunny Game. © 1970.
Cartoons, Board game. 25

8164. Whoop! © 1967. Skill, Action game. 15

8165. Winner Spinner. © 1953. Miscellaneous, Board game. 15

8166. Woody Woodpecker Up the Tree Game.
© 1969. Cartoon, Board game. 25

8167. Woody Woodpecker's Baja Rally Game.
© 1977. Cartoons, Board game. 25

8168. Woody Woodpecker's Crazy Mixed-Up Color Factory Game. © 1972. Cartoon, Board game. 25

8169. Woody Woodpecker's Moon Dash Game.
© 1976. Cartoon, Board game. 25

8170. Yosemite Sam's Treasure Hunt Game. © 1971.
Cartoon, Board game. 25

Wil-Croft

8171. Wil-Croft Baseball. © 1971. Sports, Baseball,
Board game. 30

Wilder-Hoekstra

8171a. Savings Game, The. © 1962. Economic, Board game. 22

Wildlife Games Inc.

8172. Whale Game, The. © 1985. Animal, Sea, Board game. 22

M. Wille Inc.

8173. Drew Pearson's Predict a Word. © 1949.
Personality, Word, Board game. 15

Willem Co.

8174. Limit Up, Commodity Futures Trade. © 1980.
Stock Market, Board game. 28

8175. Strike Price. © 1978. Economic, Board game. $25

Windbreaker Ent.

8176. Political Asylum. © 1993. Social Concern, Board game. 20

Windslow

8177. Quote Unquote. Circa 1990s. Word, Board game. 17

Wine Diversions Ltd.

8178. Wine Game, The. © 1978. Food, Board game. 25

Winning Moves

8179. Priceless. © 1996. Miscellaneous, Board game. 17

8179a. Judge 'N' Jury. © 1995. Audio cassette game. 20

Wizards of the Coast

8180. Great Dalmuti, The. © 1994. Fantasy, Card game. 15

8181. Robo Rally. © 1995. Science Fiction, Board game. 20

WKBW-TV

8182. Eyewitness News Game. © 1981.
Communications, Board game. 25

WM

8183. Sweepstakes, Electronic Horse Racing Game.
Circa 1970s. Sports, Horseracing, Board game. 25

Wolfe Prod.

8184. Kiddie Kards. Circa 1970s. Kiddie, Card game. 10

J. Woodlock

8185. World's Greatest Baseball Game. © 1977.
Sports, Baseball, Board game. 20

Woodmark Ind.

8185a. Down-Town Quarterback. © 1947. Sports,
Football, Board game. 35

Word Quest

8186. Tony Randall's Word Quest. © 1984.
Personality, Word, Board game. 10

World Book

8186a. Run for President. © 1988. Political, Board game. 28

World Bowling Tour
8187. Don Carter & Paula Spersel: World Bowling Tour. © 1979. Sports, Bowling, Board game. $40

World Games
8188. Steve Garvey's Super Star Baseball. © 1978. Sports, Baseball, Board game. 28

Worldwide Games, Inc.
8189. Fishing Frenzy, The Tournament Sport Fishing Game. © 1996. Animal, Fish, Board game. 17
8190. Woods and Water. © 1994. Animal, Board game. 17

Wortquest USA Inc.
8191. Domino's Pizza Delivery Game, Ad game for Pizza. © 1989. Advertising, Board game. 10

WST Inc
8192. Wall Street Trader. © 1988. Stock Market, Board game. 20

Xanadu Leisure
8193. Itinerary. © 1980. Geography, Board game. 22

Xela International
8194. Check Point. © 1988. Strategy, Board game. 15

XV Productions
8195. Set Point, Tennis Strategy Game. © 1971. Sports, Tennis, Board game. 30

Y.E.S. Inc.
8196. Techno Tycoon. © 1995. Miscellaneous, Board game. 17

Yaquinto Pub.
8197. Man, Myth, and Magic. © 1982. Mystic, Board game. 15
8198. Market Madness. Circa 1980s. Economic, Board game. 18
8199. Pirates and Plunder. © 1982. Adventure, Board game. 15
8200. Roaring 20s, The. © 1981. History, Board game. 15

A. B. Zbinden
8201. Monday Morning Quarterback Football Game. © 1963. Sports, Football, Board game. 35

Zeneth
8202. Whiz Bowl, New Bowling Game. Circa 1950s. Skill, Action game. $25

Zest
8203. Zest. © 1958. Word, Card game. 20

Zipees
8204. Power 4 Car Race. © 1964. Sport, Car, Board game. 25

"Zod" Prod.
8205. Ivy Towers The Game of Preppism. © 1981. Social Concern, Board game. 25

Zondervan Pub. House
8206. Bible Zoo Game. © 1954. Religious, Card game. 10
8207. Topic Bible Game. © 1956. Religious, Card game. 10
8208. Who Am I? © 1970. Religious, Card game. 10

Zondine Game Co.
8209. Gong Hee Fot Choy. © 1948. Mystic, Board game. 25

8210. Los Angeles Rams Football Game. © 1948. Sports, Football, Board game. 150
8211. Red Skelton's, I Dood It! © 1947. Personality, Board game. 110

Zyla
8211a.Vallco Pro Drag Racing Game. © 1975. Sports, Cars, Board game. 30

SIMULATION GAMES

Argon Games:
8212. Operation Husky (1981)................. $15

Ariel (British):
8213. Decline and Fall of Roman Empire (1972) 30
8214. English Civil War (Ariel/Philmar, 1979) 30
8215. Kingmaker.................................... 50
8216. Seastrike (1977) 15
8217. Sorceror's Cave................................ 30

Attack International Wargaming Association: (ziplock)
8218. Arms Race (1976) 15
8219. Formalhaut II (1975) 12
8220. It! (1978) 12
8221. Lam Son (1978)................................ 20
8222. Littorio (1977) 11
8223. Missile Crisis (1975) 17
8224. Rheinbung (1976)............................. 12
8225. Rift Trooper (1976) 10
8226. 7th Cavalry (1976)............................ 14
8227. Star Raider (1975) 10
8228. Victory at Sea (1977) 18
8229. War of the Star Slavers (1977) 14

Attractix Games:
8230. Arnhem Bridge (1982) 15
8231. Battle for Normandy (1982) 15
8232. 8th Army (1982) 15
8233. Fight for the Sky (1982) 15
8234. Interstellar Wars (1982)..................... 15
8235. Victory at Waterloo (1982) 18

Aulic Council:
8236. Hannibal (1984) 12

Avalon Hill

8237. Afrika Korps (1964) 20
8238. Air Assault on Crete (1978) 22
8239. Alexander the Great (1975)............... 30
8240. Alpha Omega (1977).......................... 15
8241. Arab-Israeli Wars (1977)................... 20
8242. B-17, Queen of the Skies 15
8243. Battle of Bulge (regular edition, 1981).. 15
8244. ○ extra large box 32
8245. Bismarck (1962) 25
8246. Black Spy (1981)............................. 12

8247. Blitzkrieg $18
8248. C & O/B & O (1969) 75
8249. Caesar's Legions (1975).....................35
8250. Caesar at Alesha (1976).....................35

8251. Chancellorsville (1974) 38
8252. Civilization 20
8253. Crescendo of Doom 12
8254. D-Day (1st edition, oversize box, 1961) 30
8255. ○ regular edition 15
8256. Dauntless (1981)..............................20
8257. Dilemmas......................................12
8258. Diplomacy (wooden pieces) 35
8259. Diplomacy (plastic pieces) 15
8260. Down With The King (1982).............22
8261. Dragonhunt (1982)...........................18
8262. Foreign Exchange 18
8263. Gettysburg (square, 1958).................55
8264. ○ (hex, 1961) 35
8265. ○ (square, 1964) 205○battlefield edition (unmounted map) 75

8266. Gettysburg '77 (1977) 28
8267. Gladiator (1983).............................22
8268. Gold! 25
8269a. Guns of August 25
8269. Intern 20

8270. Jutland (1967)...................................$35

8271. Kingmaker (1977) 30
8272. Little Round Top (1982).................... 16
8273. Longest Day 15
8274. Luftwaffe (1971) 16
8275. Magic Realm 20

8276. Midway 18
8277. Moonstar 12
8278. Mr. President 20
8279. Mystic Wood 16
8280. Naval War..................................... 15
8281. 1914 (1968) 42
8282. Panzerblitz (1970) 20
8283. Panzer Leader (1974) 18
8284. Point of Law 35
8285. Richtofen's War (1972) 18

8286. 1776 (1974)................................... 18
8287. Sorceror's Cave (1983)..................... 15
8288. Squad Leader (1977)........................ 15
8289. Squander 20
8290. Stalingrad (1963) 25

Avalon Hill continued

8291a.	Starship Troopers	$25
8291.	Stellar Conquest	16
8292.	Storm Over Arnhem (1981)	16
8293.	Submarine (1978)	22
8294.	Tactics II (1958)	38
8295.	Tactics II (2nd edition, 1961)	25
8296.	Tactics II (commemorative edition, 1988)	16
8297.	Third Reich (1976)	22
8298.	Titan (ziplock, 1982)	15
8299.	Tobruk	22
8300.	Tobruk: Origins II edition	35
8301.	Tuf-A-Bet	12

8302.	U-Boat (metal boats, 1961)	75
8303.	○ cardboard boats	35
8304.	UFO	15
8305.	Up Front (1983)	15
8306.	Verdict (1959)	75
8307.	Verdict II (1961)	55
8308.	Victory in the Pacific (1977)	20
8309.	War at Sea (1976)	20

8310.	Waterloo (1st edition, large box 1962)	35
8311.	○ regular edition	15
8312.	Wizard's Quest (1979)	18
8313.	Wizards	18
8314.	Wooden Ships and Iron Men (1975)	25

Battleline Games:

8315.	Air Force (1976)	20
8316.	Air Force/Dauntless Expansion Kit (1978)	25
8317.	Alpha Omega (1977)	20
8318.	Armor Supremacy (1979)	20

8319.	Circus Maximus (1979)	30
8320.	Custer's Last Sand (1976)	45
8321.	Dauntless (1977)	18
8322.	Flat Top (1977)	18
8323.	Fury In The West (1977)	18
8324.	Insurgency (1979)	25
8325.	Machiavelli (1977)	25
8326.	Naval War (1979)	20
8327.	Objective: Atlanta (1977)	45
8328.	Samurai (1979)	25
8329.	Seven Days Battles (1972)	175

8330.	Shenandoah (1975)	45
8331.	Submarine (1976)	25
8332.	Trireme (1979)	30
8333.	Viva Espana! (1977)	28
8334.	Wooden Ships & Iron Men (1974)	32

Bearhug Publications:

8335.	Bushi: Sword Vs. Sword (1979)	10
8336.	Foreign Legion: Moulay Ishmael (1979)	8
8337.	Foreign Legion: Macta (1979)	12
8338.	Gladiator: Men Vs. Animals (1979)	10
8339.	Gladiator: Men Vs. Men (1979)	10
8340.	Tournament: Jousting (1979)	$10

8341.	Tournament: Melee (1979)	10
8342.	Zulu: Rorke's Drift (1979)	14
8343.	Zulu: Isandhlwana (1979)	14
8344.	Zulu: Ulundi (1979)	14
8345.	Zulu: Naka (1979)	14

Jim Bumpas Games:

8346.	Bay of Pigs (1976)	30
8347.	Mission Aloft (1977)	30
8348.	Mission Aloft Expansion Scenarios (1977)	30
8349.	Schutztruppe (1975)	68
8350.	Tatchanka (1977)	40

Dave Casciano Company:

8351.	Formalhaut II (ziplock, 1975)	15

Cavalier Wargames:

8352.	The Desert Fox (1973)	35

CCC Games:

8353.	Charge To Glory (1983)	14
8354.	Iron Brigade (1982)	14

Centurion Games:

8355.	Alien Armada (1983)	15
8356.	Crisis in the Ukraine (1983)	20
8357.	Gela Beachhead (1983)	15
8358.	Silo 14 (1983)	14

Challenge Games:

8359.	New Orleans:1815	22

Chaosium:

8360.	Elric (1977)	26
8361.	Elric: Battle at the End of Time (1982)	20
8362.	King Arthur's Knights (1978)	20
8363.	Nomad Gods (1979)	50
8364.	Panzer Pranks	14
8365.	Reich (ziplock)	16
8366.	Stomp (1979)	10
8367.	Stormbringer (1981)	18
8368.	White Bear and Red Moon (1979)	50

Challenge Games:

8369.	New Orleans: 1815 (1977)	14

Citadel Games:

8370.	Broadsides & Boarding Parties (1982)	16
8371.	Rebels and Royalists (1983)	14
8372.	VI Caesers (later Conquest of Empire from Milton Bradley, 1982)	14
8373.	War in the South Atlantic (1984)	12

Class Struggle, Inc.:

8374.	Class Struggle (1978)	25

Columbia Games:

8375.	Quebec, 1759 (1978)	25

Combat Designs:

8376.	Zulu (1973)	16

Commando Wargames:
8377. Rolling Thunder (1979)....................$25

Command Perspectives:
8378. Beat To Quarters (1981)......................15
8379. Road To Washington (1980)...............28
8380. Sharpesburg (1979) 48

Commonwealth Games:
8381. The Boer War (1976)..........................38
8382. 1899 (1977) 38

The Control Box, Inc.:
8383. East Front (1977)...............................90

Dimension Six:
8384. Direct Conflict in Dimension
Six (1980) 16
8385. King of the Mountain (1980) 20
8386. Second Empire 15

Discovery Games
8387. Source of the Nile (1973)...................20
8388. Tributary (Source of the
Nile Expansion) 5

Dwarfstar:
8389. Barbarian Prince................................10
8390. Grav Armor (1981)............................12
8391. Outpost Gamma (1981).....................10
8392. Star Viking (1981) 8

Dynamic Games:
8393. Emperor of China (1976) 15

Eon Products:

8394. Cosmic Encounter (basic small
box, 1977)..50
8395. ○ basic large box 35
8396. ○ expansion #1-#2 15
8397. ○ expansion #3-#4 12
8398. ○ expansion #5 16
8399. ○ expansion #6-#8 12
8400. Hoax (1982) 18
8401. Quirks (1979) 20

Excalibre Games: (ziplock)
8402. Adventures In Fantasy (1978).........$12
8403. Ancient Conquest (boxed; 1975).......28
8404. Ancient Conquest II (1978) 15
8405. Atlantis: 12500 BC (1976)...................8
8406. Bog 786 (1977).....................................6
8407. Caen 1944 (1977) 11
8408. Cassino 1944 (1977) 11
8409. Crete 1941 (1976) 8
8410. Crimea 1941-42 (1977)........................11
8411. Cyborg (1978)..9
8412. Edgehill 1642 (1976) 7
8413. The Golden Horde (1978)....................12
8414. Malaya 1941 (1978)............................16
8415. Quazar (1977) 9
8416. Sidi Rezegh (1977) 11
8417. Sovereign of the Seas (boxed, 1979) .12
8418. Total War (1978) 11
8419. Tunisia 1943 (1976) 79
Venerable Destruction (1976)............18

Fact & Fantasy Games:
8420. Battle of Helms Deep (1976).............18
8421. Mind War (1976) 18
8422. Siege! (1975) 18
8423. Siege of Minas Tireth (1976).............28
8424. War of the Sky Galleons (1976) 12
8425. Warriors of the Green Planet (1976)..18

FASA:
8426. Battle Droids 12
8427. Starship Duel #2 8

Future & Fantasy Games:
8428. Hyper Battle 8

Falchion Products:
8429. William at Hastings (1977)...............28

Fantasy Games Unlimited:
8430. Citadel (1976) 10
8431. Diadem (1981) 18
8432. Lords & Wizards (1978) 18
8433. Oregon Trail (1981) 18
8434. Star Explorer (1982) 8
8435. Starships & Spacemen (ziplock).........8

Flying Buffalo
8436. Berserker 16
8437. Nuclear Destruction 18
8439a. Nuclear War 25
8438. Schutztruppe (1970)..........................27

Fusilier Games: (ziplock)
8439. Battle For Rome (1978) 38
8440. Robert The Bruce (1978)...................50
8441. Sadowa (1977) 25
8442. Warsaw Rising (1979) 40
8443. Wehrmacht (1977) 30

Gameforms:
8444. Combat: Normandy & Beyond
(1982) 18

Gameshop:
8445. Hammer of Thor (1980) $8
8446. Timelag (ziplock) 6

Game Science
8448a. Battle of Britain (1968) 80

Games Workshop:
8447. Doctor Who..20
8448. Valley of the Four Winds...................18
8449. Warlock (1980)..................................20

Game Theory & Design:
8450. Napoleon's Italian Campaign (1983)..15
8451. Napoleon's Peninsula Campaign
(1983)..15
8452. Napoleon's Russian Campaign (1983)15
8453. The Napoleonic Wars (1983) 28
8454. Napoleonic Wars Expansion
Set #1 (1983) 18
8455. Napoleonic Wars Expansion Set #2 ...18
8456. Napoleonic Wars Expansion Set #3 ...18

Gametime Games:

8457. Grand Imperialism (1978)................30
8458. Quest (1978)......................................14
8459. Sopwith (1978)..................................16
8460. Spellmaker (1979) 16
8461. Sqwyrm (1979)..................................12
8462. Star Fighter (1978) 12

8463. Strange New Worlds (1978)..............15

Gamma 2 Games:
8464. Quebec, 1759 (1972)....................... $35

GDW Assault, Double Blind & Third World War Series:
8465. Arctic Front (Third World War, 1985) 18
8466. Assault (1st edition, 1983) 18
8467. Boots & Saddles (Assault
Series, 1984)...................... 18
8468. Bundeswehr (Assault Series, 1986) ... 18
8469. Chieftan (Assault Series, 1988) 18
8470. 8th Army (Double Blind, 1984)......... 18
8471. Normandy Campaign (Double
Blind Game, 1983) 18
8472. Operation Market-Garden
(Double Blind, 1985) 18
8473. Persian Gulf (Third World War, 1986)..18
8474. Reinforcements (Assault,
softpacked, 1985) 22
8475. Southern Front (Third World
War, 1984) 18
8476. Third World War: Battle For
Germany (1984) 18

GDW Bookshelf Boxed Games:
8477. Asteroid (1st edition, 1980) 8
8478. Attack in the Ardennes (1982) 18
8479. Battle of Prague (1980) 9
8480. Dark Nebula (1st edition, 1980)........... 8
8481. 1815: The Waterloo Campaign
8482. (2nd edition, 1982)........................ 25
8483. A House Divided (1st edition,
2" box, 1981) 15
8484. A House Divided (2nd edition,
1" box, 1984) 12
8485. Invasion: Earth (1981) 9
8486. 1940 (1980) 13
8487. 1941 (1981) 13
8488. Red Army (1982) 18

8489. Soldier King (1982) 18
8490. Trenchfoot (1981) 12

GDW Boxed Europa Series:
8491. Case White (Collage Artwork
Box, 1979)...................... $25

8492. Case White (Europa Standard
Art Box, 1985) 25
8493. Fall of France (Collage Art Box, 1982) 40
8494. Fall of France (Standard
Europa Art, 1985) 40
8495. Fire in the East (1st printing, 1984)....60
8496. Fire in the East (2nd printing, 1985) ..45
8497. Marita-Merkur (Collage
Art Box, 1979) 40
8498. Marita-Merkur (Europa
Standard Art, 1986)...................... 35
8499. Narvik (2nd edition, Collage
Art Box, 1982) 30
8500. Narvik (2nd edition, Europa
Standard Art, 1987)...................... 25
8501. The Near East (Module 1983) 25
8502. Scorched Earth (1st printing, 1987) ...40
8503. Scorched Earth (2nd printing, 1988) ..35
8504. Spain & Portugal (Module, 1984) 20
8505. Their Finest Hour (2nd edition, 1982) 25
8506. Torch (1985) 25
8507. Western Desert (1983) 20

GDW Boxed Games:
8508. Air Superiority (1st edition, 1987) 15
8509. Blue Max (1983) 16
8510. The Brotherhood (1983)...................... 12
8511. Campaign Trail (1983) 15
8512. Team Yankee (1st print, brown
box, 1987) 15

GDW Conflict Game Co. Editions:
8513. The Fall of Tobruk (1976) 40
8514. The Iliad (1978)................................40
8515. Imperium (1977)................................40
8516. Kasserine Pass (1977)........................40
8517. Overlord (1977)................................40
8518. Verdun (1978)................................45
8519. Yalu (1977)................................40

GDW Draft Europa Material:
8520. Europa Air OB/OA 1941-42 (1976).....7
8521. Europa Air OB/OA 1942-46 (1977).....7
8522. Europa Air OB/OA 1941-46 (1978)...10

GDW Flat Boxed Games:
8523. Azhanti High Lightning (1981)..........45
8524. Bar-Lev (2nd edition) 25
8525. Belter (1979)................................18
8526. Bloodtree Rebellion (1979) 18
8527. Citadel (1977)................................30
8528. Double Star (1979) 18
8529. Eylau (1980) 18
8530. Fifth Frontier War (1981) 25
8531. Imperium (2nd edition, 1977) 25
8532. La Bataille de la Moskowa (1977) 45
8533. Operation Crusader (1978)................35
8534. Pearl Harbor (2nd edition, 1979)........30
8535. Red Star/White Eagle (1979) 45
8536. Road to the Rhine (1st print,
ochre box, 1979) 18
8537. Road to the Rhine (2nd print,
8538. green box, 1979).......................15
8539. Suez '73 (1981)................................10
8540. Triplanetary (2nd edition, 1981).........13
8541. White Death (1979) 18

GDW Miniatures Rules and Components:
8542. En Garde (1st edition, 1975)........... $10
8543. En Garde (revised 2nd edition, 1977) 12
8544. Fire & Steel (boxed, 1978)................ 28
8545. Harpoon (2nd edition, GDW
print booklet) 10
8546. Striker (1st edition, boxed, 1981) 24
8547. Striker (2nd edition, boxed, 1984) 28
8548. Tac Force (boxed, 1980) 28

GDW Series 120 Boxed Games:
8549. Agincourt (1978)............................... 13
8550. Battle of the Alma (1978) 9
8551. Beda Fomm (1979) 9
8552. Guilford Courthouse (1978)................ 9
8553. Lobositz (1978)................................ 9
8554. Mayday (1st edition, 1978) 8
8555. 1942 (1978)..................................... 13
8556. Ralphia, 417 BC (1977)..................... 9

GDW System 7 Counter Sets:
8557. N1: French Line I (1978) 28
8558. N2: Russian Line I (1978).................. 18
8559. N3: Austrian Line I (1978) 12
8560. N4: German Line I (1978) 12
8561. N5: French Line II (1979) 12
8562. N6: Russian Line II (1979) 12
8563. N7: Austrian Line II (1979) 12
8564. N8: German Line II (1979) 12
8565. N9: British Line I (1979) 28
8566. N10: Portugese Line I (1979) 12
8567. N11: Spanish Line I (1979) 12
8568. N12: Prussian Line I (1980) 12
8569. N13: Polish Line I (1980) 12
8570. N14: French Guards (1980) 18
8571. N15: Russian Guards (1980)............. 18

Gordonstar Publications:
8572. Titan plus Battlelands (ziplock, 1981) 50

Guidon Games:
8573. Alexander's Other Battles
(module, 1973) 22
8574. Alexander The Great (1972) 45
8575. Atlanta (1973) 45
8576. Dunkirk (1972)................................ 55
8577. Fight In The Skies (1972) 40
8578. Operation Greif (module, 1973) 18
8579. Sicily (1973)................................... 24
8580. Spirit of '76 (rules, 1973) 12

Harris Game Designs:
8581. National Liberation Front (1983)....... 12

Heritage:
8582. Demonlord (1982)............................. 12
8583. Dragon Rage 16
8584. Star Smuggler (1981)......................... 8

Histo Games:
8585. Hannibal (1972) 25
8586. Eagle Day (1974) 25
8587. Italian Campaign (1975) 25

Histo Games: continued
8588. 1944 (1973) $25

Historical Alternative:
8589. Belleau Wood (1980) 18
8590. Kampfgruppe (rules, 1979) 8
8591. Roark's Drift (1978) 20

Historical Perspectives:
8592. Siege of Jerusalem (1st edition, 1976)80
8593. Siege of Jerusalem (2nd edition, 1980) 65

Historical Simulations Ltd.:
8594. Manassas (1974)................................12

Holly Productions:
8595. Shogun (1983) 15

House of Games:
8596. 4000 A.D. (1972) 22

Icarus Games:
8597. Barbarian, Kingdom & Empire (1983) 12
8598. Iron Horse (1983) 12

Imperial Games:
8599. Friedland 1807 (1974)........................12

International Team Games:
8600. East and West 25

8601. Iliad 35
8602. Jolly Roger 25
8603. Odyssey 28

Iron Crown:
8604. Manassas, Sunday, July 21,
       1861 (1982)......................................28

Steve Jackson Games:
8605. Battlesuit 6
8606. Car Wars (small box, 1982).................8
8607. Cerberus (1979) 6
8608. Illuminati (small box)........................12
8609. Illuminati (expansion #1-#3)..............8
8610. Illuminati (deluxe)..............................6
8611. Kung Fu 2100 (1st edition, ziplock).....4
8612. ⭘ boxed..6
8613. Ogre (Deluxe).....................................5
8614. One-Page Bulge (1980)........................5
8615. Undead (ziplock, 1981)........................5

Jagdpanther Publications: (ziplock)
8616. Airborne! (1976)..............................$15
8617. Battle for Madrid (1976)....................20
8618. Fall of Bataan (1975) 20
8619. Poland, 1939 (1976)...........................15
8620. Spanish Civil War (1st edition, 1975) 24
8621. Spanish Civil War (2nd edition, 1976) ..20

Jasmine Publications:
8622. Jasmine (1983)..................................22

Lakeside Games:
8623. Score Four...11

Loren Sperry Games:
8624. Rommel: The Campaign for North Africa
       (1973)...50

Maplay Games:
8625. Guerilla (1974)..................................28
8626. Salamanca (1976) 28

Marshal Enterprises: (ziplock)
8627. La Bataille d'Auerstadt (1977)...........27
8628. La Bataille d'Austerlitz (1980) 100
8629. La Bataille de Deutsch-Wagram
       1982)..65
8630. La Bataille de la Moskowa (1975).....80
8631. La Bataille de Preussisch-Eylau
       (1978) 45

Mayfair Games
8632. Dragonriders of Pern (1983).............17
8633. Empire Builder (1982)......................22
8634. Encounters 25
8635. Forever War (1983) 18
8636. Hue (1982) 14
8637. The Keep (1983) 12
8638. Morgan's Rifles (1982) 18
8639. Red Star Falling (1983) 14
8640. Richard I, The Lion Hearted..............12
8641. Sanctuary (1983)...............................15
8642. Space Empire (ziplock)........................8
8643. Transylvania (ziplock) 6
8644. Wake Island......................................13
8645. War in the Falklands (1983)..............19

Metagaming:
8646. Air-Eaters Strike Back 12
8647. Black Hole (1978)................................5
8648. Chitin: I (2 color, 1st edition, 1977) 9
8649. ⭘ 2nd edition......................................6
8650. G.E.V. (1st edition, ziplock, 1979) 12
8651. ⭘ boxed..10
8652. Godsfire (1st edition, ziplock, 1978) . 20
8653. ⭘ boxed..24
8654. ⭘ task force edition 16
8655. Fire When Ready (1982) 12
8656. Fury of the Norsemen (1980) 10
8657. Helltank (1981) 8
8658. Hitler's War (1982) 10
8659. Holy War (1979) 5
8660. Hot Spot (1979) 5
8661. Ice War (1979) 8
8662. Invasion of the Air-Eaters 9

8663. Ogre (1st edition, 2 color,
       ziplock, 1977) $20
8664. ⭘ 2nd edition, ziplock 12
8665. ⭘ boxed..10
8666. Olympica (1978) 4
8667. Ram Speed (1980) 11
8668. Rivets (1st edition, ziplock, 1978)......16
8669. ⭘ boxed..10
8670. Rommel's Panzers (1980)..................10
8671. Starleader Assault................................8
8672. Stellar Conquest (1st edition, ziplock)22
8673. ⭘ boxed..17
8674. Trailblazer (1981)................................8
8675. Warp War (1st edition, ziplock, 1977)12
8676. Warp War (2nd edition, boxed) 7
8677. Ythri (ziplock, 1975)..........................12

Millennium Games:
8678. Air Attack (1982) 12

Ming's Enterprises:
8679. Texas Revolution (1981) 12

Mishler Co.:
8680. Nebula 19 (1977)...............................12
8681. Norad (1977) 12

David Moffet, Inc.
8682. Pigmania (1977) 10

Nova:
8683. Ace of Aces (1980) 26
8684. Ace of Aces Powerhouse (1980)........26
8685. Axis & Allies (1981).........................20
8686. Bounty Hunter 18
8687. Shootout at the Salon 12

Oldenberg Grenadiers:
8688. Battle of Brandywine (1976)..............50
8689. Battle of Camden, S.C. (1976) 50
8690. Battle of Saratoga (1976) 50
8691. Battles of Trenton/Princeton (1976)...50

On Target Games:
8692. B-17, Queen of the Skies (1982)........20

Operational Studies Group:
8693. Arcola (1979) 7
8694. Air Cobra (1980) 17
8695. Battles of the Hundred Days (1979).....7
8696. Bonaparte in Italy (1980) 28
8697. Dark December (1969).......................28
8698. Devil's Den (1980) 17
8699. Napoleon At Bay
       (1st edition, ziplock, 1978) 20
8700. Napoleon At Bay
       (2nd edition, boxed, 1978) 22
8701. Napoleon At Leipzig (1979) 28
8702. Panzerkrieg (1978) 19
8703. Robin Hood (1980) 10
8704. Rommel & Tunisia (1979) 20
8705. Starquest (1979) 18
8706. The 20th Maine (1980) 10

People's War Games:
8707. Aachen (1983)....................................15

People's War Games: continued
8708. Black Sea, Black Death (1982) $28
8709. The Cossacks Are Coming! (1982) 15
8710. Duel for Kharkov (1985) 16
8711. Gazala 1942 (1983) 15
8712. Kanev (1981) 10
8713. Korsun Pocket (boxed, 1979) 95
8714. Korsun Pocket (ziplock, 1979) 62
8715. To The Wolf's Lair! (1983) 16

Phoenix Enterprises, Ltd.:
8716. Alien Contact (1983) 15
8717. Chickamauga: River of Death (1983) 18
8718. Gettysburg: High Tide (1982) 18
8719. Remember Gordon! (1982) 18
8720. Zulu Attack (1982) 18

Phoenix Games:
8721. Alien Contact (1983) 16
8722. Streets of Stalingrad (1980) 80

Game Co.:
8723. War in Virginia (1982) 35

Princeton International
8724. Discretion (1982) 15

Quarterdeck Games:
8725. Doro Nawa (1980) 30
8726. Destroyer Captain (1982) 30
8727. Fleet Admiral (amateur
       production, 1987) 110
8728. Gallipoli (1980) 60
8729. Grant Moves (1983) 25
8730. Incredible Victory (1986) 18
8731. Ironbottom Sound (1981) 40
8732. Norway 1940 (1981) 30
8733. Rommel's War (1985) 18
8734. The Royal Navy (1983) 24

Raymond Game Co.:
8735. Fortress Rhodesia (1977) 18

Rand Game Associates:
8736. Cambrai (1974) 18
8737. Command Series #1 Complete
       (incl. Issued storage case, 1974) 135
8738. Command Series #2 Complete
       (incl. issued storage case, 1975) 35
8739. Hitler's Last Gamble (1975) 25
8740. Invasion: Sicily (1974) 18

8741. Lee vs. Meade (1974) 15

8742. Missile Boat (1974) $12
8743. Napoleon's Last Campaigns (1974)....18
8744. Omaha Beach (1974) 15
8745. Rommel: The War For North
       Africa (1975) 18
8746. Saratoga: 1777 (1974) 15
8747. War of the Worlds II (1974) 12

"Great Battles of History" Packaging:
8748. Cambrai (1975) 20
8749. Missile Boat (1975) 15
8750. Napoleon's Last Campaigns (1975)....20
8751. Omaha Beach (1975) 18
8752. Rommel: The War for North
       Africa (1975) 20
8753. War of the Worlds II (1975) 15

"Time Capsule Series" Packaging:
8754. Brandy Station (1976) 35
8755. The Great War 1914-18 (1976) 40
8756. Vicksburg (1975) 35
8757. Von Manstein & Heeresgruppe
       South (1975) 30
8758. Wellington: The Peninsula War 1808-18
       (1975) 35

"Gamut of Games Co." Boxed Editions:
8759. Lee Vs. Meade (revised edition, 1974) . 30
8760. Invasion: Sicily (revised edition, 1974) 35
8761. Saratoga: 1777 (revised edition, 1974) . 35

Research Games Inc.:
8762. Major Campaigns of Gen. G. S. Patton
       (1973) 20

8763. Major Campaigns of Gen. Douglas Mac-
       Arthur (1974) 18

Rimbald Enterprises:
8764. Frontier-6 22

Resquared Games:
8765. Starship and Empire (1976) 8

Sleuth Publications:
8766. Sherlock Holmes, Consulting Detective 12

Spence & Gabel Games:
8767. Keiserschlacht: 1918 (1978) 70
8768. Koniggratz 1866 (1977) 25
8769. Mukden 1905 (1977) 18
8770. Tannenburg (1977) 25

Simulations Canada:
8771. Assault on Tobruk 20
8772. Dark Stars 22
8773. Lee at the Crossroads (1980) 22
8774. Pelopennesian War (1971) 20
8775. Torpedo (1979) 20
8776. With Fire and Sword 20

Simulations Design Corporation:
8777. Battle for Hue (1977) 18
8778. Cromwell (1976) 18
8779. Dien Bien Phu (1977) 18
8780. Dunkerque 1940 (1972) 50
8781. Jerusalem (1975) 18
8782. Khalkin-Gol (1977) 18

Simulation Games:
8783. Dark Passage 12
8784. Defiance 16
8785. Divine Wind 18

Sopac Games:
8786. Battle With The Graf Spee (1977) 18
8787. Santa Cruz (counters pre-cut, 1976) .. 18

SPI Books, Modules, Miniatures, Accessories & Advertising Games:
8788. Air War Update Kit (1974) 16
8789. Battle of Nations Miniatures
       Set (1977) 150
8790. Napoleon at Waterloo (standard
       game, 1971) 12
8791. Napoleon at Waterloo (advanced
       game, 1971) 24
8792. Napoleon at Waterloo (updated
       edition, 1979) 12
8793. S & T Binders (each, 1973) 9
8794. Simultaneous Movement Plotting Pads
       (small or large format: per 50, 1973)... 9
8795. Strike Force One (1975) 4
8796. Tank! Expansion Kit (1974) 16
8797. 3 Games of Adventure Gaming (1981) 12
8798. Wagram Miniatures Set (1977) 150
8799. War in the East (S & T staff
       study #1, 1977) 40
8800. Wargame Design (S & T staff study #2,
       1976) 40
8801. Wargame Design (Hippocrene
       SC Ed., 1983) 40

SPI Bookshelf Boxed Games:

8802.   Across Suez (1980) $17

8803.   After The Holocaust (1977) 42
8804.   Agincourt (1978) 35
8805.   Air War (updated edition, 1979) 32
8806.   Air War (1977) 27
8807.   The Alamo (1981) 28
8808.   Arena of Death (1980) 12
8809.   Armada (2nd edition, 1979) 32
8810.   Art of Siege (quad, 1978) 100
8811.   Atlantic Wall (1978) 90
8812.   Austerlitz (1980) 16
8813.   Barbarian Kings (1980) 10
8814.   Battle for Cassino (1978) 16
8815.   Battlefleet Mars (1977) 27
8816.   Battles for the Ardennes (quad, 1978) 42
8817.   Battle for Stalingrad (1980) 42
8818.   Berlin '85 (1980) 25
8819.   The Big Red One (1980) 15
8820.   Bloody April (1979) 80
8821.   Blue & Grey (quad, 1975) 50
8822.   Bulge (1979)..12
8823.   Campaign for North Africa (1978) ..200
8824.   The China War (1979)..........................16
8825.   Citadel of Blood (1980) 18
8826.   City-Fight (1979) 32
8827.   Commando (1979) 25
8828.   Conflicts in American History (1979) 350
8829.   Crimean War (quad, 1978) 90
8830.   The Crusades (1978) 24
8831.   Dallas (1980) 8
8832.   Dawn of the Dead (1978) 28
8833.   Death Maze (1979) 12
8834.   Demons (1979) 12
8835.   Dragonquest (1st edition, 1980).........28
8836.   Dreadnought (1975) 50
8837.   Drive on Stalingrad (1977)..................40
8838.   Drive on Washington (1980) 40
8839.   East Is Red (1974) 30
8840.   Empires of the Middle Ages (1980).100
8841.   Fifth Corps (1980)...............................30
8842.   Firefight (1976) 20
8843.   Freedom in the Galaxy (1978) 17
8844.   Fulda Gap (1977) 28
8845.   Great Medieval Battles (quad, 1979) .60
8846.   Great War in the East (quad, 1978) ..100

8847.   Highway to the Reich
        (2nd edition, 1977) $120
8848.   Hof Gap (1980)....................................30

8849.   Invasion: America (1976) 48
8850.   Jackson at the Crossroads/
        Corinth (1981) 100
8851.   John Carter: Warlord Of Mars (1979) 35
8852.   The Kaiser's Battle (1980) 12
8853.   Kharkov (1978).....................................28
8854.   Kursk (1980) 100
8855.   Leningrad (1979) 14
8856.   Mech War 2 (1979) 45
8857.   Middle Earth (trilogy, 1977) 70
8858.   A Mighty Fortress (1977) 50
8859.   Modern Battles II (quad, 1977) 58
8860.   Napoleon's Art of War (1979)............36
8861.   Napoleon's Last Battles (quad, 1976) 42
8862.   Nato Division Commander (1979) 60
8863.   The Next War (1978) 60
8864.   Ney Vs. Wellington (1979)................35
8865.   Objective: Moscow (1978) 75
8866.   October War (1977) 28
8867.   Operation Typhoon (1978)..................35
8868.   Outreach (1976) 35
8869.   Panzer Armee Afrika (1973) 36
8870.   Panzer Battles (1979)..........................17
8871.   Paratroop (1979) 12
8872.   Patton's 3rd Army (1980)....................12
8873.   Pea Ridge (1980) 40
8874.   Ragnarok (1981) 10
8875.   Raid! (1977)..20
8876.   Red Star/White Star (2nd
        edition, 1979) 25
8877.   Red Sun Rising (1977).......................65
8878.   Rescue From the Hive (1981)............12
8879.   Siege of Constantinople (1978) 28
8880.   Sinai (1973) 25
8881.   Sniper! (1973) 25
8882.   Sorcerer (1975) 26
8883.   SPI Baseball (1980)............................10
8884.   SPI Football (1980)............................10
8885.   Spies! (1981) 5
8886.   Starforce (1974) 25
8887.   Starforce (trilogy, 1977)....................65

8888.   Star Soldier (1977) $26
8889.   Stonewall (1978) 28
8890.   Suez to Golan (1979) 60
8891.   The Sword and the Stars (1981).........16
8892.   Swords & Sorcery (1978)...................32
8893.   Tannenberg (1978) 17
8894.   Task Force (1981)...............................28
8895.   Terrible Swift Sword (1976) 65
8896.   Time Tripper (1980) 12
8897.   Tito (1980)..9
8898.   To The Green Fields Beyond (1978)..50
8899.   Universe (1981) 20
8900.   Up Scope! (1977) 35
8901.   Wacht Am Rhein (1977) 225
8902.   War Between The States (1977).......140
8903.   War in Europe (1976) 195
8904.   War in the East (2nd edition, 1976)..110
8905.   War in the Ice (1978).........................28
8906.   War in the Pacific (1978).................250
8907.   Wellington's Victory (1976) 135
8908.   War of the Ring (1977)......................45
8909.   Wilson's Creek (1980) 28
8910.   World Killer (1980)............................12
8911.   Wreck of the BSM Pandora (1980)... 10

SPI Cardboard Folio Packed Games: (ziplock)

8912.   Antietam (1975) 12
8913.   Arnhem (1976) 12
8914.   Bastogne (1976) 12
8915.   Battle for Germany (1975) 35
8916.   Battle of Nations (1975) 16
8917.   Battle of the Wilderness (1975).........20
8918.   Bloody Ridge (1975)...........................17
8919.   Breitenfeld (1976) 20
8920.   Bundeswehr (1977) 20
8921.   Cauldron (1976) 12
8922.   Cemetery Hill (1975) 12
8923.   Chattanooga (1975) 20
8924.   Chickamauga (1975) 12
8925.   Chinese Farm (1975) 16
8926.   Crusader (1976) 12
8927.   Dixie (1976) 12
8928.   DMZ (1977) 16
8929.   Fredericksburg (1975) 24
8930.   Freiburg (1976).................................28

SPI continued

8931.	Golan (1975)	$16
8932.	Gondor (1977)	20
8933.	Hooker and Lee (1975)	24
8934.	Hurtgen Forest (1976)	16
8935.	Jena-Auerstadt (1975)	16
8936.	Jerusalem (1977)	16
8937.	Kasserine (1976)	12
8938.	La Belle Alliance (1976)	16
8939.	Leyte (1975)	12
8940.	Ligny (1976)	16
8941.	Lutzen (1976)	28
8942.	Marengo (1975)	16
8943.	Mukden (1975)	16
8944.	Nordlingen (1976)	32
8945.	Oil War (1975)	20
8946.	Okinawa (1975)	16
8947.	Punic Wars (1975)	32
8948.	Quatre Bras (1976)	16
8949.	Remagen (1976)	16
8950.	Revolt in the East (1976)	24
8951.	Road to Richmond (1977)	20
8952.	Rocroi (1976)	32
8953.	Saipan (1975)	16
8954.	Sauron (1977)	24
8955.	Shiloh (1975)	16
8956.	Supercharge (1976)	13
8957.	Wagram (1975)	16
8958.	Wavre (1976)	16
8959.	World War I (1975)	28
8960.	Wurzburg (1975)	16
8961.	Yugoslavia (1977)	28

SPI Color Boxes:

8962.	Barbarossa (1972)	28

8963.	Leipzig (1972)	28
8964.	Normandy (1972)	28

SPI Collector's Editions, Designer's Editions and Power Politics Series:

8965.	A Bridge Too Far (1976)	$25
8966.	After The Holocaust (1977)	42
8967.	Arnhem (1976)	25
8968.	Battle for Germany (1975)	40

8969.	Battle of Nations (1975)	34
8970.	Battlefleet Mars (1977)	32
8971.	Chickamauga (1975)	32
8972.	Foxbat & Phantom (1973)	32
8973.	Golan (1975)	32
8974.	Invasion: America (1976)	32
8975.	Mech War '77 (1975)	32
8976.	Napoleon's Last Battles (quad, 1976)	32
8977.	Oil War (1975)	30
8978.	Okinawa (1975)	30
8979.	Panzergruppe Guderian (1976)	30

8980.	Plot to Assassinate Hitler (1976)	30

8981.	Russian Civil War (1976)	$30
8982.	Sinai (1973)	35
8983.	Sorcerer (1975)	30
8984.	Starforce (1974)	32
8985.	War of the Ring (1977)	30
8986.	World War 3 (1975)	30

SPI Flat Tray Packs:

8987.	Air War (1977)	24
8988.	American Civil War (1974)	24
8989.	American Revolution (1972)	24
8990.	Ardennes Offensive (1973)	24
8991.	Armageddon (1972)	32
8992.	Austerlitz (1972)	28
8993.	Barbarossa (1971)	25
8994.	Bastogne/Anzio Beachhead (1970)	40
8995.	Battle of Moscow (1970)	32
8996.	Battlefleet Mars (1977)	20
8997.	Blitzkrieg Module System (1969)	45
8998.	Blue & Grey (quad, 1975)	28
8999.	Blue & Grey II (quad, 1976)	75
9000.	Borodino (1972)	32
9001.	Breakout & Pursuit (1972)	25
9002.	Bull Run (1973)	25
9003.	"CA" (1973)	28
9004.	Canadian Civil War (1977)	25
9005.	Centurion (1970)	100
9006.	Chariot (1975)	35
9007.	Cobra (1977)	20
9008.	Combat Command (1972)	35
9009.	Combined Arms (1974)	16
9010.	Conquerors (1977)	75
9011.	Conquistador (1976)	28
9012.	Crimean War (quad, 1978)	70
9013.	Dark Ages (1971)	50
9014.	Descent on Crete (1978)	40
9015.	Desert War (1973)	16
9016.	Destruction of Army Group Center (1973)	35
9017.	Dreadnought (1975)	32
9018.	Drive on Stalingrad (1977)	32
9019.	East is Red (1974)	22
9020.	1812 (1972)	50
9021.	El Alamein (1973)	20
9022.	Fall of Rome (1973)	32
9023.	Fast Carriers (1975)	32

SPI Flat Tray Packs: continued

9024. Firefight (1976) $16
9025. First World War (Module with maps, 1977) 75
9026. Flight of the Goeben (1970)..............65
9027. Flying Circus (1972) 35
9028. Foxbat & Phantom (1973)................16
9029. Franco-Prussian War (1972)............40
9030. Frederick The Great (1978)..............24
9031. Frigate (1974) 20
9032. Fulda Gap (1977) 20
9033. Global War (1975)............................40
9034. Grenadier (1971) 35
9035. Grunt (1971) 40
9036. Highway to the Reich (1st edition, 1977) 75
9037. Invasion: America (1976)..................40
9038. Island War (quad, 1975) 50
9039. Kampfpanzer (1973) 15
9040. Korea (1971)...................................28
9041. Kursk (1971) 32
9042. La Grande Armee (1972)..................35
9043. Lee Moves North (1973) 32
9044. Legion (1975)..................................45
9045. Lost Battles (1971) 40
9046. Marne (1971)...................................36
9047. Mech War '77 (1975)........................16
9048. Middle Earth (trilogy, 1977)..............65
9049. A Mighty Fortress (1977).................55
9050. Minuteman (1976)............................32
9051. Modern Battles (quad, 1975)............40
9052. Modern Battles II (quad)..................50
9053. Moscow Campaign (1972)................32
9054. Musket & Pike (1973)......................47
9055. Napoleon At War (quad, 1975) 42
9056. Napoleon At Waterloo (1971)............28
9057. Napoleon's Last Battles (quad, 1976). 36
9058. Nato (1973) 16
9059. 1918 (1971) 36
9060. North Africa (quad, 1976)................38
9061. Objective: Moscow (1978)................70
9062. October War (1977)..........................20
9063. Operation Olympic (1974) 32
9064. Outreach (1976) 28
9065. Panzer '44 (1975)............................16
9066. Panzerarmee Afrika (1973)..............20
9067. Panzergruppe Guderian (1976) 32
9068. Patroli (1974)..................................16
9069. Phalanx (1971) 70
9070. Prestags Master Pack (1976)...........190
9071. Raid! (1977) 16
9072. Red Star/White Star (1st edition, 1973) 18
9073. Red Sun Rising (1977) 50
9074. Renaissance of Infantry (1970) 120
9075. Rifle & Saber (1973) 40
9076. Scrimmage (1973)............................25
9077. Search & Destroy (1974)..................35
9078. Seelowe (1974).................................38
9079. Sinai (1973) 20
9080. Sixth Fleet (1975)............................35
9081. Sniper! (1972) 16
9082. Soldiers (1972) 40
9083. Solomon's Campaign (1973)..............40
9084. Sorcerer (1975)................................18
9085. South Africa (1977)..........................12
9086. Spartan (1975).................................40

9087. Spitfire (1973)..................................$28
9088. Starforce (1974) 15
9089. Starforce (trilogy, 1977) 50
9090. Starsoldier (1977) 18
9091. Strategy I (1971) 60
9092. Tank! (1974) 15
9093. Terrible Swift Sword (1976)...............80
9094. Thirty Years War (quad, 1976) 100
9095. To The Green Fields Beyond (1978) . 42
9096. Turning Point (1972) 32
9097. Up Scope! (1977)..............................28
9098. U.S.N. (1971)...................................35
9099. Veracruz (1977)................................20
9100. Viking (1975)....................................42
9101. Wacht Am Rhein (1977)...................135
9102. War Between The States (1977) 120
9103. War In Europe (1976)......................150
9104. War In The East (1st edition, 1973)... 35
9105. War In The East (2nd edition, 1976) 100
9106. War In The Pacific (1978)................275
9107. War In The West (1976)....................80
9108. War of the Ring (1977) 45
9109. Wellington's Victory (1976)...............52
9110. Westwall (quad, 1976) 42
9111. Wilderness Campaign (1972) 35
9112. Winter War (1972) 50
9113. Wolfpack (1974) 35
9114. World War II (1975)..........................20
9115. World War Three (1975)....................25
9116. Year of the Rat (1972) 32
9117. Yeoman (1975) 52

SPI Moment In Conflict Series Packaging: (ziplock)

9118. MCS #1: Chickamauga (1975) 16
9119. MCS #2: Arnhem (1976) 16
9120. MCS #3: Bundeswehr (1977) 16
9121. MCS #4: World War I (1975) 25
9122. MCS #5: Kiev (1979) 16
9123. MCS #6: Rostov (1979)....................16
9124. MCS #7: Operation Star (1979)........16
9125. MCS #8: Korsun (1979) 16
9126. MCS: King Arthur (1979) 25
9127. MCS: Robert At Bannockburn (1979) 22
9128. MCS: Tamburlaine The Great (1979) 16

SPI Space, Fantasy and Magic Capsule Series Packaging: (ziplock)

9129. FCS #1: Gondor (1977) 25
9130. FCS #2: Sauron (1977) 25
9131. MGC #1: Demons (1979) 8
9132. MGC #2: Death Maze (1979) 9
9133. SCS #1: Creature That Ate Sheboygan (1979)............................22
9134. SCS #2: Star Gate (1979) 6
9135. SCS #3: Titan Strike! (1979) 6
9136. SCS #4: Vector 3 (1979) 6

SPI White Generic Flat Boxes:

9137. Battle of Stalingrad (1972) 28
9138. Lee At Gettysburg (1973) 28

Standard Games:

9139. Cry Havoc 30
9140. Out Remer (Cry Havoc)....................28

9141. Siege (Cry Havoc) $28
9142. Speed & Steel....................................19

Strategic Games Pub., Inc.:

9143. At the Gates of Moscow 1941 (1984) 18
9144. Operation Thunderclap (1985)...........18

Strategic Studies Games:

9145. Alaric The Goth (1980).....................15
9146. Army Group South (1982) 15
9147. Attila The Hun (1980) 15
9148. Battle of Salamanca (1981)...............18
9149. Battle of Vittoria (1982) 18

Strife Games Co.:

9150. Napoleon's Russian Campaign (ziplock, 1979) 18
9151. The Siege of Port Arthur, 1904 (ziplock, 1976) 18

Swedish Game Production:

9152. Dark Passage (1980).........................15
9153. Defiance (1980)................................15
9154. Holowczyn (1980).............................15
9155. Ostkrieg (1981) 18
9156. Southern Flank (1981).......................15

Tactical Templates:

9157. Deep Space Navigator (1983) 15

Task Force Games:

9158. Asteroid Zero Four 10
9159. Battlewagon (1982) 16
9160. Cerberus (ziplock, 1979)....................6
9161. Federation Space (1981) 20
9162. Intruder (ziplock, 1980) 10
9163. McPherson's Ridge (1980) 18
9164. Moon Base Clavius (ziplock, 1982)...10
9165. Operation Pegasus (1980) 10
9166. Power Play (1981)..............................10
9167. Star Fleet Battles (1st edition, ziplock, 1979) 20
9168. ○ expansion #1-#3 (ziplock) 9
9169. ○ captain's edition (boxed) 16
9170. ○ volume I (boxed)..........................19
9171. ○ volumes II & III 18
9172. Starfire (1st edition, ziplock).............20
9173. ○ boxed edition 20
9174. Swordquest (ziplock, 1979).................6
9175. Valkenburg Castle..............................6
9176. War of the Worlds 10
9177. Warriors of Batak (ziplock, 1982)........7

Taurus, Ltd.:

9178. Albania (1975) 16
9179. Battle of the Atlantic (1975) 35
9180. Crete, Gibraltar, Malta (1975)............24
9181. Egypt (1975) 17
9182. Glory Of Rome (1976) 40
9183. Raiders of the North (1975) 35
9184. Undersea Warriors (1975)..................40
9185. Warriors of the Dark Star (1975)........16

Teaching Concepts, Inc.:

9186. Space Hop 25

Third Millenia, Inc.:
9187. Breakout (1973) $25
9188. Empire I (1973) 15
9189. First Indochina War (1974) 18
9190. Flying Tigers II (1973) 15
9191. Operation Market Garden (1973) 24
9192. PBI (Poor Bloody Infantry, 1972) 24
9193. Salerno (1972) 24
9194. Search for the Graf Spee (1973) 18
9195. Sealion (1973) 24
9196. Second Galactic War (1973) 15
9197. Shiloh (1973) 28

TSR
9198. Attack Force (1982) 5
9199. Awful Green Things from Outer Space
      (1979).. 22

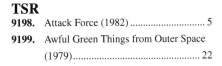

9200. Battle of the Five Armies (1975) 18
9201. Cohorts (1977) 18
9202. Divine Right (1979) 55

9203. Dungeon! (first edition; 1975) 20
9204. ○ second edition 16
9205. ○ third edition 12
9206. Empire of the Petal Throne (1975) 45

9207. Firefight (1984) $25
9208. 4th Dimension (1979) 12
9209. Icebergs (1982) 5
9210. Knights of Camelot (1980) 25
9211. Lankhmar (1976) 16
9212. Little Big Horn (1976) 28
9213. Remember The Alamo (1982) 10
9214. Revolt on Antares (1981) 5
9215. Snit's Revenge (1978) 28
9216. Suspicion (1977) 12
9217. They've Invaded Pleasantville (1981)...5
9218. Warlocks and Warriors (1971)............. 7
9219. Vampyre (1981) 6
9220. Viking Gods (9182) 5

Twentieth Century Reniassance:
9221. Gateway to the Stars (1979) 15
9222. Tokyo Express (1977)........................ 22

Ultimate Products:
9223. Battle of Stones River (1978) 40

U.S. Games Corp.:
9224. Commando Raid 16

Victory Games:
9225. Civil War (1983) 15
9226. NATO: The Next War in Europe
      (1983) 15
9227. Tokyo Express (1977)......................... 15

West End Games:
9228. Bug-Eyed Monsters (1983) 12
9229. Cosmic Encounter (1977).................. 24
9230. Imperium Romanum (1979).............. 12
9231. Junta (1979) 16
9232. KamaKura (1982) 22
9233. Last Panzer Victory (1983)............... 19
9234. Operation BADR (1983) 9

Robert Williams Games:
9235. Warlord 50

World Wide Wargames:
9236. Napoleon at Austerlitz....................... 18
9237. Saratoga 1777 16
9238. Sturm Nash Osten (1982).................. 10

Yaquinto Publications:
9239. Adventurer (album game, 1981)...........8
9240. Apache (album game, 1981).................8
9241. Armor (1981).....................................55
9242. Asteroid Pirates (album game, 1981)...8
9243. Attack of the Mutants (album
      game, 1981)...8

9244. The Barbarians (album game, 1981) $10
9245. Battle (1st edition, 1979)................... 14
9246. Battle (2nd edition, 1981) 8
9247. Battles and Leaders (album
      game, 1981) 18
9248. Beachhead (1st edition, 1980)............ 16
9249. Beachhead (2nd edition, 1981) 10
9250. Beastlord (1979)............................... 15
9251. Bomber (1982) 18
9252. Close Assault (album game, 1983) 24
9253. Combat Cards (album game, 1984) 8
9254. Commando Actions (album
      game, 1982) 10
9255. C.V. (1979)....................................... 18
9256. Dallas (album game, 1980) 8
9257. Demon's Run (album game, 1981)....... 8
9258. "88" (1980)....................................... 45
9259. The Fall of South Vietnam
      (album game, 1981) 10
9260. Fast Attack Boats (1980) 10
9261. The French Foreign Legion (1982).... 15
9262. The Great Redoubt (1980) 24
9263. Hero (1980) 10
9264. Ironclads (1979) 45
9265. Ironclads Expansion Kit (1981)......... 55
9266. Marine: 2002 (1979) 15
9267. Market Madness (album game, 1981).. 8
9268. Murfreesboro (1980)......................... 18
9269. Neck and Neck (album game, 1981).... 8
9270. Panzer (1979) 40
9271. Pickett's Charge (1980) 28
9272. Pirates & Plunder (album game, 1982) 15
9273. Raider! (album game, 1982) 10
9274. Red Storm (album game, 1983) 18
9275. The Roaring 20's (album game, 1981). 8
9276. Shooting Stars (1980) 15
9277. Solitaire Scenario Pack for Panzer '88' &
      Armor (1981) 15
9278. Starfall (1979) 15
9279. Superiority (album game, 1981) 10
9280. Swashbuckler (1980)......................... 15
9281. The Sword and The Flame
      (rules, 1979) 10
9282. The Thin Red Line (1980) 25
9283. Timeship (album game, 1983) 15
9284. Timewar (1st edition, 1979)............... 15
9285. Timewar (2nd edition, 1980)............. 15
9286. Ultimatum (1979)............................. 18
9287. United Nations (album game, 1982).. 10
9288. Wings (album game, 1981) 35

Zocchi:
9289. Alien Space (ziplock).......................... 8

ROLE PLAYING GAMES

Role Playing Games (FANTASY)

9295.	A1 Slave Pits Of The Undercity (TSR 1980).	$5
9296.	A2 Secret of the Slavers Stockade (TSR 1981).	5
9297.	A3 Assault on the Aerie of the Slave Lords (TSR 1981).	5
9298.	A4 In the Dungeons of the Slave Lords (TSR 1981).	5
9299.	Accoutery (Bearhug).	4
9300.	Advanced Melee (Metagaming 1977).	16
9301.	Adventures in Fantasy (Excalibre 1979).	10
9302.	All the World's Monsters, Vol. I (Chaosium).	20
9303.	All the World's Monsters, Vol. II (Chaosium).	20
9304.	All the World's Monsters, Vol. III (Chaosium).	20
9305.	Angmar, Land of the Witch King (Iron Crown).	8
9306.	Arduin Grimoire (Grimoire Games).	10
9307.	Arms Law (Iron Crown).	10
9308.	B1 In Search of the Unknown (TSR 1979).	5
9309.	B2 Keep on the Borderlands (TSR 1981).	5
9310.	B3 Palace of the Silver Princess (first edition; almost all copies destroyed; TSR 1981).	150
9311.	B3 Palace of the Silver Princess (later edition).	5
9312.	B4 The Lost City (TSR 1982).	5
9313.	Blackmoor (TSR 1975).	15
9314.	Blade of Allectus (SPI 1980).	10
9315.	Blue Frog Tavern (Flying Buffalo 1981).	15
9316.	Borderlands (Chaosium 1982).	24
9317.	Bunnies & Burrows (Fantasy Games Unlimited 1978).	16
9318.	Bushido (Phoenix Games).	12
9319.	C1 Hidden Shrine of Tamoachan (TSR 1980).	5
9320.	C2 Ghost Tower of Inverness (TSR 1980).	5
9321.	Call of Cthulhu (Chaosium 1980).	15
9322.	Caverns of Thracia (Judges Guild).	8
9323.	Character Law (Iron Crown 1982).	12
9324.	Chill (Pacesetter Ltd. 1983).	25
9325.	Chivalry & Sorcery (Fantasy Games Unlimited 1977).	16
9326.	Citadel of Fire (Judges Guild).	8
9327.	Cities (Midkemia Press).	16
9328.	City State of the Invincible Overlord (Judges Guild).	35
9329.	City State of the World Emperor (Judges Guild).	35
9330.	City State Warfare (Judges Guild).	18
9331.	Citybook I (Judges Guild 1982).	6
9332.	Claw Law (Iron Crown 1982).	12
9333.	D1 Descent into the Depths of the Earth (TSR 1978).	6
9334.	D2 Shrine of the Kuo-Toa (TSR 1978).	6
9335.	D1,2 Descent into the Depths of the Earth (TSR 1981).	6
9336.	D3 Vault of the Drow (TSR 1978).	6
9337.	Dark Folk (Mayfair Games 1983).	10
9338.	Death Test (Metagaming 1979).	10
9339.	Death Test 2 (Metagaming 1980).	10
9340.	Deities & Demigods, 1st edition (TSR 1980).	60
9341.	Deities & Demigods, 2nd edition (TSR 1980).	18
9342.	Dragonquest, 1st edition (SPI 1980).	25
9343.	Dragonquest, 2nd edition (SPI 1981).	35
9344.	Dungeon Geomorphs II: Caves and Caverns TSR).	6
9345.	Dungeons & Dragons Expert Set (TSR 1983).	10
9346.	Dungeons & Dragons "Old Basic Set" (TSR 1981).	14
9347.	Dungeons & Dragons Original (TSR 1973).	35
9348.	Dwarven Glory (Wee Warriors 1977).	8
9349.	Egg of the Phoenix (RPGA).	8
9350.	Eldritch Wizardry (TSR 1976).	10
9351.	En Garde (Game Designers Workshop 1975).	15
9352.	EX1 Dungeonland (TSR 1983).	5
9353.	EX2 Land Beyond the Magic Mirror (TSR 1983).	5
9354.	Fantasy Paths (Board-Craft Simulations).	16
9355.	Fantasy Trip (Metagaming).	$22
9356.	Fez I: Valley of Trees (Mayfair Games).	6
9357.	Fiend Folio (TSR 1981).	24
9358.	First Fantasy Campaign (Judges Guild).	35
9359.	Free City of Haven (Gamelords).	20
9360.	G1 Steading of the Hill Giant Chief (TSR 1978).	8
9361.	G2 Glacial Rift of the Frost Giant Jarl (TSR 1978).	8
9362.	G3 Hall of the Fire Giant King (TSR 1978).	8
9363.	G 1,2,3 Against the Giants (TSR 1981).	10
9364.	Goblin (Heritage).	4
9365.	Goblin Lake (Flying Buffalo).	4
9366.	Gods, Demi-Gods & Heroes (TSR 1976).	20
9367.	Grimtooth's Traps (Flying Buffalo 1982).	15
9368.	Grimtooth's Traps Two (Flying Buffalo 1983).	15
9369.	High Fantasy (Reston Publishing Co. 1981).	2
9370.	I1 Dwellers in the Forbidden City (TSR 1981).	4
9371.	I2 Tomb of the Lizard King (TSR 1982).	4
9372.	I3 Pharaoh (TSR 1982).	4
9373.	I4 Oasis of the White Palm (TSR 1983).	4
9374.	I6 Ravenloft.	15
9375.	Iron Wind (Iron Crown 1980).	16
9376.	Island Book I (Judges Guild).	8
9377.	Kabal (Kabal 1982).	8
9378.	Knights of King Arthur (Chaosium).	14
9379.	Secret of Bone Hill (TSR 1983).	6
9380.	Land of the Rising Sun (Fantasy Games Unlimited 1980).	12
9381.	Lord of the Rings (Iron Crown).	12
9382.	Lords of Adventure.	10
9383.	Lords of Creation (Avalon Hill 1983).	12
9384.	M1 Blizzard Pass (TSR 1983).	4
9385.	Machiavelli (Battleline 1978).	28
9386.	Man, Myth & Magic (Yaquinto 1983).	20
9387.	Masters of Mind (Judges Guild 1981).	12
9388.	Melee (Metagaming 1977).	24
9389.	Middle Earth (Iron Crown 1983).	15
9390.	Mines of Keridan (Gamelords 1983).	6
9391.	Monster & Treasure Assortment, Set 2 (TSR 1977).	6
9392.	Monster Cards (TSR 1982).	4
9393.	N1 Against the Cult of the Reptile God (TSR 1982).	6
9394.	Nanorian Stones (Mayfair Games 1983).	6
9395.	Palladium Role-Playing Game (Palladium 1983).	15
9396.	Powers & Perils (Avalon Hill 1984).	24
9397.	Q1 Queen of the Demonweb Pits (TSR 1980).	10
9398.	Quest for the Ring.	12
9399.	Rogues Gallery (TSR 1980).	8
9400.	Rolemaster (Iron Crown).	15
9401.	Runequest (Chaosium 1978).	26
9402.	S1 Tomb of Horrors (TSR 1978).	8
9403.	S2 White Plume Mountain (TSR 1979).	6
9404.	S3 Expedition to the Barrier Peaks (TSR 1980).	6
9405.	S4 Lost Caverns of Tsojcanth (TSR 1982).	8
9406.	Sea Steeds & Wave Riders (Judges Guild 1978).	12
9407.	Skull & Crossbones (Fantasy Games Unlimited 1983).	10
9408.	Snow King's Bride (Chaosium).	10
9409.	Soloquest (Chaosium 1982).	10
9410.	Spell Law (Iron Crown).	15
9411.	Stalking the Night Fantastic (TriTac 1983).	15
9412.	Swordbearer (Heritage 1982).	14
9413.	T1 Village of Hommlet (TSR 1979).	6
9414.	Tegel Manor (Jedges Guild).	18
9415.	Thieves' Guild (Gamelords 1980).	19
9416.	Thieves' World (Chaosium 1983).	16
9417.	Tollenkar's Lair (Metagaming).	9
9418.	Treasure Chest (Judges Guild).	15
9419.	Treasure of the Silver Dragon (Metagaming).	8

Role Playing Games (FANTASY) continued

9420. Tunnels & Trolls (Flying Buffalo 1975). $15
9421. U1 Sinister Secret of Saltmarsh (TSR 1981). 6
9422. U2 Danger at Dunwater (TSR 1983). 6
9423. U3 The Final Enemy (TSR 1983). 6
9424. UK1 Beyond the Crystal Cave (TSR 1983). 6
9425. Unicorn Gold (Metagaming 1981). 8
9426. Village Book I (Judges Guild). 8
9427. WG4 Forgotten Temple of Tharizdun. 10
9428. (TSR 1982). 6
9429. Wizard (Metagaming 1978). 18
9430. Wizard's Lair. ....
9431. World of Greyhawk (TSR 1980). 12
9432. World of Greyhawk Boxed Set (TSR 1983). 12
9433. Worlds of Wonder (Chaosium 1982). 16
9434. X2 Castle Amber (TSR 1981). 6
9435. X3 Curse of Xanathon (TSR 1982). 5
9436. X4 Master of the Desert Nomads (TSR 1983). 5

Role Playing Games (SCIENCE FICTION)

9437. 1001 Characters (Game Designers Workshop). 10
9438. Aftermath (Fantasy Games Unlimited 1981). 16
9439. Animal Encounters (Game Designers Workshop). 10
9440. Azhanti High Lightning (Game Designers
        Workshop 1980). 35
9441. Citizens of the Imperium (Game Designers
        Workshop). 12
9442. Darthanon Queen (Judges Guild). 8
9443. Dra'k'ne Station (Judges Guild). 8
9444. Fasolt in Peril (Fantasy Games Unlimited 1982). 6
9445. Gamma World (TSR 1981). 15
9446. GW1 Legion of Gold (TSR 1981). 2
9447. GW2 Famine in Far-Go (TSR 1982). 4
9448. Highway 2000 (Gamescience). 12
9449. Judge Dredd (Games Workshop 1983). 20
9450. Klingon D-7 Deck Plans (FASA). 25
9451. Marooned/Marooned Alone (Game Designers
        Workshop). 10
9452. Mechanoids Invasion (Palladium 1983). 16
9453. MERC (Fantasy Games Unlimited). 14
9454. Metamorphosis Alpha (TSR 1974). 24
9455. Morrow Project (Timeline Inc.). 15
9456. SF1 Volturnus, Planet of Mystery (TSR 1982). 2
9457. Space Opera (Fantasy Games Unlimited 1981). 18
9458. Space Patrol (Gamescience 1977). 6
9459. Spinward Marches (Game Designers Workshop). 12
9460. Star Empires (TSR 1977). 18
9461. Star Frontiers (TSR 1982). 10
9462. Star Frontiers Knight Hawks (TSR 1984). 12
9463. Star Patrol (Gamescience 1981). 6
9464. Star Trek (FASA). 30

9465. Starfleet Voyages (Terra Games 1982). $20
9466. TimeMaster (Pacesetter Ltd. 1984). 18
9467. Timeship (Yaquinto 1983). 18
9468. Traveller (Game Designers Workshop 1977). 20
9469. Traveller- Deluxe Set (Game Designers
        Workshop). 24
9470. Traveller Judge's Screen (Judges Guild). 8
9471. Universe (SPI 1981). 20
9472. Universe Gamemaster's Screen (SPI 1982). 12
9473. U.S.S. Enterprise Deck Plans (FASA 1983). 25

Role Playing Games (SUPERHEROES)

9474. Champions (Hero Games 1982). 8
9475. Daredevils (Fantasy Games Unlimited). 10
9476. Enemies (Hero Games). 6
9477. Enemies II (Hero Games). 6
9478. Official Superhero Game (Mayfair Games 1982). 12
9479. Super Squadron (Adventure Simulations 1983). 12
9480. Supervillains (Task Force Games 1982). 10
9481. Villains & Vigilantes (Fantasy Games Unlimited). 10

Role Playing Games (ESPIONAGE)

9482. Agent Dossiers (TSR 1983). 3
9483. Espionage! (Hero Games 1982). 8
9484. For Your Information (Victory Games 1984). 6
9485. James Bond 007 (Victory Games 1983). 10
9486. M.I.S.S.I.O.N. (Kabal). 8
9487. Top Secret (TSR 1980). 12
9488. TS 004 Operation: Fastpass (TSR 1983). 3

Role Playing Games (HISTORICAL)

9489. Behind Enemy Lines (FASA 1982). 20
9490. BH3 Ballots & Bullets (TSR 1982). 3
9491. Boot Hill (TSR 1975). 10
9492. Commando (SPI 1979). 20
9493. Dallas (SPI 1980). 12
9494. Dawn Patrol (TSR 1983). 24
9495. Elementary Watson (Fantasy Games Unlimited). 12
9496. Gangbusters (TSR 1982). 12
9497. Gangster (Fantasy Games Unlimited 1979). 12
9498. GB1 Trouble Brewing (TSR 1982). 4
9499. GB3 Death on the Docks (TSR 1983). 4
9500. Gunslinger (Avalon Hill). 4
9501. Inner City. 6
9502. Justice, Inc. (Hero Games 1984). 10
9503. Killer (Steve Jackson Games). 15
9504. Odysseus (Fantasy Games Unlimited). 8
9505. Pirates & Plunder (Yaquinto 1982). 16
9506. Recon. 15
9507. Shootout (Argon Games). 8
9508. Wild West (Fantasy Games Unlimited 1981). 12

COLLECTIBLE CARD GAMES

Magic the Gathering

		set	starter box	booster box
9509.	Alpha printing, 290 cards	$3500	$2000	$3250
9510.	Beta printing, 290 cards	3950	2500	3500
9511.	Unlimited edition, 292 cards	2500	2000	3400
9512.	Revised edition, 296 cards	275	240	295
9513.	4th Edition, 368 cards	230	85	100
9514.	5th Edition, 434 cards	255	85	85
9515.	Arabian Nights, 78 cards	900	3700	85
9516.	Antiquities, 100 cards	300	900	20
9517.	Legends, 310 cards	975	1000	35
9518.	The Dark, 119 cards	150	400	8.50
9519.	Fallen Empires, 102 cards	50	50	1.50
9520.	Ice Age, 373 cards	175	85	85
9521.	Chronicles, 125 cards	75	90	2.50
9522.	Homelands, 115 cards	72.50	70	1.50
9523.	Alliances, 144 cards	165	145	4
9524.	Mirage, 335 cards	185	90	90
9525.	Visions, 167 cards	175	100	3
9526.	Weatherlight, 167 cards	160	90	3
9527.	Portal, 200 cards	125	90	90
9528.	Tempest, 335 cards	250	90	90
9529.	Stronghold, 143 cards	175	100	85
9530.	Exodus, 143 cards	190	100	90

Star Trek

		set	starter box	booster box
9531.	Limited edition, 363 cards	750	125	175
9532.	Unlimited edition, 363 cards	250	85	85
9533.	Alt. Universe, 122 cards	150	-----	80
9534.	Q-Continuum, 121 cards	100	-----	85
9535.	First Contact, 130 cards	150	-----	60
9536.	Fajo series, 18 cards	125	-----	-----
9537.	Deep Space Nine, 278 cards	150	125	75

Star Wars

		set	starter box	booster box
9538.	Limited edition, 324 cards	$350	$125	$160
9539.	Unlimited edition, 324 cards	250	85	90
9540.	A New Hope, 162 cards	200	-----	100
9541.	Hoth, 162 cards	185	-----	100
9542.	Dagobah, 186 cards	200	-----	130
9543.	Cloud City, 180 cards	200	-----	120
9544.	Jabba's Palace, 180 cards	190	-----	120
9545.	First Anthology	22	-----	-----

Aliens Predator

9546.	TheGame, 363 cards	95	9	85

Babylon 5

9547.	Premier, 446 cards	130	85	40
9548.	The Shadows, 203 cards	-----	-----	35

Battletech

9549.	Limited, 283 cards	275	100	120
9550.	Unlimited, 283 cards	160	85	90

Xena Warrior Princess

9551.	The Game, 180 cards	-----	70	70

Doomtown

9552.	The Game, 157 cards	90	9	-----
9553.	Episode three, 52 cards	25	9	3
9554.	Episode four, 52 cards	25	9	3

Anti-Mayhem

9555.	Series "0" & "1"	-----	-----	15

Middle Earth

9556.	Limited	-----	90	60
9557.	Lidless Eye	-----	60	60

X-Files

9558.	Premiere	-----	20	20

GAMES BY CATEGORY

Action

6650. 1-2-3 Game Hot Spot!
7498. 4-5-6 Pick Up Sticks
4472. Air Trix, The Airstream Game
7075. American Pachinko
7304. Ants in the Pants
7303. Ants in the Pants, Photo cover
4494. Back off Buzzard
2390. Baggy Beans 'Goes to Town'
5895. Bang Box Game
7305. Bango! Bango!
6424. Barnstormer
6254. Barrel of Monkeys
3178. Baseball Game & G-Man Target
4500. Bash!
7076. Batman Batarang Toss
6426. Batman Shooting Arcade
6456. Bats in Your Belfry
5899. Battling Tops Game
6255. Beanbag Buckaneers
7077. Beany and Cecil Ring Toss
7078. Beany and Cecil Skill Ball
6349. Beat the Clock
5900. Bee Bopper Game
5511. Bent Outta Shape
7670. Big Blast
5236. Big Game Hunt
6188. Big Otis - Catapult Game
5901. Big Sneeze Game, The
6458. Big Thumb
6459. Blarney
5903. Block the Clock
7262. Blockhead!
5905. Blowout Game
4519. Bobbin Noggin
4522. Body English
5295. Body Talk
5906. Bop the Beetle
6427. Bops and Robbers
1886. Boston Baked Beans
7679. Bottle Buster Target Game
5439. Bowl-A-Matic
7680. Bozo Ring Toss
7681. Bozo Sling Dart Game
7683. Break-A-Plate Carnival Pitch
5910. Breaking Point
5913. Buck-A-Roo! Game
6428. Bucket Ball
4531. Bucket of Fun
6694. Buckshot!
6695. Bug Out
8042. Bug-A-Boo Game
7023. Bullwinkle Motorized Target Game
7024. Bullwinkle Target and Ring Toss
7025. Bullwinkle, Fli-Hi Target Game
7687. Burke's Law Target Game
6429. Bust 'Em Target Game
2140. Buster Brown Necktie Party
4330. Can-Doo
8048. Cap the Hat
5919. Careful
5918. Careful The Toppling Tower
6447. Cascade
7376. Charades
7375. Charades for Juniors
6541. Cheyenne Target Game
5925. Chip are Down Game
5513. Chutes Away
7641. Clock-A-Word
5930. Cold Feet
6407. Combat Tank Game
6624. Coney Island Penny Pitch
7567. Crazy Car Race
6730. Crow Hunt
6282. Dick Tracy Target Set
6733. Dig, Blue box
6734. Dig, Red box
6735. Dig, Red letters
6736. Dig, White letters
5726. Dodge Ball
7271. Donkey Party Game
5730. Don't Bug Me
7314. Don't Cook Your Goose
7316. Don't Go Overboard
7156. Double or Nothin'
455. Double Snap, (© D. Eckley Hunter)
2562. Down and Out

7389. Dr. Tangle
6221. Dragnet Target Game
4608. Drop in the Bucket
626. Duck Shooting
4610. Dynamite Shack Game
6260. Easy on the Ketchup Game
5948. Egg Race Game
4628. Fang Bang
4634. Feeley Meeley
6299. Felix the Cat Target Game
6408. Fireball XL5, Magnetic Dart game
7712. Firehouse Mouse Game
6764. Five Wise Birds, The
7163. Flap Jack
6467. Flea Circus
8070. Flintstones Break Ball, The
6430. Flintstones Mechanical Shooting
8072. Flintstones Mit-Full
7714. Flintstones Pitch 'N Bowl
7715. Flintstones Sling Dart Game
7716. Flintstones Smash-A-Roo Game
6300. Flintstones Target Set
7720. Flintstones Window
        Whacker Game
4331. Flip-It Jackpot
5739. Flying Nun Flying Maze Game
5740. Frankenstein Horror Target Game
7722. Fred Flintstones Just for Kids Target
5742. Freefall
7723. Frisky Frog
5958. Funny Finger
5658. Gabby Hays Champion Shooting
6262. Giant Barrel of Monkeys
6781. Gnip Gnop
4659. Go Back
5751. Gold Trail
6403. Gone Bananas!
5965. Grand Slam Game
4674. Green Hornet Quick Switch Game
6648. Gunsmoke Target Game
5968. Hands Down
7729. Hands Up Harry
4680. Hangman, Vincent Price on cover
7730. Hanna-Barbera Break-A-Plate
3840. Hats Off Bowling Game
6328. Heads Up
7922. Heckle & Jeckle 3-D Target Game
6796. Hip Flip
7735. Hocus Pocus
5973. Hoopla, The Game of
6203. Hop and Stomp
7738. Hop N' Pop
7739. Hopalong Cassidy Pony
        Express Toss
5466. Hopalong Cassidy Target Practice &
7410. Hopskip and Jump
7171. Hot Potato
6801. Howdy-Doody Beanbag Game
7745. Huckelberry Hound & Yogi Bear
4699. Huckelberry Hound Tiddely Winks
7746. Huckle Chuck
7747. Huckleberry Hound Lids Off
7319. Huff 'N Puff Game
5974. Hungry Henry Game
6802. Hurry Up
2823. I've Got It
6807. Jack Straws
5230. Jumble
3582. Jumbo Ring Toss Game
6477. Jumping DJ Surprise Action Game
7757. Jungle Fun
5879. Jungle Hunt
5982. Junk Yard Game, The
5983. Kaboom Ballon Busting Game
4334. Karate Men Fighting Action Game
5984. Karate Tops
5985. Ker Plunk
7321. Kick Back
3584. Kick Ball
5238. Kikit Skittles
6431. Knock It Off
6204. Knock Off
5990. Knock the Clock
5762. Knock Your Block Off
4733. Kooky Carnival Game
7176. Land of the Giants Shoot & Stick

7323. Last Straw, The
7762. Laurel and Hardy Ring Toss
5992. Leapin' Lizard
2382. Lid's Off, The (by Arthur Dritz)
4749. Limbo Legs
4755. Lolli Plop, Skill Game
7768. Lone Ranger Target Game
5996. Look Out Below Game
7769. Lucky Louie
5997. Lucky Star Gum Ball Game
6432. Magic Shot Shooting Gallery
5998. Magilla Gorilla Bowl and
        Toss Game
6000. Magilla Gorilla Target Barrel
6480. Magnatel
6435. Man from U.N.C.L.E. Target Game
6436. Man from U.N.C.L.E. Target Game
4243. Marble Raceway
6004. Marble-Head Game
7772. Master Spy Target Game
7774. Meatball the Hungry Lion Ball Toss
2639. Merry Game of Spinaroo, The
7090. Mighty Mouse Skill-Roll Game
4176. Mighty Mouse Spin Targets Game
7780. Monkey's Uncle
7327. Moon Blast off
4791. Mosquito
6145. Mr. Brain
6222. Mr. Magoo at the Circus Target
6013. Mushmouse & Punkin Puss Feudin'
6865. Never Say Die
2653. Nobby Sticks
4812. Oh No!
6022. Oh, Nuts! Game
4814. On the Ball
5163. One Arm Bandit
7787. Over the Hill
3966. Over the Top
1820. Pantaloon Target
4417. Par-A-Shoot Game
2262. Peg at My Heart
6268. Perfection
6026. Peter Potamus Target Barrel
6027. Pie Face
5790. Pie in Your Eye Game
2033. Pitch, The Game of
5166. Pitchin' Pal
2331. Play Boy Tiddledy Winks
5471. Pom Pom Game
4850. Pop Yer Top!
6438. Popcorn
7800. Popeye Ball Toss
7647. Popeye Carnival
7802. Popeye Ring Toss
7803. Popeye Sling Dart Game
6031. Poppin Hoppies Game
2037. Popular Game of Tiddley Winks, The
6487. Pop-Za-Ball Target Game
7804. Pot O' Gold
4853. Pow Cannon Game
6894. Pow Wow
7328. Pull the Rug Out Game
6901. Push Over
7329. Put & Take Game
7331. Puzzling Pyramid, The
6223. Quick Draw McGraw
        Moving Target
6032. Quick Shot Game
5526. Ramar of the Jungle
        Blow Gun Game
6037. Rebound
6038. Rebound
6439. Rex Mars Space Target Game
6044. Rock, Paper, Scissors
4228. Rocket Patrol Magnet Target Game
4244. Rocket Satellite Action Game
4877. Roller Coaster
2053. Roly Poly Game, The
8114. Sad Sam The Target-Ball Man
1166. Safety Target
4884. Sandlot Slugger
6489. Scr-unch
7819. Seven-Up Game
5179. Sharpshooter
7822. Silly Sidney Count Shoot Target

6224. Siren Sparkle Space Game
6931. Skatterbug, The Game of
7098. Skill Ball
4907. Skill-It
5183. Skip-A-Cross
4340. Skittle-Bowl
6052. Skully
4909. Slam Back
6053. Slap Happy
6054. Slap Trap Game
6208. Sleep Walker
6491. Slick Shooter Penny Arcade Game
6492. Slip Disc
6493. Smack-A-Roo
6056. Snake's Alive!, The Game of
6235. Snakes in the Grass
465. Snap, (© D. Eckley Hunter)
8121. Snare
4914. Snoopy Vs. the Red Baron
4097. Spear-Em
7826. Spider's Maze
1549. Spillikins
7827. Spy's-A-Poppin
5189. S-S-S-Scat
4938. Steady Eddie
7831. Stingray Target Game
4945. Streach-Out Sam
6165. Super Crow Shoot
7584. Super Target Dart Game
6412. Supercar Target Game
6071. Swacki Game
7038. Swingin' Sam
6619. Tantalizer
7347. Tarzan in the Jungle Target Game
7100. Temple of Fu Manchu
7337. Thing Ding
4979. Think-Thunk
5614. Tiddley-Winks Game
5817. Tie 'N Tangle
6504. Tight Squeeze
7845. Tigrrrr Score-A-Matic Ball Toss
4985. Tilt 'N Roll, Obstacle Puzzle
7338. Tilt Score
6080. Tiltin' Milton Game
8130. Tilty
4986. Time Bomb
6083. Tin Can Alley
6085. Tip It
7848. Tom and Jerry Platter Splatter
7849. Tom and Jerry Target Game
6086. Top Across Game
7851. Top Cat Shoe Toss Game
6087. Top It
7560. Top Me
6088. Top the Top
6275. Topper
6089. Tornado Bowl Game
6090. Toss Across
4991. Trip Hammer
7186. Trip Trap
5623. Tuggy
7339. Tumble Bug
6094. Tumble Bumble
345. Tumble Down Dick
4994. Tussle
7340. Twizzle Game, The
6096. Up 'N Over
4202. Ups and Downs
7341. Voodoo Doll Game
5479. Walt Disney's Davy Crockett Radar
7859. Walt Disney's Donald Duck Ring
7861. Walt Disney's Ludwig Von Drake
7862. Walt Disney's Ludwig Von Drake
7863. Walt Disney's Ludwig Von Drake
7864. Walt Disney's Mickey Mouse Top
5604. Walt Disney's Zorro Beanbag-Darts
6225. Walt Disney's Zorro Target Game
7585. Walt Disney's Zorro Target Game
6441. Wanted Dead or Alive Target Game
5025. Whirl Out Game
7342. Whirly Bird
8202. Whiz Bowl, New Bowling Game
7343. Who You? Game
8164. Whoop!
5209. Wing Ding
5041. Wow Pillow Fight Game for Girls
7875. Yogi Bear Score-A-Matic Ball Toss
7876. Yogi Bear Sling Ring Toss Game

6106. Zig Zag Zoom
5462. Zingo
5829. Zok

Adventure

4465. 4 Alarm
5672. Adventures of Davy Crockett, The
2505. Adventures of Robin Hood
4437. Adventures of Robin Hood, The
8030. Adventures of Sir Lancelot
3746. Adventures of Tom Sawyer and Huck
2813. Al Djemma
1559. Aladdin, or The Wonderful Lamp
3657. Ali Baba
5309. Ali Baba and the Forty Thieves
3249. Alice in Wonderland
3284. Alice in Wonderland Game
3747. Alice in Wonderland, Game of
6656. Annette's Secret Passage Game
7359. Arabian Knights Flying Carpet
6579. Arabian Nights, Game of
2275. Bengalee, The Game of the East
4511. Bermuda Triangle Game
2166. Blue Beard, Game of
3307. Boy Hunter, The
2889. Bring 'Em Back Alive
5911. Bruce Force, Lost in Outer Space
5912. Bruce Force, and the Treasure of
3311. Buccaneers
7684. Buccaneers, A Sea-Faring Game, The
1026. Buccaneers, Game of
1889. Buffalo Bill, The Game of
609. Bugle Horn or Robin Hood, The
4032. Buried Treasure
3611. Buried Treasure, The Game of
3040. California Mine A Million
7692. Captain Gallant
6354. Captain Kid
1895. Captain Kid and His Treasure
3322. Captain Kidd and His Pirate Crew
3323. Captain Kidd Junior, Walking the
1588. Captive Princess, Game of
1030. Captive Princess, The
2820. Captive Princess, The
3764. Cinderella
4108. City of Gold
6717. Claim to Fame
6718. Climb the Mountain
3513. Climbing Mt. Zip
6555. Count of Monte Cristo, The
7512. Cutthroat
5514. Deep Sea Diving Game
7081. Doorways to Adventure
3766. Down the Rabbits Hole with Alice in
3348. El Dorado
7395. Escape to the Casbah
4042. Fighting the Wolf Pack
3212. Four Musketeers, The
1644. Going to the Klondike, The Game of
1077. Gold Hunter, The
1939. Gold Hunters, The
2845. Gold Rush, The
2600. Gulliver's Travels
7750. Jack and the Beanstalk, Adventure
1677. Jack the Giant Killer
2896. Jim Hawkins on Treasure Island, The
4055. Jolly Robbers
5485. Kave Keepers
3380. Kismet, The Game of
1974. Klondike
5579. Klondike
1459. Klondike, Game of
5862. Legend of Camelot
1979. Life Boat Game
1108. Life Savers (4020)
1505. Lion Authors, Game of
5994. Liz Tyler, and the Mystery of the
5995. Liz Tyler, Hollywood Starlet
6825. Lost Gold, Hidden Treasure Game
6826. Lost Treasure
3767. Marooned in the South Seas
3560. Mickey Mouse Cone's Card Game
1255. Moose-Hunt
5521. Mt. Everest
3686. Nuggets The Rush to the Klondike
4237. Oh Wilderness
672. Pearl Divers, The
3428. Pieces of Eight
4842. Pirate & Traveler
4843. Pirate & Traveler
1151. Pirate & Traveler
3430. Pirate and Traveler

3970. Pirate Gold, The Game of
3155. Pirate Ship Game
3802. Pirate Treasure Hunt
6535. Pirateer
8199. Pirates and Plunder
5524. Pirate's Cove
3971. Pirate's Cove & Wild West Rodeo
2330. Pirate's Gold
4190. Pirate's Gold
2829. Pirate's Island
3768. Pirates' Raid
3431. Pirates' Treasure, The
2668. Plunder
2040. Princess in the Tower
2041. Prisoner of Zenda
3440. Prisoner of Zenda, The
7452. Prospecting
8019. Prospectors Pete's Game of Gold
6206. Raiders of the Lost Ark Game
5868. Raise the Titanic
5526. Ramar of the Jungle Blow Gun Game
8007. Ramar of the Jungle, The New Jungle
2688. Rip-Van-Winkle
4073. Robin Hood
6598. Robin Hood
5684. Robin Hood and His Merry Men
2051. Robin Hood, The Game of
3561. Robin Hood's Strong Bowman
1744. Robinson Crusoe
6385. Robinson Crusoe
1323. Robinson Crusoe for Little Boys
1159. Robinson Crusoe, Game of
1158. Robinson Crusoe, Game of, Different
3989. Royal Mounteds, The
1265. Seal Hunting in Alaska
6643. Shanghai Trader
4383. Source of the Nile
5358. Source of the Nile
7581. Span It, Climb the Mountain
4952. Sunken Treasure
6958. Sunken Treasure
6961. Survive!
8013. Tales of Arabian Nights
3701. Thief of Bagdad
3700. Thief of Bagdad, Jr. Edition, The
4980. Three Musketeers
2720. Three Musketeers, The. Three facing
2721. Three Musketeers, The. Deluxe
3763. Tom Sawyer and Huck Finn
2911. Tom Sawyer on the Mississippi
2727. Tom Sawyer, The Game of
2730. Trade Winds
6979. Trade Winds, Caribean Sea Game
3232. Traveling to Wheatsworth Castle
2774. Treasure Hunt
3530. Treasure Hunt
4201. Treasure Hunt
5200. Treasure Hunt
2733. Treasure Island
3770. Treasure Island
4215. Treasure Island
5688. Treasure Island
3000. Treasure Island, Game of
5011. Voyage to the Bottom of the Sea
1533. Wars, Game of
2913. Wild West, Wild East! Bring'em
6214. Wildcatter
5040. World of Micronauts, The

Advertising

4288. Advertizement Game, The
1483. Animals
4213. Astro World Game, Ad game for
5674. Billboard
6304. Brand Image
5059. Bud Vs Bud Light Checkers, Ad
5089. Burger King Championship Checkers
7206. Camel The Game, Ad game for
4560. Chevyland Sweepstakes, Ad game for
5718. Chiclets Gum Village Game, Ad for
1492. Color Casino, Game of
1493. Countries
4583. Cracker Jack Game, Ad game for
8191. Domino's Pizza Delivery Game, Ad
4159. Fast Freight Game (A.P.A.), Ad game
6473. Hawaiian Punch Game, Ad game for
1809. Maud or "Hee Haw", The Game of
4775. McDonald's Game, The
6547. Miller's Outpost Game, The
5319. Money Matters, Manhattan Savings
1136. National Standards

1828. Page Fence, Advertising Premium
7041. Pepsi-Cola Acrosss the U.S.A.!
7054. Polaroid's Party Pack, Ad game for
1805. Snip-Snap
7635. Store. Ad game for shoes
5818. Tootsie Roll Train Game
4162. WABC-TV's Media Careers, Ad
5022. Where's the Beef?, Ad game for

Animals - All

376. (Rabbit) that Lived in the Garden of
5884. 4 Little Pigs
8029. Adventures of Lassie
5692. Adventures with Clifford the Big Red
1001. Aesop
3798. African Hunt
7658. Alligaroo
4293. Alpha Animals Game
2516. Animal Ball Game
5387. Animal Bird Fish Card Game
4106. Animal Bowling
3250. Animal Fair
4484. Animal Fun Game
2517. Animal Grab
4107. Animal Hunting
7652. Animal Kingdom, The
7358. Animal land
6448. Animal Talk Game
3289. Animal Top Game
6564. Animal Trap Game
4485. Animal Twister
1483. Animals
3563. Animals, Game of (Learn Spanish)
7304. Ants in the Pants
7303. Ants in the Pants, Photo cover
6545. Arabian Horse Game, The
4025. Arc Dominoes
4024. Arc Dominoes, Variant cover
2378. Audubon Bird Game, The
801. Avilude, Game of Birds
1572. Baa Baa Black Sheep, Game of
1573. Ba-A Ba-A Black Sheep, Game of
2949. Baby Barn Yard
2950. Barn Yard
2999. Barnyard Swap (© H. C. Parsons)
6254. Barrel of Monkeys
2536. Bear Hunt for the Honey Pot
607. Bear Hunt, Game of
7667. Bears and Bees
901. Beast, Bird or Fish
1017. Beauty and the Beast, The Game of
5693. Berenstein Bears, Hidden Honey Pot
5694. Berenstein Bears, Hide and Seek, The
5695. Berenstein Bears, So Much To Do
980. Bible Animals and Plants
6581. Big Game
5236. Big Game Hunt
1580. Big Game Hunting
4028. Big Hunt, The
3643. Billy Whiskers
4517. Bird Barn
1453. Bird Center Etiquette, A Card Game
5260. Bird Hunt [Cheerios Box Game]
6681. Bird Watcher
1297. Birds
1798. Birds
2238. Birds
1243. Birds of North America
430. Birds, Fact & Fables about
1398. Birds, Game of
3302. Birds, Game of
1486. Birds, Game of, Premium
3749. Black Beauty
7676. Black Beauty, The Game of
3833. Black Birds (255)
5320. Black Cat
6682. Black Cat Game, The
608. Black Cat, Game of
1365. Black Sheep, The, with The Scape
3750. Blue Birds, The
564. Boa Constrictor
6245. Buck Fever
7889. Buck Skin Sam's Pennsylvania Black
1890. Buffalo Hunt
1891. Buffalo Hunt
4231. Bug Game, The
6258. Bug House
2471. Bug, The Old Army Game
6461. Bug's Life, A, Bug Collector King-
889. Bugville Games
3610. Bull Frog
1028. Bull in a China Shop

7368. Bulldog
1790. Bunny Esmond Games, Premium
7266. Bunny Ho
3009. Bunny Hunt, The
3313. Bunny Rabbit Game
6696. Bunny Rabbit Game
4031. Bunny Ring
5390. Busy Bee
5111. Butterflies
6704. Care Bears, Card Game, Which
3906. Cat & Witch
6711. Cat and Mouse
2821. Cat 'n' Mouse
5716. Catch a Chicken Torie
1589. Catching Mice, Game of
431. Cats & Mice
3324. Cats and Dogs
3077. Cats Meow
7344. Chameleon
5113. Chase, A Nature Study Game, The
3001. Cheerios Bird Hunt
3002. Cheerios Hook the Fish
4248. Chicken in Every Pot, A
5924. Chicken Lotto
4563. Chicken Out
7308. Chicken, The Game of
765. Chopped Up Monkey, The
317. Chopped-Up Monkey, The
5696. Clues with Clifford the Big Red Dog
1596. Cock Robin, Game of
5302. Cock-A-Doodle-Doo
4036. Combination Board, Animal &
1906. Comical Farm Yard Game, The
7310. Cootie, Deluxe 6, Contains 6 Cooties
7311. Cootie, Photo cover
7313. Cootie, The Game of
7312. Cootie, The Game of, Pictures 4
3333. Cottontail and Peter
2169. Country Fish Pond
3335. Crow Hunt
6730. Crow Hunt
3336. Crows in the Corn
2171. Cuckoo
1815. Daisy Fox & Geese
5335. Dalmania
7384. Decoy
7950. Dinomite, The Dinosaur Adventure
6737. Dinosaur Island
6417. Dinosaur Survival
7951. Dinosaur World
7286. Dinosaurs
4296. Dinosaurs and Things
4358. Dinosaurs of the Lost World
5354. Dinozoo
2499. Diving Fish
7386. Doctor Quack
3341. Dodging Donkey, The
6213. Dog House Game
3836. Dog Race
3835. Dog Race, Smaller box
2172. Dog Show, The
3765. Dog Sweepstakes
4602. Dolly and Daniel Whale Game
1299. Domestic Animals
1917. Domestic Animals
1494. Donkey
3919. Donkey Party
1247. Donkey Party Game
7271. Donkey Party Game
1046. Donkey Race
3920. Donkey Ring Toss
3665. Doodle-Bug Race
5732. Down on the Farm
3612. Dr. Quack, #52
3613. Dr. Quack, The Game of
1051. Duck and Eggs
7976. Duck Hunter
2565. Duck on the Rock
1052. Duck on the Rock (4136)
1052. Duck on the Rock (4136)
626. Duck Shooting
3346. Duck Shooting
3837. Duck Shooting
2175. Ducks and Drakes, Game of
2917. Electric Bunny Run
7391. Ellsworth Elephant
7606. Endangered Species
6111. Extinction, The Last Game They
627. Falconry
1624. Farmer Jones' Pigs
5120. Feed the Elephant
3670. Feed'n the Kitty

802. Ferrilude or Game of Beasts	3582. Jumbo Ring Toss Game	3879. Peter Rabbit's Race	3006. White Wings
7712. Firehouse Mouse Game	1969. Jumping Frog Game (718)	1520. Pig, Game of	1346. Who Can Mount the Donkey
1063. Fish Pond	2182. Jumping Frog, Game of	580. Pigs and Kittens, Comical Game of	7343. Who You? Game
1064. Fish Pond	3871. Jumping Monkeys	7798. Pigs in a Poke	2100. Wild Animals
1318. Fish Pond	1970. Jungle Animals	777. Pigs in Clover	1314. Wild Animals (Normal Size)
1630. Fish Pond	3010. Jungle Game	6270. Play it Cool	1414. Wild Animals, Game of. Small
2582. Fish Pond	3528. Jungle Hunt	4240. Predator - The Food Chain Card	1777. Wild Animals, Game of
2856. Fish Pond	2825. Jungle Shooting	7068. Predators & Prey	1222. Wild Birds, Game of
3525. Fish Pond	5648. Kangaroo	442. Puss in the Corner	2133. Wild Birds, Game of
4044. Fish Pond	2798. Kangaroo Race	2043. Puss in the Corner	3496. Wild Goose Hunting
6584. Fish Pond	2760. Kennel- Club Card Game	1735. Puss in the Corner, The Game of	5036. Wild Life
948. Fish Pond Game, Improved	5546. Kentucky Jones Horse Auction Game	1736. Pussy and the Three Mice, Game of	2753. Wise Old Goose (4654)
1062. Fish Pond, 10 Fish cover	1972. Kilkenny Cats, The Amusing Game	401. Quack Doctor, Game of	3170. Wolf & Sheep Game
2581. Fish Pond, 10 Fish cover	3586. Kitty Kat Cup Ball	680. Rabbit Hunt, The Game of	3171. Wolf Card Game
1929. Fish Pond, Boy on sturgeon cover	1106. Komical Kats	6595. Race of the Turtles and Hares, The	4018. Wolf Hunt and Race to Saturn
1335. Fish Pond, Game of	4236. Krill, A Whale of a Game	5170. Red Herring	1292. Wonderland Zoo
1626. Fish Pond, Game of	3383. Lame Duck	5171. Red Rover Game, The	8190. Woods and Water
1627. Fish Pond, Game of	649. Leap Frog	2806. Ring-Toss, Animal cover	1216. Zoo Game, The
1628. Fish Pond, Game of	1685. Leap Frog, Game of	7237. Ripley's Believe it or Not, Animals	2111. Zoo, Game of Animals
1629. Fish Pond, The Improved Game of	2848. Let's Fish	3562. Rippon Magic Fishing Game	
2797. Fish Quick	2978. Let's Go Shopping	3692. Rock-A-By Birdies	**Animals - Birds**
633. Fishing	1504. Lion and Tiger	5616. Rrib-Bit, Plastic frogs tokens	495. American Eagle, or Bird Chase, Game
3870. Fishing (by Arthur Dritz) (621)	5520. Lion Hunt	967. Runaway Sheep	5387. Animal Bird Fish Card Game
8189. Fishing Frenzy, The Tournament	3756. Lion Hunt, The	7457. Runaway Zoo	2378. Audubon Bird Game, The
3671. Fishing, For Compliments, by Art	7421. Little Benny	6920. Saddle Up	801. Avilude, Game of Birds
1417. Fitch's Game of Natural History	3118. Little Red Bushy-Tail	7459. Safari	4517. Bird Barn
1336. Five in a Row, Cats on a Fence	3391. Little Red Bushy-Tail	8115. Safari	1453. Bird Center Etiquette, A Card Game
3353. Five Wise Birds, The	3152. Little Red Hen (581-7)	4250. Save the Whales	5260. Bird Hunt, [Cheerios Box Game]
6469. Flipper Flips	7324. Little Stinker Game, Cards as tiles	1366. Scape Goat, The	6681. Bird Watcher
4646. Forest Friends	1116. Lively Frog	4412. Scrambled Squares Ferocious Felines	1297. Birds
4647. Forest Friends	330. Lively Monkey, The	937. Scratch	1798. Birds
1636. Fox & Geese, The New	2635. Lotto, Dressed Animal Cover	6118. Sea World Treasure Key	2238. Birds
1337. Fox & Hounds	3950. Lucky Duck	6119. Sea World, Fish Card Game	1243. Birds of North America
2417. Fox and Cheese	8088. Lucky Fisherman Game	1265. Seal Hunting in Alaska	430. Birds, Fact & Fables about
1068. Fox and Cheese, Game of	7424. MacDonald's Farm Game	2833. Shah-Shah	1398. Birds, Game of
1637. Fox and Geese, Game of. Pearl	7425. MacDonald's Farm Game	7956. Sierra Club Game, The	1486. Birds, Game of, Premium
2176. Fox and Geese, Game of	1120. Magnetic Fish Pond	7642. Silly Safari	3750. Blue Birds, The
2177. Fox and Geese, Game of. No. 2	5303. Magnetic Fish Pond	2194. Singer's Snake Game	5716. Catch a Chicken Torie
8074. Fox and Hound Game, The	1694. Magnetic Fish Pond, The Game of	2468. Sippa Fish	3002. Cheerios Bird Hunt
6773. Fox and Hounds, Game of	5145. Mammoth Hunt	2404. Skit Skat	4248. Chicken in Every Pot, A
574. Fox Chase	6533. Marlin Perkins' Wild Kingdom	7333. Skunk	5924. Chicken Lotto
2309. Frank Buck's Bring 'Em Back Alive	5147. Marlin Perkins' Zoo Park	2154. Sliced Objects, Frog cover	4563. Chicken Out
4649. Frantic Frogs Game, Windup frogs	7427. McDonald's Farm	6055. Smokey the Forest Fire Preventin'	7308. Chicken, The Game of
1070. Freddie the Frog, Game of	7774. Meatball the Hungry Lion Ball Toss	3695. Snake Eyes	1596. Cock Robin, Game of
2972. Frog Frolics	524. Meangerie or Game of Beasts	1749. Snake Game	5302. Cock-A-Doodle-Doo
1638. Frog He would a Wooing Go, Game	2185. Menagerie, Game of	3733. Socko the Monk, The Game of	6730. Crow Hunt
6585. Frog He Would A-Wooing Go, A	1701. Merry Fishing Game	4194. Space Mouse	2171. Cuckoo
2241. Frog Who Would A-Wooing Go, The	438. Merry Foxes	1280. Spider & the Bee, The	1815. Daisy Fox & Geese
1934. Fun at the Zoo: A Game	1124. Merry -Go-Round	2707. Spider and Fly Game	7386. Doctor Quack
4651. Fun on the Farm	1125. Mice and Cheese	8122. Spider and the Fly	1051. Duck and Eggs
4047. Gawara Hunters	1704. Migration, New Game of	6563. Spider's Web	7976. Duck Hunter
3554. Go Fish	4786. Mister Bug Goes to Town	1752. Spider's Web, Game of	2565. Duck on the Rock
5398. Go Fish, King Size	2640. Mister Wiskers	2709. Spot, Game of	1052. Duck on the Rock (4136)
3240. Gold Finch, Bird Game	3242. Monarch	4929. Spots	626. Duck Shooting
308. Goose, The Game of	3243. Monarch. Later Edition	2710. Spotta	2175. Ducks and Drakes, Game of
2181. Goosy Gander, or Who Finds the	2423. Monkey Face	6496. Spring Chicken	627. Falconry
933. Greased Pigs	3956. Monkey Shines	340. Squirming Fish, The	308. Goose, The Game of
5071. Greeny Grasshoppers	8096. Monkey Shines	4931. Squirt	2181. Goosy Gander, or Who Finds the
2148. Hare and Hounds, or Cross-Country	7780. Monkey Tree	584. Steeple Chase	643. Hens and Chickens, Game of
5517. Harpoon, The Real Whale Hunt	1508. Monkey, Premium	1179. Stubborn Pigs, Game of	4234. Humming Bird Game, The
2987. Hens a Hoppin	7326. Monkeys and Coconuts	6195. Super Mario Kart Choco Island	370. Jolly Game of Goose, The
643. Hens and Chickens, Game of	7781. Monkey's Uncle	1844. Tadpole Pool, The	1704. Migration, New Game of
4298. Herd Your Horses!	1255. Moose-Hunt	7251. Tail, The Donkey Game	1387. Our Bird Friends
3935. Here Comes Jumbo	4058. Mother Carey's Ducks	8128. Tally Ho!	1321. Owl and the Pussy Cat, The
6795. Hey Pa, There's a Goat on the Roof	1134. Mounting the Camel in Cairo	1182. Three Bears (4478)	401. Quack Doctor, Game of
3364. Hickety Pickety	8097. Mousey	6274. Three Blind Mice	6496. Spring Chicken
2432. Hold Your Horses	3684. Mr. Doodle's Dog, Junior Edition	5816. Three Chipmunks, Cross Country	1222. Wild Birds, Game of
1662. Home Fish Pond, The	3685. Mr. Doodle's Dog	1183. Three Little Kittens, The	2133. Wild Birds, Game of
1093. Honey Bee Game	4793. Mr. Bug Goes to Town	1184. Three Little Pigs	
1094. Honey Gatherers, The	6860. Mr. Ed	2718. Three Little Pigs	**Animals - Horses**
5262. Hook the Fish, [Cheerios Box Game]	7785. National Velvet Game	4077. Throwing the Bull	6545. Arabian Horse Game, The
5135. Hookey	1712. New and Improved Fish Pond	4008. Tiger Hunt	3749. Black Beauty
7318. Hop Pop Game	1802. New Century Busy Work-Wild Animals	1269. Tiger Hunt, Game of	7676. Black Beauty, The Game of
2894. Hot Dog Race	1341. Nimble Spider. Tokalon Series	6079. Tiger Island, The Game of	4298. Herd Your Horses!
1473. Hounds & Hares	2324. Noah Ark Fishing Game	2724. Tiger Tom, Game of	7173. Johnny on the Pony
4234. Humming Bird Game, The	5158. Noah's Ark	2726. Tip Top Fish Pond	5546. Kentucky Jones Horse Auction Game
1666. Hunt the Hare, Game of	2007. Noah's Ark, The Game of	2405. Tip-Cat	6860. Mr. Ed
2879. Hunter's Shot	960. Noah's Ark, Game of	1761. Toll Gate, Game of	7785. National Velvet Game
892. Hunting Big Game	1140. O' Grady's Goat	3635. Tortoise and the Hare, Game of	6920. Saddle Up
3581. Hunting Game, The	6622. Octopus	8132. Track & Trap	**Animals - Insects**
3031. Hunting in the Jungle	3962. Old Hogan's Goat	7477. Trap-Em	7304. Ants in the Pants
952. Hunting Match	702. Old Hunter and His Game, The	1763. Troublesome Pigs, Game of	7303. Ants in the Pants, Photo cover
1340. Hunting the Rabbit	4238. Onto the Desert	3853. Tumbling Twins, The	7667. Bears and Bees
1667. Hunting the Tiger	1387. Our Bird Friends	2860. Turtle Race	6258. Bug House
1668. Hunting Wild Animals	1368. Our Friends in Fur	5468. Turtles	889. Bugville Games
1670. Improved Game of Fish Pond, The	1321. Owl and the Pussy Cat, The	2088. Uncle Sam's Farm, Game of	5390. Busy Bee
4054. Jig-A-Roomp Frog Shooting	4825. Pass the Pigs	4999. Uncle Wiggily	5111. Butterflies
7173. Johnny on the Pony	2018. Pat and His Pigs, The Game of	5205. Undersea World Game, The	3665. Doodle-Bug Race
2620. Jolly Animal Picnic Game	1149. Peter Rabbit	6986. Undersea World of Jacques Cousteau	5071. Greeny Grasshoppers
370. Jolly Game of Goose, The	5523. Peter Rabbit	3652. Unscramble Animals (Series B)	1093. Honey Bee Game
1967. Jolly Game of Quack, The	3278. Peter Rabbit's Egg-Rolling Game	975. Visit to The Farm	4786. Mister Bug Goes to Town
1102. Jolly Tumblers		8172. Whale Game, The	4793. Mr. Bug Goes to Town

Animals - Reptiles (continued)

1341. Nimble Spider. Tokalon Series
1280. Spider & the Bee, The
8122. Spider and the Fly
6563. Spider's Web
1752. Spider's Web, Game of

Animals - Reptiles

564. Boa Constrictor
7344. Chameleon
7950. Dinomite, The Dinosaur Adventure
6737. Dinosaur Island
6417. Dinosaur Survival
7951. Dinosaur World
7286. Dinosaurs
4296. Dinosaurs and Things
4358. Dinosaurs of the Lost World
5354. Dinozoo
6111. Extinction, The Last Game They
2194. Singer's Snake Game
1749. Snake Game

Animals - Sea

5387. Animal Bird Fish Card Game
3003. Cheerios Hook the Fish
2169. Country Fish Pond
2499. Diving Fish
4602. Dolly and Daniel Whale Game
1063. Fish Pond
1064. Fish Pond
1318. Fish Pond
1630. Fish Pond
2582. Fish Pond
2856. Fish Pond
3525. Fish Pond
4044. Fish Pond
6584. Fish Pond
948. Fish Pond Game, Improved
1062. Fish Pond, 10 fish cover
2581. Fish Pond, 10 Fish cover
1929. Fish Pond, Boy on sturgeon cover
754. Fish Pond, Early wooden boxed set
1335. Fish Pond, Game of
1626. Fish Pond, Game of
1627. Fish Pond, Game of
1628. Fish Pond, Game of
1629. Fish Pond, The Improved Game of
633. Fishing
8189. Fishing Frenzy, The Tournament
6469. Flipper Flips
4649. Frantic Frogs Game, Windup frogs
1070. Freddie the Frog, Game of
1638. Frog He would a Wooing Go, Game
6585. Frog He Would A-Wooing Go, A
2241. Frog Who Would A-Wooing Go, The
5398. Go Fish, King Size
5517. Harpoon, The Real Whale Hunt
1662. Home Fish Pond, The
5262. Hook the Fish, [Cheerios Box Game]
5135. Hookey
1670. Improved Game of Fish Pond, The
1969. Jumping Frog Game (718)
2182. Jumping Frog, Game of
4236. Krill, A Whale of a Game
649. Leap Frog
1685. Leap Frog, Game of
2848. Let's Fish
1116. Lively Frog
8088. Lucky Fisherman Game
1120. Magnetic Fish Pond
5303. Magnetic Fish Pond
1694. Magnetic Fish Pond, The Game of
1701. Merry Fishing Game
1712. New and Improved Fish Pond
2324. Noah Ark Fishing Game
6622. Octopus
5170. Red Herring
3562. Rippon Magic Fishing Game
5616. Rrib-Bit, Plastic frogs tokens
4250. Save the Whales
6118. Sea World Treasure Key
6119. Sea World, Fish Card Game
2468. Sippa Fish
2154. Sliced Objects, Frog cover
340. Squirming Fish, The
1844. Tadpole Pool, The
2726. Tip Top FishPond
5468. Turtles
5205. Undersea World Game, The
6986. Undersea World of Jacques Cousteau
8172. Whale Game, The

Architecture

6228. Building Boom
2788. Building Fun, # 416
4030. Bungalow Building
6462. Cathedral, Plastic Buildings
4039. Construction
7382. Cross Roads
4694. Hotels
2397. Kastle Kwoits
6818. Let's Furnish a House
4762. Lucky Town
1230. Mountain Building
5703. New Town
1451. Philadelphia Buildings, The Game
4856. Prize Property
4855. Prize Property, 1st edition
3723. Skyscraper
3457. SkyScraper Game
4930. Square Mile

Art

7284. American Art Quiz Card Game
4428. Art Game, The
1548. Art History
427. Artists
1860. Artists
726. Artists, Game of
1396. Artists, Game of
1859. Artists, Life's Game of
2434. Damp Deck
1300. Famous Paintings
1926. Favorite Art, Game of
2578. Fine Arts
2146. Gems of Art, with Art Sale; Display
6113. In the Picture
6834. Masterpiece, The Art Auction Game
6011. Mr. Rembrandt
2325. Old Maid, by Vernon Grant
782. Painters
6237. Peter Max Chess Game
3219. Privilege
2049. Rembrandt's Playing Cards
7510. Treasures of the Smithsonian

Baseball (See Sports - Baseball)

Basketball (See Sports - Basketball)

Bicycling (See Sports - Bicycling)

Birds (See Animals - Birds)

Boating (See Sports - Sea)

Boxing (See Sports - Boxing)

Car Racing (See Sports - Car Racing)

Careers (See Occupations)

Cartoons (See TV-Cartoons)

Chance (See Gambling - Chance)

Circus

2388. Action Rolling Circus
2520. At the Circus
1869. Barnum's Greatest Show on Earth
3300. Bell Merry Go Round
3547. Bowling Bozo
6352. Bozo in Circus-Land
5908. Bozo Pop-Outs Game
7680. Bozo Ring Toss
7681. Bozo Sling Dart Game
7682. Bozo the Clown Circus Game
5909. Bozo the TV Lotto
6692. Bozo The World's Most Famous Clown
2546. Bradley's Big Top Game
2756. Bunnie's Circus
2548. Carnival
3226. Carnival, The
1902. Circus
1594. Circus Clown, Game of
1037. Circus Game

2392. Circus Lotto
1491. Circus, Game of
8054. Clown Capers
8055. Clown Checkers
4034. Clown Toss
2969. Clown Twins
2213. Comical Tivoli Game
6624. Coney Island Penny Pitch
3869. Coney Island Playland Park
7378. Coney Island, The Game of
5117. Confetti the Clown
1604. Day at the Circus
3864. Doo Dad Circus
1918. Dreamland, Wonder Resort Game
4185. Emit Kelly's Circus Game
2306. Emmett Kelly's Circus Game
1640. Fun at the Circus, Game of
3644. Greatest Show on Earth, The
709. Harlequin Circle
1657. Harlequin, The Game of the
1090. Hippodrome
1320. Hippodrome, The
7742. Hot Diggity Dog
5678. Howdy Doody's 3-Ring Circus
2621. Jolly Clown Whoopee Game (4001)
1467. Jolly Faces Game, The
2321. Ko-Ko the Clown
6816. Larry Harmon's Bozo
1992. Menagerie
4780. Merry Circus Game
1123. Merry Go Round
1253. Merry Go-Round, The
2898. Merry Merry Go Round
1994. Merry-Go-Round
5150. Merry-Go-Round
2418. Midway Ring-Over
2657. On the Midway
1820. Pantaloon Target
2665. Peck's Bad Boy with the Circus
6904. Reddy-Clown 3-ring Circus Game
5172. Ring Master
8111. Rodeo, The Wild West Game
4899. Shenanigans, Carnival of Fun Game
8118. Silly Carnival
4007. Three Ring Circus/Steeplechase
686. Tight Rope Dancing
685. Tight-Rope, Game of
3474. Tom Mix Circus Game
1770. Walking the Tight Rope, Game of
3062. Whiffle Circus

Circus - Clowns

3547. Bowling Bozo
6352. Bozo in Circus-Land
5908. Bozo Pop-Outs Game
7680. Bozo Ring Toss
7681. Bozo Sling Dart Game
7682. Bozo the Clown Circus Game
5909. Bozo the TV Lotto
6692. Bozo The World's Most Famous Clown
1595. Circus Clown, Game of
8054. Clown Capers
8055. Clown Checkers
4034. Clown Toss
2969. Clown Twins
5117. Confetti the Clown
1657. Harlequin, The Game of the
1467. Jolly Faces Game, The
2321. Ko-Ko the Clown
6816. Larry Harmon's Bozo
2898. Merry Merry Go Round
6904. Reddy-Clown 3-ring Circus Game

Cities & Towns

4179. All About (Cities) different city issues
4180. All About Cumberland, Maryland
4181. All About Minneapolis
6155. Beverly Hills
7637. Beverly Hills
4446. Big Apple
5330. Boston Game, The
5653. Boston Scene
7111. Brightonopoly
5487. Capital Edition
5654. Chicago Scene
5837. Discover Iowa
5308. Encounter at Hanover
7939. Lewisboro, N.Y., The Game of
5271. Millionare, Danbury Ct
5665. Minneapolis-St. Paul Scene

5880. New Canaan
5251. New York City's Great Blizzard
7220. New York Game
5655. New York Scene
5704. Newtown
5646. Penn-State-O-Poly
7818. See New York "Round the Town Game"
5671. So You Think You Know Maine

Classic

378. American Jack Straws
2514. Ancient Game of China
3505. Ancient Game of the Mandarins
6658. Arkansas Bluff
4026. Backgammon and Checkers
380. Backgammon, Japanese
786. Bezique
3574. Bingo
3301. Bingo or Beano
2540. Bingo, 25 Card Set
5512. British Square
3310. Broadway, The Popular Game of
420. Card Dominoes
4122. Challenge Bridge, flat box edition
4552. Charles Goren's Advanced Bridge for
4553. Charles Goren's Beginner's Bridge
4554. Charles Goren's Bridge for One
4555. Charles Goren's Bridge for Two
2391. Checkers. Avion
613. Checkers, Back-Gammon and Tousel
567. Checquers and the Game of Mill Morris
3752. Chess & Checkers
7377. Chess for Juniors
1333. Chessindia
2141. Chessindia
2552. Chinamen
6582. Chinese Checkers
3325. Chinese Checkers, Wooden board
3911. Chinese Marble Checkers
2553. Chinese Star Checkers
2554. Chinese Star Checkers
4570. Chutes and Ladders, Children at slide
4571. Chutes and Ladders, Red box
1042. Crokinole
624. Croquet
775. Croquet (© S. F. Cramer)
2874. Donkey Party
3919. Donkey Party
1615. Donkey Party Game, The
5243. Flintstones 3-D Chess, The
7288. Fourhanded Checkers
6230. Ginasta
6327. Go
6326. Go, 1st. Lowe Edition
1446. Halma, 1st. Edition
1447. Halma, 2nd. Edition
1947. Halma, 3rd. Edition
8075. Hearts
3527. Hop Ching Checker Game
1370. India Bombay
2857. India Bombay
1095. India, Game of
1673. India, Game of
6586. India, Game of
3941. India, The Game of
3942. India, The Game of
3617. Indian Backgammon
4050. Indoor Horse Shoe
1101. Jack Straws
2619. Jack Straws
4053. Jack Straws
2616. Jack Straws, Magnetic
1965. Jack Straws, New Edition
2617. Jack Straws, Royal (4095)
2618. Jack Straws, Senior (4418)
1966. Jack Straws, The Game of, (Brownies
5323. Jackpot, The Las Vegas Game
3370. Japanola
7758. Junior Bingo-Matic
5140. King Tut's Game
3842. Krokay
6284. Las Vegas Junket
1460. Magnetic Jack Straws
367. Merry Game of Old Maid, The. Hand
657. Game of Old Maid, The
1702. Merry Game of Old Maid, The. Elite
6331. Mikado, Game of Go
6192. Mini Sorry!
895. New Game of Tiddledy Winks, Earliest

7786. Nine Men's Morris
1718. Old Fashioned Jack Straws
440. Old Maid
1514. Old Maid Premium
3621. Old Maid. #50
3964. Old Maid
4064. Old Maid
5077. Old Maid
6592. Old Maid
7235. Old Maid
3620. Old Maid Thrift Game
2325. Old Maid, by Vernon Grant
666. Old Maid, Game of
1722. Old Maid, Game of
2152. Old Maid, Game of
2326. Old Maid, Nursery Rhymes & Fairy
2011. Old Maid, The Board Game
1721. Old Maid, The Game of
3963. Old Maid, The Game of
667. Old Maid, The New
544. Old Pampheezle and His Comical
588. Old Pamphezzle and His
     Comical Friends
5615. Orient, patterned after Go
4188. Pachisi
769. Parcheesi
3687. Parcheesi
770. Parcheesi (© John Hamilton)
7439. Parcheesi Jr. Edition
7440. Parcheesi, Brown Board
     and Implement
7441. Parcheesi, Gold on blue
     implement box
7442. Parcheesi, Gold Seal Edition
7443. Parcheesi, Popular edition, blue box
1726. [Parshesi] in Arabic
6237. Peter Max Chess Game
1822. Pin the Tail on the Donkey,
     Black cover
4096. Pin-Nock'l
369. Pocket Chess-Board, The
3438. Pollyanna
6890. Pollyanna, Multi colored letters
3437. Pollyanna, Blue board
     & implement box
6891. Pollyanna, Dixie
2035. Pollyanna, Red & Gold
     letters board &
2036. Pollyanna, The Glad Game
2037. Popular Game of Tiddley Winks, The
2038. Popular Jack-Straws
5525. Poucho Checkers
4071. Ride a Cock Horse and Go Bang
2050. Ring the Pin
3627. Ring Toss
4072. Ring Toss
6597. Ring Toss
6044. Rock, Paper, Scissors
8112. Ropes and Ladders
3450. Royal Game of India
1165. Rummie
3990. Rummy Card
8113. Rummy Card Game
3255. San Loo, Chinese Checkers
6925. Senet
6620. Senet Game
7332. Shake Bingo
4340. Skittle-Bowl
3629. Slap Jack
1172. Snap
1527. Snap
6937. Snap Card Game
8119. Snap Card Game, #2995
8120. Snap Card Game, #4904
2065. Snap, Game of.
     (Blue on white cover)
2195. Snap, Game of
3994. Snap, Game of
1750. Snap, Game of, Punch & Judy Series
1461. Snap, The Game
2067. Snap, The Game of. Nickel Edition
2427. Snap, The Game of
3995. Snap, The Game of
6939. Sorry, The Great Game, three-quarter
6940. Sorry, The Great Game, Dark green
6941. Sorry, The Great Game, Overhead
6942. Sorry, The Great Game, 1st edition
6943. Sorry, The Great Game, 1st edition
2449. Star Checkers, The Original
3037. Tic Tac Toe
7473. Tic Tac Toe Times 10
2077. Tiddledy Winks

4078. Tiddledy Winks
4112. Tiddledy Winks
3470. Tiddledy Winks Game, Fairie's
3471. Tiddledy Winks, Bowling, Ten Pins
3529. Tiddledy Winks, Jumbo
2348. Tiddley Winks
2722. Tiddley Winks
4079. Tiddley Winks
2347. Tiddley Winks, latter edition
2349. Tiddly Winks
3511. Tidley Winks
3702. Tidley Winks
6968. Tit Tat Toe
3472. Tit Tat Toe, Game of
2282. Tripoley © Fireside Games)
2239. U. S. Card Dominoes
2355. U. S. Rummy
7482. Ur
6621. Ur Game

Clowns (See Circus - Clowns)

Combination

2500. 12 Game Combination Board
3887. 16 Ready to Play Games
4037. 25 Game Combination Boards, Indian
904. 25 New Top Games: Cuban
     Battle Spin;
3146. 32 Games
3888. 44 Games
6577. 49ers-Round Up- Odds & Ends
3892. 8 Games in One, (Racing Themes)
999. ADT Messenger, Robinson Crusoe &
601. Ambuscade, Bounce, & Constellation
1561. Ambuscade, Bounce, and
     Constellation
6580. Arabian Nights-Triple Play-7-in One
905. Archarena Combination Boards
3605. Authors & Spin-A-Top
4026. Backgammon and Checkers
3571. Bag of Fun, A
2531. Baseball & Checkers
6669. Baseball, Football & Checkers
1582. Bobbing-Tribang-Robbing the Miller
611. Cats & Mice; Gantlope; Lost Diamond
4035. Combination Board Air & Road
     Races
4036. Combination Board, Animal
     & Spider
432. Combinaue
1482. Combinola, Combination Board,
     Large
4038. Combos, Auto, Army & Navy, Hunt
1043. Crown Cards, Inc.: Aviation; Baffle;
5122. Five Famous Favorites
906. Flag Travelette
7351. Flintstone Game Alley
2395. Flip It, Auto Race & Transcontinental
8073. Four Complete Games
7273. Frontier Marshall & Star of India
2586. Game Combination, U. S. Mail &
7399. Game Galore
324. Go-Bang, Japanese Verandah Game
635. Go-Bang, Rusian Tivoli, Fox & Geese
4049. India Home and Checkers
1096. Interchangable Combination Circus
6589. Jack Sprat-Puzzle Solitaire-Merelles
647. John Gilpin, Rainbow Backgammon
2398. Let's Play Games, Golf, Polo,
     Boots &
3947. Library of Games, (Bookshelf of 6
653. Life's Mishaps, Domino Rex and
2280. Lucky Nine, Word Bingo, Radio Quiz
1277. Marveldex Game Board
1703. Messenger Boy and Checkers
1705. Mill & Checkers
2400. My Word, Horserace
6193. Nintendo Board game
3619. Old Maid & Spin-A-Top
3622. Old Maid-Authors-Dr. Quack,
     Games of
3968. Partys and Puzzles
963. Perfection Game Board
493. Portfolio of Social Games
1164. Rummie, with: Argentina; Baffles;
2695. Senior Combination Board
2491. SportMaster, include: Backgammon
4074. Star Flight, Combo, Marketing &
1181. Telegraph Game, Bradley's (4638)
4005. Ten Playing Cards
1188. Tip-Top Four Game Combination
1357. Trail, Chase, Dogon, Red Heads

3158. Treasure Chest of Games
8133. Treasure Kit Of Card Games
1195. Twelve Game Combination Board
1764. Two Game Combination, India &
1196. Two Game Combination,
     Steeple Chase
1197. Two Game Combination,
     U.S. Mail and
2410. Whoopee, combination game board

Comics

2502. Abbie An' Slatts, The Game of
7656. Adventures of Popeye Game
2507. Adventures of the Nebbs
7355. Alfred's Other Game
3894. All Star Comics
3719. Alley Oop, Boxed Set
3603. Alley Oop, Can Edition
2515. Andy Gump, His Game
6657. Annie
8036. Archie Game, The
6449. Archies Card Game
5710. Archie's Fun Game
2530. Barney Google and Spark Plug Game
4510. Beetle Bailey, The Old Army Game
6157. Beetle Bailey's Fulough
6156. Beetle Bailey's Hilarious New Army
6158. Blondie and Dagwoods Race for the
6683. Blondie Game, The
3883. Blondie Goes to Leisureland,
     Premium
3903. Blondie Playing Card
5904. Blondie, Sunday Funnies Board Game
7677. Blondie, The Hurry Scurry Game
2931. Bringing Up Father Game
1888. Brownies and Other Queer Folk, The
1330. Brownies, Game of
2296. Buck Rogers in the 25th Century
2140. Buster Brown Necktie Party
5916. Can You Catch It Charlie Brown?
7989. Cap'n Crunch Island
     Adventure Game
6238. Captain Action Card Game, Premium
4542. Captain and the Kids
7596. Casper Electronic Adventure Game
4549. Casper the Friendly Ghost Game
7307. Casper, The Friendly Ghost, Glow in
5066. Casper's Picture Lotto
6713. Charlie Brown's All Star Baseball
2551. Chester Gump Game
2550. Chester Gump Game, In The City of
4576. Comic Card Game
6731. Curious George Game, The
7549. Dennis the Menace Game
7385. Dick Tracy
3914. Dick Tracy Card
3915. Dick Tracy Card. Variant cover
5940. Dick Tracy Crime Stopper
3916. Dick Tracy Detective
2892. Dick Tracy Detective Game
7949. Dick Tracy Game, The
5724. Dick Tracy Marble Maze
6282. Dick Tracy Target Set
5941. Dick Tracy, A Sunday Funnies Game
3917. Dick Tracy, Super Detective. Variant
     cover
6544. Doonsbury Game, The
5442. Electric Commin' Round the
     Mountain
6514. ElfQuest Boardgame, The
2570. Ella Cinders
3668. Elsie and Her Family
3667. Elsie and Her Family, Jr. Edition
7392. Elsie Game, The
4636. Felix the Cat
5068. Felix the Cat Down on the Farm
     Game
7991. Felix the Cat Rummy
6299. Felix the Cat Target Game
5854. Flash Gordon Game
2144. Foxy Grandpa an Up to Date Game
1816. Foxy Grandpa at the World's Fair
2145. Foxy Grandpa Hat Party
2237. Foxy Grandpa's Christmas Tree
2957. Funnies
3041. Funny Fellers
6779. Garfield
4445. Garfield Card Game
2587. Gasoline Alley, A Game of Walt &
4669. Good Ol' Charlie Brown Game
4670. Gordo and Pepito
5629. Great Shakes, Charlie Brown

2601. Gumps at the Seashore, The
2603. Happy Hooligan Game
1949. Happy-Hoppers
2605. Harold Teen Game, Up the Ladder
2607. Harold Teen, A Game
2606. Harold Teen, A Game, Smaller box
7993. Heathcliff, Munch Out
2315. Hi-Way Henery
1094. Hurdle Race
1966. Jack Straws, The Game of, (Brownies
5454. Jim Prentice-Electric Comin' Round
6370. Joe Palooka Boxing Game
5651. Jolly Green Giant Card Game
4725. Kigmy Game by Al Capp
3552. Kuti-Kuts (Cutie cuts): A Comic
6819. Li'l Abner Game, The
4748. Li'l Abner His Game
2628. Li'l Abner, Game of
4750. Little Lulu Adventure Game
8086. Little Lulu Game, The
1113. Little Nemo
7422. Little Orphan Annie
2630. Little Orphan Annie Game
2631. Little Orphan Annie Game
3949. Little Orphan Annie Rummy Cards
2632. Little Orphan Annie Travel Game
3273. Little Orphan Annie's Treasure Hunt
6521. Lone Wolf & Cub Game
5370. Mad, Spy Vs Spy Card Game
6406. Mad's Spy vs. Spy Combat
     Card Game
4764. Mad's Spy vs Spy
3042. Mama's Darlings
6832. Mask, The
1809. Maud or "Hee Haw", The Game of
2642. Moon Mullens Game, The
2643. Moon Mullins Automobile Race
2644. Moon Mullins Game
2645. Moon Mullins Game
2646. Moon Mullins Gets the
     Run-A-Round
2650. Nancy & Sluggo Game
2651. Nebbs, Game of the
2652. Nebbs, Game of the. Deluxe larger
3960. Og, Son of Fire
3961. Oh Blondie
3044. Oh Min
5787. Olive Oyl-I'll Catch My Popeye Game
2658. Orphan Annie to the Rescue
3274. Orphan Annie, Treasure Isle of Health
5078. Ozark Ike's Complete 3 Game Set
3646. Pals Kartoon Cards
7446. Peanuts
2424. Peg and Midget
4851. Popeye
6893. Popeye
3983. Pop-eye
6029. Popeye and His Pals
7800. Popeye Ball Toss
5412. Popeye Card Game
6892. Popeye Card game, based on the
     Arcade
7647. Popeye Carnival
5079. Popeye Games
2901. Popeye in Plunderland
5793. Popeye is the Strongest Man in the
7801. Popeye Magnetic Fishing game
3592. Popeye Pipe Toss Game
3593. Popeye Ring Toss
7802. Popeye Ring Toss
6030. Popeye Skooz-It Game
5080. Popeye Sliding Board & Ladders
7803. Popeye Sling Dart Game
2902. Popeye the Sailor Shipwreck Game
2903. Popeye to the Rescue
3978. Popeye, Party
3979. Popeye, Red Box Edition
3980. Pop-eye, Variant cover
3981. Pop-eye, Variant cover
3982. Pop-eye, Variant cover
5081. Popeye's 3 Game Set
5082. Popeye's Good Time &
     "Blow Me Down"
6160. Popeye's Old Maid
8101. Popeyes Ship Ahoy! Game
8102. Popeye's Spinach Hunt Game
8103. Popeye's Treasure Map Game
3647. Poppin' Popeye
3845. Prince Valiant
7027. Prince Valiant Cross
     Bow Pistol Game
1734. Pug and Poodle

4864. Raggedy Ann
2683. Raggedy Ann, Game of
6606. Ranger Rick and the Great Forest Fire
3988. Red Ryder Target, The
5084. Red Ryder's 3 Game Set
3691. Reg 'Lar Fellers Bowling Game
2686. Reg'lar Fellers
6041. Rex Morgan M. D. Sunday Funnies
1739. Rhymes & Chimes
4870. Richie Rich
7097. Richie Rich Big Money Game
4883. Sammy, the White House Mouse
3821. Shadow, The
2700. Skeezix
2697. Skeezix and the Airmail
2698. Skeezix Game, The
2699. Skeezix Visits Nina
2338. Skippy
2701. Skippy, Game of
3510. Smiling Jack's Victory Bombers
2702. Smitty Game
2703. Smitty Speed Boat Race Game
1805. Snip-Snap
7466. Snoopy
4914. Snoopy Vs. the Red Baron
4916. Snoopy Come Home Game
4917. Snoopy's Doghouse Game
4918. Snuffy Smith Time's a Wastin' Game
6161. Snuffy Smith's Hootin Holler Bug
2199. Social Brownies, The Game Of
6388. Steve Canyon
7468. Straight Arrow
3467. Tarzan
6503. Tarzan Comic Game
7347. Tarzan in the Jungle Target Game
3164. Tarzan of the Apes
2909. Tarzan Rescue
2910. Tarzan Treasure Island
7135. Teenage Mutant Ninga Turtles Pizza
6076. Terry and the Pirates
4006. Terry and the Pirates, The Game of
7843. Terrytoons Hide N' Seek Game
5811. Thimble Theatre Game Staring Wimpy
5812. Thimble Theatre Game, Olive Oil
7102. Tick, The
2728. Toonerville Trolley Game
6124. Toxic Crusaders Battle for Tromaville
1192. Toy Town Target with Foxy Grandpa
4162. WABC-TV's Media Careers, Ad Game
2745. Walt & Skeezix
5824. Wimpy, Where are My Hamburgers?
2750. Winnie Winkle, Game of
2751. Winnie Winkle, Glider Race Game

Communications

6649. 10-Four, Good Buddy, CB Radio Game
994. A.D.T. Messenger Boy
995. A.D.T. Messenger Boy
2508. Air Mail, Game of
2511. Airmail
563. Atlantic Telegraph
3303. Boake Carter's Game Star Reporter
1612. District Messenger Boy or Merit
1611. District Messenger Boy, Game of
1613. District Telegraph Boy
309. Errand Boy, The
1620. Errand Boy, The
8182. Eyewitness News Game
2373. Five Star Final
2583. Five Star Final
2472. Flash!-News
7397. Flash, The Press Photographer Game
2586. Game Combination, U. S. Mail &
1686. Letter Carrier, The
1980. Limited Mail and Express, The
3951. Mail Coach
3952. Mail Must Fly, Round Up, The
1121. Mail, Express or Accommodations
2186. Messenger Boy, Game of
3227. National Radio Game, The
5334. NBC-TV News Game w/Chet Huntley
959. Newsboy, Game of
7509. Newspaper Game, The
3534. Original Professor Quiz Radio Game
2759. Original Radio Game, The
2021. Penny Post, The Game of
2980. Play Post Office

2425. Play Radio Game
3760. Pony Express, The
7055. Pony Express, The Game of
4067. Post Office
5794. Post Office Game
1322. Postal Delivery Boys
2799. Postmaster
2682. Radio
3068. Radio
4069. Radio
4070. Radio
3145. Radio Amateur Hour, The
2490. Radio Ball
3231. Radio Flash
3601. Radio Flash, The Game of
2681. Radio Game
3446. Radio Game
2336. Radio Game for Little Folks
2680. Radio Game, Radio & knobs cover
2807. Radio Mike
2880. Radio Questionnaire
3542. Radio Questionnaire
3543. Radio Quiz, The
3689. Radio Ramble
3541. Radio, Game of
2484. Radio, The Game of
3448. Real Radio Game
6128. Satellite
6923. Scoop!, The Game, Publish Your Own
3452. Scoop, The Game of
6215. Scrambled Headlines
3156. Sparks-Code Game
6947. Star Reporter, Blue-grey background
6948. Star Reporter, Red and Grey box
6949. Star Reporter, Three red star cover
4003. Telegrams, Game of
1758. Telegraph Boy, Game of the
5191. Telephone Game, The
2351. Toonin Radio Game
2080. Toy-Town Telegraph Office
4393. TV Wars
1198. Uncle Sam's Mail
2736. Uncle Sam's Mail
1766. Uncle Sam's Mail, Game of
6614. Uniquely New Jersey, Ad Game for
3484. United States Air Mail, The
5822. War of the Networks

Detective

5663. 221-B Baker Street-The Master
6347. 77 Sunset Strip
6219. Badge 714 Dragnet
4497. Baretta, The Street Detective Game
4556. Charlie's Angels Game, Cheryl on cover
4557. Charlie's Angels Game, Farrah on
4574. Columbo Detective Game
1914. Detective Game
945. Detective, Game of
7699. Detectives Game, The
3916. Dick Tracy Detective
2892. Dick Tracy Detective Game
7704. Dragnet, The Game of
2599. Great Charlie Chan Detective Mystery
5975. I Spy Game
7954. Inspector Gadget Detective Kit Game
4731. Kojak, The Stake Out Detective Game
4768. Man Hunt
7040. Miami Vice
7180. Mod Squad Game, The
6863. Nancy Drew Mystery Game, The
6377. Peter Gunn Detective Game
7797. Philip Marlowe Detective Game
5180. Sherlock Holmes Game, The
6599. Sherlock Holmes, The Game of Great
2059. Sherlock Holmes
2060. Sherlock Homes. Variant box cover
2061. Sherlock Homes. Variant box cover
7278. Special Detective ane Speedwat
4934. Starsky and Hutch Detective Game
6390. Surfside 6
5666. Trivial Detective Game
5204. Undercover

Dinosaurs (See Animals - Reptiles)

Disney

5587. 20,000 Leagues Under the Sea
6142. 20,000 Leagues Under the Sea

7222. Bambi
7221. Bambi, Vol. 4, Bookcase
8061. Davy Crockett Indian Scout Game
8063. Disney Checkers
4593. Disney Presents Follow that Mouse
5943. Disney Score Around Game
7224. Disneyland Monorail Card Game
6740. Disneyland Monorail Game
6739. Disneyland Monorail Game, Blue box
6741. Disneyland Pirates of the Caribbean
6742. Disneyland Riverboat Game
6738. Disneyland, It's a Small World Game
4594. Disney's All Aboard Game
4595. Disney's Chip & Dale Rescue Rangers
4596. Disney's Darkwing Duck Game
4597. Disney's Duck Tales Game
4598. Disney's Tale Spin Game
4599. Disney's The Hunchback of Notre Dame
5396. Donald Duck
8064. Donald Duck
5592. Donald Duck Beanbag Game
6159. Donald Duck Tiddley Winx
7225. Donald Duck, Vol. 1, Bookcase
3343. Donald Duck's Party for Young Kinds
6745. Donald Duck's Party Game
3344. Dopey Bean Bag
3925. Ferdinand the Bull
3924. Ferdinand the Bull in the Arena, The
3350. Ferdinand's Chinese Checkers with the
8083. Huey, Dewey, & Louie, Ice Cream Cone
5403. Jungle Book Card Game
4751. Little Mermaid
3392. Little Red Riding Hood, The Three
7229. Ludwig Von Drake
8089. Mary Poppins Game
5408. Mickey Mouse
7232. Mickey Mouse
7233. Mickey Mouse
5594. Mickey Mouse Basketball
3180. Mickey Mouse Bean Bag Game
3181. Mickey Mouse Circus Game
8092. Mickey Mouse Club Game in
3182. Mickey Mouse Coming Home Game
3560. Mickey Mouse Cone's Card Game
7230. Mickey Mouse Funny Rummy
6836. Mickey Mouse Game Box
3183. Mickey Mouse Hoop-La Game
3521. Mickey Mouse Horseshoes
3953. Mickey Mouse Old Maid Cards
3954. Mickey Mouse Old Maid Cards
6837. Mickey Mouse Picture Matching Game
3184. Mickey Mouse Rollem Bowling Game
3185. Mickey Mouse Scatterball Game
3186. Mickey Mouse Soldier Set Bowling
4781. Mickey Mouse, Follow the Leader
7231. Mickey Mouse, Vol. 3, Bookcase
7236. Pinoccio, Vol. 2, Bookcase
3973. Pitfalls, A Pinocchio Marble, Walt
3984. Put the Tail on Ferdinand the Bull
6905. Rescuers, The
6934. Sleeping Beauty Game, Walt Disney
6935. Sleeping Beauty Game, Walt Disney
2704. Snow White and the Seven Dwarfs, The
7245. Snow White and the Seven Dwarfs, Vol
7253. Three Little Pigs, The
7252. Three Little Pigs, The, Vol. 5, Bookcase
3102. Three LittlePigs, The Game of The
5007. Visit to Walt Disney World, The
7571. Walt Disney's Zorro Slate Game
5601. Walt Disney Character Quick or Be
5533. Walt Disney Character, My First Game
8138. Walt Disney One Hundred and One
5424. Walt Disney Presents Jungle Book
6989. Walt Disney Presents Peter Pan Game
6990. Walt Disney Presents Pinoccho Game
2406. Walt Disney Snow White and the Seven
8139. Walt Disney Tiddly Winks
6276. Walt Disney World 20,000 Leagues
8140. Walt Disney World Game
6277. Walt Disney World Haunted Mansion

6991. Walt Disney, Babes in Toyland
7254. Walt Disney, Catch the Mouse
7255. Walt Disney, Catch the Mouse
8141. Walt Disney's 101 Dalmations Game
6992. Walt Disney's Adventureland Game
6993. Walt Disney's Babes in Toyland
8142. Walt Disney's Babes in Toyland Game
6994. Walt Disney's Cinderella
7857. Walt Disney's Cinderella Card Game
5602. Walt Disney's Davy Crockett
5479. Walt Disney's Davy Crockett Radar
8143. Walt Disney's Disneyland
7858. Walt Disney's Disneyland Game
6148. Walt Disney's Disneyland Tours
4011. Walt Disney's Donald Duck
8144. Walt Disney's Donald Duck Big Game
5603. Walt Disney's Donald Duck Flips His
8145. Walt Disney's Donald Duck Money Bag
7859. Walt Disney's Donald Duck Ring Toss
6149. Walt Disney's Electric Disneyland
6995. Walt Disney's Fantasyland Game
7860. Walt Disney's Game of Step 'N Slides
2407. Walt Disney's Game Parade Academy
8146. Walt Disney's Goofy Finds His Marbles
8147. Walt Disney's Goofy Finds His Marbles
8148. Walt Disney's Goofy Goes to the Sea
8149. Walt Disney's Goofy's Mad Maze
6997. Walt Disney's Jungle Book Game
7861. Walt Disney's Ludwig Von Drake
6248. Walt Disney's Ludwig Von Drake Card
7862. Walt Disney's Ludwig Von Drake Ring
7863. Walt Disney's Ludwig Von Drake Score
8150. Walt Disney's Ludwig Von Drake
8164. Walt Disney's Ludwig Von Drake
7256. Walt Disney's Marry Poppins Card
5015. Walt Disney's Mary Poppins
7257. Walt Disney's Mary Poppins
6998. Walt Disney's Mary Poppins Carousel
6151. Walt Disney's Mickey Mouse
8151. Walt Disney's Mickey Mouse Castle
7919. Walt Disney's Mickey Mouse Electric
6999. Walt Disney's Mickey Mouse Game
6150. Walt Disney's Mickey Mouse Lotto
8152. Walt Disney's Mickey Mouse Pop-Up
5534. Walt Disney's Mickey Mouse Stand-Up
7865. Walt Disney's Mickey Mouse Top Hat
8153. Walt Disney's Mickey Mouse's Pizza
8154. Walt Disney's Mickey Mouse's Tree
7866. Walt Disney's Micky Mouse Club
7000. Walt Disney's Mouseketeer Game
5535. Walt Disney's My First Game
7001. Walt Disney's Official Davy Crockett
5536. Walt Disney's Official Davy Crockett
7002. Walt Disney's Official Frontierland
6097. Walt Disney's Official Mouseketeer
3485. Walt Disney's Own 3 Little Pigs-"Who's
3486. Walt Disney's Own Game Donald
3487. Walt Disney's Own Game Ferdinand
3488. Walt Disney's Own Game Red Riding
3489. Walt Disney's Own Game Snow White
7867. Walt Disney's Peter Pan Game
5881. Walt Disney's Peter Pan Games, Food
2746. Walt Disney's Pinocchio
4012. Walt Disney's Pinocchio
3490. Walt Disney's Pinocchio Game
8155. Walt Disney's Pinocchio Game
8156. Walt Disney's Pluto's Big Bike Race
7003. Walt Disney's Presents Pinocchio Game
7004. Walt Disney's Robin Hood
8157. Walt Disney's Snow White Game
7868. Walt Disney's Steps and Chutes
7005. Walt Disney's Swamp Fox
7006. Walt Disney's Sword in the Stone
8158. Walt Disney's Sword in the Stone
2912. Walt Disney's Three Little Pigs Game
7007. Walt Disney's Tommorrowland
7008. Walt Disney's Uncle Remus Game
7010. Walt Disney's Winnie the Pooh

6098. Walt Disney's Winnie the Pooh Honey
7009. Walt Disney's Winnie the Pooh, Blue
7011. Walt Disney's Wonderful World of
5604. Walt Disney's Zorro Beanbag-Darts
7012. Walt Disney's Zorro Game
8159. Walt Disney's Zorro Game
6225. Walt Disney's Zorro Target Game
7585. Walt Disney's Zorro Target Game
8160. Walt Disney's Wonderful World of
5027. Who Framed Roger Rabbit Game
3189. Who's Afraid of the Big Wolf,
　　　Game of
5043. Wuzzles, by Walt Disney

Drinking

7625. Moonshine
7029. Pass Out, The Drinking Game
6278. Pass Out Travel Game
7030. Sip and Go Naked
7031. Sip and Strip

Economic

4468. Acme Checkout Game
4117. Acquire
4341. Acquire
4116. Acquire, Later Edition, Plastic tiles
6654. Advance to Boardwalk
4342. Air Empire
4475. Allowance Game
6249. Allowance Game, The
4482. American Dream, The
7127. American Gold
4241. Amsco Chaos
1831. Amusing Game of the
　　　Corner Grocery
4251. Anti
6573. Anti
4252. Anti-Monopoly
4256. Anti-Monopoly
6574. Anti-Monopoly II
4254. Anti-Monopoly III, Star Peace
4253. Anti-Monopoly, green box
7360. Assembly Line, The Game of, 4 car
7361. Assembly Line, The Game of,
　　　1st edition
1862. Auction, The Game of
2521. Auctioneer
5893. Auctioneer
450. Auctioneer, (© D. Eckley Hunter)
826. Auctioneer, The Game of
4455. Auto Dealership
4438. B. T. O. Big Time Operator
2930. Balance the Budget
2529. Bank Roll
451. Banker, (© D. Eckley Hunter)
1833. Banking, Game of
3297. Bargain Day
4498. Bargain Hunter
4118. Bazaar, Trading Game
5620. Big Bucks, The World of Business
3832. Big Business
7671. Big Business, National Money Game
7672. Big Business, Popular edition
7673. Big Business, Quality edition, Yellow
6256. Big Deal
6187. Big Wheel
6677. Billionaire
5670. Billionare, You Can be a, Uranium
1274. Blind Auction
2201. Board of Trade Game
6689. Boom or Bust, Game of, Square box
6690. Boom or Bust, Game of, Red box, 2nd
5907. Boss, The
2547. Brewster's Millions
6228. Building Boom
7883. Business Cycles
2212. Business Men's Series, He
1231. Business Men's Series, The
1892. Business or Going to Work, Game of
4351. Business Strategy
8046. Buy and Sell
1487. Buy and Sell, Game of
2300. Cargo For Victory
7373. Cargoes by William Longyear
7371. Cargoes by William Longyear, Box
7372. Cargoes by William Longyear, Deluxe
5920. Cars N' Trucks, Build-A-Game
5571. Cartel
5582. Cartel, 2nd Edition
2168. Cash
5255. Catchpenny, The Game of
　　　18th-century

7048. Caveat Emptor
8050. Charge It!
1352. Charge It!
4356. Collector, The
7053. Columbus! The Game of Exploration
1814. Commerce
2805. Commerce, Game of
1600. Commercial Traveler, The Game of
1421. Competition or Department Store
4218. Conrolling Interest
3912. Corner the Market
8057. Corner the Market, Two color cover
5650. Corporate Circles
1909. Country Fair, The
2557. Country Fair, The
7932. Credit Ability
4586. Cut Up Shopping Spree Game
7513. Dallas, Empire building Strategy
6732. Dealer's Choice
7028. Defend Your Capital
2891. Department Store
1605. Department Store Game, The
1913. Department Store, Game of Playing
5942. Diner's Club, Credit Card Game
4436. Dollars and Sense
2567. Easy Money
2568. Easy Money. 1st Edition
2569. Easy Money. 2nd. Edition
4613. Easy Money
2566. Easy Money, 4th Edition
4612. Easy Money, The Game of
6242. Economy Game, The
3669. Empires
6753. Encore
2143. Exchange
4127. Executive Decision
3209. Exports and Transportation, Game of
6759. Express Monopoly Card Game, Blue
4041. Factory Assembly
8066. Fame and Fortune Game
3351. Finance
6762. Finance and Fortune, The Game of
2940. Finance (1st edition)
6763. Finance, Blue cover with
　　　four houses &
2941. Finance, this edition is licensed by
3270. Financial Flurry Game
5486. First Class Farmer
4365. Foreign Exchange
7083. Fortune 500 Business Game
1302. Fortunes, Game of
1933. Frenzied Finance
6775. Fun City
6776. Fun City
4650. Fun on the Farm
6778. Gambler
1249. Geschalft or The Game of Business
4419. Give
7404. Go for Broke
2253. Going to Market
3734. Going to the Fair
4668. Going1 Going! Gone!
　　　The Flea Market
4366. Gold!
1942. Good Old Game of Corner Grocery
6630. Green Game, The
5321. Grocery Cart
1946. Grocery Store, Game of, Improved
3199. Guilty, The Funny Money Game
5237. Gusher, Win a Million
2313. Hi! Neighbor, The Trade Game of
　　　Pan-
4131. High Bid
4132. High Bid
4133. High Bid
4134. High Bid, 1st Edition, larger book-
　　　shelf
7880. High Finance
1957. I'm a Millionaire
7615. In the Chips, New York
7616. In the Chips, Silicon Valley
　　　investment
1795. Industries, Game of
6178. Inflation
3645. Inflation, The New Game
4212. Insure!
3678. Jamboree
6368. Jan Murray's Charge Account
8084. Jr. Executive
2183. Keeping Store, Game of
4728. King OlI
3384. Landlord's Game (by E. M. Philips)

1388. Landlord's Game, The
362. Laughable Game of What D'ye Buy,
　　　The
404. Laughable Game of What D'ye Buy,
　　　The
735. Laughable Game of What D'ye Buy,
　　　The
5766. Leave it to Beaver Money Maker
　　　Game
4745. Leverage
4746. Life, The Game of
4747. Life, The Game of, 100th Anniversary
1987. Little Grocer, The
1436. Little Shoppers
6313. Lose, The Game of
7423. Lottery Game
4302. Made for Trade
3396. Make a Million
6830. Make a Million
3397. Make-a-Million, New Edition
3398. Make-a-Million, Pocket Edition
4372. Management
5328. Managing Your Money
8198. Market Madness
3263. Merchant Prince
7944. Merger
1841. Merry Game of the Country Auction
3218. Middleman, The Game of
6197. Mini Express Monopoly, Premium
2256. Moneta, Game of
7325. Money Card
8093. Money Game of Junior Executive,
　　　The
8094. Money Game of Junior Executive,
　　　The
5319. Money Matters, Manhattan Savings
7495. Money Power, The Investment
　　　Strategy
8095. Money! Money! Money!
659. Monopolist, Ten Up, and Mariner's
3412. Monopoly
6856. Monopoly
3411. Monopoly
6842. Monopoly, (Deluxe), 2 color plastic
3403. Monopoly, 1st Deluxe Edition
3404. Monopoly, 1st Parker
　　　Trade Mark only
3405. Monopoly, 2nd Printing, U.S. Patent
6843. Monopoly, Braille Edition
3406. Monopoly, Deluxe
6845. Monopoly, Deluxe Edition, 50th
6844. Monopoly, Deluxe Edition, 50th
6846. Monopoly, Deluxe Edition, 60th
5506. Monopoly, Deluxe Edition,
　　　Hardwood
6847. Monopoly, Deluxe Edition, Photo of
6848. Monopoly, Deluxe Edition, Red &
6849. Monopoly, Deluxe Edition,
　　　Train cover
6850. Monopoly, Deluxe Edition, white box
3407. Monopoly, Green box, & Board
6851. Monopoly, Impliment box with Rich
6852. Monopoly, Impliment box with Rich
2864. Monopoly, Large White box
6853. Monopoly, NASCAR
6854. Monopoly, NFL
3408. Monopoly, No patent on board,
　　　Darrow
2865. Monopoly, Original large white box
2866. Monopoly, Separate red & white
6855. Monopoly, Star Wars Edition
3410. Monopoly, With metal playing pieces
7920. Monotony
7049. Moscow! Auction!
1998. My Mother Sent Me to the Grocery
1223. National Finance
7134. Oil
3418. Oil, The Game of
701. Old Curiosity Shop
6870. Option
1448. Paola
4823. Park and Shop
4822. Park and Shop, Pictue of shopping
6873. Pay Day
5610. Pay the Cashier
1843. Peculiar Game of Yankee Peddler,
　　　The
7093. Petropolis
2667. Play Safe
2666. Play Safe, Blue and Red Lable
1733. Playing Department Store, Game of
4852. Pop-Up Store Game

2039. Ports and Commerce, Game of
4191. Pot O'Gold
4854. Power Barons
7067. Power Technics, The Game of
5368. Praise the Loot?
7451. Products and Resourses, The Game of
7298. Profit
5631. Race to Riches
7095. Race to Riches
8017. Race to Riches
2832. Raffles
7649. Real Estate the Game
5845. Real Estate, Game of
7199. Resolution? The Game of Savings &
2227. Saving Game, The
　　　(by Albert H. Lewis)
3782. Saving, The (by Albert H. Lewis)
4887. Scavenger Hunt
6643. Shanghai Trader
2159. Shepherd's National Game of Finance
2193. Shop Boy, The
6247. Shopping
8117. Shopping Center Game
3229. Shopping Game
970. Shopping, Game of
2062. Shopping, The Game of
6928. Situation 4
5502. Snob, A Fantasy Shopping Spree
3458. Society or High Hat
683. Speculation
4927. Spot Cash
4930. Square Mile
4935. States, Game of the, Horozontal red
4936. States, Game of the, Vertical red,
　　　white
2345. Stop and Shop
7635. Store. Ad game for shoes
4076. Store Management
2196. Store, Game of
8175. Strike Price
989. Success, The Game of
7470. Super Market
6072. Swap, The Wheeler-Dealer Game
3217. Take Your Profit
7620. Texas Millionaire, Neiman-Marcus'
3634. Thrift Game. #55
4222. Thrift, A Banking Game, Premium
5499. Ticker Tape
343. Trade and Dicker
740. Trades or Knowledge is Power
2081. Trades, The Game of
7921. Transaction
3780. Traveling Salesman, The
4992. Trump, The Game
1811. Trusts and Busts, or Frenzied Finance
2775. Twenty Grand
6984. Tycoon
8006. Tycoon, Rag to Riches Game
7132. Tycoon, The Real Estate Game
7281. Uranium
2739. Values, The Money
　　　Management Game
4154. Venture
4155. Venture. Variant Packaging
5501. Volunteers! The Name of the GFame
2983. We Play Store (T-231)
3882. Wealth
1772. What D'ye Buy, The Game of, Banner
398. What is it or the Way to Make Money
6101. Winning Ticket
695. Yankee Pedlar
599. Yankee Pedlar
2842. Yankee Trader
534. Yankee Trader or What D'ye Buy by Dr
760. Young Banker, The, Salom's Game
5605. Your Money
5050. Zillionare

Educational

4230. AC/DC
2962. Around the Clock
552. Cabinet of Knowledge
7607. Circulation
1354. College, The Greatest Game on Earth
1234. Colors
4433. Diablo, The Safe-Driving Game
7977. Driver-Ed
5348. Drivers Training Game, Let's Drive,
　　　Old
7215. Driving Spirit Safety Game, The
637. Good and Bad Scholar
3579. Hickory Dickary Dock, Game of

5159. Offical Drivers Ed Game
5434. Productivity Management Game
8107. Ripley's Beleve it or Not! Game
5174. Rules of the Road, Driver Education
592. School in An Uproar, The Game of the
462. Schoolmaster, (© D. Eckley Hunter)
7296. Search
5551. Student Survival
3493. What's the Time
761. Young Compositor, The, Salom's Game

Ethnic

5459. African-History Discovery
7961. Afro-American History Mystery Game
2293. Bean-Em
7622. Black Experience, The
2964. Black Sambo, Game of
1894. Cake Walk
6546. Celtic Realm
1489. Chinese Game
2966. Ching Cong
1490. Chink, Game of
5927. Chop Suey Game
5114. Chutzpah
1908. Coon Hunt Game, The
1334. Coonies (101)
916. Coontown Shooting Gallery
320. Eskimo
2307. Flap Jacks
5955. Fu Manchu's Hidden Hoard
1079. Golliwogg
3616. Goof Race and Ten Pins
3936. Hitch Hicker, The Game of
5577. Honor of the Samurai
1305. In Dixieland, Game of
2973. Indian Arrow-Heads
2318. Jaunty Butler Bowl Over
2319. Jav-Lin
2438. Jungle Race
2396. Jungle Skittles
6170. Kosherland
6171. Let My People Go!
5141. Little Black Sambo
2897. Little Black Sambo, Game
3757. Little Black Sambo, Game of
6172. Magical Mitzvah Park
3590. Manchu Checkerettes
2446. Man-Dar-In
2636. Mandarins (4206)
5148. Martin Luther King Jr
3401. Mexican Pete (I-Got-It)
1471. Negro Characterism Game of
1716. Nosey
3623. Pan-Cake Tiddly Winks
2332. Poor Jenny, The Game of
2333. Pop and Plop
5843. Pow-Wow the Game
739. Round Game of the Jew, The
2337. Simba
4906. Skillets and Cakes
1412. Strange People, Game of
2076. Ten Little Niggers, The Game of
4309. Time for Native Americans, The
2350. Tip the Bell Boy
6173. Torah, Slides and Ladders
7852. Totem
6174. Tradition
2990. U Bang It
1532. Uncle Tom's Cabin
5259. Underground Railroad Game & Songs
2408. Wampum, Bub, Chen-Check
2357. Watch on the Rind
2095. Watermelon
4157. We Dunit, New Black History, Premium
4113. Zulu Blowing

Fairs

3304. Bobby & Betty's Trip to the N. Y
1552. Chicago and the World's Columbian
708. Donny-Brook Fair
1047. Down the Pike with Mrs. Wiggs at the
1816. Foxy Grandpa at the World's Fair
2595. Going to the Worlds Fair Game
1502. Jeremiah Judkin's Trip to the Fair
5410. New York World's Fair Children Card
6615. New York World's Fair Game
4808. Offical New York World'a Fair Game
4809. Offical New York World's Fair
3425. Peter Coddle at the New World's Fair

3426. Peter Coddle's Trip to the World's Fair
1199. Uncle Silas at the Fair
978. World's Columbia Exposition, Game of
5425. World's Fair Children's Game
3499. World's Fair Card Game
2102. World's Fair Game (Chicago)
2219. World's Fair, Game of; with Rivalry

Fantasy

5374. Barbarian Prince
7893. Battle of the Five Armies, boxed game
7894. Battle of the Five Armies, ziplock game
429. Beauties of Mythology
4347. Black Magic Valor Kit
5493. Citadel, ziplock bag
8053. Clash of the Titans Game
5470. Darkover
5835. Demonlord
4361. Dragonhunt
6323. Dragonmaster
6514. ElfQuest Boardgame, The
4363. Elric
6515. Elric, Battle at the End Time
5250. Elric, ziplock game, 1st edition
1054. Enchanted Forest
1496. Fairies' Palace, The
6520. Fantasy Adventers
7901. Fantasy Forest
6133. Fellowship of the Ring
8180. Great Dalmuti,The
5433. Greek Myths and Legends
4686. Hero Quest Game System
4223. Hobbit Game, The
4689. Hobbit Game, The
1304. Illustrated Mythology
6812. Krull
6813. Krull
5299. Lion and the White Witch, The
4758. Lord of the Rings, Adventure Game
8016. Masters of the Universe
746. Mythology, Game of
2233. Mythology, Game of
7906. New Dungeon, The
2830. Pixie
5300. Prince Caspian
6926. Shadowlord!
6525. Thieves' World, Sanctuary
4982. Thundarr The Barbarian
7105. Treasure Trools
5301. Voyage of Dawn Trader
6567. Warrior Quest
7019. Willow
5210. Wizard of Oz Game, The
6526. Xanth

Fantasy - Mythology

429. Beauties of Mythology
5433. Greek Myths and Legends
1304. Illustrated Mythology
748. Mythology, Game of
2233. Mythology, Game of

Farm

5449. Electric Whiz Farm Roundup

Fish (See Animals - Sea)

Fitness (See Physical Fitness)

Food

7695. Cherry Pie Fun Game
1916. Dinner
7402. Gingerbread Man
7725. Gingerbread Man Game
4401. Good Cooking, The Game of
1652. Grandma's Game of Mince Pie
3841. Hungry Willie
5453. Jim Prentice Electric Farmer's Round
5651. Jolly Green Giant Card Game
5769. Loli Pop Lane
4775. McDonald's Game, The
333. Mixed Pickles
405. Mixed Pickles
6570. Nabisco Chewza Cookie Game
6039. Reese's Pieces Game, Ad for candy
4906. Skillets and Cakes
4402. Spices of the World, Ad Game with

7836. Suger Bowl
2095. Watermelon
8161. What's Cooking
6415. Wine Celler
8178. Wine Game, The

Football (See Sports - Football)

Gambling-Chance

6240. Atlantic City Tycoon
6315. Bet a Million
2493. Deck-O-Cards Roulette
6322. Dollar Bill Poker, with TV's Odd
5731. Double Dealer, Jerry Lewis on Cover
4331. Flip-It Jackpot
6778. Gambler
7542. Gambler's Paradise
5282. Gooses Wild
2951. Jackpot
4332. Jimmy the Greek Odds Maker Poker -
7764. Liar's Poker
6402. Lucky Ten, The Money Game
3413. Monte Carlo
2885. Monte Cristo
5163. One Arm Bandit
4217. Popularity Lottery
7329. Put & Take Game
6336. Showdown Poker
5316. Splurge
5201. Tripoley, The Game of, Green molded
5202. Tripoley, The Game of, Overhead photo
5203. Tripoley, The Game of, Red box
5821. Vegas
5005. Vegas, The Family Game of Skill &

Game Shows (See TV - Game Shows)

Geography

3281. Across the Continent
5706. Across the USA
742. Alphabet of Nations, The New
2794. America
1853. American Cities
1855. American Eagle Geography
2518. Around the World with Nellie Bly
876. Boston Game, The
1218. Brewster's Educational Game Cards
1829. Buffalo, The Game of
1228. California - The Great Educator
731. Capital Fun or New Game of Geographic
698. Cards of Boston
1378. Characters, Foreign, Game of
2302. Cities
2303. Cities. Variant cover
1903. Cities Game of
1464. Cities of Our Country
1379. Cities, A Game of
596. Counties of the State of New York, A
1493. Countries
2170. Crossing the Alps
1920. East is East and West is West
2939. Farmers Electric Maps
733. Five Navigators, or A Voyage of
1631. Flag Game, The
1930. Flag, Improved Game of
1301. Flags
514. Flags of Nations
7226. Flags of the United Nations, Game of
1400. Flags of the World, Game of
1401. Flags of the World, Game of, Pan-Am
1632. Flags, Game of
3354. Flags, New Game of
1065. Flags, The Game of (4061)
5617. Geografacts
5436. Geografacts, The Game of the World
553. Geographical Cards
1641. Geographical Cards
2230. Geographical Cards, Improved
743. Geographical Game of the Old World
1642. Geographical Game, Grandma's
2136. Geographical Games: Cities; Countries
1219. Geographics
2147. Ge-O-Graph-O
2161. Geography
349. Geography and Amusement or
350. Geography and Entertainment

2222. Geography Game
4654. Geography Lotto
1936. Geography Up to Date
1428. Geography, Game of
2217. Geo-Histo
7403. Globe Trotter
640. Grandmama's Geographical Game
1081. Grandma's Geographical Game (4930)
6787. Great American Flag Game
5287. Great Game of Visiting Williamsburg
3363. Hendrik Van Loon's Wide World Game
7191. Holiday
1958. Improved Geography Game
1404. In Castleland, Game of
470. Interrogatory Geographical Game of the
8193. Itinerary
3028. Know Your Own United States
3029. Know Your Own United States
5373. Know Your States Game
3948. Little America, Antartic
1990. London Game, The
3394. Lowell Thomas' Travel Game "World
4093. Map:Pennsylvania County Seats
2474. Map-Peeno
3211. Missouri Cards
334. Most Laughable Thing on Earth, The, or
3224. Murray-Way States Game, The
792. National Game of States
6603. National Geographic, Global Pursuit
388. Nationalia
1137. Nationalia
1406. Nationalities, Game of
1710. Nations or Quaker Whist, Game of
1138. Nations, Game of
2002. Nations, Game of
662. Nations, or Quaker Whist, Game of
3640. New States Game, The
2005. New York, Game of
6289. North to Alaska
6604. On Assignment with National
2016. Panama Canal Game
64. Philosopher's Travels or Game of
5311. Pla-O-Map Game, made by Indiana
2251. Pleasant Geography of the United States
1411. Population, Game of
2039. Ports and Commerce, Game of
1361. Progressive Game of Geography, The
5869. Rand McNally Destination, Vacation
1444. Rivers
392. Round the World
1161. Round the World
393. Sam Slick From Weathersfield to Paris
3848. Sidewalks of New York
682. Six Nations, Game of
3460. South America Game
2440. Spinning Traveler
6954. State Capitals, Game of
3463. States & Cities, Game of
6955. States and Cities, The Game of
1530. States, Game of, Premium
1221. States, Hosford's Game of
1443. States, Hosford's Game of
1380. States, The
1381. States, The. Later edition
531. States, The Game of
1185. Through the Locks to the Garden Gate
5198. TOP-ography
556. Traveller's Tour Round the World, The
557. Traveller's Tour Through Europe, The
558. Traveller's Tour Through the United
3196. U. S. A. Game of
5852. UBI
7480. UBI
2220. United States Geographical Lotto
7481. United States Map Game
2483. Visual Geography, Belknap's
2742. Voyage Around the World, Game of
4310. Where in the World
1205. Which, What or Where? A Geography
2099. Wide World & A Journey Round it, The
5427. Worldwide Pen Pals World Geography
2363. X-Plor US, Large box with no planes
2364. X-Plor US, Small box with planes on
1415. Yellowstone, Game of

1784. Young Folk's Geographical Game
2110. Young People's Geographical Game
314. Young Traveller, or Geographical
Cards

Golf (See Sports - Golf)

History

5857. 50's & 60's Trivia Game- #9
3071. A1, A2:Discovery of American and
5459. African-History Discovery
1449. America
1375. American Characters, Game of
1458. American History
7285. American History Rummy
1856. American History, The Game of
540. American Story and Glory,
The Game of
3286. Americana
3123. Autographs
3072. B1,B2:Intercolonial Wards,
French and
7223. Believe it or Not, Famous People
7669. Betsy Ross and the Flag Game
730. Biographical Amusement
7622. Black Experience, The
6416. Blizzard of '77
2166. Blue Beard, Game of
355. Buried Cities
4294. By Jove
3073. C1, C2:From Adoption of the
907. Caesars, Game of
3163. Capt. Ashley McKinley W/ Bird at the
5255. Catchpenny, The Game of
18th-century
790. Centennial Games 1776-1876
699. Centennial Games of the Revolution
612. Centennial Presidential Game
780. Centennial Seventy-Six (author W. C
781. Century Game
1377. Characters Foreign, Game of
706. Chronicles of Uncle Sam's Family
453. Chronographer,(© D. Eckley Hunter)
922. Chronology (author Leavitt Bartlett)
5432. Civil War Map Game
4355. Civilization
5093. CNN The Game
1039. Columbus
3327. Comical History of America
490. Conquest of Nations, The (Game of
2122. Constitution, Game of
809. Contest for the Capital, The
1041. Costumes and Fashions, Game of
1603. Crusaders, Game of the
3074. D1,D2: Beginning of the Civil War to
7502. Dr. Livingstone I Presume
3867. Du-Ration
541. English Blood Royal, Game of
1922. English History
5256. Erie Canal Game & Songs, The
4126. Events
696. Events and Dates of U.S. Colonial
2160. Events and Dates of United States
5488. Facts-A-Nation
1923. Fame, The Game of
1924. Famous Men, The Game of
1498. Famous People
1925. Famous, The Game of
733. Five Navigators, or A Voyage of
310. Game of Kings, The
3245. Gas Rashun
2240. Gaskell's Popular Historical Game
212. Geographical Game of the Old World
2217. Geo-Histo
3012. Gnirol and the Pilgrim's Party
2597. Government
639. Grandmama's Game of Useful
1085. Grandma's Game of Useful
Knowledge
409. Great Events, The Game of
5287. Great Game of Visiting Williamsburg
708. Great Republic, The
6789. Guiness Book of World
Records Game
3852. H.V. Kaltenborn of Diplomacy, The
1086. Happy Days in Old England,
The Game
502. Helps to History
2883. Heroes of America
3500. Heroes of America
517. Heroes, The Game of
434. Heroines of History

457. Historian, (© D. Eckley Hunter)
734. Historical Amusements
1660. Historical Cards, Improved
2231. Historical Cards, Improved
921. Historical Game "Our Country"
3017. Historical Lotto, The Game of
2211. Historical Queries
425. Historical Topics
360. History for Young and Old, Games of
546. History of Philadelphia
1952. History Up to Date
3275. Histro (© Warren D. Ownby)
1092. Home History Game
374. House of Washington and the Palace of
722. House of Washington and the Palace of
3070. I.N.S.History Cards, Series D
4368. Image
1671. Improved Historical Cards
1404. In Castleland, Game of
3075. Interstate History Cards
(sold in sets of
1500. Inventions
1962. Italian History
1839. Johnny's Historical Game
3810. Kate Smith's Own, America
1682. Kings and Queens, New & Popular
1973. King's Castle
375. King's England & House that Jack
311. Kings of France, The Game of the
3381. Knights Journey, The
7417. Kommissar
4300. Land Ho/ Terra Trerra
7419. Landmarks, The Game of
2368. Liberty, Enlightening the World
7420. Life Magazine Remembers
3948. Little America, Antartic
496. Little Corporal, The World and Its
1432. Lone Star Game, or Texas History
4301. Ludi at the Circus maximus
2216. Makers of History, The
1405. Mayflower, The
1698. McAllister and the 150
2637. Men of Destiny
4779. Men of Destiny
1309. Mythology
2162. Mythology
3121. Napoleon, The Popular Advertising
526. National Game of American Eagle, The
3415. National Game of Peace for Our
Nation
413. National Game of the Star Spangled
578. National Jubilee Snake Game
6126. National Parks Wit
1511. National Rulers. Premium
1512. Nations, Game of, Premium
3501. Nations, Games of the
1139. Nations, The Game of
1793. Neutral
403. New Game of American Revolution,
The
579. New National Snake Game
3201. New U. S. Merchant Marine, The
312. New-World, A Game Of American
814. Noted People and Places
816. Old Flag or 1776, The
1425. Our Country
1515. Our Country, Premium
2014. Our Country
1311. Our National Life
1407. Our Union, Game of
4818. P.T. Boat 109
6024. P.T. Boat 109
896. Panama Canal Game
762. Parallels of History
723. Parlor Monuments to the Illustrious
5437. Passtimes, The Game of History
421. Patriot Heroes
459. Patriot, (© D. Eckley Hunter)
2118. Patriotic Game
(author Emile Pingault)
3625. Patriotic Picture Quiz Game
2114. Pearl's Historical Authors
1451. Philadelphia Buildings, The Game of
1730. Philippine, Game of
460. Philosopher, (© D. Eckley Hunter)
4305. Play 's the Thing, The, Introduction to
1418. Presidents & Historical Events,
Game of
1476. Presidents & Historical Events,
Game of
1360. Progressive Game of Biography
4307. Pyramids and Mummies

391. Queen's Guards
2415. Questo
5578. Quests of the Round Table
898. Rambles
3083. Ration Board
8200. Roaring 20s, The
7455. Roman X, The Game of the Caesars
313. Romance of American History, The
5840. Royal (author Lizzie Ballou)
917. Royal (author Lizzie Ballou)
582. Running the Blockade
3693. Salute
752. Signers of America's Independence,
The
6050. Sinking of the Titanic Game, The
583. Sociable Snake, The Game of
366. Sociable Snake, The Game of the
5527. Spiro T.Agnew, American History
972. Stanley Africa Game, The
1221. States, Hosford's Game of
1443. States, Hosford's Game of
466. Statesman, (© D. Eckley Hunter)
467. Statesman, Variant
7834. Story of the U.S. Air Forse, The
2075. Telka, Ancient Romans cover
2352. Totuum
4315. Trivia Party - People
720. Uncle Sam's Family, Chronicles of
687. Uncle Sam's History of the U.S
688. Uncle Sam's Game of
American History
5259. Underground Railroad
Game & Songs
2090. United States History
2089. United States History Illustrated, The
3104. Van Loon Story of Mankind, The
6612. Wagon Wheels to Oregon
4431. Watergate
4227. Watergate Scandal, The
7869. West Point Story, The
2101. World History, The Game of the
5876. World Trivia Game-#4
1382. World, A Game of the
2106. Yankee Doodle
594. Yankee Land, The Game of
1220. Young America's Home and School
1785. Young Folks Historical Game
5213. Your America

Hobbies

7133. Bottle Hunt
7508. Coin-Walk Coin Game
6137. Stamp Collectors Game
7829. Stampin'
3997. Stamps

Hockey - (See Sports - Hockey)

Holiday - Christmas

1899. Christmas Dinner, A
508. Christmas Game of the Months
825. Christmas Game, or "Dickens", The
1591. Christmas Goose
1592. Christmas Jewel, Game of the
1813. Christmas Mail
318. Christmas Pudding
1593. Christmas Stocking, The
1900. Christmas Tree
2237. Foxy Grandpa's Christmas Tree
8079. Hi-Ho Santa Clause Game
1122. Merry Christmas Game
1699. Merry Christmas Games, The
1700. Merry Christmas Goose Chase, The
1993. Merry Christmas Goose Chase, The
1707. Mother Goose's Christmas Party
2006. Night Before Christmas
3959. Night Before Christmas, The
1477. Night Before Christmas
5173. Rudolph, the Red-Nosed Raindeer
337. Santa Claus' Magical Box
1168. Santa Claus Game
2690. Santa Claus Game
7242. Santa Claus Game
1747. Santa Claus or Game of Presents
2057. Santa Claus, The Game of
4885. Santa's Workshop
5195. Ting-A-Ling Bingo
1760. Tobogganing at Christmas, Game of
1768. Visit of Santa Claus, Game of the

Holiday-Halloween

3906. Cat & Witch
3193. Hallowe'en
2479. Halloween Kitty Card Game
2137. Halloween Party Game
2478. Hallowe'en Spot Game
3080. Scream

Home Economics

7660. Angela Cartwright's Buttons & Bows
5894. Baby Sitter
7689. Buttons and Bows
4792. Mother's Helper
6025. Pattie Playpal
6295. Stork Bingo
7838. Taffiy's Baubles & Bangles Game
7483. Wash Out

Horse Racing (See Sports - Horse Racing)

Horses (See Animals - Horses)

Indians

4292. A Time for Native Americans
2539. Big Chief
1273. Cheyenne
1438. Council
3677. Indian Trail
1114. Little Red Men
957. Minnehaha, Game of
2189. Pocahontas
1169. Scouts and Indians
494. Travels and Sojourn of Ichabod Solo

Insects (See Animals - Insects)

International

5572. Diplomacy, Brown box, 1st edition
5573. Diplomacy, Red box, picture of board
4359. Diplomacy
5498. Nuclear Escalation
5217. Victory Over Communism
Kiddie
535. 16 Merry Face
1868. Babes in the Woods
941. Bad Boy's Little Game, The
6450. Bandersnath
7675. Birthday Cake
7691. Candy Capers
4538. Candyland
4537. Candyland Game
7693. Captain Kangaroo Parade Around the
7639. Charley 'N Me Robot Game
6715. Children's Hour, The
4573. Clickety-Clak
1598. Colors, The Game of
4584. Crocodile Dentist
2304. Dickory-Dock
4682. Happy Face Game
6472. Happy Happy Birthday
1951. Hickery Dickory Dock
1659. Hide and Seek, Game of
8078. Hi-Ho Cherry-O Game
2610. Hippety Hop, Game of
2822. Hippity-Hop
4690. Homestretch
7411. Hot Numbers
5518. It. Game of Tag
2824. Jig-A-Roo
2622. Joyland
8184. Kiddie Kards
5861. Kids Trivia Game- #7
6633. Koo Koo Choo Choo!
4732. Kookie Chicks
4743. Lets Play Tag
5143. Little Prince
6822. Little Red School House Game
1693. Lost in the Woods
6267. Lunch Bunch Easy on the Ketchup
4776. Melvin
6862. My Lucky Stars
5157. Noah's Ark, Pre- School
4813. Oh What a Mountain
2464. Peanut Party Game, inc.:Feeding the
934. Peek-a-Boo
7182. Pinhead, Game of Hide and Seek
2831. Pop-In
4866. Rainbow Game
969. School's Out

483. Shadows on the Wall
7184. Shmo
7821. Shuttle Game
5182. Skedaddle, Game of Hurdles
4211. Sniggle
4925. Splat! The Bug
6956. Steps to Toyland
8127. Swoop
5190. Tag You're It!, The Game of
6166. Toy Parade
3236. Toy Town Target Game
2354. Treasure Hunt
6980. Treasure Trail, Game of

Law & Order

7662. Arrest And Trial
7113. Attorney Power
3178. Baseball Game & G-Man Target
6676. Beggers and Thieves
3604. Black Falcon of the Flying G-Men, The
4348. Blind Justice, The Game of Lawsuits
5606. Brotherhood, The
7687. Burke's Law Target Game
6703. Caper
4206. Car 54, Where are You?
5923. Catch a Crook Game
4564. Chips Game
5926. Chips Game
5929. Cloak and Dagger
4582. Conspiracy
2556. Cops and Robbers
7882. Courtroom, America Game of Law
2460. Crime and Mystery
2461. Crime and Mystery, by J.H. Wallis
1914. Detective Game
945. Detective, Game of
3916. Dick Tracy Detective
2892. Dick Tracy Detective Game
2305. Dim Those Lights
3340. District Attorney
6746. Don't Go to Jail, Monopoly Dice Game
7702. Dragnet Maze
6220. Dragnet Radar Action Game
6221. Dragnet Target Game
2922. Electric Patrol
5950. Electronic Detective
7708. Eliot Ness The Untouchables Game
6519. Family Business
4633. FBI Crime Resistance Game
7710. FBI Game, The
2462. Four Little Mysteries
7902. Gang Busters
3930. Gang Busters (Philips H. Lord)
2592. G-Men
3931. G-Men Clues
5489. Godfather Game, The
5490. Godfather Game, The (Black Violin
2599. Great Charlie Chan Detective Mystery
7168. Hawaii Five-O
7970. Hi Jacked
8077. Hide 'N' Thief
3365. Highway Patrol
4703. Illya Kuryakin
7506. Inspector Gadget, Spin N'Match Game
3943. Inspector Wade of Scotland Yard
2317. International Game of Spy
5978. Ironside Game
4327. Jack the Ripper
4711. James Bond 007 Goldfinger Game
4713. James Bond Secret Agent 007 Game
2320. Jolly Cop Ring Toss
1679. Judges Game Cards, The
5352. Jurisprudence
7969. Jurisprudence
3372. Jury Box, The. Series # 1
3373. Jury Box, The. Series # 2
3374. Jury Box, The. Series # 3
3375. Jury Box, The. Series # 4
3376. Jury Box, The. Series # 5
6371. Justice
2473. Libel
784. Liberty, Law, Protecton, Habeas Corpus
6479. Lie Detector
5370. Mad, Spy Vs Spy Card Game
3399. Man Hunt
3400. Melvin Purvis' "G" Men
5776. Mob Strategy
1995. Mock Trial
6239. Organized Crime

3789. Outlaw Rummy
7795. Perry Mason Game
7142. Philadelphia Lawer
3815. Phililip Lord's Gang Buster Actions
3166. Philips H. Lords Gang Busters
4144. Point of Law
7447. Policeman
2334. Prowl Car
5339. Rich Man, Poor Man, Beggarman
1742. Rival Policemen
1350. Robber, Game of
1743. Robbing the Miller, Game of
3451. S. S. Van Dine's Great Detective Game
4891. Scotland Yard
2344. Stop and Go
3998. Stop and Go
2908. Stop Thief
4075. Stop Thief
4939. Stop Thief, Electronic Cops and
6644. Subway Vigilante Game, The
7582. Sue You
4975. Tell it to the Judge, The Club Game
5196. Top Cop
5353. Trial Lawyer
6440. Untouchables Target Game
4396. Verdict II
7986. Warden, The
2942. Who is Guilty? Premium American
4016. Who is the Thief

Learning (See Education)

Letters

764. Alphabet Game
775. Anagrams or Word's Alive
741. Anagrams, The Game of
1861. Auction Letters
6734. Dig, Red box
6735. Dig, Red letters
6736. Dig, White letters
1977. Letters & Anagrams
710. Letters Improved
711. Letters, Game of
1687. Letters, Game of
1978. Letters, Game of, Salem Edition
813. Letters, The Game of
824. Letters, The Game of
500. Letters, The Original Game of
712. Letters, The Original Game of
666. New Yankee Letter Cards
716. Original Game of Letters, The
484. What, the Battle with Letters
693. Yankee Letter Blocks
694. Yankee Letter Cards

Literary

2761. Adventures of Pinocchio, The
3746. Adventures of Tom Sawyer and Huck
5692. Adventures with Clifford the Big Red
475. Aesop, New Game of
1557. Aesop's Fables
1386. Albion Business Authors (Albion, MI)
5309. Ali Baba and the Forty Thieves
3249. Alice in Wonderland
3284. Alice in Wonderland Game
3747. Alice in Wonderland, Game of
497. Auteurs, Le Jeu des
755. Author's Game
428. Authors
606. Authors
1013. Authors
1296. Authors
1485. Authors
2290. Authors
3896. Authors
1327. Authors Illustrated, Tokalon Series
1863. Authors Illustrated, The Game of
379. Authors Improved
1010. Authors Improved, Illustrated Edition
3748. Authors of To-day, Game of
1864. Authors Petite Deluxe, Game of
1011. Authors William Shakespeare, Game of
3606. Authors, #51
3292. Authors, Best Edition
603. Authors, Cribbage
744. Authors, Game of, Brown Cloth Box
1569. Authors, Game of
1570. Authors, Game of

2420. Authors, Game of
2163. Authors, Game of, No. 2
1568. Authors, Game of, Red Box
808. Authors, Game of, The
3293. Authors, Great
1328. Authors, Hidden
1012. Authors, Household (4051)
1351. Authors, Improved Game of Oriental
1567. Authors, Improved, Popular Edition
605. Authors, Star
1866. Authors, The Game of
1867. Authors, The Game of
3895. Authors, The Game of
1865. Authors, The Game of, New Edition
406. Authors, The New Game of
787. Authors, The New Game of
1329. Authors, Vignette (210)
6663. Babar
5056. Babar 7 Families Card Game, The
4493. Babar and His Friends, See-Saw
429. Beauties of Mythology
5693. Berenstein Bears, Hidden Honey Pot
5694. Berenstein Bears, Hide and Seek, The
5695. Berenstein Bears, So Much To Do, The
452. Biographer, (© D. Eckley Hunter)
1023. Black Beauty
3749. Black Beauty
2964. Black Sambo, Game of
4520. Bobbsey Twins, The
354. Boston Game of Authors
609. Bugle Horn or Robin Hood, The
774. Carnival of Characters from Dickens
1896. Charles Dickens Game, The
1479. Checker Game of Classics, The
1033. Choice Thoughts from Longfellow
825. Christmas Game or "Dickens", The
1036. Cinderella
3764. Cinderella
5115. Cinderella Game, The
1035. Cinderella, A Game
1901. Cinderella, A Game
616. Cinderella, or Hunt the Slipper
979. Citations des Auteurs Francais
2890. Count of Monte Cristo
4110. David Goes to Greenland, The Game of
1836. Dickens Game
1045. Dickens, Game of
3766. Down the Rabbits Hole with Alice in
504. Dr. Busby, Game of
506. Dr. Busby, Game of
511. Dr. Busby, Game of. beige cover
512. Dr. Busby, Game of. Variant cover
2173. Dr. Busby, The Game of
6752. Elmer Wheelers Fat Boy Game
1055. English Literature
629. Familiar Quotations
1623. Familiar Quotations from Popular
628. Familiar Quotations from Popular
1621. Familiar Quotations, Game of
408. Familiar Quotations, The Game of
789. Familiar Quotations, The Game of
1622. Familiar Quotations, The New Game of
1497. Familiary Quotations, A New Game
1060. Figaro, Game of
1072. Funny Fortunes
4209. Games People Play Game, The, Based
987. Gems of Thought (author John D. Boroff
832. Gems of Wisdom
1080. Grandma's Game of Riddles (4928)
1944. Great Authors
410. Great Truths, The Game of
2600. Gulliver's Travels
641. H.M.S. Pinafore, Game of
6792. Hardy Boys Mystery Game, The
6797. Holly Hobbie Wishing Well Game
326. Humorous Authors
7904. Hunt for Red October, The
1669. Illustrated Authors, Game of
1672. Improved Star Authors, The
1469. Indiana Authors, Game of
745. Instructive Game of Authors
1960. International Authors, The Game of
1838. Ivanhoe
1677. Jack the Giant Killer
1966a. Jack the Giant Killer, The Game of
7497. James Clavell's Shogun
6476. Jonathan Livingston Seagull
5559. King Hamlet

458. Librarian, (© D. Eckley Hunter)
1505. Lion Authors, Game of
1840. Literary Salad
1981. Literary Salad, A Feast of Reason
1982. Literary Salad, A Game of Quotations
1983. Literary Women
1796. Literature Game
1506. Literature, Game of
918. Literature, The University Game of
5141. Little Black Sambo
2897. Little Black Sambo, Game
3757. Little Black Sambo, Game of
6821. Little Noddy's Taxi Game
6827. Mad Magazine Card Game
6828. Mad Magazine Game, The
3767. Marooned in the South Seas
1128. Modern Authors
6012. Murder on the Orient Express
6864. Nancy Drew Mystery Game, The
6863. Nancy Drew Mystery Game, The
815. Old Curiosity Shop, The
335. Oliver Twist
1842. Oliver Twist
817. Olympus, or A Feast with the Gods
818. Originations of Shakespeare
3419. Oz, The Wonderful Game of
7651. Paths & Burrows, World of Beatrix
7955. Peter Pan Game, The
2979. Peter Rabbit Game (T-249)
472. Pickwick Card
800. Pickwick Cards, The
799. Pickwick Cards, The, Pickwick Standing
797. Pickwick Cards, The, Cloth Cover
798. Pickwick Cards, The, Cupid Cover
476. Pinafore, Game of
6378. Pinocchio, New Adventures of
4305. Play 's the Thing, The, Introduction to
1409. Poem Illustrated, Game of
1410. Poems, Game of
2034. Poems, Game of
389. Poetical Pot Pie, or Aunt Hulda's
747. Poets, Game of
3518. Polaris, by Charles Muir, Book, Board
390. Popular Characters From Dickens
501. Portrait Authors
803. Portrait Authors
1807. Portrait Authors
422. Puck's Portfolio
2670. Put a Hat on Uncle Wiggily (by Howard
1737. Queens of Literature
927. Quotations
2205. Quotations & Characters from
491. Quotations, Game of
4862. Quotations, The Game of
1312. Quotes of Authors
4864. Raggedy Ann
4865. Raggedy Ann
2684. Raggedy Ann's Magic Pebble Game
1157. Rip Van Winkle
1344. Rip Van Winkle, Tokalon Series
2905. Rip Van Winkle's Nine Pins
2688. Rip-Van-Winkle
6598. Robin Hood
2051. Robin Hood, The Game of
1744. Robinson Crusoe
417. Robinson Crusoe and His Man Friday
1159. Robinson Crusoe, Game of
2052. Robinson Crusoe, Game of
1158. Robinson Crusoe, Game of, Different
4883. Sammy, the White House Mouse
3177. Scarlett O'Harra
7816. Screwball, The Mad Mad Mad Game
7817. Screwball, The Mad Mad Mad Game
464. Sentimental Biographer
474. Shakespeare in a New Dress
1313. Shakespeare, Game of
4379. Shakespeare, The Game of
411. Shakespearian Game, The
338. Shakespearian Oracle, The
5180. Sherlock Holmes Game, The
7957. Sleeping Beauty Game, The
2221. Sleeping Beauty Game, The
5185. Snow White and the Seven Dwarfs
1529. Spy, The Premium
1753. Standard Authors, Game of
1754. Star Authors, Game of. Red & Gold
7834. Story of the U.S. Air Forse, The
412. Stratford Game of Characters and
444. Studies from Shakespeare
4966. Sweet Valley High Game, by Francine

4972. Tarzan
4971. Tarzan to the Rescue Game
5697. Thomas the Tank Engines's, All Aboard
5698. Thomas the Tank Engines's, B-I-N-G-O
5699. Thomas the Tank Engines's, Hats Off
5700. Thomas the Tank Engines's, Railroad
5701. Thomas the Tank Engines's, Tricky
5702. Thomas the Tank Engines's, Whistle
419. Tipsy Philosophers, or Language Game
823. Tipsy Philosophers, or Laughable Game
3763. Tom Sawyer and Huck Finn
2727. Tom Sawyer, The Game of
6970. Tom Swift
2733. Treasure Island
3770. Treasure Island
3000. Treasure Island, Game of
4312. Trivia Party - Literature & Arts
6631. Tugs
3781. Ultimate Litterat, Game of
729. Uncle Tom and Little Eva, The Game of
533. Uncle Tom's Cabin
1533. Uncle Tom's Cabin
4999. Uncle Wiggily
2737. Uncle Wiggily Game
6985. Uncle Wiggily Game, The
2738. Uncle Wiggily's New Airplane Game
5000. Uncle Wiggily Game
5001. Uncle Wiggily Game
919. University Game of Literature, The
778. Vignette Authors
779. Vignette Authors. Variant cover
6996. Walt Disney's Hardy Boys Treasure
7869. West Point Story, The
6506. Where's Waldo? Memory Game
590. Willis the Pilot, or Sequel to Swiss
7020. Winnie the Pooh
3720. Winnie-The-Pooh
3498. Winnie-The-Pooh Game
5689. Wiry Dan, Adventure of Pinocchio
6398. Wizard of Oz
5210. Wizard of Oz Game, The
4017. Wizard of Oz, The Game of the
4203. Wonderful Wizard of Oz, The
7200. Yertle, The Game of
1416. Young Folks Favorite Authors

Magic
7178. Magic! Magic! Magic! Game
7735. Hocus Pocus

Marbles
6661. Avalanche
7383. Dead Pan
6466. Fast Eddie Game
6591. Marble Bowl
888. Marble Muggins
7334. Stadium Checkers, Photo cover
7335. Stadium Checkers, The Game of
6103. Wrestle Around Game
6004. Marble-Head Game
6032. Quick Shot Game

Mathematics (See Numbers)

Memory
4624. Eye Witness, What Do You Remember?
4868. Recall, The Game of Observation
6040. Remember
4928. Spots

Mental Activity
2454. After Dinner, 1st Series
2455. After Dinner, 2nd Series
2456. After Dinner, 3rd Series
2457. After Dinner, 4th Series
3722. After-Dinner
2458. Are You a Sacred Cow, 5th Series
2459. Are You a Sacred Cow, 6th Series
5343. Brain Game, The
3794. Colonial Stoopnagle & Budd's Are You
3795. Colonial Stoopnagle & Budd's Are You
3796. Colonial Stoopnagle & Budd's Are You

3797. Colonial Stoopnagle & Budd's Are You
5344. Ink Blotz
1349. Mark Twain's Memory Builder
3717. Reward
3718. Snap Judgement (by Herbert E. Marks
3777. Sunshine Funmaker Cards

Military - All
1553. 100 Soldiers on Parade
4463. 12 O'Clock High
5882. 12 O'Clock High (Paul Burke picture)
5883. 12 O'Clock High (Robert Lansing
6510. 1835
1554. 25 Soldiers on Parade
996. Across the Border
998. Across the Yalu
3203. Admirals, The Naval War Game
2441. Aerial Bomber
2867. Aero Sham Battle, The Game of
4471. Air Combat
3129. Air Combat Trainer
2442. Air Defense
2509. Air Raid Warden
2812. Air-Attack
2915. Air-Base Checkers
6655. All the Kings Men
3198. Allie-Patriot Game (© Elizabeth M
4479. America Heritage Game of Civil War
2371. America in the War
1563. American Battles
700. American Revolution
3291. Army Air Corps Game
3290. Army Air Corps Game, Variant cover
2289. Army Checkers
4089. Attack
940. Attack, Game of
5504. Avanté
4492. Axis and Allies
2817. Barrage
2533. Bataan, The Battle of the Philippines
2292. Battle
3107. Battle Checkers
4504. Battle Cry
1236. Battle for the Flag
1239. Battle for the Flag, The Game of
1478. Battle of Gettysburg, A Parlor Game
1874. Battle of Manila, The
1875. Battle of Santiago
3725. Battle of the Marne, The
2534. Battle of the Tanks
5090. Battle Stations
3898. Battle Stations, The Game of
2535. Battle Winks
3205. Battle, The Game of
5897. Battleboard
3061. Battlefield
5898. Battleline Game
875. Battles of the Republic
1576. Battles, or Fun for Boys, Game of
1876. Battles, The Game of
2868. Battleship Chess
4507. Battleship, Photo cover
3899. Battleship, The
5063. Beachhead Invasion Game
1241. Ben Hur
5284. Bicentennial Games, The
2541. Bizerte Gertie
2543. Blackout
2542. Blackout, Large Format
5902. Blast, The Game of
3827. Blaze Away
1024. Blockade
2819. Blockade, A Game for Armchair
1884. Boer and Briton
3873. Bom A Jap
3828. Bomb Sight Target
7219. Bomb Target Game
7079. Bomb the Navy
2757. Bomb Tokyo (Poph-Itt Cereal Co.)
3522. Bomb! The Navy
2809. Bombardier Bombsight
1885. Bombardment of the Fort
1583. Bombardment, The Game of
2276. Bomber Attack
2985. Bomber Ball
2295. Bomber Raid
2544. Bombs Aloft
3808. Bombs Away!
7345. Boomers, Fighters & Bombers
1586. Boy's in Blue, The

4121. Break Thru
4528. Broadside
4527. Broadside, American Heritage Series
4529. Broadsides & Boarding Parties
1029. Cadet Game (4036)
3318. Camelot
3319. Camelot
3316. Camelot, Brown Box
3317. Camelot, Two Knights on box cover
3320. Camouflage, Game of
2416. Campaign
7268. Campaign
7267. Campaign, The American "Go" Game
6639. Canoga
2246. Capture the Fort
2300. Cargo For Victory
4547. Carrier Strike!
6710. Castle Risk
3538. Champion European War Game
3537. ChampionEuropean War Game, The
3663. Champs: Land of Brauno
1332. Charge, The. Tokalon Series
3726. Chasing Villa
1812. Chateau Thierry
3267. Chateau Thierry
705. Chivalrie
1897. Chivalry
4568. Chopper Strike
3326. Citadel
6716. Civil War Game, 1863
7888. Civil War Trivia Board Game
5622. Civil War Wit
4572. Civil War, Game of the, American
2286. Coast Defense
2444. Coast Defense
3555. Coast Defense
3655. Coast Defense Game
2445. Coast Guard in Action
6725. Code Name: Sector
2787. Combat
5931. Combat at Anzio Beachead
6407. Combat Tank Game
5933. Combat, The Fighting Infantry Game
5932. Combat, The Fighting Infantry Game
424. Commanders of Our Fourses, The
3328. Commandos
6726. Conflict, Arrow cover
6727. Conflict, Black tank cover
3329. Conflict, Board and box, Pressed wood
3330. Conflict, Board and implement box
3331. Conflict, Long box
5576. Confrontation
570. Conquer, The Game To
3161. Conquest
4434. Conquest
4581. Conquest of the Empire
7696. Convoy The Naval War Game
6728. Coup D'Etat
1541. Custer's Last Fight
2393. Dave Dawson Pacific Battle Game
2394. Dave Dawson Victory Game
3754. Defenders of the Flag
3865. Defense, Game of, (Atlantic Theater)
3867. Defense, Game of, (Pacific Theater)
2796. Destroyer
1246. Dewey at Manila
1383. Dewey Game, The
1915. Dewey's Victory
3877. Dictator
3253. Direct Hit
3878. Direct Hit
3918. Dive Bomber, The Game of
5290. Dixie, 1st Bull Run
5291. Dixie, Gettysburg
5292. Dixie, Shilo
3342. Dog Fight
4601. Dogfight, American Heritage Series
2763. Down the Hatch
759. Draft Enforced, The
1050. Drummer Boy, Game of
2174. Drummer Boy, Game of
1919. Drummer Boy, The
3867. Du-Ration
7627. Electronic Battle Cry
4614. Electronic Battleship
4615. Electronic Battleship
5951. Electronic Radar Search Game
4617. Electronic Stratego
3669. Empires
4415. Escalation
6754. Escape from Colditz

3727. Escape of the Boeben
4625. F Troop Mini-Board Card game
4129. Feudal
4364. Feudal
5121. Fighter-Bomber
1927. Fighting in the Soudan
2577. Fighting Marines (4031)
1928. Fighting with the Boers
2413. Flagship
2995. Flagship
3672. Flying Aces
2851. Follow the Flag to Victory
4648. Fortress America
358. Fortress, The Game of
2310. G. H. Q
4653. G.I. Joe
5743. G.I. Joe Adventure Board Game
5744. G.I. Joe Combat Infantry Game
5745. G.I. Joe Commando Attach Game
5746. G.I. Joe Marine Paratroop Game
5747. G.I. Joe Navy Frogman Game
5748. G.I. Joe, Capture Hill 79
1837. Garrison
810. Garrison Game
1935. Garrison Game
5959. Garrison's Gorillas
3245. Gas Rashun
5960. General, The
6305. Generals
2588. Get In the Scrap
5257. Gettysburg, The Battlefield Game
5558. Grand Imperialism
727. Grand National Victory
1480. Grant's National Victory
2254. Great Allied War Game, The
3362. Great European War Game, The
812. Guerrillas, The
4676. Guided Missile Navy Game
3852. H.V. Kaltenborn of Diplomacy, The
2844. Hang the Tyrants
2803. High Command
3003. Hi-Seas
4688. Hit the Beach, World War II Game
2887. Hit-the-Deck
1091. Hold the Fort
1953. Hold the Fort
1457. Hood's War Game, U.S. vs. Spain
3150. Hornet Airplane Games
7904. Hunt for Red October, The
6264. Intercept
7943. Intrigue-Internation Game of World
2998. Invasion
2780. Jeep Board, The
3144. Jeep Board, The
6301. Jeep Patrol
1968. Jolly Tars, The Game of
3272. Junior Bombsight Game
4334. Karate Men Fighting Action Game
4299. Knights and Castles
7417. Kommissar
7417. Kommissar
2624. Kop the Kaiser
3151. Land and Sea, War Games
3514. Land and Water Battle Game
3946. Landing Force, The Game of
4738. Laser Attack Game
1250. Lee at Havana
2278. Let'em Have It. Our Fighting Rangers
7045. Liberation of Kuwait
2322. Liberty Flag Game
4056. Liberty War
1252. Little Corporal, The
1818. Little Drummer, The
1111. Little Knight, The
3139. Machine Gun Nest, Game of
518. Mahomet and Saladin (The battle of
5146. Maneuver
6833. Mask
1991. Maxfield Parish Soldier
7773. McHale's Navy Game
5386. Mega Nation
7569. Meltdown, The Nuclear Energy Conflict
1254. Miles at Porto Rico
3545. Military Checkers
5306. Military Chess
2960. Military Strategy
1126. Military Table Game, A
2383. Modern Warfare
448. Moorish Fort, Game of the
1999. Napoleon, Game of

3415. National Game of Peace for Our Nation
663. Naval Engagement
2138. Naval War Game (© 1912 by Munn &
1711. Naval War, Game of
3022. Navy Game, The
6375. Navy Log, TV Game
3416. Navy Weftup
1793. Neutral
2492. Neutral Game of War, Peace and
403. New Game of American Revolution, The
446. New Military Game, The
3201. New U. S. Merchant Marine, The
4456. Nuclear Escape
5366. Nuclear War
1144. On Guard
4374. Origins of World War II
365. Our Army, A Solders Game
3195. Our Defenders
1516. Our Navy
2015. Our Navy
1146. Over There
4818. P.T. Boat 109
6023. P.T. Boat 101Game
2447. Par-A-Shoot
2328. Paratroops
3772. Paris to Berlin, The Latest War
2017. Parker Bros. War Game
5265. Pax
8099. Phalanx
2026. Philippine War
3509. Plane Packet
4853. Pow Cannon Game
7065. Power, The Game
2904. Pre-Flight Trainer
2042. Prisoner's Base
2989. Pursuit
4337. Pursuit!
3254. Push-Em-Up-Victory Bomber
3214. Put the Yanks in Berlin
772. Quartette Union War Game
2402. Quoits Ahoy
6034. Radar Search
4226. Radaronics
4085. Radar-Salvo
3447. Ranger Commandos, World War II
7096. Rat Patrol Spin to Win Game
7808. Rat Patrol, The
3083. Ration Board
827. Rebellion, The Game of
4871. Rickenbacker Ace Game "Keep Em
7241. Ripley's Believe it or Not, War
6911. Risk and Castle Risk
6912. Risk, with plastic playing pieces
6913. Risk, with plastic playing pieces
6914. Risk, with soldier playing pieces
6915. Risk, with wooden playing pieces. 1st
1740. Rival Armies, The Game of, Pastime
1263. Roosevelt at San Juan
2055. Roosevelt's Charge
966. Rough Rider Ten Pins
1324. Rough Riders, The Game of
2414. Sabotage
1167. Sailor Boy
968. Sailor Boy Ring Toss
2242. Sailor Boy, The
1824. Sailor, The Game of
3693. Salute
3744. Salvo
6047. Salvo, The Game of Naval Strategy
1264. Schley at Santiago Bay
7973. Scramble, Air Battle Game
4892. Screaming Eagles
3092. Sea Battle
3132. Sea Battle
3775. Sea Battle
6303. Sea Battle
2947. Seige
4175. Seige
4897. Seige Game
3874. Set the Sun
1266. Shafter at Santiago
2436. Shanghai
4900. Shogun
2063. Siege of Havana, The
1170. Siege, Game of
2810. Sigs- The Game of United States Forces
2448. Sink the Invader
3849. Sink the Ship
3710. Skirmish (© Geo. A. Simon)

1748. Skirmish at Harper's Ferry, A New
4908. Skirmish, American Heritage Series
2705. Snug Harbor, Submarine Game
2496. Soldier on the Fort, The
3822. Soldiers and Sailors
6494. Sonar Sub Hunt
2068. Spanish Main
3823. Spot-A-Plane
3550. Spot'Em
2956. Spotter School
2342. Squadron Insignia
3996. Squadron Scramble
2343. Stand Up Soldiers in Action
1177. Stars and Stripes
3082. Stick the Dictator
2712. Storming the Castle
2225. Strat: The Great War Game
7835. Strategic Command Game
4944. Stratego
4941. Stratego, cameo of four at play
4942. Stratego, Man and boy at play
4943. Stratego, Two horseman one footsoldier
2836. Strategy
2837. Strategy
1756. Strategy, Game of
4949. Sub Attack Game
4950. Sub Search Game
2714. Submarine Chaser
4098. Submarine Drag
3466. Sunk
2385. Surrender of the Fort
4968. Swords and Shields
3256. Tactics
2074. Taking the Fort
4970. Tank Battle
3469. Thumbs Up, The Victory Game
2840. Tiddly Winks Barrage Game
3247. Torpedo Action Game
2369. Torpedo Attack
4990. Torpedo Run
2882. Total Victory
593. Tournament, The New Game of
2082. Trafalgar
3215. Trap the Jap in Tokyo
2087. U.S. Army Game
7854. U.S. Air Force, The Story of the
3826. V for Victory
3736. Victo
3737. Victo
3109. Victory
4010. Victory Bomber, A Target
3207. Victory Game
3868. Victory Rummy
690. Visit to Camp
1271. War and Diplomacy, Game of
1771. War at Sea or don't Give Up the Ship
3024. War Bingo
2091. War in Cuba
2092. War in South Africa, The
2093. War of 1812
1200. War of Nations
1201. War of Nations
2386. War of the Allies
2387. War of the Nations
468. War, (© D. Eckley Hunter)
1202. War, Game of
1203. War, Game of
1424. War, or American Generals and their
1542. War, The Game of
1845. War, The Game of
3266. War, The Game of
469. War, Variant, (© D. Eckley Hunter)
2945. Warfare Naval Combat
1534. Wars of the World, Premium
1533. Wars, Game of
2094. Waterloo
3771. Waterloo, The
1826. West Point
2096. West Point Cadet Game, The
1413. White Squadron -U. S. Navy Vessels
2245. World War Games (G. D. Hartlett
2255. World's War Winner
2259. Yankee Navy Game, The
586. Zouave, Game of the

Military-American Revolution

700. American Revolution
3161. Conquest
403. New Game of American Revolution

Military-Civil War

4479. America Heritage Game of Civil War
1478. Battle of Gettysburg, A Parlor Game

4506. Battle-Cry, American Heratige Series
7888. Civil War Trivia Board Game
5622. Civil War Wit
4572. Civil War, Game of the, American
424. Commanders of Our Fourses, The
5290. Dixie, 1st Bull Run
5291. Dixie, Gettysburg
5292. Dixie, Shilo
759. Draft Enforced, The
5257. Gettysburg, The Battlefield Game
727. Grand National Victory
365. Our Army, A Solders Game
829. Rebellion, The Game of

Military-Cold War

7417. Kommissar

Military-Medieval

3326. Citadel

Military-Napoleonic

6728. Coup D'Etat
1999. Napoleon, Game of
2094. Waterloo
3771. Waterloo, The

Military-Spanish American War

996. Across the Border
1563. American Battles
1874. Battle of Manila, The
1583. Bombardment, The Game of
1332. Charge, The. Tokalon Series
1919. Drummer Boy, The
1953. Hold the Fort
1458. Hood's War Game, U.S. vs. Spain
1250. Lee at Havana
2015. Our Navy
1324. Rough Riders, The Game of
1264. Schley at Santiago Bay
1266. Shafter at Santiago
1271. War and Diplomacy, Game of
1413. White Squadron -U. S. Navy Vessels

Military-WWI

3198. Allie-Patriot Game (© Elizabeth M
2371. America in the War
3320. Camouflage, Game of
3557. "Champion" European War Game, The
3267. Chateau Thierry
4601. Dogfight, American Heritage Series
2254. Great Allied War Game, The
3362. Great European War Game, The
2624. Kop the Kaiser
3514. Land and Water Battle Game
3201. New U. S. Merchant Marine, The
1146. Over There
3772. Paris to Berlin, The Latest War
2017. Parker Bros. War Game
4337. Pursuit!
4098. Submarine Drag
2087. U.S. Army Game
3207. Victory Game
2246. World War Games (G. D. Hartlett
2255. World's War Winner

Military-WWII

3203. Admirals, The Naval War Game
2867. Aero Sham Battle, The Game of
3129. Air Combat Trainer
2509. Air Raid Warden
2812. Air-Attack
3291. Army Air Corps Game
3290. Army Air Corps Game, Variant cover
2289. Army Checkers
4089. Attack
4492. Axis and Allies
2817. Barrage
2533. Bataan, The Battle of the Philippines
2292. Battle
3107. Battle Checkers
4504. Battle Cry
2534. Battle of the Tanks
3898. Battle Stations, The Game of
3899. Battleship, The
2541. Bizerte Gertie
2543. Blackout
2542. Blackout, Large Format
3827. Blaze Away
2819. Blockade, A Game for Armchair
3873. Bom A Jap

3828. Bomb Sight Target
3522. Bomb! The Navy
2276. Bomber Attack
2985. Bomber Ball
2295. Bomber Raid
2544. Bombs Aloft
3808. Bombs Away!
2300. Cargo For Victory
3538. Champion European War Game
2787. Combat
3328. Commandos
2393. Dave Dawson Pacific Battle Game
2394. Dave Dawson Victory Game
3865. Defense, Game of, (Atlantic Theater)
3866. Defense, Game of, (Pacific Theater)
3876. Dictator
3253. Direct Hit
3878. Direct Hit
3918. Dive Bomber, The Game of
3342. Dog Fight
2763. Down the Hatch
3867. Du-Ration
2995. Flagship
3672. Flying Aces
2851. Follow the Flag to Victory
2310. G. H. Q
3245. Gas Rashun
2588. Get In the Scrap
3852. H.V. Kaltenborn of Diplomacy, The
2803. High Command
3003. Hi-Seas
4688. Hit the Beach, World War II Game
3150. Hornet Airplane Games
2998. Invasion
3144. Jeep Board, The
3272. Junior Bombsight Game
3151. Land and Sea, War Games
3946. Landing Force, The Game of
2278. Let'em Have It. Our Fighting Rangers
2322. Liberty Flag Game
3415. National Game of Peace for Our Nation
3416. Navy Weftup
3195. Our Defenders
2447. Par-A-Shoot
2328. Paratroops
3509. Plane Packet
2904. Pre-Flight Trainer
2989. Pursuit
3254. Push-Em-Up-Victory Bomber
2402. Quoits Ahoy
4085. Radar-Salvo
3447. Ranger Commandos, World War II
3083. Ration Board
2414. Sabotage
3693. Salute
3092. Sea Battle
3132. Sea Battle
3775. Sea Battle
3874. Set the Sun
2436. Shanghai
2810. Sigs- The Game of United States Forces
2448. Sink the Invader
3822. Soldiers and Sailors
3823. Spot-A-Plane
3550. Spot'Em
2956. Spotter School
2342. Squadron Insignia
3996. Squadron Scramble
2343. Stand Up Soldiers in Action
3082. Stick the Dictator
2836. Strategy
2837. Strategy
2714. Submarine Chaser
3466. Sunk
3256. Tactics
2840. Tiddly Winks Barrage Game
3247. Torpedo Action Game
2369. Torpedo Attack
2882. Total Victory
3737. Victo
4010. Victory Bomber, A Target
3868. Victory Rummy
2945. Warfare Naval Combat

Military, Post WWII

5265. Pax

Mind (See Mental Activity)

Miscellaneous

3221. 400, The
4467. 4-Cyte

7354. Abbot & Costello, "Who's on First?"
6201. Alien Game
6673. Batman Returns
4171. Ben Hur, Chariot Race Game
6350. Ben-Hur
3604. Black Falcon of the Flying G-Men, The
8039. Black Hole, Space Alert Game, The
8040. Black Hole, Voyage of Fear Game, The
6551. Box Office
2547. Brewster's Millions
6461. Bug's Life, A, Bug Collector King-Size
5112. Cannonball Run, The
4566. Chitty Chitty Bang Bang
8051. Chitty Chitty Bang Bang-"Ask For"
7155. Chitty Chitty Bang Bang, Electric
8052. Chitty Chitty Bang Bang-Switcheroo
5364. Cinderfella Road Race Game, With
8053. Clash of the Titans Game
6719. Close Encounters of the Third Kind
7949. Dick Tracy Game, The
5357. Director's Choice
6464. Doctor Dolittle
7061. Doctor Dolittle, Card Game, Cereal
5725. Doctor Dolittle, Marble Maze
4285. Doctor Dolittle's Magic Answer
7390. Drive-In
6748. Dune
6750. E.T. The Extra-Terrestrial
5219. Egg and I, The
7900. Escape from New York The Game
6756. Ewok, Favorite Five
6757. Ewok, Paw Pals
6758. Ewok, Say "Cheese!"
5613. Going for Toy Story Toy Glory
3051. Going Hollywood
5276. Gone with the Wind
5277. Gone With the Wind, The Game
6783. Goodbye, Mr. Chips Game
4672. Grease
6115. Gremlins Card game
5630. Gremlins Game
6798. Hollywood "Go"
3052. Hollywood Burlesque
3937. Hollywood Movie Bingo, Female in Star
3938. Hollywood Movie Bingo, Green &
3939. Hollywood Movie Bingo, Red & Yellow
4103. Hollywood Producer
8081. Hollywood Stars, The Game of
7593. Hot Property! The Board Game
6803. Indiana Jones from the Raiders of the
4708. Ipcress File, The
4711. James Bond 007 Goldfinger Game
4712. James Bond 007 Thunderball Game
4713. James Bond Secret Agent 007 Game
5981. Jaws, The Game of
4723. Jumanji, The Game
3091. Kam-Ra! (© Josephine Q. Miranda)
5987. King Kong
6813. Krull
5404. Larry Harmons Laurel & Hardy
3682. Little Colonel
7422. Little Orphan Annie
4760. Lostworld Jurassic Park Game, The
7775. Michael Todd's Around the World in 80
5863. Movie Trivia Game- #1
5505. Movie Game, The
5463. Movie Mania
5465. Movie Mania (Trivia Edition)
2769. Movie Mart
7617. Movie Memory
3843. Movie Millions
7194. Movie Moguls
2648. Movie Picture Game, The
4059. Movie-Land Keeno
2649. Movie-Land Lotto
6374. Mr. Magoo Visits the Zoo
5234. Nightmare on Elm Street, A, The
5522. Original Little Rascals Clubhouse Bingo
2327. Our Gang Tipple-Topple Game
6024. P.T. Boat 109
4311. Party - Movies & TV
2665. Peck's Bad Boy with the Circus
5789. Phantom of the Opera Mystery Game
4841. Pink Panther Game, The
4848. Planet of the Apes

2863. Plot Cards
3435. Polly Pickles
4851. Popeye
5611. Post Doctor Dolittle Card Game
3440. Prisoner of Zenda, The
6206. Raiders of the Lost Ark Game
7493. Rasputin's Revenge, (Anastasia)
5548. Reel Schpeel
5632. Return to Oz Game
5176. Screen Challenge
5507. Screenplay
6387. Show-Biz, The Game of the Stars
5181. Sinbad
5796. Singing Bone, The
4921. Sons of Hercules Game, The
8034. Spanky and His Rascals
6953. Star Wars
6209. Star Wars Adventures of R2D2 Game
6210. Star Wars Game, Escape from Death
5802. Star Wars, Destroy Death Star
6950. Star Wars, Empire Strikes Back, Yoda
6211. Star Wars, Hoth Ice Planet Adventure
6951. Star Wars, Return of the Jedi, Battle at
6952. Star Wars, Return of the Jedi, Wicket
6121. Sting
6063. Sting Game, The
6064. Stump the Stars
4976. Terminator 2, Judgement Day
2719. Three Men in a Tub
2771. Top of the Town
4313. Trivia Party - Movies and TV
2929. Uncle Ben in Hollywood
6998. Walt Disney's Mary Poppins Carousel
7006. Walt Disney's Sword in the Stone
6505. Wayne's World VCR Board Game
7016. Wicket the Ewok
5211. Woody Woodpecker

Music
2125. Allegrando, Musical Game
604. Authors, Musical
5711. Banana Splits Game, The
4509. Beatles, Flip Your Wig nGame, The
3807. Benny Goodman, A of Musical
5460. Chubby Checker Twister
8023. Chubby Checker's Limbo
7588. Country Music "Stars on Tour"
4609. Duran Duran Game, In the Arena
1450. Educational Music Game
2126. Elementaire Musical Game
7613. Elvis Presley
6291. Elvis Presley, 'King of Rock' Game
5371. Elvis Welcomes You to His World
383. Figaro, Game of
2127. Great Composers, The
1358. Harmony, The Game of
7734. Hey, Hey, The Monkees
3248. Hi-Ho (© Wallach & Messier;
4696. How to Suceed in Business without
7172. Hulla Baloo
3018. Hymn Quartettes
7496. Jackson Five
4408. Kiss
6243. K-Tel Superstar Game, with 45 record
2984. Maestro, The Musical Bingo
3553. Melodio
3863. Modern Orchestra, The
7778. Monkees
5864. Music Trivia Game- #3
4163. Music # 1
4303. Music Maestro II
5464. Music Mania
2252. Music, Noel's Game of
2128. Musical Authors
2232. Musical Authors, Game of
3030. Musical Casino
439. Musical Composers
364. Musical Garlands and Landscape
2250. Musical Hits
1475. Musical Logomachy
3856. Musical Lotto
1431. Musical-Biography (author Margaret A
6486. Musingo
7554. My Fair Lady Game, The
4800. Name that Tune, with record, Red box
4801. Name that Tune, with record, White
4803. New Kids on the Block
1732. Pinafore Game
6568. Plays the Beats
7589. Rock & Roll, The Music Biz Game
5351. Rock and Roll

7213. Roll for the Gold Record
7183. Shindig Teen Game
6058. Solid Gold Music Trivia
5836. Song Burst
6138. Super Group
3023. Swing It, Record Game
4001. Swing, The
5816. Three Chipmunks, Cross Country Game
2129. Triads or Chords, Game of
4314. Trivia Party - Music

Mystery
4464. 13 Dead End Drive
5892. And Then There Were None
5922. Case of the Elusive Assassin, The
4559. Cherry Street
6720. Clue, The Great Detective Game
6721. Clue, The Great Detective Game, Gold
6722. Clue, The Great Detective Game, Green
6723. Clue, The Great Detective Game
6724. Clue, The Great Museum Caper Game
6792. Hardy Boys Mystery Game, The
6129. How to Host a Murder, Grapes of Rath
5976. I Spy Mini Board Card Game
6190. Mini Clue Jr.Game
7430. Mr. Ree, blue box
7431. Mr. Ree, Green box
7432. Mr. Ree, Purple and Gold cover
7433. Mr. Ree, purple box
6012. Murder on the Orient Express
7996. Murder She Wrote
4799. Mystery Mansion
6864. Nancy Drew Mystery Game, The
4148. Sleuth
3256a. Sus-Pense
4442. Trapped
5208. Who Dunit?
5823. Whodunit
7488. Whodunit
5030. Why, Alfred Hitchcock Presents
5031. Why, Mystery Game, Alfred Hitch-cock
5032. Why, Presented by Alfred Hitchcock

Mystical
6251. 25 Ghosts
5708. Amazing Dunninger Mind Reading
562. American Fortune-Telling Cards
2914. Ask Electra, The Game of Mystery
7364. Behind the "8" Ball Game
7365. Bewitch
1022. Billie's Dream
565. Bonaparte's Oraculum, Non-Portrait
566. Bonaparte's Oraculum, Portrait cover of
3220. Chi-Chi Chinese Daily Fortune Teller
615. Chiromagica
1034. Chuba
569. Comic Leaves of Fortune, the Sibyl's
5336. Dark Lore
757. Divination Cards, Salom's
1616. Eastern Fortune Telling Game
477. Expanding Fortune Teller. The
2308. Fortune Teller Cards
456. Fortune Teller, (© D. Eckley Hunter)
1066. Fortune Teller, The
3928. Fortune Telling
3929. Fortune Telling Playing Cards
749. Game of Fortune Telling
1073. Genii
1338. Gypsy Fortune Teller (102)
811. Gypsy Oracles for the Drawing Room
3007. Glob-Astral, A Social Game - Advice
8209. Gong Hee Fot Choy
3078. Gypsy Fortune Teller
591. Gypsy Fortune Teller, The Game of the
1655. Gypsy Fortune Telling Game, The
1817. Gypsy Queen
3568. Gypsy-Doodle
1656. Hand of Fate
2602. Hand of Fate
644. Hocus Pocus Conjurocus
5759. Interretation of Dreams
4714. Jeane Dixon's Game of Destiny
1226. Johnny, Pipe the Whistle Out, Fortune
7759. Ka-Bala, Glows in the Dark
4736. Kreskin's ESP
4735. Kreskin's ESP, Advanced Fine Edition

794. Ladies and Gentlemens Improved
7426. Madame Planchette Horescope Game
750. Magic Cards
1119. Magic Fortunes
4371. Magic Realm
386. Magic Squares and Mosaic Tablets
8197. Man, Myth, and Magic
6005. Mind over Matter, The Great Julian
1127. Mind Reading
387. Modern Hieroglyphics
1135. Myriopticon, The
3618. Mystic and Airplane Race
6558. Mystic Eye
3271. Mystic Maze Game
661. Mystic Thirty-One, The
4060. Mystic Writing
1709. Mystic, Cards of Knowledge
5266. Nemo
1141. Old Gypsy Fortune Teller
1142. Old Mill Fortune Teller, The
3844. Orje, The Mystic Prophet
1147. Palmistry
6895. Prediction Rod
7117. PSIKick
4895. Séance
548. Sybelline Leaves
785. Sybil's Leaves for 1833
2758. Tally Tale-Teller (a fortune telling game
342. Tom Thumb's Comical Fortune Teller
6972. Touch
478. Tyche: The Fireside Oracle (author C.B
4090. Veda the Magic Answer Man
397. Visit to the Gypsies
2747. Wheel of Fortune
3258. Wishing Well, The (© L.F.G.)
2953. Wizard, The
347. Wizard's Pack of Playing Cards, The
4399. Wizard's Quest
2107. Ye Witchcraft Game
3176. Zingari Fortune Telling Dice

Numbers
2284. Adaco
600. Addem Up and Dividem
1294. Addition and Subtraction
2288. Add-Too
1395. Arithmetic-Play, Game of
602. Arithmetical Game, Grandmama's
1232. Arithmomachy (J. Carr, author)
936. Biereley's Arithmetical Cards
1883. Block
1454. Bunco
568. Children's Arithmetic Game of 1000
732. Comic Game of Multiplication Table
1298. Constructive Geometry
7381. Crazy Threes
6747. Double Some 'R' Set, 2nEdition
5469. Entre's Fun & Games in Accounting
1422. Flinch
6766. Flinch. Variant cover
6767. Flinch. Variant cover
6768. Flinch
6765. Flinch, Three player cartoon cover
1403. Fraction Play
1303. Fractions
5481. Fun with Numbers, Deck # 9
1084. Grandma's Arithmetical Game
1651. Grandma's Arithmetical Game
3676. Hot Numbers
6799. Hot Spot! The 1-2-3 Game
6308. Las Vegas Wild
2280. Lucky Nine, Word Bingo, Radio Quiz
1308. Multiplication and Division
471. Multiplication Merrily Matched
697. Multiplication, An Arithmetical Game
372. New York Counting Cards, The
5346. Number Quest
5263. Number Tag, [Cheerios Box Game]
7435. Numberland Counting Game
1808. Numerica, Game of
5877. One Armed Bandit, Hardware Premium
670. One, Two, Three, Game of
6117. O'No 99
4849. Plus One- Electric Board Game
4861. Quizmo
1823. Rex, Game of
1423. Roodles
2054. Rook
5566. Sight Four

3597. Sixty Six, The Game of
2201. Some ' R' Set
5187. Spell It
2469. Take It and Double, 1st Series
2470. Take It and Double, 2nd Series
6509. Tally It
2228. Teddy's Multiplication Cards
3787. Teddy's Multiplication Cards.Later
4391. Tuf, A Game of Math
595. Young Peddlers, or Learning to Count in

Nursery Rhymes

1001. Aesop
1017. Beauty and the Beast, The Game of
1581. Bo Peep Game
2167. Bopeep, Game of
5719. Cobbler and the Elves, The
618. Cock Robin
619. Cock Robin. Hand painted cover
1904. Cock Robin
1038. Cock-a-Doodle-Do (4079)
2986. Dickory Dock Bowling Game
1058. Fairyland Game
1633. Fly Away Jack & Jill
1635. Four and Twenty Black Birds
6585. Frog He Would A-Wooing Go, A
3149. Game of the Three Bears
2589. Gingerbread Boy, The Game of the
5130. Goldilocks
7405. Goldilocks and the Three Bears
1647. Goosy Goosy Gander
5132. Grandmother's House We Go, To
6362. Hansel and Gretel
1951. Hickery Dickery Dock
325. House That Jack Built
645. House that Jack Built, The
1664. House that Jack Built, The
1954. House that Jack Built, The
3368. Humpty Dumpty
6365. Humpty Dumpty
5758. Humpty Dumpty Marble Game
1665. Humpty-Dumpty
951. Humpty-Dumpty, Game of
1097. Jack and Jill
1098. Jack and Jill
1099. Jack and Jill
2615. Jack and Jill
5137. Jack and Jill
5761. Jack and Jill Jacks Game
2614. Jack and Jill, or Who Brought the
436. Jack and the Bean Stalk
1963. Jack and the Beanstalk
5138. Jack and the Beanstalk Memory Game
4052. Jack and the Beanstalk, Bean Bag
6587. Jack and the Beanstalk, Game of
1100. Jack O'Lantern
6588. Jack Sprat, Game of
1676. Jack Sprat, The Game of
1964. Jack Sprat, The Game of
6367. Jack the Giant Killer
2933. Jack-Be-Nimble
3098. Kellogg's Story Book Of Games # 1
3099. Kellogg's Story Book Of Games # 2
3100. Kellogg's Story Book Of Games # 3
3101. Kellogg's Story Book Of Games # 4
6590. Little Bo Peep
1984. Little Bo-Peep
3680. Little Bo-Peep
1109. Little Boy Blue
1985. Little Boy Blue
3681. Little Boy Blue
5142. Little Boy Blue
1986. Little Golden Locks, A Game
1110. Little Jack Horner
1688. Little Jack Horner, The Game of
1112. Little Miss Muffett
1988. Little Mother Goose
653. Little Red Riding Hood
1115. Little Red Riding Hood
1989. Little Red Riding Hood
658. Merry Goose Game
363. Merry Goose Game, The
1132. Mother Goose
1510. Mother Goose
2647. Mother Goose
3957. Mother Goose (3952)
1706. Mother Goose and Her Friends
3154. Mother Goose Game
5153. Mother Goose Game

6859. Mother Goose Rhymes Games
1131. Mother Goose, Game of
1130. Mother Goose, Game of Melodious
1708. Mother Goose's Party or the Game of
3859. Mother Hubbard
660. Mother Hubbard, A Game
1513. Nursery Rhymes
3758. Nursery Rhymes
1719. Old Father Goose
2010. Old King Cole
1256. Old King Cole, Game of
1720. Old King Cole, Game of
2326. Old Maid, Nursery Rhymes & Fairy
1342. Old Maids as played by Mother Goose
1258. Old Mother Goose, Game of
1143. Old Mother Hubbard
2656. Old Mother Hubbard. Later Edition
5161. Old Mother Hubbard. Red box
5162. Old Mother Hubbard. Blue box
2013. Old Woman in the Shoe, The
441. Old Woman Who Lived in a Shoe
1259. Old Woman Who Lived in a Shoe, The
930. Our Cinderella Pary
3688. Peter Pan
4840. Peter Rabbit
4839. Peter Rabbit in the Cabbage Patch, The
4189. Peter Rabbit Rummy
2024. Peter, Peter Pumpkin Eater
1522. Polly Wants a Cracker
1153. Puss in Boots, Game of
1154. Puss, the Funny Game of (4035)
6382. Red Riding Hood
1738. Red Riding Hood and the Wolf
2048. Red Riding Hood, Game of
1267. Silverlocks and the Three Bears
5795. Simple Simon Balloon Game
530. Spanish Fairy Tale Game
684. Spider and the Fly
5419. Story Card Game
2717. Three Blind Mice, Game of (4737)
1183. Three Little Kittens, The
6601. Three Little Pigs, The
3157. Three Little Pigs, The Game of
2078. Tom, Tom the Pipers Son

Occupations

7113. Attorney Power
6455. Barbie's Keys to Fame
6454. Barbie's Keys to Fame Game
5569. Call Kelly
5235. Career Explorers
6705. Careers, Revised edition
6706. Careers, The Game, Red box
6707. Careers, The Game, 1st edition
6708. Careers, The Game, Green, red and
6709. Careers, The Game, Orange box
1595. City Life, The Game of
5944. Doctor, Doctor!
7032. Doctors Game, The
3666. Ed Wynn, The Fire Chief
2918. Electric Fire Fighters
5452. Electric Whiz Fire Fighters
7394. Engineer
8009. Farming Game, The
5737. Fearless Fireman Thrilling Game and
2971. Fighting the Flames (T-246)
3352. Fire Alarm Game
7396. Fire Chief
2580. Fire Department
2579. Fire Department, Game of
1061. Fire Fighters
4043. Fire Fighters
7272. Fire Fighters
3067. Forest Ranger Game, The
7398. Freddy the Fireman
5757. How to Succeed
6806. Inventors
1675. Jack of All Trades, The Game of
2320. Jolly Cop Ring Toss
7562. Jolly Postman, The
6311. Law School Game, The
7033. Lawers Game, The
7428. Mechanic Mac
7114. Medical Monopoly
5774. Merry Milkman Exciting Game and
2186. Messenger Boy, Game of
6841. Miss America Pageant Game, The
8025. My Son the Doctor
5285. Occupation

3565. Occupations, Game of (Learn Spanish)
5791. Police Patrol Action Game and Toy
7447. Policeman
7034. Politicians Game, The
7449. Postman
7452. Prospecting
5172. Ring Master
1741. Rival Doctors, The
3697. Stepping Stones
5353. Trial Lawyer
7484. What Shall I Be? (Boys)
7485. What Shall I Be? (Girls)
7486. What Shall I Wear?
4225. White Cover Girl, A Manpower Game
6214. Wildcatter
6401. Zip Code.995. A.D.T. Messenger Boy

Organization

1003. American Boys
1564. American Boys Company D
3308. Boy Scouts' Progress Game, The
2545. Boy Scouts, A Game
1025. Boy Scouts, Game of
1887. Boy Scouts, The Game of
3309. Boy Scouts, The Game of
3321. Camp Fire Girls
5216. Honors
3046. Scout Trail
2693. Scouting, Game of
2058. Scouts, The Game of, Variant box
4095. Sea Scouts
3005. Trupe, A Girl Scout Game

Patriotic

1643. Get There, Game of
6787. Great American Flag Game
1755. Stars and Stripes, or Red, White and

Personalities

7354. Abbot & Costello, "Who's on First?"
3283. Admiral Byrd's South Pole Game
4474. Allan Sherman's Camp Granada Game
8037. Art Linkletter's Game of "People are
8038. Art Linkletter's House Party
5834. Arthur Godfrey's Par-Tee Golf
6212. Bandit Trail Game, Featuring Gene
7223. Believe it or Not, Famous People
3303. Boake Carter's Game Star Reporter
4523. Body Language with Lucile Ball
6697. Burr Tillstrom's Kukla and Ollie
3163. Capt. Ashley McKinley W/ Bird at the
4546. Carol Burnett's Card Game
3908. Charlie McCarthy Put and Take Bingo
3909. Charlie McCarthy Rummy Card
3910. Charlie McCarthy's Game of Topper
2785. Charlie McCarthy's Radio Party
5460. Chubby Checker Twister
8023. Chubby Checker's Limbo
4569. Chuggedy Chug, Paul Winchell & Jerry
5364. Cinderfella Road Race Game, With
5568. Crusade, Lawerence Welk's All Star
3664. Dale Carnegie Game. The
4324. Dave Garroway's Game of Possesion
7125. Dave Garroway's Today Game
5937. Dear Abby Game
6465. Donny & Marie Osmond TV Show
5731. Double Dealer, Jerry Lewis on Cover
8173. Drew Pearson's Predict a Word
3666. Ed Wynn, The Fire Chief
3347. Eddie Cantor's "Tell it to the Judge"
6751. Eddie Cantor's Tell it to the Judge
3922. Edgar Bergen's Charlie McCarthy Q &
7613. Elvis Presley
6291. Elvis Presley, 'King of Rock' Game
5371. Elvis Welcomes You to His World
2306. Emmett Kelly's Circus Game
2576. Fibber Mcgee and the Wistful Vista
2875. Foolish Questions by Rube Goldberg
2309. Frank Buck's Bring 'Em Back Alive
7618. Gab, Gracie Allen's Rummy Game
5658. Gabby Hays Champion Shooting Target
7140. Garroway's Game of Possessions
5070. Gene Autry's Dude Ranch Game
2599. Great Charlie Chan Detective Mystery
5752. Great Estate, The, with Jerry Lewis on

6360. Groucho's You Bet Your Life
3363. Hendrik Van Loon's Wide World Game
3223. Howard H. Jones College Football
5491. Howard Hughes
7320. I'm George Gobel
7751. Jackie Gleason's, And Awa-a-a-a-y We
7496. Jackson Five
3246. Jimmy Durante Schnozzola Game
4332. Jimmy the Greek Odds Maker Poker -
3810. Kate Smith's Own Game, America
7760. Kennedy's, The
6478. Larry Hagman Presents Flip Out
5232. Loudmouth, Morton Downey Jr
2463. Lowell Thomas Questionnaire
3394. Lowell Thomas' Travel Game "World
7770. Lucy Show Game, The
4763. Lucy's Tea Party Game
3880. Major Bowes Amateur Hour
6533. Marlin Perkins' Wild Kingdom Game
5147. Marlin Perkins' Zoo Park
5148. Martin Luther King Jr
2638. Merry Game of Fibber Magee, The
6484. Merv Griffin's Word by Word
6485. Merv Griffin's Word for Word Game
7628. Motor Mouth
5334. NBC-TV News Game w/Chet Huntley
2187. Nellie Bly
4803. New Kids on the Block
4836. Patty Duke Game
7791. Paul Winchell & Jerry Mahoney's TV
7795. Perry Mason Game
3166. Philips H. Lords Gang Busters
1731. Phoebe Snow, Game of
8033. Pinky Lee and the Runaway
5411. Pinky's Lee's Who am I?
6488. Predicaments, Hosted by Joan Rivers
3079. Quintuplets Game
6380. Ralph Edwards' This is Your life
4104. Red Skelton's, "I Dood It".
8211. Red Skelton's, I Dood It!
4873. Ripley's Believe it or Not!
7237. Ripley's Believe it or Not, Animals
7238. Ripley's Believe it or Not, Science
7239. Ripley's Believe it or Not, Ships
7240. Ripley's Believe it or Not, Sports
7241. Ripley's Believe it or Not, War
4876. Rodney Dangerfield's No Respect
4245. Roy Rogers Magic Play-Around Game
7210. Roy Rogers Rodeo Game
7820. Sheri Lewis in. Sheriland Game
4919. Solotare, with Lucille Ball on cover
4965. Swayze
4984. Tic-Tac-Aroo with Captain Kangaroo
6967. Tiny Tim Game of Beautiful Things
3473. Tom Hamilton's Pigskin
3474. Tom Mix Circus Game
3475. Tom Mix's Game Wildcat
8186. Tony Randall's Word Quest
4996. Twiggy
6986. Undersea World of Jacques Cousteau
3104. Van Loon Story of Mankind, The
5549. W. C. Fields
3877. Waners Baseball
5030. Why, Alfred Hitchcock Presents
5031. Why, Mystery Game, Alfred Hitchcock
5032. Why, Presented by Alfred Hitchcock

Physical Fitness

6421. Funtastic Fitness Game, The, Christain
6752. Elmer Wheelers Fat Boy Game
6422. Funtastic Fitness Game, The
3875. Green's Highroad to Health &
5496. Weigh-Out

Plant

980. Bible Animals and Plants
551. Botanical Cards
2135. Botanical Game
795. Botany, The Game of
1399. Chestnut Burrs
6543. Earth Alert
5625. Eco Game
321. Feast of Flowers, A Floral Game of
1417. Fitch's Game of Natural History
368. Flower Game, The

1286. Flower Game, The
1402. Flowers, Game of
1931. Flowers, Game of
1435. Game of Know Your Vegetables, The
4232. Garden Game, The
4235. Into the Forest
3241. Larkspur, Flower Game
3650. Match It, Game of Trees
4111. Matchit, The Game of Trees
333. Mixed Pickles
405. Mixed Pickles
1419. Mothers Earth's Produce Game, by C
364. Musical Garlands and Landscape
2000. National Flower Game, The
1145. Over the Garden
1408. Pines, The
545. Planting, Game of
426. Planting, The Game of
4239. Pollination Game, The
376. (Rabbit) that Lived in the Garden of
7956. Sierra Club Game, The
2073. Sweet William and Marigold
5423. Tree Spotter Cards
1208. Wild Flowers
1468. Wonder Garden Game
7489. Wuffle Tree
4400. Yellowstone

Political

1791. Administrations
3108. All American Game of Ballots
7130. Allegiance "The Constitution Game"
2871. America First, The National Election
1005. American Politics, The Game of
1225. Anarchist (author J. W. Burdette)
2930. Balance the Budget
2291. Battle of Ballots
5484. Big Wig, The Great Game of Politics
7263. Bluff
5215. Campaign. A Game of American
5607. Campaign Trail
4352. Candidate
7491. Candidate
1590. Centennial Game of Columbia's
6636. Clintonoploy
6246. Comrades, Russian Monopoly
3809. Democracy
8014. Democracy
7387. Doondoggle, The Game of Comic
1921. Election
2229. Election
5553. Election
5317. Election '68
3105. Election, Game of
3614. Famous White House Game
1499. From Log Cabin to the White House
1639. From Log Cabin to White House
5664. Glastnost
2597. Government
6217. Hat in the Ring, Presidental Nominating
6179. High-Politix
6404. I Wanna Be President
1306. In the White House
7760. Kennedy's, The
6815. Landside
2768. Lection
3507. Let U.S. Have Peace
2121. Let Us Have Peace
5382. Lie, Cheat and Steal,The Game of
7153. Lie, Cheat and Steal,The Game of
4752. Lobby, A Capital Game
4753. Lobby, A Capital Game
4754. Lobby, A Capital Game
5657. Majority Rules
7429. Meet the Presidents
4137. Mr. President, 1st edition
4138. Mr. President
4139. Mr. President
5349. Mr. President, U.S.A
2235. National Game of Presidents
1430. National Temperance Game, The
5289. New Frontier, The Game of Nobody
2247. Political Bluff
4177. Political Influence, An America
5866. Political Trivia Game- #6
1426. Politics
1521. Politics. Premium
3140. Politics
3434. Politics
2863. Politics - The National Card Game
6888. Politics, Election Game

2190. Politics, Game of
2224. Politics, Game of
2132. Politics, or Race for the Presidency, The
6889. Politics, The Game, Election Game
1789. Politix
2249. President Game (© J. G. Bauer)
7287. Presidental Rummy
5431. Presidential Card Game
1233. Presidential Electoral Game
7587. Presidential Fever
480. Presidential Quartets, A New Game
1418. Presidents & Historical Events, Game of
1476. Presidents & Historical Events, Game of
3439. Presidents, Game of
2669. Presidents, The Game of
791. Races to the White House
1540. Red, White and Blue, The New Game of
6522. Road to the White House
2191. Road to Washington, The
5218. Running for President
6152. Save the President
442. Snake Game
5527. Spiro T. Agnew, American History
973. Stars and Stripes, Game of
7151. States and Statesman
5359. Tax and Spend
5626. Taxology
993. Teddy Bear *by Newbern H. Lewis)
884. Teddy Bear, Game of
991. Teddy's Bear Hunt
1367. Teddy's Ride from Oyster Bay to
3124. To the Aid of Your Party
1440. Uncle Sam's Cabinets. Part 2
1439. Uncle Sam's Cabinets, Part one
4431. Watergate
4227. Watergate Scandal, The
2358. Way to the White House, The
4397. We the People
5645. We Want Freedom, Elect Yourself
5384. Who Can Beat Nixon

Pool - See (Sports - Pool)

Premium

4481. American Airlines Travel Games
7124. Bewitched Hunt Game
6188. Big Otis - Catapult Game
4451. Billy and Ruth, premium
1486. Birds, Game of, Premium
3883. Blondie Goes to Leisureland, Premium
988. Boston Globe's Bicycle Game of
7056. Bugs Bunny Head Start Game
7057. Bugs Bunny Space Race
7058. Bugs Bunny Trapped
5221. Capital Air Race, Premium
5222. Cap'n Crunch's Crunch Power Game
5223. Cap'n Crunch's Hot Air Race
5224. Cap'n Crunch's Jungle Safari
5225. Cap'n Crunch's Undersea Adventure
7059. Central Bedrock U*S*A Race Game
1488. Chance, Game of
2785. Charlie McCarthy's Radio Party
3002. Cheerios Bird Hunt
3003. Cheerios Hook the Fish
1490. Chink, Game of
1385. Crystal Domino Sugar Cards. Premium
7062. Eastern Bedrock U*S*A Race Game
3238. En-Ar-Co Automobile Game
1495. Eureka, Game of. Premium
1498. Famous People
8012. Go Fish Dinos, Premium
5656. Go-Gulf Game, Gasoline oil premium
3872. Hurry Home
1501. Jack Straws
6189. Kellogg's Soccer Slam, Kellogg's Raisin
1503. Knowledge, Game of. Premium
3273. Little Orphan Annie's Treasure Hunt
6634. Lucky 3 Game, Bread premium
6290. Lunar Landing Game, Premium for
2943. Meet the Missus, Premium American
5319. Money Matters, Manhattan Savings
1508. Monkey, Premium
1509. Months
6570. Nabisco Chewza Cookie Game
1511. National Rulers. Premium

1512. Nations, Game of, Premium
5245. Nicelodeon, The Ren & Stimpy Show
5877. One Armed Bandit, Hardware Premium
3534. Original Professor Quiz Radio Game
3274. Orphan Annie, Treasure Isle of Health
1515. Our Country, Premium
1517. Our Union. Premium
1519. Patent Medicine, Premium
2437. Pigglie Wiggle, Premium
6638. Planit, The Omni Evolution Board
1521. Politics. Premium
7492. Rasputin's Revenge, (Anastasia)
3743. Red Crown, Premium
3742. Red Crown, The, Premium
7121. Sergeant Preston Gets His Man! cereal
7122. Sergeant Preston"Great Yukon River
7123. Sgt. Preston Gets His Man, Premium
3788. Snow White, Premium
3733. Socko the Monk, The Game of
1528. Spelling, Premium
1530. States, Game of, Premium
3709. Stop and Go. Premium
1531. Stop, Game of, Premium
3559. Streamlined Train Game, Premium
3778. Sunshine Mazes, Premium
3779. Sunshine Target Practice, Premium
1474. Touchdown or Parlor Foot Ball, The
2804. Trip through Columbia Network
5881. Walt Disney's Peter Pan Games, Food
1534. Wars of the World, Premium
7064. Western Bedrock U*S*A Race Game
3886. White King Game, The. Premium
2942. Who is Guilty?, Premium American
3126. Whoopo-Lifebuoy Premium Game

Puzzle

7961. Afro-American History Mystery Game
4501. Batman Jigsaw Puzzle Game
614. Chinese Puzzle
515. French Puzzle Brain Game
7925. Hexed
3160. Puzzle-Peg
2466. Puzzlems
4307. Pyramids and Mummies
6929. Situation 7, Space Puzzle Game
6619. Tantalizer

Q & A

5227. $1,000,000 Chance of a Lifetime
5228. $25,000 Pyramid
7655. 3 In-A-Row Home Quiz
5857. 50's & 60's Trivia Game- #9
5581. 6 Pack of Paper & Pencil Games, The
6143. Adventure in Science, An
7961. Afro-American History Mystery Game
5475. Amazing Mr. Nim
7284. American Art Quiz Card Game
7929. Ant Farm Game
3791. Are You a Sacred Cow?, 1st Edition
3792. Are You a Sacred Cow?, 2nd Edition
3793. Are You a Sacred Cow?, 3rd Edition
4490. Around the World
2495. Ask and Answer
2274. Be a Wiz-Play Radio Quiz
6202. Beat the Buzz
5858. Bible,Trivia Game- #10
6459. Blarney
7212. Boating Trivia
7678. Book of Knowledge Electromatic Dial
4349. Book of Lists, The
6319. Brain Storm
8049. Catchword
3206. Categories
5244. Celebrity Challenge
5539. Celebrity Challenge
7888. Civil War Trivia Board Game
6548. Clever Endeavor
5696. Clues with Clifford the Big Red Dog
5093. CNN The Game
5337. Dark Lore, The Original Horror Trivia
2937. Dr. I. Q. Jump
5385. Dream On
3922. Edgar Bergen's Charlie McCarthy Q &
2847. Electric Quiz Game
3081. Electric Quiz Game
5451. Electronic Classroom Game
6292. Escapades

4626. Fact Finder Fun
4128. Facts in Five
2573. Facts Worth Knowing Games - Fine
2574. Facts Worth Knowing Games -
2572. Facts Worth Knowing Games -Science
5488. Facts-A-Nation
2875. Foolish Questions by Rube Goldberg
3110. Ges-It
4660. Go to the Head of the Class, 10th Series
4661. Go to the Head of the Class, 11th Series
4662. Go to the Head of the Class, 17th Series
2593. Go to the Head of the Class, 2nd. Series
2594. Go to the Head of the Class, 3rd. Series
4663. Go to the Head of the Class, 5th Series
4664. Go to the Head of the Class, 6th Series
4665. Go to the Head of the Class, 7th Series
4666. Go to the Head of the Class, 8th Series
4667. Go to the Head of the Class, 9th Series
5633. Golden Quizziac, The
8015. Golden Trivia Game
7084. Groucho TV Quiz
1371. Guess Again
4675. Guess Again
1654. Guess Again, The Game of
6790. Guinness Game of World Records
7406. Heroes and Events, Game of
6233. Hi-Q
7737. Home Quiz
3940. How Good Are You?
575. Humorous Queries and Solutions
6549. I Q Game, The
5314. Info-Mania
4207. Inquizitive
5369. Intellectual Quests, The New Age Board
7299. I-Q Solitare
7086. Jeopardy
3944. Jingle Quiz, #3 Catch Questions
7415. Jotto
5861. Kids Trivia Game- #7
4729. Knock, Knock
2991. Kwiz
1976. Kwiz, Series A
2926. Let's Go to College
3711. Mental Whoopee, 1st Edition
3712. Mental Whoopee, 2nd Edition
3713. Mental Whoopee, 3rd Edition
3714. Mental Whoopee, 4th Edition
3715. Mental Whoopee, 5th Edition
3716. Mental Whoopee, 6th Edition
5773. Mentor
5863. Movie Trivia Game- #1
6145. Mr. Brain
5864. Music Trivia Game- #3
6625. Mystic Wheel Of Knowledge
2384. Opportunity Hour for Amateurs
3535. Original Professor Quiz, The
4414. Pantomine Quiz, Chocolate premium
6875. People Weekly
2465. Pictorial Mysteries
7258. Play it by Ear
7259. Play it by Ear. Volume 2
5866. Political Trivia Game- #6
5867. Potpourri Trivia Game- #12
6379. Price is Right, The
3820. Professor Wiz Partys
2270. Quest, The Game Of Knowledge
2467. Question Box, The, 1st Series
2475. Question Box, The, 2nd.Series
5839. Question of Scruples, A
4178. Questionable Integrity
3985. Quiz 4 Party
3444. Quiz Kids, Own Game Box
3986. Quiz Kids, Radio Question Bee
2671. Quiz Me, Game of Useful Knowledge
3504. Quiz of the Whiz, The. by J. N. Ding
5169. Quiz Panel
3175. Quizical Questions by Professor Quiz
2672. Quiz-Me, Game of Geography (4930)
2673. Quiz-Me, Game of Numbers (4289)
2674. Quiz-Me, Game of Numbers (4929)
2676. Quiz-Me, Game of Riddles
2677. Quiz-Me, Game of Riddles. Variant box
2678. Quiz-Me, Game of Riddles. Variant box

2675. Quiz-Me, Game of Riddles (4774)
2679. Quiz-Me, Game of Useful Knowledge
3761. Quizzer, The Game of
678. Quizzical Questions and
     Quaint Replies
4862. Quotations, The Game of
7806. Qwik Quiz Game
7454. R.S.V.P.
7603. Reminiscing, The Game for People
6146. Robot Sam the Answer Man
4886. Scatter Gories
5176. Screen Challenge
4920. Sonny Fox Fact Finder
2834. Spin-A-Quiz
5871. Sports Trivia Game- #5
6954. State Capitals, Game of
6962. Tattler Quiz Game
5873. Teen's Trivia Game- #8
5874. Television Trivia Game- #2
7626. Think
7101. Things and Places
5813. Think-A-Tron
7844. Tic-Tac-Dough, TV Game
6392. Tic-Tac-Toe Q & A Game
7631. Time
4987. Times to Remember
5197. Top Scholar
5875. Travel Trivia Game- #11
4447. TriBond
4312. Trivia Party - Literature & Arts
4314. Trivia Party - Music
4315. Trivia Party - People
4316. Trivia Party - Pot Luck
4317. Trivia Party - Sports
4390. Trivia, Game of, Set 1
5666. Trivial Detective Game
6981. Trivial Pursuit, The Vintage Years
5532. Truth or Consequences
7881. TV Guides' TV Game
6394. Twenty One, TV Quiz Game
5820. Two for the Money
7131. Ultimate Sports Trivia
6616. Ultimate Trivia Game, The
3825. Uncle Jim's Question Bee
3824. Uncle Jim's Question Bee, Jr. Series
7036. United Nations, Game About the
4460. USA Trivia
7107. Veda Magnetic Quiz Game
2741. Vox Pop
4013. What's the Answer
7487. What's Up?
7352. What's What
346. Which Is the Largest?
1204. Which, What or Where
1206. Who Knows?
3495. Who's Who
3494. Who's Who, Variant edition
6626. Wise Old Owl
2359. Witzi-Wits
5876. World Trivia Game- #4
2134. World's Educator, The. Wooden box
5213. Your America

Radio

7121. Sergeant Preston Gets His Man!
     cereal
7122. Sergeant Preston "Great Yukon River
7123. Sgt. Preston Gets His Man, Premium

Reading

1835. Billy Bumps Visit to Boston
1905. Comic Game of Sir Hinkle Funny-
1907. Comical Game of Who
2563. Down the Pike with Mrs. Wiggs at the
639. Grandmamas Games of Riddles
1653. Grandma's Improved Game of
     Riddles
385. Japhet Jenkins & Sally Jones Visit to
1975. Komical Konversation Kards
3414. Mrs. Casey Wants to Know
2019. Peculiar Game of My Wife and I, The
1729. Peter Coddle and His Trip to N. Y
1148. Peter Coddle's Trip
2022. Peter Coddle's Trip to N. Y., Nickle
2153. Peter Coddle's Trip to N. Y
3860. Peter Coddles Trip to New York
487. Peter Coddle's Trip to New York
1821. Peter Coddles, Game of
2188. Peter Coddle & His Trip to New York
2025. Petter Coddle Tells of His Trip to
2027. Picture Reading Game
3427. Picture Reading Game for Little Ones

2056. 'Round the World Joe
341. Three Merry Men
351. Three Merry Men
352. Trip to Paris
344. Trip to Paris, A
1765. Uncle Josh's Trip
1199. Uncle Silas at the Fair
1846. When My Ship Comes In
1774. Where's Johnny
1773. Where's Johnny, A Pleasing Game
1779. Wonderful Joe

Religious

7654. 3 In-A-Row Bible Quiz
2244. 66, The Game of Games
3014. Acme Bible Book Game, The
806. Ah Sin, the Heathen Chinese, The New
5298. Aliyah
7350. Becoming One
3087. Bible A B C & Promises
1543. Bible ABC's & Bible Promises
980. Bible Animals and Plants
1393. Bible Authors
4199. Bible Authors
1389. Bible Authors, Game of
981. Bible Books
1544. Bible Books
4100. Bible Boys
4444. Bible Challenge
1376. Bible Characters
1546. Bible Characters
7201. Bible Characters Game
1545. Bible Cities
6180. Bible Cities
982. Bible Customs & Ceremonies
983. Bible Events
1397. Bible Game
1877. Bible Game
1362. Bible Game Occupations
1363. Bible Game Occupations. Variant
2271. Bible Game of Facts,
     Places and Events
1577. Bible Information, Game of
1384. Bible Links
984. Bible Localities
5636. Bible Lotto, Game of
3015. Bible Lotto, The Game of
5053. Bible Match-A-Verse
1538. Bible Names for Old & Young
1018. Bible Objects, Game of
704. Bible Questions, Game of
1019. Bible Questions, Game of
3016. Bible Rhymes, The Game of
8206. Bible Zoo Game
5858. Bible, Trivia Game- #10
7208. Bold Adventure
1462. Book of Books (author W. J. Hosmer)
2248. Books of the Bible
     (author J. B. Wade)
1898. Christian Endeavor, Game of
7270. David and Goliath
1788. Eureka Bible Game
5252. Exiled - It's Dangerous in the Desert
6297. Exodus Out of Egypt
1429. Famous Scripture People
636. Going to Sunday School
1649. Grandmama's Sunday Game (New
1648. Grandmama's Sunday Game, Old
1650. Grandmama's Sunday New Testament
2598. Grandma's Game of Bible Questions
1082. Grandma's New Testament Game
1083. Grandma's Old Testament Game
4173. Happy Highway Game, The
3018. Hymn Quartettes
1537. Illustrated Game of Bible Names
6562. Jesus Deck, The
3371. Journey to Bethlehem, The
4369. Journey's of St. Paul
4101. Lemon's Bible
5435. Merit, The Catholic Game
1348. Missionary Pioneers
746. Mythology, Game of
2233. Mythology, Game of
928. N. J. Bible Game, The
6443. Never Alone, Bible Cards
1801. New Century Game of Proverbs
1713. New Pilgrim's Progress, The
2202. New Bible Cards
2004. New Testament
1364. New Testament Books, Bible Game of
985. New Testament Characters

1310. New Testament Game
664. New Testament Game, Grandma's
2007. Noah's Ark, The Game of
960. Noah's Ark, Game of
986. Old Testament Characters,
     The Game of
668. Old Testament Game, Grandma's
669. Old Testament Questions & Answers
2012. Old Testament, The
675. Pilgrim's Progress Going to Sunday
8028. Pilgrimage
676. Pilgrim's Progress, Game of the
1372. Pilgrims Progress, The Game of
7448. Possibility Thinkers Game
7544. Promised Land
4443. Revelation
371. Sabbath School Cards
6646. Saints Alive! Card Game
6635. Salvation
498. Scripture Cards
555. Scripture Cards
681. Scripture Cards
499. Scripture Characters
831. Scripture Characters
394. Scripture Game, or Who Knows?
529. Scripture History
3654. Scripture Memory Cards
5192. Ten Commandments Bible Game
1392. Tess Mads
8207. Topic Bible Game
3019. Traits, The Game of
8208. Who Am I?
4102. Who am I? Quizzes and Bible
721. Who Can Tell? The Scripture Game of
3200. Who's Who in Missions
3055. Woodard Biblical Game
1786. Young Folks Scriptural Cards
2109. Young People's Bible Game

Romance

3607. Bachelor Girl Game
6451. Barbie Charms the World Game
6452. Barbie Game, The
5627. Barbie, Queen of the Prom Game
5474. Blind Date, Magazine premium
6294. Bride Bingo
7367. Bride Game
6216. Campus Queen
793. Courting Cards
407. Courtship and Marriage, The Game of
788. Courtship and Marriage, The Game of
5723. Dating Game, The
4161. Dating Game, The, Party Pack, with
1609. Diamond Heart, Game of
7705. Dream Date
5540. Eloping
7393. Emily Post Popularity Game
6755. Escort, Game of Guys & Gals
3642. Happy Marriage Game
3194. Kissing Game
6565. Love Computer, The
5770. Love, The Game of
6508. Make-Out Game, The
2184. Marriage, Game of
332. Match & Catch
6608. Mating Game
2777. Matrimony Card Game
4797. Mystery Date Game
4798. Mystery Date Game
6876. Perfict Match Game
5563. Romantic Journey, The
2958. Seeing Nellie Home
5085. Senior Prom
4426. Sexual Trivia
5797. Spin the Bottle Game
4966. Sweet Valley High Game
7839. Taffy's Party Game

Royalty

542. English Blood Royal
310. Game of Kings, The
311. Kings of France
1523. Queen's Guards
76. Royal Comedy
1746. Royal Game of Kings and
     Queens, The
717. Royalty, Game of
2206. Tally Ho!, The Royal Game of

Schools / Universities

6288. Coloradoopoly

Science

6127. Evolution Game, The
4304. Nova True Science
7238. Ripley's Believe it or Not, Science
5599. Uranium Rush

Science Fiction

6201. Alien Game
4505. Battle of the Planets
6679. Bionic Crisis, Six Million Dollar Man
6680. Bionic Woman, The
8039. Black Hole, Space Alert Game, The
8040. Black Hole, Voyage of Fear Game,
     The
7685. Buck Rogers
7896. Buck Rogers Martian War
7897. Buck Rogers, Battle for 25th Century
6712. Centurions
6513. Dragonriders of Pern
4362. Dune
6750. E.T. The Extra-Terrestrial
6756. Ewok, Favorite Five
6757. Ewok, Paw Pals
6758. Ewok, Say "Cheese!"
4639. Fireball XL5
6408. Fireball XL5, Magnetic Dart game
5544. Flash Gordon
5854. Flash Gordon Game
6115. Gremlins Card game
4734. Korg: 70,000 B.C. The
7176. Land of the Giants Shoot & Stick
4737. Land of the Lost
7629. Land of the Lost Board game
4759. Lost in Space Game
4760. Lostworld Jurassic Park Game, The
6481. Major Matt Mason Space Exploration
6855. Monopoly, Star Wars Edition
7784. My Favorite Martian Game
4816. Outer Limits, The
8181. Robo Rally
6043. Roboforce Card Game
6919. Saban's VR Troopers
6920. Saban's VR Troopers Game
4894. Sealab 2020 Game
6523. Sim City - The Card Game
6930. Six Million Dollar Man
7609. Solar Conquest
8018. Solarquest
4923. Space:1999
7907. Star Frontiers, Night Hawks
5278. Star Trek : The Game
4933. Star Trek Game
5800. Star Trek Game
6953. Star Wars
6209. Star Wars Adventures of R2D2 Game
6210. Star Wars Game, Escape from Death
5802. Star Wars, Destroy Death Star
6950. Star Wars, Empire Strikes Back, Yoda
6211. Star Wars, Hoth Ice Planet Adventure
6951. Star Wars, Return of the Jedi, Battle at
6952. Star Wars, Return of the Jedi, Wicket
7207. Starchase
7830. Steve Scott Space Scout
6081. Time Tunnel Card Game, The
6082. Time Tunnel Game, The
7104. Time Tunnel Spin-To-Win, The
6970. Tom Swift
5609. Traveller
6095. Twilight Zone Game, The
4394. UFO
5599. Uranium Rush
6988. Voltron
7016. Wicket the Ewok

Self Help / Self-Improvement

7659. Analysis
6628. Animalysis
5508. Psyche-Paths
2740. Vita Lee

Sexual

7598. Dirty Minds, The Game of Naughty
7599. Dirty Minds, Volume Two,
     The Game of
7600. Falsies, The Game of Sexual Fibs
764. Sexual Secrets
7029. Pass Out, The Drinking Game
4426. Sexual Trivia
7030. Sip and Go Naked
7031. Sip and Strip

Skating (See Sports - Skating)

Skill

7498. 4-5-6 Pick Up Sticks
2504. Acey Deucy
2389. Aero-Chute Target Game
4472. Air Trix, The Airstream Game
378. American Jack Straws
1004. American Jack Straws
7075. American Pachinko
2377. Amos & Sandy Acrobats
1009. Animal Ten Pins
4494. Back off Buzzard
1015. Backgammon, Japanese
3571. Bag of Fun, A
2390. Baggy Beans 'Goes to Town'
2528. Balaroo
4495. Balaroo
942. Ball Toss Game
943. Balloon, Game of
5895. Bang Box Game
7305. Bango! Bango!
6424. Barnstormer
4500. Bash!
6255. Beanbag Buccaneers
2293. Bean-Em
5511. Bent Outta Shape
7670. Big Blast
5901. Big Sneeze Game, The
6458. Big Thumb
5903. Block the Clock
7262. Blockhead!
4518. Blop
5905. Blowout Game
4519. Bobbin Noggin
4522. Body English
4524. Boob Tube
6687. Booby-Trap, Horizontal box
6688. Booby-Trap, Vertical box
5906. Bop the Beetle
6427. Bops and Robbers
1886. Boston Baked Beans
7679. Bottle Buster Target Game
6460. Boundary
3306. Bowlem
5910. Breaking Point
5913. Buck-A-Roo! Game
6428. Bucket Ball
4531. Bucket of Fun
6694. Buckshot!
6695. Bug Out
8042. Bug-A-Boo Game
8044. Bullwinkle Ring Toss Game
6429. Bust 'Em Target Game
881. Button, Button (© Frank F. Honeck)
4330. Can-Doo
8048. Cap the Hat
5919. Careful
5918. Careful The Toppling Tower
6447. Cascade
3575. Catchem
4558. Chaseback
5925. Chip are Down Game
3503. Chop Suey Game
5927. Chop Suey Game
5513. Chutes Away
5275. Claymania
7309. Clean Sweep Game
4034. Clown Toss
2970. Clown Winks
5930. Cold Feet
2213. Comical Tivoli Game
2487. Cootie, The Game of
7567. Crazy Car Race
5934. Crazy Clock Game
5935. Criss Cross
3336. Crows in the Corn
7383. Dead Pan
8062. Dennis the Menace Tiddly Winks
1276. Diamond Ball
2870. Diamond baseball dart game
537. Diamond Game, The
2986. Dickory Dock Bowling Game
3339. Dig
5726. Dodge Ball
6159. Donald Duck Tiddley Winx
2874. Donkey Party
3919. Donkey Party
1615. Donkey Party Game, The
3920. Donkey Ring Toss
5730. Don't Bug Me
7314. Don't Cook Your Goose

7315. Dont Go Overboard
3344. Dopey Bean Bag
7156. Double or Nothin'
4605. Doubletrack
7389. Dr. Tangle
4608. Drop in th eBucket
3346. Duck Shooting
3577. Dwarf's Twirling Game, The
4610. Dynamite Shack Game
6260. Easy on the Ketchup Game
5948. Egg Race Game
5445. Electric Hot Potato
5446. Electric Jack Straws
477. Expanding Fortune Teller.
1359. Faba Baga, or Parlor Quoits
4628. Fang Bang
7158. Fascination Checkers
7159. Fascination Pool
7160. Fascination, The Electric Maze Game
7161. Fascination, The Electric Maze Game
7162. Fascination, The Electric Maze Game
6466. Fast Eddie Game
4634. Feeley Meeley
3517. Fiddle Stix
5954. Fish Bait Game
6764. Five Wise Birds, The
7163. Flap Jack
2307. Flap Jacks
6467. Flea Circus
4289. Flintstone Quick Score Target Game
7718. Flintstones Stoneage Tiddley Winks
1067. Forty Five
2145. Foxy Grandpa Hat Party
5742. Freefall
7723. Frisky Frog
5958. Funny Finger
6262. Giant Barrel of Monkeys
3004. Gilbert Meteor Game
6781. Gnip Gnop
4659. Go Back
5751. Gold Trail
6403. Gone Bananas!
4671. Grab a Loop
5965. Grand Slam Game
5968. Hands Down
5969. Hang on Harvey! Game
4680. Hangman, Vincent Price on cover
1087. Happy Harry Ring Toss
6231. Hat's Off
3840. Hats Off BowlingGame
6232. Headache
6328. Heads Up
882. Hearts, The Society Game
     also known as
5970. Hide & Seek
6474. High Gear Game
6796. Hip Flip
5973. Hoopla, The Game of
6203. Hop and Stomp
7738. Hop N' Pop
7410. Hopskip and Jump
7171. Hot Potato
7319. Huff 'N Puff Game
5974. Hungry Henry Game
6802. Hurry Up
5977. Incredible Hulk Smash-Up Action
4051. Indoor Horse Shoe
4052. Jack and the Beanstalk, Bean Bag
1101. Jack Straws
1501. Jack Straws
2619. Jack Straws
4053. Jack Straws
6807. Jack Straws
2616. Jack Straws, Magnetic
1965. Jack Straws, New Edition
2617. Jack Straws, Royal (4095)
2618. Jack Straws, Senior (4418)
1966. Jack Straws, The Game of, (Brownies)
2318. Jaunty Butler Bowl Over
2319. Jav-Lin
2996. Jeepers
2320. Jolly Cop Ring Toss
5230. Jumble
7757. Jungle Fun
5879. Jungle Hunt
5982. Junk Yard Game, The
5983. Kaboom Ballon Busting Game
5984. Karate Tops
2397. Kastle Kwoits
6189. Kellogg's Soccer Slam,
     Kellogg's Raisin
5985. Ker Plunk

7321. Kick Back
4725. Kigmy Game by Al Capp
5238. Kikit Skittles
7322. King of the Hill
1681. King's Quoits, New Game of
3586. Kitty Kat Cup Ball
6431. Knock It Off
6204. Knock Off
5990. Knock the Clock
5762. Knock Your Block Off
3382. Knockout Andy
4733. Kooky Carnival Game
3842. Krokay
5231. Labyrinth, Wooden
7323. Last Straw, The
953. Lawn and Parlor Ring Toss
3706. Leaning Tower of Piza Game
5992. Leapin' Lizard
4749. Limbo Legs
4755. Lolli Plop, Skill Game
5996. Look Out Below Game
7769. Lucky Louie
3395. Lucky Strike
6432. Magic Shot Shooting Gallery
6480. Magnatel
1460. Magnetic Jack Straws
5772. Marble Maze
888. Marble Muggins
8091. Merry-Go-Round Game
4791. Mosquito
958. Mother Goose Ten Pins
6007. Mouse Trap Game
6008. Mouse Trap Game
2399. Mumbly-Darts
895. New Game of Tiddledy Winks,
     Earliest
5245. Nickelodeon, The Ren & Stimpy
     Show
6532. Obsession
4812. Oh No!
6022. Oh, Nuts! Game
1718. Old Fashioned Jack Straws
3619. Old Maid & Spin-A-Top
7437. Old Shell Game, The
4814. On the Ball
7787. Oop Stix
4815. Operation Skill Game
2327. Our Gang Tipple-Topple Game
5562. Over the Hill
4821. Paddle Pool
3623. Pan-Cake Tiddly Winks
962. Parlor Floor Croquet
908. Parlor Quoits
751. Patent Parlor Bagatelle Table, pat
2262. Peg at My Heart
819. Peggy, New Game of
5788. Penguin Polo
6268. Perfection
6027. Pie Face
5790. Pie in Your Eye Game
1822. Pin the Tail on the Donkey,
     Black cover
4096. Pin-Nock'l
2329. Pipers 3
4091. Pitch Em Indoor Horseshoes
2033. Pitch, The Game of
5166. Pitchin' Pal
2331. Play Boy Tiddledy Winks
5455. Plinkety Plunk
3436. Polly Put the Kettle On
5471. Pom Pom Game
2333. Pop and Plop
4850. Pop Yer Top!
6438. Popcorn
3592. Popeye Pipe Toss Game
3593. Popeye Ring Toss
6031. Poppin Hoppies Game
3647. Poppin' Popeye
2038. Popular Jack-Straws
6487. Pop-Za-Ball Target Game
7804. Pot O' Gold
6894. Pow Wow
7027. Prince Valiant Cross Bow Pistol Game
7328. Pull the Rug Out Game
964. Punch and Judy Ten Pins
6901. Push Over
7330. Put and Take
3984. Put the Tail on Ferdinand the Bull
7331. Puzzling Pyramid, The
679. Quoits
3626. Radio Ball
6037. Rebound

6038. Rebound
3691. Reg 'Lar Fellers Bowling Game
2687. Ring My Nose
2050. Ring the Pin
3627. Ring Toss
4072. Ring Toss
6597. Ring Toss
965. Ring Toss, Game of
2806. Ring-Toss, Animal cover
2403. Rocket Darts
4877. Roller Coaster
2053. Roly Poly Game, The
1163. Royal Jack Straws (4095, 4428)
8114. Sad Sam The Target-Ball Man
1166. Safety Target
4411. Scrambled Squares
6489. Scr-unch
2906. Seaside Shooting Gallery
7819. Seven-Up Game
2156. Sharp's Shooter
5179. Sharpshooter
3454. Shell Out
3694. Shoot*A*Cak
7098. Skill Ball
4907. Skill-It
5183. Skip-A-Cross
6052. Skully
3456. Sky Shoot
4909. Slam Back
6053. Slap Happy
4910. Slap Stick
6054. Slap Trap Game
6208. Sleep Walker
6491. Slick Shooter Penny Arcade Game
6492. Slip Disc
6493. Smack-A-Roo
6056. Snake's Alive!, The Game of
6235. Snakes in the Grass
8121. Snare
3461. South American Blow Gun Game
7467. Spacewalk, The 21st
     Century Labyrinth
4097. Spear-Em
7826. Spider's Maze
2835. Spin-O
6495. Splat
339. Squails
396. Squails
822. Squails
5799. Square-It
5188. Squaresville
5189. S-S-S-Scat
4938. Steady Eddie
4945. Streach-Out Sam
5531. Sudden Death
3779. Sunshine Target Practice, Premium
6165. Super Crow Shoot
6071. Swacki Game
7038. Swingin' Sam
4967. Swivel
7837. Syncron-8
974. Table Croquet
1180. Table Croquet
7471. Tangle
4002. Target Ball
3881. Targo
4974. Tee'd off
7100. Temple of Fu Manchu
7337. Thing Ding
4979. Think-Thunk
2077. Tiddledy Winks
2723. Tiddledy Winks
4078. Tiddledy Winks
4112. Tiddledy Winks
1186. Tiddledy Winks (4455)
3470. Tiddledy Winks Game, Fairie's
3471. Tiddledy Winks, Bowling, Ten Pins
3529. Tiddledy Winks, Jumbo
2348. Tiddley Winks
2723. Tiddley Winks
4079. Tiddley Winks
2347. Tiddley Winks, latter edition
2349. Tiddly Winks
2839. Tiddly Winks Barrage Game
3511. Tidley Winks
3702. Tidley Winks
5817. Tie 'N Tangle
6504. Tight Squeeze
7845. Tigrrrr Score-A-Matic Ball Toss
4985. Tilt 'N Roll, Obstacle Puzzle
7338. Tilt Score
6080. Tiltin' Milton Game

8130. Tilty
4986. Time Bomb
6083. Tin Can Alley
6085. Tip It
2350. Tip the Bell Boy
3119. Tip-Top Boxing, Dempsey-Wills
6086. Top Across Game
6087. Top It
7560. Top Me
6088. Top the Top
6275. Topper
6090. Toss Across
2729. Toy Town Target
3236. Toy Town Target Game
1192. Toy Town Target with Foxy Grandpa
4991. Trip Hammer
7186. Trip Trap
6236. Trouble
5623. Tuggy
7339. Tumble Bug
6094. Tumble Bumble
3853. Tumbling Twins, The
4994. Tussle
4998. Twister
7340. Twizzle Game, The
6096. Up 'N Over
976. Wall Ring Game, The
8149. Walt Disney's Ludwig Von Drake
5025. Whirl Out Game
7342. Whirly Bird
8202. Whiz Bowl, New Bowling Game
8164. Whoop!
2841. Wild West Shooting Game
4084. William Tell Shooting
1283. Win-a-Peg
5209. Wing Ding
5041. Wow Pillow Fight Game for Girls
6106. Zig Zag Zoom
5462. Zingo
4113. Zulu Blowing

Soccer (See Sports - Soccer)

Social

3889. 72 Party Stunts
3890. 72 Party Stunts. Variant cover
3891. 72 Party Stunts. Variant with woman
6314. Ad-Lib
481. Age Cards
538. Amusette
763. Amusing Game of Consequences by
598. Amusing Game of Conundroms, The
1006. An Account of Peter Coddles Visit to
807. Anybody & Everybody; Somebody &
486. Anybody and Everybody; Somebody
703. Anybody and Everybody; Somebody
3298. Baron Munchausen Game, The
3609. Beano, The Popular Game of
5900. Bee Bopper Game
1240. Bell Boy Game, The
5570. Bluff
316. Bottle Imp, The
1585. Boys and Girls
507. Characteristics, An Original Game
7376. Charades
7375. Charades for Juniors
1032. Checkered Game of Life
382. Checkered Game of Life, The
6154. Chicanery
2260. Chocolate-Splash
5378. Chug-A-Lug Drinking Party Game
8024. Chutzpah
319. Colored Fires
1599. Comical Chit Chat Game
620. Comical Conversation Cards
510. Comical Converse
891. Comical Game of Atta Boy, A
621. Conundrums
571. Conversation
353. Conversation Cards
356. Conversation Cards. Large Cards
357. Conversation Cards. Small Cards
550. Conversation Cards
756. Conversation Cards, Loves & Likes
547. Conversation Game
622. Conversations on Love
623. Conversations on Marriage
766. Corn & Beans
572. Cottage of Content
2124. Courtship of Johnathan Peas, The
748. Courtship of Jonathan Peas and Salley

1601. Cousin Peter's Trip to New York, Game
2142. Dinner Party
7933. Do What is Right
707. Donny-Brook Fair
4459. Double Talk 2nEdition
625. Dr. Fusby, Game of
758. Dr. Kane's Trip, Salom's New Game
1048. Dr. Busby
2173. Dr. Busby, Game of
2564. Dr. Busby
1617. Elite Conversation Cards, Social &
1618. Elite Conversation Cards, The. Loves
1619. Elite Conversational Cards, Comical
1056. Evening Party
3349. Excuse Me!
7601. Family the Game
630. Farmer Trot and His Family
631. Farmer Trott, Game of
4424. Fart the Game
632. Fashion and Famine
433. Fashionable Boarding House, The Game
513. Fireside Game
322. Forced Confessions
4297. Friends Around the World, A Game of
323. Fun Alive
6777. Funny Bones
1071. Funny Conversation Cards, Game of
3615. Funny Frolics or 10,000 Smiles
1287. Funnyface Game
516. Fusby Cards
1937. George Washingtons's Dream
1074. Get Busy, Game of
359. Gifts, Uses and Concequences, Game of
634. Gifts, Uses and Consequences, Game of
3578. Giggles
1938. Going to the Picnic
3932. Good Neighbor
1646. Good Old Aunt, The
768. Grand Mother Haphazard's Carnival
5133. Happy Birthday Game Party Pak
1948. Happy Families
418. Happy Family, A New Illustrated Game
642. Happy Family, The New Illustrated
7602. Harassment
3673. Have-You-It
3674. Have-You-It. Yellow It. cover Variation
1658. Heraldry, A New Society Game
2157. House that Jack Built, A New Picture
1955. How Silas Popped the Question
5329. I.N.I.T.I.A.L Response
1956. I Doubt It
384. I Down Know
361. Improved and Illustrated Game of Dr
6110. In You Face
5760. It Takes Two
327. Japanese Scintillities, or Parlor
328. Joker's Bond, The
543. Jolly Exempts, The
1289. Jolly Faces Game, The
1680. Just Like Me, Game of
329. K K K, Komical Konversation Kards
482. Key to the King's Garden, The
587. King of the Golden River, or The Black
2149. Komical Konversation Kards
1107. Kornelia Kinks at Jamestown
648. Ladies & Gentlemen's Conservation
728. Lamplighter, Game of the; or Uncle True
5768. Let's Face it
650. Life
3587. Life of the Party
3588. Life of the Party. Variant
2203. Life, The Game of
651. Life's Mishaps, A Merry Game
652. Life's Mishaps, Domino Rex and
2204. Lost Heir
893. Lost Heir, Game of
1691. Lost Heir, Game of
1692. Lost Heir, Game of. Two Boy Cover
2634. Lost Heir, Game of the
331. Love Chase
656. Loves & Likes
6139. Mad Dash
2827. Man About Town
503. Mansion of Happiness
1696. Mansion of Happiness

519. Mansion of Happiness w/Selchow Righter
520. Mansion of Happiness, golden spaces, 1st
521. Mansion of Happiness, green spaces, 2nd
522. Mansion of Happiness, publihed with
576. Masquerade Game, The
523. Master Rodbury and His Pupils
437. Matrimonial Bureau
1697. Matrimony or Old Maid, Game of
2943. Meet the Missus, Premium American
956. Milk Maid
577. Miracle
503. Miser, The Game of
7778. Miss Popularity Game
7625. Moonshine
1997. Mrs. Casey Wants to Know
894. Muggins, Hand Made Game, cf. Happy
1452. New Parlor Game, Capture of Mr
402. New Centennial Game! A Trip to
4804. Nosey Neighbor Card Game
736. Odd Figures, The Merry Game of
5355. Office Party
1717. Old Bachelor, Merry Game of
2008. Old Bachelor, The Game of
902. Old Maid
1723. Old Maid and Old Batchelor, The Game
1257. Old Maid, Game of
1724. Old Time Comic Conversation Cards
7438. Opinion Poll
2401. Opportunity Hour for Amateurs
3420. Parlor Bedlam
3967. Party Fun
2770. Party Package
6278. Pass Out Travel Game
796. Paul Pry, The Game of
1728. Peter Coddle, The Improved Game of
2023. Peter Coddle's Trip to N. Y., The Game
737. Peter Puzzlewig's Mirthful Game of
1343. Petter Coddles Dinner Party, Tokalon
673. Phantoms, or Delusive Visions
1150. Pick Up, The New Game
677. Poor Old Soldier and His Dog
738. Poor Old Soldier and His Dog
4066. Pop the Question
771. Popping the Question
336. Popping the Questions
493. Portfolio of Social Games
3219. Privilege
1427. Progressive Chautauqua Cards
1155. Queer Heads and Odd Bodies
3442. Quick Wit
3443. Quick Wit.Glyvas Williams Edition
2045. Quit
528. Reward of Virture, The
492. Right and Wrong, or The Princess
7204. Rollacolor Family Game
7936. Roll-A-Role
1524. Rueben Rubberneck's Visit to Chicago
1525. Samuel Goodall's Vacation
2692. Scavenger Hunt
4893. Scruples
589. Sea of Ice, or The Arctic Adventurers
5315. Seduction
463. Sentiment, (© D. Eckley Hunter)
1171. Signs, The Game of
8000. Simon Says
2064. Sir Hinkle Funny-Duster, Comical
1526. Sir Kinkum Funny Duster
718. Snap
377. Snap Dragon
783. Snap, Game of
1751. Snip, Snap, Snorum, Game of
373. Snip, Snap, Snorum, New and Illustrated
804. Society
2708. Spoof, The Cheer -Up Game
3086. Staff Frolics
2071. Strange Game of Forbidden Fruit, The
415. Strife of Genius, By a Lady
5356. Strip Tac Toe
7605. Stupid Game, The
1825. Success, Game of
3632. Sufficient
1757. Susceptibles, The
2226. Sweet Hearts, The Game of
8026. Take It Off
4004. Telling Tommy Card

341. Three Merry Men
2725. Time
1187. Timothy Tuttle
532. Tivoli, The Game of
1356. Trail, Parlor Card Game
494. Travels and Sojourn of Ichabod Solo
2131. Trix
6982. Trust Me
729. Uncle Tom and Little Eva, The Game of
1767. Ups and Downs
1769. Visit to the Old Homestead
3703. We Wow Wang
3492. What Color is Your Car?
489. What D'ye Buy, Laughable Game of
691. Where is Johnny?
692. Where's Johnny, A Game. Painted cards
5026. Whirligig
485. Who Do You Love Best?
2158. Who Killed Cock Robin? A New Play in
7014. Who? Game of Hidden Identity
2098. Who? The Comical Game of
2748. Whoopee
1224. Wiggs
6293. Wisdom
2752. Wise Cracks
4088. Wits
915. Women are Trumps
2108. Yes or No
1217. Zum

Social Action

3540. NRA, Game of Prosperity
2356. W P A, Work-Progress-Action

Social Concern

5367. Ax Your Tax
5376. Beat Detroit
4346. Beat Inflation Strategy Game, The
7623. Beat the Draft
7624. Big Funeral
5294. Blacks and Whites
4350. Bureaucracy
5660. Capital Punishment
5240. Changing Society
4210. Chap Acquitted
7118. Cities Game, The, Urban Blight
5272. Class Struggle
7152. Compatibility
6566. Conservation
7597. Couch Potato Game, The
4221. Credibility Gap
5503. Daze of our Loans
5379. Diet, The Cheating Man's Game
7964. Dirty Water Game
4435. Divorce, of Course
7965. Ecology
4616. Electronic Mall Madness
6136. Energy Crisis Game
8010. Energy Quest
5380. Family Game, The
4209. Games People Play Game, The, Based
6405. Gas Crisis
7037. Give Peace a Chance
7975. Global Survival
7026. Group Therapy
8205. Ivy Towers The Game of Preppism
4425. Lifestyles of the Poor and Discusting
6218. Litter Bug
6153. Medical Madness
5560. Middle Age Crazy
5561. Mid-Life Crisis
7923. National Enquirer Game
5233. National Lampoon Game of Sell Out
6613. Nuke
6285. Offical Dealer McDope Dealing Game
7879. Original Preppie Board Game, The
4375. Outdoor Survival, 2nd Printing
6376. Person-alysis
4249. Peter Principle Game, The
4377. Peter Principle Game, The
6638. Planit, The Omni Evolution Board
8176. Political Asylum
4306. Pollution Solution, The Game of
7966. Population Game, The
5214. Psych-Out
5661. Public Assistance
5058. Retirement Planing System
6529. Rich-Farmer Poor-Farmer

Social Help

Space

Sports - All

3089. Casey at the Mound,
        Kamm's Baseball
3662. Cavalcade
3660. Cavalcade, Deluxe Edition
3661. Cavalcade, Separate board & box
4353. Challange Football
5717. Challange the Yankees
4354. Challenge Basketball All-Stars
4123. Challenge Golf at Pebble Beach
2301. Challenger Cup Race
7694. Champion 6 in 1 Sports Combination
1804. Champion Base Ball Game, The
1442. Champion Base Ball Parlor Game
2130. Champion Game of Baseball, The
2784. Champion Road Race, Premium
4551. Championship Baseball
5246. Championship Baseball
7634. Championship Baseball
5247. Championship Basketball
5637. Championship Flight Game
5248. Championship Golf
5591. Championship Golf
6713. Charlie Brown's All Star Baseball
6713. Charlie Brown's All Star Baseball
5267. Chex Ches Football
5274. Classic Major League Baseball
5557. Classic Major League Baseball Travel
5116. College Basketball
1597. College Boat Race, Game of
2555. College Football
3058. Country Club Golf
3913. Cowboys & Indians Also Junior Golf
5497. Crosby Derby, The,
        Bing Crosby Photo
3148. Cross Country
2559. Cross Country Marathon
2560. Crusader Horse Race Game
1912. Cycling, The Game of
4448. Dan Kerateter's Classic Football
4357. Decathlon
7528. Decathlon
6512. Demo Derby
3337. Derby Day
3523. Derby Day
5647. Derby Downs
1606. Derby Steeple Chase, The
1607. Derby Steeple Chase, The
3063. Derby Winner
2870. Diamond baseball dart game
1608. Diamond Game of Base Ball, The
903. Diamond, or The Game of Short Stop
3546. Dice Ball, Baseball Game
3252. Dizzy and Daffy Dean
        Nok-Out Baseball
2561. Dog Chase (4689)
7702. Dog Race
8187. Don Carter & Paula Spersel: World
2869. Donkey Derby
3549. Double Header, Wooden Sides
5365. Double Quarterback
4606. Drag Strip!
5849. Dribbling Around Basketball
5288. Drip Dragster, Race a Drop of Water
1441. Driver, or Parlor Golf (© J. W. Keller)
8011. Earl Gillespie, Baseball Game
7706. Eddie Arcaro Blue Grass Handicap
5440. Electric Baseball, 3 color cover'
2916. Electric Basketball (64-X)
5441. Electric Basketball, 3 color cover
2919. Electric Football
5443. Electric Football, 3 color cover
2920. Electric Golf
2921. Electric Hockey
5444. Electric Hockey
3524. Electric Speed Classic
5447. Electric Speedway
5450. Electric Whiz Raceway
2764. Elmer Layden's Scientific Football
5461. Empire Auto Race
2571. Endurance Run
2765. Eric Layden's Scientific Football, 1st
5119. Ethan Allen's All-Star Baseball Game
2381. Exciting Motor Boat Race, An
6186. Extra Innings
5841. F/11 Armchair Quaterback
5297. Face-Off
7886. Fairway Golf, Photo of Billy Maxwell
6572. Falls, Wrestling Game
1547. Fan-I-Tis, Fan's Baseball Fun
6761. Fast 111's
8068. Fast Golf
6542. Fastbreak Basketball

3056. Fireside Baseball
7621. First Down
6771. Fomula-1
6770. Fomula-1, Bold Photo cover
4186. Football
7082. Football
3133. Football As-You-Like-It
7992. Football Card Game
2285. Football game
4404. Football Strategy
6772. Football, Baseball, & Checkers
1634. Football, Game of
3927. Football, Horizontal green box
1293. Football, The Game of
1932. Football, The Game of
3360. Football, the Game of
3168. Foot-Race Game
4321. Fore
4045. Fore Country Club
4046. Fore, Game of Golf
3728. Forward Pass
5123. Foto-Electric Baseball
5124. Foto-Electric Bowling
5128. Foto-Electric Football
5125. Foto-Electric Football, Blue sky white
5126. Foto-Electric Football, Football photo
5127. Foto-Electric Football, Three players
3526. Foto-Finish Horse Race
3131. Four Horsemen Football Game
7721. Four Lane Road Racing Game
7518. Fourth and Goal Football Game
8074. Fox and Hound Game, The
1069. Fox Hunt
2781. Fox Hunt
3142. Fox Hunt
6325. Fox Hunt
7192. Fran Tarkenton's Pro Football
5241. Frank Cavanaugh's American Football
2178. Funny Game Toboggan Slide, A
2959. Fut-Bal
5220. Galloping Golf
5580. Gamblers Golf
2263. Game of Base-Ball, A
5750. Game of the Week
5510. GammonBall
6200. George Brett's 9th Inning Baseball
7166. Giant Wheel Speed Boat Game
7167. Giant Wheel Thrills & Spills Horse
7193. Gil Hodges' Pennant Fever
1437. Glenleven's New Boat Race, The
7529. Go for the Green!
5555. Goal Line Stand
5556. Goal Line Stand
7218. Gold Medal World Olympian Game
1078. Golf
1940. Golf
1941. Golf
929. Golf Bug
3088. Golf Junior
3361. Golf, Amateur
1319. Golf, The Game of
1339. Golf, The Game of
2180. Golf, The Game of
5878. Golferino
3265. Golflet
5641. Gotham All Star Bowling, Metal
5860. Grand Master of the Martial Arts
3933. Grand National, A Sweepstakes of
4242. Grand Prix
3755. Grand Slam
7507. Grand Slam
2435. Grande Auto Race
1373. Great American Game Base Ball, The
2115. Great American Game Baseball, The
2258. Great American Game Baseball, The
3502. Great American
        Game of Baseball, The
3059. Great American Game, Baseball, The
5649. Great Pennant Races
5457. Greatest Baseball
        Teams of the Century
3026. Gregg Football Game, The
6569. Greyhound Pursuit
3558. Greyhound Racing Game
5844. Hal Holiday's Football Strategy
4685. Harlem Globe Trotters Game, The
2608. Hazard's Bowling on the Green
3776. Hear and See Football
5480. Heavy-Weight Boxing
6364. Herman Hickman's Football Game
2609. Hialeah Horse Racing Game
4048. Hi-Fly Baseball

2281. Hit and Run
3117. Hit That Line Football Game
5134. Hockey
2944. Holland's Indoor Golf Game
2802. Hollywood Derby
1661. Home Base Ball Game
3580. Home Baseball Game
7407. Home Baseball Game
5847. Home Court Basketball (Charlie
2878. Home Run
3222. Home Run- With Bases Loaded!
        Johnny
6329. Home Stretch Harness Racing
5756. Home Stretch, The
7407. Home Team Baseball
7408. Home Team Baseball
3675. Home Team Baseball Game
3143. Horse Race
2612. Horse Racing
1663. Horseless Carriage Race, The
2316. Horses
3213. Horses
5842. Horseshow
8082. Hot Wheels Game
5324. Houston Astros, Baseball Challenge
3223. Howard H. Jones College Football
7412. Huggin' the Rail
1094. Hurdle Race
2613. Ice Hockey
3707. Indianapolis 500 Mile Race Game
3172. Indoor Horse Racing
4051. Indoor Horseshoe
3276. Indoor Sports Base Ball
2123. Inside Baseball
5659. In-Side Golf
6805. Instant Replay
3060. Inter Collegiate Football
1674. Intercollegiate Football
1961. International Automobile Race
5136. International Grand Prix
6411. International Grand Prix
7653. International Soccer The Game
2997. Irons and Woods
4421. Jack Bannings Putt-Pins
        (Bowling-Golf)
5642. Jackie Robinson Baseball Game
6144. Jacmar Big League Electric Baseball
6167. JDK Baseball
646. Jerome Park Steeplechase
1678. Jerome Park Steeple-Chase
5458. Jerry Kramer's Instant Replay
2974. Jim Duffer Golf Game
2923. Jim Prentice Electric Baseball
2924. Jim Prentice Electric Basketball
2925. Jim Prentice Electric Football
4333. Jimmy the Greek Oddsmaker Football
5643. Johnny Bench
        Magnetic Baseball Game
7116. Johnny Unitas Football
7051. Johnny Unitas Football Game, The
7043. Jose Canseco's Perfect Baseball Game
5073. Jr. Quarterback Football Game
3583. Junior Basketball Game
3021. Junior Hockey
6537. Junior Table Top Bowling Alley
3262. K. D. Basketball Game
7416. Kace, The Game of
3093. Kellogg's Baseball Game, Premium
3094. Kellogg's Boxing Game, Premium
6189. Kellogg's Soccer Slam,
        Kellogg's Raisin
3095. Kellogg's Football Game, Premium
3096. Kellogg's Golf Game, Premium
3097. Kellogg's Racing Game, Premium
3945. Kentucky Derby
8085. Kentucky Derby Horse Racing Game
2826. Kick-Off
2433. Kick-off Football Game
2623. King of the Turf
4416. King Pin Deluxe Bowling Alley
3111. Knapp Electro Game Set, Auto Race
3113. Knapp Electro Game Set, Baseball
3114. Knapp Electro Game Set, Football
3254a. Knockout
5763. Knuckle Busters
3544. Knute Rockne Football & World
        Series
7761. Krokay
6226. KSP Baseball
6227. KSP Basketball
7289. Las Vegas Baseball
1481. Lawson's Baseball Card Game

5338. Lazy Pool
4370. Le Mans
3811. Lester Patrick's Official Hockey
5360. Let's Bowl a Game
2952. Let's Go Golfun
5361. Let's Play Baseball
5362. Let's Play Basketball
2398. Let's Play Games, Golf, Polo, Boots &
5091. Let's Play Golf
5092. Let's Play Golf, The Hawaiian Open
5495. LF Baseball
3855. Light Horse H. Cooper Golf
1251. Lilliput Golf
6310. Line Drive
2422. Little Jack Horner Golf Course
7553. Little League Baseball
5075. Little Leaguer Baseball Game
4323. Long ball
2633. Long Green, The
6824. Long Shot
7115. Look All Star Baseball Game
5405. Los Angeles Dodgers Game
8210. Los Angeles Rams Football Game
3085. Lou Gehrig's Game
5076. Lucky "9" Race Game
2287. Lucky 7th Baseball Game
3135. Lucky Strike & Horse Race Game
3034. Magic-Race (Horse Race)
2411. Major League Baseball Game
2119. Major League Baseball Game, Wood
7994. Manage Your Own Baseball Team
5149. Match Point Tennis
7137. Mel Allen's Baseball Game
1819. Merry Steeple Chase, the
5407. Mets Baseball Game
5594. Mickey Mouse Basketball
5595. Micky Mantle's Big League Baseball
2846. Midget Auto Race
3153. Midget Auto Race
3955. Midget Speedway, The Game of
7565. Midwest Research ML Baseball
3210. Miniature Golf
3038. Monday Morning Coach
3216. Monday Morning Coach
8201. Monday Morning
        Quarterback Football
4335. Monday Night Baseball
4336. Monday Night Football with
3520. Monte Carlo Whippet Derby
2643. Moon Mullins Automobile Race
3208. Motor Race
5478. Motorace
7295. Mulligans, Pinehurst Championship
6559. Munich Decathlon
6014. MVP Baseball,
        The Sports Card Game
4802. NASCAR Daytona 500
2116. National Base Ball Game
3228. National Card Baseball Game
3235. National Football Game
1470. National Football Match, The
2852. National Game of Baseball
3641. National Game, A Base-Ball Card
5155. National Pro Football, Hall of Fame
7524. National Pro Hockey
2001. National-American Base Ball Game
3958. Navigator-A Boat Race w/ a Deck of
6016. NBA All-Pro Basketball
5156. NBA Bas-ket
6554. NBA Opoly
5781. NBC Game of the Week
5782. NBC Pro Playoff
6611. Negamo Basketball
6610. NeGamo Pro Golf
2003. New Bicycle Game, The
1714. Newport Yacht Race
7650. NFL Armchair Quaterback
7211. NFL Franchise
7910. NFL Play Action
4449. NFL Playoff, Various team s
7911. NFL Strategy
7912. NFL Strategy
6017. NHL All-Pro Hockey
2899. Nineteenth Hole Golf Game
3173. Nineteenth Hole, The
3417. Nip and Tuck, Hockey
5239. Nok Hockey
7636. Nuttsy Tennis
2779. Obstacle Golf
3187. Obstacle Golf
7645. Official Babe Ruth's Baseball Game

4807. Official Baseball Game
6534. Official Globetrotter Basketball, The
7556. Official National Football League
6021. Official NFL Football Game
7092. Official Roger Maris Baseball Game
6629. Official Skins Golf Game, The
4811. Official Baseball Card Game
4810. Official Baseball Card Game, 1st
3812. Official Basketball
7044. Official Boston Marathon Game
5619. Official NBA Basketball Game
3814. Official Radio Baseball
3813. Official Radio Football
2476. Open Championship Gold Game
5350. Original Home Jai-Alai Game, The
7195. Oscar Robertson's Pro Basketball
2877. Ot-O-Win Horseshoe Game
1551. Our National Ball Game
2210. Our National Ball Game
3729. Over the Hurdles
3277. Palley Golf Game
4065. Palm Beach Auto Race
5652. Par Golf
6593. Par Golf
6645. Par It
3624. Par The New Golf Game
4450. Par, 73
4417. Par-A-Shoot Game
6647. Pari, Horse Race Card Game
2663. Parlay
879. Parlor Base Ball
883. Parlor Base Ball
1550. Parlor Base Ball
880. Parlor Base Ball, Wooden Box Edition
1727. Parlor Foot-Ball
1261. Parlor Golf
2112. Parlor Golf
7203. Parlor Ponies
776. Parlor Race, or Dickens on the Turf
2498. Parlor-Bowl Baseball
2431. Pass "N" Punt
3730. Pat Morgan's Own Ball
7885. Paul Brown's Football Game
7530. Paydirt
4376. Paydirt!
4837. PD Cue Bumper Pool
3421. Peg Baseball
5310. Pennant Chasers Baserball Game
4165. Pennant Drive
7519. Pennant Quest
6877. Phil & Tony Esposito's Action
      Hockey
5164. Photo-Electric Football
4160. Photo-Finish
6878. Pigskin
6879. Pigskin
6880. Pigskin
3429. Pigskin, Tom Hamilton's
      Football Game
4091. Pitch Em Indoor Horseshoes
4845. Pivot Golf
4846. Pivot Pool
3508. Pla-Golf
1797. Play Ball
3233. Play Ball
3591. Play Ball
3115. Play Ball Baseball Game
7646. Play Ball Hockey
7052. Play Baseball
6594. Play Basketball with Bob Cousey
3975. Play Football
3976. Play Football
3977. Play Football
3974. Play Football, Dark blue cover
7209. Play Pace Racing Game
3433. Playing the Ponies
5322. Playoff Football
5341. Plymouth Drag Race Game
3817. Pocket Baseball
2412. Pocket Edition Major League Base-
      ball
3818. Pocket Football
4246. Pocket Football
6886. Pole Position
1262. Pool, Game of
8204. Power 4 Car Race
7214. Power Play
4857. Pro Bowling
6445. Pro Coach Football
6897. Pro Draft
6896. Pro Draft, Topps cards included
4145. Pro Football

4858. Pro Football
7217. Pro Football Franchise
5167. Pro Foto-Football
5168. Pro Foto-Football
4405. Pro Golf
6609. Pro Golf Game
5644. Pro League Basketball
4192. Pro Locker Basketball
5249. Pro Quarterback
6279. Pro Quarterback
7112. Pro Replay Football
4406. Pro Tennis
6183. Pro, Base ball,Card Game
7042. PSG Baseball
3441. Psychic Base ball Game
3539. Psychic Baseball
7119. Pug-I-Lo
4068. Punt Football (69)
7046. Pursue the Pennant
7120. Pursue the Pennant
3279. Quaddy Golf
1536. Quarterback
1810. Quarterback
7805. Quaterback Football Game
6033. Quickflip Volleyball Game
7807. Race A Car
820. Race Course
2046. Race for the Cup
4410. Race Trap
897. Race, Game of the
5083. Race-O-Rama, 4 Race Games
1156. Races
473. Races, Game of the
414. Races, The Game of the
3445. Raceway
6596. Raceway
2861. Racing Stable, The Game of
3690. Rainy Day Golf
5057. Rainy Day Golf
7619. Razzle Dazzle Football Game
3032. Razz-O-Dazz-O Six-Man Football
3570. Real Football
7138. Real-Action Baseball Game
3548. Realistic Baseball
5564. Real-Life Basketball
7149. Regal Finger-Tip Baseball Game
4147. Regatta
7066. Regatta
8105. Regatta
7188. Replay Baseball
7189. Replay Pro Football
4457. Replay Series Baseball
7586. Ride the Surf
7240. Ripley's Believe it or Not, Sports
7592. Road Race Skill Drive Game
7810. Rocky Colavito
      Baseball, Bowling Ball
7196. Rocky Gratziano, A Century of Great
4338. Roger Staubach ABC Monday Night
3569. Roller Derby
4878. Roller Derby
6334. Rose Bowl
6333. Rose Bowl, Photo cover
3648. Rotary Golf
2452. Roulette Baseball Game
3035. Rum-E-Golf
1279. Rush Punt Football
6561. Sail Away. A Racing Game
4454. Sailor's Game, The
7292. Samsonite Basketball
7293. Samsonite Football
7294. Samsonite Pro Football Game
4884. Sandlot Slugger
2691. Saratoga
2192. Saratoga Steeple Chase
7349. Scott's Baseball Card Game
4413. Scrambled Squares Soccer
7521. Scrimmage
6207. See-Action Football Game, O.J
8195. Set Point, Tennis Strategy Game
7632. SI, The Sporting Word Game
3136. Six Day Bike Race
7514. Skaters Only
1268. Skating Race Game, The
4224. Ski Gammon
7500. Skill Games, Baseball,
      Tennis, Football
6051. Skin Divers
4339. Skittle Baseball
7205. Skrimage
4381. Slapshot
2489. Slide Kelly!

3188. Slugger Baseball Game (511)
2703. Smitty Speed Boat Race Game
6057. Snap Bowling
2482. Snappy Foot Ball
7297. Sod Buster
7540. Sooperbowl Pro-Football Game
3735. Spare-Time Bowling
6273. Spare-Time Bowling
7278. Special Detective ane Speedwat
2340. Spedem Auto
2341. Spedem, Junior Auto Race Game
2706. Speed Boat Race
4149. Speed Circuit
3631. Speed King, Game of
3116. Speed Up
6147. Speed-O-Rama
6061. Speedway
3721. Speedway Motor Race
3732. Speedway Motor Race
2491. SportMaster, include: Backgammon;
1175. Sports (4143)
4926. Sports Arena
7187. Sports Arena No. 1
7525. Sports Dynasty, The Game for
7531. Sports Illustrated Baseball
7532. Sports Illustrated College Football
7533. Sports Illustrated Handicap Golf
7630. Sports Illustrated Pro Football
7534. Sports Illustrated, All Time, All Star
5871. Sports Trivia Game- #5
7503. Sports Yesteryear
7539. Sportsbet
1176. Springfield Football Game
6497. Sprint Drag Race Game
5418. St. Louis Cardinals Baseball Game
2850. Stadium Football
3656. Stadium/Big League Combination
3858. Star Baseball
4094. Star Basket-Ball
3745. Stars and Stripes, Football Gmae
4385. Statis Pro Baseball
4386. Statis Pro Major League Game of Pro-
7566. Statis-Pro Football
1325. Steeple Chase
899. Steeple Chase Game, The
1178. Steeple Chase, Game of
2070. Steeple Chase, Game of
900. Steeplechase, The Game of
8188. Steve Garvey's Super Star Baseball
3773. Sto-Auto Race
5597. Stock Car Race
8123. Stock Car Racing Game
7202. Stock Car Racing Game
      with R. Petty &
5529. Stock Car Road Race
6177. Stock Car Speedway, Game of
7469. Straightaway
6528. Strategy Manger Baseball
7572. Strat-O-Matic Baseball
7573. Strat-O-Matic Baseball
7574. Strat-O-Matic Hockey
7575. Strat-O-Matic Pro Football
7576. Strat-O-Matic Pro Football
7577. Strat-O-Matic Pro Football
7578. Strat-O-Matic Pro Football
7579. Strat-O-Matic Sports "Know-How"
7974. Stretch Call
5803. Strike Bowling
3804. Strike Three by Carl Hubble
2838. Suffolk Downs- Club Edition
5304. Suffolk Downs Racing Game
3698. Sumrun, The Great Racing Game
7535. Super Star Baseball
5805. Super Sunday Football
4389. Superstar Baseball
7536. Superstar Baseball
7583. Superstar Pro Wrestling Game
4287. Superstar TV Sports
6067. Sure Shot Baseball
6068. Sure Shot Basketball
6069. Sure Shot Hockey
4963. Swat Baseball
4197. Sweeps
4198. Sweeps
4199. Sweeps
3036. Sweepstakes
8183. Sweepstakes, Electronic Horse Rac-
      ing
5831. Swish
5086. Swish Basketball Game
7590. T.H.E. Pro Football
5685. Table Top Bowling

6538. Table Top Bowling Alley
6196. Table Top Soccer
3782. Tackle
3783. Tactical Baseball
3784. Tactical Football
6501. Talking Baseball
6502. Talking Monday Night Football
5624. Tee Off by Sam Snead
7611. Tee Off on Golf
2873. Tee Off!
4973. Tee Party
6641. Teed Off
3257. Te-Ho Hockey
3064. Ten Grand
6963. Tennis
3885. Test Your Gridiron Skill
6444. They're at the Post, Record plays the
6964. They're Off, Horse Race Game
4151. Thinking Man's Football
4152. Thinking Man's Golf
6338. Thorobred
4007. Three Ring Circus/Steeplechase
2853. Thrilling Indoor Football Game
4983. Thunder Road
7633. Time Travel Baseball
3119. Tip-Top Boxing, Dempsey-Wills
3125. Tit for Tat Indoor Hockey
4407. Title Bout
3473. Tom Hamilton's Pigskin
2840. Top Hockey
5421. Top Pro Football Quiz Game
6971. Top Ten Bowling
7638. Top Ten College Basketball
3805. Toto the New (BaseBall)
2772. Touchdown
4080. Touchdown Football
1474. Touchdown or Parlor Foot Ball, The
3039. Touchdown, The New Game
4418. Tournament Golf
7537. Track Meet
6091. Trap Tennis
2732. Traps and Bunkers, Game of Golf
7877. Traps, The Game of, Golf Game
4317. Trivia Party - Sports
7913. Tru-Action Electric Baseball
7914. Tru-Action Electric Football
7915. Tru-Action Electric Horserace
7916. Tru-Action Electric Sports Car Race
7891. TSG I, Pro Football
7917. Tudor Electric Horse Racing Game
7918. Tudor Electric Sports Car Race
3013. Tumble Golf
4993. Turbo
3065. Twenty Grand
7538. U.S.A.C. Auto Racing
3651. U-Bat-It
7927. Ultimate College Basketball
7928. Ultimate Golf
7131. Ultimate Sports Trivia
931. Uncle Sam's Game
3862. Universal Baseball
3861. Universal Baseball Playing Cards
8211. Vallco Pro Drag Racing Game
2778. Va-Lo, The Football Card Game
992. Vanderbilt Cup Race Game, The
3103. Varsitee Football Playing Cards
5206. Varsity
2776. Varsity Football Game
1270. Vassar Board Race, The
5600. Verne Gagne World Champion
7197. Vince Lombardi's Game
5009. Volley, A Volley ball game
1472. Walter Johnson Baseball Game
3877. Waners Baseball
2808. Ward Cuff's Football Game
3053. We V Nap Horse Race Game
3708. Wee-Tee Indoor Golf
2886. Whippet Derby
2872. Whippet Race
3531. Whippet Race
5456. Whiz Baseball
2927. Whiz Baseball
3705. Wicket Golf
5033. Wide World of Sports-Auto Racing
5034. Wide World of Sports-Golf
5035. Wide World of Sports-Tennis
8171. Wil-Croft Baseball
4082. Wilders Baseball
4083. Wilders Football
4156. Win, Place & Show
4398. Win, Place and Show
5037. Win, Place and Show

5690. Wiry Dan's Electric Baseball Game
5691. Wiry Dan's Electric Football Game
1792. Wizard Base Ball Game
4092. Woolsey's Football
6340. World Series
2243. World Series Base Ball Game
8185. World's Greatest Baseball Game
5042. Wrestling Superstars
5044. WWF Wrestling
2362. Wyntre Golf
3557. Yacht Club
1215. Yacht Race
1347. Yacht Race
1781. Yacht Race
3533. Yacht Race
3532. Yacht Race (930)
1780. Yacht Race at Sandy Hook
536. Yacht Race, Franklin and Great
7022. Yacht Race, Saturday Housed
1214. Yacht Race, The Pennant
1782. Yacht Racing Game, The
2103. Yachting
2198. Yachting
2197. Yachting, Game of
2104. Yachts The International Race
1783. Yale Princeton Foot Ball Game
3120. Yale-Harvard Football game
2105. Yale-Harvard Game
3639. Yankee Doodle Baseball
2365. Yatteau
1272. Young Athlete, The
2843. You're Out Baseball Game
1787. Zimmer's Base Ball Game
4114. Zweifel Card Golf

Sports - Baseball

5254. 1876 Baseball
7072. Action Baseball
7069. Action Baseball for Mickey Mantle
7070. Action Baseball for Roger Maris
7071. Action Baseball for Tom Seaver
3785. All American Base Ball
5886. All Pro Baseball
5097. All Star Baseball
5098. All Star Baseball
5099. All Star Baseball
5100. All Star Baseball
5094. All Star Baseball, Ethen Allen's
5095. All Star Baseball,
     Green background No
5096. All Star Baseball, Green background
3893. All Star Basketball
5887. All-Pro Baseball
5105. All-Star Baseball
5106. All-Star Baseball
5673. All-Star Electric Baseball & Football
2375. American Indoor Baseball Game
4257. APBA Baseball Master Game, each
4258. APBA Baseball Master Game, each
4259. APBA Baseball Master Game, each
4260. APBA Baseball Master Game, each
4261. APBA Major League Baseball Game
4262. APBA Major League Baseball Game
7547. Approved Little League
     Baseball Game
6580. Arabian Nights-Triple Play-7-in One
5618. ASG Major League Baseball
7526. Authentic Major League
     Baseball Game
914. Aydelott's Base Ball Cards, The
2527. Babe Ruth's Baseball Game
2450. Bambino
6414. Bambino Base ball Game
1872. Base Ball
3857. Base Ball Card
1374. Base Ball Game,
     Clark & Martin's New
944. Base Ball Game, League Parlor
1870. Base Ball Game, The Major League
1871. Base Ball Game,
     The Professional Game
990. Base Ball with Cards
2164. Base Ball, Game of
923. Base Balline
1834. Baseball
2532. Baseball
2754. Baseball
4182. Baseball
6671. Baseball
7665. Baseball
2531. Baseball & Checkers
4255. Baseball Action

5226. Baseball Card All Star Game
7887. Baseball Challenge
1873. Baseball Game
2428. Baseball Game
2818. Baseball Game
3130. Baseball Game
6666. Baseball Game
6667. Baseball Game
3178. Baseball Game & G-Man Target
5851. Baseball Game, The
4344. Baseball Strategy
3299. Baseball, Game of
1576. Base-ball, Game of
6670. Baseball, Green with Red Strip cover
3536. Baseball, The Champion Game of
924. Baseballitis
4322. Baseball's Greatest Moments
5388. Batter Up. Baseball Card Game
5850. Batter Up
925. Batter Up, Game of
8008. B-B Ball Players Baseball Game
7546. Bible Baseball
3137. Big League
3900. Big League Baseball
3902. Big League Baseball
4119. Big League Baseball
7564. Big League Baseball Card Game
2421. Big League Baseball Game
3901. Big League Baseball,
     by A. E. Gustafson
3141. Big League Game of Baseball
3506. Big Six:Christy Mathewson Indoor
4432. Bileth Baseball
7261. Bob Feller Big league Baseball
7264. Bob Feller's Big League
7139. Bobby Shanz Baseball Game
6199. Brett Ball
7080. Broadcast Baseball
5640. Carl Hubbel Mechanical Baseball
6184. Casey at the Mound,
     Kamm's Baseball
3089. Casey at the Mound,
     Kamm's Baseball
5717. Challange the Yankees
1804. Champion Base Ball Game, The
1442. Champion Base Ball Parlor Game
2130. Champion Game of Baseball, The
4551. Championship Baseball
5246. Championship Baseball
7634. Championship Baseball
6713. Charlie Brown's All Star Baseball
5274. Classic Major League Baseball
5557. Classic Major League Baseball Travel
2870. Diamond baseball dart game
1608. Diamond Game of Base Ball, The
903. Diamond, or The Game of Short Stop
3546. Dice Ball, Baseball Game
3252. Dizzy and Daffy Dean
     Nok-Out Baseball
3549. Double Header, Wooden Sides
8011. Earl Gillespie, Baseball Game
5440. Electric Baseball, 3 color cover'
5119. Ethan Allen's All-Star Baseball Game
6186. Extra Innings
1547. Fan-I-Tis, Fan's Baseball Fun
3056. Fireside Baseball
5123. Foto-Electric Baseball
2263. Game of Base-Ball, A
5750. Game of the Week
6200. George Brett's 9th Inning Baseball
7193. Gil Hodges' Pennant Fever
3755. Grand Slam
7507. Grand Slam
1373. Great American Game Base Ball, The
2115. Great American Game Baseball, The
2258. Great American Game Baseball, The
3502. Great American Game of Baseball,
     The
3059. Great American Game, Baseball, The
5649. Great Pennant Races
5457. Greatest Baseball
     Teams of the Century
4048. Hi-Fly Baseball
2281. Hit and Run
1661. Home Base Ball Game
3580. Home Baseball Game
7407. Home Baseball Game
2878. Home Run
3222. Home Run- With Bases Loaded!
     Johnny
7408. Home Team Baseball
7409. Home Team Baseball

3675. Home Team Baseball Game
5324. Houston Astros, Baseball Challenge
3276. Indoor Sports Base Ball
2123. Inside Baseball
5642. Jacmar Big League Electric Baseball
6144. Jacmar Big League Electric Baseball
6167. JDK Baseball
2923. Jim Prentice Electric Baseball
5643. Johnny Bench Magnetic
     Baseball Game
7043. Jose Canseco's Perfect Baseball Game
3093. Kellogg's Baseball Game, Premium
3113. Knapp Electro Game Set, Baseball
3544. Knute Rockne
     Football & World Series
6226. KSP Baseball
7289. Las Vegas Baseball
1481. Lawson's Baseball Card Game
5361. Let's Play Baseball
5495. LF Baseball
6310. Line Drive
7553. Little League Baseball
5075. Little Leaguer Baseball Game
4323. Long ball
7115. Look All Star Baseball Game
5405. Los Angeles Dodgers Game
3085. Lou Gehrig's Game
2287. Lucky 7th Baseball Game
2411. Major League Baseball
2119. Major League Baseball Game, Wood
7994. Manage Your Own Baseball Team
7137. Mel Allen's Baseball Game
5407. Mets Baseball Game
5595. Micky Mantle's Big League Baseball
7565. Midwest Reasearch ML Baseball
4335. Monday Night Baseball
6014. MVP Baseball,
     The Sports Card Game
2116. National Base Ball Game
3228. National Card Baseball Game
2852. National Game of Baseball
3641. National Game, A Base-Ball Card
2001. National-American Base Ball Game
7644. Official Babe Ruth's Baseball Game
4807. Official Baseball Game
7092. Offical Roger Maris Baseball Game
4811. Official Baseball Card Game
4810. Official Baseball Card Game, 1st
3814. Official Radio Baseball
1551. Our National Ball Game
2210. Our National Ball Game
879. Parlor Base Ball
883. Parlor Base Ball
1550. Parlor Base Ball
880. Parlor Base Ball, Wooden Box Edition
2498. Parlor-Bowl Baseball
3730. Pat Morgan's Own Ball
3421. Peg Baseball
5310. Pennant Chasers Baserball Game
4165. Pennant Drive
7519. Pennant Quest
1797. Play Ball
3233. Play Ball
3591. Play Ball
3115. Play Ball Baseball Game
7052. Play Ball
3817. Pocket Baseball
2412. Pocket Edition Major League Base-
     ball
6183. Pro, Base ball,Card Game
7042. PSG Baseball
3441. Psychic Base ball Game
3539. Psychic Baseball
7046. Pursue the Pennant
7120. Pursue the Pennant
7138. Real-Action Baseball Game
3548. Realistic Baseball
7149. Regal Finger-Tip Baseball Game
7188. Replay Baseball
4457. Replay Series Baseball
7810. Rocky Colavito Baseball, Bowling
     Ball
2452. Roulette Baseball Game
4884. Sandlot Slugger
7349. Scott's Baseball Card Game
7500. Skill Games, Baseball,
     Tennis, Football
4339. Skittle Baseball
2489. Slide Kelly!
3188. Slugger Baseball Game (511)
7531. Sports Illustrated Baseball
7534. Sports Illustrated, All Time, All Star

5418. St. Louis Cardinals Baseball Game
3656. Stadium/Big League Combination
3858. Star Baseball
4385. Statis Pro Baseball
4386. Statis Pro Major League Game of Pro-
8188. Steve Garvey's Super Star Baseball
6528. Strategy Manger Baseball
7572. Strat-O-Matic Baseball
7573. Strat-O-Matic Baseball
3804. Strike Three by Carl Hubble
7535. Super Star Baseball
4389. Superstar Baseball
7536. Superstar Baseball
6067. Sure Shot Baseball
4963. Swat Baseball
3783. Tactical Baseball
7633. Time Travel Baseball
3805. Toto the New (BaseBall)
7913. Tru-Action Electric Baseball
3651. U-Bat-It
931. Uncle Sam's Baseball Game
3862. Universal Baseball
3861. Universal Baseball Playing Cards
1472. Walter Johnson Baseball Game
3877. Waners Baseball
5456. Whiz Baseball
8171. Wil-Croft Baseball
4082. Wilders Baseball
5690. Wiry Dan's Electric Baseball Game
1792. Wizard Base Ball Game
6340. World Series
2243. World Series Base Ball Game
8185. World's Greatest Baseball Game
3639. Yankee Doodle Baseball
2843. You're Out Baseball Game
1787. Zimmer's Base Ball Game

Sports-Basketball

5061. 4 Quarter Basketball Game
2814. All American Basketball
2816. All-American Basketball Game
5888. All-Pro Basketball
5638. All-Star Basketball Bagatelle
4263. APBA Pro Basketball, 1st edition
4264. APBA Pro Basketball, last edition
4265. APBA Pro Basketball,later editions
4266. APBA Pro Basketball,later editions
4267. APBA Pro Basketball,later editions
2762. Bas-Ket
2481. Basket Ball
5109. Bas-ket, Photo cover
5110. Bas-Ket, Red Cover
1238. Basketball
3608. Basketball
3897. Basketball
7665. Basketball
7987. Basketball Card Game
2443. Basketball Game
5062. Basketball Game
4345. Basketball Strategy
2888. Basketball Tiddley Winks
1575. Basketball, Game of
4452. Big League Manager Basketball
4354. Challenge Basketball All-Stars
5247. Championship Basketball
5116. College Basketball
5849. Dribbling Around Basketball
2916. Electric Basketball (64-X)
5441. Electric Basketball, 3 color cover
6542. Fastbreak Basketball
4685. Harlem Globe Trotters Game, The
5847. Home Court Basketball
2924. Jim Prentice Electric Basketball
3583. Junior Basketball Game
3262. K. D. Basketball Game
6227. KSP Basketball
5362. Let's Play Basketball
5594. Mickey Mouse Basketball
6016. NBA All-Pro Basketball
5156. NBA Bas-ket
6554. NBA Opoly
6611. Negamo Basketball
6534. Offical Globetrotter Basketball, The
3812. Official Basketball
5619. Official NBA Basketball Game
7195. Oscar Robertson's Pro Basketball
6594. Play Basketball with Bob Cousey
5644. Pro League Basketball
4192. Pro Locker Basketball
5564. Real-Life Basketball
7292. Samsonite Basketball
4094. Star Basket-Ball

6068. Sure Shot Basketball
5831. Swish
5086. Swish Basketball Game
7638. Top Ten College Basketball
7927. Ultimate College Basketball

Sports-Bicycling

1878. Bicycle Cards, A Game
1020. Bicycle Game
1879. Bicycle Game, Century Run
1880. Bicycle Game, Junior
1881. Bicycle Game, The New
1021. Bicycle Race
1578. Bicycle Race, Game of
1242. Bicycle Race, The
1579. Bicycle Racing
1882. Bicycling
3191. Bike Race Game, The
988. Boston Globe's Bicycle Game of
2003. New Bicycle Game, The
3136. Six Day Bike Race

Sports-Bowling

5639. All-Star Bowling
4268. APBA Pro Bowling, 1st Edition
4269. APBA Pro Bowling,
      laret editioins each
4270. APBA Pro Bowling, later editions
      each
3106. Bo-Lem-Ova
6317. Bowl A Score
5439. Bowl-A-Matic
6318. Bowl-A-Strike
3305. Bowlem
3306. Bowlem
6691. Bowl-Em
2497. Bowlett
5064. Bowling, Pocket Size
5494. Bowlo
8187. Don Carter & Paula Spersel: World
5124. Foto-Electric Bowling
5641. Gotham All Star Bowling, Metal
4421. Jack Bannings Putt-Pins
      (Bowling-Golf)
6537. Junior Table Top Bowling Alley
4416. King Pin Deluxe Bowling Alley
5360. Let's Bowl a Game
4857. Pro Bowling
6057. Snap Bowling
3735. Spare-Time Bowling
6273. Spare-Time Bowling
5803. Strike Bowling
5685. Table Top Bowling
6538. Table Top Bowling Alley
6971. Top Ten Bowling

Sports-Boxing

3751. Boxing, The
4029. Boxing
5637. Championship Flight Game
5480. Heavy-Weight Boxing
3094. Kellogg's Boxing Game, Premium
3254a. Knockout
5763. Knuckle Busters
7119. Pug-I-Lo
7196. Rocky Gratziano, A Century of Great
3119. Tip-Top Boxing, Dempsey-Wills
4407. Title Bout

Sports-Car Racing

5060. 300 Mile Race
2525. Auto Race
3294. Auto Race
2523. Auto Race Game
3268. Auto Race, Game of
1571. Automobile Race Game
2784. Champion Road Race, Premium
6512. Demo Derby
4606. Drag Strip!
3524. Electric Speed Classic
5447. Electric Speedway
5450. Electric Whiz Raceway
5461. Empire Auto Race
6761. Fast 111's
6771. Fomula-1
6770. Fomula-1, Bold Photo cover
7721. Four Lane Road Racing Game
4242. Grand Prix
2435. Grande Auto Race
1663. Horseless Carriage Race, The
8082. Hot Wheels Game

7412. Huggin' the Rail
3707. Indianapolis 500 Mile Race Game
1961. International Automobile Race
5136. International Grand Prix
6411. International Grand Prix
3097. Kellogg's Racing Game, Premium
3111. Knapp Electro Game Set, Auto Race
4370. Le Mans
5076. Lucky "9" Race Game
2846. Midget Auto Race
3153. Midget Auto Race
3955. Midget Speedway, The Game of
2643. Moon Mullins Automobile Race
3208. Motor Race
5478. Motorace
4802. NASCAR Daytona 500
4065. Palm Beach Auto Race
5341. Plymouth Drag Race Game
6886. Pole Position
8204. Power 4 Car Race
7807. Race A Car
4410. Race Trap
5083. Race-O-Rama, 4 Race Games
7592. Road Race Skill Drive Game
7278. Special Detective ane Speedwat
2340. Spedem Auto
2341. Spedem, Junior Auto Race Game
4149. Speed Circuit
3631. Speed King, Game of
3116. Speed Up
6147. Speed-O-Rama
6061. Speedway
3721. Speedway Motor Race
3732. Speedway Motor Race
6497. Sprint Drag Race Game
3773. Sto-Auto Race
5597. Stock Car Race
8123. Stock Car Racing Game
7202. Stock Car Racing Game
      with R. Petty &
5529. Stock Car Road Race
6177. Stock Car Speedway, Game of
7469. Straightaway
4983. Thunder Road
7916. Tru-Action Electric Sports Car Race
7918. Tudor Electric Sports Car Race
4993. Turbo
7538. U.S.A.C. Auto Racing
8211. Vallco Pro Drag Racing Game
992. Vanderbilt Cup Race Game, The
5033. Wide World of Sports-Auto Racing

Sports-Football

4328. ABC Monday Night Football
3786. All American Football
3285. All American Football Game
2815. All Star Football Game
3234. All-American Football Game
5103. All-American Football Game
5104. All-American Football Game
5101. All-American Football Game, Photo
5102. All-American Football Game,
      single red
5889. All-Pro Football
5673. All-Star Electric Baseball & Football
5588. All-Star Football
7144. Alpha Football Game
2272. American Football Game
2376. American Football Game
3069. American Football Game
3512. American Varsity Football
3854. America's Football
4275. APBA Pro League Football,
      1st edition
4276. APBA Pro League Football,
      2nd edition
4277. APBA Pro League Football, later
4278. APBA Pro League Football, later
4279. APBA Pro League Football, later
4280. APBA Pro League Football, later
6627. Arm Chair Quarterback
6668. Baseball, Black Background and Red
2946. Benson Football Game, The
4453. Big League Manager Football
3600. Big Ten Football Game
3884. Big Ten Football, The, Premium
7594. Big Time Colorado Football
1244. Blow Foot Ball
3066. Bo McMillin's Indoor Football Game
7494. Booth's Pro Conference Football
4403. Bowl Bound
7527. Bowl Bound

1584. Boy's Own Football Game
4353. Challange Football
5267. Chex Ches Football
2555. College Football
4448. Dan Kereteter's Classic Football
5365. Double Quarterback
2919. Electric Football
5443. Electric Football, 3 color cover
2764. Elmer Layden's Scientific Football
2765. Eric Layden's Scientific Football, 1st
5841. F/11 Armchair Quaterback
7621. First Down
4186. Football
7082. Football
3133. Football As-You-Like-It
7992. Football Card Game
2285. Football game
4404. Football Strategy
1634. Football, Game of
3927. Football, Horizontal green box
1293. Football, The Game of
1932. Football, The Game of
3360. Football, the Game of
3728. Forward Pass
5128. Foto-Electric Football
5125. Foto-Electric Football, Blue sky white
5126. Foto-Electric Football, Football photo
5127. Foto-Electric Football, Three players
3131. Four Horsemen Football Game
7518. Fourth and Goal Football Game
7192. Fran Tarkenton's Pro Football
5241. Frank Cavanaugh's American Football
2959. Fut-Bal
5555. Goal Line Stand
5556. Goal Line Stand
3026. Gregg Football Game, The
5844. Hal Holiday's Football Strategy
3776. Hear and See Football
6364. Herman Hickman's Football Game
3117. Hit That Line Football Game
3223. Howard H. Jones College Football
6805. Instant Replay
3060. Inter Collegiate Football
1674. Intercollegiate Football
5458. Jerry Kramer's Instant Replay
2925. Jim Prentice Electric Football
4333. Jimmy the Greek Oddsmaker Football
7116. Johnny Unitas Football
7051. Johnny Unitas Football Game, The
5073. Jr. Quarterback Football Game
3095. Kellogg's Football Game, Premium
2827. Kick-Off
2433. Kick-off Game
3114. Knapp Electro Game Set, Football
3544. Knute Rockne Football &
      World Series
6309. Little Caesars Football! Football!
8209. Los Angeles Rams Football Game
3038. Monday Morning Coach
3216. Monday Morning Coach
8201. Monday Morning
      Quarterback Football
4336. Monday Night Football with Roger
3235. National Football Game
5155. National Pro Football, Hall of Fame
5781. NBC Game of the Week
5782. NBC Pro Playoff
7650. NFL Armchair Quaterback
7211. NFL Franchise
7910. NFL Play Action
4449. NFL Playoff, Various team s
7911. NFL Strategy
7912. NFL Strategy
7556. Offical National Football League
6021. Offical NFL Football Game
3813. Official Radio Football
1727. Parlor Foot-Ball
2431. Pass "N" Punt
7885. Paul Brown's Football Game
7530. Paydirt
4376. Paydirt!
5164. Photo-Electric Football
6878. Pigskin
6879. Pigskin
6880. Pigskin
3429. Pigskin, Tom Hamilton's
      Football Game
3975. Play Football
3976. Play Football
3977. Play Football
3974. Play Football, Dark blue cover
5322. Playoff Football

3818. Pocket Football
4246. Pocket Football
6445. Pro Coach Football
6897. Pro Draft
6896. Pro Draft, Topps cards included
4145. Pro Football
4858. Pro Football
7217. Pro Football Franchise
5167. Pro Foto-Football
5168. Pro Foto-Football
5249. Pro Quarterback
6279. Pro Quarterback
7112. Pro Replay Football
4068. Punt Football (69)
1536. Quarterback
1810. Quarterback
7805. Quaterback Football Game
7619. Razzle Dazzle Football Game
3032. Razz-O-Dazz-O Six-Man Football
3570. Real Football
7189. Replay Pro Football
4338. Roger Staubach ABC Monday Night
6334. Rose Bowl
6333. Rose Bowl, Photo cover
1279. Rush Punt Football
7293. Samsonite Football
7294. Samsonite Pro Football Game
7521. Scrimmage
6207. See-Action Football Game, O.J
7500. Skill Games, Baseball,
      Tennis, Football
7205. Skrimage
2482. Snappy Foot Ball
7297. Sod Buster
7540. Sooperbowl Pro-Football Game
7532. Sports Illustrated College Football
7630. Sports Illustrated Pro Football
1176. Springfield Football Game
2850. Stadium Football
3745. Stars and Stripes, Football Gmae
7566. Statis-Pro Football
7575. Strat-O-Matic Pro Football
7576. Strat-O-Matic Pro Football
7577. Strat-O-Matic Pro Football
7578. Strat-O-Matic Pro Football
5805. Super Sunday Football
7590. T.H.E. Pro Football
3782. Tackle
3784. Tactical Football
6501. Talking Football
6502. Talking Monday Night Football
3885. Test Your Gridiron Skill
4151. Thinking Man's Football
2853. Thrilling Indoor Football Game
3473. Tom Hamilton's Pigskin
5421. Top Pro Football Quiz Game
2772. Touchdown
4081. Touchdown Football
1474. Touchdown or Parlor Foot Ball, The
3039. Touchdown, The New Game
7914. Tru-Action Electric Football
7891. TSG I, Pro Football
2778. Va-Lo, The Football Card Game
3103. Varsitee Football Playing Cards
5206. Varsity
2776. Varsity Football Game
7197. Vince Lombardi's Game
2808. Ward Cuff's Football Game
2927. Whiz Football
4083. Wilders Football
5691. Wiry Dan's Electric Football Game
4092. Woolsey's Football
1783. Yale Princeton Foot Ball Game
3120. Yale-Harvard Football game
2105. Yale-Harvard Game

Sports-Golf

7073. Action Golf
4271. APBA Pro Golf, issued intermit-
      tently
4272. APBA Pro Golf, 1st Edition
2430. Armchair Golf
6423. Arnold Palmer's Indoor Golf Game
5051. Arnold Palmer's Inside Golf
5834. Arthur Godfrey's Par-Tee Golf
4427. Birdie Golf
7988. Break Par Golf Game
2297. Bunker Golf
7580. Call It Golf
4123. Challenge Golf at Pebble Beach
5248. Championship Golf
5591. Championship Golf

3058. Country Club Golf
3913. Cowboys & Indians Also Junior Golf
1441. Driver, or Parlor Golf (© J. W. Keller)
2920. Electric Golf
7886. Fairway Golf, Photo of Billy Maxwell
8068. Fast Golf
4321. Fore
4045. Fore Country Club
4046. Fore, Game of Golf
5220. Galloping Golf
5580. Gamblers Golf
7529. Go for the Green!
1078. Golf
1940. Golf
1941. Golf
929. Golf Bug
3088. Golf Junior
3361. Golf, Amateur
1319. Golf, The Game of
1339. Golf, The Game of
218. Golf, The Game of
5878. Golferino
3265. Golflet
2608. Hazard's Bowling on the Green
2944. Holland's Indoor Golf Game
5659. In-Side Golf
2997. Irons and Woods
4421. Jack Bannings Putt-Pins
       (Bowling-Golf)
2974. Jim Duffer Golf Game
3096. Kellogg's Golf Game, Premium
2952. Let's Go Golfun
2398. Let's Play Games, Golf, Polo, Boots &
5091. Let's Play Golf
5092. Let's Play Golf, The Hawaiian Open
3855. Light Horse H. Cooper Golf
1251. Lilliput Golf
2422. Little Jack Horner Golf Course
3210. Minature Golf
7295. Mulligans, Pinehurst Championship
6610. NeGamo Pro Golf
2899. Nineteenth Hole Golf Game
3173. Nineteenth Hole, The
2779. Obstacle Golf
3187. Obstacle Golf
6629. Offical Skins Golf Game, The
2476. Open Championship Gold Game
3277. Palley Golf Game
5652. Par Golf
6593. Par Golf
6645. Par It
3624. Par The New Golf Game
4450. Par, 73
4417. Par-A-Shoot Game
1261. Parlor Golf
2112. Parlor Golf
4845. Pivot Golf
3508. Pla-Golf
4405. Pro Golf
6609. Pro Golf Game
3279. Quaddy Golf
3690. Rainy Day Golf
5057. Rainy Day Golf
3648. Rotary Golf
3035. Rum-E-Golf
7533. Sports Illustrated Handicap Golf
5624. Tee Off by Sam Snead
7611. Tee Off on Golf
2873. Tee Off!
4973. Tee Party
6641. Teed Off
4152. Thinking Man's Golf
4418. Tournament Golf
2732. Traps and Bunkers, Game of Golf
7877. Traps, The Game of, Golf Game
3013. Tumble Golf
7928. Ultimate Golf
3708. Wee-Tee Indoor Golf
3705. Wicket Golf
5034. Wide World of Sports-Golf
4398. Win, Place and Show
2362. Wyntre Golf
4114. Zweifel Card Golf

Sports-Hockey

5890. All-Pro Hockey
4273. APBA Pro Hockey, 1st edition
4274. APBA Pro Hockey, later editions each
4120. Blue Line Hockey
6536. Box Hockey
2921. Electric Hockey
5444. Electric Hockey

5297. Face-Off
5134. Hockey
2613. Ice Hockey
3021. Junior Hockey
3811. Lester Patrick's Official Hockey
7524. National Pro Hockey
6017. NHL All-Pro Hockey
3417. Nip and Tuck, Hockey
5239. Nok Hockey
6877. Phil & Tony Esposito's Action
       Hockey
7646. Play Ball Hockey
7214. Power Play
4381. Slapshot
7574. Strat-O-Matic Hockey
6069. Sure Shot Hockey
3257. Te-Ho Hockey
3125. Tit for Tat Indoor Hockey
2840. Top Hockey

Sports-Horse Racing

6557. Across the Board Horse Racing Game
3047. America Derby, The
1854. American Derby
5107. American Derby, The
4281. APBA Saddle Racing Game,
       1st Edition
4282. APBA Saddle Racing Game, later
4283. APBA Saddle Racing Game, later
4284. APBA Saddle Racing Game, later
4329. Aurora Derby
3179. Belmont Park
6678. Bing Crosby's Game Call Me Lucky
2494. Bookie
2783. Broadway Handicap, Movies of Races
3662. Cavalcade
3660. Cavalcade, Deluxe Edition
3661. Cavalcade, Separate board & box
5497. Crosby Derby, The,
       Bing Crosby Photo
2560. Crusader Horse Race Game
3337. Derby Day
3523. Derby Day
5647. Derby Downs
1606. Derby Steeple Chase, The
1607. Derby Steeple Chase, The
3063. Derby Winner
7706. Eddie Arcaro Blue Grass Handicap
3526. Foto-Finish Horse Race
7167. Giant Wheel Thrills & Spills Horse
3933. Grand National, A Sweepstakes of
2609. Hialeah Horse Racing Game
2802. Hollywood Derby
6329. Home Stretch Harness Racing
5756. Home Stretch, The
3143. Horse Race
2612. Horse Racing
2316. Horses
3213. Horses
3172. Indoor Horse Racing
646. Jerome Park Steeplechase
1678. Jerome Park Steeple-Chase
3945. Kentucky Derby
8085. Kentucky Derby Horse Racing Game
2623. King of the Turf
2633. Long Green, The
6824. Long Shot
3135. Lucky Strike & Horse Race Game
3034. Magic-Race (Horse Race)
1819. Merry Steeple Chase, the
7044. Official Boston Marathon Game
6647. Pari, Horse Race Card Game
2663. Parlay
776. Parlor Race, or Dickens on the Turf
4160. Photo-Finish
7209. Play Pace Racing Game
3433. Playing the Ponies
820. Race Course
897. Race, Game of the
1156. Races
473. Races, Game of the
414. Races, The Game of the
6596. Raceway
2861. Racing Stable, The Game of
2691. Saratoga
2192. Saratoga Steeple Chase
899. Steeple Chase Game, The
1178. Steeple Chase, Game of
2070. Steeple Chase, Game of
900. Steeplechase, The Game of
7974. Stretch Call
2838. Suffolk Downs- Club Edition

5304. Suffolk Downs Racing Game
3698. Sumrun, The Great Racing Game
4197. Sweeps
4198. Sweeps
4199. Sweeps
3036. Sweepstakes
8183. Sweepstakes, Electronic Horse Rac-
       ing
3064. Ten Grand
6444. They're at the Post, Record plays the
6964. They're Off, Horse Race Game
6338. Thorobred
4007. Three Ring Circus/Steeplechase
7915. Tru-Action Electric Horserace
7917. Tudor Electric Horse Racing Game
3065. Twenty Grand
3053. We V Nap Horse Race Game
4156. Win, Place & Show
5037. Win, Place and Show

Sports, Pool

5338. Lazy Pool
4837. PD Cue Bumper Pool
4846. Pivot Pool

Sports-Sea

3799. America's Cup Yacht Race
1562. America's Yacht Race Game, The
2301. Challenger Cup Race
1597. College Boat Race, Game of
2381. Exciting Motor Boat Race, An
7166. Giant Wheel Speed Boat Game
1437. Glenleven's New Boat Race, The
3958. Navigator-A Boat Race w/ a Deck of
1714. Newport Yacht Race
2046. Race for the Cup
4147. Regatta
7066. Regatta
8105. Regatta
7586. Ride the Surf
6561. Sail Away. A Racing Game
4454. Sailor's Game, The
6051. Skin Divers
2703. Smitty Speed Boat Race Game
2706. Speed Boat Race
1270. Vassar Board Race, The
3557. Yacht Club
1215. Yacht Race
1347. Yacht Race
1781. Yacht Race
3533. Yacht Race
3532. Yacht Race (930)
1780. Yacht Race at Sandy Hook
537. Yacht Race, Franklin and Great
7022. Yacht Race, Saturday Housed
1214. Yacht Race, The Pennant
1782. Yacht Racing Game, The
2103. Yachting
2198. Yachting
2197. Yachting, Game of
2104. Yachts The International Race
2365. Yatteau

Sports, Skating

4878. Roller Derby
1268. Skating Race Game, The

Sports, Soccer

6189. Kellogg's Soccer Slam, Kellogg's
       Raisin
1470. National Football Match, The
4413. Scrambled Squares Soccer
6196. Table Top Soccer

Sports-Tennis

5149. Match Point Tennis
7636. Nuttsy Tennis
4406. Pro Tennis
8195. Set Point, Tennis Strategy Game
7500. Skill Games, Baseball,
       Tennis, Football
6963. Tennis
6091. Trap Tennis
5035. Wide World of Sports-Tennis

Sports, Wrestling

6572. Falls, Wrestling Game
7583. Superstar Pro Wrestling Game
5600. Verne Gagne World Champion
5042. Wrestling Superstars
5044. WWF Wrestling

Spy

7971. 007 James Bond, The Man with the
4619. Enemy Agent, The game of foreign
4620. Enter the Dangerous World of James
7570. Espionage
7709. Espionage
3923. F. B. I. Agent, The Games of
5961. Get Smart Mini-Board Card Game
8031. Get Smart, Quiz Machine
7274. Get Smart, Sorry About That Game
5962. Get Smart, Time Bomb Game
7275. Get Smart, Would You Believe Game
4706. Intrigue, Liner & Tugboat cover
4707. Intrigue, Liner,
       Key & Briefcase cover
4710. James Bond 007 Card Game
4712. James Bond 007 Thunderball Game
5980. James Bond, Message from M Game
4721. John Drake, Secret Agent
6406. Mad's Spy vs. Spy
       Combat Card Game
4764. Mad's Spy vs Spy
4766. Man from U.N.C.L.E. Card Game
4767. Man from U.N.C.L.E. Shoot Out!
5406. Man from U.N.C.L.E. Playing Cards
6001. Man from U.N.C.L.E. Game, The
6002. Man from U.N.C.L.E.
       Thrush Ray Gun
6433. Man from U.N.C.L.E. Pinball Affair
6434. Man from U.N.C.L.E. Secret Code
6435. Man from U.N.C.L.E. Target Game
6436. Man from U.N.C.L.E. Target Game
7772. Master Spy Target Game
5855. Project CIA, A Spy Training Game
7516. Robert Ludlum's Counter-Espionage
7945. Secrecy
7522. Spies
6498. Spy Detecter Game
7826. Spy's-A-Poppin
4954. Super Spy
6602. Top Secret
7908. Top Secret

Stock Market

6176. Arbitrace
5279. Beat the Market
5473. Big Board
5332. Big Board, For Juniors, The
2538. Big Board, The
5333. Big Board, The
7610. Blue Chip Stock Market Game
1420. Bourse or Stock Exchange
7520. Broker
6419. Bull and Bears
1027. Bull Board, Bradley's
7591. Bulls "N" Bears
3312. Bulls and Bears, A Stock Exchange
1587. Bulls and Bears, The Great Wall
       Street
7128. Crash! The Stock Market Game
1433. Gavitt's Stock Exchange
1434. Gavitt's Stock Exchange.
       Black & Grey
7946. Invest
7985. Investment Club, The
8174. Limit Up, Commodity Futures Trade
3225. Mutuels
5783. NBC World of Wall Street
7035. Option Game Board, The
2257. Options, The Game of
1830. Panic - The Great Wall Street Game
2032. Pit
6881. Pit, Photo cover
3432. Pit, Art cover by John Held Jr
6883. Pit, Red & Blue Color Pit
6884. Pit, Red horizontal box
6882. Pit,, Red Vertical box
6906. Rich Uncle, Blue & Grey background
6907. Rich Uncle, Deluxe Edition,
       Grey cover
6908. Rich Uncle, Orange background cover
6909. Rich Uncle, Yellow background cover
2069. Speculation
5242. Speculation
6618. Speculation
7517. Speculation, The Stock Market Game
3464. Stock Exchange
3774. Stock Exchange, The Game of
7346. Stock Market
3076. Stock Market Game
8124. Stock Market Game Deluxe edition
4387. Stock Market Game, The

5530. Stock Market Game, The
5667. Stock Market Specialist
2993. Stock Market, The
3128. Stock Market, The
4150. Stocks and Bonds
4388. Stocks and Bonds
3167. Ticker Tape
5194. Ticker Tape
3008. Ticker, The Wall Street Game
5331. Trade the Market
4216. Wall Street Game, The
2744. Wall Street The Game of Speculation
8192. Wall Street Trader
5828. World of Wall Street, The

Strategy
5342. 20 to 2
6578. 7 Peg Games
5054. 99, Game of
1556. Advance & Retreat
1000. Advance and Retreat, Game of
1850. Advance Guard
939. Arena, Game of
381. Bamboozle, Game of
1016. Bamboozle, Game of
6664. Bantu
1445. Basilinda
3573. Big Apple
6257. Blockade
4525. Brainwaves
6699. Cam, The Great Game of, shorter
3318. Camelot
3319. Camelot
6701. Camelot
6702. Camelot
3316. Camelot, Brown Box
6700. Camelot, Two knights on beige cover
3317. Camelot, Two Knights on box cover
610. Captive Princess, The
1031. Carromette, The New Game of
6462. Cathedral, Plastic Buildings
447. Chameleonoscope
6259. Chaos
8194. Check Point
2234. China, pat
3576. Chuckler's Game, The
6320. Chute-5
4580. Conect Four
1040. Conette
8020. Configurations
8021. Configurations, cardboard Hexagonal
8022. Configurations, Later editions
5538. Connect
7379. Consetta
4125. Contigo
5305. Corx
5662. Counter Ploy
8058. Counterpoint
4590. Dead Stop! Game
5938. Deduction
6744. Domain
4603. Domination
1614. Domino Rex, Game of
7614. Dotto
5846. Dragon's Teeth
5438. Dualing
1053. Eckha
5118. Egg-Citement!
5448. Electric Whiz Checkers
4617. Electronic Stratego
5859. End of the Line
6130. Ergo
4129. Feudal
4364. Feudal
5832. Final Strategy
4638. Finders Keepers
6468. Flip Flop Go
4130. Foil
6782. Go for It!
5963. Go Gin Card Game
6786. Grapple
5966. Great Escape, The
6788. Great Game Cam, The
6794. Hex, The Zig-Zag Game
7505. Hideaway
7170. Hippopotamus Electronic Puzzle Game
1803. Hub-Checkers
5668. Hunch
5428. Input Output Game
6804. Inside Moves
7414. Ipswich

6265. Isolation
3679. Jump
4136. Jumpin
1103. Junior Combination Board (4927), incl.:
1104. Kakeba, or Japanese Backgammon
6552. Karter Peanut Shell Game
1105. Kerion
6810. Kimbo
3379. Kings Men
6266. Kismet
7418. La Riga
4219. Linkup
655. Lost Diamond
1690. Lost Diamond, The Game of
713. Lost Heir, The
6330. Mandinka
5621. Mega Gammon
525. Merelles, or Nine Men's Morris
6840. Mindmaze
5318. Mystery Checkers
4373. Nieuchess
6332. Nile
6018. Nirtz, The Game is
910. No-Jump-O
4140. Octrix
5160. Oh Hell
4141. Oh Wah Ree
6869. On Guard
6872. Outwit
7445. Pass it On
4834. Pathfinder, Photo of game cover
4835. Pathfinder, White & Green cover
3969. Peg Pen, Game of
3422. Peg Top
2020. Peggity
6874. Pegity
3424. Peg'ity
3423. Pegity, The Game of
6420. Penta
7039. Pente
4142. Phlounder
6885. Plotz!
4143. Ploy
5792. Pooch
527. Pope and Pagan, Game of
4146. Quinto
7453. Qwink
6035. Ransom
6903. Rattle Battle
5586. Realm
4879. Roundabout
6046. Rubik's Race
6918. Ruffhouse
7458. Russian Roulette
6272. Score Four
6049. Sha-EE, Game of Destiny
7501. Skip-Bo
6932. Skudo
4911. Slide 5
4247. Sly
5870. Smarts
6936. Smess the Ninny's Chess
7511. Snafooey
6640. Space Checkers
6946. Square Off
5554. Sqwurm
4229. Stadium Checkers
4937. Stay Alive Game
4940. Strata 5
4947. Stump
4962. Swahili Game
8126. Switchboard
7300. Teeko
7280. Third Man
5193. Thirteen
7474. Tic Tac Tower
7103. Tigo
912. Tit-Tat-Toe, Three in a Row
6092. Trap
5819. Trap the Rat
7478. Troke, Castle Checkers
4153. Twixt
585. Uncle Sam's Game of Six Corners
6987. Universe
3202. Veuisee
5020. Whatzit?
4205. Wiff N' Proof
5038. Wipe Off Target Game
7021. Wit's End, Game of
4423. World Class Liar
1213. Wyhoo!

7504. Yesterday
5212. Yoo Doo
5049. Zero Zap

Super Heroes
2506. Adventures of Superman, The
4477. Amazing Spiderman Game with the
4478. Amazing Spiderman Game, The
5891. Amazing Spiderman Web Spinning
5709. Aquaman, Justice League of America
5713. Batman and Robin Game
5712. Batman and Robin Game, Marble
7076. Batman Batarang Toss
5896. Batman Card Game
6672. Batman Forever
5714. Batman Game
5715. Batman Game
7948. Batman Game, The
4501. Batman Jigsaw Puzzle Game
4502. Batman Mini Board Card game
6425. Batman Pinball Game
6673. Batman Returns
6426. Batman Shooting Arcade
6674. Batman, The Animated
4503. Batman, The Game of
7685. Buck Rogers
4530. Buck Rogers Game
3162. Buck Rogers Game of 25th Century
3165. Buck Rogers, 3 Game Combo
7690. Calling Superman
4540. Captain America Game
4541. Captain America Game
5574. Doctor Who
5949. Electra Woman and Dynagirl
4629. Fantastic Four Featuring Herbie the
5544. Flash Gordon
5738. Flash, Justice League of America
7227. Flash, The
5399. Green Hornet
4674. Green Hornet Quick Switch Game
4704. Incredible Hulk Game with the
5977. Incredible Hulk Smash-Up Action
5575. Judge Dredd
7771. Mandrake the Magician
4770. Marvel Comics Super-Hero
4771. Marvel Comics Super-Hero
7089. Marvel Super Heroes Game
7905. Marvel Super Heroes, Basic Set
7776. Mighty Comics Super Heroes Game
7796. Phantom Game, The
3821. Shadow, The
7145. Shazam
7243. Shazam! Card Game
7246. Super Hero, Batman
7247. Super Hero, Robin.
7248. Super Hero, Shazam
7249. Super Hero, Superman
7250. Super Hero, Wonder Woman
5804. Super Heroes Bingo
4953. Super Heroes Strategy Game
6959. Super Powers
5806. Superboy Game
6571. Superfriends Magnetic Pa'cheesie Game
4956. Superheroes Card Game
6540. Superman
4957. Superman - Fantastic Four
4958. Superman and Superboy
6065. Superman Card Game
6499. Superman Comic Game
8125. Superman Flying Bingo
5808. Superman Game
5809. Superman Game
5807. Superman Game, Search for
4959. Superman II Game
6960. Superman III
5810. Superman Marble Maze
6066. Superman Match II
2716. Superman Speed Game
7099. Superman Spin Game
7106. Uncanny X-Men Alert, The
5826. Wonder Woman Game
5827. Wonder Woman, Justice League of

Tennis (See Sports - Tennis)

Theatre
1849. Actors, The Game of Popular
3907. Charlie Chan
3090. Kam-ra, Motion PictureCard Game
1794. Moth and the Flame, The

6623. On Stage
4380. Showbiz, The Entertainment Game
1316. Stage
1317. Stage. Purple box Edition
4932. Stage II

Time
453. Chronographer
454. Chronologist
2968. Clock Lotto (T-239)
1044. Days, Game of
1509. Months
2938. Season (© Paul Lee)
7842. Terry Tell Time Game
2346. TickTock
5669. Ticky the Clown Clock

Towns (See Cities & Towns)

Toy
6451. Barbie Charms the World Game
6452. Barbie Game, The
6453. Barbie World of Fashion
5627. Barbie, Queen of the Prom Game
6455. Barbie's Keys to Fame
6238. Captain Action Card Game, Premium
6463. Chatty Cathy Game
4653. G.I. Joe
5743. G.I. Joe Adventure Board Game
5744. G.I. Joe Combat Infantry Game
5745. G.I. Joe Commando Attach Game
5746. G.I. Joe Marine Paratroop Game
5747. G.I. Joe Navy Frogman Game
5748. G.I. Joe, Capture Hill 79
5749. G.I. Joe
5628. Go Bots
7169. Heidi Elevator Game
6475. Hot Wheels Wipe Out Game
6808. Kewpie Doll Game
5989. King Zor The Dinasaur Game
6481. Major Matt Mason Space Exploration
4458. Matchbox, Traffic Game
6009. Mr. Machine Game
6025. Pattie Playpal
6490. Skipper Game, Barbie's Little Sister
7840. Taffy's Shopping Spree Game
8129. Tammy Card Game
6084. Tiny Thumbelina
5830. Transformers Card Game
7931. Uncle Milton's Exciting Ant Farm

Travel - All
6649. 10-Four, Good Buddy, CB Radio Game
2273. 3 Point Landing
4172. 3 Point Landing
2269. A & P Coast to Coast Relay Race, Leg #
2267. A & P Coast to Coast Relay Race, Leg #
2266. A & P Coast to Coast Relay Race, Leg #
2268. A & P Coast to Coast Relay Race, Leg #
2265. A & P Coast to Coast Relay Race, Leg #
2503. Above the Clouds
3280. Ace of Aces
1848. Across the Continent
3282. Across the Continent, The United States
6652. Across the Continent, Train scene cover
6653. Across the Continent, U.S. map cover
997. Across the Sea
1555. Across the Sea or Trip to Europe
3283. Admiral Byrd's South Pole Game
3057. Aero Race
2389. Aero-Chute Target Game
4342. Air Empire
7110. Air Mail
3740. Air Mail Race
2429. Air Mail, The
6298. Air Race Around the World
1558. Air Ship Game, The
7302. Air Traffic Controller Game
4174. Airderby
3830. Airdrome
7643. Airlift
6560. Airline
2512. Airmail

2097. What Color is Your Car?
7958. Where in the USA is Carmen San Diego
7959. Where in the World is Carmen
1775. Whirlpool, The Game of
7017. Wide World Travel Game, Six picture
7018. Wide World Travel Game, Yellow
3497. Wings, The Air Mail Game
3244. World Air Derby, The
3011. World Flyers
2361. World Flyers Around the World Flight
1284. World to World Airship Race, The New
2366. Zippy Zepps, Air Game
6141. Zip-Zingo- The Travel Game
2367. Zoom, Original Game of
4021. Zoom, The Airplane
4022. Zoom, The Airplane. Red & Black
4020. Zoom, The Airplane Card
1806. Zylo-Karta Games, Folding wooden

Travel-Air

2273. 3 Point Landing
4172. 3 Point Landing
2266. A & P Coast to Coast Relay Race, Leg #
2503. Above the Clouds
3280. Ace of Aces
3057. Aero Race
2389. Aero-Chute Target Game
4342. Air Empire
7110. Air Mail
3740. Air Mail Race
2429. Air Mail, The
6298. Air Race Around the World
1558. Air Ship Game, The
7302. Air Traffic Controller Game
4174. Airderby
3830. Airdrome
7643. Airlift
6560. Airline
2512. Airmail
2510. Airmail, The Game of
5707. Airpalne Game
2512. Airplane Trip
5375. Airport
5833. Airport
1851. Airship Game, The
3831. Airway
6306. Airways
4480. American Airlines Travel Game
4481. American Airlines Travel Games
2519. Around the World
5634. Around the World Travel Game
3738. Around the World with the "Graf
4213. Astro World Game, Ad game for
6662. Aviation
913. Aviation Game
2526. Aviation Game
3295. Aviation, The Air Mail Game
3296. Bailing Out
5221. Capital Air Race, Premium
2298. Capital Cities Air Derby, The
5223. Cap'n Crunch's Hot Air Race
2299. Captain Hop Across Jr
2967. Clipper Race
3801. Coast to Coast Air Race
3259. Crash, The New Airplane Game
4087. Famous Flyers Race Around the World
4640. Flagship Airfreight, The Airline Cargo
6324. Flight Captain
2584. Flight to Paris, The
3356. Flying Four, The
3260. Flying Fun
3838. Flying High
3926. Flying Jack
3358. Flying the Beam
3357. Flying the Beam, Large Transport on
3359. Flying the United States Airmail
2590. Gliding, Game of
7190. Global Air Race, with round globe as
2591. Glyder Racing Game
2311. Glydor
3839. Happy Landing
3367. Hop Off
6409. International Airport game
6410. International Airport Game
4166. Jet Aircraft
5072. Jet Race Game
6169. Jet Race Game

4716. Jet World
6181. Jumbo Jet
3112. Knapp Electro Game Set, Air Race
2625. Leap for Life Game
3389. Lindy - The New Flying Game
3388. Lindy - The New Flying Game, Wide
3390. Lindy, Improved Edition
2858. Long Flight
4057. Loop the Loop
2279. Looping the Loop
3618. Mystic and Airplane Race
3261. New Lindy Flying Game, The
2451. New York to Paris Aerorace
1715. North Pole by Air Ship, Game of to the
4062. Ocean to Ocean Flight, Blue Box, new
4063. Ocean to Ocean Flight, Red Box
2661. Parachute Jump Game
2662. Parachute Jump, The Game of
5681. Plane Parade
2859. Ski-Hi, Flight to Paris
6933. Sky Lanes
3628. Sky Trails. (Small Book Shelf Vol. II)
7244. Sky Trails
2339. Sky-Hawks
3127. Skyways
3633. Take -Off
2439. Tell-A Plane
1759. To The North Pole by Airship, Game of
2773. Transport Pilot
2738. Uncle Wiggily's New Airplane Game
3484. United States Air Mail, The
2743. Voyage Round the World, Game of
3491. We, The Magnetic Flying Game
3497. Wings, The Air Mail Game
3244. World Air Derby, The
3011. World Flyers
2361. World Flyers Around the World Flight
2366. Zippy Zepps, Air Game
2367. Zoom, Original Game of
4021. Zoom, The Airplane
4022. Zoom, The Airplane. Red & Black
4020. Zoom, The Airplane Card

Travel, Car

2268. A & P Coast to Coast Relay Race, Leg #
7356. Allstate Travel Games (Sears)
5108. Amoco's the Mileage Game, Ad game
7146. Auto Bingo
1014. Auto Game, The
2522. Auto Game, The
2524. Auto Race Game
4491. Autofun
4516. Big Town
3314. Buster Bumps Automobile Trip
3658. Cabby!
3659. Cabby!
6698. Calling All Cards
3315. Calling All Cars
4545. Car Travel Game
5921. Cars N' Trucks
8056. Collision!
4433. Diablo, The Safe-Driving Game
7977. Driver-Ed
5348. Drivers Training Game, Let's Drive, Old
7215. Driving Spirit Safety Game, The
3238. En-Ar-Co Automobile Game
3239. En-Ar-Co Automobile Tour
7147. Find-A-Car Bingo
2585. Fliver Game
6774. Free Parking
7401. Get That License
3084. Honk-Honk-Honk
5676. Hot Rod
5312. Hot-Rod
5293. Interstate
7413. Interstate Highway
6116. Land Race Card Game
3385. Leapin Lena
2977. Let's Auto-Tour (T-290)
4741. Let's Drive, Road Safty Fun Game
7148. License Number Bingo
6829. Magnificent Race, The
1996. Motor Carriage Game, The
4061. Obstacle Race
5159. Offical Drivers Ed Game
3519. Pontiac Safety Drive Game, The
4167. Racing Cars
3742. Red Crown, The, Premium

7812. Route 66 Travel Game
5174. Rules of the Road, Driver Education
2453. Speeding
4170. Sports Cars
5798. Spot a Car Bingo
6600. Squad Car
7545. Standard Oil Travel Road Game
2881. Stay Off Street, SOS Safety game
7472. Taxi!
4978. Test Driver Game, The
7563. Tollroad Turnpike
2079. Toot
2426. Tourex, The Game of
2876. Touring
3478. Touring - Famous Automobile Game
3479. Touring - Famous Automobile Game
3480. Touring - Famous Automobile Game
3481. Touring - Famous Automobile Game
3482. Touring - Famous Automobile Game
3483. Touring - Famous Automobile Game
3476. Touring - Famous Automobile Game, 1
3477. Touring - Famous Automobile Game
6973. Touring, Map box
6974. Touring, Map lertters Cover
6975. Touring, Red Car and Trialer
6976. Touring, Scene with speed limit 45
6977. Touring, Scenes with line drawing of
6978. Touring, Yellow box Modle T Ford
7136. Town and Country Traffic
2782. Traffic
6339. Traffic
2982. Traffic Jam
5686. Traffic Jam
7150. Traffic Safety Bingo
2731. Traffic, Game of
2353. Traffic, The Game of
6418. Travel America
7878. Turnpike
209. What Color is Your Car?

Travel-Rail

2265. A & P Coast to Coast Relay Race, Leg #
7306. Black Ball Express
6511. British Rails
4567. Choo Choo Charlie Game
4360. Dispacher
6307. Double Crossing
6516. Empire Builders
6517. Eurorails
6518. Express
1059. Fast Mail, The
2596. Golden State Limited
950. Great Railroad Game, The
4683. Happy Little Train Game, The
2627. Lightning Express, A Railroad Game
1980. Limited Mail and Express, The
561. New Railroad Game, or Trip Around the
6182. Orient Express
2660. Overland Limited, The
3174. Pay as You Enter, 20th Century Game
4378. Rail Baron
2685. Railroad Game
423. Railroad Game or Clear the Track
2047. Railroad Game, The
449. Railway Traffic, Game of
2713. Streamline Express Game, The
3559. Streamlined Train Game, Premium
2072. Street Car Game, The
2715. Sunset Limited
5697. Thomas the Tank Engines's, All Abord
5698. Thomas the Tank Engines's, B-I-N-G-O
5699. Thomas the Tank Engines's, Hats Off
5700. Thomas the Tank Engines's, Railroad
5701. Thomas the Tank Engines's, Tricky
5702. Thomas the Tank Engines's, Whistle
1285. Through Train (author Joseph Vail)
7476. Toot! Toot!
1190. Tourist, A Rail Road Game, The
1191. Tourist, The, A Railroad Game
4081. Toyland Railway
5422. Tracks
2083. Train for Boston
2085. Trolley
2207. Trolley
2208. Trolley. Gold Edge Box
2086. Twentieth Century Limited
2735. Twentieth Century Limited, The

Travel, Sea

2267. A & P Coast to Coast Relay Race, Leg #
4023. Al-Nav
5225. Cap'n Crunch's Undersea Adventure
5988. King of the Sea
2629. Liners and Transports (4667)
6831. Marine World
3556. Merchant Marine
4086. Navigator
2659. Outboard Motor Boat, The
7239. Ripley's Believe it or Not, Ships
3251. Rules of the Road, Seamanship Cards
3847. Save the Sailor
3453. Sea Rider
5178. Seven Seas
4169. Ships
5184. Skipper
3462. Speed Boat
6983. Tugboat
1775. Whirlpool, The Game of

Travel-USA

3282. Across the Continent, The United States
6652. Across the Continent, Train scene cover
6653. Across the Continent, U.S. map cover
6286. America in a Box
5500. America, The Great Board Game
7059. Central Bedrock U*S*A Race Game
3192. Coast to Coast
7353. Discover America
7062. Eastern Bedrock U*S*A Race Game
7612. Fun Places of the USA
5052. Go to Texas
6140. Mad Dash, Three Minutes Across
5430. Name That State
5492. New America
6109. Northwest Passage
920. Our Country (© A. M. Edwards)
5682. Play U.S.A
5177. See the USA Game
5687. Travel America
6418. Travel America
7884. Treasure Resort
7198. Weekend in Vegas
7064. Western Bedrock U*S*A Race Game
7958. Where in the USA is Carmen San Diego

Travel-World

997. Across the Sea
1555. Across the Sea or Trip to Europe
1857. Amusing Game of Innocence Abroad
5261. Brazil, [Cheerios Box Game]
7380. Cook's Tours- European Travel Game
1911. Crossing the Ocean
573. English Farm: Twenty Rural Scenes
2766. Foto World
5129. Geo-Graphy World Wide
5565. Great City Game of Rome, The
5519. J. Fred Muggs 'Around the World'
5429. Name that Country
1745. Round the World with Nellie Bly
352. Trip to Paris
828. Trip to Paris
344. Trip to Paris, A
7959. Where in the World is Carmen
7017. Wide World Travel Game, Six picture
7018. Wide World Travel Game, Yellow

TV

5227. $1,000,000 Chance of a Lifetime
4461. $10,000 Pyramid Game, The
4462. $20,000 Pyramid
5228. $25,000 Pyramid
6346. $64,000 Question Quiz Game
4463. 12 O'Clock High
5882. 12 O'Clock High (Paul Burke picture)
5883. 12 O'Clock High (Robert Lansing
5705. 2 for the Money
6250. 20,000 Leagues Under the Sea
6347. 77 Sunset Strip
6651. A Team, The, Mr. T On cover
4469. Addams Family Card Game, The
5885. Addams Family, The
7657. Adventures of Rin Tin Tin, The
8029. Adventures of Lassie
5286. Alf Game, The
4473. All in the Family Game, The

7892. All My Children
4476. Alumni Fun
8035. Amazing Chan and the
      Chan Clan, The
4486. Annie Oakley Game
4487. Annie Oakley Game. Variant Cover
5541. Annie Oakley Game
4488. Apple's Way
7661. Aquanauts Game, The
4489. Archie Bunker's Card Game
8036. Archie Game, The
7662. Arrest And Trial
4038. Art Linkletter's House Party
6659. As the World Turns
7663. Atom Ant Saves the Day
6219. Badge 714 Dragnet
4496. Bamboozle
7664. Bamm-Bamm Game,
      Color Me Happy
5711. Banana Splits Game, The
4497. Baretta, The Street Detective Game
4499. Barnabas Collins Game
      Dark Shadows
6665. Barney Miller
6348. Bat Masterson
4505. Battle of the Planets
5898. Battleline Game
6457. Beany and Cecil Match-It Tile Game
7077. Beany and Cecil Ring Toss
7078. Beany and Cecil Skill Ball
6349. Beat the Clock
4508. Beat the Clock Game
7668. Ben Casey M. Game
4512. Beverly Hillbillies Card Game, The
7548. Beverly Hillbillies Game, The
4513. Beverly Hills, 90210
5542. Bewitched
7124. Bewitched Hunt Game
4514. Bid it Right, The Price is Right
6316. Big Nuumbers
6351. Big Town
6679. Bionic Crisis, Six Million Dollar Man
6680. Bionic Woman, The
4520. Bobbsey Twins, The
4523. Body Language with Lucile Ball
6685. Bonanza, Michigan Rummy Game
8041. Brady Bunch Game, The
4526. Branded Game
4439. Break the Bank, Photo of Bert Parks
7683. Break-A-Plate Carnival Pitch Game
4530. Buck Rogers Game
5065. Buffalo Bill Jr. Cattle
      Round Up Game
5914. Bullwinkle and Rocky
7898. Bullwinkle and Rocky
5389. Bullwinkle Card Game
6280. Bullwinkle Electronic Quiz Game
4533. Bullwinkle Hide 'N Seek
6281. Bullwinkle Magnetic Travel Game
7023. Bullwinkle Motorized Target Game
8044. Bullwinkle Ring Toss Game
7024. Bullwinkle Target and
      Ring Toss Game
7686. Bullwinkle Travel Adventure Game
7025. Bullwinkle, Fli-Hi Target Game
5612. Bullwinkle's Electronic Quiz Game
8045. Bullwinkle's Supermarket Game
7688. Burke's Law
7687. Burke's Law Target Game
6697. Burr Tillstrom's Kukla and Ollie
4534. By the Numbers
4535. Call My Bluff
4536. Camouflage
6353. Candid Camera Games
5590. Captain Kangaroo Let's Build a
      House
4539. Captain Kangaroo Tic Tagaroo
5917. Captain Kangaroo TV Lotto
4184. Captain Kangaroo/ Mr. Green Jeans
4543. Captain Caveman and the Teen
      Angels
7692. Captain Gallant
7693. Captain Kangaroo Parade Around the
4544. Captain Video
4206. Car 54, Where are You?
7269. Casey Jones Game Box
7059. Central Bedrock U*S*A Race Game
4556. Charlie's Angels Game,
      Cheryl on cover
4557. Charlie's Angels Game, Farrah on
5273. Cheers
7899. Cheers

6714. Cherry Ames, Nursing Game
4559. Cherry Street
4561. Cheyenne Game, Cowboy with pistol
4562. Cheyenne Game, Picture of Ty Hardin
6541. Cheyenne Target Game
4564. Chips Game
5926. Chips Game
4569. Chuggedy Chug,
      Paul Winchell & Jerry
5928. Cimarron Strip Game
5675. Circus Boy
6355. College Bowl
4574. Columbo Detective Game
4575. Combat
5933. Combat, The Fighting Infantry Game
5932. Combat, The Fighting Infantry Game
4577. Concentration, 3rEdition, Lower blue
4578. Concentration, 9th Edition, Upper red
4579. Concentration,, 1st. Edition
6555. Count of Monte Cristo, The
7060. Critter Cards Card Game, Linus The
5568. Crusade, Lawerence Welk's All Star
7924. Crusader Rabbit Game
6531. Dallas
6312. Dallas, A Game of the Ewing Family
7513. Dallas, Empire building Strategy
4587. Dark Shadows
8060. Dark Shadows Game
4588. Dastardly and Muttley
5723. Dating Game, The
4161. Dating Game, The,
      Party Pack, with 45-
4324. Dave Garroway's Game of Possesion
7125. Dave Garroway's Today Game
5395. Davy Crockett
4589. Day with Ziggy, A
7549. Dennis the Menace Game
8062. Dennis the Menace Tiddly Winks
4591. Deputy Dawg Game
5939. Deputy Dawg TV Lotto
4592. Deputy Game, The
7699. Detectives Game, The
5583. Diamondhead Game
7550. Dick Van Dyke Game, The
7700. Dino the Dinosaur Game
6356. Discovery, Home Game
4600. Diver Dan, Tug-O-War Game
7701. Doc Holliday Wild West Game
5574. Doctor Who
6357. Dollar a Second
6322. Dollar Bill Poker, with TV's Odd
4602. Dolly and Daniel Whale Game
5727. Dondi Finders Keepers Game
5728. Dondi, Potatoe Race Game
5729. Dondi, Prairie Race Game
6465. Donny & Marie Osmond TV Show
5945. Double Exposure
6358. Dough-Re-Mi
7388. Down You Go
5946. Dr. Kildare
7703. Dragnet Maze
6220. Dragnet Radar Action Game
6221. Dragnet Target Game
7704. Dragnet, The Game of
4607. Dream House TV Home Game
6114. Dukes of Hazzard
5947. Dukes of Hazzard Game, The
4611. Dyno Mutt, The
7062. Eastern Bedrock U*S*A Race Game
7708. Eliot Ness The Untouchables Game
4618. Emergency Game
5735. Ensign O'Toole,
      U.S.S. Appleby Game
6261. Entertainment Tonight
8002. Everybody's Talking
4623. Eye Guess
5952. F Troop Game
4625. F Troop Mini-Board Card game
6359. Face the Facts
8067. Family Affair
7157. Family Affair, Where's Mrs. Beasley?
4627. Family Feud
5736. Family Game
4286. Family Ties Game
6760. Fangface
4630. Fantastic Voyage Game
5953. Fantasy Island Game
4632. Fat Albert and The Cosby Kids
4635. Felix the Cat Game
4637. Fess Parker Trail Blazers Game
4639. Fireball XL5
6408. Fireball XL5, Magnetic Dart game

7351. Flintstone Game Alley
4289. Flintstone Quick Score Target Game
5243. Flintstones 3-D Chess, The
5397. Flintstones Animal Rummy
8069. Flintstones Big Game Hunt Game
8070. Flintstones Break Ball, The
8071. Flintstones Cut-Up
4641. Flintstones Game, The
4642. Flintstones Game, The
7713. Flintstones Magnetic Fish Pond Game
6430. Flintstones Mechanical Shooting
7952. Flintstones Memory Card Game, The
8072. Flintstones Mit-Full
7714. Flintstones Pitch 'N Bowl
7715. Flintstones Sling Dart Game
7716. Flintstones Smash-A-Roo Game
7717. Flintstones Stoneage Game
7718. Flintstones Stoneage Tiddly Winks
6300. Flintstones Target Set
7719. Flintstones Tumble Race
7720. Flintstones Window Whacker Game
6469. Flipper Flips
5739. Flying Nun Flying Maze Game
4643. Flying Nun, The
4644. Fonz, Hang Out At Arnolds, The
7722. Fred Flintstones Just for Kids Target
5957. Fugitive Game, The
5956. Fugitive Game, The, Image of David
4652. Funky Phantom Game
7953. Funtastic World of Hanna-Barbera
6556. Fury, Western Bingo Game
7724. Gang Way for Fun Game (Broadside
7963. Gay Puree Board Game
5229. General Hospital, The Game of
6470. Gentle Ben Animal Hunt
7164. Gentle Ben Electric Quiz Game
6780. George of the Jungle
5961. Get Smart Mini-Board Card Game
8031. Get Smart, Quiz Machine
7274. Get Smart, Sorry About That Game
5962. Get Smart, Time Bomb Game
7275. Get Smart, Would You Believe Game
4655. Get the Message
4657. Gidget Fortune Teller Game
7551. Gidget Game
4658. Gilligan, The New Adventures of
5545. Gilligan's Island Game
7726. Gomer Pyle Game
4214. Gong Show, The
7727. Gray Ghost, The
4673. Great Grape Ape Game, The
7552. Green Acres Game, The
7084. Groucho TV Quiz
6360. Groucho's You Bet Your Life
5283. Gumby and Pokey Playfull Trails
4677. Gumby Game, The
6361. Gunsmoke
6648. Gunsmoke Target Game
4678. H.R. Pufnstuf Game
4679. Hair Bear Bunch, The
7730. Hanna-Barbera Break-A-Plate
7731. Hanna-Barbera Ruff and
      Reddy Circus
6791. Happy Days
4684. Hardy Boys Game, The, Based on the
7732. Hashimoto-Sam Game
6793. Have Gun Will Travel
7168. Hawaii Five-O
6363. Hawaiian Eye
7733. Hector Heathcote Game
5363. Hee Haw
7169. Heidi Elevator Game
4687. High Spirits with Calvin
      & the Colonel
7736. Hogan's Heroes Bluff Out Game
5971. Hollywood Squares, The
8003. Hollywood Squares, The
8080. Hollywood Squares, The
5972. Honey West
7903. Honeymooners Game, The
4692. Hopalong Cassidy
4691. Hopalong Cassidy Chineese Checkers
7739. Hopalong Cassidy Lasso Game, The
7740. Hopalong Cassidy Pony Express Toss
5466. Hopalong Cassidy Target Practice &
4693. Hoppity Hopper Game
7741. Hoppy the Hopparoo
4695. Houndcats Game
5400. Howdy Doody Dominos
5677. Howdy Doody's Electric Doodles
5678. Howdy Doody's 3-Ring Circus

5679. Howdy Doody's Electric
      Carnival Game
6800. Howdy Doody's Own Game
4697. Howdy Doody's T.V. Game
7228. Howdy-Doody
6801. Howdy-Doody Beanbag Game
4698. Howdy-Doody's Adventure Game
7743. Huck Finn Game
7744. Huckelberry Hound "Bumps" Game
7745. Huckelberry Hound & Yogi Bear
      Break
4699. Huckelberry Hound Tiddledy Winks
7746. Huckle Chuck
4701. Huckleberry Hound
5401. Huckleberry Hound
7747. Huckleberry Hound Juggle Roll
7748. Huckleberry Hound Lids Off Bowling
4422. Huckleberry Hound Spin-O Game
7749. Huckleberry Hound Tumble Race
4700. Huckleberry Hound Western Game
7172. Hulla Baloo
4702. I Dream of Jennie Game
5975. I Spy Game
5976. I Spy Mini Board Card Game
4703. Illya Kuryakin
7320. I'm George Gobel
7954. Inspector Gadget Detective Kit Game
4705. Inspector Gadget Game
7506. Inspector Gadget,
      Spin N'Match Game
5978. Ironside Game
5979. It's About Time
6366. I've Got a Secret, I'm Garry Moore.
      and
5519. J. Fred Muggs 'Around the World'
4187. Jace Pearson's Tales of the Texas
7751. Jackie Gleason's, And Awa-a-a-y
      We
4709. Jackpot!
6368. Jan Murray's Charge Account
5593. Jan Murray's Treasure Hunt
4715. Jeopardy!
7752. Jetson's Fun Pad Game
4717. Jetson's Fun Pad Game, The
7753. Jetsons Game, Out of This World, The
4718. Jetsons Game, The
7754. Jetson's Rosey the Robot Game, The
6369. Jingle Dingle's Weather Game
4721. John Drake, Secret Agent
7755. Johnny Quest Game
7756. Johnny Ringo Game
4719. Joker, Joker, Joker
4720. Joker's Wild
4722. Jonny Quest Card Game
6477. Jumping DJ Surprise Action Game
5546. Kentucky Jones Horse Auction Game
4724. Kermit the Frog
4727. King Leonardo and His Subjects
6811. Knight Rider
4731. Kojak, The Stake Out Detective Game
4734. Korg: 70,000 B.C. The
6814. Kukla and Ollie
7175. Lancer Game
5991. Land of the Giants
7176. Land of the Giants Shoot & Stick
6283. Land of the Lost
6372. Land of the Lost Bagatelle
6372. Laramie
5547. Lassie Game
7216. Laugh-In Knock Knock Jokes Game
5764. Laughin, Squeeze Your Bippy Game
7763. Laurel and Hardy
7762. Laurel and Hardy Ring Toss
6817. Lavern & Shirley
5765. Leave it to Beaver Ambush Game
5766. Leave it to Beaver Money Maker
      Game
5767. Leave it to Beaver Rocket to the Moon
4739. Legend of Jessie James Game
4740. Legend of the Lone Ranger, The
4742. Let's Make a Deal
5993. Let's Make a Deal
7765. Lieutenant, The
7766. Life and Legend of Wyatt Earp Game
7767. Linus the Lionhearted Uproarious
5074. Little Beaver's 3 Game Set
6820. Little House on the Praire
4756. Lone Ranger
6823. Lone Ranger
5537. Lone Ranger & The Silver Bullets
7087. Lone Ranger & Tonto Spin to Win
8032. Lone Ranger Silver Bullets Game

7768. Lone Ranger Target Game
4759. Lost in Space Game
5232. Loudmouth, Morton Downey Jr
7934. Love Boat, The
4761. Lucan Game
7770. Lucy Show Game, The
4763. Lucy's Tea Party Game
5144. Magic Midway
7126. Mail Run, TV's Pony Express
4765. Make a Face
4766. Man from U.N.C.L.E. Card Game
4767. Man from U.N.C.L.E. Shoot Out!
5406. Man from U.N.C.L.E. Playing Cards
6001. Man from U.N.C.L.E. Game, The
6002. Man from U.N.C.L.E.
      Thrush Ray Gun
6433. Man from U.N.C.L.E. Pinball Affair
6434. Man from U.N.C.L.E. Secret Code
6435. Man from U.N.C.L.E. Target Game
6436. Man from U.N.C.L.E. Target Game
4769. Margie, The Game of Woopee!
7154. Mary Hartman, Mary Hartman
4772. Mash Game
4441. Masquerade Party
8016. Masters of the Universe
8090. Masters of the Universe Pop-Up
      Game
6482. Masters of the Universe, Battle for
6483. Masters of the Universe, Snake
4774. Match Game
4773. Match Game, The, 1st Edition
6608. Mating Game
7773. McHale's Navy Game
6484. Merv Griffin's Word by Word
6485. Merv Griffin's Word for Word Game
6835. Miami Vice
7040. Miami Vice
4785. Missing Links
6006. Mission Impossible
7180. Mod Squad Game, The
7778. Monkees
4790. Mork & Mindy Card Game
6858. Mork & Mindy Game
4794. Mr. T Card Game
4795. Mr. T Game
6860. Mr. Ed
7091. Mr. Peepers School Bag & Game Kit
7783. Mr. Novak Game
4796. Munsters Card Game, The
7962. Muppet Show
6861. Muppet Show, The
7996. Murder She Wrote
6013. Mushmouse & Punkin Puss Feudin'
7784. My Favorite Martian Game
4800. Name that Tune, with record, Red box
4801. Name that Tune, with record, White
6864. Nancy Drew Mystery Game, The
7785. National Velvet Game
6375. Navy Log, TV Game
7434. NBC Peacock Game
7935. New Zoo Revue, The
5784. Newlywed Game, The, Wedding cake
5785. Newlywed Game, The, 3rd edition
5786. Newlywed Game, The,
      Original Edition
5245. Nicledeon, The Ren & Stimpy Show
6866. Nicktoons Doug
6867. Nicktoons Rugrats
6019. No Time for Sergeants Game
4304. Nova True Science
4805. Now You See It
6868. Number Please
6020. Nurses Game, The
4806. Off to See the Wizard Game
7789. Outlaws Exciting Western Game
7790. Overland Trail
4817. P D Q
4824. Partridge Family
4311. Party - Movies & TV
4826. Pass Word, 2nedition, Blue cloth
4827. Pass Word, 3redition, Large cartoon
4828. Pass Word, 5th. edition,
      red & blue MB
4829. Pass Word, Collectors Edition, Wood
4830. Pass Word, Fine Edition, Square box
4831. Pass Word, Original edition,
      CBS Logo
4832. Pass Word, Red & white box
4833. Pass Word, Red, white & blue box
4836. Patty Duke Game
7791. Paul Winchell & Jerry Mahoney's TV
7792. Pebbles Flintstone Game

7793. Pebbles Flintstone Magnetic Fish
      Pond
7794. Pebbles Live Wire Game
5865. People's Court, The
6437. Perils of Pauline
7795. Perry Mason Game
4838. Personality Game
6377. Peter Gunn Detective Game
8098. Peter Potamus and Yo-Yo Card Game
6026. Peter Potamus Target Barrel
7557. Petticoat Junction Game, The
5596. Phil Silvers Sgt. Bilko
7797. Philip Marlowe Detective Game
7558. Picture This
8033. Pinky Lee and the Runaway
7094. Pinky Lee Game Time
5411. Pinky's Lee's Who am I?
8100. Play Cards!
7799. Play Your Hunch
6271. Playful Trails Game, Gumby and
6887. Police Academy, The Series
7999. Power Lords Board Game
6379. Price is Right, The
4860. Quick Draw McGraw
5413. Quick Draw McGraw
4859. Quick Draw McGraw Game
6223. Quick Draw McGraw Moving Target
6380. Ralph Edwards' This is Your life
5526. Ramar of the Jungle Blow Gun Game
8007. Ramar of the Jungle, The New Jungle
7808. Rat Patrol, The
6381. Rawhide Game
4867. Real Ghostbusters Game, The
6036. Rebel Gun
4869. Restless Gun Game, The
6383. Revlon's $64,000 Question
      Junior Quiz
6384. Revlon's $64,000 Question
      Quiz Game
6042. Ricochet Rabbit & Droop-A-Long
4872. Rifleman Game, The
7809. Rip Cord
8110. Rocky and Bullwinkle
      Magic Dot Game
4875. Rocky and His Friends Game
4430. Romper Room Magic Teacher
5414. Rootie Kazootie Word Game
7811. Rosey the Robot
7812. Route 66 Travel Game
7813. Ruff and Ready at the Circus
5482. Ruff and Ready TV Favorite Spelling
4880. S.W.A.T. Game, The
4882. Sale of the Century
6921. Say When!
4888. Scooby Doo Game
4889. Scooby-Doo & Scrappy-Doo Game
4890. Scooby-Doo, Where are You?
6386. Sea Hunt
4894. Sealab 2020 Game
8116. Secret of Nimh Game, The
4898. Sergeant Preston Game
6048. Seven Keys
7820. Sheri Lewis in. Sheriland Game
7183. Shindig Teen Game
4901. Shotgun Slade
4903. Sigmund and the Sea Monsters Game
7823. Silly Sidney
7822. Silly Sidney Count Shoot
      Target Game
4904. Simpsons Don't Have a Cow, The
6930. Six Million Dollar Man
4905. Skatebirds Game
6234. Sky's the Limit, The
4912. Smurf Game, The
7824. Snaggle Puss Fun at the Picnic
4913. Snap Judgement
4915. Snoopy Card Game
6059. Soupy Sales Game, The
6060. Soupy Sales Mini-Board Card Game
6162. Soupy Sales, Funny Rummy
6163. Soupy Sales, Hearts
6164. Soupy Sales, Old Maid
4922. Soupy Sez Go-Go-Go!
7825. Space Angel
4923. Space:1999
4924. Speed Buggy Game
7828. Stagecoach West Game
4933. Star Trek Game
5800. Star Trek Game
6062. Star Trek Game
4934. Starsky and Hutch Detective Game
7831. Stingray Target Game

7832. Stingray, The Underwater
      Maze Game
7833. Stoney Burke Game
6957. Strawberry Shortcake
      Card Game, Win
6389. Strike It Rich
6064. Stump the Stars
4948. Stymie Card Game, Bewitched
7559. Supercar Road Race Game
6412. Supercar Target Game
4955. Supercar to the Rescue Game
4960. Supermarket Sweep
6390. Surfside 6
6070. Surprise Package
4964. Swat
6073. T. H. E. Cat Game, Card game
6074. T. H. E. Cat Game
4200. Tales of Texas Rangers
4969. Tales of Wells Fargo Game
6500. Talk to Cecil
6075. Tammy Game, The
4290. Taxi!
6605. Television
5874. Television Trivia Game- #2
7841. Tennessee Tuxedo Game
6077. Terrytoons Pop-outs Game
6078. Terrytoons TV Lotto
7185. That Girl
5814. Three Chipmunks Acorn Hunt
5815. Three Chipmunks Big Record
4981. Three on a Match
6391. Three Stooges Fun House Game
6966. Thunderbirds
4984. Tic-Tac-Aroo with Captain Kangaroo
7844. Tic-Tac-Dough, TV Game
6081. Time Tunnel Card Game, The
6082. Time Tunnel Game, The
7104. Time Tunnel Spin-To-Win, The
6393. To Tell the Truth
7141. Today
4325. Today with Dave Carroway
4989. Tom and Jerry
8131. Top Cat Game
7853. Touche' Turtle Game, The
6125. Toxic Crusaders Card Game
6093. Travels of Jaimie McPheeters Game
4313. Trivia Party - Movies and TV
7479. Tune-In TV Bingo
7881. TV Guides' TV Game
4995. TV Jackpot Game
6394. Twenty One, TV Quiz Game
6095. Twilight Zone Game, The
4997. Twinkles, His Trip to the Star Factory
5820. Two for the Money
5002. Underdog
8136. Underdog to the Rescue
8137. Underdog's Save Sweet Polly Game
6986. Undersea World of Jacques Cousteau
6440. Untouchables Target Game
5006. Video Village
7855. Virginian Game, The
5010. Voyage to the Bottom of the Sea
5011. Voyage to the Bottom of the Sea
7561. Wackiest Ship in the Navy, The
5012. Wacky Races Game, The
5013. Wagon Train
5014. Walk Along Sesame Street
7856. Wally Gator Game
5536. Walt Disney's Official Davy Crockett
8159. Walt Disney's Zorro Game
5016. Waltons Game, The
6395. Wanted Dead Or Alive
6441. Wanted Dead or Alive Target Game
6100. Welcome Back, Kotter
5017. Welcome Home Kotter Card Game
5018. Wells Fargo Game
5019. Wendy the Good Little Witch Game
7064. Western Bedrock U*S*A Race Game
8162. What's My Line?
6396. What's My Line?
5021. Wheel of Fortune TV Game
7108. Wheel of Fortune, Deluxe
5023. Where's Willie?
5207. White Shadows
5028. Who What or Where Game, The
5029. Whoopee! Margie, The Game of
5087. Wild Bill Hickock and Jingles Pony
5088. Wild Bill Hickock, Calvary & Indians
7870. Wild Wild West
5824. Wimpy, Where are My Hamburgers?
6397. Window Shopping
7109. Wink Dink TV Game

6102. Wonderbug Game
7872. Wyatt Earp Game
7960. Yo Yogi Card Game
7873. Yogi Bear and Huckelberry Hound
5426. Yogi Bear Card Game
6442. Yogi Bear Circus Bagatelle
5045. Yogi Bear Game
5046. Yogi Bear Game
7874. Yogi Bear Game, Go Fly a Kite
7875. Yogi Bear Score-A-Matic Ball Toss
7876. Yogi Bear Sling Ring Toss Game
5047. You Don't Say Game
6399. Your First Impression
6105. Your Surprise Package
6400. Yours for a Song

TV - Cartoon

7663. Atom Ant Saves the Day
7664. Bamm-Bamm Game,
      Color Me Happy
6457. Beany and Cecil Match-It Tile Game
7077. Beany and Cecil Ring Toss
7078. Beany and Cecil Skill Ball
7683. Break-A-Plate Carnival Pitch Game
4532. Bugs Bunny Adventure Game, Blue
7056. Bugs Bunny Head Start Game
7057. Bugs Bunny Space Race
7058. Bugs Bunny Trapped
8043. Bugs Bunny's
      "Under the Cawit" Game
5914. Bullwinkle and Rocky
7898. Bullwinkle and Rocky
5389. Bullwinkle Card game
6280. Bullwinkle Electronic Quiz Game
4533. Bullwinkle Hide 'N Seek
6281. Bullwinkle Magnetic Travel Game
7023. Bullwinkle Motorized Target Game
8044. Bullwinkle Ring Toss Game
7024. Bullwinkle Target and
      Ring Toss Game
7686. Bullwinkle Travel Adventure Game
7025. Bullwinkle, Fli-Hi Target Game
5612. Bullwinkle's Electronic Quiz Game
8045. Bullwinkle's Supermarket Game
7370. Cap-It
4543. Captain Caveman and the Teen
      Angels
7990. Cartoon Capers Game
4548. Cartoon Cards, with Flintstones,Pink
4549. Casper the Friendly Ghost Game
7060. Critter Cards Card Game, Linus The
7924. Crusader Rabbit Game
4588. Dastardly and Muttley
4589. Day with Ziggy, A
7549. Dennis the Menace Game
4591. Deputy Dawg Game
5939. Deputy Dawg TV Lotto
8065. Dudley Do-Right's Find Snidely
      Game
6760. Fangface
4630. Fantastic Voyage Game
4632. Fat Albert and The Cosby Kids
4635. Felix the Cat Game
4289. Flintstone Quick Score Target Game
5397. Flintstones Animal Rummy
8069. Flintstones Big Game Hunt Game
8070. Flintstones Break Ball, The
8071. Flintstones Cut-Up
4641. Flintstones Game, The
4642. Flintstones Game, The
7713. Flintstones Magnetic Fish Pond Game
6430. Flintstones Mechanical Shooting
7952. Flintstones Memory Card Game, The
8072. Flintstones Mit-Full
7714. Flintstones Pitch 'N Bowl
7715. Flintstones Sling Dart Game
7716. Flintstones Smash-A-Roo Game
7717. Flintstones Stoneage Game
7718. Flintstones Stoneage Tiddley Winks
6300. Flintstones Target Set
7719. Flintstones Tumble Race
7720. Flintstones Window Whacker Game
7722. Fred Flintstones Just for Kids Target
5069. Funday Cartoons Card Game, Harvey
4652. Funky Phantom Game
79532. Funtastic World of Hanna-Barbera
7963. Gay Puree Board Game
6780. George of the Jungle
4673. Great Grape Ape Game, The
5283. Gumby and Pokey Playfull Trails
4677. Gumby Game, The
4679. Hair Bear Bunch, The

7730. Hanna-Barbera Break-A-Plate
7731. Hanna-Barbera Ruff and
  Reddy Circus
4684. Hardy Boys Game, The, Based on the
7922. Heckle & Jeckle 3-D Target Game
8076. Heckle and Jeckel's Ski Trail Game
7276. Herman and Katnip Game Box
4693. Hoppity Hopper Game
7741. Hoppy the Hopparoo
4695. Houndcats Game
7743. Huck Finn Game
7744. Huckelberry Hound "Bumps" Game
7745. Huckelberry Hound &
  Yogi Bear Break
4699. Huckelberry Hound Tiddledy Winks
7746. Huckle Chuck
4701. Huckleberry Hound
7747. Huckleberry Hound Juggle Roll
7748. Huckleberry Hound Lids Off Bowling
4422. Huckleberry Hound Spin-O Game
7749. Huckleberry Hound Tumble Race
4700. Huckleberry Hound Western Game
7954. Inspector Gadget Detective Kit Game
4705. Inspector Gadget Game
7752. Jetson's Fun Pad Game
4717. Jetsons Fun Pad Game, The
7753. Jetsons Game, Out of This World, The
4718. Jetsons Game, The
7754. Jetson's Rosey the Robot Game, The
4722. Jonny Quest Card Game
6477. Jumping DJ Surprise Action Game
4727. King Leonardo and His Subjects
7763. Laurel and Hardy
7762. Laurel and Hardy Ring Toss
7063. Linus Critter Cards
7767. Linus the Lionhearted Uproarious
8087. Looney Toons Ballon Game
4757. Looney Tunes Game
8004. MGM Tom & Jerry Merry-Go-Round
5775. Mighty Hercules Game, The
4782. Mighty Mouse Game with Heckle and
7777. Mighty Mouse Presents the Game of
5680. Mighty Mouse Rescue Game
7090. Mighty Mouse Skill-Roll Game
4176. Mighty Mouse Spin Targets Game
4783. Mighty Mouse Target Game
6222. Mr. Magoo at the Circus Target Game
6373. Mr. Magoo Visits the Zoo Game
6374. Mr. Magoo Visits the Zoo
7554. Mr. Magoo Maddining Adventures
7782. Mr. Magoo's Maddening
  Misadventures
6013. Mushmouse & Punkin Puss Feudin"
4806. Off to See the Wizard Game
7997. Oh Magoo
7792. Pebbles Flintstone Game
7793. Pebbles Flintstone Magnetic Fish
  Pond
7794. Pebbles Live Wire Game
6437. Perils of Pauline
8098. Peter Potamus and Yo-Yo Card Game
6026. Peter Potamus Target Barrel
5165. Pink Panther
7998. Pink Panther Game
4841. Pink Panther Game, The
6271. Playful Trails Game, Gumby and
8104. Porky Pig's Donut Factory Game
4860. Quick Draw McGraw
4859. Quick Draw McGraw Game
6223. Quick Draw McGraw Moving Target
6042. Ricochet Rabbit & Droop-A-Long
4874. Road Runner Game
8108. Road Runner Game, The
8109. Road Runner Pop-Up-Game, The
8110. Rocky and Bullwinkle
  Magic Dot Game
4875. Rocky and His Friends Game
7811. Rosey the Robot
7813. Ruff and Ready at the Circus
5482. Ruff and Ready TV Favorite Spelling
4889. Scooby-Doo & Scrappy-Doo Game
4890. Scooby-Doo, Where are You?
7822. Silly Sidney Count Shoot
  Target Game
4904. Simpsons Don't Have a Cow, The
4912. Smurf Game, The
7824. Snaggle Puss Fun at the Picnic
7841. Tennessee Tuxedo Game
5420. Terrytoon Edition Old Maid
4977. Terrytoons Mighty Mouse Game
6077. Terrytoons Pop-outs Game
6078. Terrytoons TV Lotto

7475. Tom & Jerry Game, The
4989. Tom and Jerry
6969. Tom and Jerry
7846. Tom and Jerry Bowling Set
4988. Tom and Jerry Game
7847. Tom and Jerry Magnetic
  Fishing Game
7848. Tom and Jerry Platter Splatter
7849. Tom and Jerry Target Game
7850. Tom and Jerry, Adventures in
8131. Top Cat Game
7851. Top Cat Shoe Toss Game
7853. Touche' Turtle Game, The
5199. Travel with Woody Woodpecker
8135. Tweety and Sylvester's "I Tawt
  I Taw a
4997. Twinkles, His Trip to the Star Factory
5002. Underdog
8136. Underdog to the Rescue
8137. Underdog's Save Sweet Polly Game
7856. Wally Gator Game
7282. Walter Lanz Picture Dominoes
5019. Wendy the Good Little Witch Game
8163. What's Up Doc?, Bugs Bunny Game
4204. Woody Woodpecker
5039. Woody Woodpecker
5211. Woody Woodpecker
8168. Woody Woodpecker
  Up the Tree Game
8167. Woody Woodpecker's
  Baja Rally Game
8168. Woody Woodpecker's
  Crazy Mixed-Up
7283. Woody Woodpecker's Game Box
8169. Woody Woodpecker's Moon Dash
7960. Yo Yogi Card Game
7873. Yogi Bear and Huckelberry Hound
5426. Yogi Bear Card Game
6442. Yogi Bear Circus Bagatelle
5045. Yogi Bear Game
5046. Yogi Bear Game
7874. Yogi Bear Game, Go Fly a Kite
7875. Yogi Bear Score-A-Matic Ball Toss
7876. Yogi Bear Sling Ring Toss Game
8170. Yosemite Sam's Treasure Hunt Game

TV - Game Shows
5227. $1,000,000 Chance of a Lifetime
4461. $10,000 Pyramid Game, The
4462. $20,000 Pyramid
5228. $25,000 Pyramid
6346. $64,000 Question Quiz Game
5705. 2 for the Money
4508. Beat the Clock Game
4514. Bid it Right, The Price is Right
6316. Big Nuumbers
4439. Break the Bank, Photo of Bert Parks
4534. By the Numbers
4535. Call My Bluff
6355. College Bowl
4577. Concentration, 3rEdition, Lower blue
4578. Concentration, 9th Edition, Upper red
4579. Concentration,, 1st. Edition
5723. Dating Game, The
4161. Dating Game, The,
  Party Pack, with 45-
6357. Dollar a Second
5945. Double Exposure
6358. Dough-Re-Mi
7388. Down You Go
4607. Dream House TV Home Game
8002. Everybody's Talking
4623. Eye Guess
6359. Face the Facts
4627. Family Feud
5736. Family Game
4655. Get the Message
4214. Gong Show, The
6360. Groucho's You Bet Your Life
5971. Hollywood Squares, The
8003. Hollywood Squares, The
8080. Hollywood Squares, The
6366. I've Got a Secret, I'm
  Garry Moore. and
4709. Jackpot!
5593. Jan Murray's Treasure Hunt
4715. Jeopardy!
4719. Joker, Joker, Joker
4720. Joker's Wild
4742. Let's Make a Deal
5993. Let's Make a Deal
4765. Make a Face

4774. Match Game
4773. Match Game, The, 1st. Edition
6608. Mating Game
6484. Merv Griffin's Word by Word
6485. Merv Griffin's Word for Word Game
4785. Missing Links
4800. Name that Tune, with record, Red box
4801. Name that Tune, with record, White
4805. Now You See It
6868. Number Please
4817. P D Q
4826. Pass Word, 2nedition, Blue cloth
4827. Pass Word, 3redition, Large cartoon
4828. Pass Word, 5th. edition,
  red & blue MB
4829. Pass Word, Collectors Edition, Wood
4830. Pass Word, Fine Edition, Square box
4831. Pass Word, Original edition,
  CBS Logo
4832. Pass Word, Red & white box
4833. Pass Word, Red, white & blue box
7558. Picture This
8100. Play Cards!
4799. Play Your Hunch
6379. Price is Right, The
6383. Revlon's $64,000 Question
  Junior Quiz
6384. Revlon's $64,000 Question
  Quiz Game
4882. Sale of the Century
6921. Say When!
6048. Seven Keys
6234. Sky's the Limit, The
4913. Snap Judgement
6389. Strike It Rich
4960. Supermarket Sweep
6070. Surprise Package
5874. Television Trivia Game- #2
4981. Three on a Match
7844. Tic-Tac-Dough, TV Game
6393. To Tell the Truth
4995. TV Jackpot Game
6394. Twenty One, TV Quiz Game
5820. Two for the Money
5006. Video Village
8162. What's My Line?
6396. What's My Line?
5021. Wheel of Fortune TV Game
7108. Wheel of Fortune, Deluxe
5028. Who What or Where Game, The
6397. Window Shopping
5047. You Don't Say Game
6399. Your First Impression
6105. Your Surprise Package
6400. Yours for a Song

TV - Medical and Doctors
7668. Ben Casey M. Game
6714. Cherry Ames, Nursing Game
5946. Dr. Kildare
5229. General Hospital, The Game of
Trivia (See Q & A)

Video Game
4550. Cenepede
4993. Turbo
4604. Donkey Kong
4819. Pac-Man Card Game
4820. Pac-Man Game
5048. Zaxxon
6893. Popeye

Western
6575. 49 ers, The, Large stage coach
6576. 49 ers, The, Small stage coach
4486. Annie Oakley Game
4487. Annie Oakley Game. Variant Cover
5541. Annie Oakley Game
6212. Bandit Trail Game, Featuring Gene
7362. Bang. The Game of the Old West
2539. Big Chief
4183. Big Chief
2795. Big Chief Apache
4521. Bockaroo
7895. Boot Hill
5589. Boots & Saddles
4526. Branded Game
2961. Buckaroo
3834. Bucking Broncos
5065. Buffalo Bill Jr. Cattle Round Up
  Game

1889. Buffalo Bill, The Game of
5067. Cattle Round-Up Game
7374. Cattleman, The
1273. Cheyenne
4561. Cheyenne Game, Cowboy with pistol
4562. Cheyenne, Picture of Ty Hardin
6541. Cheyenne Target Game
5928. Cimarron Strip Game
3138. Covered Wagon, Game of
4109. Covered Wagon, The Game of
2558. Cowboy
1245. Cowboy Game, The
6729. Cowboy Roundup Game
5393. Cowboys & Indians
3913. Cowboys & Indians Also Junior Golf
5720. Cowboys and Indians
5394. Daniel Boone
7698. Daniel Boone Card Game
4592. Deputy Game, The
8027. Desperado
7700. Doc Holliday Wild West Game
947. Dudes, Game of the
4631. Fastest Gun
4637. Fess Parker Trail Blazers Game
7711. Fess Parker Wilderness Trail Card
5516. Frontier Fort Rescue Race
7273. Frontier Marshall & Star of India
6556. Fury, Western Range Game
5658. Gabby Hays Champion
  Shooting Target
5070. Gene Autry's Dude Ranch Game
7165. Giant Wheel Cowboys 'N Indians
5131. Good Guys "n Bad Guys
5967. Gunfight at O.K. Corral
4367. Gunslingers
6361. Gunsmoke
6648. Gunsmoke Target Game
3033. H - Bar -O, Mail Premium
7729. Hands Up Harry
3169. Happy Hunting Ground, The
6793. Have Gun Will Travel
4692. Hopalong Cassidy
4691. Hopalong Cassidy Chineese Checkers
7739. Hopalong Cassidy Lasso Game, The
7740. Hopalong Cassidy Pony Express Toss
5466. Hopalong Cassidy Target Practice &
2895. Indian Ambush
3677. Indian Trail
7756. Johnny Ringo Game
7175. Lancer Game
6372. Laramie
2150. Lasso, The Jumping Rag
5765. Leave it to Beaver Ambush Game
4739. Legend of Jessie James Game
4740. Legend of the Lone Ranger, The
954. Life in the Wild West
5074. Little Beaver's 3 Game Set
4756. Lone Ranger
6823. Lone Ranger
5537. Lone Ranger & The Silver Bullets
7087. Lone Ranger & Tonto Spin to Win
3393. Lone Ranger Game
8032. Lone Ranger Silver Bullets Game
7768. Lone Ranger Target Game
5055. Lot the Calf
7499. Magnetic Cowboy Roundup
7126. Mail Run, TV's Pony Express
957. Minnehaha, Game of
7979. Montezuma
7181. Notch
7789. Outlaws Exciting Western Game
7790. Overland Trail
2900. Pioneers of the Santa Fe Trail
3971. Pirate's Cave & Wild West Rodeo
3972. Pirate's Cove &
  Wild West Rodeo, The
7055. Pony Express, The Game of
7450. Pow, the Frontier Game
2044. Quien Sabe
6381. Rawhide Game
6036. Rebel The
3731. Redskins & Cowboys
4869. Restless Gun Game, The
3846. Ride 'Em Cowboy & Knuckle Down
4872. Rifleman Game, The
3237. Rodeo Toy Game
8111. Rodeo, The Wild West Game
4193. Round Up
1162. Round Up, Game of
2849. Round-Up
7980. Roundup, 64-32 Ranch

Select Bibliography

Books on Games

Brady, Maxine. *The Monopoly Book.* New York: David McKay Co., 1974.

Brown, Timothy and Lee, Tony. *Official Price Guide to Role-Playing Games.* New York: House of Collectibles 1998.

Bruegman, Bill. *Cartoon Friends of the Baby Boom Era, A Pictorial Price Guide.* Akron, Ohio: Toy Scouts Inc., 1993.

Cheney, E. D. *Social Games.* Boston: Lee and Shepard, 1871.

Collins, A. Frederick. *Boy's and Girl's Book of Indoor Games.* New York: Appleton and Co., 1928.

Cooper, Mark W. *Baseball Games, Home Versions of the National Pastime, 1860-1980.* Atglen, Pennsylvania: Schiffer Publishing, 1995.

Culin, Stewart. *Games of the Orient.* Rutland, Vermont: Charles E. Tuttle Co., 1958.

Daiken, Leslie. *Children's Toys throughout the Ages.* New York: Frederick A. Praeger, 1953.

Dennis, Lee. *Warman's Antique American Games 1840-1940.* Radnor, Pennsylvania: Wallace-Homestead Co., 1986 and 1991.

Diagram Group. *The Way to Play.* New York: Paddington Press LTD., 1975.

Freeman, Ruth and Larry. *Cavalcade of Toys.* New York: Century House, 1942.

Goodfellow, Caroline. *A Collector's Guide to Games and Puzzles.* Secaucus, New Jersey: Chartwell Books 1991.

Grunfeld, Frederic V. *Games of the World.* New York: Plenary Publications International, 1975.

Harbin, E. O. *Games of Many Nations.* New York: Abingdon Press, 1945.

Hargrave, Catherine P. *A History of Playing Cards.* New York and Boston: Houghton Mifflin Co.,1930.

Hertz, Louis H. *The Handbook of Old American Toys.* Wethersfield, Colorado: Mark Haber and Co., 1947.

Hochman, Gene. *Encyclopedia of American Playing Cards, Part 1-VI.* 1976.

Kiefer, Monica. *American Children through their Books 1700-1835.* Philadelphia: University of Pennsylvania Press, 1948.

Lane, Stephanie, and Dilley, David. *Board Games of the 50's, 60's and 70's with prices.* Gas City, Indiana: LW Sales, 1994.

Longstreet IV, William. *Name of the Game.* Plainville, Connecticut: self-published, 1991.

Love, Brian. *Play the Game, The Book that You can Play.* Los Angeles: Reed Books, 1978.

Malloy, Roderick A. *Malloy's Sports Collectible Value Guide.* Radnor, Pennsylvania: Wallace-Homestead, 1993.

Malloy, Alex G. and Wells, Stuart W. *Comics Collectibles and their Values* Radnor, Pennsylvania: Wallace-Homestead, 1996.

Mason, Bernard S., and Mitchell, Elmer D. *Social Games for Recreation.* New York: A. S. Barnes, 1935.

Matthews, Jack. *Toys go to War, World War II Military Toys, Games, Puzzles and Books.* Missoula, Montana: Pictorial Histories Publishing Co., 1994.

McClintock, Marshall and Inez. *Toys in America.* Washington D.C.: Public Affairs Press, 1961.

Mentzer, F, Ward, J. M., Black, J. B. *Game Buyer's Price Guide, 1985-1986.* 1985, Lake Geneva, WI.

Monckton, O. Paul. *Pastimes in Times Past.* London: J.B. Lippincott Co., 1913.

Morley, H. T. *Old and Curious Playing Cards.* London: Bracken Books, 1989.

Mulac, Margaret E. *The Game Book.* New York: Harper Brothers, 1946.

Opie, Iona and Robert, and Alderson, Brian. *The Treasures of Childhood.* New York: Arcade Publishing, 1989.

Orbanes, Philip. *The Monopoly Companion.* Boston: B. Adams Co.,1988.

Palmer, Nicholas. *The Best of Board Wargaming.* New York: Hippocrene Books, 1980.

Parker Brothers. *75 Years of Fun, The Story of Parker Brothers, Inc.* Salem, Massachusetts: Parker Brothers, 1958.

Polizzi, Rick, and Schaefer, Fred. *Spin Again: Board Games from the Fifties and Sixties.* San Francisco: Chronicle Books, 1991.

Polizzi, Rick. *Baby Boomer Games, Identification & Value Guide.* Paducah, Kentucky: Collector Books, 1995.

Riedel, Lisa and Hirte, Werner. *Die Schöne Kartenlegerin, Kurzweil auf Neuruppiner Bilderbogen.* Berlin: Eulanspiegel Verlag, 1984.

Rinker, Harry L. *Collector's Guide to Toys, Games & Puzzles.* Radnor, Pennsylvania: Wallace-Homestead Book Co., 1991.

Rinker, Harry L. *Guide to Games & Puzzles.* Dubuque, Iowa: Antique Trader Books, 1997.

Sams, Allen E. *The Rook Book.* Salem, Massachusetts: Parker Brothers, 1930.

Scarpone, Desi *Board Games with Prices.* Atglen, Pennsylvania: Schiffer Publishing Co., 1995.

Smith, Charles F. *Games and Game Leadership.* New York: Dodd, Mead and Co., 1938.

Whitehill, Bruce. *Games, American Boxed Games and their Makers, 1822-1992 with Values.* Radnor, Pennsylvania: Wallace-Homestead, 1992.

Whitehouse, F. R. B. *Table Games of Georgian and Victorian Days.* London: Peter Garnett, 1951.

Other Publications and Sources

American Game Collectors Association, *Game Times*, 34 Issues through 1999

American Game Collectors Association, *Game Researchers' Notes*, 28 Issues through 1998

American Game Collectors Association Convention Catalogues, Various years and Locales

Bloomfield Collection of Games (1746-1990), James International Auctioneers, Auction 12/7/91, Norwich, UK.

Bruegman, Bill, *Toy Scouts, Inc.* Mail Order Catalogue, Dealer Fixed Price List, Akron, Ohio.

Cadaco-Ellis, Sales Catalogue, Chicago, Illinois.

Collectible Toy Values Monthly Magazine, #7, Game Issue 8, Simulation Games, various other issues all contain game articles and listings, 1994 & 1995, Ridgefield, Connecticut.

Continental Auctions, Various Auctions, Sheboygan, Wisconsin.

Corey Games, Sales Catalogue, East Boston, Massachusetts.

Current Price Report, Games, 1991, Lexington, Missouri.

Curtis, Scott, *52 Girls Collectibles,* Dealer Fixed price list Marion, Ohio.

Ephemera Society of America, *Ephemera Journal, Volume # 6,* 1993, Schoharie, New York.

Exhibition at the Bruce Museum 12/2/95-2/4/96, 1995, Greenwich, Connecticut.

F. A. O. Schwarz, Sales Catalogue, Various Years, New York, New York.

Game Preserve Museum Collection, Antique American Games, Auction by Skinner, 9/17/88, The Lee and Rally Dennis Collection, Boston Massachusetts.

Hake's Americana & Collectibles, Auction & Mail Bids in 1990s, York, Pennsylvania.

Just Kids Nostalgia, Auctions Mail Bid, Huntington, New York.

Kaplan, Stuart R., Saunders, Wayne, and Darquenne, Jean, *Play Your Cards! The Stuart and Marilyn R. Kaplan Playing Card Collection, Exhibition at the Bruce Museum 12/2/95-2/4/96,* 1995, Greenwich, Connecticut.

Kayyem, Marisa and Sternberger, Paul, *Victorian Pleasures: American Board and Table Games of the Nineteenth Century from the Liman Collection, Exhibition Columbia University,* 11/13/91-1/22/92 New York.

Ketchum, Jr., William C. and Weis, Robert K., *Katonah Museum of Art, The Board Game: America at Play 1845-1945,* 12/13/92-2/28/93, Katonah, New York.

Krim, Debby and Marty, *New England Auction Gallery,* Auctions, 65 Sales through 1998, West Peabody, Massachusetts.

Malloy's Sports Collectibles, Magazine, Sports Games Issue, # 7, May 1992, Ridgefield, Connecticut.

Mc Loughlin Bros. Sales Catalogues, Various years, New York, New York.

Parker Brothers, Inc., Sales Catalogue, Various Years, Salem, Massachusetts.

Pfeiffenberger, Deborah, *Classic Comic Games from the Collection of Alex G. Malloy, Exhibition New Britain Youth Museum, 1/18/97,* 1996, New Britain, Connecticut.

Randolph, Col. Bob , *Auction of a Large Private Game Collection,* !0/5/96,11/9/96, 4/26/97, 5/3/97, Manasquan, New Jersey.

Schwarz, Helmut and Faber, Marion, *Games We Play, History of J. W. Spear & Sons., Nuremberg Toy Museum, Volume II,* 1997, Nuremberg.

Selchow & Righter Co., Sales Catalogue, Various Years, New York.

Siegal Collection of Games & Toys, Auction by Noel Barrett Antiques & Auctions, Ltd., June 5-7, 1992, New Hope, Pennsylvania.

Skinner Auctions, Various Auctions, 1990's, Bolton, Massachusetts.

Smith House, Auctions, Sales through 1998, Eliot, Maine.

Sotheby's, Auction, The Hannas Collection, 7/23/84, London, UK.

Spear's Games, Sales Catalogue, 1930, Nuremberg-Doos, Bavaria, Germany.

Stanley Gibbons Auctions, Various Auctions, 1970-1980's, London, UK.

Starr, Frederick, *Catalogue of an Exhibition of Educational Games,* 1928, Seattle, Washington.

Toys and prices, magazine, April, 1993, Vol. No. 3, Iola, Wisconsin.

Whitehill, Bruce, *The Big Game Hunter,* Various Mail Bid Sales in the 1990's.

DAS IST DES DEUTSCHEN VATERLAND

122

A Voyage through the Clouds.

The Game of To-day.

303b

Gendarmes et VOLEURS

Jeu de Société

87

FROG RACE

A HILARIOUS PARTY GAME FOR ANY NUMBER OF PLAYERS AGED 8 TO ADULT

213a

South Sea Adventures

An exciting Game

149

A Journey round the World

134

THE CLIMBING MONKEYS

120

136

THE AUST...... WOOL GAME

SQUATTER

NO. 3 ASSORTMENT

61

Aerial Attack

174

THE BIG ROLLER

115

THE GARDEN GAME

214

235

157

155

60a

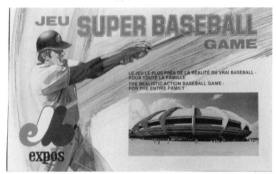

73

165

83

141

105

170

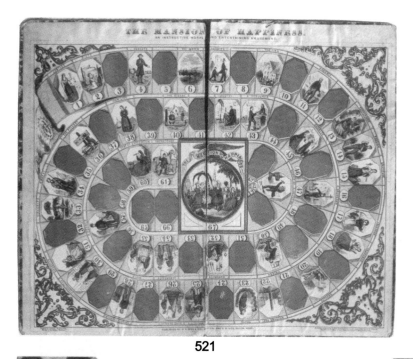

521

740

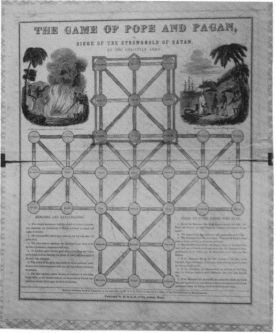

777

763

360

517

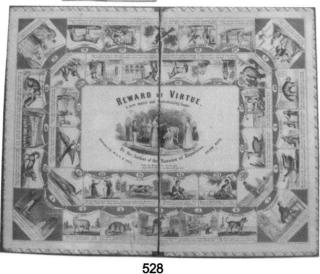

361

503

528

527

237

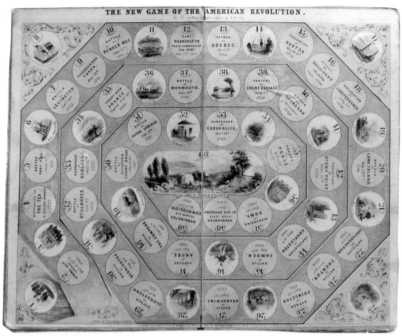

403

766

729

566

417

310

312

1806

238

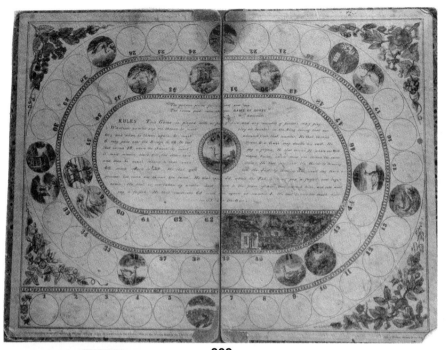

308

359

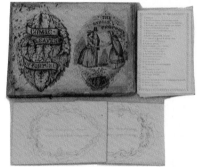

569

541

477

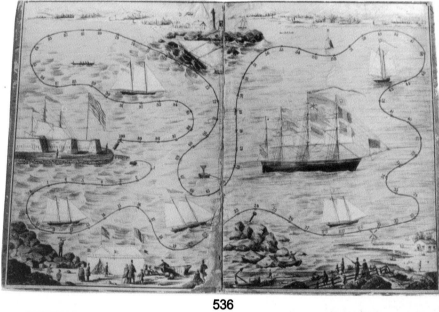

536

700

800

533

507

239

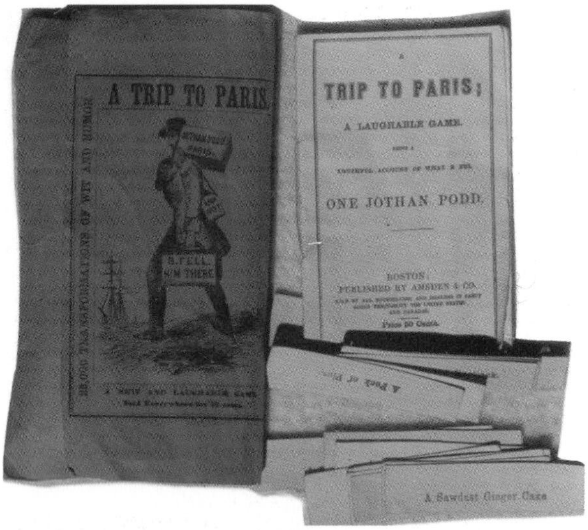

352

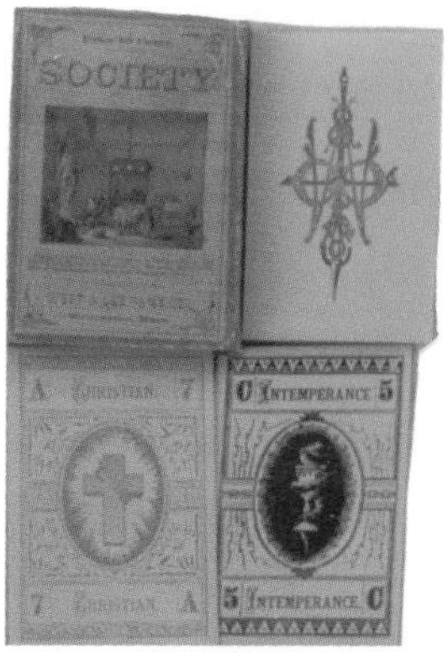

804

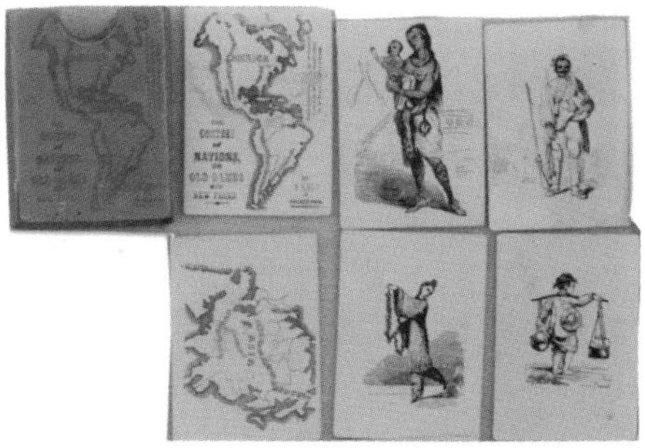
490

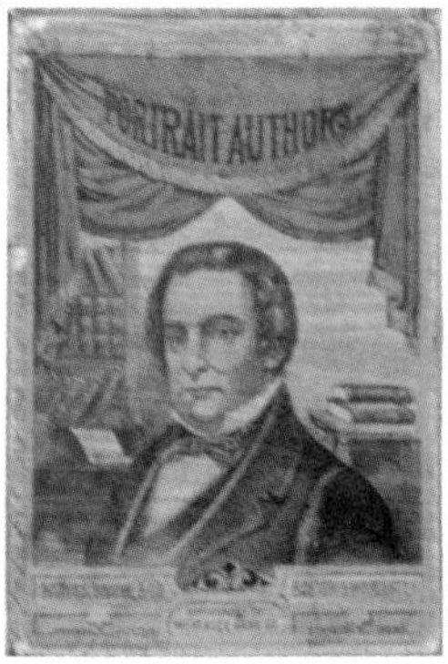

1807

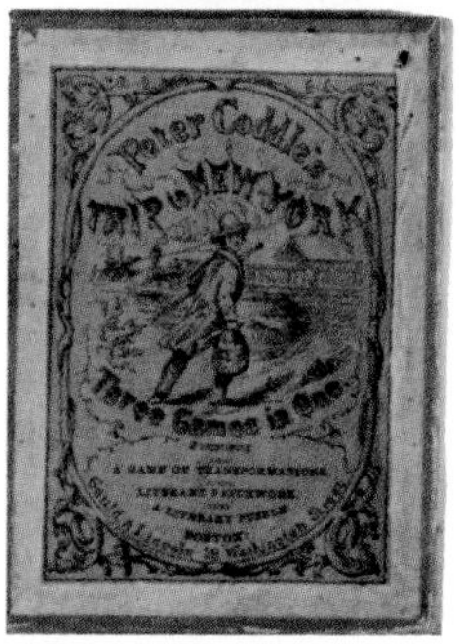

487

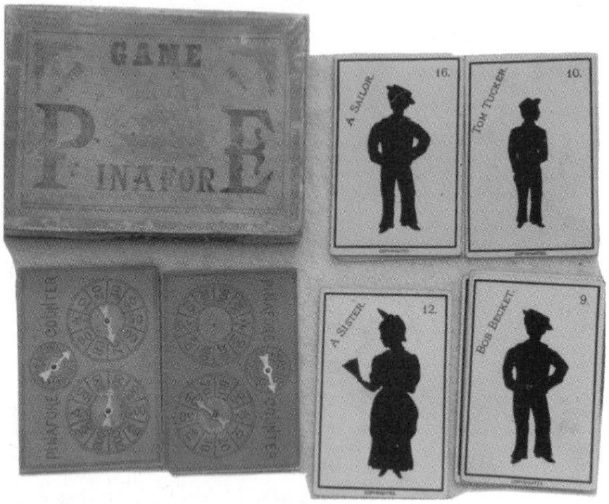

476

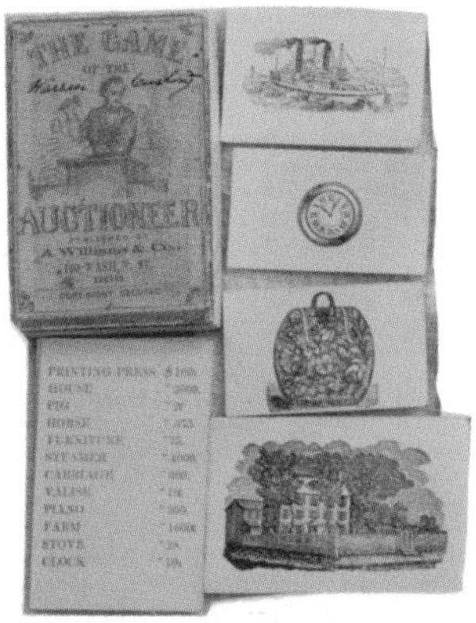

826

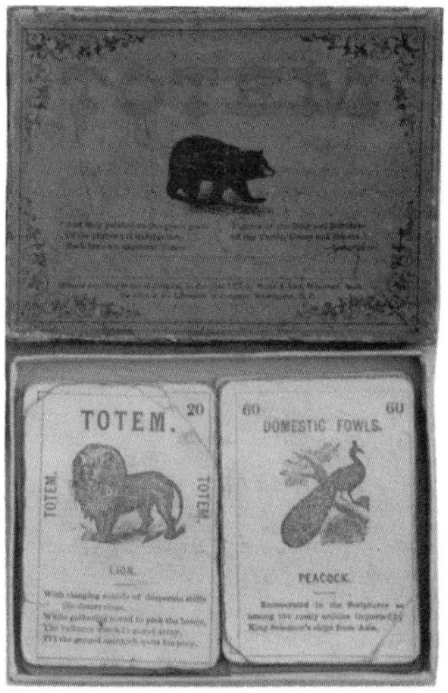

805

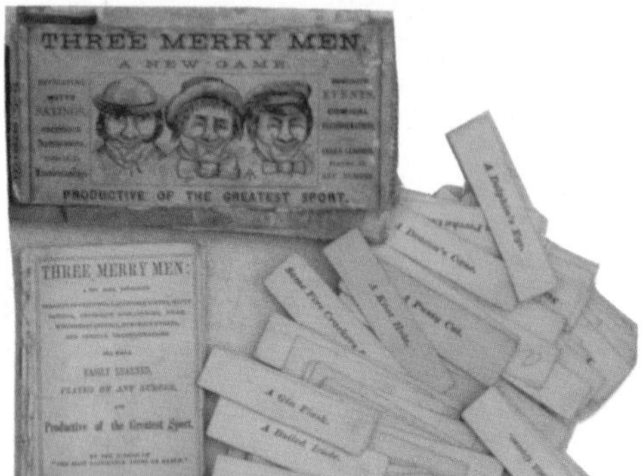

351

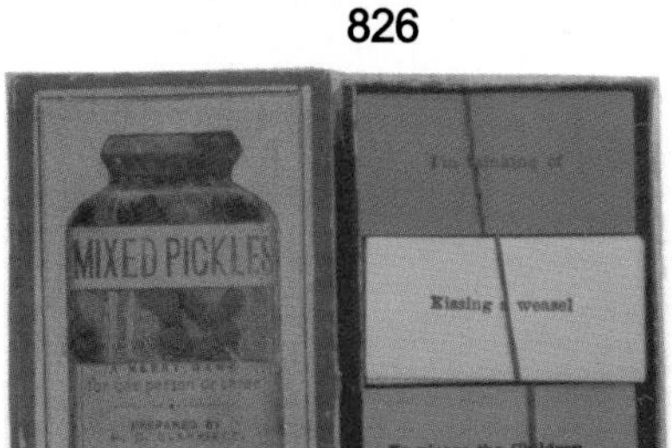

405

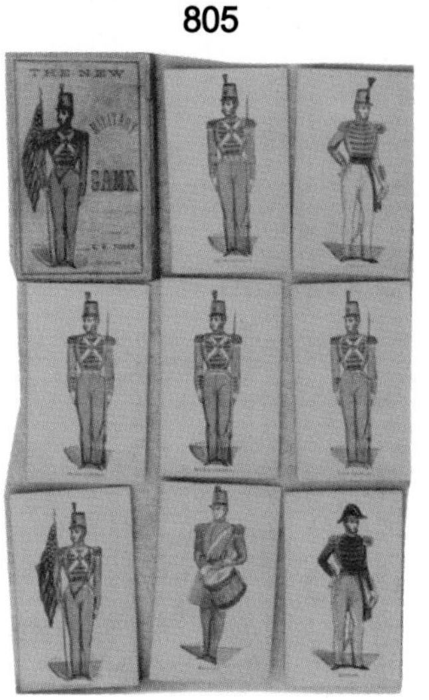

446

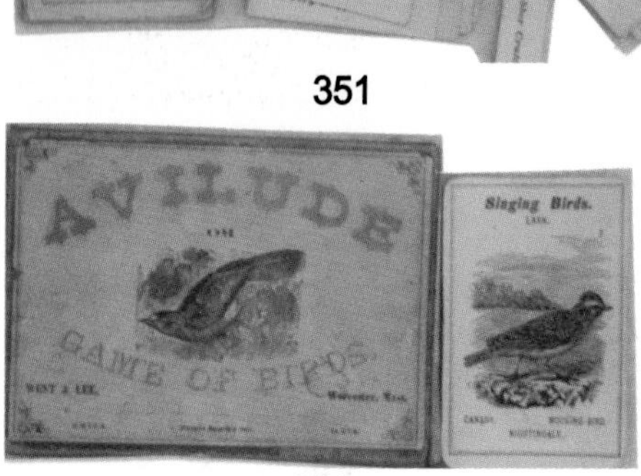

801

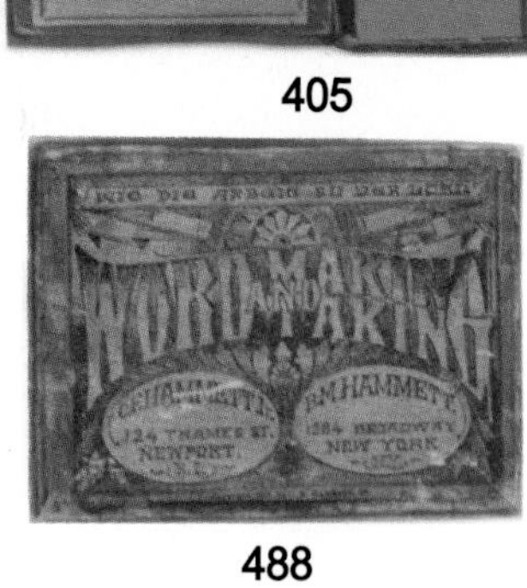

488

735

362

365

401

832

378

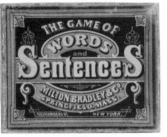

399

415

397

398

759

424

379

813

241

382

511

504

506

512a

353

382a

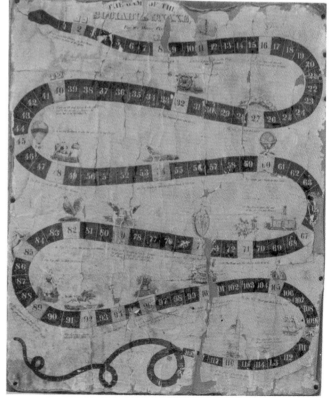

366

242

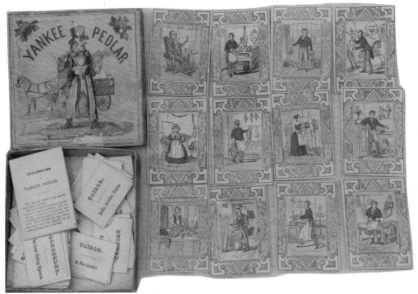

599

615

688

638

692

640

657

674

609

243

639

651

610

675

647

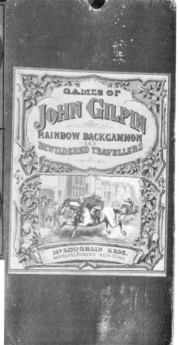

244

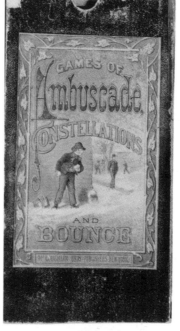

601

608a

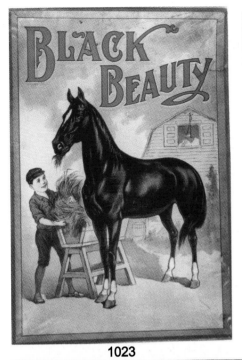

1023

1185

1117a

996

1123

1097

1013

1131

1138

1033

1050

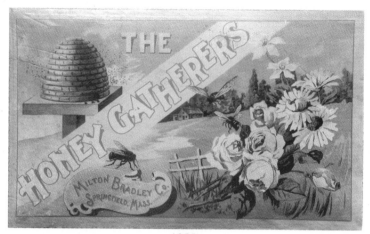

1093a

1035

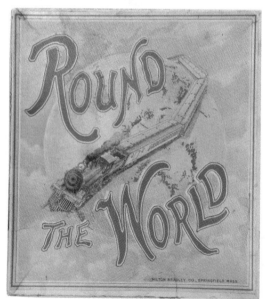

994

1049

1068

1044

1132

1160

1001

1069

1054

1102

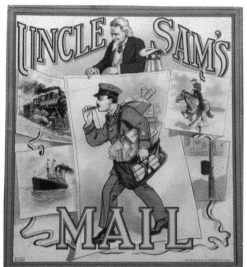

1198

1007

1014

1061

1143

1179

1092

1142

1162

1109

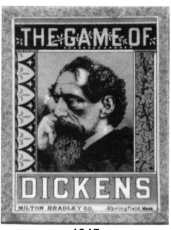

1045

995

1058

1191

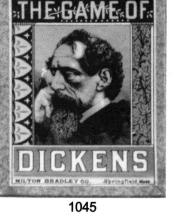

1021

1161

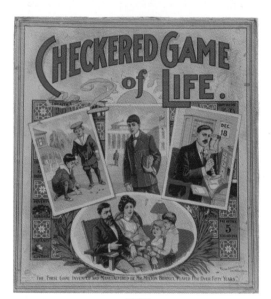

1032

1209

1172

248

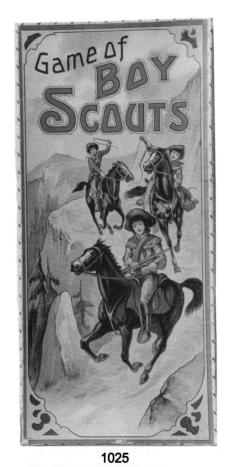

1025

1078

1094

1157

1048

1202

1030

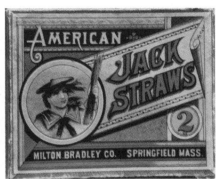

1004

1167

1994

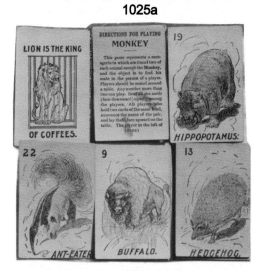

1025a

1149

1099

1508

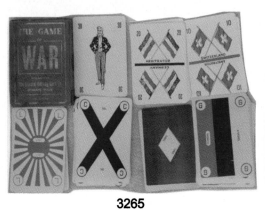

3265

1692

997

250

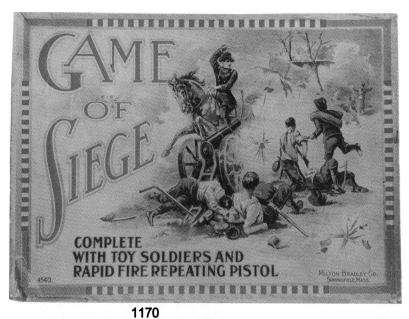

1170

1091

1111

1148

2025

1125

2011

1946

1876

2028

1891

1609

1765

1555

1691

1586

1745

1784

1671

1590

1763

1654

1764

1708

1713

1740

1715

1673

1606

1758

1776

1638

1594

1583

1683

1728

1658

253

1667

1772

1676

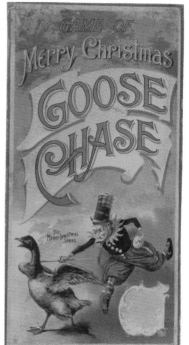

1700

1644

1624

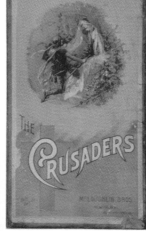

1603

1749

1773

1759

1620

254

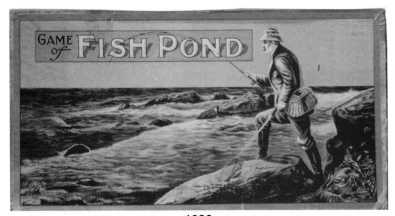

1626

1607

1675

1743

1655

1694

1553

255

1677

1761

1623

1720

1672a

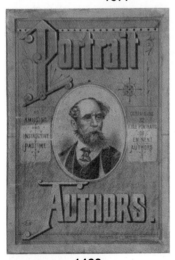

1460a

1622

1621

1669a

1569

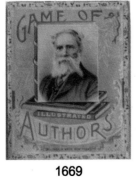

1669

1753

1672

256

1598

3201

1730

1723

1752

1631

1717

1744

1652

1632

1786

257

1756

1611

1636

1637

1614

1653

1688a

1690

1775

1764a

258

1628

1630

1628a

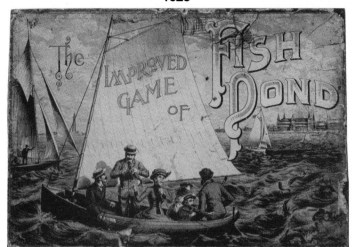

1629

1628b

1670

1662

1630a

259

1615

1560

1572

1617

1618

1554

1589

1710

1773

1585

1709

1722

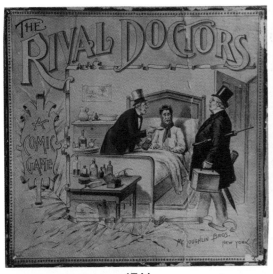

1741

1648

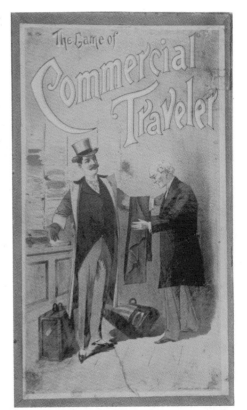

1600

1721

1675

1766

1853

1650

1697

1770

261

1999

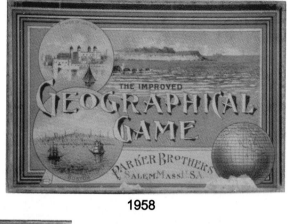

1958

1911

2071

2095

2018

2052

1856

1908a

2057

2110

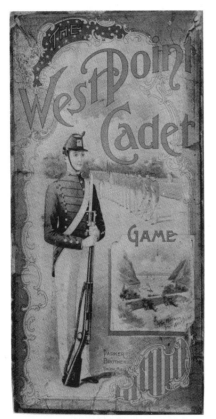

2096

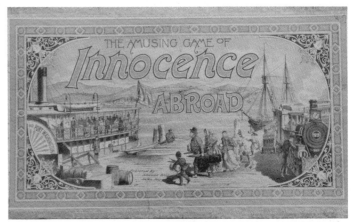

1959

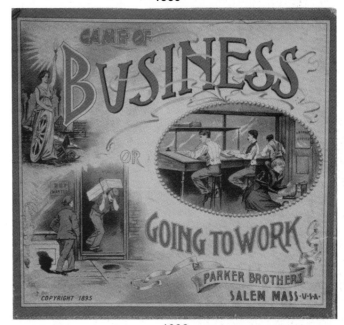

1892

1916

1853

1867

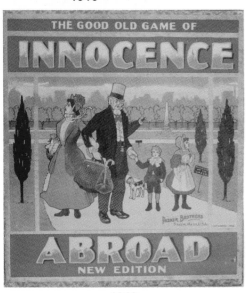

1943

2015

1865

1954

1924

2107

1988

1595

1565

1888

1904

2049

1831

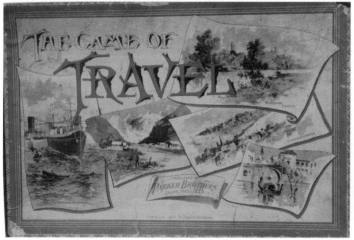

2084

1621

1839

264

2099

2069

1862

1858

1980

2052

2104

2081

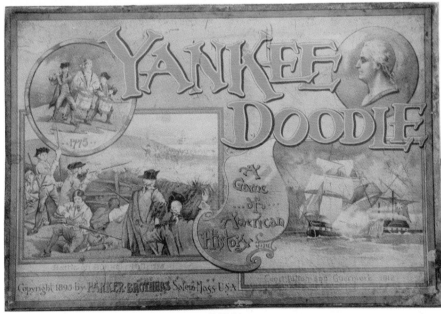

2106

2012

1881

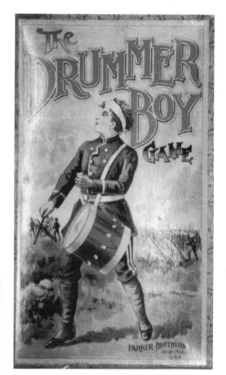

1919

2042

2030

1932

1901

2101

2064

2038

1874

266

2192

3371

2198

2168

1817

1912

2167

2195

1897

1341

4088

2134

887

1814

2196

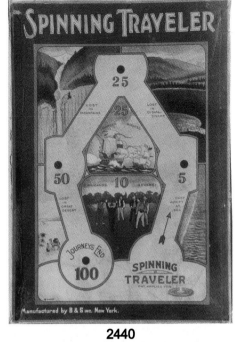

2440

1803

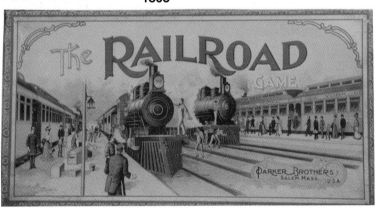

2047

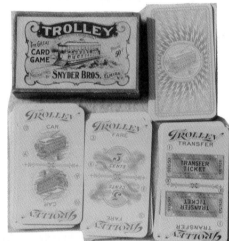

2208

2257

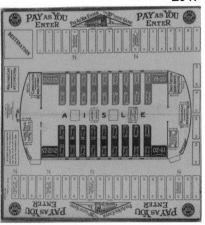

3174

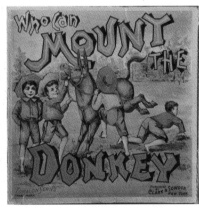

1346

268

1250

1445

2145

2237

1478

888

2144

1332

3771

1949

1793

2122

1434

269

2243

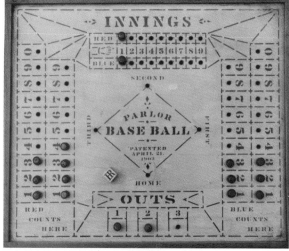

880

2195

2178

3877

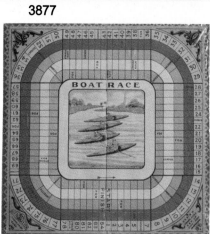

1437

890

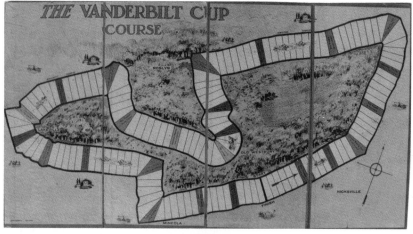

992

2452

270

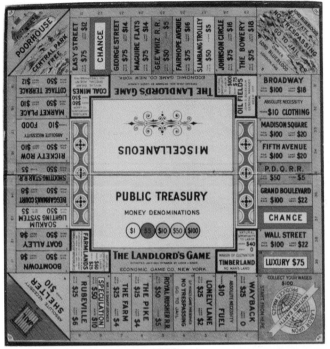

1388

1249

2185

1387

975

2187

1336

1436

1809

1324

1255

1265

2176

1340

1344

2186

1245

2366

2311

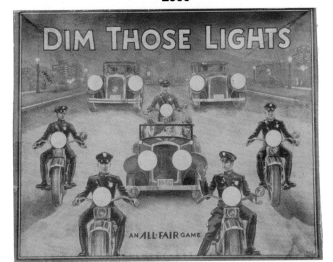

2305

2257

2330

2318

2361

2319

273

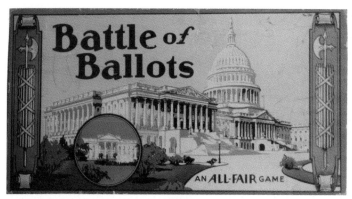

2291

2350

2332

2333

2293

2344

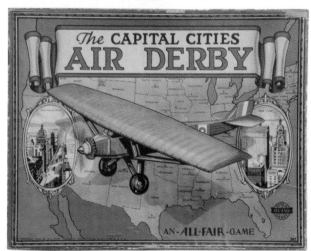

2298

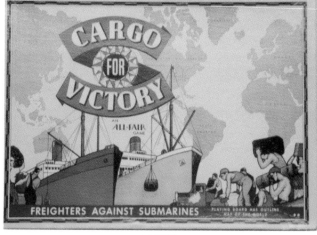

2300

2296

2342

2325

2327

2337

2302

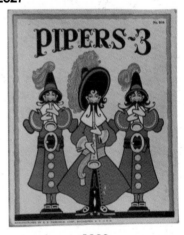

2329

2310

2358

275

2720

2583

2535

2613

2725

2709

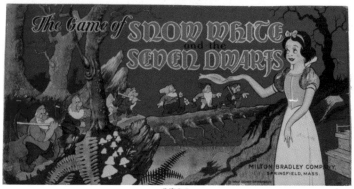

2704

2694

2590

2559

2662

2731

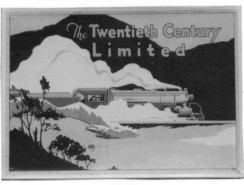

2735

2682

2511

2659

2715

2503

2580

2525

277

2550

2693

2732

2651

2527

2700

Santa Claus Game

2690

2711

Bradleys Big Tent Peg Game

2546

2731a

2614

2743

1090

2687

2717a

2668

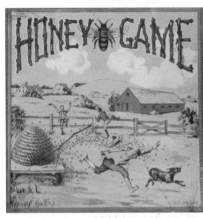

1093

1197

2688

1042

2634

2737

279

2505

2642

2727

2595

2557

2699

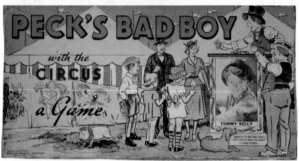

2665

2646

2722

2576

2635

2508

2579

2660a

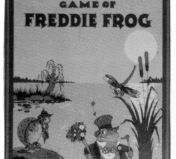

1070

2559

THE OVERLAND LIMITED

2660

2743

2716

2530

2585

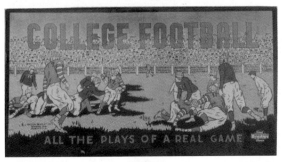

2555

2599

2740

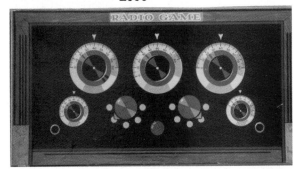

2680

2603

2541

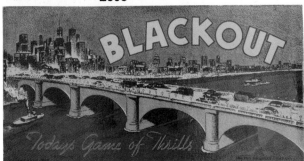

2543

2665a

2630

2584

2681

2501

3296

2601

2751

2632

2606

2706

2591

2719

2625

283

2508a

2551

2644

2697

2631

2700a

2728

2648

2587

2703

3876

2989

2803

3161

3245

3290

3539

3203

3083

2841

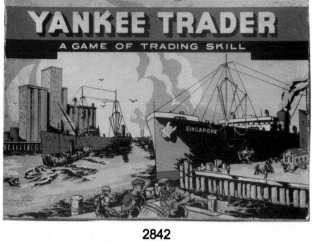

2842

2812

2822

2819

2837

2832

2840

2827

2829

2821a

2826

2818

2813

2836

287

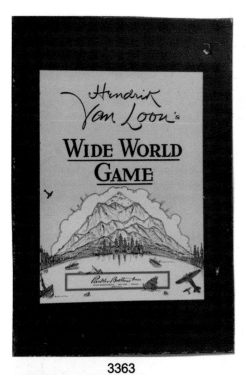

3363

3420

3285

3385

3473

3348

3457

3394

3448

3399

288

3301a

3395

3284

3336

1937

3381

6737

3351a

289

3489

3404

3405

3406

3407

3456

3409

3411

3439

3417

6852

290

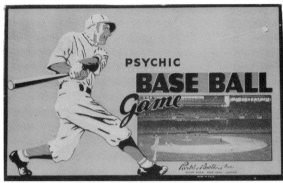

3340

3318

3484

3489

3367

3328

3487

3497

3465

3401

291

3283

1996

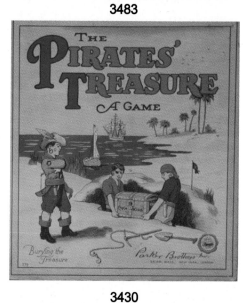

3483

3323

3496

3430

3490

3312

3383

292

3359

3281

3346

3400

3297

3486

3477a

3478

2598

3326

3476

3479

3481

3480

3482

3475

3476a

3477

3379

293

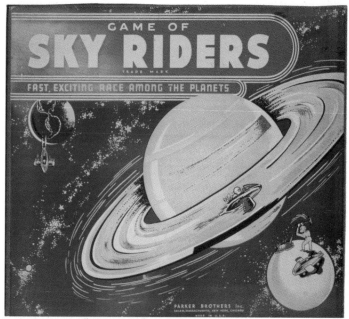

3454

3356

3452

3304

3317

3428

3464

3442

3425

3374

294

3577a

3585

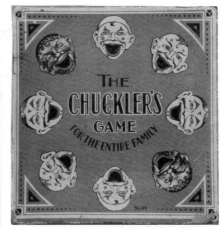

3575

3574

3580

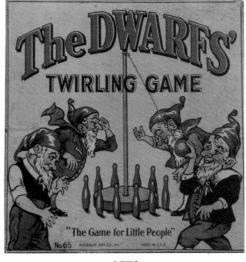

3576

3593

3590

3592

KING-HIGH

3584

3571

295

3696

3693

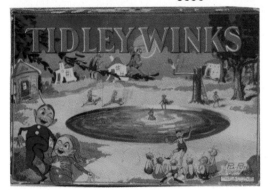

3701

3676

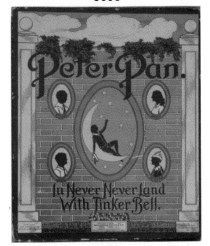

3687

3678a

3657

3672

3656

3698

296

3695

3684

3668

3670

3679

3663

3685

3690

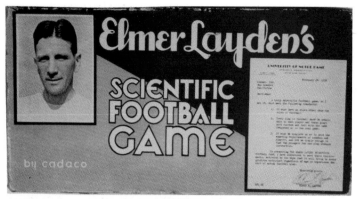

2765

2390

2762

2408

2393

2766

2394

4097

298

3756

3751a

3745

3755

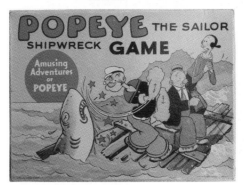

2902

3761

3759

2913

2892

3768

2907

3770

3752

3766

3768a

3617

3612

3637

3634

300

2405

3607

4098

2763

2262

3629

2396

2407

2406

2403

301

3999

4000

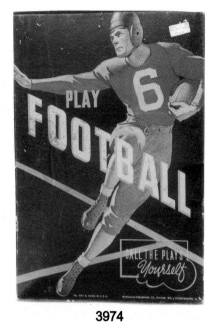

3974

3927

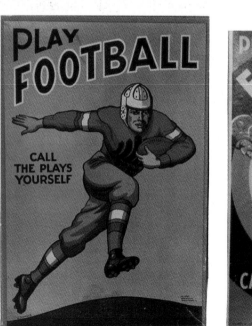

3977

3975

3976

3970

3960

3931

3902

3930

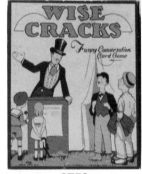

3952

3898

2752

3936

4008

3948

3928

3951

303

3962

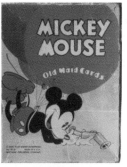

3953

4012

3954

3961

3914

3915

3917

3959

4007a

3894

3916

3908

3906

4006

4015

3913

3937

2747

4007

3978

3939

4018

3998

3989

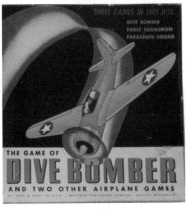

3946

3918

305

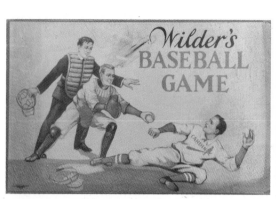

4082

4069

4034

4046

4080

4027

4055

4061

4035

4043

4063

4037

4070

4035

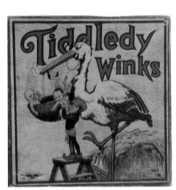

4078

4059

4030

4074

4038

4058

307

4032

4076

4052

4073

4036

4023

4035a

3162

3166

3725

1448

3821

2859

3603

3165

3773

4113

309

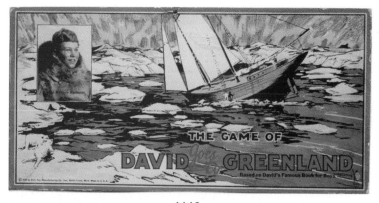

THE GAME OF
DAVID GOES GREENLAND
Based on David's Famous Book for Boys

4110

CAPTAIN ASHLEY McKINLEY
WITH
Byrd
AT THE
SOUTH
POLE

3163

2472

CHAMPION
ROAD RACE

An
EXCITING GAME
for the
WHOLE FAMILY

2784

LET'S GO TO
COLLEGE

THE FUN OF COLLEGE LIFE
PACKED IN A GAME.

2926

OCTOPUS

1 TO 4 CAN PLAY
AGE GROUP 6 AND UP

6110

A·A·MILNE'S
WINNIE-THE-POOH
GAME

3719

STREAMLINED TRAIN GAME

EXCITING · AMUSING · EDUCATIONAL

3558

Game of
"TREASURE ISLAND"
Suggested By
ROBERT LOUIS STEVENSON from
TREASURE ISLAND

3000

GOIN'
TO THE
FAIR

The "FUN ON THE FARM" Game

Another SPARE-TIME Product
SPARE-TIME CORPORATION

3733

4864

4725

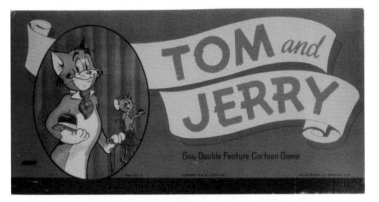

4987a

4622

2609

2588

4640

4692

311

4544

4670

4898

4612

5013

5039

4493

4842

4510

4778

4730

4875

7588

4531a

4872

4561

4533

4548a

4782

313

4463

4708

4784

4713

4658

4468

4899

4968

4949

4764

5010

314

4894

4541

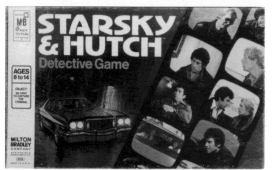

4934

4619

4549

4574

4728

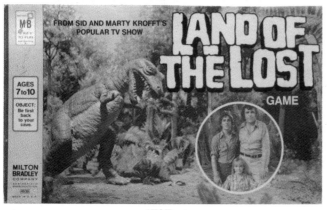

4737

4631

315

4669

4636

4996

4511

4841

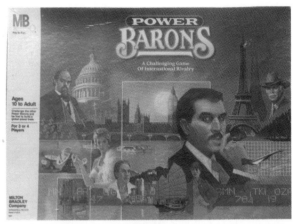

4854

4601

4823

5002

4499

316

4639

4808

4717

4897

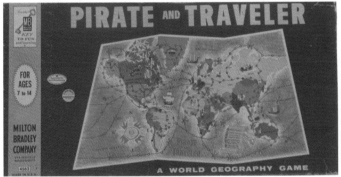

4842

4930

4572

4712

317

4196

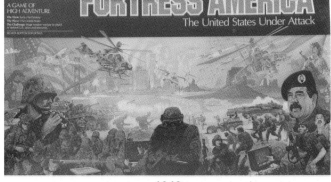

4653

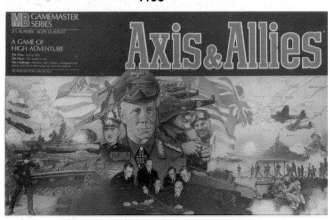

4492

4648

5027

4820

4787

4686

5189a

5184

5158

5141

5095

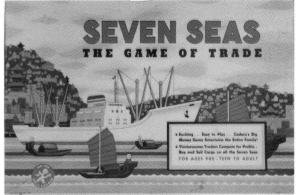

5178

5120

5170

5137

319

6581

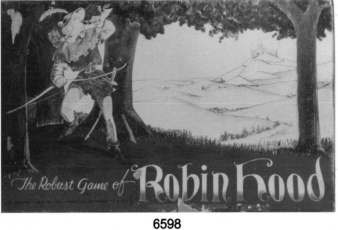

6598

6595

6593

6600

6584

6579

6585

6599

6602

6818

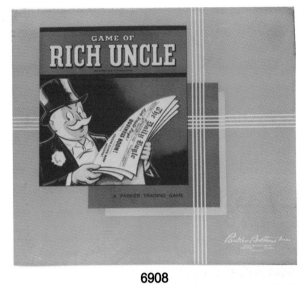

6908

6923

6762

6904

6753

6823

6970

6689

6879

3459

6915

6782a

6980

3357

6656

6765

**Parker Brothers
Leaky Pipe Card Game**

Ages 8 to Adult

7013

6965

6693

6819

Charlie Brown's All-Stars
Parker Brothers BASEBALL GAME

Ages 8 to adult

6713

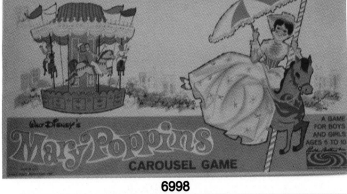

6998

6770

323

6967

6800

6653

3337

6723

6863

6945

7005

6685

324

6994

6829

6677

7010

6828

6992

6947

6995

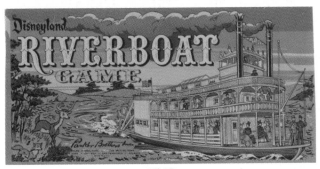

6742

6997

325

6826

6903

6703

6654

6665

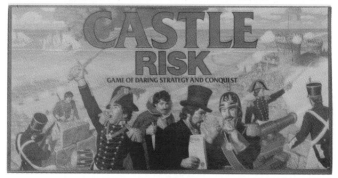

6710

6714

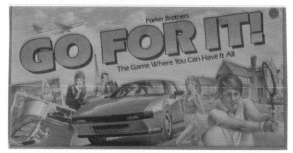

6782

6750

6817

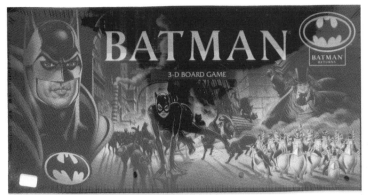

6673a

6815

6649

6988

7002a

6663

4816

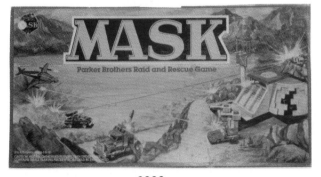

6833

6778

8044

8170

8125

8063

8157

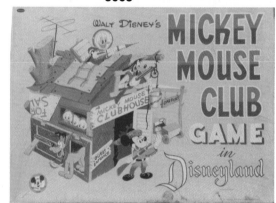

8092

8147

8101

8166

5577

8128

328

7775

5840

7268

7760

5218

4442

5980

6371

6498

7369a

7366

7468

7390

3699

7371

7419

7408

3671

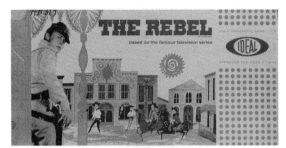

6036

7008

6095

6386

5519

8007

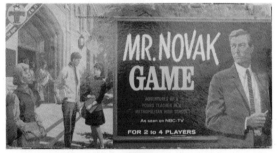

7783

7657

6375

7844

7180

6469

5885

6220

5975

5747

7557

6390

7175

4206

332

5268

7608

5269

7830

2975

6321

6481

5599

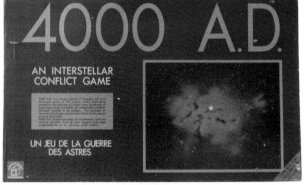

5853

6351

5956

7549

7183

5991

8031

5800

5953

7996

6006

FIGHTER-BOMBER
THE GAME OF MUSTANGS AND MESSERSCHMITTS
A MILITARY STRATEGY GAME

Cadaco

5121

THE CANNONBALL RUN!

A STAR-SPANGLED WACKY RACE GAME

FOR 2 TO 4 PLAYERS
AGES 8 AND UP

Cadaco

5112

Treasure Island

a game based on
the famous book by
Robert Louis Stevenson

SEARCH FOR HIDDEN TREASURE WITH JIM HAWKINS AND LONG JOHN SILVER

5688

A NATURE STUDY GAME

Cadaco
For Nature
Lovers...
All Ages
No. 262

THE CHASE

Wild Kingdom
of
The Everglades

5113

Travel along the Midway

HOWDY DOODY'S Electric Carnival GAME

ANOTHER Wing & Dan ELECTRIC GAME

5679

BILLBOARD
THE BRAND NAME ADVERTISING GAME

AN EXCITING
CHALLENGE
FOR 2-4
PLAYERS!

5674

Robin Hood
AND HIS MERRY MEN
of SHERWOOD FOREST

A GAME OF ADVENTURE

5684

CBS TELEVISION'S
MIGHTY MOUSE playhouse
RESCUE GAME

5680

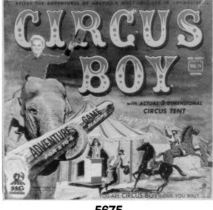

CIRCUS BOY

with ACTUAL 3 DIMENSIONAL
CIRCUS TENT

YOU ARE CIRCUS BOY...CAN YOU WIN?

5675

A "SUNDAY FUNNIES" GAME

IDEAL
2-4 PLAYERS

BLONDIE

SHARE IN THE COMIC SITUATIONS OF AMERICA'S FUN FAMILY

5904

7734

3843

8028

7544

4128

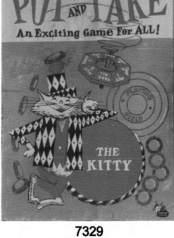

7329

5796

4369

7086

6678

336

4306

5294

5272

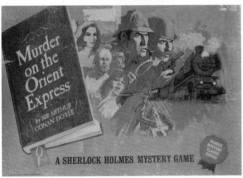

6012

8024

7970

6606

6168

6218

5660

337

5350

5051

8187

5624

WRESTLING GAME

6572

CHAMPIONSHIP

FIGHT GAME

5637

7537

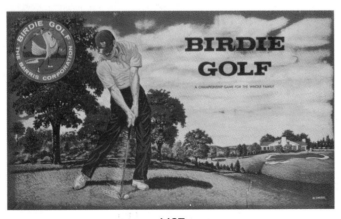

4427

8195

7136

7537

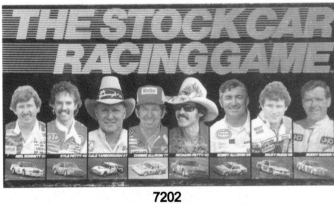

5251

5108

7202

5880

6566

5498

7706

5847

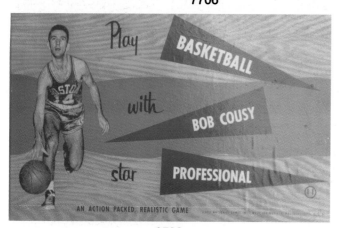

6583

7196

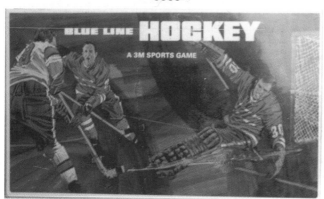

4120

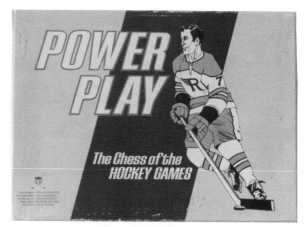

7214

5842

5600

7193

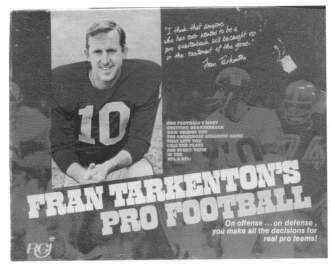

7192

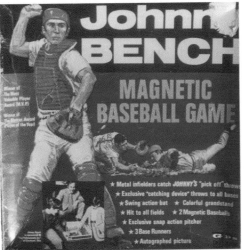

5643

5349a

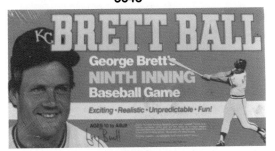

6200

7408

7261

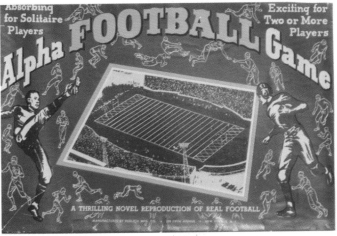

7144

341

5521

4131

5333

4134

4150

4118

7130

3819

7133

4172a

6388

342

6245

7983

5517

7980

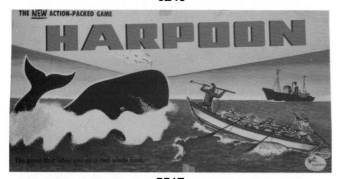

6350

7374

8076

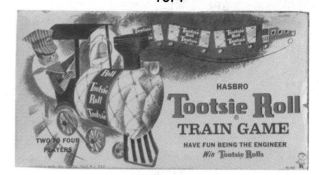

5818

4294

5514

343

7477

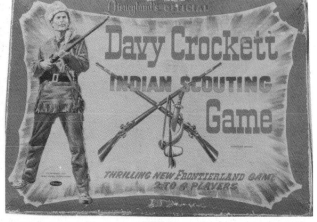

8061

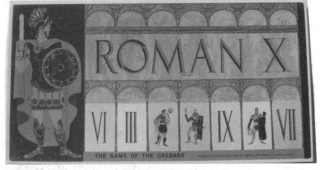

7455

7430

8071

7397

7378

8062

8131

344

7904

8258

4362

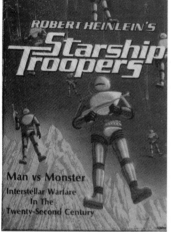

8291a

8826

8741

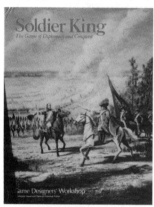

8489

8981

8286

8314

8849

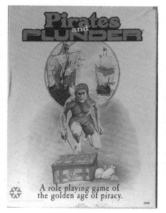

9272

8448a

8245

8290

8310

8466

8488

8269a

8439a

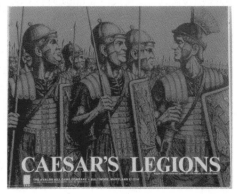

8249

8601

8247

8690

346